PAUL,

I GOT NO IDEA WHAT
THIS BOOK IS ABOUT.
IF THERE ARE ANY GOOD
BASEBALL PARTS IN IT
LEND IT TO ME.
Dan
&
LISA

Alexis de Tocqueville

1805–1859

TOCQUEVILLE

A Biography

ANDRÉ JARDIN

Translated from the French by Lydia Davis
with Robert Hemenway

Farrar Straus Giroux
New York

Because of unforeseen circumstances, Lydia Davis was unable
to complete the revision of her translation of *Alexis de
Tocqueville, 1805–1859.* The final manuscript was further
revised and corrected by Robert Hemenway.

Library of Congress
Library of Congress Cataloging-in-Publication Data
Jardin, André
[Alexis de Tocqueville. English]
Tocqueville : a biography / André Jardin ; translated from the
French by Lydia Davis with Robert Hemenway.
Translation of : Alexis de Tocqueville.
Includes index.
1. Tocqueville, Alexis de, 1805–1859.   2. Historian—France–
–Biography.   3. France—Politics and government—1830–1848.
4. France—Politics and government—1848–1870.   5. United States–
–Description and travel—1783–1848.   6. Tocqueville, Alexis de,
1805–1859—Journey—North America.   I. Title.
DC36.98.T63T3713   1988   944′.072024—dc19   [B]   88–10255

ACKNOWLEDGMENTS

Writing this biography was first suggested to me by M. le comte Jean de Tocqueville, the great-grandnephew of Alexis. His children, M. le comte and Mme. la comtesse d'Hérouville, helped me greatly by making available to me every resource at their disposal.

François Furet proposed that the biography, one that he might well have written himself, be included in the series he edits and thus enabled me to bring the work to completion.

Finally, Françoise Mélonio has been of invaluable help in the arduous tasks of verifying the citations, preparing the notes, and reading the proofs.

I would like to express here my heartfelt thanks.

André Jardin

CONTENTS

PART III

THE DEPUTY FROM VALOGNES

PART IV

TOCQUEVILLE AND THE SECOND REPUBLIC

Part I

TOCQUEVILLE
BEFORE AMERICA

AN ARISTOCRATIC FAMILY

DURING THE REVOLUTION

ON 11 THERMIDOR of the year XIII (July 29, 1805) there was born in Paris "at 987, rue de la Ville-l'Eveque, Roule division . . . Alexis-Charles-Henri . . . son of Hervé-Louis-François-Jean-Bonaventure Clérel, landed proprietor, aged 33, and Louise-Madeleine Le Peletier Rosanbo, aged 33, married in the commune of Males-herbes, department of Loiret."[1]

The certificate of birth, drawn up in the early days of the Empire, still avoids any allusion to the titles of the Ancien Régime, but the family names are enough to suggest the newborn child's noble descent on both his father's and his mother's side.

The Clérels are a very old family of the Norman nobility. One "Guillaume Clarel" fought at Hastings and was in all likelihood the progenitor of the Clarell family in England that can be traced there down into the sixteenth century. There is little doubt, in any event, that this comrade in arms of William the Conqueror belonged to Alexis's family. A branch of the Clarels or Clérels, which can be found established in the Caux region as far back as the twelfth century, owned English lands at one time and bequeathed a portion to the powerful Abbey of Jumièges, with which this feudal family had close ties. At the end of the fourteenth century, however, the family's center of gravity shifted further west, with a marriage to the female heir of

NOTE: In the citations that follow, references to the edition of the *Oeuvres complètes* being published under the direction of J. P. Mayer (Paris: Gallimard, 1951–   ) are abbreviated *O.C.* References to the edition edited by Gustave de Beaumont (Paris, 1860–1866) are abbreviated *O.C.* (Bmt).

[1] From the copy in the Beinecke Library at Yale University, Tocqueville Collection, A1.

4

꣓ ꣓

the house of Rampan, near Saint-Lô. It was yet another marriage, in 1590, that established a collateral branch of the family in the Cotentin, with its acquisition of the fief of Auville in the parish of Tocqueville. There followed lengthy disputes with the Leverrier family, who owned the other fief in that parish; in 1661, through an exchange of properties, the Clérels gained possession of the Leverrier land. And now that they were masters of the entire parish, the Clérels took the name of Tocqueville, as the Leverrier fief was called. (Even taking into account the fact that his contemporary Urbain Leverrier threw in his lot with the Second Empire, isn't it possible that Alexis's want of cordiality toward the celebrated astronomer may also have had a source in family resentments of long standing?)

The Clérels of Tocqueville willingly entered the armies of the king for a time while they were young, but their principal concern was the careful management of their properties. Few of them were drawn to the court; visits to their town house in Valognes were enough to satisfy what appetite they had for city life. The oldest son ran the estate; the younger sons often took orders and contented themselves with meager livings as curés in the nearby parishes. The Tocquevilles were on good terms with the Church and scrupulously fulfilled their obligations toward their tenants.[2] They were not mere squires, as has sometimes been said, but were counted among the lords of the western regions of France, attached to their estates and to the people who lived on them, and to a provincial world from which they were not distracted by their periods of service, brilliant though they sometimes were, in war or at the royal court.

In the eighteenth century the family's position improved substantially, and this was reflected in their practice of matrimonial politics on a larger scale: one of Alexis's great-uncles married a Faudoas; his grandfather, Bernard-Bonaventure, the "Chevalier de Tocqueville," married Catherine de Damas-Crux, from an old family of Forez in whose veins flowed the blood of Saint Louis and Cesare Borgia, a family that the genealogist Beaujon describes as "one of the oldest and most important of the kingdom."[3] These grandparents of Alexis were both of them quite striking personages: the "Chevalier," a kindly officer and a cultivated and pious gentleman, died prematurely in 1776,

---

[2]G. A. Simon, *Histoire généalogique des Clérel, seigneurs de Rampan, Tocqueville etc. (1066–1954)* (Caen, 1954).

[3]Quoted by F. Bluche, *Les Honneurs de la cour*, 2 vols. (Paris, 1958); alphabetical index of vol. 1 (*Cahier nobles*, no. 10).

while his widow, an upright and resolute soul, lived on until the year 1785, retaining the affection of her tenants during those agitated years.[4]

Alexis's father, Hervé-Bonaventure, orphaned at the age of thirteen and heir while still a child to properties from extinguished collateral lines, amassed a substantial fortune in land in the Cotentin.[5] When an attempt was made during the Restoration to recreate some sort of hierarchy of the nobility, his title as Comte was recognized by King Louis XVIII in an official document dated in 1820.[6]

At the time of his mother's death, Hervé was in Paris, at the Collège d'Harcourt, preparing for a career as a soldier; a private tutor, Abbé Lesueur, originally from Picardy, was looking out for him. At the age of fifteen, the young man was named *lieutenant de remplacement* in the regiment from Vexin in which one of his Damas uncles was a colonel, and at the age of sixteen he took part in maneuvers under the Maréchal de Broglie.

Like many young gentlemen, however, Tocqueville sympathized with the Revolution that was just beginning and sought a liberal regime, one in which the rule of law might be reconciled with loyalty to the king. When the first regiments of émigrés formed in Brussels, he was automatically assigned to old Montboissier's musketeers, but after yielding briefly to family pressure and making a short trip to Brussels, he returned to Paris and joined Louis XVI's constitutional guard. At that time he had lodgings in the faubourg Saint-Victor with a trellis-maker who was to prove unfailingly devoted to his friends.

On the morning of August 10, 1792, he set off with the section of the National Guard from his quarter, which was apparently prepared to defend the Tuileries. But en route numbers of proletarians mingled with the bourgeois contingents and caused the feeling toward Louis XVI to alter. Hervé was obliged to slip away. Now suspect, he left Paris to hide out in Picardy for a time; here he rejoined the Abbé Lesueur, who had barely managed to avoid arrest in the faubourg Saint-Victor for being a nonjuring priest. (He was one of those who had refused to swear an oath of loyalty to the Civil Constitution of the Clergy in 1790.)

By January 1793, Hervé de Tocqueville was back in Paris. Arrange-

[4]G. A. Simon, *Histoire des Clérel*, 151–55.

[5]See the pamphlet about him written by one of his descendants, Emmanuel de Blic, entitled *Hervé Clérel, comte de Tocqueville* (Dijon, 1951).

[6]For the conditions and procedure of this recognition of titles, see A. Révérend, *Titres, anoblissements, pairies de la Restauration* (1902) II, 153–54.

ments, made by an intermediary whose name is unknown, had just been completed for his marriage to Louise Le Peletier de Rosanbo, twenty years old—his own age—and a granddaughter of Malesherbes.

Now in his seventies, Malesherbes had come out of retirement at his own request to help conduct the defense of Louis XVI before the Convention. After the execution, on January 21, the defender of the king had left the capital together with his household and retired to his home in Malesherbes, in the Loiret. Tocqueville joined them there on January 31 and, even though Malesherbes had never met him before, was welcomed "like a son" by the illustrious old man.[7]

The younger daughter of Malesherbes, Madame de Montboissier, had emigrated,[8] but his other daughter, the favorite, Madame Le Peletier de Rosanbo, was there with her husband, the former *président de chambre* of the Parlement of Paris, and their children—young Louis, who was only sixteen, and the three daughters and their husbands: the oldest, who had married Jean-Baptiste Chateaubriand, the elder brother of François-René; the middle daughter, married to her first cousin, Le Peletier d'Aunay, on November 6, 1792, whose household divided its time between Malesherbes and her husband's lands in the Nièvre; and the youngest, Louise, whose marriage to Hervé-Bonaventure took place on March 12, 1793.

Tocqueville's *Mémoires* show that although the Reign of Terror was now at its height, this was a relatively happy time. The family was anxious, of course, and Malesherbes himself was prepared to defend the queen if called upon and to sacrifice his life, but he thought this crisis would pass. He had resumed the half-intellectual, half-rustic life that he liked best—alternating reading and philosophical conversations with gardening and village business. He had always been benevolent and charitable to the peasants and the poor, and they continued to treat their former lord with trust and affection.[9] When he was later arrested and removed to Paris, the municipality of Malesherbes posted a notice of protest.

The prevailing feeling at the time was that even though the king

[7]My main source, here, is Hervé de Tocqueville's *Mémoires,* which were hardly used by de Blic and which remain unpublished, except for a section relating to the period of the Revolution brought out by his son Edouard under the title "Episodes de la Terreur," in *Le Contemporain, Revue d'Economie chrétienne* (January 1861), subsequently off-printed in 1901. Useful information can also be found in Georges Collas's *La Vieillesse douloureuse de madame de Chateaubriand,* 2 vols. (Paris, 1961), which contains a summary of the correspondence rediscovered at Combourg between the father of the author of *Democracy* and the mother of the author of *Mémoires d'outre-tombe.*

[8]Comte de Leusse, *Notes sur l'émigration de la baronne de Montboissier et de sa famille* (Châteaudun, 1935).

[9]Life in Malesherbes is described not only in Tocqueville's *Mémoires* but also in Pierre Grosclaude's *Malesherbes, témoin et interprète de son temps* (Paris, 1961).

was dead the crisis would doubtless pass, and then France would return pretty much to its old ways and to a course of simple reforms. Hervé de Tocqueville's marriage actually took place within the psychological context of the very end of the Ancien Régime, and from this point of view what it meant for the Tocqueville family was another step upward in the social hierarchy.

When, in 1827, young Alexis chose to enter the magistrature rather than the army, a Normandy neighbor, the Comtesse de Blangy, would accuse him of lowering his status by refusing to wear the sword. The attitude was characteristic of the provinces, particularly in the following generation. On the eve of the Revolution, the narrow aristocracy of the *présidents à mortier*—the presiding judges in the Parlement of Paris who were entitled to wear the *mortier,* the round cap, of their high office—was inferior in rank only to the members of the Chamber of Peers and a few old, illustrious houses. Both the Le Peletiers themselves, a family from the Maine ennobled in the fifteenth century, and the Lamoignons, who could boast so many councillors on intimate terms with the crown, were related to the Molés, the Chauvelins, and the d'Aguesseaus. And the Le Peletiers were related as well to the Montmorencys, the Hénin-Liétards, and the Salignac de la Mothe-Fénelons, while the Lamoignons had ties to the La Luzernes, the Broglies, and the Caumonts.[10] For the members of the highest provincial nobility, therefore, to marry into one of these families was not to marry beneath themselves at all, but to advance themselves socially; it was to enter the antechamber of power, to achieve the highest position in the city and one of the highest in the court. The ambitious Jean-Baptiste de Chateaubriand had understood this very well, having expected to accede, through his marriage, to one of the high offices of *président de chambre* in the Parlement.[11] Hervé de Tocqueville had probably had a similar plan, in the hope that the terrorists would fall from power.

These illusions, and the apparent peace at Malesherbes, were brutally disrupted, Hervé de Tocqueville tells us, on December 17, 1793: "We were at table when the keeper of the manor came in with a thunderstruck expression and said, in an unaccustomed turn of phrase: 'Citizen Rosanbo, there are citizens from Paris here and they're asking for you.' We all turned pale. M. de Rosanbo went out immediately and we

[10]For the importance of these *familles de grande robe,* see especially F. Bluche, *Les Magistrats du Parlement de Paris au XVIIIe siècle* (Paris, 1960).

[11]Jean-Baptiste de Chateaubriand's ambitions, discreetly revealed in *Les Mémoires d'outre-tombe,* are analyzed by Collas in *Madame de Chateaubriand,* 52–53.

became very uneasy when after a little while he did not return. It wasn't long before we learned that the citizens of Paris were two workers who had been promoted to the rank of members of the revolutionary committee of the Bondy section and had come to tear the father of the family away from his children and take him to prison. They had with them a warrant for his arrest issued by the Comité de Sûreté Générale of the Convention."[12]

A house search of M. de Rosanbo's Paris residence in the rue de Bondy by the revolutionary committee of the section had indeed discovered a draft of the secret protest of the Parlement of Paris against its own dissolution by the Constituent Assembly, a protest that had been entrusted to M. de Rosanbo in his capacity as president of the *chambre des vacations* (the court that sat during a judicial recess to judge urgent cases). At Malesherbes itself, some rather insignificant letters from Madame de Montboissier, émigré, would also be found.

And it may be that Jean-Baptiste de Chateaubriand was suspected of being a returned émigré . . .[13] Here was a collection of facts or presumptions of fact more than sufficient to condemn an aristocrat's family to the scaffold, and the Bondy revolutionaries, in their stubborn hatred, seemed bent on destroying the king's defender, and his family as well.

Arrested, taken to Paris, scattered among different prisons, then reunited in Port-Libre (as Port-Royal was then called), the family was decimated in a series of hasty trials: on April 20, 1794, M. de Rosanbo was executed; the next day, Malesherbes was executed; Madame de Rosanbo and the Chateaubriands were in their turn "summoned to the office of the clerk of the court." Hervé de Tocqueville and his wife, together with the Le Peletier d'Aunays and Louis de Rosanbo, remained in prison until 9 Thermidor and Robespierre's fall from power. They were released three months later.

The upheaval of the Revolution left permanent scars; let us speak first of those to the body and mind. Hervé de Tocqueville woke one morning to find that his hair had gone completely white. His wife's health was impaired and she never recovered her emotional stability. In the various accounts of her that we possess, we see her as capricious, impatient, apparently also wasteful, a victim of recurring migraine headaches, and afflicted with a profound, constant melancholy that

[12]Edouard de Tocqueville, "Episodes de la Terreur," 32.
[13]The story in the *Mémoires d'outre-tombe* in which Chateaubriand insists that his brother was denounced by his servant (édition du Centenaire, vol. 1, 390) is strongly contested by Collas in *Madame de Chateaubriand,* vol. 2, 410–11.

must have been quite common among the survivors of the Reign of Terror. This would have cast quite a heavy pall over the atmosphere of the family during Alexis de Tocqueville's early years.

Property was affected, too. Formidable tasks awaited the twenty-one-year-old head of the family when he came out of prison. One of the most arduous is easily discerned in the rediscovered correspondence between Hervé de Tocqueville—guardian of Louis and Christian de Chateaubriand, the two children of Jean-Baptiste—and the old Madame de Chateaubriand, widow of Auguste-René. In these letters it becomes clear how difficult it was to restore a nobleman's fortune, buildings having fallen into disrepair, forests having been pillaged and goods sequestered. And in addition to the material difficulties, there were also legal difficulties: as the guardian of minors representing the senior branch of the family, Hervé de Tocqueville could only induce that branch to recognize his holdings at Combourg at the price of interminable transactions with the younger daughters, who made use of the advantages they gained from the new body of laws, as opposed to the old Breton feudal custom. Though less is known of them, the difficulties caused by the Rosanbo patrimony, the bulk of which consisted of estates with terminable leases in the vicinity of Lannion, were apparently no less severe. At Malesherbes and at Tocqueville, things must have been simpler, but the two manors had been badly damaged. However, Comte Hervé's tenacity was crowned with success: in 1826, by the time the Chateaubriands were back in possession of their patrimony again and when a partition with Louis de Rosanbo had occurred, Hervé de Tocqueville was able to declare an annual income of seventy-five thousand francs.[14]

Finally, relations within the family were affected. It had been dispersed by the emigration. Hervé de Tocqueville appealed to Joséphine de Beauharnais for help in enabling Madame de Montboissier to return, and the former obligingly promised to have her name struck from the list of émigrés. Then, in 1801, he traveled to central Germany and met with relatives who had not returned. Unfortunately, he gives us no information about that trip.

The Revolution and the First Empire had led to political disagreements in many noble families. Among the Tocquevilles, these disagreements were glaringly evident, but what was more surprising was that they hardly seem to have disturbed family relations. The Le Peletier

[14]Reported in the description form he filled out as prefect, individual files of prefects: Nat. Arch. F(1), b(1) 174(9).

cousins of Saint-Fargeau had been ardent Jacobins: Michel, a friend of Robespierre, the regicide, was murdered by a former member of the king's bodyguard, but Comte Hervé, in his *Mémoires,* convinces himself that Michel was in fact killed by revolutionaries and thus avoids the unpleasant vision of a traitor's punishment. Félix adopted Babeuf's children, was a representative in the Chamber of the Hundred Days, and was exiled in 1816. More discreetly, Le Peletier d'Aunay, *auditeur* in the Council of State in 1806, would serve "the Usurper" Napoléon as prefect and become a baron of the Empire, while the Molé cousin, Comte Louis-Mathieu Molé, was to play a leading role in the government under Louis-Philippe. The Damas branch of the family was the very picture of loyalty to the Bourbons—the uncle, Damas-Crux, was the official companion and the confidant of the Duc d'Angoulême—but in the family of the maternal grandparents, the Menous, the situation was different: in Vendémiaire of the year IV, General de Menou had yielded to Bonaparte, who had broken the Paris revolt of the royalists, but he remained Bonaparte's friend and later commanded the Egyptian army, though without special distinction.

We are unable to follow the lives of Comte Hervé and his family year by year under the First Empire, but we know their seasonal pattern: after several stays at Malesherbes, the family took up its summer residence in the Château de Verneuil (Verneuil-sur-Seine), a "gallows inheritance"[15] left by Madame de Senozan, Malesherbes's sister, of which the Tocquevilles inherited only a twelfth part, buying back the rest in whole or in part from the other heirs. Winters, they returned to the capital.

Apparently, politics was not much talked about at Verneuil. On the other hand, every new book of philosophy, history, or literature was passionately discussed and the family played parlor games just as they had in the carefree days of the eighteenth century. But politics was always on their minds, and their underlying feelings were clear: they accepted the out-of-favor Chateaubriand, they remained faithful to the royal family.[16] The liberal impulses of 1789 seem to have been quite forgotten.

It is true that Hervé de Tocqueville accepted the office of mayor of Verneuil from 1804 on. But this didn't commit him to anything—in the eyes of the big rural landowners, these municipal obligations were still regarded as quasi-feudal duties. Thus, the mayor of Verneuil had

---

[15]Chateaubriand, *Mémoires d'outre-tombe,* vol. 3, 184.
[16]Antoine Rédier, *Comme disait M. de Tocqueville* (Paris, 1925), 32.

to be reminded that in his absence the commune was to be managed by the deputy mayor and not by the steward of his properties.[17] As late as 1852, Alexis, who refused to take his seat in the departmental council of the Manche because he would not swear an oath of allegiance to the new regime of Napoléon III, came to the realization that the responsibilities of the municipal offices had altogether changed.

It is quite possible, for that matter, that Hervé de Tocqueville's apparent inaction really masked clandestine activities and that at the least he served as informer to Louis XVIII's brother, the exiled Comte d'Artois (later Charles X). In 1815, he was to stress his twenty-six years of loyalty to Monsieur (as the oldest brother of the king was called). He did not say just what this loyalty had consisted of. And at the conclusion of the *Mémoires,* written near the end of his life, he asserted that he had had the good fortune—rare among his contemporaries—of having served only one master.

It is therefore not surprising that the fall of Napoleon in 1814 should have aroused great hopes in Hervé de Tocqueville. On March 30, he returned to Paris from Verneuil with his household while the belligerent armies were still in the field. He took part in demonstrations by Parisian royalists and, with his son Hippolyte, joined the horse guard serving as escort to Monsieur and the two princes, the Duc d'Angoulême and the Duc de Berry. Here the testimony of his own *Mémoires* is corroborated by the two earliest letters written by Alexis, letters addressed to Abbé Lesueur, his father's old tutor and now his own, which give us a child's version of the events: "Good day my little *bé* . . . why didn't you come with us! How you would have shouted, 'Long live the king!' " (April 4). "My little *bébé,* I wish you a good day. I'm going to tell you something: three days ago, Papa bought Hippolyte a dappled gray horse and boots and both of them had riding breeches made . . . The statue on the column in the Place Vendôme has just been pulled down and in its place they have put a white flag with fleurs-de-lis . . ." (April 9).[18]

Comte Hervé, of course, contemplated serving the new power in a more enduring way. He went to see his uncle Damas, who tried to discourage him in his ambitions, insisting that Louis XVIII had decided to make use only of those people already in place—a royal resolve

[17]Sister Marie-Claire Tihon, Verneuil's historian, has found the record of Hervé de Tocqueville's installation as mayor on September 30, 1804. The document, the details of which she has kindly communicated to this author, would appear to invalidate the dates given by Rédier in *M. de Tocqueville,* 32–33.

[18]Tocqueville Archives, file 1.

12
⚜ ⚜

which, if it existed at all, was rapidly swept away by the tide of royalist claims.

The safety of the princes, for that matter, required that the royalists be called into service, and the royal bodyguards, including the *compagnies rouges* once suppressed by the Comte de Saint-Germain, had to be activated again. In these special corps, every trooper had a lieutenant's commission, every corporal a captain's commission, every sergeant was a major, and every sub-lieutenant a lieutenant-colonel! Crowds of young men belonging to titled families rushed to join the guard, including the two older sons of Comte Hervé, Hippolyte and Edouard.[19]

Hervé himself obtained an administrative post: the Abbé de Montesquiou, minister of the interior, appointed him prefect of Maine-et-Loire on June 18, 1814.

Since a new administration was being set in place made up of men devoted to the monarchy, it would have seemed ungrateful not to employ this faithful royalist who let no one forget for long that he was the grandson-in-law of M. de Malesherbes, the defender of Louis XVI, who had died for his king. Louis XVIII had too strong a sense of propriety and Monsieur too kind a heart for Hervé to be forgotten.

[19]See their files in the Military Archives of Vincennes.

2

THE CAREER
OF COMTE HERVÉ
DE TOCQUEVILLE

THERE ARE THOSE who have made fun of the inexperienced royalist noblemen who, in 1814, came into the government to replace the administrators of the First Empire. (They amounted to no more than a small proportion of the imperial personnel.) But this mockery is by no means always justified, and in the case of Hervé de Tocqueville the very complete archives he left, which conceal neither his flaws nor his good qualities, provide no grounds for accusing him of administrative incompetence.[1]

As mayor under the First Empire, he had not been particularly devoted to the regime—which must often have been the case with local civil servants chosen from the old nobility (in a single day in 1813 he secretly performed marriage ceremonies for thirteen boys from Verneuil so that they might escape conscription)[2]—but he had worked hard: "The necessity of studying the municipal laws gave me the preliminary knowledge that I needed to bring to a larger administration, and it bore good fruit when I began my career as prefect," he wrote in his *Mémoires*. Nor is it altogether unlikely that his association with a member of the King's Council of State like Le Peletier d'Aunay helped him grasp the spirit of the new institutions.

But at the very outset of his tenure as prefect in Angers Hervé de Tocqueville found himself confronting a serious political problem,

---

[1]This chapter is based on an examination of the archives of the Tocqueville charter room, an inventory and a microfilm of which are deposited in the National Archives under the classification 154 AP, and of Hervé de Tocqueville's partially published *Mémoires*.

[2]Rédier, *M. de Tocqueville*, 34.

14

much graver than any difficulties he may have had mastering the details of administration. The regions that had remained royalist and had all along been hostile to Napoleonic centralization now had strong aspirations to achieving full autonomy. In the South, where the royalist spirit was vigorous in both town and country, people dreamed of a *royaume d'Oc* under the rule of the Duc d'Angoulême; in the West, however, the life of the people of the *bocage*— the characteristic mixed pasture and woodland country of the region—was withdrawn and folded in upon itself; their desire for independence clashed with the Jacobinism of the towns, where the bourgeoisie were determined to preserve the gains of the Revolution, particularly the ownership of the national property. Between these two hostile currents, the representatives of the central power had to appear as impartial arbiters. Hervé de Tocqueville acknowledged that he was too well known a royalist for anyone to be convinced of his impartiality.

This reputation, though, hardly made his job any easier where the local royalist insurgents were concerned: the Vendeans on the left bank of the Loire and the Chouans—the Breton royalists—in the northwest of the department continued to form little rural, military republics, obeying only the voice of their local commanders, of whom the most important were d'Andigné in the north and d'Autichamp in the region of Beaupréau. Tocqueville attempted to win over these homegrown leaders, with the intention of subsequently dominating them, but they were distrustful and jealous of their local prestige. Hervé, a member of the noblest family in the Cotentin, also a region of mixed woodland and pasture, made the mistake of declaring upon his arrival that he was one of them. Immediately, the opposing party—the "blues," and especially the bourgeoisie of Angers, who were resigned to the return of the Bourbons but hated the nobility and the clergy—complained to Paris. Theirs was a vigorous party that had not been brought low by its temporary defeat. When the Duc d'Angoulême came to visit the department, the Vendean cavalry escorted him from Saumur to the gates of Angers; there, the National Guard of the town was waiting for him, and if the commanders had not intervened, the two companies would have engaged in a pitched battle.

Situated somewhere between these two hostile parties, the moderates—the *patauds* (clumsy oafs) as the Vendeans disdainfully called them—were too weak to be of much help to the administration. Would the peacemaking efforts of the prefect (who must be given credit for several minor victories) have been successful in the long run? It is impossible to say, for on March 8, 1815, the word of Napoléon's return from Elba began to spread throughout the department. On the fourteenth, the Duc de Bourbon, entrusted with the defense of the West, established himself in the area of Beaupréau. Tocqueville, who had remained at Angers, suggested certain defense measures—fortifying the Loire crossings, for example—but he did not get along well with d'Autichamp, who was in charge of organizing the military.

The garrisons could not be counted on, and the Vendeans were short of ammunition. Very soon, the idea of an immediate response had to be abandoned, and during the second Restoration a fairly bitter controversy took place between Tocqueville and d'Autichamp, who accused each other of being too soft. The truth seems to be that though they were devoted to the cause of the king, neither the Duc de Bourbon nor they themselves believed that an effective resistance could be mounted so quickly, and everyone accepted with secret satisfaction the safe-conducts offered by Colonel Noireau, of the gendarmerie, who had assumed command in Angers.[3]

Tocqueville withdrew with his household to Lannion, whose mayor, Guermarquer, was the business agent for the Chateaubriand family and whose sub-prefect, Billiard, was Guermarquer's son-in-law. A little later, however, Tocqueville went off to Caen, where people were not required to wear the tricolored cockade as they were in Brittany. The news of Waterloo took him back to Paris—to Pasquier, his relative, who was in charge of re-forming the government.

The latter judged it preferable not to send him back to Angers and on July 13, 1815, he was appointed prefect of the Oise.

The new prefect was immediately faced with a problem—the occupation, which had become all the more serious since the English, with whom relations had been tolerable, were soon replaced by Ziethen's corps of Prussians.

In his *Mémoires,* Tocqueville emphasizes that when he started out in the Oise, he had to deal at all hours of the day and night with the demands of the occupation authorities or with complaints about their behavior. The second Restoration and the allied occupation brought with them a kind of anarchy; one aspect of it was the surprisingly broad decision-making power given to the prefect, even though he was quite close to the capital.

Thus, for example, in order to escape direct requisitions on the

[3]In answer to d'Autichamp's allegations, Tocqueville wrote a *Mémoire justificatif,* of which there is still a copy in his private archives (154 AP I[c] 1) and which supplements the explanations in the *Mémoires.*

populace, Tocqueville concluded an agreement with a supplier who was authorized to advance to the allied troops whatever they required. As for the levies on the local inhabitants, he had them paid in short-term bonds, guaranteed by the tax revenues, whose value was to be reimbursed by the tax collectors. If these bonds were reabsorbed easily enough, reimbursement of the supplier, Saint-Just, proved much more difficult, and this gave rise to recriminations from Tocqueville's successors. Tocqueville said in his own defense that the arrangement had freed him to attend to more pressing matters and had spared the people numerous exactions.

The prefect was able to establish himself as a mediator, in the name of the king, between the local people and the allied occupation authorities, refusing to turn over a list of those under his jurisdiction who had been implicated during the Hundred Days. But the main thrust of his policy was to assign administrative responsibilities to good royalists, leaving until later any attempt to bring in the lukewarm or those in the opposition who might eventually be won over. He set about establishing the royalists in his department with a good deal of enthusiasm.[4]

Public opinion in the Oise, according to the prefect, was divided, with one party hostile to the Restoration and the other well disposed toward it but inactive and lethargic. "I knew at once that the bad party had to be stripped of all influence, the ties binding its members had to be broken, their network of relationships destroyed. At the same time, it was essential to arouse the zeal of the king's servants and make them into a vigorous body which, by taking concerted action in the department at every point, might deprive the agitators of even the hope of doing harm."

First came a purge of the mayors, then a purge of the tax collectors—this one less sweeping, but thorough enough to silence the skeptics. Tocqueville then set about removing the dangerous schoolteachers, "whose bad examples corrupt the younger generation and predispose them to disorder and further revolution," but he was not very successful with this except in the Beauvais arrondissement. He also organized the corps of rural police and put them under the strict surveillance of the officers and noncommissioned officers of the gendarmerie.

Tocqueville attached great importance to the National Guard, which was charged with influencing public morale and averting trou-

---

[4]The private archives (154 AP I[c] 2) supplement the *Mémoires* and illustrate it with concrete examples.

ble. First, he formed a horse guard recruited from among the large landowners; his intention was to organize a squad in each canton. Whenever "seditious shouts or alarming noises were heard" in a commune, "the horse guards would proceed there . . . and would, by their presence and by their words, reassure the weak, intimidate the wicked, and spread love of the sovereign and the laws."

As for the foot guards, he created units in the towns of Senlis, Compiègne, and Noyon; while he brought men he thought the regime could depend on into the elite companies of grenadiers and light infantry, he consigned the dubious cases, those one would not call upon in actual practice, to the fusiliers.

The prefect spared no effort organizing all of this; after the fashion of the intendants of the Ancien Régime, he actually rode around meeting with mayors and ordinary citizens and noting down their suggestions in a minute-book. On good terms with the deputies of the department, of whom the most important was his cousin by marriage, Kergorlay,[5] he experienced some difficulties keeping his subordinates in their places and fired de Fleury, sub-prefect of Senlis, who, being in favor at court, saw fit to prolong a leave of absence outside the department without permission.

Still, it was not because of difficulties with the allied authorities (contrary to a story that is sometimes brought up) or because of popular hostility toward him that he was transferred.[6] M. de Choiseul, prefect of the Côte-d'Or, was on bad terms with the royalists of that department because he had maintained that Napoleon's return from Elba had been willed by providence, and because he had remained in office during the Hundred Days. To humor the royalists, therefore, the minister of the interior, Vaublanc, had the prefects of Dijon and Beauvais exchange posts. Tocqueville was in the Oise only seven months altogether, an even shorter time than in Maine-et-Loire.

Though his work had only just begun, the plan was clear: to rely heavily on a strongly organized royalist party and, in point of fact, on the great wealth that existed in lands, whether in the hands of nobles or commoners (Tocqueville wrote that this distinction—between nobles and commoners—belonged to the past); to deprive the old imperial personnel of all influence; then to promote, through an upright administration, a favorable climate for winning over anyone prepared to accept the new state of affairs. He was sorry that the government

---

[5]The correspondence between Alexis de Tocqueville and Louis de Kergorlay, sons respectively of the prefect and the deputy, appears in the *Oeuvres complètes* XIII, parts 1 and 2 (Gallimard), ed. by M. Lesourd.

[6]Tocqueville's transfer provoked a protest by royalist deputies of the Oise.

of 1815 did not simply follow, on the national level, the line he had unhesitatingly adopted on the departmental level—what amounted to the practical application of an approach that Chateaubriand would soon advocate in *La Monarchie selon la Charte*.[7]

Tocqueville, appointed prefect of Dijon on January 31, 1816, was installed in office on February 24. He was sorry not to have had a little more time to finish his work in the Oise, and, all in all, showed little satisfaction with the change, though it was tantamount to a promotion. This was quite possibly due in part to his personal situation: Madame de Tocqueville, who had followed her husband to Angers and Beauvais, would be with him only briefly in Dijon and in Metz, where he was assigned in 1817; at about this time, she settled in Paris.

Tocqueville's appointment to Dijon, which was Vaublanc's attempt to placate the royalists of the Côte-d'Or, was one of the last gestures of a moribund policy: in early May 1816, the ultraroyalist Vaublanc was replaced as minister of the interior by Laîné, a moderate, and the ministry grew more markedly hostile to the ultras as the minister of police, Decazes, who sought to gain the support of the left, became more and more clearly the favorite of the king.[8] Decazes did not scruple to encroach on Laîné's responsibilities. Tocqueville, newly arrived in the Côte-d'Or, was brought to Decazes's suspicious attention by the esteem in which he was held by Vaublanc, and found himself under the watchful eye of Jollivet, the Dijon police commissioner, who took it upon himself to thwart Tocqueville's policies at every opportunity. For this, Jollivet would be rewarded with an advancement to sub-prefect.[9]

Such vexatious interference added to the local difficulties Tocqueville mentions in his *Mémoires:* the Côte-d'Or was one of the departments in which political passions were the most lively; the powerful and unified liberal party had well-known leaders there, like Maret and the brother of Lazare Carnot, and among its members were large landowners or magistrates who had been removed from office; many of the officers on half pay were politically active; Bishop Reymond, one of the conforming clergy who had signed the oath of allegiance

---

[7] *La Monarchie selon la Charte* first appeared in print on about September 10, 1816.

[8] Guillaume de Bertier de Sauvigny, *La Restauration* (Paris, 1955), 183f.

[9] There are other instances in which Decazes employed this procedure: surveillance by a police superintendent, together with simultaneous investigations by special agents, then requests for immediate explanations that elicited polite but bitter responses from the prefects—with Tournon, the prefect of Bordeaux, for example, or with Bertier de Sauvigny, the prefect of Caen. (See Jacques Moulard, *Camille de Tournon* [Paris, 1914] and Guillaume de Bertier de Sauvigny, *Ferdinand de Bertier de Sauvigny* [Paris, 1948].)

to the Civil Constitution, was now under the sway of his nephew and secretary, a former soldier of the Empire, and had filled the clergy with revolutionary elements and ne'er-do-wells;[10] while the nobility, strongly pro-dynasty to be sure, fed its own lack of discipline on memories of the old States.

The new prefect's first acts were in line with Vaublanc's instructions and with the changes already carried out in the Oise: surveillance of the sale of gunpowder and gun licenses; the repression of seditious writings; the closing of taverns where "bad" talk was heard; surveillance of peddlers and itinerants; imprisonment of "a few intriguers" under the law of November 29, 1815, which permitted the administrative internment of suspected individuals; development of the organization created by M. de Choiseul—the National Guard, and the horse guard in particular; and lastly, the purging of the ecclesiastics, which was performed with dispatch. Monsignor Reymond was summoned to Paris, and in his absence the vicar-general, Collin, got rid of the dubious elements of the clergy. The liberals cried out against the "tyrannical prefect of the Côte-d'Or." Tocqueville insisted, in his own defense, that he had sought to discourage his adversaries by taking rigorous measures in his first three months in office so that he could then conduct his administration with a much gentler hand.

There is reason to believe he was sincere: he showed that he was prepared to welcome those royalists and supporters of the Empire who now accepted the Restoration, and on a personal level he tried to win over the liberal leaders, taking the initiative, for example, of paying a visit to Carnot's brother, who did not in the least refuse to associate with the prefect.

But clearly the highest priority for Tocqueville, as for the intendants of the eighteenth century, was the prudent management of the department's economy. This is sometimes apparent from measures he took that he would later acknowledge to have been somewhat ill-considered and rash. On March 4, 1816, for example, faced with the threat of food shortages, he prohibited the shipment of grains outside his department. This measure, rigorously applied even to grains in transit through the department, earned the prefect an admonition from the government and provoked a polite but firm protest from Chabrol, the prefect of Lyon. The flooding of the Saône, interrupting navigation, allowed him to back down without losing too much face: on March 14, he with-

---

[10]Paul Viard, *L'Administration préfectorale dans le département de la Côte-d'Or sous le Consulat et le Premier Empire* (Paris, 1914), has a much more positive opinion of Bishop Reymond than Tocqueville in his papers.

20
৺ ৺

drew his decree, which he claimed circumstances had rendered unneces-sary.[11]

Early in 1817, after traveling throughout the department and listen-ing to what all its mayors had to say, Tocqueville drew up an inven-tory of the Côte-d'Or's resources, stressing the shortcomings of its traditional, inefficient agricultural practices and envisaging how a cure might be found. He gave instructions to the sub-prefects and tried to breathe new life into the agricultural association. But he had no time to do more, for the ministry now asked him to exchange posts with the prefect of the Moselle, Lachenède. This time, it was the latter who received the warm commendations, which amounted to as many indi-rect criticisms of the prefect of the Côte-d'Or: "The king has been informed of your prudent administration in the department of the Moselle, and he has decided that the man who was able to maintain a crucial harmony between Frenchmen and foreigners with such skill would be able, through his impartiality and justice, to win over to the cause of king and country the Frenchmen of the department of the Côte-d'Or, who have at this point been divided by deplorable events."[12]

Such was the outcome of the long conflict between the prefect and Decazes that had been simmering since the very beginning of Tocque-ville's tenure, and whose most intense phase came between May 1816 and the beginning of 1817.

It was on May 4, 1816, that Jean-Paul Didier led a peasant uprising in an attempt to seize the city of Grenoble. The Didier conspiracy, so-called, was easily suppressed by General Donnadieu and the prefect Montlivault,[13] but when the first news of the disturbance reached Paris it took Decazes, the minister of police, by surprise. Since he did not know the real scope of the incident, he ordered precautionary measures in the Eastern departments. When the minister's instructions reached Dijon, Tocqueville was out making the rounds of the Semur arron-dissement, and the secretary-general of the prefecture—having sum-moned the commandant of the military division, the public prosecutor of the royal court, the police commissioner, and the captain of the gendarmerie—had some Bonapartists arrested, including a former pre-siding judge and a former public prosecutor of the court of appeals, and sent a battalion of the National Guard to Auxonne. When Tocque-ville returned, he approved these spectacular measures. He sent in a

[11]154 AP I(c) 4.
[12]National Archives, Lachenède file.
[13]Grenoble conspiracy file: 154 AP I(c) 3.

report on the general situation in his department (May 17), and on June 4, asking to have certain individuals removed, said he believed that in Grenoble "a few scatterbrains started off too early," but that this had only "retarded the general conspiracy."

Decazes's inquiries had shown him that the Grenoble conspiracy was no more, in actual fact, than an isolated incident without deeper roots, and he decided to play it down in the eyes of the public. On May 20, he expressed his regret at the "fuss" made by the strict measures taken in the Côte-d'Or, deplored the prefect's "lack of prudence," and reproached him for having tried to tell the police what to do. When Tocqueville warned of the danger of a general insurrection, Decazes called him a "dreamer" and insinuated that he was "afraid."

A prefect of the Restoration, more a vassal of the king than a modern-day civil servant, two of whose relatives were ministers—one of them the minister of justice—and who was, most important, the grandson-in-law of M. de Malesherbes, would hardly be inclined to make retractions at the orders of a man like Decazes. Tocqueville, through his uncle Damas, often transmitted what were really political bulletins to the Duc d'Angoulême, the king's nephew, and now he informed him of the minister's change of position during this little crisis. Quite maladroitly, the Duc d'Angoulême, without withdrawing his favor from Tocqueville, spoke of the affair to Decazes, revealing his sources. It is easy to imagine that the minister would hold a substantial grudge against Tocqueville for this.

From July 1816 on, Decazes was clearly looking for a quarrel to pick with the prefect of the Côte-d'Or. The discovery of a tricolored flag (or, according to other reports, of a flagstaff) caused him to charge Tocqueville with negligence. A jury's acquittal of officials in power during the Hundred Days made him question Tocqueville's zeal.

Then, in September, came the dissolution of the Chamber of Deputies, that Chamber which had been elected in August 1825 with so large and unexpected an ultraroyalist majority that Louis XVIII had dubbed it the *Chambre introuvable*— the incredible Chamber. The policies of the ultras were opposed by the government and by the allied occupation forces, and the king, under pressure, was obliged to dissolve the Chamber and call for new elections. It was made quite clear to Tocqueville that he would be judged by the results of the forthcoming elections in his department.

Three of the department's deputies in the *Chambre introuvable*— all ultras—presented themselves again as candidates to the electors: Brenet, de Grosbois, and de Vauroy. The first, a doctor from Dijon, was particularly out of favor with the government, which could, in Tocqueville's opinion, have accepted the election of the third. In accordance with the system then prevailing, each arrondissement's electoral college was to propose a number of candidates equal to the number of deputies to be elected; the electoral college of the department, which made the final choice, was obliged to select two of the three deputies it chose from the lists drawn up in the arrondissements. In the colleges of both the arrondissements and the department, an election could be won only with the yea votes of a majority of the eligible electors. (There were relatively few eligible electors; only those who paid substantial direct taxes each year had the right to vote.)

Neither Beaune nor Dijon, among the colleges of the arrondissements, was able to gather a quorum; the other arrondissements put forward ultraroyalists. The departmental college convened 183 out of the 243 registered electors—111 ultras, 58 "Jacobins," and 14 pro-government ministerialists. No party by itself could muster the 122 votes needed for a majority, and behind-the-scenes negotiations were necessary. The prefect undertook these with the help of the commandant of the military division, a relative of his. For his part, Police Commissioner Jollivet endeavored to make sure their efforts came to nothing.

From Tocqueville's own account, which is somewhat vague, it would appear that Carnot, in the name of the liberals, would have agreed to support de Vauroy, together with Tocqueville himself, who had been proposed by the Châtillon college, and a bourgeois who could have had the support of the ultras. But the royalist electors insisted on de Grosbois; the only concession they would make was for Comte Wahl to replace Brenet.

In these circumstances, no representatives to the Chamber could be chosen; Tocqueville and Jollivet refused to take responsibility for the result. Decazes, of course, had no confidence in the prefect's good faith—and no doubt he was right. Tocqueville, however, was not replaced immediately. He himself—noting how much the public feeling in his department had improved—seemed to think that he would remain in Dijon for some time. But in February 1817 rumors circulating through the town hinted strongly at his replacement. Tocqueville complained to the government on the nineteenth, the very day on which, in Paris, he was appointed to Metz. He wrote a letter of resignation full of bitterness, but after consulting the Duc d'Angoulême, did not send it. He tried to obtain an appointment as state councillor in recompense for the transfer, but in vain.

Laîné, whose relations with the prefect had always remained courteous, refused his colleague Decazes's request for a pure and simple dismissal, and though there was certainly some disfavor involved, the punishment remained light, Metz being a prefecture of the same class as Dijon. Tocqueville had deceived himself in thinking he could brave the animosity of the minister of police. Nevertheless, he had solid backers in the court and in the entourage of the Duc de Richelieu, the first minister: his aunt Montboissier; the Damases, who had the confidence of the dauphin and the dauphine; his brother-in-law Rosanbo, a peer of France; and his friend Madame de Montcalm, the Duc de Richelieu's sister. Naturally, these protectors did not let anyone forget that the prefect of Dijon was the grandson-in-law of M. de Malesherbes. To dismiss him, therefore, would not have been an easy undertaking, and of all the ultraroyalist prefects of 1814 and 1815, Tocqueville remained the only one, in 1820, who had not been discharged by Decazes.[14]

Tocqueville was installed as prefect in Metz on March 25, 1817, in the midst of a food supply crisis.[15] The department of the Moselle was particularly hard hit: it was trying to support the weight of a heavy Prussian occupation, and hailstorms had practically wiped out the harvests in the cantons of Longwy, Longuyon, and Sarreguemines. The people living in the countryside were in some cases reduced to eating grass.[16]

Lachenède had made no attempt to ward off the famine, which had already been threatening the year before. But in Metz, the mayor, M. de Turmel, had taken initiatives in November of 1816 that could serve as an example: he had appealed to the investors in the town and they had lent him 187,000 francs at five percent, a loan guaranteed by municipal securities. He had thus been able to buy grains, set up *ateliers de charité,* and give out soup. Tocqueville extended these measures to the whole department. A new company of investors advanced 410,000 francs, guaranteed by an additional ten centimes on the tax rate. With this working capital, Tocqueville contracted for 1,100,000 francs' worth of provisions including rice, whose nutritive value he praised, as well as the more familiar grains. He also obtained a grant from the

---

[14]Private archives, correspondence with the ministers. On the dismissal of ultra prefects by Decazes, see Nicholas Richardson, *The French Prefectoral Corps, 1814–1830* (Cambridge, 1966).

[15]*Mémoires* and private archives (154 AP I[c] 11 and 12).

[16]On the state of the department at that time, see H. Contamine, *Metz et la Moselle de 1814 à 1870* (Nancy, 1932).

royal purse. He endeavored to funnel the grains toward the less well provisioned markets, selling them at or below cost depending on the situation. These measures and his surveillance of the way they were carried out were a provocation to the merchants who supplied the occupation forces, and they threatened to suspend deliveries of oats to the Prussians: But very soon they realized that the new prefect was not the man to back away from enforcing his arbitrary measures and that they would quickly find themselves in prison. They gave in.

On the local level, Tocqueville had organized this effort to manage the crisis with a good deal of care. He prohibited the free movement of beggars—illegal but tolerated in practice—and in each commune formed a commission made up of the curé and three taxpayers to tax the well-to-do. Within the cantons, the visitors to the poor apportioned relief and kept the administration informed. In addition, the prefect arranged for the able-bodied poor to be employed in large-scale repair projects on local roads. By the end of the year, the crisis had been contained and the investors repaid, and by 1819, the Moselle was exporting grains. Nevertheless, Tocqueville was sorry to see the relief organization he had begun, and which he had hoped to turn into a permanent institution, fall into disuse because of lack of zeal on the part of the leading citizens. He also expressed his regret that he could not impose his plan for repairing the roads on the communes without first negotiating their acceptance.[17]

The energy Tocqueville displayed appears to have won the new prefect the respect of certain powerful men in the department. The most important of these, too eminent not to be independent—even in the departmental council to which they had been elected—understood that Tocqueville was a man to be reckoned with. For some of them, like de Wendel, monarchical loyalism made good relations easier; it is more surprising to see that an unshakable opponent like Bouvier-Dumolard managed to maintain good relations with him and actually contributed money to the construction of a road—though it is true that the road served his own lands.

For the rest, even the smallest measures taken by the administration were frustrated at a lower level by the mediocrity of the local officials in the communes. The Moselle, like many other departments, suffered from the ineptness of its mayors, a malady aggravated in this case by the fact that the district of Sarreguemines was German-speaking (which didn't stop the government, despite Tocqueville's warnings,

[17]154 AP I(c) 9 and 10.

from appointing to the district a sub-prefect who didn't know a word of the language!). Shortly after his arrival, Tocqueville appointed several prominent citizens as inspectors, with the intention of throwing some light on municipal accounting procedures and putting a halt to illegal police arrests. He would have liked to make permanent inspectors of them—benevolent overseers of the mayors—and Laîné had to remind him that this would be against the law. Whether it was a matter of the communal roads or the municipal police, Tocqueville's projects sometimes seemed to require and attempt to create a rural aristocracy in the English mold, which neither the institutions nor the social milieu of the Moselle appeared to permit . . .

Even though he asserted the contrary, his experience at Dijon had not made the impetuous prefect any more circumspect, and when Decazes—who was now minister of the interior—began getting rid of Tocqueville's colleagues, he had to be rescued once again by the Duc d'Angoulême from the resentful minister, who would have been happy to add him to his game bag. But thereafter Decazes stopped hounding Tocqueville and sought a reconciliation; the minister began to confide in him. Shortly before Decazes's fall from power he met privately with Tocqueville in Paris, confessed that he had been wounded by the denunciation the prefect had made to the Duc d'Angoulême at the time of the Didier affair, and invited him to dine with Abel François Villemain, the man of letters, then a brilliant young professor at the Sorbonne. Nonetheless, Tocqueville was relieved when Decazes fell from power, after the murder of the Duc de Berry in February 1820, and Richelieu returned. Under the Villèle ministry, when Chateaubriand attained a position of power, Tocqueville conceived great hopes of a peerage, hopes that were dashed by a trip to Paris in January 1823. "I should have been able to look upon M. de Chateaubriand's coming into power as a happy event for me . . . but I knew he would turn his attention only to what concerned him personally," he was to write bitterly in his *Mémoires*. Eventually, against his will, Tocqueville left the Moselle in July 1823, after six years. Transferred from the Côte-d'Or in 1817 because he did not get along well with the people under his administration, he was removed in 1823 because he got along too well with the people of the Moselle. Villèle wanted to avoid the possibility that in the elections of 1824, de Serre, then ambassador to Naples, would be elected in this department, where his powerful friend de Wendel was working for him. Villèle needed a prefect who would consent to fight energetically against the de Serre candidacy; the ties between Tocqueville and de Wendel made it doubtful that, despite his

26

ultra convictions, Tocqueville would apply himself to this task, which was subsequently performed with success by Balsac, who followed him in the position.[18]

Not without a feeling of bitterness, Tocqueville thus witnessed the exhumation of an earlier request he had made, to be closer to Paris; he was appointed prefect of the Somme.

Tocqueville was the only Restoration prefect of Metz to leave his personal mark on the regional administration. Nevertheless, although the Moselle did not display the lively passions of the Côte-d'Or, it was not, for all that, a "good" department: the population as a whole was more resigned to the monarchy than enthusiastic about it. The presence of garrisons and numerous half-pay officers (about nine hundred) made constant surveillance necessary. Tocqueville's stay there was at a period of great activity on the part of the secret societies, and the prefect suspected the local elements of having liaisons with Paris by way of the stagecoach drivers. He sometimes went to bed wondering if Bouvier-Dumolard would take his place in the prefecture during the night.

But with the large landowners, the iron merchants, and the industrialists in the department Tocqueville shared common ground in their mutual concern for economic prosperity. Tocqueville, with the help of the departmental council, did his best to repair the damage done by the occupation and develop the various sectors of the economy.

At that time, agriculture was by far the most important. Tocqueville resurrected the agricultural association that had been created in the year X; although it was short-lived, the association did recommend measures which the prefect tried to put into practice: establishing the boundaries of the common land, importing better vine stocks for the vineyards, distributing seeds for reforestation, selecting stud horses to improve a decimated stock. Tocqueville also recommended introducing forage crops and chemical fertilizers, and expanding the cultivation of potatoes and beets—and he would have liked to introduce the growing of tobacco. He also wanted customs duties to be modified to allow wines to be exported to the Prussian provinces. He encouraged the introduction of insurance against hail and fire, for which the liberal industrialist Chédeaux was an active propagandist.

Though agriculture was the most important activity in the Moselle, industry was much less negligible here than in the Côte-d'Or. The iron merchants played a significant role in the society. François de Wendel,

---

[18]154 AP I(c) 11 and the *Mémoires*.

the most prominent figure in the departmental council, mined iron ore, relied on coal, and used the recently discovered technique of rolling iron. The cloth industry, on the other hand, was in decline as a result of the sharp reduction in the sheep population at the time of the rains of 1816 and because the coming of peace had slowed down the manufacture of uniforms and shakos; Chédeaux's embroidery shops employed eight hundred workers and exported goods as far away as America; the crystal glassworks and the potteries established in Sarreguemines by the Bavarian Urtzschneider sometimes lacked outlets.

Although Tocqueville could do no more than suggest the measures the government might take to facilitate exports, he endeavored, with the consent of his departmental council, to develop the transportation system. He was not able to bring to completion the plans he had for connecting the Moselle to the Marne or the Saône. But with the help of an active chief engineer, Bouquet, he applied himself to improving the roads; he formed a network of more than two hundred kilometers of departmental roads, and subsidized the construction or maintenance of numerous smaller ones. He would have liked these work projects to be inspected by the neighboring large landowners—once again, in emulation of the English; to carry these projects out, he reestablished the *prestations en nature,* a direct tax in labor imposed on the inhabitants of the communes, who were required to work several days each year maintaining the roads. It would appear that where the road system was concerned his administration achieved important results that did not have the "sporadic" character sometimes pointed to by his critics.

Under Tocqueville's administration, too, and through his initiative and that of Turmel, the mayor of Metz, a savings bank was established, the third in France.

There was another area of particular interest to Tocqueville—primary education.[19] This was the time of the polemical debates between the proponents of *enseignement mutuel,* reputed to be "liberal," in which older pupils called monitors taught the less advanced pupils under the guidance of the instructors, and the proponents of *enseignement simultané,* practiced in particular by the brothers of the *Doctrine chrétienne,* in which the instructor taught the pupils himself and had them all do the same exercises at the same time. The controversy did not stop Tocqueville from supporting and subsidizing, in 1818, a society that established a *mutuel* school in Metz; in his *Mémoires* he insists that his mind had not been made up and that he supported both

[19]154 AP I(c) 11 and the *Mémoires.*

of the rival teaching methods. He also concerned himself with the education of the Jews in Metz, who were still not well assimilated into the nation, and tried to give them the means to escape the ignorance and poverty of the ghetto. And in 1821 he established a normal school, the second teacher-training institution in France. He seems to have taken the matter of popular education very much to heart: he scolded the minister of the interior, Corbière, roundly for having deliberately tried to make sure the people remained uneducated. Well disposed as he was to the University (as the entire lay establishment of secondary and higher education in France was called) Tocqueville nonetheless kept up good relations with the clergy, retaining a very fine memory of Bishop Jauffret as "wise and tolerant toward everyone."

He could, for that matter, plume himself in the eyes of the government for his electoral successes, the criterion by which the ministers of every regime judged their prefects.

It is true that the first elections during his tenure in the Moselle were not at all favorable. In 1818, two liberals, Rolland and General Grenier, were elected along with the moderates Wendel and Simon. As in the Côte-d'Or, Decazes's agents seem to have schemed against the prefect, whom they suspected of supporting Turmel, the ultraroyalist mayor of Metz. With Decazes's fall from power, the expectations of the ministry were once again satisfied by the prefect's choices. Thanks to the double-vote law of 1820, which gave the richest electors (the top twenty-five percent) two votes, one in the college of their arrondissement and one in the departmental college, not only the three deputies from the department (Turmel, d'Hausen, and Ducherray) but soon the deputies from the arrondissements as well were "good royalists."

To obtain such satisfactory results, the prefect embroiled himself deeply in the electoral battles—to the extent that, in 1817, he wrote a pamphlet anonymously and had it published without observing the required legal formalities. There followed the tracking down of the printer and the discovery of the author, who had written his manuscript on paper from the prefecture . . . All of which led to a reprimand from the ministry. As for the civil servants, under threat of punishment they were obliged to promote the government's candidates in the elections: "A government that wishes to preserve itself must . . . endeavor to steer the choice in the direction most conducive to the good of the State and it has the right to require that all civil servants dependent on it contribute to achieving its goals." A district in which the electors voted the wrong way could expect to be punished. Such was the case with Sarreguemines after the election of Semellé in 1820: the town's garrison of horse guards was withdrawn and with it the profits the town derived from the troop (naturally, as Tocqueville wrote in this connection, "the Germans must be guided with a firm hand"). The secretary of the Metz prefecture, Viville, writing to Tocqueville after his departure, paid him the following tribute: "The best things you did for us here were things that you were not ordered to do and that were not even pointed out to you by the government, and for a long time to come we will continue to feel the happy effects."[20] Tocqueville's administration appears to have benefited the department in spite of the arbitrary acts that La Minerve, the journal of liberal opinion, denounced—and perhaps exaggerated. Certainly it resembled the administration of an intendant of the Ancien Régime more than it did that of a prefect dutifully following the instructions of his ministry.

The Somme, to which the prefect was now assigned against his wishes, was reputed to be a "good" department. Tocqueville found it apathetic; he appears to have been somewhat bored there. The only electoral problems were the struggles of the ministerialists against the defection from the ultraroyalist party of Chateaubriand's partisans. Tocqueville loyally served Villèle, the ultra minister of finance who was now effectively head of the government, though he didn't much care for him.

But he cared even less for Corbière, the minister of the interior, and disobeyed him openly: he refused to withdraw a decree that prohibited laying straw roofs on new houses, issued by Tocqueville because of the danger of fire. Although he could not stop Corbière from discontinuing all subventions for teacher training in his department, he obtained from Monsignor Frayssinous, the minister of church affairs and public education, an equivalent amount under another rubric of the budget.

But the most paradoxical aspect of the administration of this prefect, a royalist and a good Catholic, was his almost total lack of rapport with the Congrégation, the powerful lay Catholic society with ties to the Jesuits.[21]

He grumbles that a mission preached by Père Guyon has extolled the "intolerant zeal" of women and that the government officials have

[20]154 AP I(c) 14.
[21]See Guillaume de Bertier de Sauvigny, Ferdinand de Bertier et le mystère de la Congrégation.

been made to feel morally obligated to take part in the mission's grand religious procession. "I took a little trip to Paris myself," he adds, "and became rather seriously ill there." His relations with the Jesuits of Saint-Acheul—who sought to force the school of medicine in Amiens to take on the doctor of their house as a teacher even though he had a clouded legal record—were far from perfect. And he endeavored to clear the Duc d'Angoulême and even Charles X from the suspicion of having sympathies for the *Congrégation*, though the general opinion was that they did.

The accession of Charles X gave Tocqueville strong reason to hope that he might leave Amiens, and the sudden death of the prefect of Versailles, Destouches, made it possible. Tocqueville was immediately, in June 1826, appointed to replace him.

Tocqueville took up his duties in Seine-et-Oise at once: "For the first time in twelve years, a change of prefecture was gratifying to me. I had always wanted to be at Seine-et-Oise; it brought me closer to my own interests at the same time that it permitted me to continue in a kind of work that I enjoyed, with occupations necessary to my turn of mind."

For that matter, this change satisfied a desire of long standing. Chateaubriand, who thought he was already the prime minister, had promised Tocqueville the post at the time of Field Marshal Gand's return from exile in 1814. Versailles was no ordinary prefecture; it was sometimes called the first in France. Baron Capelle, Tocqueville's successor and one of the most respected of the king's councillors, left the Versailles prefecture to join the Polignac ministry. Tocqueville himself was considered for this ministry at the time it was being formed, but was passed over—it was felt that he would be "afraid"— in favor of Baron d'Haussez, who had, moreover, acquired some familiarity with maritime problems when he was at Bordeaux.

The Seine-et-Oise's importance was due not only to the fact that it was a large and prosperous department; its prefect was also a sort of amphibian—half administrator, half courtier. The title of *gentilhomme de la chambre* bestowed on Tocqueville simply validated the existing state of affairs. Even though the dilapidated château was not suitable for long visits, the king came here every year to renew his ties with his good town, in the manner of the Ancien Régime: "Everyone in the town was admitted to greet him upon his arrival . . . He reviewed the garrison, went out for a drive through the park in an open barouche, and ended the day with a dinner at the Grand Trianon.

The people were allowed to walk around his table during the meal."[22]
In the autumn, the king hunted in the Versailles woods. There were
other princely residences in the department: Villeneuve-l'Etang, which
the Duchesse d'Angoulême had bought from Maréchal Soult; Rosny,
which belonged to the Duchesse de Berry and whose chapel contained
her husband's heart; and above all Saint-Cloud, the monarch's summer
residence, to which the prefect would come every Sunday to pay court
and perform a semblance of his official duties.

What was more, not only was the prefect now closer to his properties in Normandy and Brittany, and to his wife, who continued to
make her home in Paris, but he was far from being a stranger in his
new department. He had once owned the Château de Verneuil—as we
have noted—and had been mayor of the commune. His brother-in-
law, Louis de Rosanbo, a member of the Chamber of Peers with whom
he had ties of affection, owned the Château du Mesnil near Fontenay-
Saint-Père, not far from Mantes; his other brother-in-law, Le Peletier
d'Aunay, lived in Mareil, near Montfort-l'Amary; while his cousin
Molé's residence was the magnificent Champlâtreux. Thus the sessions
of the departmental council were also the occasion for family reunions.
The majority of the council was of liberal tendencies, but all its
business was conducted by people of the same social milieu and the
head of the opposition was none other than Le Peletier d'Aunay. At
the end of the 1827 session, the departmental council sang the prefect's
praises.

For that matter, Tocqueville's partisan zeal had cooled: his ultra
sentiments had been moderated by disappointment and misgivings, and
he was now fifty-five years old. In spite of his age, however, he made
his traditional tour on horseback, was struck by the development of
the department he had left twelve years before, particularly by the
number of factories built over rivers and streams, and noted that the
functioning of the administration was, on the whole, satisfactory. He
was therefore able to devote some time to the pleasures of society, and
he entertained in the prefecture with the sort of ostentation he enjoyed.
Despite his efforts, however, the two societies of Versailles—the nobility of the *quartier* Saint-Louis and the bourgeoisie of the *quartier*
Notre-Dame—gathered, by tacit consent, in different salons.[23]

For the moment, the prefect's main preoccupation was with the
preparations for the election of November 17–24, 1827, Villèle having

[22]*Mémoires.*
[23]Duchesse d'Abrantès, *Mémoires sur la Restauration ou Souvenirs historiques sur cette époque, la révolution de Juillet et les années du règne de Louis-Philippe Ier* (Paris, 1835–1836), vol. 6, 460–62.

appealed to the country to support him in his fight against the liberals who sided with Chateaubriand in his defection. Tocqueville had no illusions about the electoral colleges of the arrondissements, which would be certain to name liberals. He thought, however, that the departmental college would favor the government. But here, too, the opposition triumphed (though by only one vote, it is true, for one of the seats). A crowning disgrace was the fact that one of the men elected was an old gentleman who had refused to accept the support of the administration and had become a turncoat on the eve of the election.[24]

Tocqueville had been elevated to the peerage on November 4. The duties of a prefect having been declared incompatible with those of a peer, he gave up his post, in January 1828, to Baron Capelle.

He was sorry to leave Versailles; he liked his job and the idea of public debate intimidated him. He no longer had much desire for a political career, after having considered, in 1821, becoming a candidate for deputy from the Manche and, in 1823, from the Moselle, and having sought the peerage itself at the time of his appointment to Amiens and then at the time of Charles X's coronation. His son Alexis concludes in a melancholy tone: "Now my father has his peerage. He badly wanted it and earnestly requested it four years ago. This time he didn't seek it at all and now he finds himself thrown in with a whole batch of others. Such is the way of this world. He expressed his disapproval of the measure before it was taken; he hasn't changed his opinion since, and I'm convinced he's right."[25]

One fact underlines the change in him. In the Chamber of Peers at that time there were three groups, one made up of the pure royalists (led by the Duc d'Havré), the second of the right center (led by the Duc de Mortemart), and one of the left (led by Barbé-Marbois). Tocqueville refused to join the first, allying himself with the second instead (he didn't join it formally because of scruples concerning Villèle, who had raised him to the peerage).

For that matter, he had no intention whatsoever of being inactive or silent in the Chamber. He frequently spoke, either on economic problems (the works in the ports of Le Havre or Cherbourg, for example) or on political questions. A member of the committee charged with drafting municipal and departmental laws, he published a pamphlet expressing his own opinions.[26] He told the Chamber that public education should be in the hands of the sovereign. He fought

---

[24]154 AP I(c) 15.
[25]Letter to Kergorlay dated November 23, 1827, *O.C.* XIII, 1: 118.
[26]*De la Charte provinciale* (Paris, 1829).

the Villèlists on the matter of regulating elections. He was not against Charles X's "Martignac experiment"—when Martignac, an ultra turned moderate, was appointed minister of the interior and became, without having the title of prime minister, head of the government. He was upset to see Polignac, "ultra of the ultras," come to power, though he had some faith that the more moderate ministers, Chabrol and Courvoisier, would restrain him.

But despite everything, a Tocqueville had to remain a loyal vassal of the king. In 1829 he agreed to go to Valognes as president of the electoral college and his speech, which has been preserved, is an appeal for loyalty to the monarch. But he was not able to prevent the college of Valognes from electing a Bonapartist, Colonel de Bricqueville, his son Hippolyte's brother-in-law. In the departmental college, two rightists out of four just barely managed to get elected . . .[27]

The revolution of 1830 deprived him of his peerage. "After seeing so many hopes disappointed, so many changes in my way of life, and so many illusions destroyed, I felt the need to withdraw into the gentleness of family feelings in order to rest from the disappointing spectacle of human passions." Since he was to live until 1856, he would enjoy a long retirement. Widowed in 1836, he alternated between visits with his children and stays in Paris, in Lannion, and then in Clairoix, not far from Compiègne, in a modest residence where his household was managed by Madame Guermarquer, whom he secretly married at the end of his life. Intellectual concerns were important to him, and centered on the great drama of his life, the French Revolution. They resulted in the publication, in 1847, of his *Histoire philosophique du règne de Louis XV,* followed by his *Coup d'oeil sur le règne de Louis XVI* —works of a cultivated man, but informed by a rather commonplace and tedious philosophy. The *Mémoires,* also written at the end of his life and still largely unpublished, best reveal the liveliness of the former prefect.

"What distinguishes the nobility of the Restoration from that of the latter part of the nineteenth century is the role it played in the service of the State, a role regarded as both a privilege and a duty." This comment by Guillaume de Bertier de Sauvigny about the prefects of that time is certainly applicable to Comte Hervé. Having entered, through his marriage, what was by the end of the Ancien Régime the

---

[27]Tocqueville's speech to the electoral college is in the Tocqueville Archives (unnumbered file).

very small class of *ministrables*— those whose rank in the nobility gave them some prospect of being named ministers of state—he saw his bond as vassal to the Bourbons strengthened by the sacrifice of the Malesherbes. And this gentle, courteous man claimed for himself and his family the right to serve the State in his proper position in the hierarchy of public office. Ambitious and ostentatious, he freely spent his fortune in the service of the king. But the government interposed itself between him and the sovereign, a government that sometimes included cousins or peers but sometimes also upstarts whose orders he was quite prepared to disregard. Even when he was willing to work with the ministers, he could not stomach simply being their tool. These prefects of the early years of the Restoration kept alive the spirit of independence of the intendants of the Ancien Régime, or of Napoleon's prefects—"those little despots." Around 1820 they would be replaced by docile civil servants in the modern style.

What was unusual about Tocqueville was that he preserved this independence almost to the end of the Restoration. Insofar as the ultraroyalism of 1815 was more a matter of temperament than of doctrine, mingling love for the sovereign with a love for the old aristocratic freedoms, he was essentially an ultraroyalist. But when the ultras dwindled to no more than a clique of the court and the Church he lost his enthusiasm for public service and retired, disenchanted, in 1830.

There has been some attempt, and with good reason, to discover to what extent Alexis de Tocqueville owed his ideas to his father. The question is not an easy one to answer: as he distanced himself intellectually from his family, Alexis was all the more affectionate and respectful toward them, and tended to conceal any differences. He was not at all a man to nurse grievances.

Some analyses have maintained that Comte Hervé's *Charte provinciale* appears to be the source of his son's ideas about decentralization. This seems unlikely, for the genesis of these ideas can be traced during the course of his trip to America.[28] And it was King Charles X, uneasy about the plans to decentralize the royal administration, who had the elder Tocqueville appointed a member of the study commission created by Martignac. In the booklet in which he sums up his ideas, Hervé de Tocqueville asserts that one must refrain from creating new institutions and be content with "bringing the existing institutions into harmony

[28]See Chapter 10 below, 148–63.

with the principles of the political Charter." This proved to mean the election of local bodies of prominent figures whose only function would be to deliberate, and all of whose deliberations would be submitted to the representative of the king. The king alone could determine what action was to be taken. The royal power would thus remain intact, but in the case of a conflict with the Chambers, the king could perhaps look to these secondary, local bodies for support. In all of this, the former prefect is clearly visible.

As we have already said, in 1847 Comte Hervé was to publish his *Histoire philosophique du règne de Louis XV* and after it his *Coup d'oeil sur le règne de Louis XVI.* His intent was obviously to try to understand the origins of the Revolution; certain themes seem to foreshadow his son's *Ancien Régime:* the evolution of the mores, the role of the *philosophes,* the decline of the nobility. But these similarities are superficial. The work, largely narrative and written in the style of the eighteenth century, gives a prominent place to the court and foreign affairs. Above all, it is typical of what Alexis was to call in the *Democracy* "aristocratic history": the king and the governors, their virtues and vices, play the central role. Thus, for example, it was the amorality of the regent—Philip, Duc d' Orléans—that gave rise to the Mississippi Bubble of John Law, the Scots financier, in the years 1718 to 1720. In replacing respect for birth by the love of gold, Law's scheme with its dazzling prospects that ended in widespread disaster perverted the nation and corrupted the nobility. This is a far cry from the rigorous and coherent analyses of Alexis's *Ancien Régime.*

In the moral realm, too, there are perceptible differences between father and son. Although he claimed to be a lover of freedom, Comte Hervé felt no remorse for the arbitrary arrests he had authorized in 1815: "It was the style in those days," he says matter-of-factly in his *Mémoires.* The prospect of a possible illegal order from the Polignac ministry, on the other hand, confronted his magistrate son with the problem of having to refuse to obey. Comte Hervé did not like Polignac but out of obedience to his sovereign urged others to vote for him. A note he wrote on July 30, 1830, shows that he felt his son did not agree with him: "Whatever decision you make, do not make it without careful consideration, because the ministry will respond with harsh measures."

For all that, though it is difficult to perceive and though it is diffused, the influence of father upon son was strong. There was, first of all, his fundamental conception of life. Comte Hervé's career was devoted to public service; on this he spent himself (and his wealth) freely. For his son, this was the true virtue, inherited from aristocratic times—without it, life was tainted with a kind of moral decay.

All things considered, Comte Hervé was, in his youth, as profoundly marked as was Chateaubriand by his association with Malesherbes, whose speech and actions were governed by an endlessly fertile mind. His love of the intellectual life, his requirement of himself that he express this intellectual life in the form of clear ideas and use these ideas to form rules by which to live—this was what Comte Hervé received from Malesherbes and passed on to his son. Alexis de Tocqueville was proud of his grandfather and planned to write his biography. "It is because I am M. de Malesherbes's grandson . . . that I have written these things," he was to say one day. The consciousness of his lineage evolved into his need for a more than ordinarily rigorous intellectual life and this in turn evolved into the recognition that he was thereby in a better position to exercise the public virtues. This ethic was the essence of what he inherited from his father.

3

THE FAMILY MILIEU

HIS *MÉMOIRES*, together with the archives accumulated during his career as prefect that have been handed down to us, help to throw some light on the character of Alexis de Tocqueville's father. We possess only scanty information concerning his mother, Louise de Rosanbo (1772–1836). Her letters were not preserved and we have very little that was written by her. References to her are brief.

"Poor woman—often sick, always melancholy and discontented, a flower too rudely shaken by the tribulations of the Reign of Terror," writes Antoine Rédier![1] And he was probably right to stress the horrible trial she had undergone at the age of twenty—prison, the daily roll call of the condemned, most of her own family taken off to the scaffold. We have already described her incurable nervous agitation.[2] And yet with the strength of her youth she fought back during the years that followed, and it was not until she was close to forty that she became unremittingly subject to a tendency to neurasthenia and withdrawal into herself which lasted until the day in January 1836 that "she succumbed after twenty years of misery," as Alexis wrote to his cousin de Grancey.[3] But the sadness of the family home, to which Alexis alludes in a letter from America to his brother Edouard,[4] was only intermittent during the First Empire. At Verneuil, the chatelaine visited the poor, arranged for her doctor to treat the sick,

[1]Rédier, *M. de Tocqueville*, 31.
[2]See page 8.
[3]Unpublished letter to Madame de Grancey dated January 11, 1836, de Grancey Archives.
[4]Letter to his brother Edouard dated January 20, 1832, in the Beinecke Library, Yale University.

and generally involved herself in the lives of the people. The château was the scene of gatherings that were not exclusively plunged into a gloomy contemplation of the past. New books were discussed passionately, there were games of charades, and Hervé de Tocqueville's *Mémoires* describe Chateaubriand as a merry guest disguising himself as an old woman to await the return of the master of the house. In 1814, Madame de Tocqueville followed her husband to the prefecture at Angers after the second Restoration at Beauvais. She settled in Paris around 1817, and it was at about this time that she began to appear chronically ill. In 1831, Alexis thanked her for two letters she had written to him in America, as though this had been an effort almost beyond her strength,[5] and Louis de Kergorlay admired her for tending the aged Abbé Lesueur in his last illness. The fragile health of both Edouard and Alexis could well have been inherited from their mother, along with the former's tendency to neurasthenia and the latter's constant anxiety. The ever-alert sensitivity of the author of the *Democracy* appears to have very little in common with Comte Hervé's bold confidence.

Like her brother Louis de Rosanbo, Madame de Tocqueville was apparently animated by a royalism and a Catholicism that were ardent and closely interrelated, her kind of royalism being that of the Restoration salons—much less subtle than that of the politicians, comments Hyde de Neuville, who was very probably a frequent visitor at the Tocqueville house. Quite naturally, she was at the center of a family scene that struck young Alexis and that he described on two occasions many years later, once to Lady Thereza Lewis and once to his friend Corcelle:

As though I were back there again now, I remember a certain evening in the château where my father was living at the time and where a large number of our close relatives had gathered for a family party. My mother, who had a strong, sweet voice, began to sing a song that was famous at the time of our civil disturbances and that told about the misfortunes of King Louis XVI and his death. When she stopped, everyone was crying, not so much over the many individual afflictions all had suffered, not even over the many relatives lost in the civil war and on the scaffold, but over the fate of this man who had died more than fifteen years before and whom most of those shedding tears for him had never seen. But this man had been the king.[6]

[5]Letter to his mother dated June 19, 1831, Beinecke Library.
[6]Letter to Lady Lewis dated May 6, 1857.

The ballad was the *Troubadour béarnais,* which dated from the captivity of Louis XVI in the Temple. That it was still being sung sometime around 1808 attests to a loyalty of feeling that stands well above mere fashion in this closed world of the nobility:[7]

> *Un troubadour béarnais*
> *Les yeux inondés de larmes*
> *A ses montagnards chantait*
> *Ce refrain, source d'alarmes:*
> *Louis, le fils d'Henri,*
> *Est prisonnier dans Paris.*

> *[A troubadour of Béarn,*
> *his eyes filled with tears,*
> *sang to his mountain people*
> *this alarming refrain:*
> *Louis, son of Henri,*
> *is captive in Paris.]*

This scene created lasting memories in the mind of a child not yet three at the time—fifteen years after the king's death—and only eight when the family left Verneuil, where the scene took place. But in 1853 he would also remember that in those days people had "generous and disinterested political passions and wanted something more than peace and quiet at any price,"[8] and that he himself shared his family's enthusiasm during the first Restoration, helping to knock over Napoleon's statue and shouting "Long live the king!" He was not yet nine years old.

Madame de Tocqueville believed in the possibility of a religious and legitimist reconquest of France. Her confessor was Abbé Legris-Duval, chaplain of the *Congrégation* and father of the Faith—that is to say, a clandestine Jesuit. She was delighted with a sermon preached at a mission at Angers that assumed the character of a ceremony of atonement for the crimes of the Revolution.[9] Later, in 1830, Henrion, the son of a secretary of the exiled Comte de Provence and a friend of Alexis's who had been more or less adopted by his father in Metz, wrote him a vehement letter urging him to refuse the oath required

---

[7]Tocqueville also wrote of this incident in a letter to Corcelle dated December 3, 1853, *O.C.* XV, 2: 86.

[8]Letter cited, to Corcelle.

[9]Tocqueville cartulary.

of magistrates by the government of July. Alexis was furious that Henrion had sent this letter by way of his mother, and Henrion himself admitted that he had seen this as a way of giving more weight to his objurgations:[10] Madame de Tocqueville—like her brother Louis de Rosanbo, who resigned from the peerage—must have been hostile to any compromise with "Philippe"—the Bourbon loyalists' contemptuous sobriquet for Louis-Philippe of the House of Orléans, who supplanted Charles X, last of the Bourbon kings, after the revolution of July 1830. The following year, she repeated in a letter to her son some derogatory salon talk about Americans and he, in his reply, strongly objected to this superficial and false view of the people he was living among.[11]

It seems, then, that Tocqueville's mother was more intransigent in religion and politics than Comte Hervé. As we have seen, the senior Tocqueville disapproved of the missions and did not like the Jesuits, whom he accused of being intriguers and morally lax (reserving his admiration for the members of the Society of Jesus who brought civilization to Paraguay). Yet Comte Hervé, in his *Histoire philosophique,* was just as severe toward the Jansenist excesses of the preceding century. In essence, he maintained the gallican tradition of the men of the Parlement in the eighteenth century, jealously guarding the independence of the French Church and the French King against any ultramontane encroachments from Rome. The tradition was still alive for many of his contemporaries, the "good royalists."

His father's various occupations and his mother's withdrawal into herself certainly must have meant that the sickly and sensitive child Alexis de Tocqueville was to some extent deprived of love. But the old tutor attached to the family, Abbé Lesueur, treated him with a tender care to which he responded with deep affection. When Alexis, in Boston, learned of the Abbé's death at the age of nearly eighty, he shut himself up in his room and wrote a heartrending letter to his brother Edouard, the only one who would understand it: "I felt . . . the most lively and painfully sharp grief I have ever felt in my life . . . I loved our good old friend as I loved our father; he always shared our concerns, our worries, our affections, and yet nothing tied him to us but his own wish . . . There is no getting accustomed to the idea of having the support of one's childhood, the friend (and what

[10]Unpublished letters, Beinecke Library.
[11]Letter to his mother, Philadelphia, October 24, 1831, unpublished passage.

a friend!) of one's whole life disappear, just like that . . . a man whose every thought, whose every affection turned on us alone; who seemed to live only for us." And, ending his letter two days later: "I have lost one of the greatest goods in this world. Ten years may pass and this will be just as true as it is today. The more I compare his friendship for us with everything else I know of the same kind, the more I find that it was like nothing else in the world, and yet now it is no longer anything more than a memory."[12]

We have already encountered Abbé Lesueur. Originally from Picardy, in the last years of the Ancien Régime he was young Hervé de Tocqueville's tutor; he looked out for the orphan, who had been entrusted to him by the boy's mother before her death. He was one of the nonjuring priests and had to emigrate, but once he was back in France he attached himself to the family of his old pupil and, so far as we know, never left it. After having brought up Comte Hervé, he became the tutor and confidant of his three sons, and there is no doubt that his favorite was Alexis. He had high ambitions for this youngest son of his adopted family, predicting that he would make himself known as an "enlightened magistrate . . . distinguished orator or . . . celebrated diplomat." When Louis de Kergorlay, Alexis's cousin and friend, attempted to persuade Alexis to adopt a military career as he himself had done, the Abbé protested that it would be a great shame to put such a head under a helmet and resolved to "request Monsieur Loulou to mind his own business."[13]

The Abbé is reputed to have been too old-fashioned, and too indulgent a teacher; he is supposed to have spoiled his pupil. Without mentioning the Abbé specifically, Chateaubriand observed that the future author of the *Democracy* had a more pampered childhood than his own. Given what Chateaubriand says of his childhood at Combourg, this hardly proves that there was excessive laxness at Verneuil. Beaumont is more severe, and perhaps reflects the confidences of his friend.[14] Though if it is possible that this delicate child was allowed to play more than was usual in those days, it would be unfair to blame Abbé Lesueur for the whimsical spelling of the future member of the Academy, which was more a consequence of his casual attitude than of his ignorance. The old tutor denied in advance the imputation that he had neglected his pupil's primary education. When Alexis won the highest prize in rhetoric at the Metz lycée, the Abbé said with assurance

[12]Letter to Edouard dated September 10, 1831, Beinecke Library.
[13]Tocqueville Archives, file 9.
[14]Preface to vol. 5 of his edition of the *Oeuvres Complètes*, 6.

42

że że

that for a long time now he had been preparing the boy for a successful school career. Whatever the case, the tutor himself wrote elegantly in the style of the eighteenth century, knew Greek, and had traveled (during his youth or during his emigration?) in Italy and Germany. It is perhaps thanks to him that Alexis had some early familiarity with Italian, which was not taught at the Metz lycée.

Before all else, of course, this particular tutor would have sought to give his pupil some religious training. And here it would be good to know something of the Abbé's own leanings within the Catholic family. Although there is very little we can be sure of, we can gather something from the Tocqueville library, in which old works survive despite certain losses, works that antedated or were contemporary with Alexis's youth. There are, of course, editions of the great orators (Bossuet, Fléchier, Bourdaloue, Fénelon) and of the moralists of the *grand siècle* (Pascal, La Rochefoucauld, etc.), though there is only one Church Father (St. Augustine) — but the books of Christian education form an austere, if not a Jansenist, group. Abbé Lesueur probably did not instruct his pupil in the Latin commentary to the fourth Gospel of Jansénius, the copy of which bears the Abbé's signature.[15] Among the more clearly educational works, we find the *Idée de la religion chrétienne* by Hersan, a teacher at the Sorbonne, where his Jansenist tendencies caused problems for him; *Les Instructions générales en forme de catéchisme,* which is nothing other than the catechism in four volumes approved by Colbert, the Jansenist bishop of Montpellier; and *La Doctrine chrétienne . . .* by Abbé Lhomond. Though this priest, the long-famous author of *De Viris Illustribus,* does not seem to have been a militant Jansenist, he can hardly be accused of lax morals: "Original sin has cast a heavy darkness over our spirits, and a deep corruption in our hearts. We are born in ignorance and with a strong inclination to evil: these are the two general sources of all our sins. We sin only because we are ignorant of our duties, or because, knowing what they are, we would rather follow our inclinations than our lights."[16] If the young Alexis meditated on this treatise or listened to these lessons and was inspired by them, this could have been the source of a certain pessimistic view he had of human nature, in which our instincts lead us toward evil when the enlightened but difficult exercise of freedom fails to combat them with the support of a conscious recognition of the dignity of man.

---

[15]This fact was pointed out by R. P. Gilbert.
[16]Abbé Lhomond, *Doctrine chrétienne en forme de lectures de piété* (1783), 348.

In any case, the good Abbé was no more concerned with keeping   43
the throne and the altar separate than was Madame de Tocqueville, nor
did he extend Christian charity to the liberals, about whom he wrote,
on September 13, 1822:

All of Europe is infested with this cursed race . . . Ways must be invented
to stop the contagion. There ought to be a leper house in the frozen seas of
Siberia where the sowers of the plague would be shut up; there they would
be subjected to a quarantine lasting not for days but for years. I am convinced
that not one of them would ever return. They would poison one another,
kill one another, eat one another . . . In the middle of the night I would put
them aboard a river steamer that would swiftly take them to Le Havre. There
a ship would be waiting to receive them and take them to their destination.
If a good storm came up, that would cut short the trip . . . Sharks, which
are said to love rotten meat, would make a very good meal of this foul cargo
and then the poor things would die of it . . . [17]

The Abbé may have been deliberately outrageous in this letter in
order to amuse the person it was addressed to. Certainly it could not
serve as a model of tolerance or moderation.

What we know of the three figures who dominated the family
circle, therefore, reveals considerable differences. In Madame de
Tocqueville, a rejection of the present and a passion for a crusade that
would restore everything to the way it was in the past. Comte de
Tocqueville, servant of the king, a good Christian but a gallican,
displays a more pragmatic flexibility. The Abbé remains locked in
anti-liberal spite and an austere piety that are softened, however, by
the man's own tenderness. But these are no more than individual
variations within a milieu that was ultraroyalist, aristocratic, paternalistic toward the people, and little affected by the trends of the time.

We must also remember that Alexis de Tocqueville, being the
youngest son, may have been subject to the influence of his older
brothers. "M. de Tocqueville's father was one of the most reactionary
prefects of the Restoration . . . But there is more: M. de Tocqueville
has a brother who is quite alive, very much alive, and a model of
Carlism." This is how *Le Globe,* on July 5, 1842, introduced its readers
to Alexis de Tocqueville's oldest brother.

Born on October 1, 1797, Hippolyte entered the élite troops of the
king's bodyguard on July 1, 1814, and under the Restoration made a

[17]Tocqueville Archives, file 9.

career for himself in the army. He took part in the Spanish campaign with the rank of captain of dragoons. When he was not posted to the Algiers campaign, he approached the dauphine—Thérèse, wife of the Duc d'Angoulême, the eldest son of Charles X—as she was stepping into her carriage one day and persuaded her to recommend him to General Louis Auguste de Bourmont as an aide-de-camp. Bourmont, however, did not take him, and out of spite Hippolyte quarreled with those of his comrades lucky enough to be a part of the expeditionary force. He left the service on October 15, 1830, having waited, before handing in his resignation, to find out if the July days would start a war in Europe. He was to try in vain, in 1840 and again in 1848, to reenter the army. By his marriage to Emilie Evrard de Belisle de Saint-Rémy, he became the owner of the Château de Nacqueville in the Cotentin, and he was to occupy himself with husbandry, take an interest in maritime problems, occasionally advising his brother in these matters but also harassing him with recommendations for protégés who do not appear, from an examination of the dossiers in the archives, to have been uniformly judicious choices.

His fiery spirit sometimes reminds one of the beginnings of Comte Hervé's career. An ardent legitimist, in 1833 he published the *Lettres aux Normands,* a pamphlet against the July regime which radiates horror of the middle-of-the-road—"the party of hate and fear"—and shows him to be friendlier both to the Bonapartists, whose patriotism he acknowledges, and to the republicans, who own the future but whom he begs to return to the ranks of the legitimists where they will make a place for themselves. This small text to some extent explains, though it doesn't justify, Hippolyte's subsequent political fluctuations. In 1834, he pressed Hyde de Neuville to stand as a candidate in the legislative elections at Cherbourg against his own brother-in-law, Colonel de Bricqueville, an old soldier of the Empire and a fierce enemy of the Bourbons under the Restoration, who had joined the ranks of the dynastic opposition under Louis-Philippe. Nevertheless, in 1842, at a time when he had just induced his brother to take steps to get him back into the army, Hippolyte supported the aged Chateaubriand on his arm when the latter led the French legitimists associated with the young pretender to the throne—Henri, Comte de Chambord and Duc de Bordeaux, the grandson of Charles X—to the meeting with him that Guizot, the conservative constitutional monarchist, caused to be stigmatized by a vote in the Chamber. "What a man!" Alexis groaned, upset by such indiscretions. But the Republic of 1848 allowed Hippolyte to start on a political career. Having converted to the Republic, placing himself firmly to the left within it, Hippolyte, elected a member of the departmental council with the support of his brother, ran in a special legislative election for the Constituent Assembly against Comte Daru, Alexis's political ally and esteemed neighbor, who was the candidate of the party of order, a right-wing party made up of Catholics, Bourbon legitimists, and adherents of Louis-Philippe. He lost rather miserably, garnering only the votes of the "reds"—the left-wing republicans—and particularly those of the workers at the Cherbourg arsenal, whereas the great majority of the peasants in this conservative department voted for his opponent.[18]

Although he insists in a letter that he witnessed the reestablishment of the Empire with joyless resignation, Hippolyte would soon move close to the new power. His two brothers having quarreled after Edouard's public adherence to the regime, he vehemently sided with the latter, and was seen even more frequently than Edouard in social circles close to the imperial court. "Citizen Tocqueville burns to become a senator," Alexis said derisively, though he was furious when, at the Cherbourg fêtes in 1856, his sister-in-law Emilie opened the ball dancing in the same quadrille as His Majesty and was on this occasion called by the title of "Comtesse de Tocqueville," his own wife's title. And it was Emilie, it was this "race of Belisles" whom he blamed: "As far as she's concerned, her husband is like a tenant farm. He has to be made to yield a certain revenue in some way or other. But these days, men in Hippolyte's position don't bear fruit that way except sporadically."[19]

Despite these misadventures, relations between the two brothers remained affectionate. In 1849, when Alexis was minister of foreign affairs, Hippolyte was transformed into a benevolent and zealous secretary. When he was living alone, Alexis had a good deal to do with "the Hippolytes." And before Alexis's death, at Cannes, his brother paid him an extended visit and nursed him attentively. "My poor Hippolyte, what a sorry character, but what a heart of gold!" he wrote in one of his last letters.[20]

The fall of the Empire roused Hippolyte's faith in the Republic. More prudent than he had been in 1848, and using the memory of his

---

[18]On January 7, 1849, in the special election necessitated by the resignation of Reibel, Daru obtained 15,514 votes and Le Marois, another conservative, 9,713, while the progressive republican candidates, Henry and Hippolyte de Tocqueville, obtained only 3,525 and 2,417 votes respectively.

[19]Letter to Beaumont dated January 22, 1858, *O.C.* VIII, 3: 536.

[20]Letter to Beaumont dated February 3, 1849, *O.C.* VIII, 3: 613.

brother to enhance his own position, he became part of the group of senators for life elected by the National Assembly thanks to the alliance of the republicans and the legitimists under Gambetta.

The second brother, Edouard, born in 1800, was closer to Alexis not only in age but also in temperament. For a long time, the brothers were bound to each other by an intellectual intimacy which they did their best to preserve despite their diverging paths in life, and this intimacy was not entirely destroyed by their lively disagreements under the Empire. At the age of sixteen, Edouard, like his older brother, entered upon a career in the army and continued in it until his bad health (he suffered in particular from rheumatoid arthritis) forced him to resign in 1822, when he had just attained the rank of lieutenant. This reverse evidently left him with a crippling spiritual distress that lasted for some years, until his marriage in June 1829. This marriage was a very rich bourgeois one: his bride, Alexandrine Ollivier, was the daughter of a governor of the Bank of France who was first a deputy, then a peer of France under the Restoration. Descended from a line of Paris merchants, "Baron" Ollivier, Alexandrine's father, had married the daughter of a Le Havre shipowner with connections not only in the world of high finance but also among the Breton nobility—the Duchesse de Duras, who maintained one of the principal salons of the faubourg Saint-Germain, was a cousin whose influence at the court would have facilitated the financial success of Ollivier's bank. Through his marriage, Edouard de Tocqueville became one of the two hundred largest shareholders in the Bank of France and, even more important, the manager of a large agricultural estate in the Oise called Baugy, whose château was surrounded by a park of a hundred hectares.[21] Edouard de Tocqueville showed himself to be resolute and hardworking, with a great devotion to his family duties and an inclination to melancholy that was perhaps related to his health. His younger brother poked fun at him for his thrift and his growing piety as the years passed. However, he was not completely absorbed in the management of his property. Economic and social problems, the customs regulations, and the fight against pauperism were constant intellectual preoccupations for him. He published several booklets on agricultural economy and collaborated on the *Annales de la Charité*. He appears to have been more indebted for his ideas to Alban de Villeneuve-

[21]R. Szramklewicz, *Les Régents et censeurs de la Banque de France nommés sous le Consulat et l'Empire* (Geneva, 1974), 286–94.

Bargemont's *Economie politique chrétienne* than was his brother. He was
anxious to temper the natural laws of economy with measures favorable to the agricultural sector, and to preserve Christian principles in
the society of the day.

Although Alexis de Tocqueville preferred Alexandrine to his other
sister-in-law, he nevertheless reproached her for making her husband
live in a bourgeois atmosphere and for narrowing his horizons. In his
Souvenirs, he recalls with irritation her fear during the day of February
24, 1848, when Louis-Philippe, confronted by the prospect of civil war
and with an angry crowd threatening the royal palace, decided to
abdicate:

My sister-in-law had lost her head, as usual. Already she saw her husband
dead and her daughters raped . . . What made me most impatient was that
she did not dream of including the country as a whole in the lamentations
that poured from her over the fate of her own family. She was a woman
of a demonstrative sensibility rather than a profound or broad one. Very
good, for all this, and even very intelligent, but someone who had narrowed
her mind a little and chilled her heart, squeezing them into a sort of pious
egoism in which she lived solely preoccupied by the good Lord, her husband,
her children, and especially her health, not taking any interest in others. The
best woman and the worst citizen one could ever encounter.[22]

Edouard's candidacy for the Legislative Assembly in 1852 caused a
sharp conflict between the two brothers. Yet Edouard was not the
official candidate. His primary concern was to defend religious interests, but he did declare his adherence to the newly proclaimed authoritarian regime of Napoléon III. And Tocqueville, who, though he
denied it, may have been afraid that public opinion would confuse him
with his brother, wrote him a very vehement letter: "Freedom's ruin,
my renunciation of public life, my country's humiliation, my friends'
exile or voluntary dispersal—I believe that none of these has caused
me such a feeling of bitterness as this profound disagreement between
us."[23] Edouard feared there would be a complete break with his
brother. Yet Alexis assured him he still felt the same affection for him,
though it was henceforth impossible for them to talk about the most
important event of the time. The fact that Edouard was so roundly
defeated by the official candidate probably helped smooth over this
difference of opinion.

[22]*Souvenirs, O.C.* XII: 61–62.
[23]Letter to Edouard dated February 14, 1852, Tocqueville Archives.

Toward the end of his life, Tocqueville, who had no children of his own, extended his paternal affection to his nephews, Edouard's sons. Their education, entrusted by their pious parents to the *petit séminaire* of Paris, the Catholic secondary school, had borne different sorts of fruit. René, an officer in the regiment of the Empress's guards, was a "very likable boy, but much too ready to let pretty women love him . . . and what's more, to kick his rivals in the seat of their pants, including even the women's husbands."[24] René's uncle, in 1853, had to make the trip from Saumur to settle an annoying affair with legal repercussions caused by this bad habit of his. Alexis took advantage of the occasion to "haul him over the coals . . . but it was no use. For nothing sticks in that head. He is a twenty-year-old Hippolyte all over again, brave as thirty-six devils, but without any more brains than a sparrow." Again and again we sense his indulgence for this nephew, whose boisterousness must have awakened some echo of his own youth. But it was to René's brother Hubert, who was also his godson, that Alexis de Tocqueville tried to transmit a sort of spiritual family heritage. He reproached Hubert for being too serious, too regular in his habits, too unworldly for the position of attaché to the embassy in Berlin which he had helped him obtain. But it was to Hubert that he confided his faithfulness to the family tradition of being a lord of the West living in symbiosis with his peasants. Thus, after exploring the Tocqueville collection of deeds, he wrote to Hubert on February 23, 1857:

I have traced the line of our ancestors back over nearly four hundred years, finding them always at Tocqueville and their history intertwined with that of the population that surrounds me. There is a certain charm in thus treading the earth that one's forebears walked on and in living among people whose very origins are mingled with our own. I am waiting for you before I finish this research, which is interesting only to us, but which for us has a very great interest. I was also curious enough to glance at the old baptism and marriage certificates of the parish; some of them go back to the sixteenth century. I saw, as I read, that three hundred years ago we served as godfathers to a very great number of the inhabitants of the village.[25]

Yet Alexis de Tocqueville seemed to have repudiated these traditions by his marriage in October 1835 to Mary Mottley, an English-woman who was not at all "wellborn."

[24]Letter to Beaumont dated December 5, 1853, *O.C.* VIII, 3: 172.
[25]Letter to Hubert de Tocqueville, *O.C.* (Bmt) VII, 433–36.

This marriage caused some scandal, as we know from a letter Edouard wrote to Beaumont after the death of Madame de Tocqueville, and the family resigned themselves to it without enthusiasm.[26] Tocqueville's best friends tried to dissuade him from it—Kergorlay, who, it seems, never entirely forgave him for it, and Beaumont, who was more accommodating and, thanks to the approaches made by his wife, Clémentine de Lafayette, completely won back Mary's trust. Mary had known Tocqueville in 1828 or 1829 at Versailles when he was a magistrate there. She lived near him with her aunt, a Mrs. Belam, and during Alexis's trip to America, Ernest de Chabrol, who continued to live in the apartment in the rue d'Anjou that he and Tocqueville had rented together, acted as his neighbor's "mailbox." The marriage in 1835 regularized a liaison that already been going on for some time. Very little is known about Mary Mottley's youth; biographers are unsure of her age, believing her to be from six to nine years older than her husband. It appears that she was born in Stonehouse, just outside Plymouth; her parents were George Mottley and Mary Martin, whom she left when she was quite young to live in France with an aunt. What is certain is that a large part of her family lived in Portsmouth in 1857, and that she had brothers who served as officers in the British navy. She was perhaps related to a British admiral named Sykes. J. T. Schleifer, in his study of Tocqueville, insists plausibly that one of the purposes of Tocqueville's trip to England was to meet his future in-laws.[27]

Traditional accounts, collected by Rédier, have it that she was ugly, and cursed with large yellow teeth. Certainly her husband alludes to "her strong dentition," but a medallion now at Yale shows features that are not without grace. Her sisters-in-law, it seems, would burst out laughing at her mistakes in French and make fun of her excessive love for dogs of all kinds; in this, Tocqueville shared her tastes. His letters when he is far from home are full of concern for their dogs' health.

It is sometimes said that Mary Mottley "didn't have a penny to her name." True, she prevented Alexis de Tocqueville from marrying a rich woman. But she was to leave Beaumont a sum of money of her own that was not insignificant and at the time of her marriage she enjoyed an income of from eight thousand to ten thousand francs. In sum, Madame de Tocqueville came from a middle-class English family that was perhaps burdened with too many children. To all appearances,

[26]Letter from Edouard to Beaumont, Tocqueville Archives.
[27]J. T. Schleifer, *The Making of Tocqueville's Democracy in America* (Chapel Hill, 1980), 20.

this marriage seemed to be in contradiction to the advice Tocqueville was soon to give his friend Louis de Kergorlay when he was looking for a wife: "I would hold firmly to one general rule if I were in your place: only choose a woman from a family that on both sides belongs to what we would have called *our class* fifty years ago."[28] He would have intimated, no doubt, that there are women who by their "loftiness of mind" or their "loftiness of soul" are an exception to this rule. Was this the case with Mary Mottley?

The question is not easy to answer, partly because of the limited sources available to us. In order to present an image of herself in keeping with her views, after Madame de Tocqueville was widowed she sorted through the family archives very thoroughly, and of course her husband's letters to her were especially carefully expurgated. In the case of quite a large number of his letters, we have only copies in her handwriting, which reproduce the praises he lavished on her but not the reservations that may have accompanied them. Almost nothing remains of all the correspondence from before the marriage. Very few opinions of her have been handed down: Beaumont, her heir, wrote that she was an excellent woman, though unequal to the task of being Tocqueville's wife, which, he conceded, was not an easy one.[29] Louis de Loménie, upon her death, wanted to write an article showing that she was not the "insignificant" person she was sometimes thought to be, but friends of Madame de Tocqueville, unfortunately for the historian, saw to it that this notorious blunderer was kept quiet. She herself, in a letter written after the death of her husband, grieved over the fact that he should have died just when she was beginning to enjoy his company, but in another letter insists that she had a much greater influence on him than people thought. None of this is very precise, but it strikes a slightly more subdued note than the anthology of praises taken from her husband's letters.

It is clear, nevertheless, that Tocqueville was very attached to her, and that for a long time the attachment was sensual. But more than anything else, she was and remained for him a calm, soothing refuge. "You reconcile me with the world and with myself," he wrote to her.[30] He felt that this calm, and the confidence he had in her, provided support that was essential to his very life. People who knew them sensed that there was a maternal side to this woman, years older than

[28]Letter to Kergorlay dated July 5, 1838, *O.C.* XIII, 2: 36.
[29]Unpublished letter from Beaumont to Kergorlay, Kergorlay Archives.
[30]Unpublished letter to his wife dated July 1832.

her husband, that complemented his unstable nature—for there would always be something of the spoiled child about him.

She was not uncultivated, read German and Italian, and showed, like her husband, a predilection for tales of travel in distant lands. Her natural inclinations led her to seek the solitude of the country; she loved beautiful landscapes much more, it seems, than the atmosphere of the salons of Paris. Clearly, she had enough good judgment and uprightness of character to make her scorn the petty advantages of an opportunistic career. Tocqueville harked back more than once to these good qualities of hers, which he contrasted, for example, with the maneuvers of her compatriot, Madame de Lamartine (*née* Marianne Birch), when she sought to push the poet into the presidency of the Chamber.

But her good judgment and her common sense were combined with a fragile equilibrium. She did not have much physical stamina: she suffered from attacks of lumbago, followed later by rheumatism. Her health would be shaken by, for instance, a minor illness of her husband's or a slightly extended trip. And her physical ailments were accompanied by mental disturbances; in these cases her reason would come unhinged, Tocqueville noted, and at the time of his last illness he asked Beaumont to come to Cannes, confessing to him: "My wife frightens me." During her last years (she died in 1864) she seems to have sunk into a melancholy prostration that made her a plaything in the hands of her domestic staff.

With an impatient husband whose moods alternated between liveliness and depression, her day-to-day life could not have been very restful. Tocqueville was easily exasperated by his wife's slow ways. According to one anecdote, she was taking an endless time eating some pâté one day, and he threw a plate at her; her only reaction was immediately to help herself to more pâté. This was the image of their relationship: Tocqueville would become irritated, fume, and then seek to work his way back into her good graces when faced with her fits of sulking. Her obstinacy gave her the last word and she ruled the domestic roost. The language of the household was English. She herself dealt directly with the farmers in renewing their leases. Tocqueville was sometimes uneasy about her relations with the servants or the tenants, which were less indulgent than those of his own family had been. And like many husbands who feel they are being ruled by a despot, he apparently took his revenge secretly several times, though all traces of this were carefully obliterated by his widow.

He had always had a passionate temperament, and in 1843 he confessed somewhat pitifully to Kergorlay, who was acting as peacemaker between Mary and him: "How can I make my blood stop boiling like this every time a woman comes near me, no matter what kind of woman she may be, just as it did twenty years ago?"[31]

Growing old with a woman older than he was, he hardly seems to have reconciled himself to his situation, nor did he manage to soothe her fits of jealousy.

Other differences of temperament brought Tocqueville and his wife into conflict. To Kergorlay, again, he wrote: "In our hearts we understand each other, but we cannot in our minds. Our natures are too different. Her slow and gradual way of experiencing things is completely foreign to me. And she will never know to what extent I, acting on the impulse of a moment, can do the most contradictory things and depart suddenly, by an abrupt deviation, from the path that was leading me to the thing I desired the most passionately in the world."[32] To put it more simply, if the two were alone together for too long, they soon became bored, whence their desire to have someone else with them: Kergorlay, because he was a bachelor, and later the charming Ampère, a kindly and eloquent guest, whom Tocqueville in his last years resentfully saw spending more and more time with the Cheuvreux family in Rome.

In the end, it seems to us that Mary Mottley's influence did not extend beyond the couple's domestic life. Her husband treated her with consideration, never failing, when he had gone to visit some aristocratic relative, to tell her how sorry everyone had been that she had not accompanied him. She clearly picked and chose among the family relations, having some associations with the Beaumonts or the Corcelles, but inclining more toward the middle-class Dufaures or Freslons. She maintained fairly close connections with her fellow countrymen: in Cherbourg, the family of the consul, Hammond; in Paris, the Lagden sisters, who were companions to the aging Mérimée and whose graves actually still flank his in Cannes. She had her own ideas. Politically, she was liberal and sometimes wanted her husband to be more clearly liberal, too. As for religion, she had been baptized in the Catholic faith prior to her marriage and was a sincere convert, even pious in a spiritually narrow way. She threatened to sue Falloux if he published the letter in which her husband revealed his metaphysi-

[31] Letter to Kergorlay dated September 27, 1843, O.C. XIII, 2: 121.
[32] Letter to Kergorlay dated October 19, 1843, O.C. XIII, 2: 127.

cal doubts to Madame Swetchine, and spoke without indulgence of "his heroine" with a sort of retrospective jealousy for the spiritual influence the latter had exercised on Alexis. She had no tolerance for the weaknesses of other women of her generation, and we have been handed down some quite ferocious opinions of her.

Misfit that she was in the Tocqueville social circle, did she try to break all ties with her husband's family? She had never felt the least sympathy for her sister-in-law, Emilie, and at the time they resumed relations in 1856, upon the death of Comte Hervé, she had not been to Nacqueville in ten years. In the years that followed her marriage, she spent periods of time at Baugy, the home of "the Edouards," where a large part of the second *Democracy* was written, but contacts gradually became less and less frequent; when she was widowed, she closed her door to them and left Alexis's papers to Beaumont.[33] With his father, whose perfect courtesy was universally known, relations were not simple. She got along badly with his companion, Madame Guermarquer, and refused, for instance, to inconvenience herself by going to wait for her father-in-law at the diligence station in Valognes. We are left with the impression of a persistent hostility, more or less veiled, provoked originally no doubt by the family's own hostility toward the marriage and probably sustained by the fact that she was not very comfortable or well liked in the family circle, though her own bitter obstinacy also seems to have played a large part in it.

But here, too, her influence on her husband remained secondary: he had a few fits of ill humor toward his sisters-in-law, but he never broke with his family, whom he would see, during the Second Empire, whenever he passed through Paris, and she caused no notable change in his behavior or his intellectual life.

At Tocqueville, to which he was not tied by his childhood memories, he took the place set out for him by his lineage, and, in a letter written in 1828, said to Beaumont: "All this . . . tickles the pride in my weak heart and sometimes provokes in me fits of childish enthusiasm which I am ashamed of afterwards."[34] And later, writing to Royer-Collard: "Here I enjoy . . . an esteem which I can talk about because it is accorded not to me but to the memory of my grandmother who, left a widow very young, lived in this place fifty years ago, and whose memory is still venerated here."[35] There, the Ancien Régime seemed to endure still: the heir of the old lords was in the château, the

[33]Tocqueville Archives, file 53.
[34]Letter to Beaumont dated October 5, 1828, *O.C.* VIII, 1: 50.
[35]Letter to Royer-Collard dated June 29, 1837, *O.C.* XI, 34.

54

heir of the old syndics was in the town hall; the only victims of the Revolution were the feudal pigeons, whose tower was still in ruins. A discreet almsgiving was still practiced here, as in the old days. But in actual fact, the relationship between chatelain and people had substantially changed. Although Tocqueville attempted to win their affection, he refrained, as we will see, from any interference in the life of the town and rejected outright any offers of special favors.[36] Some years later, in the days of the conservative reaction under the presidency of Marshal MacMahon, his brother Edouard found to his cost that paternalism had become completely anachronistic. His gamekeeper, charged with passing on the correct list of candidates in the municipal elections, took advantage of the means put at his disposal to make sure the republican candidates triumphed. Dismissed, he loudly insisted on his right as a citizen, when it came to the elections, to act as he saw fit. We will also see what pains Tocqueville took, as deputy under the July monarchy, to develop the civic spirit in his district. The heir to a family that was at the head of the nobility of the Cotentin wanted to maintain his position through the free choice of his fellow citizens.

But it was within his family milieu that Tocqueville's intellectual and moral principles took shape.

His preference for a "classical" clarity of literary form, one that would express ideas elegantly and soberly, was a family heritage. Before the *Democracy* was published, the father and brothers of the young writer weighed every turn of phrase, down to individual words, and all three required the sort of exactness that gives Alexis's style, in places, a crystalline purity.

For them, as for him, form had to be strictly subordinate to the idea, but the idea in turn had to serve the sort of social usefulness that appeared to them to be the only legitimate aim of intelligence. Although Alexis de Tocqueville experienced periods of lassitude when, with his invalid's sensitivity, he wanted to withdraw, he had only scorn for the selfish epicureanism that brings a man to shut himself up with his private pleasures, even legitimate ones, and live sheltered from the risks and the turbulence of public life. His father's eagerness to embark on his prefectorial career in 1814 was the expression, typical of the man, of a devotion to the state and to society bequeathed to him by

[36]Louis de Loménie, "Ecrivains et publicistes modernes de la France: Alexis de Tocqueville," *Revue des deux mondes;* May 15, 1859, 419–21.

Malesherbes. A like conviction was the motivating force for Alexis de Tocqueville throughout his life.

Comte Hervé's thoughts remained turned toward the past—toward the duty and honor of faithfully serving the king, performing the function of an élite that mediated between legitimate authority and the people's well-being. His son became conscious of an inexorable historical movement that was obliging men to rebuild the entire structure of society on new foundations. His thoughts turned toward the future, and he found his personal challenge in proving that an heir to the past could maintain his position during the time that the future was being prepared. His break with the old monarchical loyalties and his conversion to new values were made gradually over the course of a development whose very beginnings we must now examine.

4

EDUCATION

AND EMANCIPATION

ALEXIS DE TOCQUEVILLE was about twelve when Madame de Tocqueville decided to stop following her husband to the various different residences he occupied in his career as a prefect. From 1817 to 1820, Alexis lived with her in Paris under the easygoing tutelage of Abbé Lesueur. But in April of 1820, the Comte de Tocqueville sent for his son to come to Metz. During a separation that was painful for him, the old tutor wrote to Alexis that out of consideration for his future, he should henceforth have a more competent teacher than the Abbé to develop his mind, but that the Abbé would continue to reserve for himself the guidance of Alexis's soul.[1] Apparently, not only did the Comte de Tocqueville want a better education for his son, he also felt isolated from his family and wanted to have one of his children with him.[2] As we have already seen, the two older sons were at that time pursuing military careers, Hippolyte in the garrisons of the East (Lunéville, Maubeuge, Sélestat) and Edouard in Paris.[3]

At Metz, Alexis was first given into the care of M. Madelaine, a teacher of the third class at the secondary school. Then, in November 1821, he entered the rhetoric class of the *collège royal,* as the lycée in Metz was then called, and the next year he followed the course in philosophy. This institution, directed at the time by an ecclesiastic,

[1]Unpublished letters from Abbé Lesueur to Alexis de Tocqueville dated April 20 and 27, Tocqueville Archives, file 9.

[2]Letter from L. de Kergorlay to Alexis de Tocqueville dated August 13, 1821 or 1822, *O.C.* XIII, 1: 55.

[3]Army files, in alphabetical order, War Archives at Vincennes.

Abbé Sainsère, who had only a *baccalauréat,* was reputed to be one of
the best in the provinces, particularly for its teaching of the sciences
and its preparation for the entrance exam to the Ecole Polytechnique;
its teaching of literature was also on a very respectable level.[4]

It was just as his son was completing his course of study at Metz,
in August 1824, that the Comte de Tocqueville left for Amiens, to
which he had been appointed on June 27. Alexis paid only a few visits
to Amiens, because at this point he returned to Paris to study law, and,
except for a period in which he rented a room in the Latin Quarter,
he lived with his mother in the faubourg Saint-Germain. He finished
his law studies in August 1826. His father had been prefect of Versailles
since June 14.

This chronology emphasizes how important Alexis's stay at Metz
was: up to then, he had lived in the closed milieu of his aristocratic
family. His father's industrious habits, his long trips around the department, left Alexis to himself in the vast residence of the prefecture. At
the *collège,* he could choose his own friends. Abbé Lesueur wrote him
from Paris to be civil to all his comrades but not to form a special
friendship with any one of them.[5] The Abbé was probably afraid of
the homosexual friendships that were apparently fairly common in the
lycées of those times. But though his pupil paid no attention to the
advice the Abbé sent from so far away, the ardor of his temperament
did not incline him in that direction in any case.

The large garden of the Metz prefecture would later awaken tender
memories in him; passing through Metz with his wife in July 1836,
he went back to see it: "Having gone out early one morning, I stopped
by the prefecture and asked if I could walk around the garden. I can't
tell you what a feeling it gave me to see those places again after thirteen
years, places which had remained so clearly in my memory that I
instantly noticed the slightest changes that had been made during the
course of those years."[6] In the summer of 1821, he had had a little
summerhouse built for himself there which had amused his father and
the Abbé very much. The latter wrote to Alexis on June 21: "Your
papa talks to us about your little house in a way that isn't very
respectful at all. He says it's only nine feet long when it's really sixteen.

[4]Carriez, "Le Lycée de Metz," *Revue du Rhin et Moselle* (1924).
[5]Unpublished letter from Abbé Lesueur to Alexis de Tocqueville dated November 3, 1821, Tocqueville
Archives, file 9: "My dear child, your papa has surely advised you to be very civil to all your comrades
and not to form any special friendships. I know better than anyone how dangerous they are, especially
today when morals are so lax. Those young men seem the most beautiful on the outside who are rotten
within."
[6]Letter to Louis de Kergorlay dated July 16, 1836, *O.C.* XIII, 1: 185.

58

Where did he get the idea that one could only get into your second floor on hands and knees?"[7] The Abbé did not notice that his pupil had passed from the age of playing childish games to that of setting up bachelor's quarters.

We don't know very much about Tocqueville's relationships with his fellow students at the *collège royal* or the associations he formed in Metz society. He would later talk about the adventurous ardor of his youth. An episode that is hard to clarify dates from that time: on a day that we can't pin down, Tocqueville fought a duel. He actually announced that he was going to fight in a letter to Kergorlay, who answered it on May 16, 1823. But already on February 12, 1823, Abbé Lesueur had written: "Your papa has sent word to us that you have wounded yourself severely enough so that you can't leave your room." In April, there was the matter of a threat of pneumonia and on May 3, 1823, he had to spend the day lying down on his couch.[8]

These pieces of information seem to indicate the existence of one or more episodes that the prefect kept secret, hiding them even from the rest of the family. It certainly appears, in any case, that there was a violent conflict with Henrion, the future ultraroyalist lawyer and journalist, still later a magistrate, and the author of a very pious *Histoire ecclésiastique*. He was more than a school friend; he himself was to say later that during that period he had been raised by Tocqueville's father, and he was to reappear several times in Tocqueville's life, though the latter found him to be without charm.[9] Eugène Stoffels refers to Henrion's quarrel with Tocqueville, insisting that the latter was completely in the wrong, but we have no idea what the actual nature of the quarrel was—it could well have been caused by an indiscretion or a blunder on Henrion's part rather than a romantic rivalry.

In any case, Stoffels's statement has to be taken seriously, since he was in fact Tocqueville's best friend in Metz.[10] He came of undistinguished bourgeois stock, his parents at odds with each other, his father apparently somewhat unstable. He was to take his grandfather's place as municipal tax collector at Metz. His letters show him to be undeni-

[7]Unpublished letter from Abbé Lesueur dated June 21, 1821, Tocqueville Archives, file 9.

[8]Unpublished letters from Abbé Lesueur dated February 12, 1823, April 1823, and May 3, 1823; letter from Kergorlay to Tocqueville dated May 16, 1823, *O.C.* XIII, 1: 60.

[9]Concerning Henrion, see Begin, *Biographie de la Moselle* (1829).

[10]More than a hundred letters from Eugène Stoffels are preserved in the Tocqueville Archives (file 21), as well as a few letters from Madame Stoffels to Madame de Tocqueville and from Alexis Stoffels, and these help us to trace the friendship's history, as does the supplementary material in Alexis de Tocqueville's correspondence with Charles Stoffels, Eugène's brother, in the possession of Mademoiselle Stoffels d'Hautefort.

ably intelligent, but a little ungainly, of a rather Germanic sentimental-
ity, very dependable in friendship. His big-heartedness and his sincerity
could always disarm the moody irritations and the ill-founded suspicions of his touchy friend. Right up to the time of his death in 1852,
Stoffels would remain a somewhat subordinate confidant, dominated
by the demanding friend whose superiority was an article of faith for
him; prepared to help Alexis in his contacts with others, he was one
of those intermediaries whom Alexis, in his anxious and mistrustful
shyness, would always need. In return, Tocqueville, in the midst of the
agitation of his political career and his literary successes, would never
forget the modest friend in Metz, whose letters always gave him great
pleasure. After Stoffels's death, he counseled Stoffels's son Alexis, who
was also his godson, in his studies.

At the *collège,* Alexis immediately showed himself to be a good
student. In the rhetoric class, a good one filled with a healthy spirit
of competition, he won the honors prize and five other prizes or
honorable mentions. We don't know if his year of philosophy was as
brilliant, since he was confined to his bedroom for so long. In any
event, all three votes were favorable at his *baccalauréat.* [11]
    There were lacunae in the curriculum at Metz, compared with that
of the Parisian lycées. English was not taught, though it was offered
as an elective in the capital at that time, and would not be introduced
at Metz until 1829, but we know from Abbé Lesueur's letters that
Tocqueville acquired at least some English. It seems, too, that the
collège did not provide even the most rudimentary teaching of history,
though it had been introduced into the educational system in 1818 by
Royer-Collard, the intelligent and eloquent moderate royalist who
was the central figure in the Chamber of Deputies under the Restoration. Instruction in history was usually entrusted to special teachers.[12]
Tocqueville's school notebooks, fragmentary and ill-kept though they
are, do give us some information about the general spirit of that
teaching. Notions of arithmetic, geometry, and algebra are fairly elementary; these subjects were taken up only in the higher grades. Greek
translations were short and easy. Latin, on the other hand, occupied an
important place. Appropriately enough for the study of rhetoric, the
art of oratory was featured prominently: the dictated lecture on literary genres paid particular attention to oratory, and orators were given

---

[11]Letter from Abbé Lesueur dated September 1824.
[12]See Gerbod, *La Vie quotidienne dans les lycées et collèges au XIXe siècle* (Paris, n.d.), and, on life in
Metz, Contamine, *Metz et la Moselle,* op. cit., vol. 2, 170–75.

more time than the other authors studied. Of course Horace and Racine (even as he expresses himself in *Athalie*) contributed some notions of the poetic art, but Cicero, Demosthenes, and even Quintilian were studied in depth. Only a few composition topics have been preserved: for example, in Latin, *"De laudibus Demosthenis,"* and in French, "The Importance of Eloquence in Man."[13] Of the latter essay, we possess an exposition that seems to have been a fair copy of a version corrected by the teacher; it sets out to demonstrate that a good orator must have gifts, must exploit them through hard work, and can only invest them in the service of the public virtues. These commonplaces show how rigid the teaching remained, rerunning old Ciceronian themes but at the same time proposing service to the State as an ideal, which did not in the least contradict Tocqueville's family ethics. The teaching of the humanities led quite naturally to the bar or to politics.

Tocqueville, in later life so caustic, was apparently a docile student. M. Mougin, the instructor in rhetoric, was a resolute partisan of the classics, seeing nothing good in the new literary or political tendencies. He had no fear of embracing large subjects and had composed essays on "morality" and "history" which he showed to his student. After Tocqueville left Metz, as he was beginning his law studies, he asked his old teacher for advice. M. Mougin's answer, which has been preserved,[14] is not without interest, since it indicates the direction Tocqueville's studies were to take after he left the lycée.

First, M. Mougin congratulates his old pupil on following his law courses so assiduously, but agrees that they are not indispensable to his success in earning a degree. He goes on to say: "Public courses in history, literature, and other subjects will occupy you or amuse you for a little while. Knowing you, I don't think there is much chance that they will engage you." This chance of being "engaged by a public course" did occur in the case of the course offered by Guizot, of whom we will say more later. But then M. Mougin recommended the study of history: "Now I come to history, the most necessary and the most difficult of all your studies. This study appears to be the same for everyone and yet each person must approach it in his own way. Aside from general considerations—the progress of events, the origin of our laws, the evolution of the arts, etc.—it seems to me that you should pay particular attention to France's relations with her neighboring

[13]Tocqueville Archives, file 46.
[14]Tocqueville Archives, file 9.

states and note the influence she has exercised and suffered during each epoch in which there has been some change in the political system of Europe."

History conceived as helping to explain the present, viewed as beginning with the comparative study of several states—these were precepts that Tocqueville would not forget and which perhaps only confirmed ideas that he himself had submitted to his former teacher.

His exploration of his father's library in the Metz prefecture played a much more important role in the adolescent's intellectual development than the traditionalist teaching of the lycée. Up to then, Alexis had spent more time playing than reading; he had not questioned the convictions acquired in his childhood. Suddenly let loose in the world of ideas, he felt his own universe totter: he retained a painful and exact memory of this shock which he confided thirty-five years later to Madame Swetchine, the Russian mystic living in Paris who became his close friend and spiritual adviser in the last years of his life:[15]

I don't know if I've ever told you about an incident in my youth that marked me deeply for the rest of my life; how when I was enclosed in a kind of solitude during the years just after childhood, when I was prey to an insatiable curiosity whose only available satisfaction was a large library of books, I heaped pell-mell into my mind all sorts of notions and ideas which belong more properly to a more mature age. Until that time, my life had passed enveloped in a faith that hadn't even allowed doubt to penetrate into my soul. Then doubt entered, or rather hurtled in with an incredible violence, not only doubt about one thing or another in particular, but an all-embracing doubt. All of a sudden I experienced the sensation people talk about who have been through an earthquake, when the ground shakes under their feet, as do the walls around them, the ceilings over their heads, the furniture beneath their hands, all of nature before their eyes. I was seized by the blackest melancholy, then by an extreme disgust with life—though I knew nothing of life—and was almost prostrated by agitation and terror at the sight of the road that remained for me to travel in this world. Strong passions drew me out of this state of despair; they turned me away from the sight of these intellectual ruins and led me toward tangible objects. But still, from time to time, these feelings experienced in my early youth (I was then sixteen) take possession of me again. Then once more I see the world of ideas revolving and I am lost and bewildered in this universal motion that upsets and shakes all the truths on which I base my beliefs and my actions.

[15]Letter dated February 26, 1857, *O.C.* XV, 2: 315.

Judging by what has been preserved at Tocqueville, this library included the classics of the seventeenth century and translations of ancient authors; there were few moderns, Chateaubriand being an exception because of family ties; there were many travel accounts, which seems to indicate that the curiosity Tocqueville would have all his life about the appearance and the customs of different countries in the world was already present in the family before he came along; with the exception of the Encyclopedists, who may have disappeared from the library after Alexis's time, the great *philosophes* of the eighteenth century are here: Voltaire, Montesquieu, Buffon, Rousseau, Mably, and Raynal. It isn't easy to know which of these and other authors Tocqueville read, or when he read them, but it was obviously his reading of Voltaire and Rousseau that caused doubt to enter his mind. A few years later he wrote that doubt was one of mankind's three great evils: "If I were asked to arrange in order of gravity the grand miseries of mankind, I would do it in this way: 1. disease; 2. death; 3. doubt."[16]

In the letter quoted above, Tocqueville is quite specific about the date of this crisis: he was sixteen years old, the age he reached in July 1821, at the beginning of his stay in Metz, when he was left to himself for the first time.

This "all-embracing doubt" also turned on the social values revered by the world of the aristocracy. To Henry Reeve, his English translator, he later confided that at a very early age he had become aware that these values were anachronistic, an awareness that probably arose from his alternation between attendance at the lycée and solitary reflection. Though in a form different from the one it took in the family's memories, we can see in this the omnipresent shadow of the French Revolution, which was really the most intense phase of a movement that had begun earlier and was still actively working to eliminate the last of the ruinous values of the past.

This awareness, then, led to his gradual discovery of the great problem which would become central to his entire thought, the substitution of a democratic world for the aristocratic world. Whence his eagerness to learn history during this period—to throw light on the problem.

Yet the most serious aspect of his crisis, at that time, was the loss of his religious faith. Tocqueville was never particularly bent on discovering metaphysical certainty. Perhaps he was too steeped in

[16]Note quoted by Beaumont in *O.C.* (Bmt.) V, 14, taken from *Carnets d'Amérique.*

Jansenist morality to see faith as anything but a gift from God; perhaps, even, his religious education had given him the notion of the distant God of the eighteenth-century Jansenists, predisposing him to evolve toward a deism impregnated with Christian morality. Jesus, both as man and as God, was apparently absent from his thinking, appearing only as the faceless symbol, quite stripped of any mystery, of an important step forward in the history of civilization. Acceptance of the universal agreement that God exists and that there is a future life was as far as Tocqueville would go, and this can perhaps be seen as a distorted reflection of the apologetics of Lammenais, the popular theological writer of the early nineteenth century, who held that only collective thought, which finds its expression in the universal consent of mankind, can be considered infallible, because in it one discovers the original divine revelation. His *Essai sur l'indifférence en matière de religion*, published in 1817, was being widely read and discussed at the time.

Tocqueville spoke openly of his doubts to his cousin Louis de Kergorlay. We don't have his letter, but we do have Louis's answer, dated May 16, 1823:[17]

You had not talked to me before about the doubts, the uncertainties that are tormenting you. I can easily imagine them arising in your mind. But what I don't understand at all is how they can be reinforced by example. The fact is that I became accustomed, much earlier than you, to mistrusting those around me, because I found myself in bad company when I was quite young . . . Here you're reverting to a fault that I've always seen in you . . . which is to give too much consideration to the opinions of the mass of men . . . Will you believe a foolish unbeliever more than Christian[18] or your *bébé* [Abbé Lesueur], whose opinions you and I often flatly condemn in private?

And so he dwells on the fact that Tocqueville had discovered that the values acknowledged by the family milieu were rejected by the society of his time. But he only hints at Tocqueville's reading of the *philosophes*, which, to judge from what Tocqueville says in his letter to Madame Swetchine, was what led to the crisis.

As for Abbé Lesueur, he was not alerted to this crisis until 1824, when he found out that Alexis had not performed his Easter duties. Questioned by his old tutor, Alexis wrote him that he believed, but

[17]*O.C.* XIII, 1: 60–61.
[18]Christian de Chateaubriand, who was going to take orders.

could not practice.[19] Tocqueville's reply to Abbé Lesueur was a confession of youthful passions that he had no clear intention of correcting. It contained only a part of the truth and was, in the end, misleading: as far as we can tell from their incomplete and abridged correspondence, Alexis was avoiding an argument about faith that could only be painful for the old man as well as for him.

In the passage from the letter to Madame Swetchine that we have quoted, Tocqueville states unequivocally that it was the intellectual crisis he underwent when he was sixteen that brought about the liberation of his physical passions, and not the reverse. In his papers we can note evidences of this liberation from 1821 on. But these transient encounters were not enough to quiet his restlessness. He was too human, his feelings ran too deep, for him not to seek full participation, soul and body, in these youthful ardors. He could not be satisfied with brief affairs. These were replaced by a romance that we know about from the publication of Kergorlay's correspondence and whose course we can follow in Stoffels's unpublished letters.

The documentation, however, is incomplete: none of Tocqueville's letters of the time speaks of his passion, and Kergorlay destroyed the ones he received then, preserving only a copy of a few innocuous fragments. Tocqueville's letters to Stoffels seem definitely to have been lost, as have the love letters between Tocqueville and the young woman from Metz.

From the registers of births, marriages, and deaths, we can identify this woman, designated by either her initials or her first name: she was Rosalie Malye, born in Bitche on September 15, 1804. She was the daughter of a retired *commandant,* the archivist of the Metz prefecture. The father is never mentioned in any of the papers, and he appears to have been a widower; Rosalie lived with an older sister, Amélie. We know nothing of her physical appearance, only that she was charming, delicate, frank, free of coquettish affectations, with a willful and lively character. She very quickly won Stoffels's friendship and dispelled the prejudices of Kergorlay, who, having left the Ecole Polytechnique to enter the Artillery School of Instruction in Metz, spent the most pleasant times of his stay in the city in the two sisters' drawing room.

The intense, mutual love of Tocqueville and Rosalie lasted about five years. After Tocqueville left Metz, in 1825, Rosalie visited Paris;

[19]Unpublished letter in the Tocqueville Archives, file 9. This letter has been mutilated, probably by Madame de Tocqueville, and the date has disappeared: it was written in answer to a letter from Abbé Lesueur dated September 8, 1824.

Tocqueville himself returned to Metz several times. The affair was
reported to the Comte de Tocqueville, but we do not know how he
reacted.

Was this strong passion to end in an unsuitable marriage? Kergorlay
feared as much, and Tocqueville let himself be persuaded, around 1826,
to turn the love affair into a friendship.

Rosalie was harder to convince. Perhaps she was nursing certain
illusions, though she claimed the contrary, and was not willing to give
up the great love which she believed would be the only one in her
life. She received other proposals of marriage, and Kergorlay and
Stoffels advised her to accept one of them. In the end, she resigned
herself, and on April 9, 1828, she married François Begin, a man of
modest independent means who, since she had no fortune at all, credited her with a fictive dowry, which was the custom in those days in
such cases. Kergorlay and Tocqueville tried to secure the revenues of
a post office for him, a service that was occasionally distributed at that
time the same way tobacconist's shops were later. We don't know if
they succeeded. Rosalie remained very sad during the early period of
her marriage; she received letters from Tocqueville written in lemon
juice. Later, he sometimes thought of her, but it appears that she sent
one of his letters back to him.

As for Tocqueville, now a *juge auditeur* in Versailles—making the
novitiate as a junior magistrate that was the usual prelude to promotion
to higher offices in the judiciary—he flitted from one woman to the
next, as his letters to Beaumont in 1828 and 1829 show.[20] He became
acquainted with Mary Mottley, the woman he was to marry, sometime
before the 1830 revolution. As we have seen, this marriage was to
arouse the same indignation in Kergorlay as the possibility of a misal-
liance with Rosalie Malye. It, too, was a bourgeois marriage to a
woman without a large fortune and one he had been having an affair
with for some years. In 1828, at least, Tocqueville yielded before the
threat of scandal. Whatever he thought then of marriages arranged in
the French manner, joining for life a couple who hardly knew each
other, he had not yet had a chance to witness how American marriages
were arranged, or to admire the freedom with which relations among
young people across the Atlantic were conducted. In 1835, when
he was thirty, he rejected several so-called "good matches." By this
time, his great literary success had made him a public figure, and
he "followed his inclination" (as he would later say ironically of

[20]For example, the letter dated October 5, 1828, *O.C.* VIII, 1: 47–49.

Napoléon III's marrying Eugénie!), something he had not dared or wanted to do seven years before.

Though it is a secondary aspect of the episode, the romantic affair between Tocqueville and Rosalie Malye clearly put love in dramatic conflict with friendship. We find Alexis's best friend, Louis de Kergorlay, whom we saw visiting the two Malye sisters in Metz, advising Tocqueville to break with Rosalie and, by urging Rosalie to marry, seeking to make sure that the break would be unavoidable. For Alexis, Louis was a lifelong friend, the only one he trusted completely, as he wrote in 1847.[21] "As I gained more experience of life and saw the political world from closer up, I became more certain that you were the only friend I could count on, the only one whose feelings were never, and never could be, infested by those petty passions that eventually untie the tightest knots of ordinary friendships." Louis de Kergorlay's life, however, was to be very different from that of his friend, and it is useful to recall it before trying to measure his influence.

His father was César de Kergorlay, deputy from the Oise, then a peer of France, one of the strictest ultraroyalists in the political circles of the Restoration, and his mother was Blanche de la Luzerne, the daughter of Malesherbes's nephew. Madame de Kergorlay and Madame de Tocqueville, then, were cousins. Born in August 1804, Louis de Kergorlay was a brilliant student (a prizewinner in the competition among all the lycées at the *baccalauréat* level) and went to the Polytechnique, then to the Artillery School of Instruction in Metz. He took part in the Algiers expedition, but left the service after the 1830 revolution rather than swear an oath of loyalty to the new Orleanist regime. He then became absorbed in managing his family's holdings and in looking for a wife, which occupied him for fifteen years. He toyed with the idea of leading a more intellectual life, and began a study of the development of the German nation that he never finished. In 1849, he collaborated with Arthur de Gobineau in publishing *La Revue provinciale,* of which only a few issues appeared. Under the Second Empire, obliged to look for a lucrative occupation, he became a member of the Administrative Mines Council in the region between the Saumure and the Meuse. After Tocqueville's death, he helped Beaumont publish their friend's posthumous writings, his advice in-

clining toward severity in choosing which texts to offer the public. In
1871, deputy to the National Assembly and a fervent legitimist, he was
profoundly distressed by the failure of the attempt to restore the
Comte de Chambord, the Bourbon heir, to the throne. Although
Kergorlay had ambitious plans for a book on the Constitution, he died
in 1880 leaving on this subject only notes that were never written up.[22]
In short, after a brilliant beginning, with possibilities of accomplishing
great things, his life was wasted because of his refusal to accept the
changes his country was undergoing and because of his incapacity to
break out of a set framework of ideas and traditions.

Since his childhood, he had visited his cousin Alexis de Tocqueville
and spent vacations with him; the two adolescents were friends even
before Alexis came to Metz. Louis was older by one year, farther along
in his studies, and seems to have been more intellectually mature. He
had an influence over his cousin that awoke Abbé Lesueur's suspicions—wrongly, for no mind was less subversive than Louis's, or more
respectful of the values he had inherited from his family. But Tocqueville was to say quite correctly that Louis had been "his teacher." He
had acquired the habit of consulting Louis about his intellectual uncertainties and would continue to do so while he was writing the *Democracy*. Tocqueville's method, which consisted of untangling complex
facts and attaching them to some great principle, seems to have been
worked out, in part, during discussions with Kergorlay. In this way,
Louis helped Tocqueville clarify his own ideas: "I continue to consider
you the *only* man in the world who understands every last nuance of
my thinking when I express it and who knows how to complete it and
make it fertile, by adding all that can be offered by a mind cast in the
same mold as my own," Tocqueville wrote Kergorlay a few months
before his death. In 1838, during the writing of the second *Democracy,*
in which Louis seems to have been a particularly active adviser, Alexis
wrote to Beaumont: "Louis spent four days here; at the time I was
embroiled in a system of ideas from which I could not extricate myself.
It was a real intellectual dead end, and he helped me to find my way
out of it in a matter of hours. This boy has a veritable mine inside him
and he alone cannot, does not know how to, exploit it." He lamented
the fact that his friend was unable to write some great work: "Yours
is one of the most distinguished minds I have ever encountered—the
experience of my riper years has only confirmed the impressions of my

[22]Kergorlay's notes are deposited in the Bibliothèque de l'Arsenal, numbers 14091 to 14097.

68

𝒦 𝒴

youth on this point. Where, then, can the invisible defect be found, the hidden weakness that has prevented this incontestable superiority from producing its natural fruits? Nothing has preoccupied me more in my life than this question," he wrote to Louis in 1856.[23]

Nevertheless, the friendship had its ups and downs. Although their affection and intimacy remained constant—the Kergorlay who came to attend his friend in his last days at Cannes was no different from the man who had traveled to Switzerland with him in 1829—their intellectual exchanges were not maintained at a consistently high level. Thus, at the end of the July monarchy, their correspondence became anemic, less frequent and more banal. Under the Second Empire, Kergorlay's preoccupation with industry had reduced their letters to a mere exchange of news, when the publication of *L'Ancien Régime* abruptly restored its fecundity and vigor. While Kergorlay was still a bachelor, he stayed with the Tocquevilles, but apparently Madame de Tocqueville's relations with Madame de Kergorlay were limited to satisfying the proprieties, and the former has left us a very harsh letter about the latter. After Alexis's death, she withdrew into isolation, and Beaumont reproaches her for not leaving Louis any keepsake of Tocqueville when Freslon, a sincere but much less intimate friend, is bequeathed a portrait of him.

In addition to his intimate influence on Tocqueville's thought and writings, Louis de Kergorlay also tried to help his friend through the vicissitudes of his daily life. An intransigent Carlist, he did not hesitate to give Tocqueville practical advice for bettering his parliamentary position. Like Tocqueville, he took a great interest in Algeria, and in this area he may have been the one to initiate projects and ideas.

He sometimes tried to exert a more direct influence. When Alexis returned to Paris from Metz, Louis urged him to adopt a military career, and in fact, during 1823–1824, Alexis continued to study mathematics with the intention of entering Saint-Cyr. But here, Louis's influence was counteracted by Abbé Lesueur's: "That character Louis de Kergorlay is the one who has crammed this idea into his head. They are going to meet again and I certainly intend to beg M. Loulou to leave us in peace."[24]

Yielding to his family's wishes, Alexis de Tocqueville studied law from 1823 to 1826. During these years, he probably started the studies

---

[23]*O.C.* VIII, 1: 279, and *O.C.* XIII, 2: 302.
[24]Tocqueville Archives, file 9.

that M. Mougin spoke of in his letter and that he would continue after he received his degree in 1826. But until 1826, most of his time was evidently spent preparing for this degree.

The study of law had undergone a thorough reform in 1819, stimulated by Royer-Collard. The three years of preparation for the degree could be done in either of two sections; each section included the Napoleonic Civil Code, the *Institutes* of Roman law, and civil procedure, along with the subjects proper to it: commercial law in the first; public and administrative law, the philosophical history of Roman and French law, and political economy in the second. The reform was complete by 1820, except for the introduction of political economy. But the ordinance of September 6–December 1, 1822, suppressed everything in these reforms that was oriented toward the study of human societies. In its preamble, the new ordinance stated that its purpose was to "encourage the development of the study of Roman law" and to arrange the other courses in the Paris law school so that "the students there would acquire only commonsense knowledge of the prevailing legal practice." Except for a few notions of legal history, the material taught was reduced to the *Institutes* and *Pandects* of Justinian, along with the commentary on the Civil Code, civil and criminal procedure, and commercial law.[25] This reactionary measure was typical of the narrowed horizons of the Villèle ministry. It was tied, no doubt, to the changed state of mind of the law students in the years just preceding the ordinance's enactment. Fervent royalists during the Hundred Days, welcoming Monsieur with enthusiasm in 1816, they had for the most part become liberals, providing membership for the secret societies. Next to the medical school, the law school was reputed to be the "worst."

Did Alexis de Tocqueville associate with the students who belonged to this liberal or revolutionary bourgeoisie? We have no evidence of it. He was getting some training in public speaking and debate in one of those private discussion groups where half-legal, half-political questions were broached. For a time, he was secretary of it, and his minutes provide us with some of the subjects of the debates (the abolition of the death penalty, ministerial responsibility, the law of primogeniture, whether the debts contracted by the king while he was in exile and heir to the throne should be paid back from the *Liste civile* that provided the annual budget for the personal expenses of the sovereign,

[25]Jean Imbert, "Histoire des études de droit," *Le Monde,* January 13, 1963; L. Liard, *L'Enseignement supérieur en France* (Paris, 1888–1894).

etc.) as well as the names of the participants, a majority of whom belonged to the nobility, and a summary of the speeches, which were characterized by a banal conformity.[26]

Except for brief "dictations by M. Delvincourt" on legal history, the most important part of the courses was civil law and procedure, studied in the most pragmatic way: a completely utilitarian education "abandoning intellectual training, the opening of the mind to the problems of the development of law and of legal philosophy." Tocqueville, it appears, was not at all inspired by this dry curriculum, and even though he worked hard, at least in the beginning of his studies, he was awarded only one favorable vote out of three at his doctoral exams. In accordance with custom, this diploma required the presentation of two theses, one in Latin and the other in French: the first, *"De usurpationibus aut de usucapionibus,"* in a correct and flat Latin, and the second, "The Suit for Annulment or Avoidance of Contract," form a text of thirteen pages in which it is hard to discern the future author of the *Democracy*.

Once his law studies were finished, Alexis went off to Italy and Sicily with his brother Edouard. The latter had been at loose ends ever since he had left the army, and both of them liked traveling. In 1823, Edouard had visited Switzerland and written an account of his wanderings which he had had carefully copied. For Alexis, to visit the evocative land of classical antiquity provided a sort of climax to his studies—and this was not unusual in those days.

The facts about this trip cannot all be pinned down exactly: the two brothers left in December 1826 and didn't return until after Alexis's appointment as *juge auditeur* in Versailles on April 6, 1827. In January 1827 they were in Rome, and early in March they left Naples to go to Sicily by sea.

Tocqueville's impressions, reflections, and notes filled two thick quarto manuscripts, the second of which, on Sicily, was 350 pages long. They were lost sometime after Beaumont's publication of the *Oeuvres.*[27] It seems clear that Beaumont borrowed the two volumes from Stoffels's widow and gave them back to her afterwards. Unfortunately, they were never found again.

Beaumont wrote that this manuscript allowed him "to study the course of Tocqueville's thinking, his tentative advances, his mistakes,

---

[26]Tocqueville Archives, file 47.

[27]Beaumont, *Notice* on Tocqueville, introduction to vol. 5 of the *Oeuvres complètes.*

his backtrackings, and the roundabout ways by which he returned to his true path." In sum, according to this astute judge, the true personality of Tocqueville began, little by little, to emerge in this account of his travels. At first he played the conscientious tourist, visiting museums, admiring paintings or medals, seeking an understanding of the great canons of ancient architecture. Having arrived in Rome, he attempted an essay that is somewhat reminiscent of Volney's *Ruines*. In it, he falls asleep on the Capitoline Hill, and as he is dreaming of Rome's great men, of her glory and her liberty, he is awakened by a procession of monks and a cowherd's horn. He then meditates on the fragility of empires . . . All that we now possess that was written by him during this stay in Rome is the fragment of a letter that describes the desolation of the Roman *campagna* and its ruins, evoking Chateaubriand in its substance and perhaps even more in its form.[28]

Chateaubriand's influence is also perceptible in the few fragments published by Beaumont:[29] the storm on the way from Naples to Sicily, the island landscapes, including a description of climbing Mount Etna that takes a more personal turn. (Tocqueville was strongly drawn to majestic, wide-ranging landscapes. His first descriptive essay, "Le Jardin," written a few years earlier, has for its subject the Sea of Ice at Chamonix. The descriptions of Sicily are a marked improvement.)

But it was in another passage published by Beaumont, the dialogue of a Sicilian with a Neapolitan, that Tocqueville returned to "his true path"—the conditions and the effects of freedom. Sicily, rendered sterile by defeat and despotism, was degraded not only by the conquered aristocracy of the island but also by the aristocracy of the conquerors. The dialogue ends on a note of hope: Europe, with the freedoms she enjoys, will not be able to tolerate this corner of despotism, which is all the more insecure because of its exceptional nature.

In these brief fragments, one digression throws a curious light on the uneasy memory of the torment of revolution that was still vivid in the mind of this young aristocrat, who had every reason to hope for a smooth career now, early in the year 1827. After reflections, already characteristic of the man, on the evils of exile, he adds that he is "thinking of the possibility of going to prison, for the experiences of the past forty years prove that it isn't ridiculous to prepare oneself

[28]Fragment of letter to Louis de Kergorlay, *O.C.* XIII, 1: 96.

[29]These fragments are reprinted in the *O.C.* V, 1: 37–54. A study of them has been made by Nina Facon, "La Question méridionale," in *Saggi di Letteratura italiana in di Gaetano Trombatore* (Milan, 1972), 187–200.

72

in advance." It was not the 1830 revolution that first gave Tocqueville his sense of the instability of the present age. His misgivings had been there just under the surface ever since the "Metz crisis," and the events of 1830 would only reopen the wound.

5

VERSAILLES AND

THE 1830 REVOLUTION

THE POSITION OF *juge auditeur* at the Versailles court of law to which Alexis de Tocqueville was appointed on April 6, 1827, had been specially created for him, as is clear from a memorandum from the king's attorney general to the minister of justice:

I think there would be a great advantage in attaching a fourth *juge auditeur* to the Versailles court of law and with the hope that Your Highness will approve this proposal, which I believe is consistent with the good of the service, I have the honor of presenting to him M. Charles-Alexis Clérel de Tocqueville, a young lawyer and the son of *M. le préfet* of Seine-et-Oise, who ardently desires this appointment. M. de Tocqueville, the son, did very well in his studies. He is full of enthusiasm, and it seems to me extremely suitable to do his father a favor that would amount to creating a veritable bond, in Versailles, between the administration and the judicial system, very advantageous in many respects.[1]

In June, the new magistrate assumed his post and moved into the prefecture. But in January 1828 the Comte de Tocqueville had to give his quarters up to his replacement, Baron Capelle. Alexis then took an apartment in the rue d'Anjou where he lived, first, with the young deputy public prosecutor Gustave de Beaumont, then, after Beaumont was transferred to Paris (September 27, 1829) with his successor, Ernest de Chabrol.

The law court of Versailles, divided into two chambers, was com-

[1]Personal file, National Archives.

posed of a *président* (the presiding judge) and a *vice-président;* seven judges, two of whom were examining magistrates; the public prosecutor and two deputy public prosecutors; and the four *juges auditeurs.* Three generations of men came together here: those who were already middle-aged under the Ancien Régime, those who had lived through the time of troubles as children, and those born under the Consulate or the First Empire.[2]

Jacques Brunet, the *président* of the court, born in 1745, had been an attorney attached to the Parlement of Paris, then had become a district administrator under the Revolution, then a deputy in the Council of Five Hundred, then a magistrate under the Consulate. One of the judges, Leleu-Lafontaine, had almost as long a record. Under the Ancien Régime he had been a musketeer for twelve years in Custine's regiment. Elected justice of the peace at Jouy-en-Josas in 1791, he too had become a magistrate in 1800. Now completely deaf, he refused to leave the bench unless his pension was increased to twice that he drew from the Cross of St. Louis. Of the second generation, the most prominent figures seem to have been Douet d'Arcq, born in 1787, who had begun his career in Italy at the end of the Empire and had been a public prosecutor, and Bernard de Mauchamp, born in 1793 and appointed a deputy public prosecutor in 1818, who was now one of the examining magistrates, suspended from his duties under the Villèle ministry for having supported the candidacy of Le Peletier d'Aunay and then reinstated by Martignac. The young generation consisted of the deputy public prosecutors and the *juges auditeurs.* The two deputy public prosecutors, Raudot[3] and Gustave de Beaumont, would find a place in the history of their times. Of the four *juges auditeurs,* two have no distinguishing features as far as we are concerned, and the other two were Elie de Beaumont, Gustave's cousin and the brother of the celebrated geologist Léonce-Elie de Beaumont, who would later marry one of Le Peletier d'Aunay's daughters, and Tocqueville himself.

The actual work of the law court required extensive legal knowledge. Not only because both civil and criminal lawsuits were tried there, Versailles being the seat of the court of assizes, but also because one had to be prepared to apply either the custom of Paris (the traditional common law that obtained under the Ancien Régime), the laws of the Revolution, or the Napoleonic Code, depending on when

---

[2]Personal files, National Archives; *Almanach Royal,* 1828, 1829, 1830.
[3]Cougny and Robert, *Dictionnaire des parlementaires.*

the events to be judged had taken place. Given the lengths of the trials, there could easily be, for instance in lawsuits involving the statute of limitations, ambiguities or conflicts among the successive laws. The interpretation of these laws in the light of the changes of regime and the changes in social conditions thus imposed itself on anyone capable of enough reflection to refer concrete cases to general principles.

The role of the *juges auditeurs* was not well defined. Unpaid, they were actually serving an apprenticeship. The public prosecutor or a deputy prosecutor could give them a brief to study and defend before the law court; they could also be brought in to sit as surrogate judges.

Among the tasks required of them were occasional hearings of witnesses, which brought them into direct contact with the popular hostility to the regime. Thus, in May 1828, Tocqueville was sent to conduct an investigation in Saint-Germain, where about fifty young men had made tricolored cockades for themselves out of handkerchiefs and formed a procession shouting "Long live the Emperor!" In his report, the young magistrate stressed the fact that the silent complicity of the witnesses had made his inquiry difficult. He dismissed the idea of a plot or a riot touched off by extreme poverty: it was simply that after a fair amount of drinking in various taverns, the young men had dared to say out loud what they had been thinking to themselves.[4]

Every year, when the law court reopened, a young magistrate would give a speech on an assigned topic. In 1827, Gustave de Beaumont had been assigned a perilous subject, "The Discretion of Magistrates in Political Matters." In 1828 or 1829, it was Tocqueville's turn, and he was assigned a more traditional subject, "Dueling." In this speech, we can already see what was to be a constant concern in his work, the relation between the mores and the laws. Early in the speech, he seeks to show that dueling is not punishable by the laws currently in force. In a later part, he adds that the laws cannot punish the practice effectively because the laws are nothing without the support of the mores and the mores do not formally condemn dueling—which is related to the fact that the idea of honor remains one of the basic principles of society. Nevertheless, Tocqueville considers dueling to be an evil which can be cured only by a moral or religious sentiment superior to the idea of honor: "Let the idea of having merited a divine reward and not the idea of escaping the scaffold be each man's consolation for the loss of other men's good opinion, and this opinion will change of its own accord. Let religion, that divine support of human

[4]Tocqueville Archives, file 68.

virtue, reassume its place in the souls from which it has been driven out so energetically. Remake the man before remaking the citizen . . . And then you will have effective laws."[5]

It was without enthusiasm, in deference to the wishes of his family and to the voice of good sense, that Tocqueville had taken this post. There was every indication that he could make a very good career for himself, for, as Beaumont tells us,[6] the memory of Malesherbes still had considerable weight in the magistracy of the Restoration. But it is all but certain that Tocqueville already envisaged a political career for himself beyond the magistracy. Such was the case for Raudot, deputy public prosecutor at Versailles, son of a deputy in the Chamber and a large landowner in the Nivernais, whom Tocqueville would encounter again in 1849, when he was a prominent figure in the party of order, and who was the last defender of decentralized administration in the National Assembly in 1879. It was very probably the same for Beaumont, to whom Tocqueville wrote in 1829: "Now we see ourselves face to face with our ambitions." And he insisted: "What we must fashion in ourselves is the political man." The possibility was open for Tocqueville to reach high political office, which was, in the provinces at that time, linked to a family's rank in society. The nobility of the Cotentin were "accustomed to seeing us at the head of the procession," he would soon write, and the Comte de Tocqueville, a peer of France, was sent in 1829 to preside over the electoral college of the department of the Manche and to try to ensure that the elections there had the right results.[7] Comte Hervé dreamed of reserving the position due to his family for his youngest son, whose gifts he recognized—in the same spirit, Alexis would be given the Château de Tocqueville in the division of property in 1836. The two older sons had been led to adopt military careers, but the third had been prevented from doing the same because he was to move by the shortest route to achieve what had always been the Comte's own ambition, one that, he thought, took on concrete shape too late in his own life: a parliamentary role. But Alexis was barely twenty-two when he became a junior magistrate, and he could anticipate a long wait—thanks to the legislation in force under the Restoration that required deputies to be at least forty years of age—before he could be elected to the Chamber. The judiciary was, in the meantime, a career and, should things not work out as one hoped, a possible substitute for the political life.

[5]Ibid.
[6]Beaumont, *Notice,* op. cit., 7.
[7]His speech is preserved in the Tocqueville Archives. See above, p. 33, and Note 27.

The young man thus found it necessary to resign himself to the thought of a lifetime in the judiciary. It appears, from what Blosseville says and from Tocqueville's own admission, that he did not hide his distaste for his situation very well. At that time he was slight and thin; his face was at once childish and rather sickly, framed by long, silky black hair and brightened by large, sparkling black eyes. He was often silent, with a sort of stiffness that was taken for pride and disdain, though distrust, shyness, and distraction also entered in. He himself agreed that he was "icy" and "not especially outgoing." He grew animated when the conversation turned to a subject that interested him. Blosseville attributes to Beaumont the remark that the most useful conversations were always, for Tocqueville, the most interesting.[8] His manner became a little gentler with time, not only because Beaumont taught him to "unbend" but also because in a part of the law court there was an atmosphere of friendly camaraderie that allowed him to show that, despite appearances, he was basically a "pretty good fellow." By July 1827 he could write to Kergorlay that the prejudices against him had crumbled: "My companions, who all have more or less the air of conceited pedants, nevertheless have more to offer than I thought at first. They almost all treat me now with a friendliness and a good spirit of camaraderie that I find . . . quite agreeable . . . Among them I have found one or two young men who are truly honorable, conscientious and filled with worthy sentiments." Humiliated by his relative weakness in applying legal principles the abstract study of which had inspired him with "disgust,"[9] he took a great interest in the actual judgments, which filled his mind as a love object fills the heart. However, he had persistent difficulties in speaking: he groped for words and truncated his ideas, and with a feeling of "rage" envied people who could speak eloquently on no matter what. And at about the same time he wrote to his brother Edouard: "Although the work is tedious, it has the interest of something that is indispensable to learn . . . This isn't the life one imagined at the age of sixteen, full of emotions and illusions, but it is unfortunately the most natural life for man and the one, still, in which he can most tranquilly make his journey to the great abyss."[10]

But although Tocqueville resigned himself to his job and did the best he could in it, and although he had warm relations with many

---

[8]Louis Passy, Le Marquis de Blosseville (Paris, 1898), 107; letter to Beaumont dated May 8, 1830, O.C. VII, 1: 98.

[9]Letter to Kergorlay dated July 23, 1827, O.C. XIII, 1: 107.

[10]Letter to Beaumont, O.C. VIII, 1: 86.

of his colleagues, he was not able to win the favor of the presiding judge of the law court, Brunet. Did Brunet take exception to his lack of eloquence, or was it that Tocqueville had not very successfully concealed his disdain for "the circumspect and shriveled souls hidden under the black robes"? We don't know, but in one letter we learn that Brunet prevented Tocqueville from becoming a deputy public prosecutor and thereby attaining the next level of advancement, despite the fact that the minister of justice was favorably disposed toward him and despite his family's connections in the Court—an episode that shows there were certain legal limits to favoritism in the time of the Restoration even under the Polignac ministry.[11] After 1830, Tocqueville would become a *juge suppléant,* or surrogate judge—the new name given by the revolution to the *juges auditeurs*—but would leave the magistracy in 1832 without having been confirmed in his appointment and without having received any salary at all.

Important though it was in forming his mind, since he would always be interested in the legal aspect of social problems, his stint in the magistracy did not monopolize Tocqueville's attention during his time in Versailles. His real intellectual activity took place within the framework of the friendships he formed at that time with Blosseville, Chabrol, and especially with Beaumont. All four men had similar backgrounds, being of the Catholic and legitimist nobility. Strangely, Blosseville, Beaumont, and Tocqueville, even though they had first become acquainted at Versailles, were all three cousins of Le Peletier d'Aunay, who was at that time the leader of the liberal opposition party in the departmental council.

Ernest de Blosseville, who was born in 1799 and died in 1886, was the oldest. Louis Passy wrote a book about him (*Le Marquis de Blosseville* [1898]) which contains certain confidences he made at the end of his life and is not very well disposed toward Tocqueville in the Versailles period. In 1854, Blosseville had asked Tocqueville, by then a member of the Académie Française, to present his candidacy for a place as a corresponding member of the Institute, and Tocqueville had evaded the request. This cast a pall over Blosseville's memories of the Versailles period, when their relations had been very warm. Blosseville belonged to a legitimist family from the Eure; at the age of twenty, he had made his first appearance as a writer in Chateaubriand's *Le Conservateur* and the latter, who was then minister of foreign affairs,

[11]Letter to Beaumont, *O.C.* VIII, 1: 86.

had sent him to Spain during the expedition of 1823, serving under his friend Talaru, the ambassador to Madrid. In June 1827, appointed councillor in the prefecture of Versailles, Blosseville had been made welcome by Tocqueville's father; he became secretary-general under Tocqueville's successor, Baron Capelle. Interested in archaeology as well as in literature and politics, he had a predilection for everything relating to his native Normandy. At the beginning of the July monarchy he would write his *Histoire des colonies pénales de l'Angleterre dans l'Australie*. For several years he was preoccupied by the penitentiary system and it may have been he (as Passy seems to suggest) who drew Tocqueville's and Beaumont's attention to the separate-cell system he had gone to see in Geneva, providing them with the pretext for their trip to America. He was actually the most obliging of friends and, from America, Tocqueville would consult him on the subject of French administrative law.

In September 1829, Ernest de Chabrol-Chaméane replaced Beaumont as deputy public prosecutor at Versailles, a position Tocqueville had sought in vain, and moved in with Tocqueville; he was the nephew of Villèle's old minister of the navy. Tocqueville had known him since childhood and had encountered him again while he was studying law. Chabrol was more than a jurist; he was also interested in German philosophy. Although Tocqueville didn't think much of his intellect, he agreed that his frank and easygoing nature made him a very tolerable friend.

The friendship between Tocqueville and Beaumont was to last all their lives, except for a few cool periods at the end of the July monarchy.[12] Beaumont was a little older, born in 1802, and he had been appointed deputy public prosecutor at Versailles on February 22, 1826, after exercising the same functions at Bar-sur-Aube.

Tocqueville and Beaumont had many traits likely to draw them together, first of all the similarity of their backgrounds. The Beaumonts were one of the best families of Touraine. Very prolific, they had increased from marriage to marriage and from château to château through the Normandy countryside and into the Maine. It was to the south of this province, in the pleasant Loire valley, that Jules, Gustave's father, had moved, leaving Beaumont-la-Ronce, the family's cradle in Touraine, to settle in another Beaumont, Beaumont-la-Chartre. Like Alexis among the Tocquevilles, Gustave belonged to the part of the

---

[12]For more about Beaumont, see not only their correspondence published in vol. VIII of the *O.C.*, but also G. W. Pierson's classic volume, *Tocqueville and Beaumont in America* (New York, 1938), and the introduction to Beaumont's *Lettres d'Amérique* (Paris, 1973).

family that had remained unshakably attached to the legitimate king. His father, Jules, was only a departmental councillor, but one of his uncles, Armand, was a prefect and a more dedicated member of the ultraroyalist party than Tocqueville's father. Other members of the family, however, had served the Empire, like Marc-Antoine, a handsome cavalry officer and the husband of the sister of Davoust, or André who, connected by marriage to the Tascher de la Pagerie family, was chamberlain to the emperor and elicited a famous reply from Madame Sans-Gêne.[13] Among the Beaumonts, as among the Tocquevilles, there was an interest in intellectual matters, as witness the letters Gustave wrote to his family from America (although the Beaumonts later seem to have become bogged down in the humdrum routine of provincial life).

But perhaps it was the contrast in their personalities that sealed their friendship. Heine compares them to the oil and vinegar in a salad.[14] Indeed, Gustave de Beaumont was a decent fellow, warm and easygoing, with a touch of the cunning of a man of the West which didn't in the least tarnish his fundamental honesty. Beaumont's gift of gab may have irritated Tocqueville at first, but he was won over by a friendly service. Beaumont, in the public prosecutor's office, simply suggested that Tocqueville might make whatever use he thought appropriate of his dossiers and briefs. "A friendship sprang up between us that was already mature, I don't know how," Tocqueville would write in 1828 or 1829. Perhaps it was actually less spontaneous than that, but it is true that Tocqueville trusted Beaumont as he rarely trusted anyone.

Their friendship had two features common to most of Tocqueville's, for he needed someone to be an intermediary between him and other people and he also needed someone who would counter his self-distrust and offer him reassurance. Beaumont played both these roles, the first with zest, the second with scrupulousness. In the eyes of others, Beaumont was the genius of the prosecutor's room at Versailles, and his spontaneous eloquence, brilliant and occasionally glib, seemed to guarantee him a great future. Tocqueville was a little overshadowed by him.

But though he was sometimes superficial, Beaumont was a shrewd man of sound judgment. He knew how to behave with Tocqueville, recognizing the latter's intellectual superiority and graciously deferring

[13]Comte de Beaumont, *La Maison de la Bonninière de Beaumont* (Paris, 1907).
[14]H. Heine, *Français et Allemands* (1868), 314.

to it. This was what made possible the most intimate part of their friendship, the intellectual pursuits that brought them together.

After completing his secondary school studies, as we have seen, Tocqueville undertook to supplement them, particularly by his study of history. Beaumont joined him in his reading and the two of them discussed what they learned. Thus, for example, Tocqueville wrote a long letter concerning the history of England, inspired by the English Catholic historian Lingard, and briefly analyzed Barante's *Histoire des ducs de Bourgogne,* while Beaumont took notes on Thiers's *Histoire de la Révolution.* Together, they learned the laws of political economy through J.-B. Say. In an important letter dated October 25, 1829, Tocqueville explains to his friend what the goal of their studies should be: "What we must fashion in ourselves is the political man. And to do this, we have to study the history of mankind and especially that of our immediate predecessors. The only value of general history is that it gives us a few broad notions about humanity as a whole and prepares us for this particular history."[15] Then Tocqueville goes on to specify that this history centers upon revolutions, the condition of the people at the moment these revolutions come into being, and the situation they are left in afterwards. He adds—he has just returned from a trip to Switzerland—that he has been very struck recently by the influence of geography upon the "political divisions" of nations. Here, beside the explanation in temporal terms, a spatial, geographic dimension takes shape that foreshadows Tocqueville's approach in *Democracy in America.*

One would be wrong to take at face value the disdain that Tocqueville seems to profess in this passage for "general notions" about the history of humanity. Though they may not be enough in themselves to form the political man, they are indispensable to the process of forming him. For years now, Tocqueville had been looking to history for an explanation of man; he had been disappointed by the narrative style of men like Thiers and the pedantic style of the "cold fish" Lingard. Then he found his guide and teacher in the person of Guizot.

Guizot's course of lectures, which had been suspended in 1822, was resumed on April 11, 1828, when his topic was the *History of Civilization in Europe,* a broad introduction to the *History of Civilization in France,* the subject of his teaching from December 1828 to May 1830.[16] We have the notes written up by Tocqueville for some of the lectures

[15]*O.C.* VIII, 1: 93.
[16]Ch.-H. Pouthas, *Guizot sous la Restauration* (Paris, 1923).

given between April 11, 1829, and May 1830, but he also attended earlier lectures or had read the notes Beaumont took during them. In a letter to Beaumont dated August 30, 1829, the latter part of which is lost, so that we don't know how his comments end, he writes: "We have to reread that this winter, my good friend, it is extraordinary in its analysis of ideas and in the precision of its language, truly *extraordinary.*" Similarities have been pointed out that show Guizot's influence on the larger themes of *L'Ancien Régime:* the class struggle, the decline of the feudal system, the judgment on the *Lumières* (the leaders of the Enlightenment), etc.[17] But what Tocqueville discerned at once in Guizot was the concept of an all-embracing history of civilization, as his notes on the lecture of July 18, 1829, show:

The history of civilization . . . should and does try to embrace everything simultaneously. Man is to be examined in all aspects of his social existence. History must follow the course of his intellectual development in his deeds, his customs, his opinions, his laws, and the monuments of his intelligence. History must descend into him, must judge the value of the foreign influences that come to him from outside his own milieu. In a word, it is the whole of man during a given period that must be portrayed, and the history of civilization is nothing other than the summary exposition of all these relevant ideas.[18]

If we replace the "given period" by a given geographical area, don't we see a similarity between this description of Guizot's method and the meticulous analysis of American society that continually linked the social relationships and the inner life of democratic man?

And there was probably even more in the lesson Guizot taught: though subject to external circumstances, man nonetheless made his own history, and was thus obliged to submit to moral judgment. In Tocqueville there was to be a more fatalistic, more providentialistic tendency, derived perhaps from Bossuet or from a somewhat Jansenist education, but within this tendency he still stressed the collaborative role of man, who could make his fate either beneficent or harmful. In this, Tocqueville, who always waxed indignant over Thiers's amoral history, was close to Guizot, who confirmed him in a tendency that already existed in his nature.

·　　·　　·

[17]Hoeges, "Guizot und Tocqueville," *Historische Zeitschrift* 227 (1974), 328–53.
[18]Tocqueville Archives, file 69.

Beaumont's appointment to Paris in September 1829 seemed to Tocqueville to be a real catastrophe. He knew that Beaumont was quick to make friends and "forgetful," and Tocqueville was afraid of being isolated. These fears proved groundless. Beaumont spent all his free time at Versailles—though since he had romantic involvements there, we probably should not make too much of his pure devotion as a friend. In any event, the four friends met for discussions in which, during these years of 1828 and 1829, political developments occupied an important and already rather disquieting place. If one is to believe the *Souvenirs* of Carné,[19] who knew them and showed them a goodwill that Tocqueville did not reciprocate, they accepted the Martignac ministry with some sympathy, then with growing uneasiness the Polignac ministry, whose royalists, "mad" about Versailles, were rejoicing, foreseeing the day when the king would be "going horseback riding" again.

At that time Versailles was a town of thirty thousand inhabitants, the twenty-fourth largest in the kingdom. It wasn't in the least an artificial town with a preponderance of nobility. Although we don't know much about its activities or its lower classes, we can see that the bourgeoisie had solid positions and dominated the National Guard; they lived in the *quartier* Notre-Dame, in rivalry with the nobility of the *quartier* Saint-Louis. Before 1830, our friends frequented the bourgeois salons as regularly as the aristocratic ones. Several of these salons were quite serious in tone, answering a need found at that time, toward the end of the Restoration, in other provincial towns as well—the need to create literary and scientific societies. Tocqueville had become acquainted with two teachers at the *collège royal* in Versailles who were among the most active organizers. One was Bouchitté, then a teacher of the third class, later a school inspector, but, most important, a Catholic philosopher who was to write a history of the proofs of the existence of God, and also an art critic who was to publish works on Philippe de Champaigne and Poussin. Bouchitté was to remain in touch with Tocqueville all his life. His brother-in-law, Baudry de Balzac, a teacher of natural history and medicine, started a series of enterprises that were to grow under the July monarchy: an ephemeral newspaper, *La Presse de Seine-et-Oise,* in which Tocqueville was to publish his first studies on Algeria; a Natural Sciences Society that included, besides Baudry de Balzac, Dr. Edwards, brother of Milne

[19]For the thoughts and feelings of young people in 1829, see Louis de Carné, *Souvenirs,* chap. 5.

Edwards, the geologist Huot, the entomologist Berger, and the Abbé Caron, among others; a Society of Sciences, Arts, and Letters, started in December 1834, that was to organize a series of less technical lectures to which ladies would be admitted and where Bouchitté and Vacherot would speak. In the review this society put out there appeared the first part of Ballanche's *Palingénésie sociale* [social regeneration] and the introduction to the second edition of Beaumont and Tocqueville's *Système pénitentiaire*. Chabrol, Beaumont, and Tocqueville were among its corresponding members.

Actually, little had been achieved so far, but the impetus had been given. "In Versailles, toward the end of 1829 and the beginning of 1830 . . . several attempts had been made to arrange for public courses to be offered, to start literary circles—small meetings at which drafts of philosophical or literary works would be read to just a few friends. None of these attempts succeeded very satisfactorily, either because people's minds were not ripe for it, or because these timid ventures were not advertised . . . No authorization was necessary, because none of these ventures had grown large enough to require an application to the authorities for their consent . . . The revolution of 1830, the subsequent agitation in people's thinking, contributed to making a seed germinate that needed only a more fertile earth and a more vitalizing sun."

A provincial town with its own active society, Versailles obviously felt the pull of the nearby capital. There were numerous means of transport for getting to Paris, though these often consisted of uncomfortable two-wheeled post chaises which left at unpredictable hours. When the necessity arose, the young men did not hesitate to walk the distance separating them from the faubourg Saint-Germain to attend a dinner party, a dance, or one of Guizot's lectures. An equilibrium of a kind was established among work, social life, excursions, family life, and Paris connections—one that was to be shattered by the revolution of 1830.

We know what Tocqueville's state of mind was as he confronted the crisis that led up to the revolution, because of some letters he wrote telling his brother Edouard, then on his honeymoon in Italy, what was happening. The first of these letters, which cover the period from August 9, 1829, to May 6, 1830,[20] was written during the formation

---

[20]Letters to Edouard dated August 9, 1829, and March 15 and 24, April 6 and 29, and May 6, 1830, in part unpublished.

of the Polignac government. Polignac could neither obtain a vote of confidence in the Chamber nor persuade the Chamber to change the electoral law; new elections would simply return the same deputies to their seats. "And so they have embarked on a system of coups d'état, of laws by ordinances; that is to say, the choice is between the royal power and the power of the people, and a battle will be joined in the lists—a match where, in my opinion, what will be at stake for the people will be only its present, while the royal power will stake both its present and its future." And if, faced with the Chamber's hostility, the king dismissed his ministers, he would be weakened, because guarantees for the future would then be required of him. Tocqueville saw, with perfect clarity, the situation that the initiative of Charles X had created.

The following March, the king responded haughtily to a statement by 221 deputies expressing the nation's concern: "All of this smells a little of Louis XIV, but to all appearances the French people of his time have died along with him." In reality, the monarchy had placed itself in a desperate situation in order to rally its supporters. But the Chamber, which had been laying the blame on individuals, would end by blaming the way things were.

On April 6: "The king talks only of force, the ministers of firmness, the more cautious royalists are uneasy about the future, the crazy ones—and that includes most of them—are in seventh heaven. They talk only of coups d'état, of changing the election law by ordinance."

The royalists were turning on each other, as at Coblenz, but no one had any confidence in Polignac.

On May 6: "To put oneself above the Charter is to ask to be toppled from the throne." Tocqueville foresaw that the courts would refuse to enforce illegal ordinances, and he approved. He predicted "the fall of the reigning House."

This perspicacity and this pessimism did not, however, draw Tocqueville into an unshakable opposition. He was critical of Chateaubriand's opposition, as well as that of the *Journal des débats,* and seemed to approve of his father, who, as president of the departmental college of the Manche, was trying to win over the electors.

He was to confess in his *Souvenirs:* "Right up to the end I had felt a vestige of hereditary affection for Charles X, but this king fell because he violated rights that were dear to me."[21] This, no doubt, expresses Tocqueville's dilemma just before the Three Glorious Days

[21]*Souvenirs, O.C.* XII, 86.

(July 27, 28, and 29 of 1830) that put a decisive end to this "vestige of hereditary affection" with the overthrow of the Bourbon regime and the exile of Charles X.

The July revolution in Versailles has been described to us by Passy, who takes his information from Blosseville, a well-placed witness since he was at the prefecture, and in a more fragmented way by the irrepressible Beaumont, who was at the law courts in Paris in the morning, then made his way through the Paris riots, went on to visit the royal army, in which one of his uncles was serving, and by evening had reached Versailles, where a hospitable bed awaited him. He returned to Paris at dawn.[22]

In Versailles itself, confused rumors were going around on the twenty-seventh about the publication of the ordinances, then the garrison was sent to the capital. On the twenty-ninth, the population seized arms at the barracks of the king's bodyguard and invaded the town hall.

At that point the National Guard intervened to prevent bloodshed and the possible massacre of the royalists. A lawyer, an officer in the guard, led the insurgents back and forth in marches and countermarches under the pretext of keeping watch over the gates. When, exhausted, they bivouacked and fell asleep in the streets during the night of July 29–30, the National Guard retrieved the arms.

On July 27, Comte Hervé sent a note to his son urging him to be prudent, whatever his opinions might be. On the twenty-ninth, Alexis helped his parents get to Saint-Germain, where they took refuge in the home of Baron Ollivier, but by evening he was back in Versailles. On the morning of the thirty-first, Blosseville, who was in the town hall, saw Alexis de Tocqueville come in: "He was bringing back . . . a service gun which he had been given two days earlier as a volunteer in the National Guard. He took me aside and said to me with a mixture of pain and humiliation: 'There's nothing more to be done; it's all over. At the Saint-Cloud gate I just saw the convoy of the monarchy go by, the king, the princes and princesses, the ministers in carriages surrounded by the bodyguard. And the coats-of-arms on the royal carriages were hidden by spatters of mud!' "[23]

He had already written a note to Mary Mottley the night before, saying: "All of this—the bloodshed in Paris, the shouts of alarm—haunts me relentlessly. As for the Bourbons, they have behaved like

---

[22]This account by Beaumont is in the Beinecke Library at Yale University.
[23]Passy, *Le Marquis de Blosseville*, 129–30.

cowards and do not deserve a thousandth part of the blood that has been spilled over their cause."[24]

The tone in which Tocqueville speaks of the king here is a radical change from the tone of the letters he had written to Edouard not long before. Nevertheless, Tocqueville and Beaumont did not yet consider themselves liberals, and they spoke ironically of "cousin" Le Peletier d'Aunay. And yet they too placed the law above the king; they saw the revolutionary July days just past as an event that could bring about an orderly freedom. This orderly freedom was already a political ideal of Tocqueville's, and apparently only his loyalty to his family's ideas prevented him from seeing the similarities between his feelings and those of the moderate liberals surrounding the new sovereign, Louis-Philippe.

[24]Tocqueville Archives, file 18.

6

THE DEPARTURE

FOR AMERICA

ON AUGUST 1, 1830, just after his accession to power as the lieutenant general of the realm and a few days before he was proclaimed King of the French by the liberals sitting as a rump Chamber, Louis-Philippe appointed a new prefect to the department of Seine-et-Oise. Baron Capelle, who had become minister of public works in the Polignac ministry, had remained prefect of the department as well. Now he was in flight, like the other ministers, and his successor as prefect, d'Aubernon, who had already held the post in the last days of the Empire, was pleased that he would not be asked to dismiss anyone. d'Aubernon's intentions were conciliatory. He wanted to retain all the civil servants willing to serve the new monarchy, but he was required by law to ask them to swear an oath of loyalty. A platform was therefore built on which each person had to stand in turn and reply to a question concerning his loyalty to the new king and the Charter with the words: "I swear it!" D'Aubernon tactfully sent Blosseville, the secretary-general of the prefecture, away on vacation during the few days during which this obligation was to be fulfilled, but he could take such a measure only for a close associate. It was not possible to offer the magistrates an exemption.

Tocqueville had a very harsh opinion of Charles X's conduct and did not regret his fall, but he would have liked to see the Duc de Bordeaux, Charles X's grandson and of course a Bourbon, accede to the throne under the regency of the Duc d'Orléans. This was a futile hope, and Louis-Philippe, who was suspected of not doing anything to help bring it about, tried on more than one occasion to show that it was impossible. Such a solution would have preserved old monarchical loyalties and eased the scruples of men who were tied to the sovereign by an allegiance of very long standing. Nevertheless, as it was established the new regime seemed the only rampart—and at the moment a very fragile one—against revolutionary anarchy. Like his friends Beaumont and Chabrol, and also like his brother Hippolyte, who believed Europe would probably go up in flames, Tocqueville decided on August 16 to swear the oath of loyalty demanded of the Versailles magistrates. (In October, when the title of his office was changed by the new regime from *juge auditeur* to *juge suppléant,* he had to renew this oath.) He did not swear his loyalty to the new Orleanist king without great inner turmoil, as he says in a note to Mary Mottley:

"I have at last sworn the oath. My conscience does not reproach me, but I am still deeply wounded and I will count this day among the most unhappy of my life . . . I am at war with myself, this is a new state for me, and it horrifies me. At the moment the sound of my voice altered when I said those three words, I felt my heart beating hard enough to burst my chest." And in the same note, Tocqueville added: "I have to avoid the company of people I respect, though at the same time disapproving of them."[1] In his own family, his father, named a peer only recently by Charles X, was ipso facto excluded from the upper Chamber; his uncle, Rosanbo, and Louis de Kergorlay's father chose to give up the title of peer rather than submit to taking the oath. Henrion, who continued to hover about the family and who had become one of the hotheaded journalists of the ultraroyalist press—he was called into court for his excesses—addressed a menacing letter to Alexis urging him to refuse to take the oath too. The latter wrote a sharp reply asking him to mind his own business.[2] Within the family, mutual affection imposed toleration. The same was not true for society in general.

As we have seen, on July 30 and 31 in Versailles the National Guard protected the nobility against any aggression from the populace; this solidarity with the upper classes was no more than a passing reflex. Hostility and bitterness between the aristocracy and the bourgeoisie had never been so intense, and it was no longer possible to frequent the salons of both the *quartier* Saint-Louis and the *quartier* Notre-Dame. In October, a moderate friend of Blosseville's from Normandy spoke of "Versailles, that odious place where one is so disagreeably

[1]Tocqueville Archives, file 18, quoted by Rédier, *M. de Tocqueville,* op. cit., 85–86.
[2]Tocqueville Archives, file 18.

crushed between the two opposing parties, each just as exclusive and unreasonable as the other."[3] In the impassioned atmosphere of the period following the Three Glorious Days, young magistrates who had sworn the oath were accused of having sordid ambitions that violated their families' tradition of honor. If they wanted to avoid being snubbed by society or even suffering the more polite scorn of the old liberals, wisdom cautioned them to give themselves a little room and take the time necessary to let people calm down.

As early as August 1830, Tocqueville was posing to himself a question that, as he saw it, was tied to the abandonment of a career he now regretted having adopted: "If I must give up this career and if nothing obliges me to stay in France, I am determined to flee the idleness of private life and take up again for some years the more turbulent life of the traveler. For a long time now, I have had a very strong desire to visit North America. I will go there and see what a great republic is," he wrote on the twenty-sixth of that month to Charles Stoffels, Eugène's brother. And on October 4, again writing to Charles, he said that these travel plans were motivated by concern for his career. At the time, Tocqueville was pessimistic about his future. If the current regime remained in place, he would be able to advance himself only by showing an eagerness to serve that he did not feel. If it collapsed, a new revolution could open a career for him only at a low level within one of the political parties:

Suppose I go over to America now, still remaining a magistrate and retaining my seniority rights. Fifteen months pass. In France the various parties take shape. It will be possible to see clearly which is incompatible with France's greatness and with continuing peace. And it will be possible to return with clear, decisive opinions, altogether uncommitted to anyone.

In itself, the trip has taken you out of the most commonplace class. The knowledge you have gained in such a celebrated nation has separated you from the crowd. You know exactly what a vast republic is, why it is practicable in one place, impracticable in another. All aspects of public administration have been examined one by one. When you return to France you certainly feel a strength that you didn't have when you left. If the time is favorable, some sort of publication on your part can alert the public to your existence and turn the attention of the parties to you.[4]

The preoccupations with career that Tocqueville expresses here were Beaumont's as well. In his position in the public prosecutor's office, he

---

[3]Letter from Le Prévost to Blosseville (October 1830) in Passy, op. cit., 153.
[4]Unpublished letter, Stoffels d'Hautefort Archives.

felt caught on the horns of a dilemma, obliged either to demonstrate his zeal for the new regime or to have it be suspected that he was still a Carlist at heart. And since he spent most of his free time in Versailles, he had the same anxieties about the society there that Tocqueville did. It was therefore necessary to hit upon a professional excuse for the long absence that the trip to America would require, a pretext that would disguise the deeper intellectual reasons for this study of the New World.

Their pretext was a question which enlightened opinion had been raising for several years now: how to reform the French system of penal incarceration. There were several categories of prisons and houses of detention in France, but in practice a disorder and anarchy prevailed that was described with great energy by the writers of the time, especially Balzac. Most of the prisons were "cesspools" and "schools of crime." One found in them an astonishingly promiscuous mixture of criminals, old offenders, young petty thieves, even people who were simply emotionally unbalanced. Our two magistrates were acquainted with this, having paid visits to the laxly disciplined house of detention in Versailles and the central prison of Poissy. For several years, they had been talking with their friend Blosseville about the question of deportation and the methods of punishing and reclaiming convicts. The statistics showed that in France the proportion of recidivists was higher than in other countries where such statistics were available.

In October, Beaumont wrote a report to the minister of the interior noting these facts and stressing France's interest in following the example of England and Switzerland, where model prisons, built at considerable expense, had succeeded in reducing the crime rate. But Beaumont, who clearly knew how to argue a brief, added that the experience of their neighbors had been too recent to enlighten the minister in a useful way. It would be necessary to seek intelligence farther off, in the United States: here, a variety of penitentiary systems had been in place for much longer and were so effective that in the country as a whole not more than one out of every thirty-two convicted criminals was a recidivist. French criminal jurists like Charles Lucas had studied these American systems, of course, but because they had not seen them in action, they had not been able to explain clearly either the surprising moral rehabilitation of the convicts, or the low cost of the new prisons (Beaumont insisted on this point, which would impress the thrifty, "budget-minded" people in the bourgeois Chamber). It was therefore urgent to send two English-speaking observers

92

to conduct an on-the-spot investigation and compare notes over several months.[5]

The results of these observations could lead to the reform of the penal code (Beaumont did not add that they could also bring fame to the minister who accomplished the reform, but this went without saying). Referred to the minister in January 1831, and warmly supported by their cousin Le Peletier d'Aunay, who was now vice-president of the Chamber and one of the prominent figures among the moderate Orleanists, this report procured for the two young members of the magistrature the mission they had requested from the minister of the interior, Montalivet, together with a leave of absence of eighteen months from the minister of justice (February 6, 1831). Their readiness to pay for the trip out of their own pockets had facilitated the decision. They tried to hold the cost of the trip down by requesting free transportation on a warship, but when the minister of the navy refused they resigned themselves to sailing as private citizens.

As we have seen, however, this trip was motivated by broader and deeper considerations. The liberals of the Restoration had proposed English institutions as models, and not only had these institutions been somewhat shaken in England itself but France had been taken much farther, almost to the point of becoming a democratic republic, by the Three Glorious Days of 1830. The political class had checked the movement, but the new monarchy, set in place through a piece of hocus-pocus, seemed to have an uncertain future, and there was still the danger of another republican revolution. This idea of a republic, at the forefront of everyone's worries, evoked confused and contradictory images: ancient cities cemented by the civic virtues, Swiss cantons conforming to the eighteenth-century dogma which held that democracy was possible only in small states—but also the great upheaval of 1793, dictatorship and political clubs, the Reign of Terror and the guillotine, all of this finally degenerating into anarchy. Yet these concerns also brought renewed attention to bear on the great republic across the Atlantic, to which the French had long been warmly disposed.[6] The legitimists felt none of the bitterness toward the United States of the old British leaders—it would have been an offense to the memory of Louis XVI—and they contented themselves with ascribing the country's stability to unusual circumstances and prophesying that

[5]*Note sur le système pénitentiaire et sur la mission confiée par M. le ministre de l'Intérieur à MM. Gustave de Beaumont et Alexis de Tocqueville* (Paris, 1831).

[6]On the renewal of interest in the American republic at that time, see René Rémond, *Les Etats-Unis devant l'opinion française, 1815–1852* (Paris, 1962).

such stability wouldn't last forever. The liberals felt that this unusual democratic regime was well suited to a country that had remained rather primitive. It was the political expression of a rustic golden age already past in Europe. Yet a generation earlier Lafayette, now an old man brought back out of the shadows briefly by the 1830 revolution, had predicted, as had his friends the *idéologues*— the early historians of ideas, men like Destutt de Tracy—that one day Europe would have institutions in the American style. The revolution of 1830 thus presented a dilemma: did life in America portray scenes from the future or pictures of the past?

We don't know how familiar Tocqueville was with the tradition of the *idéologues,* but he did share their view of the future and it inspired him to write a letter in 1835 in which he described, at much greater length than in the letter of October 4, 1830, to Charles Stoffels, the underlying reasons for his trip to America, confirming the fact that he had it in mind well before the 1830 revolution. This letter, of which we have only a copy and which can be definitely dated as from 1835, has been published in the volume of Kergorlay correspondence (on the strength of information in the Yale archives) but we are inclined to think it was intended for Eugène Stoffels, since Kergorlay was too familiar with the inception of the *Democracy* to be enlightened by this declaration of principle:

"I am as profoundly convinced as one can be of anything in this world that we are irresistibly drawn by our laws and our mores toward an almost complete equality of social conditions. Once social conditions are equal, I no longer see any intermediary stage between a democratic government (and by the word democratic I mean not a republic but a state of society in which everyone, to a greater or lesser degree, takes part in the political process) and the unchecked rule of one man. I don't doubt for a moment that in time we will arrive at one or the other."

And farther on he links this conviction to his trip to America: "For almost ten years now I have been thinking some of the things I've just set forth to you. I went to America only to clarify my thoughts on these matters. The penitentiary system was an excuse: I used it as a passport that would allow me to go everywhere in the United States. In that country, where I encountered a thousand things I didn't expect, I also found some that were related to the questions I had so often asked myself. I discovered facts that seemed useful to know. I didn't go there with the idea of writing a book at all, but the idea of the book came to me. I said to myself that a man is under the same obligation to offer up his mind in the service of society as he is, in time of war, his body."[7]

What Tocqueville sought knowledge of, then, was the way of life in a democracy, a prototype of the future for France. But the explanation he gives of how his book came into being—born of his American experience and not planned in advance—doesn't fit the facts very well. In the letter of October 4, 1830, quoted earlier, he saw himself coming to the attention of the public with a work on American political life. He had told Beaumont about this project and Beaumont thought that as they were already collaborating on a study of the penitentiary system, they could also collaborate on a more significant work about the government and customs of the American people. On April 25, 1831, when they were on the boat sailing toward New York, Beaumont wrote to his father:

We have ambitious plans . . . We will see America as we survey its prisons. We will survey its inhabitants, its cities, its institutions, its mores. We will learn how the republican government works. This government is not at all well known in Europe . . . Wouldn't it be good to have a book that gives an accurate notion of the American people, that paints a broad portrait of their history, boldly outlines their character, analyzes their social state, and corrects the many mistaken opinions on this subject?[8]

What we have here is a plan for a book about America that already includes themes contained in the *Democracy* but which would have been the fruit of a collaboration between Tocqueville and Beaumont. The decision to write such a work had probably not been finally made, but it had clearly been envisaged for a long time.

According to Beaumont, whose testimony is corroborated by all the facts we know, it was Tocqueville who first conceived of the plan of going to America.[9] No doubt the tradition of Franco-American friendship that had been revived by Lafayette's trip to the United States in 1825 was not unknown to Beaumont. He was a distant cousin of the "Hero of Two Worlds," would later marry his granddaughter Clémentine, and was probably already a visitor to his salon. But in the Tocqueville family, interest in America was also a family tradition that had remained alive. Malesherbes had taken an interest in the young republic and his nephew La Luzerne, maternal grandfather of Louis de Kergorlay, had been the first French ambassador there. The old man

[7] *O.C.* XIII, 1: 373–75.
[8] Gustave de Beaumont, *Lettres d'Amérique,* 28.
[9] Beaumont, *Notice,* op. cit., 17–18.

had also advised Chateaubriand when he thought of going there to look for a northern passage between the two great oceans. Besides Chateaubriand, two other visitors to the Tocqueville house were Hyde de Neuville, exiled to the United States under the Empire and then ambassador to Washington under the Restoration, and Monsignor de Cheverus, the archbishop of Bordeaux, who came to Paris for the sessions of the Chamber of Peers and had been Bishop of Boston for a long time, an almost legendary character associated with the growth of Catholicism in the United States whose visits to the house may explain the care Alexis took to inform his family of the situation of Catholics in America.

It would be interesting to know what Tocqueville and Beaumont had read about the United States before their departure. Certainly they had read Chateaubriand's *Atala* (they were to have some difficulty freeing their styles from his influence), the *Leather-Stocking Tales* of James Fenimore Cooper, and the more serious *Tableau du climat et du sol des Etats-Unis d'Amérique* of Volney. They knew the former American consul David Baillie Warden, had dined with him shortly before their departure, and had perhaps leafed through his five-volume *Statistical, Political and Historical Account of the United States*. They may have read a book by the American political philosopher Thomas Cooper entitled in its French translation *Renseignements sur l'Amérique*. But were they acquainted with the *Itinéraire pittoresque du fleuve Hudson et des parties latérals de l'Amérique du Nord* [pictorial itinerary of the Hudson River and the coasts of North America] by the naturalist Jacques Milbert, published in thirteen booklets between 1826 and 1829, and then in two volumes of texts accompanied by a beautiful book of plates, or the more modest *Tournée à la mode aux Etats-Unis ou Voyage de Charleston à Québec et d'Albany à Boston* [a fashionable tour of the United States; or, a trip from Charleston to Quebec and from Albany to Boston] by Bourgeois, published in 1829? The fact that there are similarities between their itinerary and the recommendations of this last work, which was a true guide in the modern sense of the word, and that their impressions are analogous to those of the first work are not enough to prove it.

As far as works by English authors went, they knew the recently published *Travels to North America in the Years 1827 and 1828* by Captain Basil Hall, quoted in Beaumont's report, but had probably read no more than the section devoted to the penitentiary system, the only part translated into French. On the whole, though they had planned out itineraries ahead of time, they apparently made their decision too hastily to be able to do a great deal of research before leaving. It was after they returned that they supplemented what they had seen on their excursion with accounts by other travelers or pioneers. For the moment, they concerned themselves with collecting numerous letters of introduction to Americans they wanted to meet and with outfitting themselves for the long journey.

The two friends embarked on April 2 at Le Havre, Alexis's father and brothers having accompanied them this far. The ship on which they booked passage, the *Le Havre,* was American—as, on the evidence of the ship's registry at the port, were almost all those making the Atlantic crossing. It was a brig of five hundred tons that had come in ballast from Liverpool on March 20. It had a crew of 18, along with 163 passengers and a cargo of goods from the silk mills of Lyons.[10] Unfortunately, the list of the ship's passengers is missing; the letters from Tocqueville and Beaumont are our only source of information about the "ship's aristocracy," the thirty first-class passengers who had cabins: a few French and English, a Spanish family and some Swiss, with Americans in the majority. The voyage started badly, the vessel coming to ground in the port as it was trying to leave in the middle of the day; the next high tide freed it and it sailed out of Le Havre toward midnight. These brigs with their imposing sails were really no more than unwieldy nutshells that responded to the slightest motion of the sea, and the crossing was sometimes calm, sometimes rocky. During the first few days, most of the passengers were seasick. Beaumont was not, but Tocqueville didn't leave his bed until the fourth day out, and the passengers got to know one another only after six days. The length of the crossing could vary tremendously, on some occasions taking three times as long as on others. This time the *Le Havre* made it in thirty-eight days, a longer than average trip.

The passengers were moderately comfortable. Their food supply came in part from cattle and poultry brought on board along with the other provisions. But the captain's lack of foresight led to the rationing of sugar and flour by the end of the trip. A certain sociability existed on a voyage under sail that was an expanded version of the stagecoach camaraderie of the nineteenth century and whose last vestiges disappeared from the working-class milieu in France when third-class cars were eliminated from the national railway. Our two travelers took a dislike to a wine salesman from Bourgogne de Saint-Malo who was given to bawling the *Marseillaise,* but were on friendly terms with the

---

[10]According to information in the Le Havre ship's registry.

son of General Schérer (of the Italian campaign in the wars of the
Revolution) and made special efforts to speak English in daily conversations with a young American woman, Miss Edwards. Their first
informants about America were Palmer, an English landowner and
former member of the British Parliament, and especially the rich New
York businessman Schermerhorn. They would see both men again in
New York.

Sensitive though they were to the fact that in the midst of this
monotonous and reclusive life they looked out on the romantic and
ever-changing spectacle of the sea, they imposed on themselves a
rigorous work schedule: they would get up at 5:30 A.M. and work until
breakfast, which was served at 9, go back to work from 11 until 3
P.M., which was the hour for dinner, and retire at about 7 P.M. without
joining the others for supper. Except for the fact that they became
accustomed to having afternoon tea and would go out for the evening
at about the teatime hour, this was their work pattern in America as
well. On the ship, they translated an English writer on penitentiary
systems, read a history of the United States, and together studied the
Cours d'économie politique of J.-B. Say.[11] They also started taking notes
on American society, deriving most of their information from conversations with Palmer and Schermerhorn.

In many respects, the *Le Havre* was a transition between two worlds
and an apprenticeship in American life.

On May 9, the lookout shouted: "Land ho!" The American continent was in sight.

---

[11]The source of these details is the letter from Beaumont dated April 21 quoted earlier and also copies
of Tocqueville's letters to his parents dated April 25 and May 8 in the Beinecke Library at Yale, to be
published in the O.C. (volume of family correspondence).

Part II

FROM AMERICA
TO THE *DEMOCRACY*

7

AMERICA: THE BEGINNING

OF THE VISIT

ALEXIS DE TOCQUEVILLE and Gustave de Beaumont landed in New York on May 11, 1831; they embarked for Le Havre at the same port on February 20, 1832. The primary goal of their trip was the direct observation of a new kind of society and the forces that moved it and held it together. They were also sensitive to the exotic attraction that America still exerted on Europeans. If they didn't have time to prepare for their stay on the other side of the Atlantic through extensive reading, this didn't mean that they were ignorant of the literary tradition that descriptions of America now represented. It is inconceivable that Tocqueville, who had been nursing plans for this trip since he finished his studies,[1] and who had always been in the habit of thinking his plans through by himself in a coherent way, would not have made use of this tradition—even if only through newspaper articles or drawing-room conversations—to try to form some picture of the United States for himself. The tradition was alive, fed by the stories of a succession of travelers, their commentators or their plagiarists, sometimes lively, sometimes dull, in England as well as in France. It determined both the direction of the two travelers' research and the welcome they would be given by their American informants.[2]

Actually, there were two parts to this tradition, English and French. But the English part was well known to the France of the Restoration,

[1]See above, p. 90.

[2]See B. Fabian's good synthesis, *Alexis de Tocqueville Amerikabild* (Heidelberg, 1957), and also J. L. Mesick, *The English Travellers in America, 1785–1835* (New York, 1922), and E. M. Rodrigue, *Les Voyageurs français aux Etats-Unis pendant la première moitié du XIXe siècle*, thesis, Radcliffe, 1946.

where a mania for things English caused translations of books and articles to proliferate and where the *Revue britannique* had been following all aspects of intellectual activity across the Channel closely since 1825. With the exception of a few marginal figures—such as Frances Wright, who, with Robert Owen, attempted to found socialist colonies in the New World[3]—the British tradition was an unfriendly one. The old bitterness toward the rebellious colonies had been revived by the War of 1812, an episode whose importance to relations between the two Anglo-Saxon nations French historians have often misunderstood. Most of the men who took part in or witnessed that second war of independence (1812–1815) were still alive at the time of the two young magistrates' journey.

Of course, the works of literature most characteristic of this wave of disparagement on the part of the English had not yet been written. In 1829, Mrs. Trollope failed in her efforts to create a great fancy-goods bazaar in Cincinnati, and it was during the travels of the two young Frenchmen that she was writing her *Domestic Manners of the Americans* (1832), in which she vented her bitterness and snobbery. The following year, Major Hamilton discussed the same themes with more restraint in his *Men and Manners in America,* some features of which Beaumont used in *Marie.* It was only in 1842 that Dickens would in turn display, in the account of his travels, his hostility to American society.[4] The old tradition of polemics against the United States had been revived in 1829 by Captain Basil Hall. That year, the sailor turned professional traveler had published his *Travels in North America in the Years 1827 and 1828.* In the first few pages of this book he insists on his concern for objectivity, but this concern is soon swept away by his Tory prejudices. He asserts the indisputable superiority of the Anglican Church over American sects; defends English institutions, which truly represent the British nation without leading it to the edge of the abyss, as American democracy does the people of the New World; indignantly censures the freedom of American women, who have no manners; and denounces with horror the bastardization of the English language as it is spoken across the Atlantic. The captain, his wife, his whining child, and his servants had been warmly welcomed, as his account in fact attests. His book immediately created a scandal, and a lasting one (as late as 1922, an American historian called the captain an archtraitor to American hospitality!). Some of the captain's hosts

---

[3]Frances Wright, *Views of Society and Manners in America; in a Series of Letters from that Country to a Friend in England during the Years 1818, 1819, and 1820* (London, 1821). French translation, Paris, 1822.
[4]Charles Dickens, *American Notes* (London, 1842).

swore they would never receive another Englishman. Before they left France, the two young Frenchmen had become familiar with the part of the *Travels* devoted to the penitentiary system of Auburn, New York, which had been immediately translated into French, and for a part of the way they followed Hall's itinerary. It is certainly conceivable that the warmth of their reception owed something to the resentment the Englishman had aroused.

For that matter, Basil Hall was only giving new life to opinions of America that were implied in a good deal of English writing: the manners of Americans were coarse, they were returning to barbarism, they were a childish people consumed by demagogic passions who would eventually split up into several separate countries, they had no art or literature. This scorn for their primitiveness and lack of refinement could only exasperate the Americans, who were proud of their progress and their freedom. Certain journalists reacted sharply to the English attacks; such was the case with Timothy Dwight and Robert Walsch,[5] whom the two Frenchmen would meet in Boston and Philadelphia. Walsch, moreover, had distant relatives in France whom Tocqueville knew, and a permanent friendship formed between them.

The French tradition, which was much more favorable to American society, had come into being very early. Volunteers and officers in the Revolutionary War had looked with sympathy upon the events and people across the Atlantic and had praised the simplicity of customs, sometimes quite eloquently. This was the case with Chastellux, and with Ségur, the son of a king's minister and an habitué of Marie Antoinette's circle. For these liberal noblemen, the war in America remained a great memory, combining revenge against England with the emancipation of a people. Toward the end of the Ancien Régime, they celebrated the Fourth of July in Paris every year, gathering at the home of Admiral d'Estaing. Their successors went even farther in their enthusiasm. The Norman Hector St. John Crèvecoeur painted an idyllic picture of the life of the colonial, praising his inventiveness and his desire to improve his mind. Jacques-Pierre Brissot seems to have been the inventor of a triad that was destined to have great success: Protestantism-moral purity-cleanliness *(protestantisme-pureté des moeurs-propreté)*, the means by which American citizens had raised themselves above the subjects of the king of France. And Volney, though he had a bone to pick with government officials in the United States, was not resentful. His *Tableau* is a physical description of the United States, but

---

[5]See Mesick, *The English Travellers*.

his sympathy for the society shows through nonetheless, and if he gave up his plan to describe the latter in a second volume,[6] it was no doubt because his praise of American society would not be appropriate for a senator of the Empire. Condorcet saw the American people as a prefiguration of future societies and Lafayette certainly seems to have believed the same thing; these were opinions developed by their *idéologue* friends, like Destutt de Tracy, who also had ties with Jefferson.

The émigrés in America were not out of harmony with this tradition. Those who went there were mostly from the liberal nobility (when they came back to France in 1815, Bonapartists, especially old soldiers, emigrated to America in their turn). La Rochefoucauld-Liancourt traveled all over the country, noted its different aspects, and was the first to praise its penitentiary system.[7] Talleyrand, who had taken refuge in Philadelphia, threw a few darts at his hosts, but his days there were peaceful ones. His friend Moreau de Saint-Mery did indeed describe American society in a caustic fashion, but his work only saw the light of day in 1913.[8] Men like the Marquis de Gouvernet or Hyde de Neuville readily became accustomed to American life. But all these reactions are thrown into the shadow by the response of Chateaubriand.

He set out in 1792, armed with Malesherbes's advice and probably also his financial support, with the chimerical plan or the excuse of looking for a northern passage between the two great oceans. He spent only five months in America and very quickly gave up the notion, if he had ever really had it, of adding his name to the list of the great explorers of the eighteenth century. His itinerary has been a subject of controversy[9]—it is quite doubtful that he ever saw the Mississippi, even if it appears to be proved that he was at Niagara Falls. The world of the Indians no doubt attracted him for a time, as did that of the trappers, absorbed in the life of the wild. Whatever the case, America was to be one of the great themes of his work, a theme that would keep reappearing from *Atala* to the *Mémoires d'outre-tombe*. Combining what he had seen, what he had read, what he imagined, he recreated an America in unforgettable colors, juxtaposing the magnificence of

---

[6]See Rodrigue, *Les voyageurs français.*

[7]La Rochefoucauld-Liancourt, *Des prisons de Philadelphie, par un Européen* (Paris, 1819). See the analysis by Rémond, *Les Etats-Unis devant l'opinion française,* 563.

[8]Moreau de Saint-Mery, *Voyage aux Etats-Unis de l'Amérique, 1793–1798,* ed. S. L. Hims (New Haven, 1913). See Rémond, ibid.

[9]On these polemics, which have given birth to an abundant literature, see the overview by J. A. Bédé, *L'Itinéraire spirituel de Chateaubriand en Amérique,* bulletin nos. 14–15 of the Fédération internationale des professeurs de français, 292–304.

the forest, the mysteries of life in the wilderness, the bold gesture of the white man pushing the ideal frontier of the untamed land farther and farther west. His thoughts about the meaning of a democratic society are particularly evident in the *Voyage d'Amérique,* which appeared in 1827. Ambiguous in its implications, democracy has roots plunged deep in the outworn history of past societies, but it will perhaps flourish once more in the course of mankind's future development. A new freedom, daughter of the Enlightenment, will take the place of the old freedom, daughter of custom. How could the two young travelers, close to Chateaubriand as they were, not have been aware of this, the great man's verdict on the future of democracy?

In more general terms, the French tradition combined the old passion for investigation with avid curiosity concerning the only republic of any size to appear in modern times. The sympathetic response that the United States inspired, however, was not altogether unmixed. True, its existence represented a revenge against the English, but it was also the fruit of an Anglo-Saxon victory. There was regret at seeing the collapse of the old dream dating from the years before 1763 that envisioned an America under the sway of an alliance of the French and the Indians, and there was remorse over consigning the latter to inevitable destruction and over abandoning compatriots in Canada to domination by the English. Though American society had freed itself from the English, it had grave faults along with its virtues. There was the existence of slavery, unacceptable to those who held to the principles of 1789, and there was the danger, often pointed out, of a tyranny of the majority which risked imposing conformity and uniformity. The feeling of sympathy won out, however, even in ultraroyalists like Hyde de Neuville or Moré.[10] They were quite incapable of engaging in the ill-natured banter of the English travelers.

Lafayette's trip in 1825 had awakened shared memories in the two nations. And in 1830, France had just missed forming the second great democratic republic; only the skill of the political class had succeeded in appropriating power by pushing Louis-Philippe onto the throne, but it was impossible to predict how long they could keep it. The advent of a French republic would change attitudes toward the United States. From being the sort of political system that was suitable for a still primitive society, the American republic would once again become —as people had thought it would in the time of the *idéologues* and the

[10]Hyde de Neuville, *Mémoires et souvenirs* (1888–1890). See Rémond, *Les Etats-Unis devant l'opinion française,* 324, and A. Moré, *Mémoires du comte de M.* (Paris, 1828).

106

Directoire—a political system that anticipated the future. For all these reasons—as the two young magistrates had stressed in their request to be given the mission of studying the penitentiary system—nothing could be better than an on-the-spot investigation.

They could only stay in America nine months. This was not very much time in which to observe such a vast and varied country, especially since part of their efforts had to be devoted to studying prisons and since at first their lack of experience in speaking English was a problem and led to misunderstandings.

We can follow the activities of the two Frenchmen during their visit almost day by day with the help of G. W. Pierson's book *Tocqueville and Beaumont in America.* [11] The primary sources which this classic work draws upon have not been significantly supplemented since the book was written. They consist of Tocqueville's notebooks, the entries occasionally scribbled in a stagecoach or on a steamboat —notebooks whose contents are sometimes alphabetically arranged and sometimes not and that group together important conversations or the more carefully worked up notes, now and then masking an inevitable disorder under rather formal headings—and the correspondence of the two travelers with their families and friends. There are gaps in the documentation, the most serious perhaps being the loss of the journal that Gustave de Beaumont kept. It is also unequally spread over time. At the end of the stay, notes are often replaced simply by headings without comment, and letters are less frequent, as though the unavoidable return date had obliged the travelers to garner their impressions hastily. Finally, there is a surprising silence about the return itself, not a single letter or note written on board ship, as though the ocean had lost all novelty and grandeur, their fellow passengers all interest. We don't even know exactly when Tocqueville landed, though we find him in Paris at the end of March 1832.

As for the time they spent in the United States, it is divided into periods of research, when the two friends were settled in large cities in the East, and periods of traveling. In all, there were three periods in which they stayed put, in New York and its environs (May 11–June 30, 1831); Boston, Philadelphia, and Baltimore (September 9–November 22, 1831); then Washington and once again New York (January 18–February 20, 1832), framing two extended trips, the first to the Northwest and Canada, the second into the South, going down the

[11]G. W. Pierson, *Tocqueville and Beaumont in America* (New York, 1938).

Mississippi and then northward through the old South, from New Orleans to Washington. Out of the 286 days they spent in the New World, 271 of them in the United States, 140 days, or half the visit, were spent in cities. Despite the variety of misadventures we will be describing, the big trip into the South (the itinerary gave them stops in Nashville, New Orleans, and Washington) lasted only forty days, and even if we count the time spent in Baltimore as part of the Southern tour we reach a total of less than fifty days. In this visit to the United States, then, which was brief enough to begin with, the South especially was sacrificed, too much so for the visitors to be able truly to penetrate the spirit of the old South, with its complex society whose aristocracy had played such a large role in the young republic's history. It was during these years that Michel Chevalier made the distinction, which has remained classic, between two types of Americans, the Yankee and the Virginian.[12] Tocqueville observed and listened to the first much more than the second. This was not deliberate—the latter part of their stay was disrupted by the fact that the Ministry of Justice was threatening to reduce their leave from eighteen months to twelve, and unforeseen incidents forced them to change their plans so that they were not able to remain in Charleston, where they had intended to study Southern society, or to visit James Madison, the former president, now in retirement at Montpelier, his home near Charlottesville, Virginia.

Once they arrived in New York, Tocqueville and Beaumont moved into a family boardinghouse on Broadway, which was then the fashionable avenue. Palmer, the former member of the British parliament with whom they had become friends on shipboard, was staying there too, and introduced them to his American connections. They made contact with the French ambassador to Washington, Serurier, and the consul in New York, Durant-Saint-André, but the former pointed out to them that the prisons were in the domain of the particular states and not the federal government, and the latter lived very much on the fringes of American society. They also had seventy letters of introduction, but found it so easy to enter New York social circles that the letters were almost unnecessary.

On May 12, the *Mercantile Advertiser* printed a news item that was quickly picked up by the other newspapers:

[12]Michel Chevalier, *Lettres sur l'Amérique du Nord* (Paris, 1836), vol. 2, 222. See Rémond, *Les Etats-Unis devant l'opinion française,* 725–28.

108

꒭ ꒭

We understand that two magistrates, Messrs. de Beaumont and de Tonqueville [*sic*] have arrived in the ship *Havre,* sent here by order of the Minister of the Interior, to examine the various prisons in our country, and make a report on their return to France. To other countries, especially in Europe, a commission has also been sent, as the French Government have it in contemplation to improve their Penitentiary system, and take this means of obtaining all proper information. In our country, we have no doubt that every facility will be extended the gentlemen who have arrived.[13]

This notice had an almost immediate effect. There was a feeling of goodwill toward Frenchmen, who were not in the least objects of the scorn felt for the British, and the French government's desire to learn about American penitentiary systems, whose superiority it thus acknowledged, was flattering to the national pride, especially since the penitentiary system was the subject of public controversies and lively passions of which the two members of the French commission were quite unaware.

Professionals—judges, jurists, lawyers—were the first to receive or pay a visit to the young Frenchmen. The notice in the newspapers "has resulted in a zeal that surprises us daily; not only are all public places open to us, all documents made available to us, but the directors of the establishments seek us out to go look at them," Tocqueville wrote to Abbé Lesueur on May 28. Out of simple fraternal loyalty, apparently, Judge James O. Morse put himself at their disposal right away and introduced them to the mayor of New York on May 15. The latter wanted not only to make their task easier, but also to mark its importance by an official act. Thus it was that, at 10 A.M. on May 25, the two members of the commission took their places with the mayor of the city and the aldermen, twenty-five or thirty people in all, in a procession of five carriages and visited in turn a home for young delinquents, the Bloomingdale insane asylum—where the two Frenchmen were taken up to the belvedere to admire the panorama of the city—the institution for the deaf and dumb, and the almshouse for the poor, where a banquet was held in their honor. After that, the two visitors and their escort went by boat to the prison on Blackwell's Island. Describing the dinner to Abbé Lesueur, Tocqueville added: "I confess that during this august ceremony, I couldn't keep from laughing up my sleeve when I thought of the difference that fifteen hundred leagues of sea makes in men's situations. I pictured to myself the extremely minor role that

[13]Pierson, op. cit., 58.

I played in France two months ago and the comparatively elevated situation in which we found ourselves here; the little noise our mission made at home and what it is making here; and all of it thanks to that little bit of sea I have just mentioned."[14]

But it wasn't only the professionals who welcomed the young Frenchmen. New York society was wide open to them. At first they were afraid people would see them as emissaries of a country leaning toward becoming a republic, and that during the dinners they would be toasted in honor of the regime born in 1830 or of Lafayette. But their hosts were too aware of their social backgrounds to make a blunder like that. Sympathy for the "Hero of the Two Worlds"— whose ideas about politics, they were surprised to discover, were not usually taken seriously on the other side of the Atlantic—prejudiced them in favor of his two compatriots, whatever their political preferences might be.

In the France of the Restoration, the salons brought together men in public office, men with not very taxing civilian or military functions, but most of all men of leisure, who sometimes devoted themselves to disinterested scholarship, living off the income from their lands—for the Revolution, far from eliminating a taste for the way of life of the nobility, had probably spread it further through the bourgeoisie. Only a few businessmen or industrialists would be found in the salons. One of the first surprises for Tocqueville and Beaumont in New York was that at gatherings during the evening one would rub shoulders with men who had spent the day in an office or bank— lawyers, businessmen, bankers. The pleasures of society came at the end of a day in which they had waged a fierce battle for profit. This New York social milieu (which, in their letters, they hesitated to characterize as "society" in the sense of a disinterested elite) adopted them very quickly. Their companion on the sea voyage, the businessman Schermerhorn, brought together all the people who had been in the ship's first class. Their banker, Nathaniel Prime, invited them to his daughter Mathilda's wedding reception. But the most brilliant of these parties did not always take place in homes in the city, for this was the season when people moved out to their country houses on the banks of the Hudson or the East River.

In this rich New York society one encountered plenty of parvenus, but there were also descendants of the Anglo–Dutch colonial aristocracy, even authentic European nobility, whom Tocqueville was wrong

[14]Letter to Abbé Lesueur dated May 28, 1831, O.C. (Bmt) VIII, 17 (corrected from the manuscript).

110

爱 业

to make fun of for what he thought was their pretentiousness in adopting coats of arms. The Livingstons, who were so immediately friendly, had come from a feudal family of Scotland, and the great man of the family, at that time General Jackson's secretary of state, had married a Creole noblewoman from Santo Domingo, Louise Davezac de Castera. The Cruger family had its origins in the German nobility. Albert Gallatin, formerly the secretary of the treasury, came from a prominent Swiss family.[15] During the course of their trip, the two Frenchmen met other Americans who were proud of their nationality but for all that had not forgotten the old Europe and its hierarchies. Gallatin had been ambassador to Paris and London, and knew the best society of the two capitals. Tocqueville and Beaumont may not always have perceived how easily some of the people they talked to could understand the amazement of the two young European aristocrats confronting the New World.

Be that as it may, they saw the worldly life of New York as the best way for them to reach an understanding of American society: first, they would improve their English, and then, through the observation of manners, they would gain insights into social psychology—and, above all, they would treat the rather elegant gatherings to which they were invited as fish ponds. At them, they would request private interviews with men who appeared able to enlighten them concerning American institutions and mores. The notables of New York City seem to have been quite obliging; some even consented to write up notes for the two visitors.

For their study of America had a direction from the very beginning. On February 21, a few days before their departure from Le Havre, Tocqueville had written to Stoffels: "It isn't a question of our seeing the great cities and beautiful rivers. We are going with the intention of examining in detail and as scientifically as possible all the motivating forces behind this vast American society which everyone talks about and no one knows."[16] Thus, as Pierson notes, their observations about the city itself were cursory: it had no remarkable monuments; the brick

---

[15]The most notable figures in that generation of the Livingston family were Robert R. Livingston of Clermont (1746–1813), who negotiated the purchase of Louisiana from France, and Edward Livingston (1764–1836), a great jurist, senator from Louisiana in 1829, secretary of state from 1831 to 1833, then ambassador to Paris (1833–1835). See W. B. Hatcher, *Livingston* (New Orleans, 1940).

Albert Gallatin (1761–1849), secretary of the treasury from 1801 to 1814, then ambassador to Paris (1816–1823) and to London (1826–1827), was president of the National Bank of New York from 1831 to 1839.

[16]Letter to Eugène Stoffels, *O.C.* (Bmt) V, 412.

or marble houses had "neither cornices, nor balustrades, nor carriage gates"; the streets had sidewalks, but were badly paved.[17]

If Tocqueville also happened to be interested in the furnishings of country houses near New York, he had a particular reason for that: his sister-in-law Emilie wanted to do over their Nacqueville residence and might get some ideas from a description illustrated with a sketch by Beaumont.[18] As for the people he talked to, though he noted down details that made their statements credible, Tocqueville never described their personalities or appearances. There is no hint of the vivid portraitist of the *Democracy*. If he observes a judge picking his teeth while questioning a prisoner, for him this is a feature of American manners and not a particular characteristic of this judge.[19] Beaumont would occasionally free himself of so harsh a discipline. He is inclined to be moved by the charms of the very pretty daughter of the celebrated Robert Fulton, and his landscape sketches in particular are not ungraceful. But his companion's influence would soon bring him back to serious matters and the useful aspect of their observations.

These observations were actually part of a systematic investigation in which France was already an inevitable term of comparison. Tocqueville wrote to his father in June 1831:

Ever since we arrived here, we have really had only one idea: to learn about the country we are traveling through. To do this, we are obliged to analyze society *a priori,* to find out what elements our own society is made up of so that we can ask useful questions here and not leave anything out. This work of ours, which is very difficult but full of enticements, makes us notice a host of details which get lost in the shuffle when one hasn't done any prior analysis, and suggests to us a great many observations and practical ideas we never would have thought of otherwise. It has already resulted in a set of questions which we are ceaselessly occupied in trying to answer. Since we know exactly what we want to ask, the briefest conversations are instructive, and we can say that there isn't a single man, no matter what rank in society he may occupy, who can't teach us something.[20]

Their investigation centered on the social structure and its relationship to social and political institutions. Economic matters played no part in the study except as they affected the way people conducted their

[17]Letter of Tocqueville to his mother dated April 26, 1831, *O.C.* (Bmt) VII, 10.

[18]Letter to Emilie dated June 9, 1831, *O.C.* (Bmt) VII, 26.

[19]See P. Lambert White, "American Manners in 1830," *The Yale Review* 12 (1923), 118–31.

[20]Letter to his father dated June 3, 1831, *O.C.* (Bmt) VII, 22.

lives. Observing the port of New York and the Hudson, Tocqueville confined himself to saying that they were intensely active. But the high cost of manual labor changed relations between workers and employers, as did the system of ownership; the ease with which natural resources could be exploited encouraged the civic virtues by attaching the citizen to his country. Economic phenomena were of interest mainly because of their effect on the social and political structure. Even on board the steamboat that took them from Newport to New York—the first time in their lives they had been on a steam-powered vessel—their main interest lay in the general characteristics of the social arrangements improvised by the passengers.

This period in New York was also the part of the trip in which they spent the most time on their study of the penitentiary system. They displayed some haste in getting a disagreeable task out of the way, a task in which "we are buried a hundred feet deep,"[21] one that was "coming out of our ears," but they saw it through with exemplary conscientiousness, trying to make up for the absence of statistics on recidivists which, because of the American decentralization of administrative functions and records, had not been adequately established. They did an enormous amount of work in New York itself studying the home for juvenile delinquents, because they thought it would be easier to correct young offenders than experienced criminals. But most important, they were able to study at close range the Auburn system, where prisoners worked together during the day and were isolated at night, a system strongly recommended by French experts on the problem. From May 29 to June 6 they stayed at Sing Sing on the banks of the Hudson, amazed to see nine hundred prisoners working out in the open under the supervision of only thirty guards. They learned what the secret was and Beaumont wrote to his family about it on June 7: the secret was absolute silence and strict discipline. After visiting the "mother house" at Auburn, Tocqueville described their impressions more precisely in a letter to Chabrol:

It is very true . . . that at Auburn the health of the prisoners is unbelievably good, the discipline is admirable, and the prisoners' labor more than pays the costs of the establishment: all this is true, but they [the French *philanthropes,* as these early humanitarians were called] neglect to say that all this is obtained, not through persuasion, but with the help of an instrument the Americans call "the cat" and that we call a whip . . . A whip—that's what

[21]Unpublished letter to Chabrol dated June 20, 1831, copy in the Beinecke Library.

M. Lucas has been recommending for ten years, that's what he is so tenderly requesting in the name of philanthropy.[22]

In the midst of a whirlwind of appointments and readings, the life of the two young Frenchmen in New York retained an ascetic monotony. Not only because they swore they would live the lives of "good monks" (they would proudly reaffirm this resolution for the first few months of their visit), but also because they imposed a daily discipline on themselves that Beaumont describes in a letter to his brother Jules dated May 26.[23]

We always get up very early . . . We breakfast at 8 o'clock, as is the custom. Then we go to the Atheneum, a sort of public library where there are French, English, and American newspapers. This establishment was opened to us free of charge, as was another library of the same kind where there are even more interesting works [this was no doubt the New York Society Library]. We spend as much time there as we can researching statistics on the condition of the population, on public institutions, and on all the political questions that concern us.

If we can escape from our many friends, we scribble down on paper our ideas about what we've seen, we give ourselves questions to answer, and we lay the foundations of a great work that must one day make our reputations. When the dinner bell sounds we have never done half of all that we had to do.

We take our places at a table that is always laden with dishes more substantial than they are well prepared . . . In the evening we go out.

In a letter written a few days earlier to his mother, Tocqueville had given a few more precise details about how they spent their time and pointed out some difficulties they were having adapting to the American diet:[24]

We come back and dine at three o'clock; at five, we usually go to our rooms and put our notes in order until seven, the hour when we go out into the world and have tea. This kind of life is very pleasant and I think it's very healthy, but it throws all our usual habits into disorder . . . The absence of wine at meals seemed a great loss at first, and we could hardly conceive then of the quantities of things one does manage to stuff into one's stomach here. Do you know that besides breakfast, dinner, and tea—with which the

[22]Unpublished letter to Chabrol dated July 16, 1831, copy in the Beinecke Library.
[23]Letter from Beaumont to his brother Jules dated May 26, 1831, *Lettres d'Amérique,* 47–48.
[24]Letter to his mother dated May 14, 1831, *O.C.* (Bmt) VII, 12.

Americans eat ham—they also have a very copious supper and often an afternoon snack.

About Tocqueville's and Beaumont's state of mind during the time before their departure for Sing Sing on May 29 we have information from texts dating mostly from the middle of the month, but it seems clear that their impressions did not vary much between the days just after their landing in New York and the point at which they adopted a somewhat detached attitude toward the society of the great port. Quite naturally, at first they were aware of the differences between life in America and life in France without trying to locate them in any larger systematic explanation. Subsequently, however, their discoveries grouped themselves into several larger themes which were enriched by further reflection during the month of June.

American manners immediately revealed a society in which classes were much less distinct than in Europe. There was no elegant élite with a refined education, but Tocqueville also observed that even the most ordinary sales clerk did not have the "bad form" of the lower classes in France. All Americans had manners that were "grave, deliberate, reserved," and all wore the same kind of clothing. On May 16, Beaumont concluded: "This is a *commercial* people" and he saw it "consumed by a thirst for riches that brings in its train many of the less honorable passions, such as cupidity, fraud, and bad faith." Tocqueville enlarged upon the idea: "The entire society seems to have melted into a middle class." A statement which was to take him a long way, for it seems to have been the first rough sketch of his vision of a democratic society.

The two friends were struck by one fact in particular: how close the conditions of men and women were, whereas in French high society at that time they were quite distinct. Here the women were up and about at seven in the morning and dressed for the whole day. Girls had a very free life, going for walks alone for a part of the day, being approached without scandal by young men they knew, and, should it so happen, entertaining them alone in their fathers' drawing rooms. When they became engaged, it was with full awareness of what they were doing, and to young men whom they would hardly ever be apart from when they went out during the period before the wedding. Marriage was motivated, then, more by inclination than by social convention, and one can imagine that this aspect of American mores aroused in Tocqueville some bitter memories. Whatever the case, when Kergorlay acted as intermediary in the offer of a rich and brilliant

match that could be arranged for him and that would be awaiting him   115
upon his return to France, he replied that he would not marry a young
woman he did not know.[25]

These Simon-pure mores, which left no room for any faults whatsoever, also governed the life of the married woman, but by confining
her to her home. With "no more dances, no more social life," she spent
her time "admiring her husband," Tocqueville wrote to his sister-in-
law Emilie, quite possibly with the ulterior motive of giving her an
example to follow. In sum, he added, "there is no question of playing
the butterfly here, of flitting about the candle, for one would very soon
get burnt in the flame."[26]

Beaumont, quite struck by the purity of the mores, ascribed it to
the scarcity of people with time to kill, and evoked by contrast the
garrison towns in France where morals were extremely lax. As for
Tocqueville, he looked at the society as a whole, observing, along with
the vices of the middle classes, their virtues: their seriousness and their
submission to a moral law that was acknowledged by the American
people as a whole. This was tied to the power that religion had over
the mores, perceptible even on first contact, in contrast to the antireligious spirit of a large proportion of the republicans or the liberal Left
in France. And in this Tocqueville saw one of the keys to an understanding of the spirit of the democratic society in the United States.

Another feature of this society was also immediately apparent: the
absence of government. Beaumont was struck, upon his arrival, by the
absence of any military force, Tocqueville by the fact that the civil
servant was not the object of any particular respect, as he was in France:
he had his job, but in his relations with his peers he was a man like
any other. "This society runs by itself and lucky for it that it doesn't
meet with any obstacle; government here seems to me to be in the
infancy of the art."[27]

The fact that society ran by itself, under a government that was all
but nonexistent, seems to have posed a problem for the first time that
was to continue to plague Tocqueville: Was centralization a good
thing or a bad?

But this absence of government went hand in hand with the absence
of distinct parties. The two young Frenchmen thought that such parties
were of their nature implicated in a struggle to seize power. They came

[25]Unpublished letter to Kergorlay, Tocqueville Archives.
[26]Letter to Emilie dated June 9, 1831, *O.C.* (Bmt) VII, 27–28.
[27]Fragment of letter to Kergorlay, *O.C.* XIII, 1: 224.

from a country where, since the Glorious Days of 1830, the legitimists, the Jacobin republicans, and the middle-of-the-road bourgeoisie had been tearing one another apart with bitter violence in the hope of gaining possession of the State apparatus. In the decentralized United States, on the other hand, political life seemed to amount to no more than conflicts between individuals or small-town squabbles. An exaggerated view of Andrew Jackson's America it may be, but one that can be accounted for by the marked contrasts between the two countries.

And yet American society "worked," it was even full of feverish activity, "a universal movement" with profit as its goal, that could be explained by the seemingly unlimited possibilities nature offered man:

If a lifetime career in politics is more or less out of the question, still there are a thousand, ten thousand other careers open to a man. Here the entire world seems to be a malleable substance which a man can turn and shape as he likes. An immense field, of which not even the smallest part has yet been fully explored, lies open to human effort here. There isn't one man who can't reasonably hope to attain the comforts of life; there isn't one who doesn't know that if he loves hard work his future is secure.[28]

The fact that it was so easy to get rich resulted in the development of a devotion to hard work and an uneasy mobility in the very heart of society: "An American takes on and puts off ten different states in his life; he constantly moves from house to house and keeps creating new enterprises."

This country, particularly fortunate in its natural resources, whose face was being changed through the efforts of each and every one of its citizens at a rate unknown elsewhere—were its institutions of the sort that could be transplanted to Europe? Tocqueville had his doubts on that beautiful evening of June 3 when, perched in a tree overlooking the Hudson landscape that Beaumont was doing his best to sketch, he tried to sum up for his father with something like detachment his experiences of the past three weeks in America: "The more I see of this country, the more, I confess, I am convinced of this truth: that almost no political institution is altogether good or bad in itself, and that everything depends on how the people fare who are governed by the institution. It depends on their social condition."[29] And in the letter to Chabrol written six days later, Tocqueville went on to say that for this "society without roots, without memories, without prejudices,

---

[28]Unpublished letter of Tocqueville to Chabrol dated June 9, 1831, copy in the Beinecke Library.
[29]Letter to his father dated June 3, 1831, published with significant changes by Beaumont, *O.C.* (Bmt) VII, 24, and corrected here according to the Beaumont copy in the Tocqueville Archives.

without routines, without shared ideas, without a national character,   **117**
a hundred times happier than our own," a republic, grounded upon
the private interest of each citizen,[30] "very different from the republics
of ancient times," was probably the most suitable form of government.

We have lost one letter that Tocqueville sent by way of his mother
to his favorite confidant, Louis de Kergorlay. But a short text preserved
in his notebooks and dated May 18 could well be the fragment of a
copy. Here Tocqueville notes: "Up to now, I haven't been roused to
enthusiasm by anything I've seen because I know it's due more to the
nature of things than to the will of man."[31] Clearly he was also
offended by the "stinking" American arrogance; he was just as sensitive
as the English travelers to a certain crudeness of manners illustrated by
the fact that people would chew tobacco or spit during a conversation,
or the demagogical habit of shaking hands with everyone and his
brother.[32] On a deeper level, the Americans' exclusive love of profit
and absence of interest in literature and the fine arts (which he exaggerated a little) made it difficult for him to feel a spontaneous sympathy for America.

Aside from this, from his very first days there, Tocqueville was
impressed by the spectacle of the free activity of the Americans. In the
fragment of the letter to Kergorlay from which we quoted the reservations he had about the American way of life, he adds: "The spectacle
I have before my eyes is nonetheless an immense spectacle . . . Here,
mankind's freedom acts in all the fullness of its power, and its energy
is fed by everything that is useful to each person without harming
anyone." In truth, Tocqueville had been induced to come to America
much more by a profoundly uneasy desire to attempt to predict
whether future societies would be capable of preserving mankind's
freedom than by the project of observing how the American institutions operated. Certain of the defects that were so evident in American
society—even the pride at being a part of it—might simply be the
other side of the love of freedom. And couldn't this freedom, instead
of resulting in an instinct for anarchy, induce a reasoned patriotism,
a permanent foundation for the State's existence?

One event seemed to provide him with an answer. The two friends
had left New York for the modest state capital of Albany to consult
some administrative archives. They happened to be there on July 4 and
because they were close to the seat of the government of the state of

---

[30]Unpublished letter to Chabrol dated June 9, 1831.
[31]*O.C.* XIII, 1: 224.
[32]See White, "American Manners in 1830."

118

慫 愀

New York, they were able to watch and participate in the celebration of the anniversary of the Declaration of Independence. It was a ceremony that made them want to smile. The trade associations and the militia marched past with an entirely spontaneous gravity and order, then the procession surged into a church where everyone sang verses to the tune of the *Marseillaise* accompanied by a single flute. The speech made by a lawyer foundered in rhetorical commonplaces. But the reading of the Declaration of Independence gave rise to a unanimous feeling that Tocqueville describes in the following way: "It was as though an electric current moved through the hearts of everyone there. It was in no way a theatrical performance. In this reading of the promises of independence that have been kept so well, in this turning of an entire nation toward the memories of its birth, in this union of the present generation with one that is no longer and with which, for a moment, it shared all these generous feelings, there was something profoundly felt and truly great."[33]

In the course of their stay in the United States, Tocqueville and Beaumont were to observe and note down democracy's shortcomings and failings. But they now had an answer to their initial question about whether man's dignity could be preserved in a democracy. The arm of the scale had already tipped toward sympathy and hope.

---

[33]Unpublished letter to Chabrol dated July 16, 1831. See also the letter from Beaumont to his sister Eugénie dated July 14, 1831, *Lettres d'Amérique*, 90–91.

8

THE FRONTIER

AND THE GREAT LAKES

THE TRIP TO ALBANY marked a transition for Tocqueville
and Beaumont in their American experience. During May and June in
New York, they had led a regular and austere life, dividing their time
among the penitentiary establishments, the interviews they needed for
their projected book, and the social occasions where they were introduced to the American way of life. Now they entered a period of
vacation and adventure that would last until September 7, when they
would resume the same sort of discipline. Of course, some of their
activity was reminiscent of the previous period: their interviews with
Elam Lynds, the creator of the Auburn prison system, now fallen from
favor and a hardware merchant in Syracuse, and the five or six days
they spent at Auburn itself from July 9 on were concessions to the
demands of their investigation of the penitentiary system. Much more
important for the study of American institutions was their stay with
John Canfield Spencer, whom they had met in Albany and who was
their host in his home in Canandaigua from July 16 to 18. This former
lawyer and attorney was on his way to becoming a very prominent
figure: he had already been a member of Congress, then one of the
drafters of the revised statutes of the state of New York; he would later
be secretary of war, then secretary of the treasury; he would be the first
American translator of *Democracy in America*. This was the first time
in their trip, as Pierson notes, that the two friends had been the guests
of an important American. Though Spencer's two daughters provided
them with some entertainment, they obtained useful information from

this astute jurist on several aspects of American life: the influence of the freedom of the press on society, the role of religion in counterbalancing democratic excesses, the function of the judiciary power and the conservative tendencies of the bench, and the usefulness of having two Houses in a democracy—topics on which Spencer's influence would be evident in the future *Democracy*. Between conversations and outings on the lake, Spencer also took up a problem they were curious about, the fate of the Indians.[1]

For, once they left New York, Tocqueville and Beaumont had encountered the classic visions of the French explorers: the forests—the "wilderness"—but also the life of the Indians, the original inhabitants, and this brought with it a feeling of guilt at having abandoned these former allies and, tied to that, the memory of the great colonial empire lost in the Treaty of Paris. Certainly, what was original about their trip was their very new concern with arriving at an objective judgment of a society emancipated from the traditions of the Old World, but it was mainly in the larger cities that they would attempt to pursue their investigations: in New York, the principal port; in Boston, the religious and intellectual capital of New England; in Philadelphia, which held to the moral traditions of the Quakers; in Charleston, the brilliant center of Southern society (which they would regretfully have to sacrifice); and in Washington, the federal capital. This would not mean, however, that they would neglect to do some touring—- their objectives were already fixed: Niagara Falls, the beauty spots of the Hudson Valley, a boat trip down the Mississippi. But this submission to what was already a traditional tour plan was accompanied by a quest for the unexpected which combined a taste, inherited from the eighteenth century, for discovering primitive worlds, and an attraction to exotic sensations more characteristic of the romantic generations. "One of the things that piqued our curiosity most when we came to America was the idea of exploring the far limits of European civilization and even, if time permitted, visiting a few of the Indian tribes that preferred to flee into the wildest solitudes rather than adapt to what the White Men call the delights of social life," Tocqueville wrote at the beginning of a brief narrative entitled *Two Weeks in the Wilderness,* which he did not publish because he didn't want to compete with Beaumont, who took up the Indian question in *Marie,* and which

[1]On Tocqueville's and Beaumont's stay at Canandaigua, see Pierson, *Tocqueville and Beaumont in America,* 216–24.

Beaumont himself had published in the *Revue des deux mondes*[2] shortly
after Tocqueville's death.

They also decided to study briefly the situation of the French
population in Canada. They apparently had had no intention of doing
this before they left France. A letter from Tocqueville to his mother
written June 19 shows that it was the vicar-general of New York,
Powers, an Irishman who had been educated in France and had lived
in Canada, who pointed out to them how interesting a short trip into
that country would be. At that point they thought they would go by
way of the valley of the St. Lawrence to get from Auburn to Boston:

We expect to leave New York at the end of the month. Our original
intention was to go to Boston, but we have changed our plans completely.
Instead of starting in the north, we're going to go west as far as a small town
called Auburn which lies a little below Lake Ontario on the map. Auburn
has the most noteworthy prison in the United States. We will stay there about
ten days, as we did at Sing Sing, then we will go see Niagara Falls, which
is very close by. We will take the Lake Ontario steamer, which will get us
to Quebec in two days. From there, it will be very easy for us to make our
way to Boston and then return to New York . . . This is a fashionable trip
at the moment, but we will take our time, because we plan to stop in Albany,
Auburn, Montreal, and Quebec. We are very curious about Canada. The
French nation is preserved intact there; people retain the customs and speak
the language of the time of Louis XIV. It was Mr. Powers, the vicar-general
of New York . . . who especially advised us to make this trip. He lived in
Canada for a long time and has given us letters of introduction to people
there.[3]

Vicar-General Powers also led them to advance the date of their
departure: "It was in part he who made us change our first plan, which
was to go west in the autumn. At that season, one often catches the
tertian ague because of the marshy land there, only a part of which
is dried up by the summer sun. On the other hand, the coast and
Pennsylvania are the most healthy places in the world all year long."

On the very eve of their departure from New York, Beaumont was
still settling the details of an itinerary little different from the one
described by Tocqueville ten days before.[4] First, a brief stay in Albany,
then Saratoga, a watering place frequented by high society—they gave

[2]*Quinze jours dans le désert* was published by Beaumont in the *O.C.* (Bmt) V, 173–258. This text was
reprinted in *Voyage en Amérique, O.C.* V, 336–41.

[3]Letter to his mother dated June 19, 1831, Beinecke Library.

[4]Letter from Beaumont to his father dated June 29, 1831, *Lettres d'Amérique*, 68–74.

up the plan, probably because of their visit to Canandaigua—then Syracuse, then the Trenton waterfalls near Utica, New York, that had so excited Mrs. Trollope and Milbert, then Auburn, then Niagara, and—by way of Lake Ontario—Montreal and Quebec. This was a plan for a pleasure trip following a well-defined itinerary, and apparently the two friends did not spell it out in their letters merely to reassure their families. But the spirit of adventure awakened in Tocqueville once they were on the road. Drawn by the wilderness and the Indians, he led his companion, who was somewhat unwilling because he feared that Tocqueville would exhaust himself, to Michigan, then to the Great Lakes. This was an extensive detour to the west and the north—to the very frontiers of the civilized world.

The trip did not start off well: they wanted to pay a visit to the Livingstons in Yonkers, but the family was away. The two friends went up the Hudson as far as Cornwall-on-Hudson, where they got on the steamer for Albany. But they were taken on board with a haste that should have aroused their suspicions. The ship sent out a rowboat for them "into which we were thrown like a couple of packages and we found ourselves being towed along behind the steamer until we were hauled up to it."[5] The steamer was the *North America,* engaged in a race against one of its rivals of the New York–Albany line. The two Frenchmen could not arrange to be taken off the boat in the middle of the route and they thus missed seeing West Point. In compensation, however, they were able to watch the fireworks with which the *North America* celebrated its victory. The next morning, July 2, they were in Albany, and they left the city the night of July 4–5 after taking part in the celebration of the national holiday, as we have already seen.

Traveling over bad roads, they then went up the Mohawk River Valley toward the Great Lakes. The countryside they passed through was the setting for *The Last of the Mohicans,* which James Fenimore Cooper had published in 1826 and which the indefatigable Dufaucompret had immediately translated into French, but the Indians, the main characters in the story (which took place during the Seven Years' War) had disappeared; all that remained was Oneida Castle, a village now submerged by the European settlement. And the first Indians they saw ran after the carriage begging.[6]

But two days later, on July 8, Tocqueville and Beaumont went on

---

[5]Letter from Beaumont to his brother Jules dated July 4, 1831, *Lettres d'Amérique,* 77.
[6]On Oneida Castle, see *O.C.* V, 1: 223 and *Lettres d'Amérique,* 94.

a surprising and romantic pilgrimage. They were at Fort Brewerton, close to Lake Oneida. One of the two islands in the lake, which had reverted to its wild state, had been the home of a young Frenchman of gentle birth from a family that today is no more, the La Croix de Watines of the neighborhood of Lille. Having come to America in 1786, the young man had settled on the island in Lake Oneida in 1791 with his wife and two children, and they had had a third child there. About two years later, the Frenchman and his family had moved on to the northern shore of the lake, to the newly cleared site of a village called Rotterdam. It was here that Fritz von La Roche, son of the German novelist Sophie von La Roche, met him, as did, in 1795, La Rochefoucauld-Liancourt. Using what her son told her in his letters, Sophie von La Roche wrote a tale called *Erscheinungen am See Oneida* that appeared in 1798.[7]

At that time the tirelessly prolific German writer and pedagogue Joachim-Heinrich Campe was bringing out the little volumes of his *Geographical and Pedagogical Stories for Young People*—eventually twelve in all—which were immediately translated into French. In Volume 10 he retold the story of Sophie von La Roche's novel, adapting it for his readers, and this plagiarized tale was the main feature of the book, which appeared in 1803. In the same year, Volume 11 appeared, containing the list of subscribers to the whole collection, including one Hippolyte Tocqueville, who can have been none other—even though he was only five years old at the time—than Alexis's older brother. There is hardly any doubt that Alexis himself, who wasn't yet born, found Campe's story in his older brother's library a few years later. He probably also read, with passionate interest, Volume 6 of the same series, on the customs of the Indians according to Jonathan Carver.

In any case, Campe's story, which was written in the "sensitive" style of the eighteenth century and was also something of a tearjerker, made a profound impression on him: "This book left a deep and permanent mark on my soul. I can't say whether the effect was due to the author's talent, the real charm of the events, or my own tender years. But I have always remembered the two French people on Lake Oneida."[8]

The young Frenchman called Watines in Sophie von La Roche's

---

[7]The Lake Oneida episode has been examined by Victor Lange in his "Visitors to Lake Oneida; An Account of the Background of Sophie von La Roche's Novel 'Erscheinungen am See Oneida,'" *Symposium* 2 (May 1948), 48–74. See also Pierson, 197–205.

[8]*Voyage en Amérique*, in *O.C.* V, 1: 338.

and Campe's stories had very little resemblance to the real Watines, who was shallow and greedy, a ruined gentleman who had come to make a fresh start in America. He was not successful in this, but an improvement in his fortunes at home took him back to France toward the end of the Directoire. If Tocqueville had read La Rochefoucauld-Liancourt's *Voyage dans les Etats-Unis* before he left France, he would have been disenchanted or at least enlightened. Here is what La Rochefoucauld-Liancourt said of his meeting with the man:

Even as he was gathering potatoes and onions, we could see in his features and manners something distinguished, and we soon learned from him that he had once been seigneur of a *vicomté* near Lille, that his father had squandered part of his wealth and that he himself was a spendthrift, having sold his little domain even before the Revolution for 80,000 *livres* so that they might prosper in America, then squandering everything in foolish expenditures and rash business ventures in the towns, so that for the past three years he had been reduced to tilling the soil. His name was Watines. He had been living by Lake Oneida for three years, the first year with the Indians, for which he was very pleased with himself; then on an island in the middle of the lake, where he lived alone with his wife and where he had cleared about twenty acres; and lastly, for the past fifteen months, he had been settled in Rotterdam where Mr. Screiber had sold him one hundred acres, being most kind in the terms of the sale. Even by his own admission, it was the instability of M. de Watines's character rather than any deliberate plan that led him to keep changing his home.[9]

Sophie von La Roche and Campe had changed Watines into an émigré driven out by the French Revolution along with his wife, whose parents had been guillotined under the Reign of Terror. The suffering of exile and grief had led them to seek solitude far away from contact with their fellow human beings. The figure whose traces Tocqueville and Beaumont were looking for, then, was one who had been transformed into a symbol of the suffering of the French émigré nobility. They went off from Fort Brewerton on horseback, and on the shore of Lake Oneida questioned a fisherman's wife. She showed them which of the two islands still bore the name Frenchman's Island. She hadn't known him, since she had lived there only twenty-one years; but she added the dramatic and, of course, inaccurate piece of information that the Frenchman's wife had been buried on the island. She lent them a boat so that they could go there themselves. The island appeared from a distance to be no more than a clump of trees floating

---

[9]La Rochefoucauld-Liancourt, *Voyage dans les Etats-Unis.* See Pierson, op. cit., 201–203.

on the water. After landing, they pushed their way through the under-brush and found the old clearing, which was now a wood—the spot was clearly marked by the fact that the trees were so young. A half-dead apple tree showed them where the orchard had stood, next to the few remnants of the house, buried in grass. "Nearby, a plant which we at first took for a liana was growing up the tallest trees, twining around their slender trunks or hanging like a garland of leaves from their branches; examining it more closely, we saw that it was a vinestock" (strangely enough, this vine had already made its appear-ance in Campe's story!). But of course they didn't find either Madame de Watines's burial place or the clay urns Campe said she had put up in memory of her guillotined parents. Yet Tocqueville concluded the summary of his visit to the Frenchman's island with this remark in the notebook he carried with him: "This excursion has been the most intensely interesting and moving one in my experience, not only since I've been in America but since I first began traveling." And he made it the subject of the very romantic story Beaumont published in his edition of the *Oeuvres*. [10]

In it we see the same anxiety that Tocqueville had expressed in his *Voyage en Sicile,* the fear of someday being forced into exile because of the mere fact that he had been born into the nobility. This obsession, revived by the revolution of 1830, is also evident in several of his letters from America and was shared by Beaumont.

One of the great disappointments of the two visitors when they landed in America had been to find that there were far fewer trees in the landscape than they had expected. But from Albany on, they were surrounded by the great American forest. Although it was being attacked on all sides by settlers clearing the land, there nevertheless remained very impressive stretches of virgin forest, traversed by only a single road in terrible condition. But as we have seen, the original inhabitants of this wilderness, the Indians, were gone. "Ten years ago, we were told, they were here; over there, five years ago; over there, two years . . . Here . . . the great council of the confederation of the Iroquois was held." And finally, when they reached Buffalo on July 19, the town was full of Indians who had come to get the allowance the government of the United States was paying them for the sale of their lands. "I don't think I've ever before experienced such utter disappointment," wrote Tocqueville. The Indians he saw that day were small, with thin arms and legs, "their skin bronzed and oily, their black

[10]*Voyage en Amérique,* in *O.C.* V, 1: 162, and in *O.C.* (Bmt) V, 1: 161–71.

126

ℳ ℳ

hair long and stiff, their dress European, which they wore in the style of savages." This was a "population brutalized by our wines and liquors, more horrible than the equally brutalized populations of Europe." In their faces there wasn't a "trace of any of those lofty virtues born of the spirit of freedom."[11] The collapse of the Iroquois empire had resulted in the decay of the miserable remnants of the tribes which had formed it. This was a lesson Tocqueville the politician would not forget.

For the present, if they wanted to meet Chateaubriand's and Cooper's Indians, they would have to go farther west, toward the white men's advancing frontier. This idea revived Tocqueville's old longing for a trip through the West. Beaumont raised some objections because of his companion's delicate health, but then, since he was equally curious to observe the life of the Indians, he let himself be won over. On July 19 they embarked at Buffalo and, going by way of Lake Erie and the Detroit River, reached Detroit on July 23. From the steamship they admired the majesty of the forest and noted the contrasts between civilized and primitive life, symbolized by a Scottish soldier in full uniform mounting guard on the English bank while naked Indians with rings in their noses camped on the opposite shore. Detroit itself was a village in the French style, quite different from the clearings of the American settlers. The two travelers attempted to make the Americans understand that they wanted to go to the very limits of settlement, but in this they were only partly successful; they resigned themselves to riding on horseback as far as Saginaw, on the Saginaw River, a tributary of Lake Huron.

It would have been quite easy for them to reach this little post by way of Lake Huron and the river; they were mistaken in thinking that the steamboat only stopped there once a year.[12] But the land route offered other attractions: a ride over 110 miles of more and more difficult paths through the fringe where civilization mingled with the life of the wild—a fringe which in fact constituted the "frontier." At the end of three days, on July 26, they reached Saginaw after stopping overnight at Pontiac and then at Flint River. They spent two days there and then went back by the same route to Detroit from July 28 to 30.

Tocqueville, sensitive to the spectacular sights of nature, tried to put down his impressions in *Quinze jours dans le désert*. He describes, for

[11] *Voyage en Amérique,* in *O.C.* V, 1: 223.
[12] Pierson, op. cit., 285.

example, the unreal feeling of the landscape at night: "The darkness
then gave the forest a new and terrible aspect. The eye now perceived
around it only confusedly clumped masses without order or symmetry,
strange and disproportionate forms, incoherent scenes, fantastic images
which seemed borrowed from the sickly imagination of a feverish
mind." He retrieved ideas and images from Chateaubriand, who had
depicted a very similar forest in his *Journal sans date:* the immensity
of the forest, comparable to that of the sea, the successive generations
of trees where the dead slowly rot among the living until there is
nothing left of them "but a long stripe of red powder traced in the
grass."[13] When Tocqueville's essay was published, Sainte-Beuve, with
his usual malice, wrote that it "gives us in very nice prose what
Chateaubriand has already given us in daring and sublime poetry."[14]
The truth was that the two writers experienced the grandeur of this
virgin world in very different ways. Chateaubriand, slipping through
it in his canoe, celebrated the creation with joy and gave thanks to the
Creator: "Primitive freedom, at last I find you again! Here I am as God
Almighty created me, sovereign over nature, carried in triumph on the
waters, while those who dwell in the rivers go with me on my way,
and the nations of the air sing me their hymns, and the beasts of the
earth greet me, and the forests bend their treetops over my passage."

For Tocqueville, this imaginative delirium of a man who has escaped the constraints of society is merely "false coloring" and fails to
acknowledge the "absurd smallness of man." The forest is dark, damp,
unvarying. "The idea of immensity assails you. The endless reiteration
of the same scenes, their monotony, astonishes and overwhelms the
imagination." When it is frozen in silent immobility, the forest is
particularly heartrending. "When, in the middle of the day, the sun
shoots its rays into the forest, one often hears reverberating in its depths
a sort of long moan, a plaintive cry that reaches far into the distance.
This is the wind's last effort before it dies. Then everything around you
returns to a silence so deep, an immobility so complete that the soul
is penetrated by a kind of religious terror . . . It is as though the creator
has turned his face away for a moment and the forces of nature are
paralyzed."[15]

Would it be going too far to imagine that when he describes this
God turning away from his creation, this "religious terror" before the

---

[13]See Eva Doran, "Two Men and a Forest; Chateaubriand, Tocqueville and the American Wilderness," *Essays in French Literature* 13 (November 1976), 44–61.
[14]Sainte-Beuve, *Causeries du lundi* 15 (1862), 98.
[15]*O.C.* V, 1: 370.

incomprehensible laws of providence, Tocqueville is harking back to his Jansenist education?

But providence has another, more consoling face: it has prepared this wild solitude to be the cradle of civilization. Even in Saginaw itself, a gunshot that awakens echoes in the valley seems to Tocqueville to be "a long and fearsome war cry from civilization as it advances." It is because the forest is a prelude to the coming of mankind that people are moved by it, even saddened at its disappearance. And the emotional well-being Tocqueville feels in Saginaw has its source in the fitting equilibrium he senses between the wilderness of the present and a future of human conquests.

The expedition to Saginaw was richly instructive in other ways. First of all, it erased the disappointment felt by the two travelers over the Indians in Buffalo. From Flint River on, they had a young Indian guide from the Chippewa nation. They admired the animal grace of his bearing and the sharpness of his senses, adapted to life in the forest and aware of the presence of birds and animals which the Frenchmen never suspected, but they also admired his gravity, his endurance, and his love of freedom, qualities he shared with the other Indians they met along the way. They avidly inquired into the Indians' customs and became convinced that, though ferocious in battle, they were gentle and kindly in their daily life. It was their anxiety to preserve their liberty as hunters and nomads and their scorn for the various forms of servitude that the white settler imposed on himself that were bringing about their irremediable decline. And Beaumont, who had perhaps read *Les Soirées de Saint-Pétersbourg* [16] of de Maistre, was particularly eager to find out if indigenous civilizations represented the childhood of mankind or were a decline from more civilized ages, a question that troubled so many of his contemporaries of the romantic era. He even went so far as to believe that the Indians could be a separate branch of the European races that had gone its own way. In any event, for neither Beaumont nor Tocqueville were the Indians an inferior race that could be cast out of the human fraternity. Their lineage, too, was ancient, going back to the creation of man.

Tocqueville and Beaumont encountered the problem of the relations between civilizations and races once more, in an acute form, in Saginaw, which numbered no more than about thirty inhabitants—one of those minuscule posts along a road frequented by the Canadian voya-

---

[16] J. de Maistre, *Les Soirées de Saint-Pétersbourg; ou Entretiens sur le gouvernement temporel de la Providence,* 3 vols. (1821).

geurs dealing in furs that had become a center for settlers. Yet among these thirty inhabitants, within this microcosm, three different races coexisted and preserved their distinct characteristics. There were the Frenchmen, most of them hunters, living in country they had been making themselves at home in now since the eighteenth century; a few American settlers, the advance guard of the inexorable march west; and those occupants of long standing, the Indians, who lived in several wigwams on the edge of the village.

The two travelers felt a close kinship with the Frenchmen, who were from the West of France and spoke with Norman accents (a characteristic which they seem not to have taken note of in Detroit, even though it was found among most of the population there as late as 1860). And the French and English of Saginaw were as different from one another as those who lived on the banks of the Seine were from those who lived on the banks of the Thames.

The Frenchman in America, they learned, had the characteristic virtues and vices of his heritage. A passionate hunter, always ready to venture into the wilderness, he remained a Frenchman—"merry . . . enterprising, vainglorious, proud of his origins, a passionate lover of military glory, not so much selfish as conceited, a man of instinct who obeys his first impulse rather than his reason, preferring the excitements of an active life to money." He could adapt effortlessly to life in the wild, treating the Indians with a cordiality in which there was no contempt, copulating with Indian women without any sign of prejudice, sometimes recreating with one of them the sort of domesticity for which he still had an atavistic attachment in spite of his nomadic life. The Anglo-Saxon emigrant, on the other hand, was "cold, stubborn, mercilessly argumentative." He attached himself to the land and wrested from the wilderness everything he could take from it. He struggled against it ceaselessly, every day stripping it of some of its attributes. "He holds," Tocqueville wrote, "that glory is an empty noise and that man is in this world for no other reason than to acquire the comforts and conveniences of life."

The differences between their religions increased, clearly, the distance between the Frenchman and the Englishman, but there were also essential differences rooted in the characteristic temperament of each nation. The sharp divergences between them, as well as the possibility of bringing about a reconciliation through the dogma of the equality of all men, would remain an important topic for Tocqueville's reflections, and he seems never to have resolved its contradictions. In Saginaw itself, he is drawn to the *bois-brûlés,* the Franco-Indian métis.

130

❧ ❧

(*Bois-brûlé*, an argot word, means literally "charred wood"; the French word *métis*, for persons of French and Indian ancestry, has passed into English.) Their life is not an easy one, it is made up of tragic contradictions: "Proud of his European origins, he scorns the wilderness, and yet he loves the primitive freedom that reigns there. He admires civilization and is unable to submit completely to its rule. His tastes are in contradiction with his ideas, his opinions with his habits. Not knowing how to find its way in this uncertain light, his soul struggles painfully in the swaddling-clothes of an all-embracing doubt." We shouldn't be misled by the pessimistic tone of this note. Tocqueville was in favor of the intermingling of races and, though he himself does not say so more explicitly in his writings, it was clearly the indignation aroused by racial segregation that inspired the most beautiful pages of Gustave de Beaumont's *Marie*. And in Tocqueville's eyes the contradictions in the soul of the métis did not mean that his life was doomed. They were only a particular instance of the painful conflicts that divide every human soul, the unavoidable price that man pays for his freedom.[17]

In sum, their trip into the wilderness had rehabilitated the Indian in their eyes, now that they had seen him in his natural surroundings; but it also led them to discover another free man, more dear to them because he was closer kin—the French Canadian. We have no testimony from Tocqueville, but Beaumont tells us that the French Canadian hated the domination of the English and hoped to achieve autonomy within the American federation. It may be that the two friends took for gospel truth some complaints concerning English domination in the country to the north. In any case, the trip to Saginaw was a prelude to the visit to Canada, a prelude whose theme grew more expansive during another unplanned event, an excursion on the Great Lakes.

On August 1, the two visitors, back in Detroit and after taking a quick look at the Michigan state prison, were preparing to embark for Buffalo, as Beaumont wrote to Chabrol, "when someone came to tell us that a big steamship, the *Superior*, with two hundred passengers on board, had just arrived in Detroit from Buffalo and was going to Green Bay at the far side of Lake Michigan, stopping on the way at Sault Sainte Marie, which separated Lake Huron from Lake Superior, and

[17]On the opposition between the French and the English, and on the *bois-brûlés,* see *Voyage en Amérique,* in *O.C.* V, 1: 378–80. See also André Jardin, "Alexis de Tocqueville, Gustave de Beaumont et le problème de l'égalité des races," in *L'Idée de race dans la pensée politique française contemporaine* (Marseilles, 1977), 200–19.

at Michilimackinac, situated between Lake Michigan and Lake Huron.
Nothing equals the beauty of the Great Lakes. The regions I have just
mentioned are almost unknown and for the first time a steamship
loaded with *fashionable* travelers was venturing into these wild places
where no vessel of any size had ever gone before. At first we said: 'We
won't go,' then the temptation was so great that we gave in."[18]

The *Superior*, built in 1821, was forty-two meters long and seven
wide. It was a comfortable boat: the upper deck served as a promenade
or ballroom, the food was excellent, and there was a small orchestra
to entertain the passengers.[19] This orchestra played the *Marseillaise* in
honor of the two Frenchmen and the anniversary of the July regime,
which did not give them any pleasure at all.

The society on board consisted mainly of Americans and English
indulging in the pleasures of tourism. There were a good many young
people "pretty much of no account" and some exceptionally interesting personalities: the Englishman Vigne, a former barrister who had
become one of those travelers of the romantic era who published tales
of their wanderings in various parts of the world, veritable precursors
of the globe-trotting journalists of the end of the century. In his *Six
Months in America,* Vigne did not omit to tell of his trip on the Great
Lakes, in an account that is neither brilliant nor exaggerated. His
relations with the two Frenchmen were very cordial. There was also
an ardent, fanatical American Catholic priest named Mullon who had
come from Cincinnati with the vital aim of engaging in debate with
the Presbyterian pastors of Mackinac Island and of administering the
sacraments to the Catholic population, Canadian or Indian, of Sault
Sainte Marie and l'Arbre-Croche. Tocqueville had conversations with
him[20] in which he returned to the theme of relations between Church
and State, a subject he had already broached, when he first went to
Detroit, with an old priest of French origin, Abbé Richard,[21] a former
representative in Congress. He was also able to see that religious
passions were becoming more heated in the West, and to gain some
insight into the hold of the Jesuits over the Indians. The great majority
of the passengers did not seem to him to merit being interviewed. With
them, one could confine oneself to dancing and exchanging polite

---

[18]Letter from Beaumont to E. de Chabrol dated August 2, 1831, *Lettres d'Amérique,* 116.

[19]The *Superior* was in service from 1821 to 1835, having replaced the older Great Lakes steamship, the
Walk in the Water, which had sunk in 1821.

[20]*O.C.* V, 1: 72–74.

[21]On Gabriel Richard, see Beaumont's letter to E. de Chabrol dated August 2, 1831, *Lettres d'Amérique,*
107–8.

remarks. One beautiful night Beaumont took up a flute and played Tancrède's celebrated cavatina, *Di Tanti Palpiti,* which all Europe was singing. The lakes with their limpid waters, the forests surrounding them on almost every side, were a grand, if monotonous, spectacle. Whenever the boat made a stop, Beaumont would paint and Tocqueville would hunt; both of them went down the Sault Sainte Marie rapids in a birchbark canoe, guided by métis singing old French songs. But they were eager to talk to Frenchmen and, through them, to Indians. They would turn up at people's homes, visit wigwams, or take their places by campfires.

They discovered that the Frenchmen of Canada were a cordial, gay people who seemed to them to have preserved the traditions of the Ancien Régime and were prepared to revolt against the English master (they instinctively shared these resentments and perhaps exaggerated their significance). When they reached the heart of Lower Canada they were already biased witnesses.

It is a pity that they did not make any note of these conversations on the shore or in the homes of Sault Sainte Marie or Mackinac Island, especially since Tocqueville talked with John Tanner in Sault Sainte Marie. Settled there since 1830, Tanner had lived among the Indians for thirty years. In the *Mémoires* he was to publish soon and which would be translated by Blosseville, he described vividly the dreadful miseries that accompanied the decline of life in the wild and the savor it still retained, harsh though it might be, for those who had experienced its freedom.[22] This was an important source, as Tocqueville himself admits, for his reflections on the "probable future of the three races," with which the first volume of *Democracy in America* closes.

Before they went into Canada, they had to make a brief detour to see Niagara Falls, which it apparently would have been unthinkable to omit. Together with Vigne and an old Englishwoman who seems to have pursued Beaumont with unremitting attention, they rented a carriage on August 17 and spent the following two days at Niagara.

The grandeur of the spectacle appeared to them to defy description. They could not come up to Chateaubriand, even though he had failed to do justice to the marvel. They made their way under the Falls on the narrow strip of land overhanging the gulf, a walk that was not dangerous, Tocqueville assured his mother. But to a former colleague in Versailles, he confessed that the violence of the wind and the rarefied

---

[22]E. de Blosseville, *Mémoires de John Tanner ou trente années dans les déserts de l'Amérique du Nord*, French translation (Paris, 1835).

air nearly made him lose consciousness.[23] As in the forest, he was

overwhelmed by the grandeur of nature: "The whole river formed a crystal arch almost impenetrable to the rays of the sun, the day appeared to be a white and uncertain light. Surrounding one was a damp darkness and a feeling of destruction and chaos that truly had something fearsome about it." He added that it was a spectacle one wouldn't be able to see for much longer, since the forest was already being cleared by settlers around Niagara: "The Romans put bell towers on the Pantheon; I wouldn't give the Americans more than ten years before they build a sawmill or a flour mill at the foot of the cataract."

On August 20, they were back in Buffalo embarking on the steamship *The Great Britain,* bound for Montreal by way of Lake Ontario and the St. Lawrence.

[23]Unpublished rough draft of letter to Dalmassy, Tocqueville Archives, file 2.

9

CANADIAN INTERLUDE

ON SEPTEMBER 7, 1831, Alexis de Tocqueville, back in Albany after his trip to Canada, wrote a letter to his old tutor, Abbé Lesueur. This was the last letter he would write him: two days later he learned that the old man had died in June.

In this letter, in which he described the life of the French Canadians, Tocqueville expressed his surprise at the ignorance of the French about the events and people of their former colony: "I'm astonished that this country should be so unknown in France. Not six months ago I believed, like everyone else, that Canada had become completely English. I was still back at the 1763 survey, according to which the French population was only sixty thousand."[1]

We can only share Tocqueville's surprise. The public in France, attentive to the development of the United States, knew nothing of Canada's. Relations with the former New France, after the repatriation of part of the upper classes, had been difficult. There was no direct transatlantic liaison, no possibility of settling as colonists (after 1830, when it became possible, French emigration still remained infinitesimal), no consuls to represent French interests until 1850.[2] The English colonial authorities could prohibit a simple traveler from entering, as was the case for La Rochefoucauld-Liancourt in 1796. Whereas so

[1]Letter to Abbé Lesueur dated September 7, 1831, O.C. (Bmt) VI, 56.
[2]Denis Brunn, "Les Relations entre la France et le Canada de 1830 à 1850," in Les Relations entre la France et le Canada au XIXe siècle (symposium of April 26, 1974), Cahiers du Centre Culturel Canadien 3, 14–17.

many countries had welcomed thousands of émigrés (an estimated ten to twenty-five thousand to the United States, for instance), the fifty-five ecclesiastics who entered Canada between 1793 and 1802 formed the bulk of the Frenchmen taking refuge there.[3]

In Canada, therefore, one doesn't find those intellectually active centers of Frenchmen abroad that brought to France new views of the world beyond its borders. The Canadian clergy, for its part, had abandoned the narrative traditions of the Jesuits, who during the seventeenth and eighteenth centuries had taught the French so much about the Indians, the colonists, and their own efforts at evangelization. The national historian of the French Canadians, François-Xavier Garneau, wrote in 1845 that Canada had been forgotten by the mother country. Later, after 1870, the pamphleteer Buies noted that, with the Treaty of Paris, "intellectually, politically, historically, Canada was separated from France."[4]

Yet Canada remained present in French minds, though as an empire lost through the "shameful Treaty of 1763," the national disgrace which journalists and historians exorcised by casting the blame for it on Louis XV or even on la Pompadour. Shame over the past and ignorance of the present can be found also in Chateaubriand's *Mémoires d'outre-tombe,* written in 1822: "We hardly even hear the language of Colbert and Louis XIV spoken in some straggling village in Louisiana or Canada under foreign domination. It exists there only as testimony of the reverses of our fortune and the mistakes of our policy."[5]

Chateaubriand, like the Tocquevilles, was a relative of Madame de Montcalm, the widow of the grandson of the hero of the Plains of Abraham, and, like them, frequented her salon. He had gone to America, but no one had enlightened him about the vitality of New France.

For New France, the Treaty of Paris had caused widespread "pain" and "amazement," attenuated by the thought that the new status might not be final, since the territory had changed hands several times during the preceding wars. Canada had been quiet during the American Revolution. After that, public opinion in Canada, despite some reser-

---

[3]Galarneau, *La France devant l'opinion canadienne* (Quebec, 1970). Canada is not included in the classic book by Fernand Baldensperger, *Le Mouvement des idées pendant l'émigration* (Paris, 1925).

[4]Sylvain Simard, "Les Relations intellectuelles," in the symposium cited in note 2, p. 130.

[5]Chateaubriand, *Mémoires d'outre-tombe,* vol. 1, 317. The study by Abbé Yon, "Les Canadiens français jugés par les Français de France," in the *Revue d'histoire de l'Amérique française* 18 (1964–1965), 321–42, shows the scantiness and inaccuracy of information about Canada around 1830.

136

vations on the part of the clergy, had followed the events in France from afar with sympathy until 1793, and thereafter with disapproval.[6] In 1791, Pitt had soothed resentments by giving Canada certain freedoms and representative institutions.

Henceforth there were two distinct colonies, Upper Canada and Lower Canada. The latter included the French population, dense in the St. Lawrence valley, and the towns of Montreal and Quebec. Quebec was the capital of the province, with a governor who represented the King of England. The governor was assisted by an appointed executive council. The legislative power was exercised by two Houses: a Legislative Assembly, elected with a very large electoral body, and an appointed Legislative Council. To a certain extent, people's rights were protected by the freedom of the press, the application of habeas corpus, and the continued observance of French law, to which they were attached. However, these institutions did not ensure the harmonious conduct of political life. The annual vote on all subsidies and the direct allocation of certain revenues to a Civil List were longstanding subjects of dispute. Around 1830, the French Canadians wanted to transform the appointed Legislative Council into a second elected House representing the counties. Conflicts died down temporarily whenever a conciliatory governor succeeded an authoritarian one: this was the case in 1831, when Lord Aylmer replaced Lord Dalhousie.

In the case of conflict or threats to the institutions, the French Canadians sent deputies to London, where the arbitration of the mother country was not always hostile to them. It was thus that in 1828 they were able to keep off the threat of the merging of the two Canadas, which would have been accompanied by anglicization.

The vicar-general of the Diocese of New York, the Irishman John Powers, who had been educated in France and had then been assigned to Canada before settling in the great port city, was the first to draw the attention of Tocqueville and Beaumont to the French Canadians, probably in the course of an interview on June 9, 1831. He advised them, as we have noted, to make their projected trip to the West before the autumn to avoid the fevers and also to combine that trip with a visit to Canada.[7] The uneasiness that the situation in France at that time caused them—no doubt the difficult beginnings of Casimir Perier's ministry—almost made them give up this side trip. But when they were on their way they had more reassuring news, per-

[6]Galarneau, *La France devant l'opinion canadienne.*
[7]Letter from Tocqueville to his mother dated June 19, 1831, unpublished.

haps that of the relatively satisfactory elections of July 5. After visiting Niagara Falls, they therefore returned to Buffalo to go on to Montreal.

When they were in the West of the United States, as we have seen, they had met French Canadians, probably even among the inhabitants of Detroit, but especially the *coureurs des bois,* the fur trappers. This was no longer the age of the independent trappers, and after bitter rivalries the Hudson's Bay Company had absorbed its French competitor from Montreal. But although it was under British management, the company had taken back into its service a good many French Canadians. The English were willing to establish themselves in little trading posts and wait there for propositions from Indians who had furs to sell, but the French went far off in their birchbark canoes, plunging into the forest and living the life of the Indian tribes for months at a time before bringing back their haul.[8] The intermingling of the races continued, the daughters of chiefs marrying white men. Tocqueville's first contact with one of the métis of mixed ancestry took place on July 25 in the evening, when he was getting into a pirogue to cross the Saginaw River:

The man squatting at one end of this fragile vessel wore Indian dress and had every appearance of being an Indian. As I prepared ... to get in, the presumed Indian came toward me, put two fingers on my shoulder and said to me in a Norman accent that made me jump, "Pray do not make too much haste, here sometimes people get drowned." If my horse had spoken to me I don't think I would have been more surprised. I stared at the man who had spoken to me and whose face, struck by the first rays of the moon, shone then like a copper bowl: "Who are you," I said to him. "Your language seems to be French and you look like an Indian." He answered that he was a *bois-brûlé,* that is to say, the son of a Canadian man and an Indian woman.[9]

The next day, Tocqueville met Canadians and *bois-brûlés* in Saginaw. During the excursion on the Great Lakes that he and Beaumont began on August 1, they found a French-speaking population of Canadians and métis in Sault Sainte Marie, at the entrance to Lake Superior, on August 6, and at Mackinac, at the entrance to Lake Michigan, on August 12. Tocqueville's feeling of sympathy for these

[8]B. Brouillette, *La Pénétration du continent américaine par les Canadiens français 1763–1846: traitants, explorateurs, missionnaires* (Montreal, 1979).

[9]*O.C.* V, 1: 374–75. All of Tocqueville's texts on Canada were republished by M. Jacques Vallée under the title *Tocqueville au Bas-Canada* (Montreal, 1973).

people and their fate was strong.[10] He also went to talk to the trappers by their campfires. He and Beaumont took strong exception to the Anglo-Saxon colonists' horror of racial intermingling, and Beaumont was to expand on this feeling in *Marie*. In one of his letters, he expresses their shared opinion of the *bois-brûlés:*

These half European, half Indian people are not at all unpleasant. There is something fierce in the physiognomy of the Indians that is softened by the mixture. The savage's eyes have a natural vivacity that I've never seen in any white man; their defect is to be harsh and severe as well, but the fire that burns in their eyes is of great beauty when, without ceasing to be just as bright, it loses something of its primitive harshness. This is what happens when the Indian and the European come together.[11]

As for Tocqueville, he became passionately excited over the inner drama of the métis, torn between pride in his civilized ancestry and the instinct for freedom characteristic of the savage. It was from his civilized heritage that his worst failing came—the ease with which the Frenchman, a "man of instinct" more readily swayed by his imagination than his reason, returned to a savage state:

Left to himself, he is naturally inclined to be a stay-at-home. No one loves the domestic hearth more than he, none loves more to delight his eyes with the sight of the homely village church tower. But despite himself he has been torn from his tranquil ways, his imagination has been struck by new vistas, he has been transplanted beneath another sky. This same man has all at once felt himself to be possessed by an insatiable need for violent emotions, for changes, for risks. The most civilized European has become an adorer of life in the wild. He will henceforth prefer the savannahs to the city streets, hunting to agriculture. He will make light of his existence and live without any concern for the future.[12]

Before going to Canada, then, Tocqueville and Beaumont had been able to observe the behavior of the French in the New World, though the conduct of the French in Saginaw was carried to a kind of extreme because of their uprooted condition. In Canada, they would once again see a stable French society, tied to the land, but it was the society of a conquered people.

On August 10, they left Buffalo to cross Lake Ontario. The next day, they entered the St. Lawrence River and found themselves in

---

[10]M. J. Hoog, *Tocqueville et les bois-brûlés*, Actes du 3e Congrès de la Fédération internationale des professeurs de français, 1976–1977, 327–36.

[11]Beaumont, letter to his brother Achille dated August 14, 1831, *Lettres d'Amérique*, 122–23.

[12]*O.C.* V, 1: 378.

Canada. They probably landed in Montreal on the twenty-third, and
left the next evening on board the steamer *John Molson,* the jewel of
the St. Lawrence fleet, reaching Quebec in about twenty hours. They
stayed in Quebec until August 31, making trips out into the surrounding countryside. Returning up the St. Lawrence, they were back in
Montreal on September 2. They immediately left again, this time
heading toward Albany, embarked at Saint Jean on Lake Champlain
on the third and then took a carriage at Whitehall which allowed them
to reach Albany on the fifth.[13] Their stay in Canada thus lasted from
August 21 to September 3 and more than half the visit was spent in
Quebec, the capital of Lower Canada, but also the center of the French
population with a smaller English minority than in the larger city of
Montreal. In his letter to Abbé Lesueur, Tocqueville wrote of Lower
Canada: "We felt quite at home and we were received everywhere as
compatriots"—a feeling echoed in their notes. These notes, however,
completely ignore Upper Canada, which Tocqueville and Beaumont
crossed from Kingston to the gates of Montreal, an itinerary which,
according to Pavie, was not without interest.[14] In a sense, they treated
British Canada with a scorn that anticipated that of General Charles
de Gaulle.

When they arrived in Lower Canada, they set out to study it using
the same methods they had used in the United States: personal interviews with selected individuals on particular topics, direct observation
of the things and people of the country, and extemporaneous conversations from which they could derive additional insights.

In Montreal, they had a letter of introduction from Vicar-General
Powers to Abbé Quiblier, the director of the theological seminary
there. This seminary dated from the beginning of the colonization and
was a true daughter house of Saint-Sulpice of Paris, which, to found
it and keep it going, had been given the resources of a large landed
estate. It had not only trained priests but also educated a number of
cultivated Canadians. Abbé Joseph-Vincent Quiblier (1796–1852),
who seemed to Tocqueville to be an enlightened man, was not originally from Canada: born in the region of Lyons, a priest at Saint-
Sulpice, he had come to Montreal in 1825; he ran the seminary from

[13]During their stay in Lower Canada, Tocqueville and Beaumont dated the same events with one day's
difference between their dates, Tocqueville's being earlier than Beaumont's. Beaumont was correct: when
the two friends went to meet the farmers coming out of church in Beauport, Tocqueville noted this
excursion as taking place on August 29, which was a Monday, while Beaumont dated it the twenty-eighth,
a Sunday.

[14]Théodore Pavie, *Souvenirs transatlantiques* (Paris, 1833), vol. 1, 128–30.

1831 to 1846, after which he was a parish priest in England, then went back to die in France. He was thus a man able to judge the Canadians from the outside and without bias against the English.[15]

Tocqueville and Beaumont also met the Mondelet brothers in Montreal. Pierson thinks it was J. C. Spencer who had recommended them: sons of a town notary, they were at that time both lawyers. The older one, Dominique (1799–1863), had just been elected to the Legislative Assembly, but in 1832 the governor appointed him to the executive council and his seat was declared vacant by the Assembly. In 1834, he ran against Louis-Joseph Papineau and lost. In 1842, he was made a judge along with his younger brother Charles (1801–1876), who had published a work on elementary education. The Mondelet brothers thus belonged to the fraction most conciliatory toward the English administration, most disposed to allow itself to be won over by it.[16]

In Quebec, Tocqueville's and Beaumont's main informant was John Neilson (1776–1848), with whom they had several interviews and who had them visit the Huron village of Lorette, founded earlier by the Jesuits. John Neilson, born in Scotland, had come over at the age of fourteen to join his uncle, who was running the *Quebec Gazette,* and in 1797 had taken over from him. He very quickly became friends with Papineau and despite his Scottish and Protestant background appeared to be his ally for a long time in the Legislative Assembly, where he sat from 1818 to 1834. In 1822 and 1828, he made two missions to London, representing the French party, to stave off the merging of the two Canadas and the anglicization of the country. But he inclined toward conciliation with the administration, while Papineau became increasingly hostile to him. The two men quarreled in 1834.[17]

Through Neilson, they met Papineau's cousin, Denis-Benjamin Viger, who belonged to a more lively opposition. But the notes of the two Frenchmen have no precise information about these conversations.

Neither do they say anything specific about those with Jean-Thomas Taschereau (1778–1832), whose cousin in Touraine they knew. The only judge with French nationality at that time, he was certainly no adversary of the English administration.

In short, of the more important people they interviewed, most were well-informed men who wanted to maintain the status of 1791 but hoped for harmony with the English administration. They don't even

---

[15]*O.C.* V, 1: 77–78.
[16]*O.C.* V, 1: 78–79.
[17]*O.C.* V, 1: 80–85.

mention Louis-Joseph Papineau, who was the embodiment of resistance at that time—a more and more lively resistance which ended in an uprising. And except for an unnamed English tradesman whose hostility to the French is evident despite what he says, there is no one who represents the feelings of the English minority, there is nothing in particular either from the governor or from a civil servant of his entourage, whose point of view under the conciliatory administration of Lord Aylmer would have been interesting to know and quite possible to summarize.

The two young Frenchmen had made their concession to tourism by going to see Niagara Falls, and now they took up other concerns again in their trip to Canada. Nevertheless, they remained sensitive to the beauty of the countryside around them: they admired the St. Lawrence and went up the right bank as far as St. Thomas, twenty-five miles to the east of Quebec, where the river was more than seventeen miles wide. Tocqueville wrote to Abbé Lesueur: "It is as though the English Channel had been moved inland." The famous waterfalls where the Montmorency River joined the St. Lawrence disappointed them a little, and we don't know if they went to visit the nearby Plains of Abraham, where Montcalm had played the French Empire's last card. They say very little about the way the towns looked. Beaumont limits himself to the commonplace that Montreal is an island and Quebec a fortress; Tocqueville notes that Quebec is picturesque but that it is much closer in appearance to a French provincial town than to a town in the United States. In Quebec, he remarks, everyone speaks French even though English is the language of business, of the rich classes, of the theaters.

But the two Frenchmen were eager, above all, to observe the country people, in order to see in what ways they differed from the American pioneers, and especially to discover analogies with their native West of France. From the deck of the steamship they admired the harvests and all the activity attendant upon them within the fertile land the great river flowed through: "The banks of the St. Lawrence thoroughly cultivated and covered with houses and villages very like our own. All traces of the wilderness have disappeared; it has been replaced by cultivated fields, bell towers, a population as numerous as in our own countryside."[18] It was no longer an American settler who awaited you on the threshold of his log cabin, but a villager who would usher you into a properly appointed room of a house "that

[18]*O.C.* V, 1: 210.

142

ℳ ℳ

exuded comfort." The churches were richly but tastefully ornamented. Tocqueville and Beaumont confirmed Neilson's opinion that the Canadian was "an admirable race": "The farmer is strong, well formed, well dressed. His manner has a frank cordiality that is lacking in the American; he is polite without being servile and receives you on a footing of equality, but with consideration . . . All in all, this race of men seemed to us inferior to the American in mental capacities, but superior in qualities of the heart. Here, one has no sense of the *mercantile* spirit that was evident in every action as in every word of the American. The Canadian's mind is not very cultivated, but it is simple and upright; the Canadians have indisputably fewer ideas than their neighbors, but their sensibility seems more developed; they live a life of the heart, the others of the head."[19] And a little later Tocqueville wrote to his brother Hippolyte: "The French in America had everything in themselves that is necessary to make a great people. They are still the handsomest offspring of the European family in the New World."[20]

These men were cordial, loved to talk, laugh, sing, dance, and for this reason were very different from the Americans with their taciturn individualism. The Canadians' sociability was expressed in the spontaneous solidarity they evinced whenever one of them suffered some catastrophe. They would band together to replace livestock which had been wiped out by a disease, they would work together to rebuild a barn that had been struck by lightning and burned down.

In actual fact, the village formed a local cell which the government hardly penetrated, its only representative being the head of the militia. The village was governed by its collective public opinion: someone who offended the mores or committed a crime was showered with such disapproval that he had to leave. The parish priest, who had come out of the farming population and shared its deepest concerns, was everyone's adviser: "And what is more, the French Canadians are religious on principle and out of political passion. For them, the clergy forms the upper class, not because the law ordains it but because of public opinion and the mores, which place the clergy in a position of leadership in society.[21] In the eyes of the English government, the Catholic clergy appeared demagogical. In actuality, Tocqueville found it enlightened and liberal, quite free of the superstitions and pious practices of the South of France, which he abhorred.

[19]*O.C.* V, 1: 213–14.
[20]Letter to Hippolyte, November 26, 1831, *O.C.* (Bmt) VII, 87.
[21]Letter to Abbé Lesueur, September 7, 1831, *O.C.* (Bmt) VI, 57.

This society, which seemed to Tocqueville much closer to the old France than the society of the mother country, which, ever since the Revolution, had in reality become the real New France, still had a feudal regime, but an attenuated one: there was a very small ground rent, a requirement that wheat be taken to the landlord's mill—though at a rate for grinding lower than that in the United States—and heavier property-conveyance duties (one twelfth of the price), though such duties were virtually nonexistent because of the stability of the population. Besides these charges, the farmers paid a tithe, in actuality one twenty-sixth of the harvest, to the parish priest. Although Neilson asserted the contrary in their conversation, Tocqueville found that the landlords were not very popular and that there was a certain reluctance to pay the tithe. Looked at from another point of view, though, the Canadian farmer had no taxes to pay whatsoever.

On the whole, the French Canadians were a happy, healthy people who lived in large part in a closed economy but who were indisputably well off. And yet their lives were shadowed by the intimidation that was inherent in their status. They were a conquered people.

Tocqueville, whose profession still was that of a magistrate and who took the time to observe court proceedings whenever he could, was made aware of this aspect of the French Canadians' situation at the beginning of his stay in Quebec, when he attended a judicial hearing. He happened to walk in on a ludicrous trial in which the defendant was being accused, by his adversary, of having insulted him by calling him a "good-for-nothing" and "filthy." The proceedings, and the counselor's speeches, were in two languages; people only half understood one another and Tocqueville concluded: "I have never been more certain than I was leaving there that the greatest and most irremediable calamity that a people can suffer is to be conquered."[22]

What the French had to endure was made clear by the relative position of the two peoples. Tocqueville estimated the population of Lower Canada at 600,000 and the proportion of French Canadians at about ninety percent (according to the official statistics for 1831, these figures are too high; there were 553,134 inhabitants, of whom about 400,000 were French). Nonetheless, nearly all the civil servants were English, as were the upper classes and practically all members of the professions. English was the language of commerce, and thus the signs over the shops and inns were in English—in Quebec, where practically the entire population was French. The newspapers were English except

[22]O.C. V, 1: 212–13,

144

妖 光

for *Le Canadien,* published in French—its motto was "our religion, our language, our laws"—which unceasingly opposed the English administration. Neilson thought that the French language was doomed to disappear from Canada. Tocqueville sometimes came close to believing it, though Beaumont remained skeptical.[23]

In Tocqueville's opinion, for Canada to resist anglicization there would have to be a certain animosity between the races. It did exist, but it was not very strong among the upper classes, even though at that point the French and the English still led quite separate lives. As Tocqueville saw it, the ethnic separation between the two peoples, each of whom had preserved different mores and different habits of thought, had to be strictly maintained, even in political life:

In Quebec there already exists a class of men who are closing the gap between the French and the English. These are Englishmen associated with French Canadians, Englishmen discontented with the administration, and Frenchmen in responsible positions. This class is represented in the press by the *Gazette de Québec,* published in a mixture of French and English, and in the political assemblies by Mr. Neilson and probably several others whom we don't know. It is this class that I most fear when I consider the future fate of the French Canadian population . . . Should it ever take the place of the upper classes and the enlightened classes among the French Canadians, their nationality would be irretrievably lost. They would vegetate like the poor Bretons of the lower Loire valley in France. Fortunately, their religion poses an obstacle to marriage between the two races and creates in the clergy an enlightened class that has a strong interest in speaking French and in sustaining itself with French literature and ideas.[24]

Tocqueville carefully studied the progress of public education and hoped that it would help the Canadian masses to become more aware of their originality. But he always thought that a freedom movement of a people or a class had to be led by a social and intellectual elite.

At heart, he remained disappointed that the enlightened French and even the clergy did not prove to be more actively hostile to the English government. Even the text we have just cited shows that although he recognized the man's merits, he didn't trust his main informant, Neilson, and explains why he and Beaumont went off on August 29 to meet the people of the village of Beauport, five miles from Quebec, as they were coming out of Sunday mass.[25]

[23]See Beaumont's excellent objections in *Lettres d'Amérique,* 134.
[24]*O.C.* V, 1: 215–16.
[25]*O.C.* V, 1: 214–16.

This was not merely for the pleasure of conversing with compatriots without intermediaries. They wanted to know if these people were conscious of the great danger that threatened them: encirclement by emigrants who came principally from Scotland and Ireland. There had been twenty-eight thousand emigrants to Canada in 1830 and there were to be sixty-six thousand in 1832. They were established at no cost to themselves on vacant lands in Lower Canada that had been State or Church property; a large number as well settled in Upper Canada. During this period, the surplus French-Canadian population was heading for the towns. The French-Canadian people, from whom had come in the eighteenth century the *coureurs des bois,* the trappers, with their unheard-of daring, now saw the other side of the French temperament, home-loving and timorous, become dominant in their very midst. Only a small number of French went out to clear the land. In America, as Tocqueville put it so strikingly, the fate of the French Canadians ran the risk of becoming that of the poor Bretons in metropolitan France.

Tocqueville and Beaumont saw that their ideas met with the approval of the farmers they talked to, but naturally one conversation on a Sunday was not going to change entrenched habits. The two visitors, however, clearly recognized the missed opportunity with which so many historians later reproached the French Canadians, whose surplus population, dispersed not only into the cities of Canada but also into those of the United States, soon became anglicized.

The two friends eventually came to believe that what the French Canadians lacked most was an eloquent spokesman who would fight relentlessly to win their independence. The idea was suggested by Tocqueville on the very evening of August 28: "They have in them everything they need to create a living memorial of France in the New World . . . A man of genius who would understand, feel, and be capable of developing the national passions of the people would have an admirable role to play here." And Beaumont drew up the plan which this Canadian O'Connell should follow:

In Canada there is a great role to be played, at once noble, honorable, and dangerous. It is that of a man who dedicates himself entirely to the French-Canadian people, living for their interests, exciting their passions in order to preserve their existence, making himself the disinterested and free counsel of all, mingling his life wholly with theirs, the adversary of the government each time an occasion for attack presents itself, obtaining a thousand concessions from those in power, always asking for more and, when the passions

146

涎涎

of the master and his subjects are aroused, when the people are enlightened as to their true interests, proclaiming loudly the words independence and *liberty*!!![26]

Tocqueville says that unfortunately he doesn't see any sign of this man appearing on the horizon. Yet this was precisely the ambition of Louis-Joseph Papineau, whose influence over the French-Canadian people was great at that time and whose opposition to English rule led to the uprising of 1837. But his name is strangely absent, as we have already remarked, from Tocqueville's and Beaumont's notes.

To tell the truth, though Tocqueville might believe in the survival of the French-Canadian people, he hardly thought it possible for them to achieve independence, with the English of Upper Canada on one side and the United States on the other. In 1838, just after the uprising, when Henry Reeve asked him for his opinion, one that could be communicated to members of the English government, Tocqueville refused to make any statement, either openly or in private. He did, however, counsel mistrust of the opinions of the English Canadians, whose prejudices were "incredible." Though the French Canadians had neither the cunning as merchants nor the singleminded enterprise as farmers that the English did, and though it was therefore unavoidable that they would be enveloped by the English race, "they nonetheless make up an energetic little clan, capable of enthusiasm, of devotion, of sudden and violent exertions . . . that will never be forced to remain attached to an English Canada against its wishes for very long."[27]

The psychological traits Tocqueville saw in the French here he also attributed to the French of the old France . . .

Tocqueville's brief stay in Canada could not give him more than some hastily acquired and incomplete information, especially since he hadn't prepared for the visit with the extended reflections that had preceded his observation of the United States. Even his choice of the people he met owed more to chance in Canada than in the United States. A published study of the trip clearly brings out the areas of ignorance: his absence of information about the economic crisis the colony was going through and about the situation in Upper Canada, which was entering a period of unrest and revolt that paralleled Lower Canada's, and his very summary knowledge of the institutions and of the substance of the political conflicts between the governor and the

[26]*O.C.* V, 1: 212; Beaumont, *Lettres d'Amérique*, 137.

[27]Letter to Henry Reeve, January 3, 1838, published by E. McInnis, *Canadian Historical Review* 11 (1938), 394–97.

elected assembly.[28] But on the ethnic originality of the French Canadi- **147**
ans and the prospects for the future of the "French race," which formed
the central object of his interest, Tocqueville's insights were perceptive.

He did not publish either his letters or his notes, of which the public
was to gain only very limited knowledge through Beaumont's edition
of the *Oeuvres*. [29] But for that matter the pleasant but superficial book
by Théodore Pavie, who had visited Canada in 1829 and who published his *Souvenirs transatlantiques* in 1833, attracted hardly any attention. It was only after 1851 that the French public began to become
interested in Canada. The most spectacular example of this was the visit
of the corvette *La Capricieuse* to Quebec and Montreal in July 1855,
and the triumphal welcome given to Commandant de Belvèze. But
Xavier Marmier's *Lettres d'Amérique* (1851) and Jean-Jacques Ampère's
La Promenade en Amérique (1855), of which fifty-two pages were
devoted to Canada and which was brought out in several successive
editions, clearly marked this awakening of interest. All the same, it
would be easy to demonstrate the influence—which was in fact
acknowledged—of Tocqueville's conversations on Ampère's impressions, even if we assume that he did not read Tocqueville's travel notes,
which is not certain. Tocqueville therefore indirectly contributed to
the renewal of interest in the former New France.

The two weeks he spent in Canada left a mark on Alexis de
Tocqueville's thinking. Convinced of France's need to have colonies,
in Canada he picked up some intimations of the failings of the colonial
tradition of the Ancien Régime, and upon his return, comparing it
with the British tradition, he was to write the text *Quelques idées sur
les raisons qui s'opposent à ce que les Français aient de bonnes colonies* [a
few ideas concerning the reasons that work against the French having
good colonies.][30] Even more important, he would later endeavor to
draw lessons from Canada that would apply to the colonization of
Algeria, which became one of the major concerns of his political career.

[28]Jean-Michel Leclerc, "Alexis de Tocqueville au Canada," *Revue d'histoire de l'Amérique française* 22
(1968), 353–64.

[29]*O.C.* (Bmt) VIII, 252–67, and *O.C.* (Bmt) VII, 47–58.

[30]*O.C.* III, 1: 35–40.

10

FROM BOSTON

TO BALTIMORE

A LETTER FROM Gustave de Beaumont to his father dated September 5, 1831, gives us the itinerary the two Frenchmen followed from Montreal to Boston: "[Starting from Montreal on September 2,] a steamship bore us to La Prairie; there, we took a carriage to Saint Jean, where we embarked on a steamship on Lake Champlain. On September 4, we arrived at Whitehall and there we took a carriage which brought us to Albany today."[1] Tocqueville and Beaumont left Albany on the evening of the fifth or on the sixth, stopped at Stockbridge to meet Catherine Maria Sedgwick, a novelist famous at that time, missed her, and arrived in Boston on the seventh or eighth of September, to stay until October 3. Between Albany and Boston they had passed through the countryside of New England, whose landscapes, by contrast with those of the West, reminded them of Europe: "Massachusetts . . . is obviously an old region: I call old a region that has been in existence for two hundred years . . . One doesn't see . . . tree trunks in the fields or log cabins being used as dwellings. The fields are carefully enclosed. The crops are varied and everything indicates that the inhabitants make the best use of the land that they can, because even the rows are very close together there."[2]

Not only did their return put an end to their interlude in Canada, it also brought the two members of the commission back to the

[1] *Lettres d'Amérique,* 142.
[2] Letter from Beaumont to his brother Jules dated September 16, 1831, *Lettres d'Amérique,* 144.

problems of penitentiaries and the two future authors back to their study of the customs and institutions of the United States.

The society of Boston was markedly different from that of New York. On September 20, Tocqueville made a note of it:

Boston is a pretty town, situated picturesquely on several hills surrounded by water . . . The society, at least the society we have been introduced to, and I think it's the best, is almost completely similar to the upper classes of Europe. Here luxury and refinement prevail. Almost all the women here speak French well, and all the men we have seen so far have been to Europe. Their manners are distinguished, their conversations turn on intellectual subjects. One feels one has left behind the commercial habits and financial spirit that made New York society so common.[3]

The two Frenchmen were staying at the famous Tremont Hotel, the first large luxury hotel in the United States, which had opened two years before. It had been built with the financial support of rich patrons who were anxious for their city to be able to offer guests a splendid welcome. Each room had a private parlor. Each guest was provided with slippers while his boots were being polished. An army of bellboys were at his beck and call. This was a far cry from the rough hospitality of the inns in the interior, where travelers had to share the same bed. Boston took pride in its sumptuous homes, built by well-known architects who had also designed some of the public monuments, and in its collectors of paintings and its rich bibliophiles. A multimillionnaire like David Sears lived in a real palace and the two friends swore they had never eaten as well as they did when they were invited to dinner at his house.

Their first contacts in Boston, however, had been more difficult to establish than contacts elsewhere; here people did not throw themselves on foreigners as they did in New York. Trusting in the good-heartedness of the American welcome, Tocqueville and Beaumont had not armed themselves with any letters of introduction at all, since they had not known what to do with the seventy letters they had carried to New York four months earlier. The result was that they encountered closed doors, though this lasted only a few days. Once people came to know of their position and their mission, Boston society opened itself to them without reserve and they were caught up in a social whirlwind. "There

[3]*O.C.* V, 1: 227. On the whole of their stay in Boston, see Pierson, *Tocqueville and Beaumont in America,* 351–439.

isn't a minute of our time that isn't accounted for; they hound us with their invitations; we almost never dine at our hotel and every evening we have been to a dance or a political meeting," wrote Beaumont on September 25.[4]

Of course we should not take literally all that Tocqueville wrote about the society he and Beaumont frequented in New York. Along with merchants and bankers, they met judges and lawyers who were not at all uncultivated, along with a few very prominent figures, men like Chancellor James Kent, Livingston, and Gallatin. But in Boston they were in daily contact, it appears, with men who played an important part in American life. There was Joseph Coolidge, for instance, who did them many favors. He was, it is true, a prosperous merchant (he traded with China) but he was also married to the granddaughter of Thomas Jefferson.

The old Puritan city was still a very active religious center, with sixty houses of worship and lively controversies between the different sects. Their study of the penitentiary system put Tocqueville and Beaumont in touch with ministers of the gospel who were highly cultivated as well as zealous—men like Louis Dwight, secretary of the Society of Prisons, and the frail Joseph Tuckerman, a man of good works and also the author of interesting pamphlets on public education. Most important, they were received by William Ellery Channing, who because of his eloquence and his writings was unquestionably the pride of the Unitarian movement. Jared Sparks, whom Tocqueville already knew—they had first met in Paris in 1828, where Sparks had come to consult some archives—was another Unitarian minister, but he had told Tocqueville nothing of Unitarian doctrine. It is true that Jared Sparks was a historian first and foremost, already famous for his life of George Washington, and was at the time working on a biography of Gouverneur Morris and a history of the United States. He showed the two commissioners his rich collection of manuscripts and, in his conversation, opened historical perspectives to them that they had lacked. But Boston also possessed university professors like Harvard's George Ticknor and its president, Josiah Quincy; publicists like Alexander Everett, formerly the ambassador to Spain, who edited the *North American Review,* and Nathan Hale, editor-in-chief of the *Boston Daily Advertiser;* and a young German American named Franz Lieber who, after being severely wounded at

---

[4]Letter from Beaumont to his brother Achille dated September 25, 1831, *Lettres d'Amérique,* 156. See Pierson, op. cit., 355–56.

Waterloo, taking part in the Greek War of Independence, and later being imprisoned in Prussia for his views, had found it opportune to quit the Old World for the New. Lieber, who now led a more settled life, had published the first seven volumes of the *Encyclopedia Americana* within a few years and he made a gift of them to his new friends; later, he would translate their *Système pénitentiaire*. And there were famous political figures in Boston—Daniel Webster, known as the greatest orator in Congress and one day to be a candidate for the presidency of the United States (they found him disappointing), and John Quincy Adams, the former president, "a sort of dethroned king," who seemed to them at the height of his intellectual powers and whose conversation Tocqueville, seated next to him at a dinner in Alexander Everett's home, noted down carefully.[5] At last, then, they had found a society in America that, though small, was dominated by intellectual preoccupations, and they could not have come to a better source for general views of the people, the social life, and the government of America. But this elite belonged to the opposition, did not like President Jackson, and was sometimes contemptuous of him. Because *Democracy in America* did not take this bias into account, it failed to touch upon certain new trends in American life.

Tocqueville and Beaumont applied the same sort of maieutic method to these very competent informants that they had to others in New York: they subjected them to series of questions whose precise terms were fixed in advance. But in the case of several of the people they talked to, they encountered such willingness to help that they altered their method somewhat and presented a series of questions that could serve as the basis of a written account—as with Nathan Hale, from whom they wanted to find out about the problems faced by the press. Although we have neither the questions nor the answers, we do have Jared Sparks's description of decentralized government in Massachusetts, one he did not complete until January 1832.[6] At the same time, so as to have a point of comparison, Tocqueville asked for descriptions of the French system of centralization from Blosseville, Chabrol, and his father (whose ideas as expressed in his brochure of 1828 Tocqueville apparently was not familiar with).[7] It was really

---

[5]*O.C.* V, 1: 97–99.

[6]Letter from Beaumont to his mother dated October 7, 1831, *Lettres d'Amérique,* 160.

[7]Tocqueville's questionnaire can be found in the Tocqueville Archives. Sparks's answer was published by H. B. Adams, *Jared Sparks and Alexis de Tocqueville* (Baltimore, 1898). Tocqueville asked his father for an account of centralization in France on October 7; he asked the same of Chabrol on the same day, and of Blosseville on the eleventh.

Jared Sparks who showed him how important America's "point of departure" was for the development of American society.

There were a great many serious authors in Boston. They saw the two Frenchmen as potential readers, and every evening the two returned to the Tremont Hotel with their pockets stuffed full of pamphlets. Only a part of this serious literature has survived for us to inspect; in some cases, the pages have not been cut; in others, they have been devoured by the worms in the Château de Tocqueville.

The visit to New York had ended with a statement of fact and a question: American society was made up of middle-class people, independent of one another, among whom the government was more or less invisible. And yet this society "worked," it was animated by a coherent life.

What interested Tocqueville was the structural analysis of this egalitarian society. First of all, he wanted to understand more clearly how a society of small, independent landowners, which seemed to him the very foundation of American life, had been formed. Livingston had explained it by the fact that property was inherited in equal shares by the children. Adams was to point out to him that the ease with which one could procure land in the West, be one's own master there and acquire wealth, would prevent there being very many tenant farmers or agricultural workers. Other people he talked to would come back to what Livingston had said, that is, to the classical explanation of the liberal economists, which was probably not very applicable to America. But there was another factor that made fundamental equality the basis of this society: great fortunes could be amassed quickly, and they were fragile. Tocqueville considered this phenomenon to be linked to the fact that these fortunes were essentially based on commerce or banking, without foundations in landed property. Though there were very rich people in America, therefore, there were no stable fortunes, at least in the Northern States—where it would often happen that a businessman would become rich and his son would ruin himself—or, consequently, any class that expressed the aristocracy of wealth.

But the animating spirit of this society seemed to him even more worthy of attention. On September 20, he wrote this important note:

One of the happiest consequences of the absence of government (when a people is fortunate enough to be able to do without it, which is rare) is the development of individual strength that inevitably follows from it. Each man learns to think, to act by himself, without counting on the support of an outside force which, however vigilant one supposes it to be, can never answer all social needs. Man, thus accustomed to seek his well-being only through his own efforts, raises himself in his own opinion as he does in the opinion of others; his soul becomes larger and stronger at the same time.[8]

There were only two kinds of societies that dispensed with government, and they stood at the two extremes of civilization: primitive societies in which man is content with the satisfaction of his elementary needs, and very highly developed societies in which man, discovering that there are improvements to be made in society, calls for the willing collaboration of his fellow men, which presupposes "that he should have arrived at the social state in which his intellect allows him to have a clear perception of what is useful to him."

The key to this social state was a high level of education among the people as a whole. As Joseph Coolidge had said to him, Americans were the best educated in the world; here no one doubted, as some did in Europe, the usefulness of popular education. Tocqueville added a number of questions to his list; they concerned the freedom of teachers in the schools and the degree to which individual communities had a role in establishing the curriculum.

Popular education did not run the same risk it did in Europe, of producing an embittered people hostile to society, since society was too mobile and had no clearly demarcated classes—though Tocqueville did not use that phrase. Most important, American education remained Christian and conformed to the moral norm that regulated American society.

"[Here] everyone takes it for granted that education will be moral and religious. There would be a general outcry, a kind of popular uprising against anyone who tried to introduce a contrary system, and everyone would say that it would be better to have no education at all than an education of that sort. It is from the Bible that all our children learn to read," the minister Louis Dwight told Tocqueville.[9] Tocqueville thought that the American civic sense was based on the religious spirit, which called for both pure morals and the performance of civic duties. Whence the interest he showed in the country's religious evolution. Of course there were conflicts among the different sects, sometimes bitter ones, but the differences over dogma existed within a system of morality that was held in common. And Tocqueville thought that this morality would remain intact while religion in

[8]*O.C.* V, 1: 89.
[9]Ibid., 85.

154

America developed in two main directions: toward Unitarianism—which, in spite of Channing's protestations, would perhaps evolve into deism—and toward Catholicism, with its rigorously uniform discipline, which was gaining more and more ground among the masses. But the religion which molded the citizens' minds drew its strength from an almost complete independence from the State, even as it accepted the principles of democracy.

At this stage of his trip these two themes—an educated people, a religious people—were of the first order of importance for the future author of the *Democracy*. Education and religion enlightened and guided public opinion, without which republican institutions could not function.

The American institutions were not to be understood, Jared Sparks wrote in the descriptive account alluded to above, without keeping in mind "the mode in which the country was originally settled. The first establishment was at Plymouth, and consisted of only one hundred and one persons, surrounded by a vast wilderness, uninhabited except for a few savages. As far as the rights and forms of government were concerned, the new settlers, when they landed, were in a state of nature. For mutual convenience and security, they agreed on a system of social and political regulations, which had the effect of laws. This was the simplest form of a republic."[10] It was thus that Sparks explained—in a way that still has a flavor of the eighteenth century about it—the formation of the township. The townships then grouped themselves into counties, the counties into states, and later, at the time of the fighting against England and the Revolution, the states that the different colonies constituted joined in a federation. In this way, the American republic was built from the ground up, the powers of the higher levels being delegated by lower and earlier levels. This natural framework for a democracy, based on the sovereignty of the people, did not exist in Europe. To regain its freedom, the French State would have to shift responsibility onto the lower authorities, creating decentralization by law: "In America, free mores have made the political institutions free; in France, it is up to the free political institutions to create the mores."

To return to the situation in America, Tocqueville was then in a good position to witness the creative power of the base, the normal workings of a spontaneous democracy. The big political issue at that

[10]Adams, *Sparks and Tocqueville*, 17. See also the conversation with Sparks in *O.C.* V, 1: 95–96.

time was the customs tariff. The South, exporting cotton and importing manufactured products, wanted to lower the tariff while the
North, anxious to protect its young industries, wanted to keep the
tariff where it was. Now Theodore Sedgwick, a confirmed free trader
whom Tocqueville had met at Stockbridge, had initiated the idea,
through the press, of an association to demand the lowering of the
customs duties. The success of this idea had led to the creation of
private assemblies, often called conventions, which organized opposition to the tariff. Did this spontaneous demonstration of democracy
pose a threat to legal institutions, or would it confine itself to attempting to win over public opinion? Tocqueville was deeply interested in
the question.[11]

Sometimes such oppositions between the South and the North
reminded him of the old eighteenth-century axiom that a republic
cannot be a suitable form of government for a large state, and he had
doubts that the federal form was an adequate remedy. Nevertheless, the
greatest risk of an explosion in the United States came from the
problem of slavery. Tocqueville and Beaumont conducted interviews
on the subject in Boston, most importantly with a planter from
Georgia named Clay, who happened to be in town. Tocqueville even
tried to sound out John Quincy Adams on the problem and thought
he detected pessimism on Adams's part about the future of the Union.
Already, during their stay in Boston, the two visitors seem to have
foreseen that emancipation would be an ineffectual cure, given the
absolute distance and the hostility between the two races. They therefore had to ask themselves a new question about the future, and they
would later hark back to the problem.

By the time they left New England, then, they had come to have
a broad picture of the way American democracy worked. Of course
they still had to study its mechanisms, its links to the "mores," and the
various ways in which it functioned in this or that part of the country.
Though the following note was written on October 25, some time
after their departure from the city, it seems to sum up their Boston
experience:

The admirable effect of republican governments (where they can continue
to exist) is not to offer a glimpse of *regularity,* of *methodical order* in the
administration of a people, but *a picture of life itself.* A free form of govern-

[11]*O.C.* V, 1: 237–38. Similar reactions can be found in Beaumont's *Lettres d'Amérique,* 131.

ment does not carry out each of its undertakings with the same perfection as an intelligent despotism, but in the long run it yields more . . . It imparts to the entire social body an activity, a force, an energy that never exists without it and that brings forth wonders.[12]

In spite of its reservations concerning the universal value of democracy, this judgment of the American republic was much more favorable than the conclusion they had reached during their period in New York.

Tocqueville and Beaumont left Boston on October 3 for Hartford, where they stayed three days. There, they embarked on the Connecticut River and reached New York on the morning of the eighth. This time, they hardly did more than pass through, and were in Philadelphia on the twelfth.

In Boston, they had resumed their study of the penitentiary problem, having abandoned it for a few weeks: "This is why we are in America and no one has any doubt about it," Beaumont wrote to his brother Jules.[13] In Boston itself, they had visited the home for juvenile delinquents, which seemed to them an even more useful and well-conceived institution than the one in New York, as well as the Charlestown prison. The latter was based not on the Auburn system (isolation of the prisoners at night only), but on the Pennsylvania system of isolation in cells day and night. It is interesting to note that whereas in their book on penitentiaries, the two authors make no formal pronouncement on the Auburn system, Beaumont, in his letter of September 16, 1831, declares himself in favor of it: "People everywhere recognize the incontestable advantages of this system, which is now generally adopted in all the states of the Union. I haven't the slightest doubt about its superiority. The only question in France will be that of the expenses involved in introducing it."[14] Beaumont's opinion is largely based on the psychological experiment performed by Tocqueville in the Charlestown prison, where he conducted private interviews with prisoners who had been subjected to solitary confinement.

They found the Auburn system in effect at the prison in Wethersfield, which they had gone to Hartford to visit. Here they noticed that discipline was gentler than in the mother institution, and wrote in a report to Paris that this prison "offered all the guarantees of security and salubriousness that one could wish." In fact, they did not see any

[12] *Voyage en Amérique*, 184.
[13] Letter to his brother Jules dated September 16, 1831, *Lettres d'Amérique*, 149.
[14] Ibid.

signs of the poor treatment—including insufficient food and heat—to which a head warden, guilty of the misappropriation of funds, was subjecting the prisoners. A judge who had inspected the prison had already denounced this and would later create a scandal over the matter.[15]

Philadelphia, the old Quaker city, was the capital of American humanitarianism. The visit by the two French commissioners caused a sensation even before they appeared in person, and their initial welcome had none of the coolness of their reception in Boston. To the enthusiasm of the city's humanitarians for the Auburn penitentiary system, there was joined the rivalry between theoreticians and practitioners. On October 18, Tocqueville wrote to his sister-in-law Alexandrine:

There is a conflict over who will monopolize us more completely. A week before our arrival, the chief warden of the establishment came and left his card with the French consul, asking to be notified the very moment we arrived . . . while the society set up to examine penitentiary theory met at the same time and appointed a commission to help us in our investigation. The same day, we received an invitation to dine at the home of the warden and a letter from a Quaker (a man of theory par excellence) who, without using the word *Monsieur* and addressing us as "thee"—engaged us to dine with him and a few of his friends.[16]

The two Frenchmen were soon being commandeered to visit charitable institutions more often than they liked. The recently constructed Cherry Hill prison looked like a medieval castle from the outside and the individual cells were arranged in a radial plan that allowed them to be watched from a central point. For the last time in their trip, then, the two Frenchmen spent most of their days observing prisons and interviewing humanitarians, especially Quakers—even though the latter's influence in the city was on the decline and they had split into different factions. Yet the city had other interesting features besides the Society for Alleviating the Miseries of the Public Prisons.

Tocqueville and Beaumont had arrived in Philadelphia in early autumn, a time in the American East when summer seems to be prolonged and the gradual and unequal turning of the leaves colors the landscape with variegated yellows and reds. The city, with its brick

[15]Pierson, op. cit., 446–47.

[16]Letter to his sister-in-law Alexandrine dated October 18, 1831, a copy of which is in the Beinecke Library. On the eager reception they were given in Philadelphia, see Pierson, op. cit., 458–59 and 461.

158

houses that had no carriage gates but were sometimes fronted with marble porticoes, did not seem without charm to them, and they admired its cleanliness. Of course, it was rather monotonous. Penn had designed it in the form of a rectangle on the low terrace of land separating the Delaware from the Schuylkill, with two avenues intersecting in the middle, one of which, Broad Street, was the longest straight street in the world. All the other streets, numbered, intersected at right angles. The city was much larger than Boston, with 168,000 inhabitants, according to the 1830 census.

French travelers and former émigrés were biased in favor of Philadelphia. Its society, which was more hospitable and more tolerant than that of Puritan Boston, remained aloof from the commercial preoccupations that dominated New York. Tocqueville and Beaumont's visit apparently confirmed this general impression. They were entertained by the American Philosophical Society, where Beaumont was very bored, and in 1842 it appointed Tocqueville a member. But if they both enjoyed several dinners given by the Quakers, they most often attended the dinners and balls given by the most wealthy Philadelphians, where they encountered an elite society. Here they were introduced to the most prominent local lawyers and to politicians who were among the country's leaders—men like Benjamin W. Richards, who was the city's mayor, Governor George Howard, and Nicholas Biddle, the famous director of the Federal Bank—and to people who knew Europe well, among them the former ambassador James Brown, a very cultivated Frenchman named Peter Duponceau, who had been in America for the past fifty years, and, most important, Robert Walsh. The latter, from an Irish family with branches in France (and he may have come from one of these branches, since he had lived in France under the Empire), had written numerous pamphlets and his salon had the unusual attraction of providing excellent music. He was later to be appointed consul general in Paris, and Tocqueville would be a frequent visitor to his mansion on the rue de Rivoli.

According to Tocqueville,[17] it was in Boston that his desire to go to Philadelphia had been quickened. His interest was aroused there in the tariff question and in the convention that was to be assembled to fight for tariff reductions, and Philadelphia was where the convention would gather—one that, in his opinion, was carrying the practical application of popular sovereignty to a dangerous extreme, capable of threatening the institutions of the republic. But when he reached the

[17]Letter to his father dated October 7, 1831, copy in the Beinecke Library.

city he found that the convention had just been dissolved after ten days of debates open to the public, having composed an incendiary statement in which it was asserted that Congress had no right under the Constitution to fix tariffs. A lawyer in the city calmed Tocqueville's fears by pointing out to him that in a democracy one could not take all verbal violence at its face value and that this statement was no more, in actual fact, than an appeal to public opinion.

But if Tocqueville was concerned about the possible dangers in the privately organized associations for which the Americans displayed so strong a predilection, he was also attracted by the moral force such associations could exercise. After he discovered the temperance societies, he noted on October 10 that "one of the most remarkable things about this country" was "the association of men who mutually commit themselves to abstain from a vice and who find collective life to be a help to them in resisting what is most private and most peculiar to every man, his own inclinations."[18]

Another problem worried Tocqueville here, and though this was the first time it appeared in his notes, it was to remain with him in his future political career. Were the voters reluctant to elect members of the old established families to office, as had proved to be the case in France? (Here, Tocqueville was thinking of the First Republic.) When he interviewed the mayor of Philadelphia, he was assured that in Pennsylvania the people's votes seemed to go to candidates from the middle classes, and that they were just as capable of governing as those from the upper classes. Other people he talked to said that bad choices could alternate with good. But there was no systematic animosity against the rich or the older families.

On another front, Tocqueville, being a magistrate, had given a good deal of thought to the influence of the judiciary power in politics. In the United States, the dominant feature of the legal system—complex though it was, and varying from state to state—was the trial by jury, in civil cases as well as criminal. Tocqueville set out to study in detail the functioning of the American courts, which corresponded in their main principles to those in England.

He described the legal system as clearly as possible in a letter to his friend Chabrol.[19] The fact that America remained a country governed by common law at first seemed to make justice more arbitrary. In reality, judiciary democracy was restrained by the presence of the judge

[18]*O.C.* V, 1: 236.
[19]Unpublished letter to Chabrol dated November 26, 1831, copy in the Beinecke Library.

presiding over the trial, who still had the power to annul decisions, not only for de jure reasons, but also de facto—and he himself could not be dismissed except for "ill behavior," a finding that could result only from a trial instituted against him. The popular power that the jury embodied was therefore in practice checked or moderated by the power of the judges. And though the guarantee of impartial or enlightened justice might not be absolute, this system did introduce the people to juridical problems. The institutions of democracy contributed to the education of the citizens, as this example showed, and Tocqueville thought that the few slips in the way it functioned were largely compensated for by this fact.

The two Frenchmen had recognized in Boston the internal workings that give rise to the dynamism of democratic society. In Philadelphia, they analyzed the mechanisms of this process: on the whole, in this Pennsylvania setting, their conclusions remained favorable. Democracy could produce specific remedies for its own defects. Was this the case for the Union as a whole?

They were hounded by another concern that had taken shape in Boston. The problem of slavery was the Union's festering sore. Was it possible to eliminate slavery without making this sore burst open, and if the remedy was applied, what would be its effect?

Before their visit to Philadelphia, the problem was still an abstract one for Tocqueville and Beaumont. Though Philadelphia was no longer a slave state, it still had a large black population. They saw in concrete terms that the problem of slavery in America was above all else a racial problem that emancipation of the slaves alone would not solve.

As soon as they arrived, they were able to witness, at the theater, how the two races were separated, as Beaumont was to describe it in *Marie:* if a woman, even "with lily-white skin," was known to have had a mulatto ancestor, she was relegated to the gallery reserved for blacks.[20] Free blacks could not vote—public opinion was against it—and they could not send their children to the same schools as the whites, or bury their dead in the same cemeteries.

Tocqueville and Beaumont could hardly have been unaware of the fact that they were carrying out their investigation of the relations between whites and blacks, and between masters and slaves, in a dramatic context. On August 21 and 22, in the county of Southampton in Virginia, Nat Turner, a visionary slave, had led a group of blacks

[20]See Gustave de Beaumont, *Marie; ou l'esclavage aux Etats-Unis* (Paris, 1835).

in an uprising against their masters, and more than fifty whites had been massacred. On October 30, Nat Turner was captured and sentenced, with sixteen of his companions, to be hanged; he was to be executed November 11. In Philadelphia, the people the young Frenchmen talked to saw no solution to the race problem: the elimination of slavery would solve nothing. Duponceau carried his pessimism to the point of predicting that a war would have to be fought between the two races in which the blacks, who were less numerous, would be wiped out.

No doubt it was their eagerness to see a state in which slavery still existed that made the two French commissioners decide to visit Baltimore, which they did from October 28 to November 6. Slavery was on the decline there, but freed blacks were kept strictly segregated. On November 29, at a horse race, the two friends saw a black venture onto the track with some white men. When one of the whites drove him away by beating him with his cane, no one was surprised, not even the black.

Beaumont writes that he made many observations in Baltimore, but because of the unfortunate loss of his *Journal* we have no detailed record of them. He was also to make Baltimore the setting of his novel *Marie; ou l'esclavage aux Etats-Unis,* a novel whose subtitle is deceptive, because the subject of the book is really the conflict between the races.

On a different front, Baltimore was the city in the United States most given to luxurious display in festivals, horse races, and elegant dress. Here, Southern custom revealed its prodigality, frivolity, and generosity. As soon as they arrived, the two Frenchmen were invited to a dance for which there was a five-dollar entry fee, and during their stay in Baltimore they went from dinner to dinner. Another noticeable feature of Southern society besides slavery, which was very much on the decline, was what remained of the old colonial aristocracy, itself slowly disappearing as the large estates were parceled out among the heirs. Tocqueville and Beaumont dined at the home of the largest landowner in the Union, Charles Carroll, who at the age of ninety-five was the last surviving signer of the Declaration of Independence. Distinguished travelers paid visits to him as a historic monument, but he retained an accurate enough memory to be able to describe the days of the Revolution. In Baltimore, Tocqueville found confirmation for his feeling that the members of the great families who had accepted independence and democracy instead of sticking fast to the defense of their old privileges were sometimes elected by universal suffrage (which did exist in Maryland) to perform public functions. Baltimore society had been in part injected with new life by the influx of French

162

following the revolt of the people of Santo Domingo against French rule in 1808–1809. Seat of the only archbishopric in America, Baltimore was the intellectual and political center of Catholicism in the United States. Catholicism had been the religion of the poor classes and democracy favored its spread, yet it was gaining ground not only because of the influx of poor Irish immigrants, but also through the conversion of middle- and upper-class Protestants.

Tocqueville allowed the ideas he heard expressed to ripen before judging them and coming to his own conclusions. It was not until November 30, nine days after he had left Philadelphia, as he was going down the Ohio River and approaching Cincinnati, that he put down on paper a series of notes that took stock of the conversations he had had in Philadelphia and Boston.

In these notes he analyzed the essential criterion of social distinction in the American society of social equality. This equality, he concluded, in no way ruled out distinction based on wealth, which created "a true privileged class which keeps itself apart." But the criterion of wealth was more flexible than the criterion of birth and did not prevent, as did the latter, the "joining of families" through marriage.[21]

But two other facts also seemed certain: "America demonstrates invincibly one thing that I had doubted up to now: that the middle classes can govern a State. I don't know if they would extricate themselves creditably from really difficult political situations. But they are adequate to the ordinary business of society. Despite their small passions, their incomplete education, their vulgar habits, they can obviously provide a practical sort of intelligence and that turns out to be enough . . ."

Montesquieu's criterion, by which virtue was the foundation of the old republics, was not suited to modern democracies:

Another point that America demonstrates is that virtue is not, as has been claimed for so long, the only thing that can maintain a republic. Enlightenment, more than anything else, makes this social state possible. The Americans are no more virtuous than other people, but they are infinitely more enlightened (I'm speaking of the great mass) than any other people I know . . .

The mass of people who understand public affairs, who are acquainted with laws and precedents, who have a sense for the interests, well understood, of the nation, and the faculty to understand them is greater here than in any other place in the world.[22]

[21]*O.C.* V, 1: 278–80.
[22]Ibid.

The society of the South, with its vestiges of aristocratic elites and 163
its more ignorant masses, seemed less suited to the republican regime ⚘ ⚘
than the North. At the end of his stay in Baltimore, Tocqueville wrote
the following important note:

As far as I can judge, the republic doesn't seem to me to be a social state
as natural and appropriate to the South as it is to the North of the United
States. Is this because of the difference that exists between education in the
North and in the South, between the different physical makeup and resultant
differences of character in the two parts? Or rather, do the educated classes,
which are as yet not very familiar with democratic government in the South,
reveal their secrets more readily than the same classes in the North? This is
what I don't yet know. What I am certain of is that I have quite different
impressions of the two parts of the Union. The North presents, at least from
the outside, the image of a government that is strong, consistent, durable, and
perfectly suited to the physical and moral state of things. In the South, there
is something feverish, disordered, revolutionary, impassioned in the way
things are run that doesn't leave the same impression of strength and durabil-
ity.

But if, in the South, the preexisting aristocratic traditions might be
in conflict with democracy, did the latter not present other difficulties
in the West, where society was born spontaneously with the arrival
of settlers who had no previous ties to one another, where democracy
was in a sense chemically pure, with no admixture of tradition or social
distinction? It was to the West that the following reflection, also
written aboard the Ohio steamboat, more particularly applied: "What
is extremely interesting in America is to examine the tendencies and
instincts of democracy when it is altogether on its own, and to discover
the social state to which it must necessarily bring the society that it
dominates."

It was unthinkable for a traveler on a voyage of discovery in the
New World not to take a trip through the West and the South, which
were different from the North. And a political sociologist could not
judge the harmony of America's mores and its laws without having
some experience of those other societies, one of them older and one
younger than the Yankee society.

11

THROUGH THE WEST AND SOUTH

TOCQUEVILLE and Beaumont very probably left Philadelphia on November 21, 1831. Their intention was to go to Cincinnati, the active center of the state of Ohio, a mushrooming city in a territory that was growing particularly rapidly, where they could inform themselves about the problems of the West more effectively than they had during their brief excursion toward the frontier the previous August. From Cincinnati, they would cross through Kentucky and a corner of Virginia and Tennessee, and then stay for a fairly long time in Charleston. There they would find people well worth interviewing—some of the members of Charleston's high society were French in origin—who would enlighten them concerning life in the South. After studying the "Yankee" world, which they judged to be the dominant element in the American federation, they would thus resume contact with the rustic society of the West, then with the slave-owning society, less democratic in its ways, that they had already glimpsed in an attenuated form in Baltimore.[1]

But as soon as they left Philadelphia, they were confronted with the rigors of a winter such as had not been seen in living memory, one that involved them in difficult or dangerous situations that made them change their plans several times. They were brutally assaulted by the weather as they crossed the Alleghenies, and reached Pittsburgh only after three exhausting days and nights en route in bad carriages, on execrable roads, through an unending snowstorm.

[1]Letter from Beaumont to his brother Jules dated December 4, 1831, *Lettres d'Amérique*, 191.

When they were in Boston, they had not been at all interested, as most visitors were, in visiting the textile manufacturing center of Lowell. Nor did they stop now in Pittsburgh, the great center of American metallurgy. They got off their stagecoach and got right on a steamboat. Beaumont confined himself to writing his sister Eugénie that Pittsburgh was the "Birmingham of America," that the sky there was dark with smoke from the factory chimneys.[2] As for Tocqueville, he resumed the reverie he had begun in Canada on what the consequences of a great French empire in America might have been had its establishment been achieved, and wrote to his brother Hippolyte:

Pittsburgh is the former French Fort Duquesne, one of the causes of the war of 1745. In America, the French gave proof of an extraordinary genius in the way they arranged their military posts. At a time when the interior of the North American continent was still entirely unknown to the Europeans, the French established posts in the midst of the wilderness from Canada to Louisiana—a succession of small forts which, now that the country has been thoroughly explored, have been recognized to be the best places one could have chosen to found the most flourishing cities and the most favorable situations for attracting commerce and commanding the navigation of rivers ... Had we been successful, the English colonies would have been surrounded by an immense arc of which Quebec and New Orleans would have formed the two extremities. Pressed from behind by the French and their allies the Indians, the Americans of the United States would not have revolted against their mother country ... There wouldn't have been any American Revolution, and perhaps no French Revolution—or at least the circumstances would not have been the same.[3]

Tocqueville wrote that letter on November 26 on board the steamer *Fourth of July* on the Ohio River. The following night, the boat struck a reef at Burlington Bar slightly upriver from Wheeling: "The cry 'we sink!' immediately rang out; the ship, crew, and passengers together began their journey toward eternity. I have never heard a nastier noise than the noise the water made as it rushed inside the boat," Tocqueville was to write Chabrol two days later.[4] Beaumont, in notes whose dramatic tone and uncertain chronology lead us to suspect that they were reworked at a later date (even though Beaumont had some difficulty with dates even in his letters) but which are certainly basi-

---

[2] Letter from Beaumont to his sister Eugénie dated December 1, 1831, *Lettres d'Amérique*, 187.
[3] Letter dated November 26, 1831, to Hippolyte, published by Beaumont, O.C. (Bmt) VII, 86–89, and corrected on the basis of the copy in the Beinecke Library.
[4] Unpublished letter to Chabrol dated November 28, 1831, copy in the Beinecke Library.

cally truthful, shows us the two friends shaking hands before departing for the beyond, then describes to us the miracle that kept them in this world: "The hull of the boat caught on the very reef that had broken it; what saved it was the very depth of its wound and the rapidity with which the water filling it caused it to settle on the reef."[5] There was nothing exceptional about the accident. The captains of these first steamboats ran great risks—of having the steam engine explode, of running their boat aground. They would overload a vessel without taking even the most elementary precautions. The *Fourth of July,* with two hundred people on board, carried only two rowboats with room for ten each! A few hours later, another steamer came by, the *William Parsons,* and was able to extricate the passengers from their uncomfortable position by transshipping them there in the middle of the river. On December 1, Tocqueville and Beaumont landed without further mishap at Cincinnati.

The Cincinnati of those days is well known to us from the descriptions of Mrs. Trollope, who had left the city only the year before; the site was remarkable—a sort of basin in the form of an amphitheater lying between the right bank of the Ohio and the hills that bordered the river. The humble village that had come into existence twenty-five years before was now a city of more than twenty thousand inhabitants in which the construction of more than three hundred houses a year was hardly sufficient to lodge the newcomers. A large commercial depot supplying the material needs of the pioneers and shipping out their products, Cincinnati was also a manufacturing city, specializing in building steamboats. This did not mean it was without its archaic aspects: for example, its only waste disposal system was the heavy rainfalls on the sloping streets and, even more important, its roving herds of pigs.[6] Concerning these aspects of the city, Tocqueville was as restrained in his comments as he had been in his descriptions of New York: "A city that seems to want to grow up too fast for anyone to maintain order here. Big buildings, cottages, streets choked with rubbish, houses under construction. No names on the streets, no numbers on the houses, no external luxury, but offering a constant picture of industry and labor." And in a letter to his mother, he was more specific: "a rough sketch of a city rather than a city. But . . . the sound of life, a population whose activity has something feverish about it."[7] Tocque-

[5]*Lettres d'Amérique,* 200. The shipwreck that took place during the night of November 26–27 is wrongly dated December 1.
[6]*O.C.* V, 1: 284–85.
[7]Unpublished letter to his mother dated December 6, 1831.

ville and Beaumont stayed only four days, but, as we shall see, the interviewing work they did here was particularly fruitful.

In Cincinnati, they were dissuaded from taking the old route to the South across the Alleghenies, which was made impracticable by the harsh weather. They would not consider going back the way they had come. They therefore decided to go to Charleston, from which they would travel on to Washington in time for the opening of Congress in January, by making an immense detour via New Orleans. In Louisville, regular boat service took passengers from that city to the capital of Louisiana in one week. By going south, they hoped to enter a gentler climate soon, and so they embarked for Louisville.

But the following day, December 5, their boat was caught in the ice. The passengers were unloaded in the little cove of Westport, about twenty-two miles upriver from Louisville. A pioneer agreed to the risky proposition of loading their baggage into his cart and going to the city by way of roads that hardly existed. The two French commissioners followed the cart on foot through snow that sometimes came up to their knees. Once they reached Louisville, they ascertained that the Ohio was entirely blocked by ice. They were assured that this sort of thing never happened on the Mississippi and were advised to go overland to Memphis, about 210 miles north of New Orleans (and on the same latitude as Tangiers). Memphis was a regular landing stage for steamboats, which stopped there every day to replenish the supplies of wood needed for their engines. At Memphis, it would be easy for the two travelers to get on a boat for New Orleans. They therefore took the stagecoach for Nashville.

In Nashville, however, all they could find for continuing on to Memphis was an open, light one-horse carriage. This miserable vehicle, traveling over abominable roads, broke a leather strap supporting the body of the carriage as well as an axle, and only limped on after emergency repairs had been made. The expedition almost came to an end on the banks of the Tennessee, which was full of ice floes. The ferryman could not be persuaded to take on the carriage until he was assured that the vehicle and the black slave driving it were both insured in case of loss.

But Tocqueville was shivering with fever. They were in a region with almost no villages. At Sandy Bridge they were offered the hospitality of the postal relay station, a plain, isolated log cabin; the nearest doctor was thirty miles away. The round logs did not fit tightly together and let in the icy air from outside as well as the moonlight;

Beaumont, having poured himself a glass of water, found shortly afterwards that it had turned to ice. The owners of the house showed their visitors great but totally ineffectual courtesy. Their slaves attended to the guests, for the owner would have found it beneath his dignity to do anything but hunt and smoke.

This evening, the evening of December 12, was undoubtedly the most dramatic of their trip: Beaumont had a large fire built up, in which an entire tree was burned, and he smothered Tocqueville under a pile of blankets. By the fifteenth Tocqueville was better, though weak, and he was bundled into the stagecoach bound for Memphis, which was passing that way.[8]

Having arrived in Memphis, the two friends were treated to an unparalleled spectacle: the Mississippi frozen over, with steamboats caught in the ice. A small town with one inn which Mrs. Trollope has described for us,[9] Memphis was surrounded by forest. The tributaries of the Mississippi were also frozen over and it was therefore impossible to go back up north. Tocqueville and Beaumont were patient about their misfortune, hunting parrots in the forest in the company of Chickasaw Indians, one of whose villages was nearby.

At last, on Christmas Eve, the cold spell ended and a steamship coming from New Orleans appeared on the river. When it stopped at Memphis, the captain was assaulted by travelers bound for New Orleans who had been stranded in the little town and tried to persuade him that since the Mississippi was frozen farther north, he ought to turn around. And in fact, the passengers bound for the north were disembarked at Memphis and replaced by those bound for New Orleans. An unexpected incident had finally convinced the captain: "As we were parleying . . . on the river bank, we heard an infernal music resound through the forest; drums were beating, horses whinnying, dogs barking. At last a great troop of Indians appeared, old men, women, children, baggage, the whole led by a European . . ." It was a tribe of the Choctaw nation that an agent of the American government, under the authority of the "Indian Removal Act," was conducting to the right bank of the Mississippi after having persuaded them to abandon the land of their ancestors, which had been invaded by white men. They required steamboat passage to the mouth of the White River, farther south, where they would be released. That very day, in a letter to his mother, Tocqueville described with bitter irony

[8]See Beaumont's letter to his mother dated December 1831, *Lettres d'Amérique,* 197–98, and Pierson, op. cit., 572–74.

[9]Frances Trollope, *Domestic Manners of the Americans* (1832).

the pitiful spectacle of the embarkation of these poor people. He concluded:

There was a general air of ruin and destruction in this sight, something that gave an impression of a final farewell, with no going back; one couldn't witness it without a heavy heart. The Indians were calm, but gloomy and taciturn. One of them knew English. I asked him why the Choctaws were leaving their country. "To be free," he answered. I couldn't get anything else out of him. Tomorrow we will set them down in the Arkansas wilderness. I must confess it is an odd coincidence that we should have arrived at Memphis in time to witness the expulsion, or perhaps the dissolution, of one of the last vestiges of one of the oldest and most famous American nations.[10]

At the mouth of the White River, they took on a man riding a superb stallion who was going to New Orleans. Tocqueville engaged him in conversation about the Indians. He was one of the great adventurers of the United States at that time, Sam Houston. The future president of the ephemeral republic of Texas, the former governor of Tennessee, discredited because of his controversial marriage, was at that time the son-in-law of an Indian chief and an Indian chief himself.[11]

Another annoying incident occurred while they were going down the Mississippi. Because the upper part of the river and its tributaries were frozen, the level of water in the river was very low, and the boat went aground on December 26. For two days it could not be moved. Tocqueville also noted down that on the thirty-first, the day before they arrived in New Orleans, he visited a sugarcane plantation with seventy slaves, fifty miles to the north of the city.[12] This could not have been more than a boat landing where they stopped to take on more wood—giving the passengers ten minutes to stretch their legs, according to Mrs. Trollope's testimony. It certainly appears that this was the only time the two Frenchmen saw a large plantation and, if such was really the case, they could only have had a very superficial look at it.

Tocqueville and Beaumont landed at New Orleans on the morning of January 1, 1832. As with his *Visite au lac Oneida* and *Quinze jours dans le désert*, he wanted to make use of the notes in his notebooks to write a brief essay called *Vingt-Quatre heures à La Nouvelle-Orléans*. But he only managed to make a rough draft of this account, which

[10]Unpublished letter to his mother dated December 25, 1831.
[11]Pierson, op. cit., 607–15.
[12]*O.C.* V, 1: 191.

is now lost: the text has been preserved only in the translation of it done by the American Lambert White.[13] He intended to devote part of it to a *Coup d'oeil de La Nouvelle-Orléans,* but got only as far as writing the title, so that here again Tocqueville's impressions are available to us only in the form of brief daily notes and a few passages in letters.

The notes reflect his first contact with the city: "Arrival at New Orleans. Forest of ships. Mississippi, 300 feet deep. Outer appearance of city: Beautiful houses. Cabins. Muddy unpaved streets. Spanish architecture: flat roofs; English: bricks, small doors; French: massive carriage gates. Population just as mixed. Faces all shades of color. French, English, Spanish, Creole languages. General appearance French, and yet posters, commercial advertisements generally in English. Industrial and commercial world *American.*"

The two commissioners could not help being interested in the behavior of the French here, who were descendants of the French of colonial Louisiana. These French still constituted the majority of the white population, and, though they had not forgotten their old homeland, whose political developments they continued more or less to follow, they felt perfectly at ease in their status as American citizens. They did not have the complexes of a conquered people that the French Canadians had. But society in New Orleans also differed from Canadian society in its laxness of morals. Young men would live with charming mulatto women until they married white women, at which time they would leave the mulatto, who would be given a dowry and in turn marry a black man. Only in these immoral unions did the two races intermingle. Tocqueville and Beaumont, going to hear Daniel Auber's *Le Maçon,* found the concert hall divided into three parts: one white, one mixed, one black; they observed the customs from closer up at a quadroon ball, about which they unfortunately provide us with no details. Giving Chabrol a summary of his impressions a few days later, Tocqueville concluded:

The visit to New Orleans . . . has been very strange and very pleasant. When you hear people say that climate has nothing to do with people's makeup, assure them they're wrong. We saw the French of Canada; they are a calm people, moral, religious. We left behind in Louisiana quite different Frenchmen, restless, dissolute, lax in all things. Between them there are fifteen degrees of latitude: this is in truth the best reason I can give for the difference.

[13]This translation can be found in the Beinecke Library.

What morals! My dear friend, they are the morals of a Southern land into
which slavery was introduced. It is a picture that confounds the imagination.[14]

Having been inspired by the charms of New Orleans to extend their
stay there, Tocqueville and Beaumont resolved to give up their visit
to Charleston, whose most prominent men, in any case, could be found
in Washington when Congress was in session. The stretch of countryside to be traveled was rough, nevertheless; the stagecoach route from
New Orleans to Norfolk, where they embarked on the Chesapeake for
Washington, went by way of Mobile, Berkeley, Montgomery, Knox-
ville, and Augusta, covering a distance of a thousand miles. They made
the journey in twelve days (January 4–15, 1832), averaging better than
eighty miles a day. The bad luck that had been hounding them during
this harsh winter hardly let up at all now: "Bridges out . . . impassable
roads . . . carriages breaking down," wrote Beaumont to his father, and
Tocqueville, fully recovered from the scare at Sandy Bridge, gave the
following advice among his prescriptions for staying in good health:
"Eat corn and pork. Dine poorly, well, or not at all according to the
occasion. Sleep on the floor, fully dressed. In the course of a week go
from icy cold to warmth and from warmth to icy cold, put your
shoulder to the wheel, wake up in a ditch."[15] This undertaking, "almost impracticable but in which we were nevertheless successful," was,
however, marked by one piece of good fortune—the meeting with
Joel Roberts Poinsett, whom they had already seen in Philadelphia.[16]
This meeting probably took place on January 12, in a tavern where
they were seeking shelter after an accident on the road. Poinsett,
descended from Huguenots from La Rochelle, former ambassador to
Mexico, knew South America and Europe well. In South Carolina, he
had just been organizing the fight against the nullifiers (as those who
favored easing the system of tariffs set up to protect native industry
were called), a mission President Jackson had entrusted him with, and
he was now on his way back to Washington. He had all the qualities
needed to respond to the eager questions Tocqueville put to him and
submitted to them with good grace.

All in all, the two commissioners had little more than a panoramic

[14]Unpublished letter to Chabrol dated January 16, 1832, copy in the Beinecke Library.

[15]Letter from Beaumont to his father dated January 16, 1832, *Lettres d'Amérique*, 206, and unpublished
letter from Tocqueville to Emilie dated January 16, 1832, copy in Beinecke Library. See also *O.C.* V,
1: 282.

[16]On Poinsett, see *Lettres d'Amérique*, 211. Tocqueville summed up the conversations he and Beaumont
had with Poinsett (*O.C.* V, 1: 143–51).

172

𒀱 𒀱

and inevitably superficial view of the old South. Tocqueville was aware of this; he wrote his brother Edouard that a stay of six months would be necessary to understand this part of the United States.[17] The fact that they had had to skip Charleston, in particular, which they had been looking forward to for so long, left a gap in their understanding of the country.

On January 16, the two commissioners arrived in Washington. They were received by the French ambassador, Mr. Serurier, who gave them a very nice welcome, held a big ball in their honor, and thought it created an excellent impression to have two such distinguished young men entrusted with an official mission. Serurier presented them to President Jackson on January 19. "When we went into his drawing room, he was alone, though it was the day for the public reception . . . We chatted about fairly insignificant things. He gave us a glass of Madeira wine and we thanked him, calling him *Sir* as though he were just anyone." The mediocre impression left by this visit confirmed the two friends' inaccurate opinion that the powers of the president were not very great.[18] But in Washington, among the eminent political figures gathered there, they renewed their acquaintance from the previous year with John Quincy Adams, the former president, and met Edward Livingston, the senator from Louisiana who was now secretary of state in the Jackson cabinet, and Louis McLane, the secretary of the treasury. They were given every freedom to attend the sessions of Congress and acquire useful documents. Joseph Coolidge, who had done so much for them in Boston, gave them a letter of introduction to Nicholas P. Trist, a Virginian who was a senior official in the State Department, who helped them collect a mass of printed matter on the workings of the federal government.

We have noted in passing the importance of the brief visit to Cincinnati, an ideal observation post from which to gain a view of the West. The people Tocqueville found to talk to there were equally well chosen: Bellamy Storer, a journalist friend of Adams, and Timothy Walker, a jurist of great learning, both educated in the East and for that reason suited to act as guides to Tocqueville in the new part of America he was entering with the intention of comparing it with the states of the East.

Ohio had been recognized as a state in 1802. At that time a conven-

---

[17]Letter to Edouard dated January 20, 1832, copy in the Beinecke Library.
[18]Letter to his father dated January 24, 1832.

tion had given it institutions that were more democratic than those in the Eastern states, with universal suffrage and short terms for the legislative and judicial offices. Now it had a million inhabitants and seemed to be the symbol of the West, a West that was growing so rapidly that one could predict that the Union's center of gravity would settle there. Whence the importance of studying the workings of democracy in this new setting. Was democracy capable of organizing and stabilizing it?

The institutions and customs of New England had developed gradually from roots in the townships. In Pennsylvania and elsewhere in the East, the young democracy had great respect for certain eminent families who had distinguished themselves during the Revolution and, at least in some states, was quick to bring them to office. This was not at all the case in Ohio. Here the population included hardly any emigrants from Europe, almost all of whom stayed settled in the Eastern states, but was made up instead of uprooted elements from these states, particularly from New England: the younger sons of small landowners, dissatisfied with their lot in life, sometimes men whose reputations had been ruined and who wanted to make a new start somewhere else . . . This part of the population, for that matter, remained unstable. The original settlers who had cleared a patch of forest would sell it and begin the same work again farther on, as though sucked along by the frontier moving ever westward, and it was often only the third occupant of a piece of land who would settle there for good. What resulted from this was a society that was atomized and mobile: "Those who live here arrived only yesterday. They came here without knowing one another, with different mores, with different ideas. Most of them are only passing through. There is no common bond uniting them."[19]

In such a society, the institutions and customs of New England, already a distorted reflection of those of the mother country (which itself had altered the existing ancient Saxon heritage by the invasion of the British Isles) underwent further distortion here in the direction of a more absolute political democracy. There was no counterbalance to the principle of the sovereignty of the people. Electoral practices had more to do with whim than reflection; in order to be elected, it was necessary to spend some time drinking in taverns with ordinary citizens, to come out of the ranks of the people like the young lawyer who had once sold cakes in the streets of Cincinnati. And yet, this

[19]O.C. V, 1: 257.

174

society was active and prosperous. Was this because of democracy or in spite of it? Tocqueville did not answer the question directly, contenting himself with observing that the government, involving itself in very few things, did not obstruct the enterprising spirit of individual citizens, who were spurred on by the desire to get rich. And later he noted that people in this roughhewn democracy of the American West remained aware of political problems and took an interest in public life, and that a free press could lead public opinion, still subject to the impulsive passions of a half-ignorant society, to more reflective ways of thought.

On the other side of the Ohio River was Kentucky, and farther south, Tennessee, where Tocqueville was to work more through direct observation. Comparing the first of these states with Ohio, he wrote: "On both sides, the soil is equally fertile, the situation just as favorable." However, Kentucky was populated by a "people without energy, without ardor, without a spirit of enterprise."[20] Inhabited for a century now, Kentucky had made almost no progress. The problem was that it was a slave-owning state and that slavery not only degraded the slave but also discouraged all activity in his master. In Sandy Bridge and in Memphis, Tocqueville and Beaumont had had time to explore the psychological makeup of these poor whites, pioneers who had come mostly from Virginia. They lived miserably in inadequately sealed log cabins, oversaw the mediocre cultivation of their patches of earth by a few black slaves, and spent their leisure smoking and hunting; they were impoverished, but had the mind-set of a wellborn Frenchman living in reduced circumstances. Yet Tocqueville also discovered in them, side by side with their indolence and improvidence, virtues of cordiality and hospitality that drew his sympathy. Theirs, however, was a microcosm doomed by the very dynamism of the world of the Yankees. All of this reinforced the two Frenchmen's opinion that slavery was the greatest impediment to a happy future for America.

Although, as far as we can tell, they did not study relations between master and slave on a big plantation, in New Orleans they once again encountered the race problem. Tocqueville was especially intrigued by the position of the mulattoes. In the rough draft of a text that we have mentioned, he sketched out the main points of a dialogue concerning their destiny:

[20]Ibid., 283.

"Don't you intend to make these white black men your equal one day?"

"Never."

"Then I truly fear they will one day make themselves your masters."[21]

Louisiana elected to its legislature representatives of unquestionable mediocrity, and according to what the French consul in New Orleans said, confusion and disorder reigned in this assembly. At any moment any piece of legislation might, for the *n*th time, be thrown open for discussion from the floor. In reality, the legislature took very little action, and the state of Louisiana thrived. Tocqueville expressed some doubt about this pessimistic talk, pointing out that the two senators from Louisiana, Edward Livingston and Joseph Stoddard Johnson, were remarkable men.

As soon as he left New Orleans, Tocqueville intended to spend his days in the stagecoach reckoning up what he was sure of and what he was doubtful about, while sifting out what he had learned of the mores peculiar to the South, the "spirit of chivalry," the coarse habits, the absence of popular education. Once he arrived in Washington, he endeavored to fill in the gaps in his knowledge and gain a better understanding of how the central government worked. It was perhaps because he was too absorbed by this problem that he did not, so far as we know, see the great conflict looming up between Jackson and his opponents over the renewal of the charter of the Bank of the United States.

Tocqueville was fully aware that after such a brief trip he would not be able to judge the American regime as a whole. He was simply bringing back valuable material that he would have to try to work up.

As early as October 24, 1831, he had written to his mother: "If I ever write a book about America, I will write it in France using the documents that I am bringing back. When I leave America I will be in a position to understand the documents I haven't yet been able to study. That will be the most manifest outcome of the trip."[22] By January 24, 1832, although he had not yet made his choice of subject, he had rejected the notion of a general description of America, a project that would be impracticable for someone who had spent less than a year there. "One might, on the other hand, in choosing one's materials

---

[21]Based on the copy of Lambert White's translation in the Beinecke Library.

[22]Unpublished letter to his mother.

present only topics that have a more or less direct bearing on our own social and political condition. In this way, the interest of the work could be both immediate and enduring. That is my outline. But will I ever have the time and will I ever find in myself the capacity to fill it in?"[23]

Tocqueville was turning his attention, then, to the future of Europe, which was being drawn toward democracy through an evolution of which one could predict neither the limits nor the rhythm. Would the future democracies of Europe be able to unite freedom and popular sovereignty? Despite all its defects, America was successful in this, but she had no dangerous neighbors and was in the process of conquering a continent full of unexplored riches, both of which circumstances were very different from those of the nations of the Old World.

Tocqueville was inclined to think, however, that if the American system could not be exported just as it was, a similar system, when associated with a certain level of civilization, could be established elsewhere. After his conversations with Joel Poinsett, he wrote:

> There is one major reason that dominates all the rest and, when one gives them all careful consideration, tips the balance: the American people, taking them all in all, are not only the most enlightened in the world, but (something I place well above that advantage) they are the people *whose practical political education is the most advanced.*
>
> It is this truth, of which I am firmly convinced, that gives me the only hope I have for the future happiness of Europe.[24]

Only one conclusion could follow from this: that public opinion had to be educated, a civic spirit had to be created through the laws. As soon as he returned to France, this loomed, for Tocqueville, as the program for his political life, beyond the writing of the work that was to reveal the lessons France could learn from the American model.

Tocqueville and Beaumont had intended to complete their trip by a stay of three weeks in England. The spread of cholera in that country made them decide not to take the Liverpool steamship and they put off this plan to the next year.

They returned to New York on February 6, 1832, prepared to sail on the tenth, but their ship's departure was delayed until the twentieth, when they at last embarked, saying a final goodbye to the New World. For them its role had been to throw light on the future of their own

---

[23]Letter to his father dated January 24, 1832.
[24]*O.C.* V, 1: 257.

country, which had been a constant and deeply felt preoccupation for
them during their entire trip.

Because pages have been lost from the Le Havre ship's registry, we do not know the date of their arrival there. We have no notes, no mention of this return voyage, and we can only assume it was a happy one.

THE RETURN TO FRANCE
AND THE *SYSTÈME*
PÉNITENTIAIRE

THE FIRST SIGN we have of Alexis de Tocqueville's return to France is a letter he wrote Gustave de Beaumont on April 4, 1832. Alexis was at that time in Paris, Gustave in the Sarthe, where he had probably hurried to see his family, keeping the promise he had made while still in America. This letter indicates that they had been out of touch for at least a week, and yet it was written in answer to a letter from his friend asking him to study several points relating to the penitentiary system; Gustave de Beaumont was therefore hard at work somewhere around March 25, and had most likely arrived in France a few days before.

Of course, the first job they had to do was to write a general account of the American penitentiary system. Beaumont, almost always in good form, wrote easily, eloquently, fluently, and was sometimes a little long-winded. Tocqueville, on the other hand, could only put down on paper those ideas that he had fully matured by reflection. In America, he had been a meticulous investigator, taking it upon himself to question the prisoners in the Cherry Hill prison in Philadelphia—a very important stage in the investigation—concerning their reactions to solitary confinement. By turns, he and Beaumont had written eleven interim reports to keep the government informed concerning the progress of their work. But before drawing general conclusions, Tocqueville, much more than his friend, needed a period of solitary reflection to separate out the most striking ideas from their experiences and the documentation they had collected. This had always been his way, and his inactivity during the first few days after he returned should not be surprising: "[In the morning] I get up and immediately sink down into the vast armchair my father was imprudent enough to give me; next to me I put a chair and on the chair an escritoire. On my knees I have a notebook, a thick pad of paper, and close by a pile of books. Thus prepared, I lie back in my armchair and with my eyes half closed, I wait for the spirit of the penitentiary system to appear to me."[1]

It was true that when he returned to Paris there was nothing about the times to induce a feeling of calm in Tocqueville. That spring of 1832 and the summer that followed were among the more uneasy times of the July monarchy. To the widespread misery brought about by a prolonged economic crisis, there was added the great fear of cholera. The various parties of the opposition, their animosities newly exacerbated by the current anxieties, sought to profit from the conjunction of plague and poverty to bring on a new revolution.

For the first time, cholera morbus had left the banks of the Ganges, where it was endemic, to spread throughout the Western world. For two years, one had been able to follow its inexorable progress. In 1830, it had invaded Russia, and the next year, no doubt carried by the troops sent to suppress the Polish revolt, one found it in Poland, then in various parts of Germany. In October 1831, it crossed to Sunderland in the northeast of England, and from there it slowly traveled to London and the south coast.[2] From America, the two friends had anxiously followed the progress of the scourge. In October 1831, in Philadelphia, they had heard that oil of cajeput—whose only property, in fact, was to bring on a sweat—was a sovereign remedy. They had rushed to send two bottles of this oil by way of the faithful Chabrol to their respective families. The rumor that the cholera epidemic had reached southern England had made them decide not to stop there on their way back to France. On March 26, it made its appearance in Paris: there is the well-known passage of Heinrich Heine's that describes the mid-Lent ball where, suddenly, a sprightly harlequin, feeling ill, tears his mask off and reveals a ghastly pale face to the horrified crowd before dropping dead.[3] In April, the cholera spread with such fury that it caused the death of 12,733 people in the capital—especially in the working-class quarters of the city's center, where people were underfed and living conditions were filthy and squalid, but also, for reasons that

[1]*O.C.* VIII, 1: 112.
[2]See Lucas-Dubreton, *La Grande Peur de 1832; le choléra à Paris* (Paris, 1932), and the collaborative work devoted to the *Choléra de 1832* (La Roche-sur-Yon, 1958).
[3]Heinrich Heine, *Lutèce* (1854).

180

ℋ ℋ

are hard to discern, in the Saint-Thomas-d'Aquin quarter off the boulevard Saint-Germain, where the Tocquevilles lived. There was panic, and there were bloody riots, like the revolt on April 3 of more than ten thousand ragmen who were trying to live off the city's rubbish and who were enraged when the Seine prefecture decided, for reasons of hygiene, to have the rubbish carted away from the city. Troops had to be called in to suppress this riot. On April 5, 6, and 7 the rich inhabitants of the faubourg Saint-Germain fled the city. On the sixth, Alexis was already with his brother Edouard at Saint-Germain-en-Laye, at an estate owned by Edouard's in-laws, the Olliviers. His parents would take refuge there soon after and Beaumont, who arrived in Paris on the tenth, was invited to join them there.[4]

But the cholera epidemic was not the only source of trouble. The parties hostile to the new dynasty tried to take advantage of the popular anxiety, which was expressed from the outset by abrupt and savage outbursts of anger. The actions taken by the secret republican societies in response to this are well known. On June 5, shortly after the death from cholera of the prime minister, Casimir Périer, they tried to drag Paris into a new revolution on the occasion of the funeral of General Lamarque, a popular hero of the Napoleonic wars who had also died of the plague, and created the uprising whose remnants were crushed two days later in the cloister of Saint-Merry. But the legitimists were becoming agitated along with the republicans, sometimes allying themselves with them.

Though the aging Charles X seemed to have given up any thought of new adventures, his daughter-in-law the Duchesse de Berry had clearly been determined, ever since the beginning of 1831, to land in France and give the signal for an insurrection. In April of that year she decided upon Marseilles, and the center of the conspiracy moved to Nice and Genoa. Even though he was a secret accomplice, the King of Piedmont must have begged Marie-Caroline to leave his territory. She then settled nearby in Massa, in the territory of the Duke of Modena. The moment of action was postponed several times, but accompanying her, besides her main adviser, Bourmont, she had the former ambassador Saint-Priest and the Comte de Kergorlay, Louis's father.[5] The landing at Marseilles was delayed while they awaited the results of the plot of the rue des Prouvaires in Paris.

This was a romantic adventure which involved kidnapping the king

---

[4]*O.C.* VIII, 1: 114–15.

[5]Louis-Paul-Florian de Kergorlay (1769–1856), peer of France in 1823, deputy from the Oise (1820–1823).

and his entourage in the midst of a carnival ball in the Tuileries (February 1–2) and had been devised jointly by legitimists, Bonapartists, republicans, and also, it appears, by the police. Its failure was followed by a vast roundup by the police in which Louis de Kergorlay was arrested on February 28. We do not know when he was released, but Alexis probably did not find him in Paris when he returned, because he had most likely already rejoined the little group at Massa which was preparing to join the Duchesse de Berry. We will hear more of him very soon.

During his trip, Tocqueville had followed the Carlist scheming with uneasiness. It is almost certain that he had wind of the first plans for an uprising before he left. In any case, on June 29, 1831, he wrote to Louis de Kergorlay: "The latest news has worried me very much. I thought I saw in it very serious indications of agitation in the West. You know that I have never believed an uprising would succeed. I would therefore be worried to death if I learned that it had taken place."[6] And later he expressed his delight that his brother Hippolyte had not made the long journey that Tocqueville had feared he would make. He repeated that he did not approve of this kind of journey.[7] But Louis's absence and the prospect of an intrigue which, in his eyes, could only end badly, weighed on Tocqueville's mind during the first few weeks he was back, no doubt making these bonds of affection painful, since they were not strengthened by common aspirations.

The wisest thing to do, in the meantime, was to overcome his own uneasiness or laziness and collaborate on the account of the penitentiary system. In the minds of men of that time, this was not a small problem, nor was it a new one.

In 1819, the Duc Decazes had founded a Royal Society of Prisons which brought together philanthropists (as those with active humanitarian sympathies were then called) of various political opinions. A series of remarkable reports were issued that denounced the existing system in which criminals, minor offenders, those waiting for trial, and the insane were all thrown together in extremely poor hygienic conditions. These philanthropists concentrated above all on the moral rehabilitation of prisoners through isolation and work, and on establishing a system of earnings payable to the convict upon his discharge. They were already aware of America's example, and one of the most eminent

---

[6]*O.C.* XIII, 1: 235–36.
[7]"I fear . . . that you will make a long trip whose usefulness does not seem clear to me." Letter to Hippolyte dated December 4, 1831.

members, La Rochefoucauld-Liancourt, had praised the Walnut Street prison in Philadelphia, which in the opinion of Tocqueville and Beaumont did not deserve this praise in the least. The Society's program had not affected actual prison discipline, though workshops had been started and the practice of paying convicts established. At the end of the Restoration, the Society itself became dormant. Often investigators who probed the "open sore" of the existing prisons, as had Tocqueville and Beaumont, found their right to judge the system being challenged by the Ministry of the Interior. It seems clear that in this area as in others the influence of Jacques-Joseph Corbière, an ardent royalist and the minister of the interior in the Villèle ministry under Charles X, was in opposition to all humanitarian initiatives. In 1830, the prisons came within the province of inspectors like Charles Lucas, who claimed they could reform the convict by means of group work and a system of categories rewarding the most docile prisoners—who were often, in actuality, the most skillfully hypocritical ones.[8]

Tocqueville and Beaumont were severe critics of that "penitentiary riffraff" whose "industry" was prison philanthropy, who were "obsessed with the penitentiary system, which seems to them the cure for all of society's ills," who believed (or pretended to believe) that an individual, "however experienced he may be in crime, is always capable of being restored to virtue." Tocqueville's bête noire in the penitentiary world was Charles Lucas, who felt an equal antipathy toward him and caused him to fail the first time he stood as a candidate for the Academy of Moral and Political Sciences. But Tocqueville and Beaumont also claimed to be able to reform the criminal and their remedies were the same as those of the philanthropists: isolation and work.

For them, however, reform of the prisoners was not the main goal of prison. Its social function was to punish, and for that the offender must be made to suffer more than those on the other side of the prison walls who were impoverished but law-abiding. Though Beaumont and Tocqueville acknowledged that poverty and ignorance might be at the root of crime, their ideas had something in common with those of Balzac, who believed that one entered into delinquency just as one entered the priesthood, to remain marked by it *in aeternum.* This was a Jansenist way of thinking that echoed a certain deep-seated pessimism in Tocqueville. From this point of view, solitary confinement had a preventive function; insofar as possible, it was to be imposed both by day and by night, rather than by night alone, especially in a country like France where the mores made use of the whip repugnant. In exceptional cases, this silence could perhaps lead the convict to examine his conscience and raise himself with the support of an intelligent chaplain who would bring him the assistance of religious faith. But the most important function of solitary confinement was to check the propagation of evil, whose hold on corrupt natures was so strong—to destroy the "schools of crime" that most prisons were.

In May and June of 1832, when Beaumont sent Tocqueville to investigate the Toulon convict prison and the new prisons in Geneva and Lausanne, the latter wrote some reports that were especially characteristic of his attitude.[9] In the Swiss prisons, he deplored the absence of strictness, which allowed the prisoners to read in a common room on Sundays and to talk freely among themselves, though he did praise the absence of common eating rooms. The Toulon convict prison shocked him, of course, by its corruption, but he did not protest against the vestiges of the system of chains and shackles, while what he faulted most of all was the lack of strict observance of the rules, the mingling of the convicts with workers from the arsenal, their hopes of escaping, and the fact that it was possible for them to obtain the cruder pleasures. Admittedly, the Toulon convict prison was not as terrible as that of Rochefort, as it is described by Appert,[10] but Tocqueville in his study was hardly moved to pity by the prisoners' lot.

Strict discipline and an austere life, with no unnecessary cruelty— these were for Tocqueville the essential attributes of a penal institution.

Du système pénitentiaire aux Etats-Unis et de son application en France appeared in early January 1833.[11] As we have seen, Beaumont had begun writing it at the end of March. In mid-April he was in Paris and Tocqueville was able to work with him. But on May 17, Tocqueville left for Toulon and was not back in Paris until sometime around June 10. It was therefore Beaumont who went on writing, and Tocqueville, who prepared the notes, apparently played only a secondary role in the main part of the work. No doubt he read over the text Beau-

[9]These notes are published in vol. IV of the *O.C.*

[10]See B. Appert, "Séjour au bagne de Toulon du 8 au 13 décembre 1827," *Journal des prisons* (1828), 4–101, and "Voyage de 1828; Bagne de Rochefort, bagne de Lorient, bagne de Brest," *Journal des prisons* (1828), 398–487. On the convict prisons, see A. Zysberg, "Politiques du bagne, 1820–1850," in Perrot, *L'Impossible Prison*, 165–205.

[11]A second edition of the work appeared in 1836 and a third in 1844. It is included, edited and annotated by Michelle Perrot, in *O.C.* IV.

184

꿀 꿀

mont had written and made comments, and they corrected the first draft together. We could be more precise about their collaboration if we possessed the draft of the manuscript they sent to the printer. Unfortunately, it was not preserved among either Tocqueville's papers or Beaumont's. True, we have one precise piece of evidence from Tocqueville in a letter he wrote to François-Auguste Mignet, the permanent secretary of the Academy of Moral Sciences, on June 26, 1841:

> There is one detail you may not know. The one who actually wrote the first work M. de Beaumont and I published together, on American prisons, was M. de Beaumont. All I contributed were my observations and a few notes. I never concealed from my friends the fact that even though both our names were attached to the book—which, it is now easier for me to say, has had considerable success—M. de Beaumont was really the sole author.[12]

Two exceptions can be taken to Tocqueville's statement. One is that he did not hesitate to accept half the amount of the Montyon Prize that was awarded to the work—though this could be considered a reimbursement for the expenses of their expedition to America, which was not funded by any subvention, and the added expense, for Tocqueville, of the trip to Toulon and Switzerland which he took by himself.

Secondly, in the same letter to Mignet, Tocqueville asks his support for Beaumont, who was a candidate for the Academy of Moral Sciences, and for that reason he may have been inclined to exaggerate Beaumont's qualifications. If we attempt to resolve these doubts by examining the style of the work, although such an examination must be uncertain and subjective, it seems to us that the work does show the rather relaxed, wordy style of Beaumont, with its terms pushed somewhat to extremes. We would nevertheless make an exception in the case of the chapter on the reform of criminals in the first part of the book and the brief description of the French system in the second part, where the writing is denser, suggesting some recasting by Tocqueville.

However this may be, the work as a whole is primarily a description of the American penitentiary system. It does not offer as models American prisons in general, some of which were cesspools, worse than French prisons, but it does endeavor to give an accurate account of the two competing reform systems: the Auburn system, with isolation by

[12]Unpublished letter, Beinecke Library.

night and group work during the day, carried out in silence thanks to 185
the strict discipline, and the Pennsylvania system, with solitary confinement by day and night. Clearly, the two young authors preferred
the second system. But they were well aware of the accusations made
against solitary confinement, accusations against which they attempted
to defend the Pennsylvania system. If it did not include a work
program, visits to the prisoner, and an exercise yard where he could
get some fresh air, it ran the risk of impairing the prisoner's physical
and mental health. They also knew that the construction of a prison
of the Pennsylvania type was more expensive. Thus their book main-
tains the appearance of objectivity concerning the two systems, aside
from which there were then no other attempts at prison reform. In this,
they went along with the advice of their cousin Le Peletier d'Aunay,
an expert on the subject, not to bank everything on a system whose
shortcomings might be revealed by experience after several years had
gone by. The work concluded with a hope that was, in sum, modest:
that an attempt would be made to create a model prison in which the
penitentiary system could be tested, a hope that the philanthropists of
the Royal Society of Prisons had never been able to see realized.
Tocqueville and Beaumont themselves, for that matter, provided plans
that were too fragmentary to show the government how to organize
the prison space, and in order to obtain more precise information on
this point the ministry would later send another commission to America, consisting of the magistrate Demetz and the architect Blouet.

Honored with the Montyon Prize in 1833, reissued in 1836 and
again in 1844, the *Système pénitentiaire* clearly was a critical success.
Because of it, the two authors acquired a reputation as experts. This
was no small matter in a world where members of the upper classes
did not as yet ordinarily adopt a professional life. Specialization in
scholarship, agronomy, political economy merited the consideration of
society and attention from the men in power. The two young men
certainly nourished vaster ambitions, but now they had in some sense
crossed a threshold, and they would subsequently endeavor not to let
it be forgotten. It was also, in a way, compensation for leaving the
magistracy.

On May 16, 1832, indeed, Gustave de Beaumont was abruptly
dismissed from his duties as deputy public prosecutor in the superior
court of the department of the Seine. His leave of eighteen months had
not expired, but on several occasions there had been some question of

186

𝕶 𝕸

cutting it short. This time, he was asked to represent the public prosecutor in one of the actions for libel arising from an incident that had aroused political passions, the death of the Duc de Bourbon.

On August 27, 1830, Louis de Bourbon, the last Prince de Condé, had been found hanging from an espagnolette, one of the long, vertical iron bars that served to close the tall casement windows in his bedroom in the Château de Saint-Leu.

In a will dated August 20, 1829, the deceased had named as sole legatee the young Duc d'Aumale, son of Louis-Philippe, who thereby became the owner of Chantilly, the seat of the Princes de Condé, while other possessions, including Saint-Leu, were left to the Baronne de Feuchères, the old man's beloved mistress, an Englishwoman with a more than dubious past. The Rohans, the Duc de Bourbon's closest relatives, were thus disinherited altogether. It was well known that Louis-Philippe had not hesitated to treat the adventuress with courtesy at the end of the Restoration and had tried to introduce her to the court so that she would influence the duc in Aumale's favor. Thus the new King of France had connived with a demimondaine in order to make one of his sons wealthy. The legitimists did not hesitate to accuse la Feuchères of having murdered her lover. The affair was never entirely cleared up, even though suicide remained the most probable hypothesis—unless one adopts Emile Lesueur's solution, that an accident happened during an erotic game the old man was playing with his mistress.[13]

The attacks of the legitimist papers brought about a first trial before the court of Pontoise which decided in favor of suicide, but the Rohans obtained an additional judicial inquiry. The case was called before the royal court of Paris on November 1, 1830. The judge entrusted with the inquiry proved hostile to the hypothesis of suicide and was replaced. It was at this point, apparently, that Beaumont became involved and refused to remove from the dossier assembled in the public prosecutor's office two documents relating to Madame de Feuchères's past.

In June 1831, the office of the director of public prosecutions of the court of appeals decided in favor of suicide, but the affair was still not closed. It had engendered a whole series of trials, including an action asserting that the inheritance was obtained by improper means, in which the Rohans' case was rejected in February 1832; a libel action brought before the court of the Seine chamber by the old chaplain of

[13]See Emile Lesueur, *Louis-Henri-Joseph de Bourbon, le dernier Condé* (Paris, 1937).

the deceased against Madame de Feuchères and tried on May 4; and
lastly, the action brought by Madame de Feuchères and an ecclesiastic
close to the Duc de Bourbon against the Rohans, which began June
8, 1832, and resulted in the sentencing of Louis de Rohan to three
months in prison and a fine of one thousand francs.

This was undoubtedly the trial at which Beaumont had refused to
sit as public prosecutor. Had he been selected because of his merits?
Possibly, since the best legitimist lawyers pleaded in those trials in
which the king was morally compromised, and Beaumont's eloquence
had been noticed in several difficult trials before he left for America.
But it could also have been due to some perfidy on the part of the
attorney general or the government. Beaumont came from the very
legitimist circles who were hounding Madame de Feuchères; to defend
her would be to come into conflict with them and show one's servility
toward the new order of things (later, Louis de Kergorlay's father
would be prosecuted for having tried to rekindle this affair). It was
thus not only the complexity of the case that made Beaumont hesitate
to take it. Yet he thought the fact that he was writing the *Système
pénitentiaire* was a good excuse, since it was connected to his duties,
and the brutality of the retribution took him by surprise.

On May 21, as soon as he found out about it, Tocqueville made
common cause with his friend and sent in his resignation as magistrate
to the attorney general:

Being at the present time in Toulon, where I am devoting myself to an
examination of the convict prison and the other prisons in this city, I have
only this very day, through the May 16 *Le Moniteur,* learned of the harsh
and, if I may say so, supremely unjust measure which M. the Minister of
Justice has imposed on M. G. de Beaumont.

Having long been a close friend of the man who has just been afflicted
with a dismissal, sharing his opinions and approving of his conduct, I feel
I must voluntarily join him in his fate and, with him, abandon a career in
which service and conscience cannot protect one from an unmerited disgrace.[14]

In truth, though Beaumont might have hoped for a brilliant career
in the judiciary, Tocqueville had been disillusioned by his experience.
After being appointed a *juge auditeur* in 1827, he had become a *juge
suppléant* in 1830, but this was simply a change of label. He still

---

[14]This letter was published by Beaumont at the front of his edition of the correspondence, *O.C.* (Bmt)
V, 136.

performed the same unpaid duties without having advanced a single rank in the hierarchy of the judiciary. On January 24, 1831, he had written to Chabrol from America: "I don't know if I should withdraw completely, as I am often tempted to do, or try to advance. What I am at least clear about is that I will definitely not put on the robe of the *juge suppléant* again."[15] For Tocqueville, Beaumont's dismissal was the occasion to do something he had been on the edge of doing in any event.

At this point, they both had themselves registered at the bar. Beaumont was never to plead a case, it appears, and Tocqueville did so only once, on March 9, 1833, in the Montbrison court of assizes, before which appeared Louis de Kergorlay.

For Louis de Kergorlay had suddenly turned up as a minor character in the Duchesse de Berry's incredible escapade. On April 24, 1832, a little Sardinian steamship, the *Carlo Alberto,* chartered by the Comte de Saint-Priest, had left Leghorn and shortly afterwards, out at sea, taken aboard the duchesse and her chambermaid, Mademoiselle Lebeschu. Fourteen loyal supporters, including the Comte de Kergorlay and his son Louis, were already on board the ship under false identities. After putting in at Nice on April 27, the steamship was approached by another boat during the night of April 28–29 a short way beyond Marseilles, and several of the passengers—including the Duchesse de Berry and the Comte de Kergorlay—were taken off and made their way into an isolated inlet. At that point the *Carlo Alberto* proceeded to Rosas, on the Spanish coast, then turned back east and broke down on May 3 at La Ciotat, its boiler having been damaged by the rough weather.

In the meantime, on the morning of April 30, the legitimists had attempted an uprising at Marseilles; the white flag had been raised on the bell tower of Saint-Laurent. Their failure was a pitiful one, the leaders of the movement being arrested by the picket of troops guarding the Palace of Justice. The duchesse, meanwhile, went on to the West to organize the uprising that had failed to take shape in Provence. As we know, this last effort of the Vendée was crushed by the military, the entire West was put under a state of siege, and the duchesse was finally arrested in Nantes on November 6. Back in Marseilles, the comings and goings of the *Carlo Alberto* during the attempted uprising in April aroused the suspicions of the authorities. The boat was seized,

[15]Unpublished letter, Beinecke Library.

towed to Toulon, then to Ajaccio, and finally to Marseilles, where it arrived May 8. The Marseilles police, who had already arrested the Comte de Kergorlay and seized notes in code, deduced from them that the Duchesse de Berry could well be on board the *Carlo Alberto* with her son, the Comte de Chambord. As late as May 15, they thought they had seized the duchesse in the person of Mademoiselle Lebeschu, who allowed the misunderstanding to stand so that her mistress could gain time. They even thought they had seized the prince in the person of a young black man who was serving as cabin boy without his name being down on the list of the crew. A lawyer in the Montbrison trial would recall the blunder of the Marseilles police in these words: "They immediately grabbed the unfortunate Negro: they made fervent use of water mixed with soap and vinegar; vigorously they rubbed his shining skin, endeavored to uncoil his rough and woolly hair. But nature, stronger than the police, resisted this new variety of judicial investigation."[16]

The passengers of the *Carlo Alberto,* thrown in with the supposed perpetrators of the Marseilles uprising, had been imprisoned in Marseilles, then in Aix, then transferred to Montbrison, at that time the chief town of the department of the Loire, to be brought before the court of assizes of that city, for fear of public demonstrations in Carlist Provence. Side by side with the aristocratic passengers of the *Carlo Alberto* (Saint-Priest, the son of Bourmont, Sala, Kergorlay), and the local nobility arrested in Marseilles (Colonel de Lachau, MM. de Bermond and de Candole), were the humble confectioner Esig, a certain Garrail, and more modest bit players, one of whom was known only by his nickname of "Belle Viande" ("Body Beautiful"). The trial lasted from February 25 to March 15, 1833. The picturesque parade of Marseilles witnesses can be divined through the gray disguise of the pamphlets that reprinted the proceedings. A number of witnesses for the prosecution turned into witnesses for the defense, contradicting their own statements with admirable unselfconsciousness and proving the hold the legitimists had on the humbler people and the clergy of Marseilles. If the Duchesse de Berry's adventure was to be engulfed in ridicule once its heroine's out-of-wedlock pregnancy was discovered, if the repression in the West was bloody and merciless, the Marseilles episode smacked of opera buffa and when all was said and done left no victims. The eminent men who formed the Montbrison

---

[16]The speeches for the defense were published under the title *Défense devant la Cour d'assises de Montbrison, dans le procès du "Carlo Alberto" pour MM. les comte et vicomte de Kergorlay par Me Genton, avocat, Me Guillaumin, avocat, Me Tardif, avocat (9–14 mars)* (Lyons, 1833).

190

jury (landowners, notaries, doctors, a rural mayor) came to this conclusion, after having heard the highly specious addresses by the defense
lawyers (most of the accused refused to answer questions), and declared
that all the accused were innocent.[17]

We do not know whether Alexis de Tocqueville stayed till the end
of the trial or whether he took part in the festivities at Lyons that
celebrated the release of the accused. But when Louis de Kergorlay was
first imprisoned, Alexis was concerned about his fate and visited him,
in mid-May 1832, on his way to study the Toulon convict prison, then
attempted to visit him again on his way home.[18] When Louis published, in his own defense, a booklet entitled *Question du droit des gens;
Saisie du bâtiment sarde le "Charles Albert" par ordre du gouvernement
français,* in which he attempted to demonstrate that the seizure was
illegal and that the passengers should be released, just as the émigrés
tossed up on the Calais beach by storms had been released under the
Directoire, Tocqueville saw to the distribution of the 850 copies to
prominent people and to Carlist newspapers scattered throughout
France. And on March 9, 1833, as one of Louis de Kergorlay's lawyers,
he spoke for the defense before the Montbrison court of assizes.[19]

He was speaking only as the secondary lawyer. The principal lawyer, Genton, from the Lyons bar, had tried to clear Louis of the charge
that he had plotted against the State; Tocqueville therefore confined
himself to drawing a picture of this accused man who was "threatened
with a penalty involving the loss of his civil rights." Louis, told the
evening before that Alexis would be speaking, had expressed the hope
that he would also speak of his father, and Tocqueville, whether this
was already his intention or whether he revised his text, did not fail
to do so. Addressing the jury, he said: "If only I were permitted to
take you with me into the home of his venerable father, into that
sanctuary of honor and ancient virtue!" The Comte de Kergorlay was
the "fountainhead of male virtues," of the heroism that had won for
his son Louis during the Algerian campaign the esteem of the wisest
and best of his leaders. What Tocqueville idealized in Louis de Kergorlay was the aristocratic tradition whose morality consisted of serving
the State, defending the liberty of all, hating tyranny. He showed his
contempt for the king's attorney, who had spoken of the "arrogance

---

[17]On the entire *Carlo Alberto* affair, see Guillaume de Bertier de Sauvigny, "La Conspiration des
légitimistes de la duchesse de Berry contre Louis-Philippe," Société d'Histoire moderne et contemporaine,
Etudes, vol. 3, (Paris, 1950) and the collection of speeches cited above.

[18]See letter to Madame de Kergorlay, *O.C.* XIII, 1: 251–54.

[19]This speech appears in *O.C.* XIII, 1: 321–27.

of the nobility" and created an incident in the courtroom. This was one of the most emotional speeches he had ever made. Though he reproved the Carlist escapade, he felt deeply attached to the moral tradition of his own kind, and now that they were once again running the risk of persecution, loudly affirmed his solidarity with the accused.

The entire Tocqueville family, for that matter, was in a state of agitation over the affair. Comte Hervé addressed a petition to the two Chambers concerning the Duchesse de Berry.[20] At the same time, Hippolyte published the *Lettres aux Normands,* which we have already touched on. Tocqueville and Beaumont joined the protest movement of former magistrates against the duchesse's captivity. Tocqueville's protest, which appeared on February 2, 1833, was against the fact that the government treated the duchesse as a prisoner of war, whereas the insurgents of the West were tried in the courts of assizes. Tocqueville concluded: "[The government] is openly violating all the political principles that have governed us now for sixteen years. The captivity of Madame the Duchesse de Berry is an unconstitutional measure if ever there was one; it is an odious act of violence, a flagrant and palpable illegality; it threatens not only Madame the Duchesse de Berry, but also every single Frenchman and the liberty of all."[21] Tocqueville was undoubtedly right, but the government, in prolonging the captivity of the duchesse, knew what it was waiting for—at the end of this arbitrary confinement would come the birth of her illegitimate child—and knew that it would have the last laugh.

In protesting the captivity of the Duchesse de Berry and in addressing the court in Kergorlay's defense, Tocqueville, though he did not approve of the attempts to overthrow the regime, nevertheless manifested a certain solidarity in spirit with the Carlist loyalties of his family and his kind. At that point he clearly must have suspected that these acts might be held against him later in the political career he was planning for himself.

But there is another indication of his feelings at that time.

On August 7, 1833, when Tocqueville was in England, Beaumont wrote him from Paris that on the following Friday they were each going to receive three thousand francs upon the announcement of the Montyon Prize, which was being given to the *Système pénitentiaire.*

---

[20]Comte de Tocqueville, *Pétition aux deux Chambres relative á madame la duchesse de Berry* (Paris, 1832). In the Chamber of Deputies, M. Sapey delivered a report on this petition on January 5, 1833.

[21]Beaumont's protest appeared in *La Quotidienne* on January 30 and Tocqueville's in the same paper on Saturday, February 2.

Beaumont added that he had discussed with their friend the statistician Guerry (who was to be honored by the Institute the following year) a plan to start a review of economics and politics. They would have to assemble ten associates or so, each of whom would put up a thousand francs for the enterprise, thus providing funds adequate to keep it alive for the first year. On August 13, Tocqueville responded, agreeing to join in, and undertook to make contacts in England.[22] In a subsequent letter to Tocqueville, dated August 24, Beaumont lists possible associates: besides Blosseville and Chabrol, there was an "English lady" who wrote novels, and there were two Italians, one of whom was Pietro Maroncelli, who had been imprisoned with Silvio Pellico, the hero of the Carbonari, and was carrying on his work. Charles de Montalembert, who had been sounded out, had declined. (He had been, with the Abbé Lammenais and Henri Lacordaire, one of the editors of *L'Avenir,* the Catholic journal founded in the autumn of 1830 that advocated as matters of principle the absolute separation of Church and State, total freedom of education, total freedom of association, and universal suffrage. Shaken by the Pope's condemnation of the journal—it had ceased publication by the autumn of 1831—Montalembert was to remain in Germany and Italy until 1835.)

Tocqueville and Beaumont did not meet again before November (Beaumont was traveling in the South of France at the time of Tocqueville's return to Paris). In October, Tocqueville shut himself up in the rue de Verneuil to write the first part of the *Democracy;* during his trip, Beaumont was sketching out his novel, *Marie.* Even though many of their letters have been lost, we can assume the plan for the review conceived in August 1833 did not live beyond the end of the month. But a rough draft in Tocqueville's handwriting can only be a manifesto for the launching of this review and its most likely date is undoubtedly a short time after his return to England.[23]

This text states that the traditional parties have leaders but very few followers. Outside of them, there exists "an immense crowd . . . uneasy, disillusioned . . . of heterogeneous elements, strangers to one another," whether they have been disappointed by the July revolution, or whether, while regarding the revolution as a great misfortune, they accept as a given fact the government that emerged from it.

Tocqueville thought one would be able to rally these different

[22]*O.C.* VIII, 1: 124–26.
[23]Unpublished rough draft, Tocqueville Archives.

elements by reconciling the spirit of liberty with the spirit of religion, by defending both social progress and Catholicism. This was to be the stand taken by the future review.

One paragraph clarifies his position in relation to the new monarchy and also seems more favorable to the legitimists than the judgments he made at the time of the July revolution, which had been particularly hard on the senior branch of the Bourbons:

If the free expression of the will of the nation returns the senior branch of the Bourbons to the throne, if a Restoration could take place that ensured the nation the rights due to it, the editors of the review would witness this event with pleasure. They would consider it a favorable omen for future social progress, but they do not want a Restoration except under these conditions, and if it were to come about in any other way and lead to contrary results, they would regard it as their duty to oppose it.

The most moderate Carlist party, that of *La Gazette de France,* hardly asked for more than this. The future contributors who had been approached—Guerry, Blosseville, Chabrol, even Montalembert—had legitimist ties, and Beaumont had been careful not to appeal to Lacordaire, who, in his opinion, adhered to the radical program of reform advocated by the now defunct *L'Avenir.* Though the business of the review came to nothing, this draft of a prospectus revealed a secret desire, one whose realization Tocqueville must surely have known was quite unlikely and one that he no doubt let himself entertain only now and then. But we will encounter it again later on in another manifestation.

13

THE FIRST *DEMOCRACY*

AS WE HAVE SEEN, at the time of the announcement that the *Système pénitentiaire* had received the Montyon Prize, in August 1833, only Beaumont was able to be present at the meeting of the Institut de France.[1] On July 15, Tocqueville had left Paris for Normandy. First he visited his family estate, came into contact there with the tenants and a few of the officials of the town, took advantage of his meeting with these people again after several years' absence to consider what his chances were for a political future, and noted with pleasure that his family "was very much esteemed";[2] then he visited his brother Hippolyte at Nacqueville. On August 2, he was in Cherbourg trying to find a way to get to England. The owner of a yacht took him to the island of Guernsey, and from there he embarked for Weymouth and reached London overland by way of Portsmouth, arriving on August 10.[3]

During the writing of the *Système pénitentiaire,* the prospect of the future work on America had weighed on Tocqueville's mind. It was hard for him to escape the preoccupation of a dominating idea. The rudimentary idea had been in his mind before he left for the United States, but, though we cannot follow its maturation step by step, it had been evolving, during and after the trip, both in content and in form.

There is no doubt that he and Beaumont had planned to write a

[1] Records of the Institut de France.
[2] Tocqueville to Mary Mottley, August 2, 1833, unpublished letter.
[3] Tocqueville to Mary Mottley, unpublished letter dated August 11; letter to Beaumont of August 13, *O.C.* VIII, 1: 124; *Voyages, O.C.* V, 2: 25.

collaborative work about the New World just as they had planned to
write one about the penitentiary system. Starting in 1828, they had
undertaken parallel studies, exchanged notes on their reading, and
discussed the world of their time, then together drafted the memorandum in which they requested their mission. They had planned to
intensify this collaboration, as Beaumont attests formally in a letter to
his father, from which we have already quoted in part. It was written
on April 25, 1831, on board ship en route to the United States:

Tocqueville is a truly distinguished man; his ideas are very lofty and his
soul is very noble. The better I know him the more I like him. Here our
lives are joined together; clearly we share the same fate and always will
... We have ambitious plans ... We will see America as we survey its prisons.
We will survey its inhabitants, its cities, its institutions, its mores. We will
learn how the republican government works. This government is not at all
well known in Europe. People talk about it endlessly, making false comparisons between it and countries that don't resemble it in the least. Wouldn't
it be good to have a book that gives an accurate notion of the American
people, that paints a broad portrait of their history, boldly outlines their
character, analyzes their social state, and corrects the many mistaken opinions
on this subject?

In letters dated May 16 and May 26 Beaumont again alludes to this
collaborative work: "We are laying the foundations for a great work
which will one day make our reputations," he wrote at that time to
his brother Achille. Then on July 14 to his sister Eugénie: "I am
making many observations on [political institutions] which you will
read someday in our great work."[4]

Soon after, however, Beaumont's tone changed. On November 8,
in connection with slavery, he mentioned the "great work which will
immortalize me." As for Tocqueville, on January 23 he answered
Chabrol, who had suggested a plan for a book about America, in a
letter which has unfortunately not been preserved, although we have
a copy:

I haven't forgotten the idea of publishing something about the United States.
I even have in mind the idea of a book, much less complete, it is true, than
the one you outlined in one of your letters, but perhaps more practicable,
for I have not been able, during the past year, to collect the immense number
of documents that would be necessary to carry out your ideas. Moreover,

[4]Beaumont, *Lettres d'Amérique*, 27–28, 45, 51, 92.

everything I say to you here is still a great confusion in my mind. Nothing is settled. I don't know if I'll have the will to do it, nor if I can procure the leisure necessary, nor, most important, if I will have the means to undertake anything. I am leaving this question (and so many others) to the future.[5]

Tocqueville's "I" is all the more noteworthy because in the following paragraph he returns to "we" when speaking of the work he is doing with Beaumont on the penitentiary system.

It seems that in the course of their trip, the two friends became aware of the difficulties presented by a joint work on America such as they had at first envisaged it. They probably planned that each of them would take a more limited subject to study. Beaumont was attracted by the problem of the inequality of the races; Tocqueville, without losing his interest in observing the mores, found a more powerful center of interest in the rules by which the political society of America functioned.

We have seen the way in which they collaborated on the *Système pénitentiaire* when they returned: Beaumont wrote the main part of the work, Tocqueville most of the notes, and each criticized the other's portion. The cover of the first edition of the book announced a book by the same authors on the *Institutions et les moeurs en Amérique* [American institutions and mores].[6] If we allow that they had explained themselves unambiguously (which was not always the case in their subsequent relations), we can assume that Tocqueville intended to write about institutions, Beaumont about mores, and that these two studies would be joined in a single volume. Whereas Beaumont's greatest talent was as an observer content with a critical description of American life, Tocqueville's genius could not reflect on the institutions without connecting them to other aspects of American society, and thus not without a deeper analysis of the mores. They had perhaps not realized this at the beginning of the year 1833. But the very tendencies of their minds necessarily led Beaumont to write *Marie,* whose form as a novel was decided upon by the summer of 1833, and to write the notes, which accompanied the novel with parallel sociological observations. Tocqueville, for whom synthesis was a congenial habit of thought, was led to draw up a reasoned explanation of the political and social life of the United States, consolidating its various aspects

---

[5]Beaumont, *Lettres d'Amérique,* 176; Tocqueville to Chabrol, January 23, 1832, unpublished letter, copy in the Beinecke Library, Yale University.

[6]Seymour Drescher, *Tocqueville and Beaumont on Social Reform* (New York, 1969), 210–11.

around one fundamental principle. The need for a coherent overall
explanation was an enduring, deep-seated one in Tocqueville.

They had planned, early in 1832, to return to France by way of
England in order to explore the roots of American democracy more
thoroughly. Most important, as Beaumont wrote again in 1833, they
wanted to catch a glimpse of whatever heritage "John Bull, father of
Jonathan" had been able to transmit to his son.[7] As we have seen, they
were deterred from that plan by the cholera epidemic in England.

At first, it might seem surprising that Tocqueville, who was in such
a hurry to be finished with the penitentiary system so that he could
begin his real work, did not give up the idea of taking this trip. But
the center of interest of his intellectual life was the transition from the
aristocratic society to the democratic one. America had presented him
with a picture of a stable democratic society, while for forty years
France had been floundering in a transitional revolutionary state. England, on the other hand, in the eyes of many observers, seemed to be
offering a different example, of an abrupt change from the aristocratic
state to the democratic one. Tocqueville was reflecting this opinion
when, on July 3, 1833, asking his cousin Madame de Pisieux[8] for a
letter of introduction to Lady Stuart de Rothesay, the wife of the
former ambassador to France, he wrote the following lines: "They say
that [the English] are definitely on the edge of revolution and that one
should hurry over to see them as they are now! I am therefore making
haste to go to England as though it were the last performance of a fine
play."[9]

England's old electoral system, which had ensured that the rural
aristocracy would predominate politically, had indeed just been toppled by the first Reform Bill. Presented to the House of Lords in
October 1831, it had not been passed until December 1832, after
vigorous resistance. But this defeat of the Lords was only one aspect
of the deep-seated changes in society that were stirring up the English
people. The Tory government of the Duke of Wellington had foundered in 1830 amid agrarian troubles. It was the imminent threat of civil
war that had forced the Lords to give in. The prominent Whig lords,
Grey and Russell, who had brought about the reform, seemed on the

[7]Beaumont to Tocqueville, August 7, 1833, *O.C.* VIII, 1: 119.
[8]Tocqueville to Madame de Pisieux, July 3, 1833, unpublished letter at the Beinecke Library.
[9]On the situation of England just after the reform, see Elie Halévy, *Histoire du peuple anglais*, vol. 3:
De la crise du Reform Bill à l'avènement de Sir Robert Peel (Paris, 1923; republished, 1974).

198

卍 卍

point of being outflanked on their left by partisans of an egalitarian republic, or of a democratic society, which the radicals favored—or at least a faction among them. Of course the new House of Commons had not eliminated the Tory party, which still had 150 deputies out of 650, with the majority of the others still being large landowners. But more than the Whig majority, it was the thirty or so radicals —considered the avant-garde of the future—who were attracting everyone's attention. Tocqueville thus had reason to "make haste"—to observe both the traditional forms of the aristocracy and the revolutionary process under way.

We know about this visit to England (from August 3 to September 7) from Tocqueville's letters to the future Madame de Tocqueville and his brief travel notes,[10] which were, like the ones taken in America, divided into conversations, an alphabetized notebook, and impressions, but were more fully developed than the notes he had scribbled down in the United States.

The letters reveal Tocqueville as the romantic traveler—for example, in one he tells of his visit by night to the ruins of Kenilworth Castle, clearly showing that he was spellbound, like so many of his contemporaries, by the novels of Sir Walter Scott:

It was truly a great and solemn spectacle: in the middle of this solitary place there reigned a silence and an air of inexpressible desolation. I went into the halls of this magnificent manor; the upper stories were destroyed, I could see the sky above my head, but the walls still stood and the moon, penetrating in every part through the gothic windows, cast a sepulchral light that was in harmony with all these things. Was I not truly in the realm of the dead there? After exploring the ruins in every direction and with my footsteps awakening echoes that had probably been mute for many years, I came back to the center. Here, I sat down on a rock and fell into a sort of somnambulism during which it seemed to me that my soul was pulled into the past with an inexpressible force. But now, can you guess exactly which moment my imagination would light upon, of all the numberless centuries that had elapsed? I made vain efforts to put back within these walls, covered with ivy and falling into ruin, most of the great figures of the sixteenth century that had been here when Elizabeth came with her brilliant court. It wasn't Raleigh, nor any of the great historical figures of that era that the ruined towers of Kenilworth had the power of bringing back to life before my eyes, but rather Amy Robsart, the delicious creation of Walter Scott's genius. The

---

[10]The letters to Mary Mottley, with one exception, are still unpublished. The *Voyage en Angleterre* has been published in full in the O.C. V, 11–43. See also the study by Seymour Drescher, *Tocqueville and England* (Cambridge, 1964).

image of that charming and so very unhappy creature appeared to me
associated with each of the stones of the immense edifice, and at times I
thought I could hear echoing from the tops of the walls her last cry as she
fell over the precipice that had been prepared for her.[11]

The journal kept during this trip contains images characteristic of
traditional England: a session of the House of Lords, an election in
London, Oxford with its colleges and its fellows, a day in the court
of a justice of the peace. The alphabetical headings show once again
the author's fundamental preoccupations: decentralization, the social
role of religion, etc. As for the people he talked to whose conversations
were noted down, they were radicals, or important liberal noblemen
whose leanings were similar to those of the radicals: Bulwer-Lytton,
Hume, Roebuck, Lord Radnor, whom Tocqueville visited for four
days at his country estate, Longford Castle. The *Journal*'s conclusion
was all the more remarkable for that.[12] Although Tocqueville had very
probably gone to England with the notion, widespread at that time,
that a violent revolution was at hand, he now believed that such a
revolution would not take place.

The conviction was based on his observations of social psychology.
Unlike the France of the Ancien Régime, where the middle classes
sought to put an end to the aristocracy's privileges, in England the
middle classes sought access to the aristocracy's rights. The fact that the
English aristocracy remained an open class, with vague boundaries,
based on wealth that was accessible, encouraged this hope on the part
of the middle classes. Tocqueville did not think that the lower classes
alone, without some guidance from the classes above, could make a
revolution. The inevitable evolution toward democracy would therefore take place gradually and slowly, unless the Lords lost their compo-
sure and became frozen in hidebound hostility to any reform, which
would alienate the middle classes from them and isolate the upper
aristocracy. His last impressions of the trip ended with a lovely image.
On the Irish coast at Carrick-a-rede there was a rope bridge slung high
above the ocean. A stranger, watching, would fear that the fisherman
he saw venturing on it would be certain to fall and be killed. But the
fisherman made his way across without much risk; it would take a
sudden hurricane to make him lose his balance. The English people
were like this fisherman, Tocqueville noted: they would pass from
aristocracy to democracy without falling into the abyss of revolution.

[11]Slightly different version in the *O.C.* (Bmt) VI, 117–19.
[12]*O.C.* V, 2: 42–43.

Tocqueville was back in Paris toward mid-September 1833, and could at last, nearly eighteen months after his return from America, devote himself to writing his book. At his parents' house at 49, rue de Verneuil, he moved into an attic room where he could live apart from family life and the life of society. In a letter dated November 1, he wrote to Beaumont, who had gone off to spend his share of the Montyon Prize money on a trip to Spain and the South of France, and who was dallying in the Basque country in the company of a woman: "Upon arriving here, I threw myself on America in a sort of frenzy. The frenzy is still going on, though now and then it seems to die down. I think my work will benefit more than my health, which suffers a little from the extreme exertion of my mind; for I hardly think of anything else as I fire away." Ten days later, he described the life he was leading to Kergorlay: "I work as much as I can on my America and I find I am in good spirits . . . From morning until dinner time my life is altogether a life of the mind and in the evening I go to see Mary . . . The next day I start again and so on and so forth with a surprising regularity, for since my return from England, my books and Mary have been exactly my whole life."[13]

This voluntary privation bore fruit. The first part of *Democracy in America* was written in less than a year, and on August 14, 1834, Tocqueville left to go hunting at Gallerande, in the Sarthe, where he stayed at the home of Madame de Sarcé, Beaumont's sister, "his rifle slung over his shoulder and his manuscript under his arm."[14] He remained there until the middle of September. In October, he was correcting proofs of the book. His publisher, Gosselin—he was also Lamartine's publisher—planned to bring the book out in November, but copies of *Democracy in America* were not put on sale until January 1835.

Tocqueville had begun his task by reviewing his notes on America, which remained the basis of his documentation, and by drawing up an index with sixty-four headings which made it easier to consult them. Then he had undertaken a vast program of reading, which gave him a better understanding of American life and constituted a veritable "second trip to America."[15] In January 1834, feeling it was rather

---

[13]Tocqueville to Beaumont, November 1, 1833, *O.C.* VIII, 1: 136; Tocqueville to Kergorlay, November 11, 1833, *O.C.* XIII, 1: 344.

[14]Tocqueville to Beaumont, July 14, 1834, *O.C.* VIII, 1: 14.

[15]See James Schleifer, *The Making of Tocqueville's Democracy in America* (Chapel Hill, 1980), and G. W. Pierson, "Le Second Voyage de Tocqueville en Amérique," in *Alexis de Tocqueville; livre du centenaire (1859–1959)* (Paris, 1960), 71–85.

difficult for him to master this superabundance of documentation, he
decided to get help. Young Theodore Sedgwick, whom he had met
in America, was in Paris then and Tocqueville renewed his acquaintance with him, asking him to make extracts of books, but also discussing with him the problems of American democracy. Tocqueville also
applied to the United States legation for the help of a young man with
a liberal education who could devote several hours a day to a study
of American laws and their history. It was thus that he recruited Francis
Lippitt, twenty-two years old, who had been acting as a temporary
secretary at the legation while awaiting the arrival of the staff that
Edward Livingston, who had been appointed ambassador, would bring
with him. Sixty-three years later, Lippitt described his relationship
with Tocqueville. He worked for him every day from nine to five for
three or four months. His job was to summarize treaties and pamphlets
in French. Tocqueville would then question him about the content of
these summaries. Although he was very courteous, he did not display
the same confidence in Lippitt that he did in Sedgwick. He never let
him know that he was writing a book about the United States or even
that he knew English.[16]

The brevity of its references may not allow the reader of the
Democracy to appreciate fully the amplitude and variety of the book's
documentation. Tocqueville made use of eighteenth-century travel
accounts and individual histories of the states by scholars anxious to
glorify their little world, but also of collections of documents that
show the care Tocqueville took to resort to original papers, ethnolo-
gists' observations of Indian life, biographies of great men, and the like.

But there were three exceptionally important sources. When he was
writing an opinion on the conflict, in 1835, between the French
government and President Jackson, Tocqueville himself singled them
out, and what he said on that occasion holds true for the whole of the
Democracy: "I have consulted the three most respected commentaries:
the *Federalist,* a work written by three of the principal authors of the
federal Constitution, Kent's *Commentaries,* and those of Justice
Story."[17]

A federal convention, meeting in Philadelphia from May 25 to
September 17, 1787, had drawn up the Constitution of the United
States. It was a matter of transforming the confederation of the thirteen
colonies freed from British domination into a true federal state. But

---

[16]Pierson, *Tocqueville and Beaumont in America,* 732–34; D. Gilman, "Alexis de Tocqueville and His
Book on America," *Century Magazine* (September 1898), 703f.

[17]Unpublished manuscript in the Pennsylvania Historical Society Library.

only thirty-nine delegates out of fifty-five had signed the draft drawn up by the convention. The ratification of the project had run up against the self-interest and independence of the states. In the state of New York, only one of its delegates to the convention, Alexander Hamilton, approved the project, while Governor Clinton wrote letters attacking it, signed "Cato." Hamilton joined with John Jay and James Madison to counter this trend of opinion; under the joint signature of "Publius," the three men published ninety-five letters, the first of which was printed in the *Independent Journal* on October 20, 1787. These ninety-five letters were then collected in one volume which appeared in May 1788 under the title of *The Federalist*. [18] Translated into French, the collection was admired by the Girondist Convention and won the French citizenry over to its authors. The book brought out with admirable clarity what was new in the American Constitution and Tocqueville took inspiration from its analysis of the distribution of powers between the individual states and the central government, stressing the innovation of entrusting the executive power to a president and the importance of federal law.

Tocqueville had met the other two commentators. James Kent, a combative member of the Federalist Party, had been chief justice and then chancellor of the state of New York, and in 1823 had been led by the defeat of his party to devote himself to teaching, at Columbia University. He published, between 1826 and 1830, four weighty volumes that were the fruit of his teaching. The first of these, after opening with some general remarks on constitutional law, continued with a commentary on the United States Constitution; it was this part that Tocqueville drew from most heavily. Kent's position was essentially a conservative one in spirit; he finished off his texts by loyally appealing to the British common law. [19] The clear and precise *Commentaries* of Joseph Story, an associate justice of the United States Supreme Court from 1811 to his death in 1845, manifested a similar point of view. [20]

These sources gave a conservative version of American democracy that was not compensated for by a secondary source like the *Mélanges politiques et philosophiques extraits des Mémoires et de la correspondance de Thomas Jefferson,* published in 1833 by L.-P. Conseil, in which the

[18]Hamilton, Madison, Jay, *The Federalist on the Constitution Written in the Year 1788* (Washington, D.C., 1831). This, according to Schleifer, was the edition used by Tocqueville.

[19]James Kent, *Commentaries on American Law,* 4 vols. (New York, 1826–1830).

[20]Joseph Story, *Commentaries on the Constitution of the United States,* abridged edition (Cambridge, Mass., 1833). This was the edition used by Tocqueville.

people's will was affirmed without any counterbalance other than
decentralization.

In a letter to Franz Lieber, Story expressed some bitterness over
Tocqueville's borrowings from him.[21] But Tocqueville transfigured
them by linking political and juridical facts to the American social
state.

The principal source for the *Democracy*, however, remains the notes
made by Tocqueville while traveling in America. But in his notes
Tocqueville tended to filter out regional differences in his concern to
present a homogeneous picture of American society while at the same
time stressing its originality in comparison with the French society of
his time. Anxious to justify this approach, he even affirmed that the
"difference in civilization between Maine and Georgia is less than that
between Normandy and Brittany."[22] There was one main, governing
idea underlying this representation of American society and all its
permutations. Tocqueville had at first planned to make the theme of
his book the "sovereignty of the people" in America, but this theme
was too narrow, too uniquely political. Writing to Beaumont on
November 1, 1833, he noted: "My ideas have expanded and generalized," which probably indicates that he had grasped the central idea
of "the sovereign power of democracy in the United States," which
would remain the provisional title of the book right up to its publication. It encompassed a larger field—the social state of democracy, that
equality of conditions of which the sovereignty of the people was
merely the political corollary. Tocqueville was thus returning to the
method of Montesquieu: corresponding to the republic, the "nature"
of the United States, was a "principle" which found its support in a
certain state of society, but also created a collective mentality that gave
that society its direction: "Love of democracy is love of equality."
And, even more than Montesquieu, Tocqueville believed that societies
were directed by one single principle. When they departed from it, this
was because they were overcome by the instability of a revolutionary
state of transition, as in the case of France, where the democratic

---

[21]A. Pierson, op. cit., 730–32.

[22]*O.C.* I, 1: 172. *Democracy,* 168. Citations to the French edition of the *Démocratie en Amérique* are
to the first part of vol. I of the *Oeuvres Complètes* (Paris: Gallimard, 1951), abbreviated *O.C.* I, 1. Citations
to the English translation, abbreviated *Democracy,* are to *Democracy in America,* ed. J. P. Mayer, tr. George
Lawrence (New York: Doubleday Anchor Books, 1969), originally published by Harper & Row, 1966.

The passage from the *Democracy* quoted in the text is all the more striking in that it appears to be
written in response to Conseil (in the *Mélanges politiques* of Jefferson's writings referred to above, vol.
1, p. 43), who writes: "There is less conflict between the interests of the department of the Bouches-du-
Rhône and those of France's northern border than there is between the interests of the state of Vermont
and, I need not say those of Georgia, but those even of the state of New York."

204

羊 羊

principle would one day triumph, but which, nevertheless, continued to camp in the ruins of the aristocratic state.

What Tocqueville observed in America, then, was a plausible image of the future of France. For him, it was a matter not simply of describing this potential future through an account of America's history or its mores, but of judging whether such a society could maintain human freedom. Tocqueville the historian and sociologist was also a moralist. (As was Montesquieu, whatever Rousseau may have said.)

In a note quoted by James Schleifer[23] and unfortunately not dated, Tocqueville projected a work in three parts: he would discuss the *political society,* including the relations between the federal government and the individual states and the relations between the citizens and the Union; the *civil society,* considering the relations of the citizens among themselves; and the *religious society,* covering the citizens' relations to God and the religious sects' relations among themselves. In the two volumes that made up the first part of the *Democracy,* Tocqueville confined himself to examining the political society. In his preface, he evinces some hesitation at resuming his examination of the civil society later, because someone else (Beaumont) will be doing this while "casting a thin veil over the seriousness of his purpose," that is to say, in the novelistic form of *Marie.* [24] And if he broached religious problems, he took great care to point out that he was not studying them in themselves but in terms of the political significance of the religious spirit.

This study of the political society was divided into two parts: the first dealt with the institutional structures such as they were established by the American democratic society. The second, more complex, studied the mode of action of the popular power, its instincts, and the future that lay in store for it.[25] The two parts were clearly distinct enough for Tocqueville to have thought of publishing the first separately, no doubt in June 1834.[26] But it was only in July that he started negotiations with Gosselin, Lamartine's publisher, who suggested bringing out the two parts together. It was perhaps because Tocqueville wanted to have not only Beaumont but also his father and his brothers read the manuscript that publication was delayed until January 1835.

---

[23]Schleifer, *Making of Tocqueville's Democracy,* 7.
[24]*O.C.* I, 1: 12. *Democracy,* 19.
[25]*O.C.* I, 1: 179. *Democracy,* 174.
[26]Letter to Senior dated March 24, 1835, quoted by Schleifer, op. cit., 13.

Before approaching American institutions, Tocqueville devotes a brief preamble to the configuration of the country—a few pages in which the physical appearance of the land is carefully suggested by this great reader of the geographers, pages which owe nothing to Volney, or to Warden, or to Malte-Brun. A few more picturesque descriptions inspired by his trip or by Chateaubriand's add touches of color. The conclusion is that of a believer in divine providence: "Those coasts so well suited for trade and industry, those deep rivers, that inexhaustible valley of the Mississippi—in short, the whole continent—seemed the yet empty cradle of a great nation,"[27] a cradle on which the Indians had only a precarious and temporary claim. There are no conclusions about the diversity of the climate and its influence on the people, something Tocqueville had speculated about in his letters. Starting with this preamble, the emphasis is on unity. There is no allusion, either, to the pull of the empty continent on human society, though he had sensed some of the distortions to which it subjected the American civilization and though Frederick Jackson Turner was to make it a determining factor in the development of the country.[28] Because this is not essential to his argument, Tocqueville passes over it.

The second chapter, on the other hand, brings us to the heart of the subject: "Concerning Their Point of Departure and Its Importance for the Future of the Americans." In the same way that "the whole man is there, if one may put it so, in the cradle"—that is, Tocqueville says, permanently influenced by his first contacts with the outside world —so, with nations, "circumstances of birth and growth affect all the rest of their careers."[29] It is not easy to discover what is reflected in "the still hazy mirror" of the intelligence of the child in the cradle; it is scarcely easier to imagine what the circumstances or the forms of, say, the ancient Germanic liberties were for the people of Europe. But through a unique chance, we can follow from the beginning of the seventeenth century the adventure of these civilized men who, having broken with the old Europe, "had to try to build a society on new foundations."

The status and condition of these groups of emigrants varied considerably, of course, since there were crown colonies, colonies under charters granted to large landowners, and, in New England, the collective colonies of Puritans, who had left because they felt the air of their

[27]*O.C.* I, 1: 25. *Democracy,* 30.

[28]Frederick Jackson Turner, *The Frontier in American History* (New York, 1920).

[29]*O.C.* I, 1: 26–27. *Democracy,* 31. In the way Tocqueville describes the American people there is a sense of national identity reminiscent of Herder, though it is unlikely that Tocqueville had read him.

206

𝕏 𝕏

mother country was unbreathable, while they were allowed to go because it was easier to breathe without them. These colonies remained loyal to the king, but as Justice Story pointed out in his *Commentaries,* they ceased to be part of the kingdom. This notion had already struck Tocqueville when he wrote a small text for the *Système pénitentiaire* which could not be included in it—that essay mentioned earlier that dealt with "a few reasons that work against the French having good colonies."[30] These colonies of Puritans, of "Pilgrim fathers," fleeing Europe for moral reasons, were, Tocqueville tells us, "the seed of a great people which God with his own hands is planting on a predestined shore."[31] At the beginning, they are isolated little islands on a hostile soil in a harsh climate, confronting immense forests, exposed to attacks by Indians. A spirit that is at once religious and republican animates them. Each cell is a democracy of small landowners, free of any aristocratic element. They submit themselves to penal laws inspired by the Bible, which does not trifle with sin and multiplies the number of capital offenses. Tocqueville observes that custom was gentler than these laws and that capital punishment was rarely imposed, which seems quite sanguine on his part, since they were actually quick to burn people at the stake, particularly "witches." Their intolerance toward Quakers and Anglicans, not to mention Catholics, and the fanaticism of the ministers excluded from all social life anyone who was not a Congregationalist.

For that matter, this society was not, in its beginnings, as egalitarian as Tocqueville assumed it was: only the landowners, in other words a minority made up of the leading citizens, took part in the public assemblies.[32] The rigorousness of these measures detached swarms from the first colonies who established others that were, perhaps, more popular in character than the original ones. Nevertheless, these Puritans, all members of the elect and seeing in worldly success a pledge of salvation, had in common an egalitarian cast of mind and a sharp sense of their civic duties. In the heart of the township was born a *homo democraticus* who was unlike the Englishman of old Europe, even if he had preserved some features of the latter's customs and national character.

Freed of the aristocratic hierarchies that governed the peasant societies of Europe but subject to the spirit of religion whose "moral

---

[30]*O.C.* III, 1: 35–40.

[31]*O.C.* I, 1: 32. *Democracy,* 37.

[32]See Cestre's observations in "Tocqueville témoin et juge de la civilisation américaine," *Revue des cours et conférences,* 1933–1934.

steadiness" led him to "political freedom," he felt an obligation to participate in the affairs of his town and to escape from "Satan's weapon," ignorance. Through the participation of all its members, the modest township would become an administrative entity, managed by the direct democracy of the assembly of its inhabitants, in which a number of officials, elected for short terms to carry out the most varied duties, performed the community's necessary tasks.

These were the institutions characteristic of New England. To the southwest of the Hudson, one encountered large landowners, a more cultivated class that made up an aristocracy, but one that was "weak and unlikely to last," hiring menial day labor to cultivate their estates and lacking the old aristocracy's sense of responsibility for the welfare of their less fortunate neighbors. For the most part, they shared the popular feelings against the mother country, and from among them came most of the remarkable men who carried the American Revolution to its successful conclusion. But the Revolution brought individuals to the fore, not the large landowners as a class. What was more, their wealth was being undermined, in Tocqueville's view, by the laws of succession that called for an equal division of property among all the children inheriting an estate—an explanation challenged today by American historians.[33] Since the ownership of land brought no privileges with it and was much less lucrative than commerce or banking, the rich were turning to the acquisition of other forms of property.

The large landowners were therefore much too unsubstantial as a class to be able to hold back the spread of the principles of New England, which reached the neighboring states in a process of rapid democratization and then the whole of the Union, like "beacons on mountain peaks whose warmth is first felt close by but whose light shines to the farthest limits of the horizon."[34] Local cells of democracy formed throughout America, with some variations. In the South, the vital entity was the county rather than the township. In the new states in the West, the egalitarian spirit was taken to an extreme. But everywhere the generating principle was the same, and was in keeping with the American "point of departure"; despite regional variations, democracy in America came into flower at the level of the local community, which liberal writers of the time made out to be a primordial natural society that preceded all other human groupings. This was in striking contrast to France, where the Napoleonic adminis-

[33]*O.C.* I, 1: 48–50. *Democracy,* 51–54.
[34]*O.C.* I, 1: 30. *Democracy,* 35.

tration had recreated all the administrative cadres of the Ancien Régime, from bottom to top. In America one found a normal organic order, the work of history: "The local community was organized before the county, the county before the state, and the state before the Union."[35]

A natural consequence of this was administrative decentralization. One of the first facts Tocqueville and Beaumont had become aware of after their arrival in the United States was the absence of any conspicuous show of public power and, more concretely, of any public official who embodied that power in his person. It was these first observations that oriented Tocqueville's investigations toward decentralization. He saw that administrative paternalism, the trusteeship that was the golden rule of French administration, barely existed in the United States when it was not altogether absent. A Frenchman might observe with some surprise that, for example, in New England "it is a township's assessor who fixes the taxes and its collector who receives them; the treasurer of the township hands over the money raised to the public treasury."[36] This administrative decentralization led to a lack of uniformity and sometimes to inefficiency. It was slower than centralization to "assemble, at a given time and place, all the available resources of the nation." But, adds Tocqueville, centralization "militates against the increase of those resources" because it discourages citizens from settling their affairs themselves and if, in a serious crisis, it wants to appeal to them for assistance, it will find no response. In this observation, there is already an idea that the author will develop and amplify in *L'Ancien Régime et la Révolution*.

In America, for example, if a road is washed out, the neighbors, without calling on the public authorities, will come together to repair it. If a murder is committed, they will join forces to track down the murderer, who is considered an enemy of mankind, whereas in France the public gathers to witness the spectacle and follow the ups and downs of the contest between the police and their quarry. In essence, centralized administration is a form of despotism, and Tocqueville remembers what Montesquieu says of despotism: it cuts down the tree to get the fruit. The problem is all the more serious in a democratic system because there is no middle ground between having men stripped of all power under a tyranny, on the one hand, and having each citizen take an equal part in collective decisions, on the other. Decentralization

[35]*O.C.* I, 1: 42. *Democracy*, 44.
[36]*O.C.* I, 1: 89. *Democracy*, 89.

is thus bound up with one of the essential themes of Tocqueville's
thought, and when he discusses it, he does so with passionate eloquence:

What good is it to me, after all, if there is an authority always busy to see
to the tranquil enjoyment of my pleasures and going ahead to brush all
dangers away from my path without giving me even the trouble to think
about it, if that authority, which protects me from the smallest thorns on my
journey, is also the absolute master of my liberty and of my life? If it
monopolizes all activity and life to such an extent that all around it must
languish when it languishes, sleep when it sleeps, and perish if it dies?[37]

Despite the faults of a decentralized administration, it had the
immense merit of making the conduct of public life dependent upon
the free will of its citizens, and this gave it universal value. In America,
the mores of the original settlers and the way in which the nation had
developed brought about this state of affairs. In Europe, traditions
hostile to liberty would have to be overcome through changes in the
laws, and public opinion would have to be altered through education,
before a similar development could occur.

The administrative decentralization in the United States, Tocqueville insisted, did not stand in the way of centralized government. The
domain covered by the laws was broad, and the laws were enforced.
The power of the State, however, was shared between the twenty-four
individual states and the Union. The first states had been the thirteen
colonies that formed an alliance to free themselves of the mother
country. This federated State, in Tocqueville's eyes, made it possible
to join the happiness fostered by the small republic to the power of
a great national State. But it was a combination peculiar to Anglo-
Saxon America. Even Mexico, next door, which had imitated the
American system, had been unable to escape instability and anarchy.

The individual states were organized as fully functioning political
entities, with a legislature consisting of two assemblies, a House of
Representatives and a Senate, both elected by the people, and an
executive entrusted to a governor who was also elected. Everything
was subordinated to the principle of the sovereignty of the people; the
restrictions on universal suffrage were very limited, the mandates short
term. In general, the more recent the state, the more markedly democratic its institutions.

But important responsibilities, such as foreign policy, were reserved

[37]*O.C.* I, 1: 93. *Democracy*, 93.

for the federal government. The Congress also consisted of two Houses, but although the House of Representatives was elected by the people and represented the states proportionally by size, the Senate was the representative of the states and had the same number of representatives from each state. The president of the republic was chosen by an electoral college, itself elected by the public. He was the real head of the American democracy, elected for four years and, according to custom, running for office only once—a great novelty in the history of republics, in which the executive had formerly always been entrusted to a committee, as was the case with France's Directoire.

The federal Constitution seemed to Tocqueville a more adequate document than the constitutions of the individual states. But it owed this to exceptional circumstances. The first Confederation, which had conducted the War of Independence, had revealed the gaps in a simple alliance among the states. The Convention that met in Philadelphia in 1787 to fill in the gaps had among its members those great citizens who had come to the fore during the struggle against England. They were able to take advantage of the fact that the individual states, equally enlightened and animated by much the same passions, had not yet grown accustomed to acting independently as a national government. With more or less good grace, the representatives of these states agreed to share their powers with the federal government.

The newest and most original feature of this Constitution was that the people governed by the Union were simply citizens of the United States. Orders of the federal government could be given them directly without going through the individual states as intermediaries. Rather than a federal government, Tocqueville writes, this was an incomplete national government, in which many matters were under the sole jurisdiction of the states.

The American institutions thus formed a complex system—one of interlocking wheels, and wheels within wheels, in which the direct line of command of a centralized regime was not to be found. Such institutions could function only if there could be arbitration at every level from that of the township official coming into conflict with the county and refusing to carry out its orders, to the state legislature that passed a law contrary to the federal Constitution. The remedy lay in the fact that every citizen could have recourse to the law courts. American law knew nothing of the laws giving civil servants immunity from prosecution that had been permanently established in France by Article 75 of the Constitution of the year VIII of the French Revolution, and American courts were able to make political decisions

through the legal process, such as the suspension from his duties of a
man holding public office.

The most serious conflicts were those in which two states or a state
and the Union were in opposition. Every citizen was able to appeal,
in such cases, to the Supreme Court of the United States, composed
of judges nominated for life by the president, and their decision,
though occasioned by a particular case, would have the authority of
precedent in a system of jurisprudence which remained essentially that
of the common law.

Tocqueville greatly admired this system of arbitration by the
American courts. It was one of the subjects on which Federalist sources
had influenced him profoundly. The Democratic Party, however, condemned the conservative spirit of the judges; Senator Thomas Hart
Benton, in a letter to Martin Van Buren, was to challenge the *Democracy*'s optimistic conclusions.[38]

There was another subject about which it is clearer that Tocqueville
had mistaken the real situation of his time. Tocqueville felt that though
President Jackson was granted certain important powers by the Constitution, his powers were inferior to those of a constitutional monarch.
It was certainly true that Jackson had been lifted up to the presidency
by a wave of opinion hostile to the federal state. But this authoritarian
had quickly recovered his balance; he came to terms with public
opinion in ways that enraged his adversaries but definitely strengthened
his position, and this Tocqueville failed to recognize.[39]

In the first part of his book, Tocqueville examined institutions, that
is to say, "the present shape of political society." He stressed the spirit
of those laws adapted to the principle of the sovereignty of the people.
But because of the very fact that American democracy was a free
society, it possessed a dynamic capable of abolishing or changing the
existing legal structures. A sovereign people influenced public life in
its own ways and was moved in its depths by collective passions and
instincts. But "secret springs" urged on, retarded, directed its irresistible
course.[40] Democratic mores (taking the word "mores" in its broadest
possible sense) could intervene in public life with redoubtable force,
enough to endanger the very future of the republic. Tocqueville
undertook an analysis of the various aspects of democratic mores in
order to arrive at a judgment on the question that is the key to his

[38]Quoted by Pierson, op. cit., 735–36.

[39]On this point see the pertinent critiques of H. V. Brogan, "Tocqueville and the American Presidency,"
Journal of American Studies 15, 3 (December 1981), 357–75.

[40]O.C. I, 1: 170. *Democracy*, 171.

whole book: will democratic societies of the future be capable of governing themselves freely? What can be learned, from this point of view, from the only great republic in existence, the United States?

There were three principal channels for the assertion of popular power in America: the political parties, the press, and associations.

In general, at this stage of his life, Tocqueville did not favor political parties. The time had not yet come when he would think it necessary to attach himself, even if with reservations, to a major liberal party. The violence of the struggles at the end of the Restoration, the partisan manipulations that followed the establishment of the July monarchy, had left their mark on him. In the 1835 *Democracy*, parties are an "inherent evil of free governments"; they attempt to attract to themselves the peaceful citizenry. After the bitter contentions in France in 1830, after seeing that the parties remained small in-groups of the leaders in spite of the brutal interventions of the masses in the political process, how could he not have failed to anticipate the broad, popular appeal of American political movements?[41]

This was no doubt one of his first surprises when he arrived in America: the parties were moribund, and the candidates for election were obliged to take great pains to differentiate themselves from one another. However, there had once been large parties, just after the War of Independence, when the principles and the workings of the Constitution had to be settled: the Federalists wanted to limit the people's scope for action and strengthen the central power, the Republicans primarily wanted to leave the initiative to the impetus of the people and respect local differences. If the first played a role in the construction of the State, the second lodged themselves there definitively in 1801 with the accession of Jefferson to the presidency.

Afterwards, the Federalist Party died as a political power. In a country where the society was entirely democratic, it had only been a historical accident and, because of its role in drafting the federal Constitution, a happy accident, in Tocqueville's opinion. The strength of the Federalists was based on the lucidity and character of the great landowners who had led the fight against the English, and they had only survived, for a time, because of the gratitude felt by the democracy for a flowering of great citizens who turned out to be the leaders

---

[41]On Tocqueville's attitude toward parties see Matteuci, "Il problema del partito politico nelle reflessioni d'Alexis de Tocqueville," *Il pensiero politico* 1 (1968), 39–92.

it needed in a great national crisis. For the two parties to continue to exist, what was necessary was a rich class, who would be supported by those dependent on them, and a poor class. Today, the great body of common people dominated unchallenged, animated by the ideals of the small proprietor, and as soon as an institution appeared to be taking on, suddenly, the character of aristocratic authority, a flame of political passion would flare up. Such was the case with the Bank of the United States, whose power, suddenly denounced by Jackson, aroused the people's anger. But the normal state of America, as Tocqueville saw it, was that of a country in which democracy would progress slowly, almost imperceptibly: it was the age of the "little parties," with their shadowy intrigues and their petty feuds, that had replaced the great parties associated with strong, nonpartisan principles.

The role of the press in America must even more certainly have been a source of astonishment for Tocqueville. He came from a country where, because they could not bring back censorship now that it had been discredited by the use the Restoration had made of it, the ministries of the new regime doggedly prosecuted a subversive press in the law courts. This was an exhausting guerrilla warfare with various episodes in which, even when one had ruined an adversary, it was only to see him come back to life under a different name with fresh resources. This subversive press was, at the beginning of the July regime, the nightmare of the government, which thought the press capable of bringing it down.

Now in the United States, as soon as he looked at the newspapers, Tocqueville found them at least as violent as the French papers. And no one dreamt of prosecution; unlike the situation in France, there was no impediment to becoming a printer or a newspaper editor. Certainly the situations were not entirely comparable. There was no capital city like Paris in America, from which the journalist's words as they traveled out to the provinces would take on a sort of oracular prestige. Most of the papers were read less for their political articles than for their ads and local news. Yet large press campaigns waged by a number of papers could influence opinion, and Tocqueville had noted the interest aroused by the campaigns for the penitentiary system. But in general, the most scurrilous political rhetoric had no effect on a public grown blasé and made skeptical by the very proliferation of periodicals. Hence the conviction acquired by Tocqueville (who, before his arrival, may not have been opposed to prosecutions of the newspapers, for he confesses to us that he did not have any natural liking for

214
☙ ☙

freedom of the press) that the harmful effect of newspapers resulted primarily from the fact that the public was not yet accustomed to them—had not, so to speak, been vaccinated. In any case, he became definitively convinced that it was useless to suppress the excesses of the press, a conviction that would make him oppose the repressive laws of September 1835 and later cause him, conservative though he was, to vote against martial law. In a very fine passage, he expresses this conviction:

> First you bring writers before juries; but the juries acquit, and what had been the opinion of only an isolated man becomes that of the country. You have therefore done both too much and too little and must try again. You hand the authors over to permanent magistrates, but judges have to listen before they can condemn, and things which men fear to avow in a book can be proclaimed with impunity in pleadings; and what would have been obscurely said in one written work is then repeated in a thousand others . . . Your courts may arrest the body, but the soul escapes and subtly slips between their fingers.[42]

A third means by which the expression of popular opinion could be channeled and take on the form of law was the association.

The spirit of association took many forms in America and Tocqueville limited himself here to studying the ways in which it intervened in political life. These ranged from the simple collective petition to the election of a private assembly, or convention, whose delegates were chosen as advocates of a principle or an interest. In the latter case, there came to be a sort of rivalry with the legally constituted assemblies. At the time of the meeting of one such convention in Philadelphia, Tocqueville had thought there was a danger of the Union's breaking apart. In actuality, although there were violent resolutions these were not followed by any action. For the aim of such associations might well be to win over a majority of the electorate, but no matter how strong their hold on public attention might be, there was one infallible way of knowing whether or not they were successful—the exercise of universal suffrage which approved their proposals or rejected them.

This marked their difference from French political societies, particularly the secret societies that were plotting the overthrow of the existing regime. These could argue that the electoral system, which now limited the franchise to those paying direct taxes of at least two hundred francs a year, was in opposition to popular feeling, which ran

[42]*O.C.* I, 1: 185–86. *Democracy,* 180–81.

in their favor. Within a democracy, where the majority consisted of the greater part of the entire population, an association that called upon citizens to join together in order to bring about a political reform constituted a peaceful and normal way to submit the reform to the judgment of all. The example of America convinced Tocqueville that the right of association was an essential freedom.

Once Tocqueville had described the means by which a democracy acted to effect internal change, he could get to the heart of his subject and the instincts, ideas, and passions that were stirring there. But he had first to clear from his path two false problems and an old illusion.

The first of these false problems was the matter of the democratic system's bargain price. The *budgétaires* of the various parties in France argued endlessly with real or fake figures over whether a democracy was more or less expensive than a monarchy. Tocqueville had no trouble showing the inanity of comparisons with the ways and means of the American regime, so different from that of France in both situation and structure. As for the second false problem, whether a democracy was more or less corrupt than an aristocracy, he reverted to general considerations about the different possible modes of corruption without coming to any definite conclusion.

But there was also a stubborn prejudice that had originated with the eighteenth-century *philosophes,* that the people, although incapable of governing themselves, were admirable in their choice of men to govern them. This idea was linked to the Rousseauist picture of a people whose honesty had not been corrupted and whom providence had furnished with natural good sense. Tocqueville reacted to this myth with a mixture of irony and distrust for the sincerity of those who professed it, a reaction he would have again in 1848, when Hippolyte Carnot said to him that one should always trust the impulses of the people . . . He countered with a concrete fact: the American people, in the most enlightened democracy in the world, generally chose as their representatives good but thoroughly mediocre individuals whose horizons were scarcely broader than those of the average voter. It was not that the people in this democracy felt a class hatred for the rich, since they remembered that the rich had played a part in the struggle for the country's independence. But they were drawn to what resembled them, what did not overshadow them.

The relationships of social life, more than man's inherent good or bad nature, determined the political orientation of the masses. They were not at all fond of overly brilliant successes, who, in a society

216

𝄆 𝄇

where everyone theoretically had the same chance, aroused their envy; they were unstable in their desires; they were incapable of "silencing their immediate needs with a view to the future"; they readily listened to flatterers . . . All of this resulted in legislative action that was often ill conceived, disorderly, and subject to constant change.

Tocqueville also saw in the majority a collective being whose deepest instinct was to behave despotically. He denounced the "tyranny of the majority," a notion he had discovered in the *Federalist* but which he expanded on from various points of view. Few of Tocqueville's assertions aroused so much controversy, starting with the response of Jared Sparks, who immediately said he disagreed, and including most lately H. V. Brogan, who tries to show its unsubstantiality.[43]

For Tocqueville, the most important aspect of this tyranny was the more and more exclusive, tighter and tighter stranglehold of popular power on the institutions of government: legislatures elected for a very short term; judges, too, elected for a limited time instead of being guaranteed independence through a long tenure in office; in the functioning of the institutions, subordination of the executive to the legislative, which was closer to the source of popular power, but also the existence of peremptory mandates imposed by the voters on those they elected. Sole source of the law's authority, the popular power incarnated in the majority was intervening directly in the law's drafting and execution.

Another aspect of this tyranny was that the majority constituted a force of opinion intolerant of minorities. In his letters from America, Jacquemont, the friend of Stendhal, vigorously denounced the intolerance of the Christians of all sects toward "infidels" and wrote that the Bible was the "bane" of America. Though he dealt with the subject only incidentally, Tocqueville thought the same: an atheist in America could play no part in public life. Tocqueville, a magistrate by training, was particularly sensitive to the fact that the opinion of the majority could obstruct or violate the law. For example, legislation governing bankruptcy was not passed because instances of bankruptcy occurred frequently and many citizens felt themselves potentially liable. Taxes on strong liquors were not imposed, even though there was a close tie between public drunkenness and crime. A journalist who, in the face of public opinion, had opposed the idea of war against England saw his house looted and was himself thrown into prison and beaten.

[43]H. V. Brogan, *Tocqueville* (Bungay, 1973), 40–45.

During Tocqueville's trip there were anti-Catholic riots and convents were burned down. In such cases, the militia, instead of upholding the law, lent its support to the rage of the people. As for the freed blacks who had received their rights as citizens, there was no question for them of trying to exercise these rights, since the racism of the masses would bring terrible reprisals down on them and they could not even plead their cause in the courts.

Even if there were not a great many cases of such injustice, when the popular will was in a dominating position the few cases that did occur could have irremediable effects:

When a man or a party suffers an injustice in the United States, to whom can he turn? To public opinion? That is what forms the majority. To the legislative body? It represents the majority and obeys it blindly. To the executive power? It is appointed by the majority and serves as its passive instrument. To the police? They are nothing but the majority under arms. A jury? The jury is the majority with the right to pronounce judgment; even the judges in certain states are elected by the majority. So, however iniquitous or unreasonable the measure which hurts you, you must submit.[44]

A gloomy view of democracy: the ineluctable evolution toward equality of conditions brings with it the risk of a new type of despotism. But providence, which intended the evolution of the Christian world toward equality among men, left to free will the possibility of reconstructing forms that would ensure freedom. It was in the arduous struggle against a fatalistic submission to his destiny that the very dignity of man lay.

In America itself, weapons existed with which to fight tyranny.

Institutions, first of all, some of which were rather ambiguous. Decentralization might favor oppressive local measures, but within the limited setting of his community the citizen could make himself heard. The jury system sometimes expressed the predispositions and the biases of the majority, but it taught the citizens who were a part of it the true hierarchy of values: above the immediate passions of the people was the law, and above even the law was the innate sense of justice in every man. Though occasionally delinquent, for the most part the American citizen respected the law; in Tocqueville's eyes, the jury system, which fostered an association between the magistrate and the people acting as judges, was in large measure responsible for this.

[44]*O.C.* I, 1: 263. *Democracy*, 252.

218

𝕴 𝕴

More generally, in this country where there was no hereditary aristocracy, not even an aristocracy based on wealth, jurists formed a sort of spontaneous aristocracy that imposed a certain respect for tradition. British common law remained at the basis of the legal system, regulating property law, transactions, and the security of the citizens. But the interpretation of common law was a subject requiring specialized knowledge and a study of precedents which predisposed those who engaged in it to a conservative position, as much in the United States as in England. Tocqueville saw the jurists of America as being a little like the priests of Isis in ancient Egypt, the repositories of a secret knowledge. We have considered the role played by judges as arbiters in conflicts between different constitutionally established authorities. This role was supported by the true social reality of a class which had the nation's respect and because of this could act as an effective brake on the erratic impulses of popular democracy.

But the great counterbalancing force to the instability and tyranny of democracy was religion. Tocqueville was very conscious of living in a time of doubt, when the dogmas of Christianity were being challenged. But he did not conceive that man could limit his curiosity or his anxiety to the few years of his appointed life. He seems to have considered religion a permanent factor that would perhaps continue to evolve—whence the somewhat uneasy curiosity aroused in him by his discovery of Unitarianism—but whose influence on society could best be judged by the current state of the various denominations. Their role in a democracy was to provide a stable zone in the psychological makeup of the citizen, and in this respect it seemed to him that the Catholic religion, with its clearly defined dogmas and its discipline, was preferable to the Protestant sects. More generally, the congregations of the Christian religions were taught by their faith that it was an obligation of conscience to concern themselves with the general interests of society. That their political choices should be in keeping with moral law was the only obligation Christianity imposed on them. Christianity exalted man's freedom, it had been the first in the world to proclaim equality among men, and therefore, even when appearances were to the contrary, there existed profound affinities between Christianity and democracy. It was through a real aberration, due to the vicissitudes of France's long Revolution, that the clergy sided with the supporters of the Ancien Régime and social inequality. The presence of the clergy in the camp of the defeated was at once contrary to nature and disastrous for religious ideas themselves. In America, the very separation of Church and State was accompanied by a general respect for religion on the part of the masses, and religion, without itself becoming embroiled in partisan battles, gave another dimension to the spirits of those who did become involved.

For certain foreign observers, the American State was a fragile construction. A republican form of government was unsuited to a large nation, as the eighteenth-century writers had demonstrated, and centrifugal forces would one day shatter the Union. Tocqueville, who, contrary to a tenacious legend, had no taste for prophecy and always saw several possible potentialities in an actual situation, was guarded about the future of the Union. But for the present he noted a correspondence between the mores and the laws that assured the American democracy a life at once active and stable. His depiction of America as a united country was justified and expressed by the strong patriotic feeling common, in an identical form, to all its citizens.

This patriotic feeling was not an instinctive outpouring of sentiment or a deep love of the land of one's ancestors. These had apparently been left behind in old Europe, although one could find them, to a degree, across the border in Quebec. In the United States, a rational love of well-being was mingled with an attachment to those institutions that permitted each and every one to try his luck, to have a chance at success. A feeling of solidarity in a great adventure that was both individual and collective uplifted the American citizen to the point of being proud and arrogant. Here, the virtue that had animated the ancient republics was replaced by a sentiment of self-interest properly understood which was convinced that the interest of each individual was closely linked to the interest of all. This was a powerful new bond.

America was fortunate in having no neighbors and thus no armies, and in having new land whose economic conquest sustained the high standard of living of its people. But South America was also isolated and fertile, and there the inhabitants fought among themselves, with many of them living in misery. What fed the rational civic feeling of the inhabitants of the Union was a clear vision of the country's destiny, and that vision itself arose from the spread of enlightenment among the masses. American civic-mindedness no doubt had roots in the Anglo-Saxon race (the problem of national identity was one that Tocqueville hesitated to try to solve), but the essential fact was that the people of the United States were the best educated in the world. This enlightened patriotism, this reasoned and rational good citizenship, were crucial for the existence of American democracy.

In spite of some gloomy passages, then, the first part of the *Democracy* seems to give a fairly optimistic assessment of America. But

220

🍂 🍂

Tocqueville belatedly added a chapter that went beyond the analysis of the Union's public life but whose absence his readers would not have failed to notice, on the "Future of the Three Races That Inhabit the Territory of the United States." On the fringes of Anglo-American society, indeed, lived the Indians and the blacks brought in from Africa as slaves to farm the plantations.

The Indian race interested Tocqueville: he tried to understand what it had once been, felt pity for its fate, sometimes thought it might have been possible to integrate it into American life. Now it was too late. The rapid decline of the original inhabitants was accompanied by their physical and moral degeneration. But this was a marginal problem, and he would soon leave it behind.

Slavery, on the other hand, was one of the essential torments of American life. The partisans of slavery were on the defensive against the attacks of those who advocated emancipation. But Tocqueville was one of the first to stress that emancipation would not solve anything. Giving the slaves their freedom was a solution in the ancient world, where only conquest separated citizen from slave. In the United States, the real problem was the problem of race. The freed blacks remained a people apart, despised and living in misery. During his visit, Tocqueville felt a bond of sympathy with the métis and the mulattoes. Of course the *bois-brûlé* in Canada was a man often divided, even torn, but he was still a citizen. The mulatto in the United States was considered merely a consequence of licentious behavior; there could be no mulatto class, nor was there any way for the mulattoes to free themselves from the malediction cast on those who were black.

It was an impossible situation. Once the black masses were free (for sooner or later emancipation was inevitable), what would become of them and what would their relations be with the whites? It was not realistic to think of sending them back to Africa or rounding them up in one state. The hatred was deepening and Tocqueville, though he was not resigned to it, could hardly see any prospect other than genocide.

At the center of this first part of the *Democracy* is a picture of America that remains incomplete, since certain social phenomena, for instance that of associations, appear here only through their effect on political life, as though one were to judge an iceberg only by the part of it that sticks up above the water. Reference is often made to the future second part, in which *homo democraticus americanus* will be seen stripped of his function as citizen. In the preface to the first part, as we have already said, Tocqueville appears hesitant about writing it: 221

I had intended in a second part to describe the influence in America of equality of conditions and government by democracy upon civil society, customs, ideas, and mores, but my urge to carry out this plan has cooled off. Before I could finish this self-imposed task, it would have become almost useless. Another author is soon to portray the main characteristics of the American people and, casting a thin veil over the seriousness of his purpose, give to truth charms I could not rival.[45]

This was a gesture of friendship toward Beaumont, and *Marie* was more or less finished when he wrote this preface. He was acquainted not only with the scope of it, but with the content too, for he had given his friend advice and criticism. He was well aware that Beaumont had painted part of the picture, but had not drawn the great sociological fresco of democratic life with which he himself wanted to attempt a composite picture of these new societies, and this allows us to express some doubt about the sincerity of his friendly words.

As it stands, this first part of *Democracy in America* nonetheless presents a vivid portrait of American public life. An America "of cockcrow and morning star." Was this really Andrew Jackson's America? The historian is hard put to say, because of the very fact that there exists no comparable document about America at that time. Certainly errors may be found in it. Tocqueville did not see the augmentation of the presidential power. There are omissions—for instance, he did not mention either the early attempts at socialism or the proliferation of unions beginning in 1825. We know that interpreters of Jacksonian democracy disagree over its essential characteristics. Tocqueville chose an interpretation that remains quite plausible: the ideal of a rural republic, with small landowners, the encouragement of free enterprise, and the ascendancy of the middle class and the average American. And, as well, the compromise between unending social mobility and a conservative ideal.[46]

In *Democracy in America*, the author saw "more than America" and his study of the Union's political institutions and customs is often

---

[45]*O.C.* I, 1: 12. *Democracy*, 19.

[46]Lynn L. Marshall and Seymour Drescher, "American Historians and Tocqueville's Democracy," *Journal of American History* 55, 3 (1968), 512–32; Marvin Meyers, *The Jacksonian Persuasion* (Stanford, 1957).

222

interlarded with digressions on more general subjects. In the introduction he wrote after the book was complete, Tocqueville revealed the breadth of his preoccupations.

For seven centuries, the Christian world had been the theater for a "providential movement" that was leading society toward equality of conditions, and its inexorable course struck the author with a "kind of religious dread."

The substitution of a democratic world for the aristocratic one had been the overriding historical reality since the Middle Ages. In America, special circumstances had permitted the direct implantation of democracy without a struggle, and here it "attained its natural limits." In Europe, the fierce, vain resistance of the aristocratic principle, wrongheadedly supported by religion, had prolonged the revolutionary period which marked the watershed between the two worlds, and here democracy grew up among the ruins of the past "like those children deprived of parental care who school themselves in our town streets and know nothing of society but its vices and its wretchedness." The study of America thus gave Europeans the example of a free and ordered democratic society, a kind of system that was altogether unknown to them.

This did not mean it was a model that should be followed blindly. Its situation in the world gave it, in the last analysis, the advantage of being able to make "reparable mistakes," something that France, which was competing with the other nations of Europe, could not allow itself with impunity. There were institutions of general value that could and should be adopted—for instance, decentralization and freedom of the press. But, Tocqueville writes, "I do not think that American institutions are the only ones, or the best, that a democratic nation might adopt."[47]

And he later says more specifically, obviously thinking of France in 1833:

Is it, then, impossible to imagine a government founded on the genuine will of the majority, but a majority which, repressing its natural instincts for equality for the sake of order and stability of the state, would consent to invest one family or one man with all the attributes of executive power? Can one not imagine a democratic society in which national strength would be more centralized than in the United States and in which the people exercised a less direct and less irresistible sway over public affairs, but yet where each

[47]*O.C.* I, 1: 241. *Democracy*, 231.

citizen, invested with certain rights, would take part within his sphere in the   223
proceedings of the government?[48]

If such a program, requiring the political education of the people
and laws capable of reforming the mores, could not be carried out,
democracy would end in the impartial subjection of all to despotic
power.

"It is the political man that we have to develop in ourselves,"
Tocqueville had written Beaumont in the Versailles days. His book,
which was also addressed to himself, was a preparation for action: to
educate his fellow countrymen in their civic responsibilities, to show
them what was at stake in the game of politics, and to assume a role
in the making of laws. This was a political program—and why not?
thought the young Tocqueville, whose urgent and almost naive ambition underestimated the force of inertia in men and in custom. Why
not become a statesman? The immediate inference to be drawn from
the first part of *Democracy in America* was the necessity of entering the
Chamber in order to put the book's directives into effect.

[48]*O.C.* I, 1: 324. *Democracy*, 309–10.

14

FROM THE FIRST

DEMOCRACY

TO THE SECOND

DEMOCRACY IN AMERICA, published on January 23, 1835, was the book of the year. Its young author emerged from his attic room in the rue de Verneuil to find that he was now a public figure, much sought after in literary salons and political circles.

Gosselin, his editor, had anticipated nothing more than one of those ephemeral worldly successes in which a nobleman and amateur might win some esteem among a limited group of people. He had refrained from reading the manuscript and, when confronted with the public's reception, expressed delighted surprise: "Well! It seems you've written a masterpiece!"[1] He hadn't wanted to print more than five hundred copies—perhaps seven hundred in reality, if we are to believe that, as Viel-Castel said, he had a habit of stealing from his authors for his own disposition two hundred copies out of every printing. In any case, the first printing was very small. Gosselin had to set about at once preparing a second edition, which came out in June and was followed by a third later in the same year. A fourth and fifth came out in 1836, a sixth in May of 1838, and a seventh in June of 1839. The appearance of the complete work in 1840 thus constituted the eighth publication of the first part. Unfortunately, we don't know how many copies were printed of any of these editions.[2]

Could it have been its subject that led to the book's success? Only to a very small extent. The preceding years had seen a number of

[1]Tocqueville to Beaumont, *O.C.* VIII, 1: 151.
[2]*Journal de la librairie.*

deserving books appear that were quite capable of satisfying the public's curiosity about America. And interest in the United States was much less lively than it had been just after the July revolution. President Jackson's message in December 1834, in which he threatened to seize French property if France did not pay back its old debts —Tocqueville thought this a good omen for the success of his book[3] —caused only an ephemeral revival of public attention. The real cause of the book's success was the broad recognition in the press of the author's talent and, above all, the high praise he received from critics whose opinions were respected by the cultivated public.

The book had been launched in the way that was usual at the time: a descriptive notice in the principal newspapers, and a prepublication article to arouse curiosity. The article was written by Léon Faucher and published in *Le Courrier français* on Christmas Eve, 1834. It was a clear and solid review, but Faucher, a born polemicist and an envious man, was stingy in his praise and concluded the piece with an attack on Tocqueville's concept of the tyranny of the majority.[4]

After its publication, the *Democracy* was quite widely reviewed in the press. It caused enough excitement to provoke heated debates like the one between *Les Débats* and *Le National*. But from the Right to the Left there was general agreement on the author's "wisdom," his "gift for observation," and his "philosophical nature."

The legitimist *Gazette de France*[5] published the only article that was generally malevolent, though a few compliments were tacked on at the end:

Monsieur de Tocqueville is a lawyer and, as such, he pleads the cause of democracy in America. It is with a very special partiality that this author offers to the admiration of the people of Europe . . . a country with people of three different colors where red men, who are the natives, see themselves being exterminated by white men, who are the usurpers; where black men are sold along with the livestock in the town squares.

Another legitimist organ, *L'Ami de la religion et du roi,*[6] challenged the information given by Tocqueville on the position of American Catholics and the relations between Catholicism and democracy, but with

[3]Tocqueville to Beaumont, *O.C.* VIII, 1: 149.

[4]*Le Courrier français,* December 24, 1834. Information concerning this review and most of those that follow has been provided by Françoise Mélonio, who is preparing a doctoral thesis on the reception given to Tocqueville's book.

[5]*Gazette de France,* anonymous article, February 2, 1835.

[6]*L'Ami de la religion et du roi,* August 25 and 29, September 8, 1835.

226   kind words for the author and recommendations that people read the
ध्ये ध्ये   book. The pro-government *Journal des débats*[7] returned to the book
several times. In particular, it devoted two long articles to it which
expressed the doubt that the United States was a true democracy, but
concluded that the author was "the Blackstone of America . . . Our
pen almost wrote an even greater name." A similar respect for the
author shows through in another article in the *Débats* written by
Salvandy, who predicted that the American republic would be engulfed in a civil war. *Le Constitutionnel,* for its part, made a distinction
between a democracy and a representative regime, putting off to
another article, which apparently never appeared, any moral judgment
of the republic across the Atlantic. It particularly praised the author's
objectivity. *Le National* stressed the "lofty significance" of a book
which brought France so much understanding of today's America and
tomorrow's Europe, although it expressed "reservations" concerning
the mediocrity of American politicians as affirmed by Tocqueville.[8]

Le Temps,[9] in an article by Sainte-Beuve, was also unstinting in its
praise: "One would have to look far and wide among us to find
another book of science and political observation that would arouse
and satisfy the attention of thoughtful minds to this extent." The
article by Sainte-Beuve was clearly the most important of the reviews
that appeared in 1835. Its understanding of the author's purposes, the
stress it placed on the larger topics and their interrelationship won him
the respect of Tocqueville, who wrote him: "I can't help believing that
there exist many points of contact for us and that a sort of intellectual
and moral intimacy would quickly spring up between you and me, if
we had the occasion to know each other better."

Because of its density and its richness, *Democracy in America* would
seem to have been perfectly suited for those long articles full of
"extracts" that were so beloved of the reviews of the time. But this
was not the case: the brevity of the presentation in the *Revue de Paris*
and the silence of the *Revue britannique* are surprising, and the studies
that did appear are disappointing: *L'Européen,*[10] which Buchez had just
started, launched into a violent attack against Protestant individualism

[7] *Le Journal des débats,* March 23 and May 2, 1835.
[8] *Le Constitutionnel,* May 18, 1835. *Le National,* June 7 and 29, 1835.
[9] *Le Temps,* April 7, 1835. Tocqueville's letter to Sainte-Beuve, written after the appearance of this
article, was included in Sainte-Beuve's *Nouveaux Lundis* IX (1868) as an appendix to the article "New
Unpublished Correspondence of M. de Tocqueville."
[10] *L'Européen,* November 25 and December 25, 1835.

and America's foolishness. It used the work of Beaumont—his novel *Marie* also appeared in 1835—and Tocqueville as a source of ammunition, praising them highly but reproaching Tocqueville for not having passed judgment categorically enough. The *Revue républicaine*[11] published a long and verbose study by Louis Blanc in which he showed, in passing, respect for Tocqueville but at the same time expressed the suspicion that Tocqueville lacked a firm belief in the progress of mankind; in the *Revue européenne,*[12] Champagny wrote that Tocqueville attached too much importance to the institutions in America and not enough to the social aspects.

The *Revue des deux mondes*[13] was the only review to print a long, focused study of the book. Although he did not share certain of Tocqueville's pessimistic views, Francisque de Corcelle carefully developed the two panels of the diptych: the stability of American democracy on the one hand, the revolutionary state of Europe on the other. As in the case of the article by Sainte-Beuve in *Le Temps,* Tocqueville felt that here he was understood, and Corcelle's article was the beginning of a long friendship.

These critiques, though they disagreed and were often second rate, nevertheless created a composite portrait of the author: he was a serious, profound man, something of a prophet (the comparison he made between Russia's future and America's, though not in the least a new idea, was brilliantly set forth and made an impression), and anyone who aspired to understand the trends of his time had to study him or at least pretend to have read him.

But the immediate success of the *Democracy* owed more, perhaps, to support from a few important people.

We have described the family ties that linked the Tocquevilles to Chateaubriand. Now the great man appointed himself patron of his young relative, and although the mistrustful Tocqueville ascribed this to whim on Chateaubriand's part, it could well have been the expression of a sympathy that was sincere, though it was never adequately returned. Chateaubriand introduced Alexis to Madame Récamier's salon, that small but prestigious circle in l'Abbaye-aux-Bois where, on March 31, 1835, he was invited to hear the author read fragments of the future *Mémoires d'outre-tombe:* "M. de Chateaubriand introduced

[11]*Revue républicaine,* May 10, 1835.
[12]*Revue européenne,* April 1, 1835.
[13]*Revue des deux mondes,* 739–61.

me . . . in such a way as to make great friends for me out of those who don't write and sincere enemies out of those who do. But all of them showered me with compliments."[14] Still, one of "those who write" whom Tocqueville met that day was Jean-Jacques Ampère, who soon became one of his most faithful friends.

Royer-Collard, the most prominent figure in parliament during the Bourbon Restoration, now a man in his middle seventies, already knew Alexis de Tocqueville. Among his political associates were Tocqueville's cousins Le Peletier d'Aunay and Molé, and he had helped to see that the Montyon Prize was given to the *Système pènitentiaire*. Although he was already biased in its favor when he first opened the book, his reading of the *Democracy* fired his enthusiasm. He copied out more than fifty pages of extracts from it, which are now lost. In the Academy in 1836, he defended the work against the insinuations of Viennet, who insisted that the author, in his fourth edition, had changed his text to make it more favorable to republican ideas. He took Tocqueville to the home of the Duchesse de Dino, Talleyrand's niece, while Molé took Tocqueville to the home of his confidant, Madame de Castellane, where Tocqueville became a favored visitor, going there to talk in the morning and having his own special seat by the fire. Tocqueville thus had access to two great political coteries of the time, and his relations with Royer-Collard were soon those of disciple and master.

Democracy in America won other kinds of patronage for him as well. The Academy gave him a Montyon Prize of twelve thousand francs and, although Royer-Collard had something to do with it, it was Villemain who convinced the Academy with a highly laudatory report.[15] Tocqueville had asked the illustrious permanent secretary of the Academy for his literary patronage without having the close relationship with the man that he had with Royer-Collard. At this time too, most probably, Tocqueville entered into a relationship with Lamartine that was to prove both enduring and tempestuous.

The young Cavour, who was spending the first quarter of the year 1835 in Paris, was struck by the author's success and the freshness of the work. In a letter of March 20, he does not hesitate to write: "It is certainly the most remarkable work of modern times. In my opinion, it throws more light than any other on the political questions of the future. De Tocqueville is a young man, he has a splendid future before

[14]Tocqueville to Beaumont, *O.C.* VIII, 1: 152.

[15]See *Correspondance de Tocqueville avec Royer-Collard, O.C.* XI, introduction. Unpublished letter from Tocqueville to Villemain, rough draft in the Tocqueville Archives.

him." Quite probably, he met the author of the *Democracy* at that time, and he then saw him a few weeks later in London, frequenting the same salons, listening to a long discussion between him and Senior, going with him to an Anglican service. Like many others, he immediately found Beaumont very amiable and was to be disconcerted by Tocqueville's coldness, reproaching him with wrapping himself in the reserve of a great man.[16]

These relationships led Tocqueville even more directly toward the Academy than toward the Chamber of Deputies. Almost immediately after the publication of the *Democracy,* Tocqueville's ambitions turned toward the Académie Française.[17] Well-intentioned friends, especially Mignet, its permanent secretary, wanted to open the doors of the Academy of Moral and Political Sciences to him. He failed to be admitted the first time and easily consoled himself, writes Madame de Dino, because he felt the company to be found there "very poorly arranged," by which he meant that it was full of men of the Revolution.[18] The prison reformer Charles Lucas had shown a "penitentiary" animosity toward him that was to last all his life. But after the death of Laromiguière, Tocqueville was elected, on January 6, 1838, by twenty votes out of twenty-two. He felt almost no satisfaction about this because he was afraid it would put an obstacle in the way of his candidacy for the "Française." The next day he wrote to Mignet: "I still believe . . . that my nomination to the Academy of Moral and Political Sciences, however honorable the circumstances that accompanied it may have been for me, will delay my entrance into the Académie Française, whereas my nomination to the latter would not have presented any obstacle to my joining you."[19]

In October 1839, Tocqueville prepared to start his campaign. At that time two candidates were fighting over the seat left vacant by the death of Michaud, the historian of the Crusades—Victor Hugo and Casimir Bonjour. But before Tocqueville could make up his mind, Pierre-Antoine Berryer abruptly decided to stand as a candidate and Tocqueville then chose to withdraw so that he would not have to oppose the great legitimist orator with the backing of what he called the "castle flunkies." On December 19, after seven rounds of voting, none of the three candidates had managed to win a majority. At this point, Tocqueville thought of standing as a candidate for the seat of Népomucène

[16]A. J. B. Whyte, *The Early Life and Letters of Cavour 1810–1848* (London, 1925).
[17]Unpublished letter to Villemain of 1836, draft in the Tocqueville Archives.
[18]Duchesse de Dino, *Chronique,* vol. 2.
[19]Private archives.

230

卍卍

Lemercier, but gave way to Pierre-Simon Ballanche, who, seeing that he was being pushed forward to block Hugo, stepped aside in his turn, thanks to which, on January 7, 1841, Hugo was elected by seventeen votes against fifteen for Jacques Arsène Ancelot. On January 28, Ancelot stood against Ballanche for Louis-Gabriel-Ambroise de Bonald's seat, but again no one received a majority. On February 25, Tocqueville replaced Ballanche against Ancelot, though his relations with the latter were very cordial, and was beaten by him, Ancelot receiving eighteen votes out of thirty-four. For a few months now, the Académie fever had been rising in Tocqueville; he kept himself informed about the health of its oldest members. On the eve of Ancelot's election, he had sent one voter an urgent appeal: "The information I have received during the day gives me the vexatious certainty that my election hangs on one vote . . . I confess that it would be painful to fail because you refused to give me your vote over M. Ancelot when you gave M. Ballanche your vote over him."[20] The death of the old Lacuée de Cessac, and the fact that once again the good Ballanche stepped aside in favor of a younger colleague, permitted a painless election. On December 23, 1841, twenty votes went to Tocqueville as against eight to Vatout and two to Aimé Martin. Ballanche was picked at the next election, Berryer was deferred for a long time, Vatout began a seven-year marathon to get into the Académie, and Casimir Bonjour was left out of the running. During the episodes of this battle, the author of the *Democracy* had evinced an impatience that proved that under his grave exterior there was still something left of Abbé Lesueur's spoiled, capricious pet.

Marie was also an immediate success and, like his friend, Beaumont was obliged to prepare a second edition almost right away. But both needed some diversion. Tocqueville felt incapable of going back to work without a long period of solitary reflection; only after that would he be able to take up his pen again. So the two friends decided to carry out the old plan they had made, when they were in America, to visit England together. True, Tocqueville had made a brief trip there in the summer of 1833, but the rapid developments in English political life kept it at the forefront of the world's news.

The Reform Bill of 1832 had changed parliamentary life, as Tocqueville had been able to see during his first trip. But it had since

---

[20]Unpublished letter, in the New York Historical Society collections.

brought in its wake progressive administrative reforms that had changed the political, aristocratic, and decentralized structure of the country as a whole. Thus, for instance, the application of the factory law limiting the length of time children could work and making their education compulsory had created a body of state inspectors. And the Poor Law Amendment Act of 1834 (whose reporter in parliament was Nassau Senior, from whom Tocqueville received a copy of the report) created poor-law boards, each elected by qualified taxpayers, each dealing with a group of parishes, that were put under the control of a central commission. Long-entrenched local bodies were thus being replaced by new authorities, elected by large numbers of voters and governed by a central administration. The status of the established Church was also being challenged and in Ireland, where abuses were conspicuous, ten bishoprics had been eliminated.

Moreover, the great Whig aristocracy which had triumphed after the Reform Bill now found it difficult to maintain control of political life. The new elections to the House of Commons in January 1835 had revealed two trends: the resurrection of the Tories as a conservative party under the leadership of Sir Robert Peel, coming within thirty seats of obtaining a majority in the House; and the doubling of a radical extreme left which, with O'Connell's Irish, numbered more than one hundred fifty members. This second phenomenon was the most striking, because it appeared to be a swift step on the road to revolution. Early in April 1835, after a brief interlude, the Whigs had taken power again with the very moderate Lord Melbourne, but he could only govern with the tolerance of the radicals and by negotiating with O'Connell. Mérimée, who knew England well, was visiting London from mid-May to mid-June in 1835, and he met Tocqueville and Beaumont at aristocratic dinners and no doubt also at the Athenaeum Club. Mérimée, who went to London every two years, noted then that England was becoming democratic "in a geometric progression" and that it was currently "in 1789" but he hoped it would have too much sense to go "as far as 1793."[21] Tocqueville was thus able to compare, with his own eyes, the democratization now in progress with the situation he had witnessed during his first visit in 1833. Whereas at that time he had not only visited London but also made a trip into the countryside to see the castles and the great estates, in 1835, besides visiting the capital, he would go to see the new industrial England of

[21]Prosper Mérimée, *Correspondance générale*, vol. 1, 431. Letter to Requien dated June 19, 1835.

the North and the West, regions toward which the national balance was tilting.[22] This trip was such a logical one that Cavour was following the same itinerary at the same time. Tocqueville and Beaumont then went to observe the relations between the Irish peasant democracy and the English aristocracy in Ireland, in order to gain an understanding of a problem that was poisoning political life. The second part of the *Democracy*, published in 1840, was to bear numerous traces of all these observations.

Tocqueville probably had other, personal reasons for making this trip. Schleifer observes that he was to marry Mary Mottley when he returned and, even though letters written at that time show some hesitations, assumes that he probably wanted to meet the family of his future wife.[23] This is quite plausible; and one incident in the journey seems to support the idea. On June 15, Tocqueville made a quick trip from London to Boulogne-sur-Mer to meet Mary Mottley.[24] According to Rédier, who does not give his source or the date of the event, Mary Mottley renounced her Protestantism in Boulogne. It was indeed the case that the diocese of Arras specialized in receiving British renunciations of Protestantism. Unfortunately, the diocesan files for renunciations made before 1851 have been lost.[25] But it seems very probable that Mary Mottley renounced her faith in June 1835. It facilitated the marriage that took place a few weeks later and it would have been very natural for Tocqueville to be present at this ceremony.

Beaumont also thought of getting married, and one can speculate that the two friends saw their trip as a period of relaxation between the austere life required for writing their books and the orderly life that marriage seemed to imply. London, during the romantic period, was not only an aristocratic city but a capital of pleasure. Jules Taschereau recommended them to Sutton Sharp, a most obliging Englishman who during his visits to Paris joined in the convivial gatherings of Stendhal, Mérimée, and their friends and, when they came to London, helped them amuse themselves there. This excellent jurist was a notorious reveler and Taschereau sent him the following letter of introduction for Tocqueville and Beaumont:

[22]The notes taken by Tocqueville during this trip are published in the *O.C.* V, 2: 45–70. The entire trip is annotated by Seymour Drescher in his book *Tocqueville and England* (Cambridge, Mass., 1964), which we should be citing here constantly.

[23]Schleifer, *Tocqueville's Democracy,* 20.

[24]Letter from Tocqueville to John Stuart Mill dated June 13, 1835, *O.C.* VI, 1: 295; letter to Kergorlay dated July 6, 1835, *O.C.* XIII, 1: 377.

[25]According to information supplied by the diocesan archivist.

Two of my friends, Messieurs de Beaumont and de Tocqueville, are about to spend some time in England and Ireland. I am counting on you in your very amiable kindness to give them some good pointers that will allow them to see London as it ought to be seen. These gentlemen, who went to America three years ago, have, since their return, published three very successful books. They are going to England with purposes that are just as serious and with more hope of amusing themselves than in America; I know you will be happy to give them your informed advice so that they can achieve that precious result.[26]

233
𝒦 𝒴

There was nothing incompatible between studying the progress of democracy and quietly burying one's youth!

However that may be, the two friends left Paris on April 21, 1835, and reached London on the twenty-third. They stayed there until June 24 (with Tocqueville taking ten days of rest at Hampstead because he was ill), were in Coventry on the twenty-fifth, in Birmingham on the twenty-sixth, in Manchester on the thirtieth, and in Liverpool on the third of July.

They then went to Ireland, staying in Dublin from the sixth to the seventeenth of July, then traveling through the middle, the south, and the west of the country until August 9, the date they returned to Dublin to be present at a scientific conference. At that point they separated. Beaumont left to visit Scotland, while Tocqueville headed for Southampton. He had arrived by the eighteenth, and embarked there for Cherbourg by way of Guernsey.

In 1833, Tocqueville had written Beaumont from London that he was wandering over the surface of the city like a gnat on a haystack. He was exaggerating, because he had an introduction to Lord Radnor, had made some contacts by introducing himself on his own initiative, for example to the English economist Nassau Senior, and *Le Système pénitentiaire* was known and respected by men like Whately, the Bishop of Dublin. Nevertheless, in 1835 the situation was certainly no longer the same. The success of the two young authors was well known in London. Their books were still being talked about; the very conservative *Quarterly Review* made Beaumont out to be a republican in order to give more weight to Beaumont's reservations about democracy, while *Blackwood's Edinburgh Magazine* misrepresented Tocqueville as a dedicated Tory. The welcome they were given, in any case, was no longer addressed, as it sometimes had been for Tocqueville in 1833, to the offspring of legitimist families who were supposed to be

[26]Letter quoted by Doris Gurmell, *Sutton Sharp et ses amis français* (Paris, 1925).

mainly interested in balls and society events. Henry Reeve, then twenty-two years old, was in the midst of translating the *Democracy* into English. We do not know who asked him to do this initially, and when Reeve first encountered the book he thought his Tory convictions were incompatible with the job. But he read it more attentively, met its author on March 16 in Paris, and was won over by him. He became not only the official translator, but also Tocqueville's friend. In June, when Tocqueville was not feeling well and retired from London to rest in Hampstead, Reeve and his mother, who lived there, did him many services, since Beaumont—at the urging of Tocqueville, who did not want him to sacrifice precious time for his sake—had stayed in London, on Regent Street, where they had first established themselves.

On May 5, Tocqueville wrote to his future wife: "We are very anxious to mingle with all classes and try to come into contact with all sorts of people." As an example of this principle, he told her he had dined in succession at Holland House and at the home of a manufacturer. But in fact, he hardly left the circle of a certain social elite and had no personal contact with the representatives of the workers' movement, who were so active at the time. Although he and Beaumont frequented Tory salons, they also received the warm welcome that the great Whig lords reserved for eminent Frenchmen. Lord Lansdowne, a member of the cabinet, came to see them himself; Lord Holland invited them to several dinners; Lord Brougham, the chancellor of the exchequer, went to some trouble to meet them several times. In letters to Madame Ancelot, Tocqueville describes a few episodes in this society life: festive parties in crowded rooms, a sit-down banquet for two hundred people presided over by Lord Brougham, a meeting with Lady Ada Byron, the poet's daughter.[27] But, strangely, the people they talked to the most came from the radical circles and even sometimes represented the extreme left in the House of Commons: Roebuck, Hume, the Grotes.

John Stuart Mill had read the *Democracy* with enthusiasm and was to write a remarkable review of it in October.[28] He had just started

---

[27]Letter to Madame Ancelot dated May 27, 1835, published in *Un Salon de Paris (1824–1864)* (Paris, 1866).

[28]In the *London Review* 2 (1835), 85–120. Several studies of the relations between Mill and Tocqueville have been done, including particularly I. W. Mueller's *John Stuart Mill and French Thought* (Urbana, 1956), 134–39; H. O. Pappe's "Mill and Tocqueville," in *Journal of the History of Ideas* (April–June 1964), 217–34; T. H. Qualker's "John Stuart Mill, Disciple of Tocqueville," in *Western Political Quarterly* 13 (1960), 1880–89; and Joseph Hamburger's "Mill and Tocqueville on Liberty," in *James and John Stuart Mill: Papers of the Centenary Conference* (Toronto, 1976), 111–25.

the *London Review,* which would soon become the *London and West-*
minster Review. He asked Tocqueville if he would like to become a
regular contributor and write whatever he liked for the magazine. We
will see how limited that contribution was to be, but it is striking that
Tocqueville, who was always so cautious when asked to commit
himself to anything, did not try to refuse this invitation but affirmed
his sympathy for English radicalism, which he contrasted to the party
that occupied a similar position in France:

Everything I have seen of English democrats leads me . . . to think that
if their views are often narrow and exclusive, at least their goal is the true
goal that friends of democracy must aim for. Their final object really seems
to me to be to place the majority of the citizens in a position to govern and
to make them capable of governing. Faithful to their principles, they do not
seek to force the people to be happy in the fashion they consider the most
appropriate, but want to arrange things so that the people will be able to find
that out for themselves, and, having found it out, to act accordingly. I myself
am a democrat in that sense. To bring modern societies to this point by
degrees seems to me the only way to save them from barbarism and slavery.[29]

Tocqueville's welcome by important figures was of some help to
him in his attempt to untangle the rather complex situation in England.
When he arrived, he wrote to his father: "So far this country seems
to me, still, to be one vast chaos. This is certainly a different sort of
difficulty to overcome than in the study of America. Here, there is not
that single principle which tranquilly awaits the working out of its
consequences, but instead lines that cross one another in every direction, a labyrinth in which we are utterly lost."[30]

The notes taken by Tocqueville during his visit to England in
1835—more cursory than those taken in 1833—bring out two facts
that surprised or struck him: in politics, the progress of centralization;
in the area of social structures, the formation of an aristocracy of
money that gave English life its own special character.

Tocqueville had observed the decentralized democracy of America,
and had glimpsed similarities between it and the old decentralized
administration of aristocratic England. He thought the latter would be
replaced, without a great change of structure, by new local organs
more democratic than the squires who administered English counties
as benevolent amateurs. But he noted, not only in the opinions of his

[29]Letter of June 13, 1835, *O.C.* VI, 1: 293–95.
[30]Unpublished letter dated May 7, 1835, Tocqueville Archives.

radical friends but even in that of a great Whig lord like Lord Minto, how discredited the traditional system, now felt to be absurd, had become. As early as May 11, 1835, he made the following note: "Centralization, democratic instinct, instinct of a society that has succeeded in pulling itself out of the system of individualism of the Middle Ages, preparation for despotism"; and a month later (June 20) tried to analyze this instinct more closely: "Mania for centralization that has taken hold of the democratic party. Why? Feelings similar to those of France in '89 for rather similar reasons: peculiarities of the institutions of the Middle Ages, hatred of the aristocracy which has superstitiously preserved them and which uses them to its own profit. Innovative spirit, revolutionary tendency to see only the abuses of the present state: general tendency of democracies."[31] Would this trend toward centralization, which, as we have seen, had taken concrete form in several recent laws, invade the entire administrative system? John Stuart Mill, to whom he had expressed his uneasiness, was confident that it would be held within limits by the English empirical spirit, which never took a principle to its ultimate consequences. Tocqueville adopted his opinion, believing that centralization would be accomplished to the benefit of Parliament and not of the executive power, and noted especially the counterbalances that the institutions contained:

1. The creation of local elected bodies whose effectiveness was consistent with the traditional spirit of association.

2. The supervisory authority of the judiciary power, which could intervene between an injured party and a civil servant. Civil servants in England did not enjoy the immunity from prosecution guaranteed their French counterparts by Article 75 of the Constitution of the year VIII—for Tocqueville a symbol of administrative arrogance for which he, like most liberal writers of the nineteenth century, professed a stubborn hatred.

But Tocqueville also had questions about the structure of English society. The starting point of his meditations seems to have been landed property. In the democratic United States, as in France, which was in the process of becoming democratic, most landholdings were small. Senior had pointed out to him in a letter written before his visit that in England, property continued to be concentrated in the hands of a relative few. In a discussion that took place in Nassau Senior's garden in London, at which Cavour was present, Senior defended large landholdings, asserting that a landless worker on a well-run estate was

[31]*O.C.* V, 2: 69.

better off than the small rural landowner. For his part, Tocqueville   237
believed in the human value of owning one's own land. But he noted
that in England the ordinary man did not seek to invest what he had
in land. The amount of land a man owned was not the indication of
his rank in the social hierarchy; extensive landholdings were an ostentatious display of large fortunes that had already been amassed.

What directly dominated English society was the power of money.
Money was indispensable for a political career, but also for a career
as a lawyer or churchman; one had to be rich even to plead in the law
courts. Tocqueville noted: "Money is the mark not only of wealth, but
also of power, of esteem, of glory."[32] England was still an aristocratic
country, but its new aristocracy was that of wealth, which had replaced
or absorbed the old aristocracy:

Because the English nobility had the idea and the need, early on, to turn to
the middle classes for support, and because they were able to do this only
by granting them some political power, an aristocracy of money was soon
established, and as the world became more civilized and the means of acquiring wealth more readily available this aristocracy grew while the old aristocracy, for the same reasons, steadily shrank. It is fair to say that this revolution
was completed in England about fifty years ago. Since that time, birth has
been a mere ornament or, at the very most, a help to money.[33]

This aristocracy acquired its wealth from commerce and manufac-
tures. It dominated the life of the industrial centers which were, for
people of that time, the salient feature of English civilization. Tocqueville went to see the metal-working city of Birmingham and the
cotton-manufacturing city of Manchester, where he visited the foul
neighborhoods of "Little Ireland" which abutted the "palaces of industry," and stressed the contrast between the big factory owners, at the
forefront of progress, and the "half-savage" workers. This contrast
would later lead Tocqueville to wonder about the possibility of an
industrial feudal system in the future that would be even harsher, even
more merciless to man than those of the past. He was to return to this
problem in the second part of the *Democracy*.

All the same, he admired another aspect of English industrial society. Material factors were less important as a stimulus to commercial
activity than the institutions that guaranteed liberty and thereby en-

[32]*O.C.* V, 2: 63.
[33]*O.C.* V, 2: 89.

couraged men to take all sorts of risks. He was quite conscious of the English presence throughout the world—Englishmen sailing every sea, penetrating every continent. Soon the politician in him would say that France, if she was to ensure her own rightful expansion, must combat a system that was creating a British hegemony over the entire world.

Tocqueville found, then, that England was still an aristocratic country, thanks to its aristocracy's suppleness and ability to change. Nevertheless, the democratization of the laws that had begun with the Reform Bill was continuing with the plans to reform municipal bodies and to establish the secret ballot:

If the democratic process has come to a halt so far as the mores and the ideas of the rich classes are concerned, it continues to move forward rapidly in the laws. What will be the final result of these opposing trends? It is very hard to say. Whatever the outcome, I see opportunities for this country to avoid the crises of a violent revolution and succeed in changing its institutions gradually. Both parties have a real respect for the will of the majority and a habit of obedience that one may consider a great guarantee of order. There is nothing to indicate, in either of them, any thought of coming to the point of using violence. The radicals believe they are sure of succeeding in due course by legal means; as for the aristocracy, it does not seem to me to be in a position to resort to the use of force and, even if it could, I am convinced it will not attempt it.

As we have said, Tocqueville and Beaumont were in Ireland from July 7 to August 16. The laws and the government were those of England, but here the aristocracy that controlled the land had arisen from conquest and spoliation. It had no bond except mutual hatred and fear with a miserably poor peasantry, crushed that summer of 1835 by their hunger as they waited for the first harvests. Aristocracy and peasantry differed in both race and religion. Tocqueville and Beaumont witnessed the awakening of that spirit of rural democracy expressed in London by Daniel O'Connell's eloquence and political maneuvering, but which, in Ireland, was officered and disciplined by a Catholic clergy that had come out of the peasantry themselves.

Tocqueville's notes on Ireland are relatively abundant compared to his notes on England. They sometimes begin to look like sketches for stories or essays the author thought of publishing. When Beaumont found them among Tocqueville's papers after his death, he wrote that Tocqueville had refrained from publishing them out of a feeling of delicacy toward him, the author of a book on Ireland.

If Tocqueville developed these notes to such an extent during their trip together, it was because Beaumont had not yet decided to write his book. For Tocqueville, not publishing these notes was simply keeping his promise. Beaumont had perhaps forgotten by 1860 that they had actually entered into a formal agreement. On May 5, 1835, Tocqueville mentioned it to his father: "I believe . . . I sent you the arrangement I made with Beaumont, an arrangement that is advantageous to [both of us], giving him the prerogative of writing about England, if he wants to, and me about America, if I'm inclined to."[34]

Even if Tocqueville had briefly thought of writing a modest piece about Ireland, he never dreamed of writing a book about England, although a rumor to that effect was circulated around Paris, apparently started by Gosselin, seeking publicity for his authors. Molé became upset about it, fearing that his young relative was plunging into the venture very rashly. At the beginning of September 1835, Tocqueville set his mind completely at rest. He was perfectly aware of the difficulty of analyzing English society. "One could compare America to a large forest crossed by a great many straight roads all leading to the same place. The only thing one has to do is find the spot where these roads come together, and everything is revealed in a flash. But in England the roads cross each other and it is only by following each one of them to its end that it is possible to form a clear idea of the whole."[35] On the other hand, he had never abandoned the idea of writing a sequel to the *Democracy* and he had taken "care . . . to plant the seed [for it] in advance at the end of the introduction" of the book that was already published.

When he got back from England, however, he was absorbed by other concerns. His relations with Mary Mottley could not continue as they were, and he was faced with a dilemma—marriage or breakup. Tocqueville had been painfully tormented by this during his trip, wavering between a solution his family did not approve of and his attachment to Mary. On August 23, he landed at Cherbourg, went to Nacqueville, where he apparently opened his heart to his sister-in-law Emilie and asked her advice, then, after a stop at Balleroy (he had family connections with the Marquis de Balleroy) he reached Paris at the beginning of September. We have no information about his private life from then until October 26, when he married Mary Mottley at Saint-Thomas-d'Aquin. Tocqueville's mother was not present at the

239

---

[34]Unpublished letter dated May 7, 1835, Tocqueville Archives.
[35]Unpublished letter to Comte Molé, Tocqueville Archives.

240
ᵶᵶ

ceremony, either from illness or ill humor. Beaumont and Kergorlay were witnesses for the groom, the chaplain of the expiatory chapel of Louis XVI, Abbé Girardet, officiated.[36] On November 15, the newly married couple were at Baugy, near Compiègne, staying with Edouard de Tocqueville, and Alexis expressed his eagerness to get to work.

As with the first part of *Democracy,* he started by making a list of topics to be covered. At this point he envisaged only a single volume that would examine the Americans' ideas and attitudes. The following spring he expanded this plan to the size of the work, in two volumes, he eventually published.[37]

Whereas he had written the first part of the *Democracy* in a single "burst" that took barely a year, working in his attic in the rue de Verneuil with his door and his mind closed to all outside preoccupations, the writing of the second part was interrupted by all sorts of distractions, and this accounts in some measure for the fact that it took four years, from mid-November 1835 to mid-November 1839, though a first version was completed by October 1838. The longest interruptions were, first, a pause of four months, from June to October 1836, the main cause of which was the need for Madame de Tocqueville to take the waters at Baden in Switzerland, for reasons of health; then a long electoral campaign in 1837; another electoral campaign at the beginning of 1839, which resulted in the election of Tocqueville as deputy; and lastly, his drafting, during the 1839 session, of a sizable report on the abolition of slavery.

In addition to these interruptions, Tocqueville, contrary to the rule he had imposed on himself while he was writing the earlier work, produced and published several studies on other subjects.

Tocqueville found that the peace and quiet of the country provided the best conditions for writing his big book and the less important texts. As a bachelor, he had been very happy in his brother's house at Baugy and had thought of enticing Beaumont to join him there so that they could go on with the dialogue they had begun in Versailles, continued in America, and resumed again with several interruptions while they were writing their books:

It is a charming thing to see the "happiness" that arises from courtesy and order. Throughout this house there is an atmosphere of reason, of morality, that gradually penetrates you. There is comfort everywhere, luxury nowhere.

[36]Archives of the sacristy of Saint-Thomas-d'Aquin.
[37]J. Schleifer, *Tocqueville's Democracy,* 21–34.

Everything runs easily, as though by itself, and without one ever noticing
the master's hand. On all sides one sees content faces, and one meets kindly
glances. In short, one is as well off as any featherless, two-legged creature
would like to be. They took me to the castle keep (which they've finished
clearing up), and there they showed me Alexis's room and next to it Gustave's. The whole thing, which is very small, is a very agreeable place. It's
a little airy world, where I hope we can both perch next year.[38]

These bachelor plans were spoiled by the loss of bachelorhood.
Tocqueville married and then, at the beginning of July 1836, Beaumont married Clémentine de Lafayette, granddaughter of the general.
The prospect of this marriage seems to have dried up, for a few months
before it took place, all of Gustave's activity as an author. Once he
was married, he emerged from this lethargy and went off with his wife
to the British Isles to finish the documentation of the book *L'Irlande,*
which he published in 1839, an unequal work in which passages full
of banal rhetoric alternate with brilliant and lucid pages that even
today deserve to be brought back out of the quite excessive oblivion
into which they sank.[39]
Once Tocqueville was married, he and Mary settled in at Baugy
during the years 1835 and 1836. They came back several times in 1838,
but these were the last of the long visits they paid here. Madame de
Tocqueville had only a moderate affection for "the Edouards," and
Baugy's pastoral setting, with its canals of stagnant water, caused
attacks of bronchitis and rheumatism. More important, in 1836 Alexis
de Tocqueville's financial situation changed.
In January 1836, his mother died and there followed a division of
the property among her sons, by virtue of which Alexis received the
château and lands of Tocqueville (along with the title of comte, which
he would always refuse to use). The following year he lived at Tocqueville from June to November. The projects undertaken by his wife,
about which he sometimes grumbled, made the château habitable for
long visits. Henceforth, a new rhythm was established for the pair:
winters in Paris, summers (which sometimes lasted until the end of the
autumn) in the Cotentin. Because he put down roots here, the rather
abstract attachment Alexis had professed until then for his family's
birthplace evolved into a profound attachment to its things and people,
and this was perhaps the happiest passion of his life. He liked to have
good friends come to Tocqueville. The Beaumonts came here in

[38]Tocqueville to Beaumont, January 12, 1835, *O.C.* VIII, 1: 150.
[39]Gustave Beaumont, *L'Irlande sociale, politique et religieuse,* 2 vols. (Paris, 1839).

242

August 1837, when they returned from England and Ireland; the Corcelles had visited before them; Kergorlay spent the end of the year 1838 here. Of course, Beaumont and Kergorlay heard fragments of the book in progress. It seems clear that the Tocquevilles never went to visit Kergorlay at the family estate in Fosseuse, Louis's father perhaps not caring to receive a traitor to Carlism. On the other hand, from Paris Tocqueville sometimes went to La Grange, the principal country residence of the La Fayette clan, to see the Corcelles, the Rémusats, and the Beaumonts. It was inevitable that he should spend less time with Gustave now, but their intellectual exchanges were never broken off.

Tocqueville now had another "conversational instrument"—Jean-Jacques Ampère, who, for the first time, spent a month at Tocqueville in 1839, where he read the manuscript of the second part of the *Democracy* with an enthusiasm that was sincere, since he expresses it in his private journal. He was subsequently to return for long visits, living in one of the two towers that flanked the facade of the château.

There were other interruptions to the writing of the book besides those brought on by the author's entry into public life and by Madame de Tocqueville's poor health. Between the appearance of the first part of the *Democracy* in 1835 and the second part in 1840, Tocqueville published substantial essays on three quite different subjects.

We know little about what occasioned the first of these, the *Mémoire sur le paupérisme,* published in the *Mémoires de la Société académique de Cherbourg* in 1835.[40] It seems to us that it must have been written between January and April of that year—that is, between the publication of the first part of *Democracy in America* and the second trip to England. The archives of the Cherbourg Society unfortunately do not contain any covering letter for the manuscript. But Tocqueville, speaking of his experience of English life, uses a long passage from his 1833 *Notes de voyage,* without the slightest reference to those of 1835, which would be quite surprising if he had written his text after his return from England in September.

The two most important sources of the *Mémoire sur le paupérisme* were, on the one hand, the investigations and reports made before the new poor law was passed by the English Parliament on February 15,

---

[40]The *Mémoire sur le paupérisme* was published again in the *Bulletin des Sciences economiques et sociales du Comité des travaux historiques et scientifiques* (Paris, 1911), 17–37.

1834, along with the text of the law itself, and, on the other, the three-volume *Traité d'économie chrétienne* by Villeneuve-Bargemont, subtitled *Recherches sur la nature et les causes du paupérisme en France et en Europe et sur les moyens de le soulager et de prévenir,* published in 1834. It was most likely the critical reflections suggested to Tocqueville by these two series of works that led him to establish his own position on the problem of pauperism.

This 1835 *Mémoire* was meant to be no more than the first part of a larger work: the Academic Society of Cherbourg announced that the sequel would follow in 1838. The second part never appeared and scholars have assumed that either it was never written or it was lost. Now, by collecting some scattered papers in a file of the family archives, we have been able to reconstruct a written text whose length is three-fifths that of the first report. This text, written after the promulgation of the law on savings banks of February 1837, is accompanied by variants and by indications of possible further development. The piece is clearly unfinished. Why did the author not complete something he had already done so much work on? Was it because he wanted to devote himself exclusively to writing his long book, or did he have doubts about the solutions he was proposing? It is impossible to decide.[41]

In the text of the first report, the phenomenon of pauperism is amply described within the framework of civilization's development, and linked to the fact that men are not equal. "If one examines what has happened in the world since the origin of societies, one will easily discover that equality exists only at the two extremes of civilization. Savages are equal among themselves because they are all equally weak and ignorant. Very civilized men may all become equal, because they all have at their disposal similar means of attaining material comforts and happiness. Between these two extremes we find inequality of conditions, the wealth, knowledge, and power of a few contrasting with the poverty, ignorance, and weakness of all the others." It was when men quit the woods to devote themselves to agriculture, it was when men began to own land, that inequality and also battles for the possession of land first appeared, an example of which Tocqueville saw even in the conquest of the Roman Empire by the barbarians, a conquest that created the feudal society that legalized inequality. (The influence of Rousseau, particularly of his *Discours sur l'origine de*

---

[41]File in the Tocqueville Archives; the text is to appear in vol. XVI of the *Oeuvres Complètes.*

244

染 災

l'inégalité parmi les hommes is perceptible here, and even the style shows the effects of Tocqueville's reading him;[42] this influence can also be seen in the second part of the *Democracy,* but it was absent from the first.) But the proliferation and diversification of needs linked to human perfectibility had created industries to satisfy them. These industries were more unstable than agriculture, whose only aim was to provide the necessities of life. The more industrialized, the more splendid a society was, the more widespread its pauperism would become, the number of indigents being, for example, higher in England than in the Iberian Peninsula. Moreover, in a more industrialized society, presenting more striking contrasts between opulence and misery, the collective conscience was more sensitive to the need to alleviate the misery.

The age-old remedy for extreme poverty was charity, which Christianity had made one of the theological virtues. In England, the Protestants, who had suppressed the monasteries in the sixteenth century, had organized public charities to act alongside private ones. Currently, this country had the most acute problem with poverty, because its land was in the hands of the big landowners and because England's industry was trying to meet the needs of the entire world, which put its working class at the mercy of the fluctuations of those needs. The poor law, though it helped the indigent, had the serious drawback of not distinguishing between the unfortunate and the lazy, thus offering a reward for idleness. Costly to the rich, it was humiliating to the poor, imposing restrictions on their liberty, and did not even have the advantage of creating bonds of gratitude between the social classes. It was destructive both financially and morally. One should not look to this sort of State organization, then, to relieve social miseries when private charity was not adequate.

The unpublished article would have endeavored to point out other solutions possible for France.

First, Tocqueville made a distinction between the agricultural and the industrial classes. In France, the dividing up of landed property was the best cure for extreme poverty. Even the smallest rural landowner was protected from the vagaries of chance, and could acquire "habits of order, activity, and thrift." The dividing up of landed property, "which these days is such a great guarantee of material order, may therefore be the greatest guarantee of moral order, when all is said and done."

[42]Michel Bressolette, "Tocqueville et le paupérisme," in *Littératures; Annales publiées par la faculté des lettres de Toulouse* V, 2 (June 1969).

The condition of the industrial proletariat was very different. It was constantly exposed to crises, either because the number of workers grew while production remained stable, or because a lessening of demand led to a slump in production. Now, if landed property was being broken up into smaller holdings, industrial property on the other hand was becoming more concentrated and less democratic, because factories required capital and employers did not want to "give the worker an interest in the factory," which "would produce among the industrial classes effects similar to those produced among the agricultural classes by the dividing up of landed property."

Tocqueville adds:

I am led to believe, nevertheless, that a time is coming when it will be possible for a large number of industries to be directed [by associations of workers]. As our workers acquire broader intellectual capacities and as progress is made among us in the art of forming associations for honest and peaceful ends, when politics no longer becomes mixed up with the industrial associations and the government, reassured about their intentions, no longer refuses such groups its good will and its support, we will see them multiply and prosper. I think that in democratic centuries like ours association in all things must little by little replace the preponderant influence of a few powerful individuals.

The idea of associations of industrial workers seems to me, therefore, to be a necessarily fertile one, but it is an idea whose time has not yet come. For the present, remedies have to be sought elsewhere.

This leads Tocqueville to an examination of the workers' savings accounts permitted by the organization of savings banks.

These offered depositors an interest rate of four percent, when the rate of interest on money borrowed by the State was established by law at no more than two and a half or three percent. In Tocqueville's eyes, this system had drawbacks that would become more serious as the total of people's savings increased. It encumbered the State with an unproductive burden, and it did not offer the necessary guarantees to lenders who, in case of a political or economic crisis, could lose their capital if the State went bankrupt.

There was another agency, the pawn-offices operated by the State, where poor people could borrow on pledges in time of trouble, but where they paid an interest rate that amounted, in Paris, to twelve percent. This profit allowed the State to maintain hospitals and shelters for the poor—and by this means to make the poor pay for their own care. But it was the nation as a whole, that is to say the State budget itself, that ought to bear the cost. In Tocqueville's opinion, it would be possible to extend a system already in operation in the city of Metz to the rest of the country. In Metz, the savings bank provided capital to the pawn-offices, and a single administration ran both establishments. This administrative simplification made it possible to offer a five percent rate of interest to those loaning money to the State and to reduce the interest charged borrowers from the pawn-offices to seven percent. Only when the pawn-offices were supplied with capital by such means could the surplus of the people's savings be put to other uses. Tocqueville apparently planned to say what those uses were, but here his manuscript breaks off.

The origin of Tocqueville's second essay, *L'Etat social et politique de la France avant et après 1789,* is much better known. As we have mentioned, Mill had asked Tocqueville to work with him on the review he was founding, the *London Review,* which was to merge with the *Westminster Review* starting with its fifth issue and be known as the *London and Westminster Review.* In answer to Tocqueville's request for more specific information, Mill wrote on June 11 that what he had in mind was a collaboration whose terms and direction Tocqueville himself would decide, but Mill hoped Tocqueville would write a series of articles on the United States or France. On September 12, Tocqueville agreed to contribute to the review and suggested a series of articles "on France's political and social position." But in order to make sure the English public understood "the present state of our country," he wanted first to describe "what it was before the French Revolution broke out."

This depiction of the last days of the Ancien Régime actually did appear, but the sequel to it was never written. The finished manuscript was sent to England on February 10, 1836, translated under Mill's supervision, and published on April 1, 1836, in the *London and Westminster Review.* [43]

The heart of Tocqueville's analytical description of the life of French society on the eve of 1789 is the place occupied by the nobility. A collection of individuals who had lost their sense of solidarity, a class which, as such, no longer performed any real public function but continued to enjoy fiscal and honorific privileges and collect fees that

[43]*London and Westminster Review* 8, 137–69. The complete French manuscript has been reprinted in *O.C.* II, 1: 33–66.

had been established in feudal times, the nobility had been transformed
into a closed caste that hardly anyone could enter any longer except
by being born into it.

Confronting this class was the third estate, a new and rival group
that rubbed elbows with the nobility but did not mingle with it, whose
rise went hand in hand with the development of industry and commerce, from which the nobility were excluded by their prejudices. The
third estate grew richer while the nobility grew poorer, to the point
of liquidating a part of its landed fortune to the profit, in particular,
of a small landowning peasantry. These factors worked in favor of a
social democratization that had an influence even on the mentality of
the privileged: the *grands seigneurs* accepted a sort of make-believe
democracy of minds in which, in the realm of ideas, they associated
with literary men who might come from out of the commonalty. At
all events, against inequalities underwritten by law and tradition that
were becoming more and more of a fiction, the third estate preached
democratic principles.

Politically, the king proved to be their de facto ally. His jurists had
broken up the local bodies that were in the hands of the nobility in
order to establish an authoritarian and leveling centralization that did
not, however, go so far as to become despotic. But the traditional sense
of what liberty was had itself changed: it had once meant the tang of
independence for a particular social class, and now this aristocratic
conception had become the idea that each individual had a right to
liberty. This was a democratic idea—and, Tocqueville added, the
"just" meaning of liberty.

The Revolution was simply a violent process that developed the
seed of this idea, accelerating a mutation of the aristocratic society into
a democratic one, a transformation that affected all of Europe. It had
burst out first in France, because it was there that equality of conditions
was the most advanced, that centralization had made the most progress,
that opinion had most thoroughly systematized the new principle of
equality. But all of Europe was in labor—in a more or less confused
way—under the impulsion of similar movements, and for this France
was not so much the inspiration as she was, in a sense, the midwife.

The whole of this article was written in such a way as to convey
to the English reader how original French society was. The idea of the
transition from an aristocratic regime to a democratic regime was the
essential underlying notion, and it was this transition, with its different
modalities, that Tocqueville studied with such passion in England,
though in fact the problem troubled him practically all his life. He was

to resume his study of the origins of the French Revolution in more detail and depth twenty years later, but this rough draft already shows a knowledge of French society of the Ancien Régime whose sources are not easy to discern. Guizot's influence is undeniable: like Guizot, Tocqueville saw the Revolution as simply the dénouement of a conflict between the nobility and the third estate that led to modern society, and had the same view of the role of the monarchy, but he differed from his old teacher in that he believed feudalism had constituted a true social order, with shortcomings, of course, but also with guarantees of order and security.[44]

This essay was Tocqueville's one contribution to Mill's magazine. But he apparently did not want to break with Mill: when Beaumont, who was supposed to review Bulwer's book on France, did not come through, Tocqueville sent his reflections on his own reading so that they could be used.[45] It was thus the second part of the *Democracy* and his entrance into political life rather than any falling out with the English radicals that put an end to his contributions.

Tocqueville's third piece of writing between the two parts of *Democracy* was his *Deux Lettres sur l'Algérie,* published on June 23 and August 22, 1837, in a modest and ephemeral Versailles newspaper, *La Presse de Seine-et-Oise.*[46]

This was not his first sign of interest in the newly conquered territory. As early as 1828, he had been in favor of the Algerian expedition and had followed it eagerly, especially since his friend Louis de Kergorlay was taking part in it. In 1832, after his return from America, he took an interest in the first attempts at colonization. In 1833, he and Kergorlay even contemplated buying an estate in the Sahel and Tocqueville expressed the intention to learn Arabic.

In 1837, he thought of entering political life and presenting himself at Versailles in the legislative elections, so it is not very surprising that he should want to discuss this subject of current interest. Although his articles are not signed, an author's identity can easily be revealed to the small number of those qualified to be electors by their substantial tax assessments. In any case, as we have seen, he had not broken the connections he had made with Versailles society before he left for America, and he was a shareholder in *La Presse de Seine-et-Oise.*

[44]François Furet, *Penser la Révolution française,* particularly 173–82.
[45]These notes were published in *O.C.* II, 1: 318–24. Henry Bulwer's book, *La France sociale, politique et littéraire,* appeared in its French version in two volumes in 1834.
[46]*O.C.* III, 1: 129–53.

In the first of these articles, Tocqueville drew a picture of Algeria
on the eve of the conquest, described the country, distinguished carefully between the Kabyles—the Berbers of the coastal mountains—and
the Arabs (a distinction rarely made at the time), emphasized the
religious aspect of Arab society, and undertook an analysis of the
Turkish regime. In the second, after deploring the mistake made just
after the conquest in brutally eliminating the Turkish regime, he
showed himself to be in favor of an occupation that would be limited
but would control the country as a whole. He favored gradually
establishing commercial relations with the Kabyles without trying to
crush them militarily. He favored maintaining both the Arab tribes'
authority and the divisions among them, while leaving them their own
laws. At that time France had just signed the Tafna Treaty and was
on the point of taking Constantine. Tocqueville was worried about the
power France had recognized and confirmed in the young Abdel-
Kader, which would only be increased by the overthrow of the Bey
Ahmed at Constantine.

On the other hand, he had hopes for colonization. The Arabs
occupied the land in the plains in a very scattered way, so that there
was room for Europeans to settle between the tribes and farm the land.
He did not think it fanciful to believe that in the long run this
overlapping would give rise to a new people.

In these two articles, Tocqueville shows that he has a command of
precise information and a clear view of the Algerian problem. Though
he does not give his sources, one senses that he was aware of all that
was being published on the question. He also had information that was
more direct—certainly through Lamoricière, whom he had known
since 1828, and perhaps through a former intendant of Algeria, Genty
de Bussy, Royer-Collard's nephew.

We would be mistaking the significance of these three pieces of
writing to see them simply as occasional works. They were all connected to longstanding preoccupations in their author's life. His study
of poverty set forth, in part, the social program he would seek to
develop for a new party at the close of the July monarchy and that
he would propose in his speech on the right to work given in the
Constituent Assembly of 1848. The articles on Algeria were the first
manifestation of a concern that would be a constant of his political
career until 1851. And we have already pointed out the link between
L'Etat social et politique de la France and *L'Ancien Régime et la Révolution,* which appeared twenty years later.

Much more important, it is clear that none of these writings was

250
𝕸 𝕸

the manifestation of gratuitous curiosity, a mere pretext to avoid work on the *Democracy*. It was through a comparison with the conquest of America's land by the Europeans, which indirectly eased poverty in the Old World, that Tocqueville undertook his study of the remedies for poverty that might be found on a country's native soil. For France the danger of extensive poverty seemed less acute because, without her having to conquer new territories, a more general division of property into small holdings had limited the problem to the industrial proletariat, whereas for England, where large holdings of landed property were the rule, poverty would reach catastrophic proportions if it were not for that nation's worldwide commercial empire. At all events, the same question was raised by the situation in the United States, England, and France: Would industrial society prove the exception to the gradual equalizing of conditions? Tocqueville was also comparing the French conquest of Algeria to the situation in the United States: in Algeria there were new lands where a surplus of the French or European population could form a rural democracy like that in the West of America. Lastly, America was an example of a society which was democratic in its very origins, England presented the spectacle of a prolonged transition between an aristocratic society and a democratic society, and as for France, it had gone beyond that period of transition at a time and in ways that would have to be identified. In France, therefore, one could judge what might be new about the democratic world, and also how it resembled the old world—a third example of an intellectual quest that in fact constituted the germ of the author's work. He wanted to elucidate this in a series of "letters" promised to the *London and Westminster Review* and it is indeed unfortunate that he wrote no more than the prologue.

15

THE SECOND *DEMOCRACY*

THE *DEMOCRACY IN AMERICA* of 1835 took up, above and beyond the New World experiment, several problems of a more general nature linked to the advent of democratic societies. The author's deep concern with these problems became more and more apparent as one read on in the book. Nonetheless, his observations on the institutions and political life of America formed the book's main substance. In the second *Democracy,* which appeared in April 1840, observations on the mores and the mentality of the Americans occasionally serve as points of departure for generalizations about democratic societies; but often, through a sort of shifting of perspective, Tocqueville's abstract reflections on these societies make use of his remembrances of the United States as no more than illustrations of a particular line of reasoning. If we tally the amount of space that facts about America take up in the second *Democracy* as a whole, we see that they amount to only about twenty percent of the pages in the first three parts and two percent in the fourth.

Tocqueville's interpreters have often been disconcerted by this, as though in going from a study of the first *Democracy* to a study of the second they were leaving terra firma for shifting sands. One of the first of these was Major Guillaume-Tell Poussin. This French soldier, exiled in 1815, had worked as an engineer in the United States for twenty-one years. In 1841, he published his *Considérations sur le principe démocratique qui régit l'Union américaine,* in which he worked his way through Tocqueville's book chapter by chapter with the intention of teaching a lesson to this greenhorn who was judging a country he had

252
卍 卐
lived in for only nine months; when he reached Chapter 21 of Part 3 of the 1840 *Democracy*, "Why Great Revolutions Will Become Rare," Poussin stopped short. He found no more observations about America to correct, only general considerations that were beyond his competence.[1]

The titles of the four parts into which the 1840 volume is divided are somewhat deceptive in this respect: "Influence of Democracy on the Intellectual Movements in the United States"; "Influence of Democracy on the Sentiments of the Americans"; "Influence of Democracy on Mores Properly So Called"; "Influence of Democratic Ideas and Feelings on Political Society." Even in the parts whose titles refer expressly to America, the analysis bears on an ideal type of democratic society, which existed only in embryonic or imaginary form in 1840. It was not until Max Weber's work became widely known that people appreciated how original the second *Democracy* was for its time and saw in Tocqueville an admirable precursor of the great sociologist.[2] In constructing the democratic society that he proposes to us, Tocqueville borrows a good deal from the American Union, the only example then in existence of democracy in a large country, while endeavoring to separate the uniquely democratic features from traits particularly characteristic of the Anglo-Saxons. But he draws comparisons between the American actuality and the democratic tendencies that were beginning to appear in Europe. As it was in France that the progress of democracy was most marked, there are comparisons, often implicit, between America and France to support the author's conclusions, whereas in the first *Democracy* the natural parallel was between America and England, "Jonathan" being the emancipated and democratized son of John Bull—a parallel that reappears, logically enough, when he takes up in the 1840 volume certain aspects of mores or of manners.[3]

The point of view of the second *Democracy* is no less original than its structure. It thoroughly explores the new man of the egalitarian society, reveals his thoughts and the motivations for his acts, describes his relations with his fellow men, shows his free will grappling with

[1]G.-T. Poussin, *Considérations sur le principe démocratique qui régit l'Union américaine et de la possibilité de son application à d'autres Etats* (Paris, 1841).

[2]Max Weber, *Essais sur la théorie de la science* (Paris, 1965). On the ideas shared by Tocqueville and Max Weber, cf. Dorrit Freund, "Max Weber und Alexis de Tocqueville," *Archiv für Kulturgeschichte* 56, 2 (1974), 457–64.

[3]On the comparison of France and America, see J.-C. Lamberti, *Tocqueville et les deux démocraties* (Paris, 1983). On Tocqueville's relations with England, see Drescher, *Tocqueville and England*.

the new trends or the unfamiliar pitfalls of the new society.[4] This is where we find the underlying, anguished question that unifies the two parts of the *Democracy:* Will *homo democraticus* be a free man in his inner life and in his public one, and will he be able to carry forward the intellectual and moral progress that has characterized the Christian civilizations? Two kinds of approach, often linked, attempt to throw light on this large problem. One is a static, sociological analysis of the new society. The other is a diagnosis of the social ills that may develop, with an indication of the possible antidotes.

Nevertheless, everything is based on a fundamental postulate expressed in the introduction to the first *Democracy:* an irreversible movement of providence that was impelling Christian nations toward the equality of conditions. This movement was doing away with the structures and the guiding spirit of the societies which had succeeded one another in the West since antiquity and which had all—including the Greek democracies, with their slave labor—been essentially aristocratic.

This irreversible movement was thus the negation of an inegalitarian tradition whose roots went back to the time when mankind first abandoned the life of the savage. Now, the mark of every aristocratic regime was the fact that its inequality was established and sanctioned by the existence of privileges: a small group of powerful, rich, educated men stood out from the weak, poor, and ignorant mass. Society was based on the twofold idea of hierarchy and stability. And so it was that in the old France all men were joined together by a long chain, from the most lowly serf to the sovereign ruler, the inferior having the duty to obey his superior, the latter having the duty to protect his inferior. Each man's place was not only fixed at a given moment, but had been for a long time back, since each man inherited his status from his forebears.[5] This social order, doomed to disappear, was not by any means always based on force alone; it fostered human relationships of which Tocqueville seems to speak with some nostalgia, particularly in the chapter on the relations between servant and master:

[4]On the democratic man, see Pierre Manent, *Tocqueville et la nature de la démocratie* (Paris, 1982), chap. 6.

[5]J.-J. Chevallier, "De la distinction des sociétés aristocratiques et des sociétés démocratiques en tant que fondement de la pensée politique d'Alexis de Tocqueville," paper read before the Academy of Moral Sciences on April 23, 1956, *Revue des travaux de l'Académie des sciences morales et politiques, et comptes rendus de ses séances* 109 (1956), 116–36.

In aristocratic societies, not only are there hereditary families of valets, as there are of masters, but the same families of valets are settled for generations with the same families of masters (they are parallel lines which never meet and never separate); and that makes prodigious modifications in the mutual relations between the two orders.

Thus, though under an aristocracy there is no natural resemblance between master and servant, though fortune, education, opinion, and rights set them at great distance apart on the ladder of existence, yet time in the end binds them together. Long-shared memories unite them, and however different they be, yet they grow alike.[6]

In the aristocratic society, the inferior man could thus come to identify his own destiny with that of his superior, and the superior, through an "excess of egoism," to consider the inferior as an ancillary extension of his own person.

But in such a society a nation was broken up into classes and castes each of which had its own rules, its virtues and its vices. Thus the "great ones" obeyed a code of honor peculiar to their caste alone, one that could lead them to perform deeds of extraordinary heroism.[7]

If Tocqueville's heart was sometimes filled with longing for this past greatness, his reason showed him that the morals of the castes were so limited in range that they became inhuman. He cited the example of Madame de Sévigné, tender with her own people, lenient toward her vassals, and yet inclined to make atrocious jokes about the repression, by hanging and the wheel, of the Breton farmers who took part in the stamped-paper riot.[8]

Democracy, then, broke the chain of the hierarchical bonds and in a sense laid the links down on the ground, one beside the other. Men regained their social mobility, they became free and equal. They received these natural rights through a historical process in which providence continued its work of creation with the collaboration of men. God's unfathomable justice imposed greater equality among men, but left to them the business of organizing the society on which He had imposed that fundamental principle. In Tocqueville, then, there is none of that sense of a determinism imposed by the past epochs of human history that one finds in Comte, or of a dialectical movement implacably regulating society's development. Man, through the free

---

[6] *O.C.* I, 2: 187. *Democracy,* 574.

[7] *O.C.* I, 2: Part III, chap. 18, and correspondence between Tocqueville and Kergorlay in 1838, *O.C.* XIII, 2: 12–18.

[8] *O.C.* I, 2: 173–74. *Democracy,* 563–64. See also the discussion of this example with Ampère in 1839, *O.C.* XI, 128–30.

will enlightened by reason that he retains, is able to exercise moral
choice within the confines that fate traces around him.

By taking up in the initial chapter of the second *Democracy* the way
in which man exercised his reason in the new society—"the philosophical approach of the Americans"—Tocqueville made clear the orientation of his entire work.

The citizen of the United States, Tocqueville noted, put no trust in
anything, when it came to making judgments, but the individual effort
of his own reason. This "unconscious Cartesianism" was not a specifically American phenomenon, but rather a democratic one. When
conditions were equal, no one valued another's judgment more than
his own. And the progress made in freedom of thought between the
sixteenth and the eighteenth centuries had gone hand in hand with the
progress of democracy. "This method was discovered at a time when
men were beginning to grow more equal and more like each other.
It could not be generally followed except in centuries when conditions
had become more or less similar and people like each other."9

The phenomenon had its own dangers. First and foremost, these
judgments by individual men, most of whose activity was taken up
with material occupations, were inevitably superficial. They were
content with general, attractively simple formulas. Tocqueville denounced, for example, the temptation offered to such minds by panthe-
ism, a unitarian doctrine which, to his mind, confused the creator and
the creation, and which could only result in a suppression of free will.

Furthermore, no single individual's judgment could be applied to
the entire realm of knowledge. No more than man in general could
a man in a democratic society have convictions based solely upon his
own reason concerning everything that mattered to the human condition. He might resist accepting anyone else's judgment, but he would
later go along with the opinion of the majority, which had, in his eyes,
the strength of numbers. One could arrive by such a path at the tyranny
of the majority that Tocqueville had denounced in his 1835 volume.
On the other hand, general opinion could be of benefit when it was
that of a religion, for all religions imposed "duties toward mankind."
Here we again encounter ideas Tocqueville sketched out in 1835: the
Christian religions, especially Catholicism, laid down for their members certain moral obligations toward mankind and thereby drew them
away from purely selfish concerns. Tocqueville went so far as to say
of man in a democracy: "If he has no faith, he must obey a master,

9*O.C.* I, 2: 13. *Democracy,* 431.

256

灰 災

and if he is free he must believe."[10] But if it was to be credible, a religion like Catholicism would have to purify itself of secondary observances and superstitions and reduce its dogma to the essentials. This was an astonishing piece of prescience, at least where Catholicism was concerned. The immediate development of the Church was in the opposite direction, and it was not until the twentieth century that it made an about-face.

The intellectual level of a democratic society could be deduced from the state of its sciences, arts, and letters. In the first of these areas, Tocqueville observed that Americans were more interested in practical applications than in disinterested research. He refrained from inferring from this that in the end progress would come to a stop in democratic society and the society would go into a decline:

> Not only will the number of those who can take an interest in things of the mind be greater, but the taste for intellectual enjoyment will descend step by step even to those who in aristocratic societies seem to have neither time nor ability to enjoy them.
>
> When there is no more hereditary wealth, class privilege, or prerogatives of birth, and when every man derives his strength from himself alone, it becomes clear that the chief source of disparity between the fortunes of men lies in the mind. Whatever tends to invigorate, expand, or adorn the mind rises instantly to a high value.[11]

There will thus be a broader segment of society interested in scientific questions, and within it one will find men inclined to devote themselves to theoretical studies. Tocqueville adds: "I believe in scientific vocations." But such men will have to be encouraged and not allowed to go to waste; otherwise, Christian civilization would in time become immobilized just as Chinese civilization had. This social encouragement for disinterested research appears to have been a new idea.

For a deeper understanding of Tocqueville's thoughts on the arts in a democratic regime, it would be very useful to know something about his aesthetic notions. He was not at all indifferent to the arts, and had studied architectural styles when he was young. Unfortunately, his *Voyage d'Italie,* which was his main text on this subject and contained his impressions of monuments and museums, is lost. We therefore

[10]*O.C.* I, 2: 29. *Democracy,* 444.
[11]*O.C.* I, 2: 44–45. *Democracy,* 457–58.

cannot throw light upon his remarks in the second *Democracy* by 257
referring to other texts. 近近

In an aristocratic society, Tocqueville wrote, the artist worked for
a very small and very rich clientele. He could aim for perfection. In
a democratic society, he had to produce at low prices and increase his
production. For the palaces of the great *seigneurs,* the architect would
substitute country houses like those on the outskirts of New York,
where the white-painted brick and the wooden columns of the porticoes endeavored to give the impression of marble. A host of elegant
little pictures would replace the large canvases created for the residences of the *seigneurs.* The spirit of art would also change: Raphael
attempted to evoke the human soul, David wanted to reproduce the
human body in a realistic way.

Nevertheless, the democratic state had built grand public buildings,
raised colossal monuments. Tocqueville had been very struck by the
sight of Washington, with its Capitol, its grand avenues, and the spaces
still unfilled of a capital city conceived for the future, whose population in those days was no greater than that of Pontoise.

One subject that Tocqueville did not take up was that of music in
a democratic society, even though it was a topic of particular interest
in that year, 1840, when Berlioz was to celebrate the anniversary of
the July days in Paris with hundreds of instrumentalists and choral
singers performing his *Symphonie funèbre et triomphale.* But it would
be a mistake to conclude from this that Tocqueville did not care for
music: he admired Mozart's *Don Giovanni* and knew Rossini's operas.[12]

He did endeavor to point out the new tendencies in the literature
of a democratic society. Here the example of America was not useful,
since America was still too dependent on English literature. Those
commentators who have tried to see him as a "prophet" of the American literature of the future (he appears to have known little of that
of his own time) seem to us to have misunderstood the essence of these
pages.[13]

Tocqueville tried to define the new tendencies in oratory and theater, and pointed out the birth of an industrial literature—a problem
that had also preoccupied Sainte-Beuve—but his most suggestive chapter, it seems to us, is devoted to the evolution of poetry.

The poetry of aristocratic times obeyed fixed rules and attached

[12]Tocqueville-Kergorlay correspondence, *O.C.* XIII, 1: 82–83.
[13]K. Harrison, "A French Forecast of American Literature," *South Atlantic Review* 25 (1925), 350–60.

great importance to form. The poetry of democratic times no longer cultivated style for its own sake. Style was a means of attracting public attention, by showing itself to be "strange, violent, incorrect"; in any event, it had the boldness to break with established traditions. And the old sources of inspiration had gone dry: mythology, the intervention of supernatural beings, the evocation of the past, the depiction of great destinies outside the common condition. But new sources were springing up: the love of nature, in Tocqueville's eyes a transitory taste, and, more important, man himself, "not tied to time or place, but face to face with nature and with God, with his passions, his doubts, his unexpected good fortune and his incomprehensible miseries." These were the great qualities of the human heart that the new literature would magnify: Tocqueville cited as examples *Childe Harold, René, Jocelyn.* [14]

This preoccupation with the relations between literature and society was not at all new at the time; to cite only men of the generation before Tocqueville's, it was shared by Guizot, Villemain, Chateaubriand, and Fauriel. The great initiator in this realm had been Madame de Staël, and it is hardly possible that Tocqueville was unfamiliar with *De la littérature considérée dans ses rapports avec les institutions sociales.* However discreet he may have been about acknowledging his sources, and with *L'Ancien Régime* twenty years later bearing traces of the *Considérations sur la Révolution française,* we can only be surprised that he almost never mentioned in writing Madame de Staël's name.

However that may be, the chapters on literature in the second *Democracy* hardly demonstrate the indifference that has sometimes been gratuitously attributed to Tocqueville where the literature of his time is concerned.[15] If he himself mentions Byron and Lamartine, he also had Schiller and Goethe in his library. What he contrasts, roughly, under the name of aristocratic literature and democratic literature, are classicism and romanticism. It has been noted, quite rightly, that he betrays some nostalgia for a clear, orderly literature and for the precise language of the eighteenth century. But, as he himself said, one only becomes attached to what is alive. Now, he was aware that the living literature was romanticism, which was adapted, in his eyes, to a democratic society. Although he repudiated certain of its excesses and agreed with Beaumont that Hugo was an "unruly genius," he admired Lamar-

---

[14]*O.C.* I, 2: Part I, chap. 17. *Democracy,* 482–87.

[15]The source of this accusation is Antoine Rédier. R. Virtanen has shown definitively how his sketch of an ideal literature revealed that he himself had read the romantic literature; see R. Virtanen, "Tocqueville and the Romantics," *Symposium* 13, 2 (1959), 167–85.

tine as the greatest French poet of their time. And the idea that the
destiny of man would henceforth be the source of all poetry was
expressed in the preface to *Jocelyn:* "The interest of the human species
is drawn to the human species itself," because man had learned "that
he was only an imperceptible part of an immense and interdependent
unity, that the work of his perfecting was a collective and natural
work,"[16] a phrase one can find echoed in Tocqueville: "Seeing the
human race as one great whole, they [the writers of the democratic age]
are led to recognize in the actions of each individual a trace of the
universal and consistent plan by which God guides mankind."[17] Other
examples no doubt influenced Tocqueville just as much, including,
probably, Quinet's *Prométhée.* Tocqueville may have been thinking of
Lamartine and Quinet when he expressed his concern over the panthe-
ist tendencies of the democratic age. But the opposition between
classicism and romanticism was a topic of conversation in the salons
of the Empire and the Restoration, of which Tocqueville would
always retain radiant memories. He himself emphasized, in his conversations with Senior, the fervor with which new literary works were
discussed in his family circle. It would be a distortion of the reality
to think that Tocqueville was altogether absorbed by political questions before his departure for America.

This notion of an opposition between aristocratic and democratic
literatures had its weaknesses. For Tocqueville, the last state of classicism was the French eighteenth century; it would be difficult to find
a place for the *Sturm und Drang* there; Tocqueville seems unaware of
the strains of fantasy and legend so characteristic of German and even
French romanticism.[18] Following his mind's natural bent, he envisaged
the practical consequences of the tastes of the new society which he
had noted. It would be dangerous, he thought, to impose a classical
education on men of democratic times "for the state of politics and
society would always make them want things which their education
had not taught them how to earn, and they would trouble the State
in the name of the Greeks and Romans."[19] But alongside the great
battalions of those who would receive a scientific, commercial, and
industrial education, a small group belonging to the literary elite

[16]Lamartine, *Jocelyn*, prefatory note to the first edition, included in the Garnier edition (Paris, 1960),
xxviii.

[17]*O.C.* I, 2: 80. *Democracy*, 486.

[18]On this subject see H. N. Fügen, "Demokratie und Literatur, Literatursoziologie bei Alexis de
Tocqueville," *Kölner Zeitschrift für Soziologie und Sozialpsychologie* 17 (1965), 106–18.

[19]*O.C.* I, 2: 68. *Democracy*, 476–77. See also the article by M. Bressolette, "Tocqueville et la culture
universitaire," *Etudes* 332 (January 1970), 5–13.

260

㞢 㞢

would have to "master the ancient literature perfectly." And Tocqueville adds this astonishingly lucid reflection: "A few excellent universities are a better means to this end than a multitude of bad schools in which the classics are an ill-taught extra, standing in the way of sound instruction in necessary studies."

The first part of the 1840 *Democracy* was a sociological picture of the level of learning within a democratic society. The second, which explored sentiments and passions more directly, led to the fourth, which dealt with their intrusion into political life. But between these parts was inserted a more static picture of the "mores properly so called" in a democratic society. Strangely enough, the construction of the book reminds one of a classical sonata in which two slow movements are each followed by a fast movement.

The third part is a sociological study of relationships in a democratic society: relationships within families, and those between landowners and tenants, employers and workmen, masters and servants.

Within the small society of the family, the democratic spirit breaks up the subordination of children to their parents based on respect and sometimes fear. As soon as the children come of age, these ties are loosened, and they make decisions for themselves. This, within the small society of the family, is an emancipation analogous to that of the citizen in a city that restores to each individual his natural rights. "Relations between father and sons are more intimate and gentle."[20] Far from creating anarchy in family life, the democratic society gives it a more human quality, which is also true of relations between brothers, because of the suppression of the privileges of the firstborn and the shared interests that result from this; attachments are therefore based on "common memories and the unhampered sympathy of thoughts and tastes."[21]

As we have seen, Tocqueville was sometimes nostalgic for the aristocratic society, and his preference for the democratic society was sometimes purely intellectual; but head and heart agreed in preferring the new family, the advantages of which were so obvious that aristocratic circles hostile to democracy allowed themselves to be won over by the natural and human aspects of its affective foundations.

He also admired the freedom of young American women, so ex-

[20]*O.C.* I, 2: 203. *Democracy*, 587. See also P. Manent, *Tocqueville et la nature de la démocratie* (Paris, 1982), 100–101.

[21]*O.C.* I, 2: 204. *Democracy*, 589.

traordinary compared to the situation of their contemporaries in France. This freedom allowed marriage to be based on the mutual attraction of the future husband and wife, and Tocqueville generally showed himself to be hostile to the negotiations which, in France, resulted in the subordination of intimate human feelings to considerations of family lineage and patrimony.[22] In all this, Tocqueville's own experience supported his general formulations.

But he remained hostile to an emancipation of the woman that would make her the equal of the man. There was a natural division of tasks that should be respected. In America, the woman, in consenting to be married, also agreed to be cloistered in her home and to be pure in her morals, according to the norms of Puritan morality and a society devoted to commerce. Here Tocqueville seems to come close to praising bourgeois respectability in the Victorian style!

Outside the family circle, aristocratic societies saw their relationships governed by the social caste to which an individual belonged. In the democratic society, individual affinities tended to create intimate circles of friends that were often no more than merely an extension of domestic life.

Yet within this society as a whole, where considerable social mobility was the rule, there were many ambitious people seeking to raise themselves above their condition. But because of the very fact of competition they did not find it easy to raise themselves high:

When great fortunes have been divided up and education has spread, no one is absolutely deprived of either education or property. When both the privileges and the disqualifications of class have been abolished and men have shattered the bonds which once held them immobile, the idea of progress comes naturally into each man's mind; the desire to rise swells in every heart at once, and all men want to quit their former social position. Ambition becomes a universal feeling.

But equality, though it gives every citizen some resources, prevents any from enjoying resources of great extent, and for this reason desires must of necessity be confined within fairly narrow limits.[23]

This striving after small goals made democratic society both "agitated and monotonous," but at the same time conservative and an

[22]Thus, in a letter from America that has not yet been published, he cut short a matrimonial negotiation engaged upon, in his name, by his friend Kergorlay.
[23]*O.C.* I, 2: 251. *Democracy,* 629.

enemy of revolutions. Aside from bringing with it somewhat gentler mores, democratic society weakened those who supported revolutions, who had always been among either the very poor or the very rich. There might be poor people in a democratic society's midst, but they were not united "by bonds of an irremediable misery," and the rich, for their part, were "scattered and powerless." The middle class, made up of modest landowners, of merchants, of industrialists, formed the most numerous class, and it was this class that clung the most tenaciously to its bit of wealth and most feared the upheavals that a revolution would bring in its train.[24]

Social mobility that stops short of real upheaval was a feature specific to the democratic society. It resulted directly from the dominating passion which caused *homo democraticus* to act, as Tocqueville expresses it at the beginning of the second *Democracy*: "The first and liveliest of the passions inspired by equality . . . is love of that equality itself." This sentiment was not, like that of liberty, one that couldbe found in certain men in every period and in every civilization —it was the distinguishing mark of democratic societies: "Do not ask what singular charm the men of democratic ages find in living as equals or what special reason they may have for clinging so tenaciously to equality rather than the other advantages society offers. Equality forms the distinctive characteristic of the age in which they live. That is enough to explain why they prefer it to all the rest."[25]

Man in the aristocratic society could forget himself in his devotion to his superior or his protection of his inferior. The man of democratic times no longer had anyone about him but his equals, other creatures like himself, and quite naturally he was then most interested in himself. Democratic society encouraged individualism. "Individualism is a calm and considered feeling which disposes each citizen to isolate himself from the mass of his fellows and withdraw into the circle of family and friends; with this little society formed to his taste, he gladly leaves the greater society to look after itself."[26]

The very goals of human life were transformed by this. In the aristocratic society, rich and influential men concerned themselves quite naturally with public affairs without having to worry about the stability of their fortunes. The masses, with no hope of bettering their material situation, obeyed the powerful men placed above them. These

---

[24]*O.C.* I, 2: Part III, chap. 21, "Why Great Revolutions Will Become Rare." *Democracy*, 634–45.
[25]*O.C.* I, 2: 102. *Democracy*, 504. See also Manent, *Tocqueville et la démocratie*, chap. 6.
[26]*O.C.* I, 2: 105. *Democracy*, 506. See also J.-C. Lamberti, *La Notion d'individualisme chez Tocqueville* (Paris, 1970).

social ties were relaxed in the democratic society: similar, autonomous men competed with one another. They could aspire, not to great social power, but to an improvement in their material situation. The taste for material well-being, characteristic of the middle classes, then took hold of all members of society. But, since equality was never entirely realized because of differences in natural talents or the effect of circumstances, social mobility was accompanied by an anxious desire for success and by an uneasy envy of one's neighbor. Paradoxically, the man who aspired to well-being could be led to endure astonishing privations, like the merchant seaman who was willing to sail his ship in the most strenuous conditions so that he could sell a pound of tea for a penny less than his competitor. For it was hard to go very fast in this race for wealth in which so many men were taking part: "When men are more or less equal and are following the same path, it is very difficult for any of them to walk faster and get out beyond the uniform crowd surrounding and hemming them in."[27]

Benjamin Constant had already pointed out that in modern societies, as opposed to ancient societies, private affairs were becoming a greater preoccupation than public affairs.[28] He had seen this as evidence of the increased freedom for individuals in these societies. Tocqueville was much more pessimistic about the social dangers that could result from this competitive isolation of the citizens and their consequent depoliticization. He considered once more the antidotes he had studied in America: the religious spirit, which deflected man from his single-minded concentration on material enrichment; the spirit of association and all that it implied; the freedom of the press, which created new bonds within community life; the doctrine of self-interest properly understood, which associated the fecundity of private activity with the healthy functioning of the State and replaced the virtues of the "great ones" of earlier days with a morality that was less lofty but more useful for the middle classes. He would take up the problem again more amply in the last part of his book, after examining along the way two more particular dangers that could also threaten the new societies: the birth of an aristocracy created by large-scale industry, and the danger within the very heart of democracy posed by the presence of an army.

The evolution toward equality of conditions, such as Tocqueville conceived it, improved the lot of the farmer and the worker and raised them to the condition of free contracting parties with the landowner

---

[27]*O.C.* I, 2: 144. *Democracy*, 537.
[28]Benjamin Constant, *De la liberté des anciens comparée à celle des modernes* (Paris, 1819).

and the employer. Yet in England, particularly in Manchester, he had seen factories employing hundreds of workers in which the distance between the owner and his workers had, on the contrary, increased. In the *Democracy,* he gives an explanation of this phenomenon, which went hand in hand with the increased proportion of industrial goods and the diminished proportion of agricultural products in the total production of the country:

It is acknowledged that when a workman spends every day on the same detail the finished article is produced more easily, quickly, and economically.

It is likewise acknowledged that the larger the scale on which an industrial undertaking is conducted with great capital assets and extensive credit, the cheaper will its products be.[29]

While the worker, in his specialized task, acquires habits of mind and body which, by rendering him incapable of any other employment, attach him to his particular job and immobilize him in the midst of widespread activity, the employer looks out upon an increasingly vast horizon. One resembles "the administrator of a vast empire" and the other "a brute beast," and between them a link is forged that resembles those of the aristocratic society.

Tocqueville sought to demonstrate that such links were nevertheless different from those of the aristocratic societies of earlier days. The class of employers was unstable and did not form an organized body, the workers were not subject to the authority of a single man but rather to the owners of a factory, and they regained their freedom when they left the factory. But Tocqueville no longer proposed as a future remedy the workers' associations that he had suggested in his *Mémoire sur le paupérisme.*

This development of large-scale industry, which was proceeding in a direction contrary to that of the social development he had posited, worried him. He wanted to be able to determine its social dimension. But, as was very often true, the prediction he ventured was colored by uncertainty and doubt:

I think that, generally speaking, the manufacturing aristocracy which we see rising before our eyes is one of the hardest that have appeared on earth. But at the same time, it is one of the most restrained and least dangerous.

In any event, the friends of democracy should keep their eyes anxiously

[29]*O.C.* I, 2: 164. *Democracy,* 555. The most precise exposition of Tocqueville's thought on this subject can be found in the as yet unpublished part of his *Mémoire sur le paupérisme.*

fixed in that direction. For if ever again permanent inequality of conditions   265
and aristocracy make their way into the world, it will have been by that door   ⚶ ⚶
that they entered.[30]

Yet democratic societies harbored another danger, the presence of
an army. The situation of American democracy, which had no dangerous neighbors, was special in this respect. However pacific a democratic
society might be in Europe, it had to think of its defense, and it
therefore would have to have an army.

Now, in an aristocratic society the army was easily integrated into
the social structure: the nobleman was an officer, the soldier a bondman
whose trade it was to bear arms. What counted for the officer was not
his rank in the army but his position in civilian society, and the esteem
this position inspired was carried over into military society. In a
democratic society, essentially pacific, the army was not well liked. The
soldier called up from civilian life for his tour of active duty often
remained alienated from his military job. The officer was generally a
proletarian who had no other resources than his pay and no other
prospect than that of promotion. This promotion, for which competition was lively, was based on seniority alone in time of peace. The
regular army officers, commissioned and noncommissioned, thus hoped
for war because, although it involved risks, it also offered the chance
of rapid promotion. This desire was most intense among the noncommissioned officers, whose new role and direct influence on the soldiers
Tocqueville stressed, struck perhaps by memories of the armies of the
Revolution but also by the events of August 1836 in Spain, which he
had followed closely, where the regent had had to yield to an ultima-
tum delivered by noncommissioned officers.[31] This dangerous and
paradoxical role of the small military society within the great democratic society thus constituted a real danger, whether the army rose up
in revolt or—a more probable, indirect threat—led the nation into a
war whose consequence could be the restriction of individual freedoms. Tocqueville did not point out any specific remedy other than
to inculcate good citizenship in the regular army cadres.[32]

But the democratic society, by its very nature, carried within it the
seeds of a much more pernicious evil. It placed modern man at a
crossroads: "Two tendencies in fact result from equality; the one first
leads men directly to independence and could then suddenly push them

---

[30]*O.C.* I, 2: 167. *Democracy,* 558.
[31]Tocqueville left notes on the events in Spain which are included in the *O.C.* III, 2.
[32]*O.C.* I, 2: Part III, chaps. 22 and 23. *Democracy,* 645–54.

right over into anarchy; the other, by a more roundabout and secret but also more certain road, leads them to servitude."[33]

Tocqueville declined to give much attention to the risk of anarchy. It was, all in all, merely the excess of a good thing, that of insinuating "deep into the heart and mind of every man some vague notion and some instinctive inclination toward political freedom."[34] He was pleased to find democratic society "indocile." The greatest evil that fear of anarchy produced was the panic of orderly people, who would throw themselves into the arms of authority, resigning themselves to the loss of their freedom.

For by his own testimony it was for the sake of enlightening his contemporaries about this danger that Tocqueville had written his second *Democracy*. The pictures he painted of the life and mores of a democratic society and the analysis he made of men's motivations in a democracy were oriented toward this end. In the last part of his book he summed up and brought together these characteristics in order to warn more explicitly of the threat of despotism.

Centralization was the step that led to despotism, and centralization was consistent with egalitarian societies. Older societies had also known despotism, of course. To demonstrate this, it was enough to recall the arbitrary tyranny of the Roman emperors. But the peoples subjected to that tyranny preserved the diversity of their customs even down to the lowly power of the *municipium,* which retained its authority in the local sphere. Indeed, every aristocracy was characterized by the complexity of the ties between men, a complexity which gave rise to autonomous bodies and secondary powers. Democratic society, on the other hand, set the individual man, weak and isolated, in opposition to the powerful State. And this man's egalitarian cast of mind, his tendency to oversimplify, led to State centralization. At the time of his second trip to England, Tocqueville had been struck by the fact that many of the English radicals saw nothing but a private bailiwick of the aristocracy in the local institutions that he considered the guarantors of freedom.[35] If this could be the case during a nonviolent revolution in a country where freedom was of long standing, what would happen in countries where equality had been established before freedom? Napoléon, when he organized administrative centralization in France, had followed the line of least resistance. The consequence

[33]*O.C.* I, 2: 295. *Democracy,* 667.
[34]*O.C.* I, 2: 296. *Democracy,* 668.
[35]See his conversation with Lord Minto, *O.C.* V, 2: 52–53.

of centralization was uniformity of the laws, which applied to every- 267
one. It made the work of government easier and won over the support ꗥ ꗥ
of the great mass of the citizenry. Of all the lessons of the French
Revolution, this was the one that the sovereigns of Europe remembered, because it permitted them to reinforce their authority.

But it also permitted a considerable extension of the powers of the
state. The citizen of a democratic society was loath to ask help of his
fellow men, preferring to turn to the State, and the modern State had
a sphere of action that extended far beyond those prerogatives that the
aristocratic State, together with its secondary powers, had possessed:

I assert that there is no country in Europe in which public administration
has not become not only more centralized but also more inquisitive and
minute. Everywhere it meddles more than of old in private affairs. It controls
in its own fashion more actions and more of their details, and ever increasingly takes its place beside and above the individual, helping, advising, and
constraining him.[36]

Everything taking place in Europe not only sped this progress toward
equality, but also reinforced the power and the range of authority of
the State.

The movement toward centralization occurred, as we have said,
with the complicity of the citizens, and their complicity, though it was
not responsible for that change, permitted its harmful effects. No doubt
homo democraticus had aspirations to independence. But this desire for
freedom was thwarted by the kind of life he led and by his tastes: "In
times of democracy private life is so active and agitated, so full of
desires and labor, that each individual has scarcely any leisure or energy
left for political life."[37] His love of comfort also made him avoid the
troubles and frustrations of political life and gave him, as his dominant
political passion, a liking for public tranquillity. He was therefore
prepared to accept a strong central power. A caricature of this would
be the regime of Muhammad Ali, a despot who ruled over the
egalitarian society of the fellahs of Egypt and had turned the country
into his private factory and the inhabitants into his workers. The new
kind of despotism that could be established in Europe would be, on
the contrary, benevolent and gentle. But it would undertake and
succeed in carrying out great material works as it pared down the

[36]*O.C.* I, 2: 313. *Democracy*, 682.
[37]*O.C.* I, 2: 300. *Democracy*, 671.

human person, and through this would become anemic, though only in the long run. Tocqueville describes the new despotism in a famous passage:

I am trying to imagine under what novel features despotism may appear in the world. In the first place, I see an innumerable multitude of men, alike and equal, constantly circling about in pursuit of the petty and banal pleasures with which they glut their souls. Each one of them, withdrawn into himself, is almost unaware of the fate of the rest. Mankind, for him, consists in his children and his personal friends. As for the rest of his fellow citizens, they are near enough, but he does not notice them. He touches them but feels nothing. He exists in and for himself, and though he still may have a family, one can at least say that he has not got a fatherland.

Over this kind of men stands an immense, protective power which is alone responsible for securing their enjoyment and watching over their fate. That power is absolute, thoughtful of detail, orderly, provident, and gentle. It would resemble parental authority if, fatherlike, it tried to prepare its charges for a man's life, but on the contrary, it only tries to keep them in perpetual childhood. It likes to see the citizens enjoy themselves, provided that they think of nothing but enjoyment. It gladly works for their happiness but wants to be sole agent and judge of it. It provides for their security, foresees and supplies their necessities, facilitates their pleasures, manages their principal concerns, directs their industry, makes rules for their testaments, and divides their inheritances. Why should it not entirely relieve them from the trouble of thinking and all the cares of living?[38]

The danger of the establishment of despotism, even if not imminent, was "formidable" in Tocqueville's opinion. It increased when an egalitarian society was established by a violent or prolonged revolution. In this case, the two contradictory tendencies of the democratic spirit came into play one after another. First to appear was the spirit of independence which brought about the destruction of the aristocratic society but proved itself, in doing this, to be more turbulent than truly liberal. Then, once the aristocratic privileges were destroyed, lassitude descended on the new society and it yielded to the other tendency, the desire for a strongly centralized social power. This was the recent history of every country in Europe.

Through a sort of natural inclination whose danger was masked from the citizens of a democracy by the "lack of attention" that characterized them, the egalitarian societies would slip toward despo-

[38]*O.C.* I, 2: 324. *Democracy,* 691–92.

tism. To cause freedom to prevail side by side with equality in such societies could therefore be only an "effect of art"—a deliberate, reasoned undertaking.

For Tocqueville, it was not enough, in establishing a liberal society, to dress up a centralized administration with a government drawing its power from popular sovereignty. This was at the same time an inadequate palliative and an unstable compound. What was necessary, above all, was to arouse the attention of the entire citizenry and make them aware of a danger which in the long run would threaten their own interests. To do this it was necessary to organize associations, to institute absolute freedom of the press, to provide for the direct election of local officials, and to awaken the religious conscience. All these remedies, whose usefulness Tocqueville had witnessed in America— less threatened by despotism than Europe because it had neither experienced a violent social revolution nor attained equality before attaining freedom—should be appropriate ones in a democratic Europe free of the spirit of revolution, a stage that Tocqueville then considered all but achieved.[39]

Racial, climatic, or historical determinism were so many "cowardly doctrines" in Tocqueville's opinion. He declared that he would not have taken the trouble to write his book if he had not believed that it was possible for man, in his freedom and with his powers of reason, to deal with the grave dangers to society that he had diagnosed. As he wrote at the very end of the second *Democracy*, "Providence . . . has drawn a predestined circle around each man beyond which he cannot pass; but within those vast limits, man is strong and free; and so are peoples."[40]

The fundamental question of the second *Democracy* remained that of the first: Was it possible to maintain human freedom in an egalitarian society? But the range of the second book was broader, its conclusions more universal, its analysis of passions deeper and tied with greater care to the human condition. Through his reading of Pascal and Rousseau, to whom he had returned in the years since 1835, Tocqueville had reflected more deeply on the nature of man and of human societies. Furthermore, he was better acquainted with England thanks to his trip there in 1835, and he had become familiar with the day-to-day problems of politics during the early stages of his parliamentary career.

[39]On Tocqueville's opposition to Guizot in this regard, see Lamberti, *Tocqueville et les deux démocraties.*
[40]*O.C.* I, 2: 339. *Democracy,* 705.

270

㸚 㸚

On certain important points, his thinking had changed. He no longer identified democratic despotism solely with the tyranny of the majority. It could also be incarnated in a man or be the moving force behind an anonymous state organization, for Tocqueville now saw the link between democracy and centralization, having drawn conclusions from his observation of the new tendencies in English society. He was also struck, more and more, by the significance of the European revolutionary tradition and the years of upheavals it had engendered. It was this tradition that led people to want order at any cost, out of their fear of anarchy. When added to the desire for comfort and to the individualistic spirit created by equality of conditions, it prompted the citizen to withdraw from political life and live within a circle of family and friends, preoccupied with his own private concerns. It was this withdrawal of the individual from political life, more than the pressure of the fanatical masses, that risked bringing on tyranny and the very paralysis of civilization itself. The entire book is a warning against this danger, a struggle upstream against the strong currents of history, and because of this the second *Democracy* often takes on a darker tone than the first.[41]

Tocqueville's health had already begun to decline by 1835, and it may be that his frequent attacks of gastritis and his bad liver heightened his irritability and pessimism.[42] Nevertheless, the goal of the book remained the same: to awaken France's conscience and continue her civic education. A hard task for a young philosopher brought up in the political seraglio who was unable to conceive of the possibility that some electors might not know the name of the prime minister—harder, perhaps, than combating the crude sectarianism of the extremists!

Since 1836 he had been returning frequently to his compatriots in Lower Normandy, to whom he was attached by sincere and enduring affection. He was filled with a determination, by no means an immodest one, to restore his family's paternalistic tradition, to respond to a call of duty first sounded several centuries before. Royer-Collard, his mentor since 1835, failed to recognize the depth and seriousness of this feeling, and with all the pride of a bourgeois intellectual saw in it only banal ambition. Tocqueville surely had no illusions about his fellow Normans. This was how he described them in a letter of June 23, 1838: "These people are honest, intelligent, fairly religious, passably *moral*,

[41]See Seymour Drescher, "Tocqueville's Two *Democracies*," *Journal of the History of Ideas* 25 (April–June 1964), 201–16.

[42]See Schleifer, *The Making of Tocqueville's Democracy in America*.

very orderly. But they are rarely disinterested. The egoism in this part
of the world is a gentle, peaceful, stubborn sense of one's own best
interest that gradually absorbs all other feelings."[43] And Royer-Collard answered him: "Your *Normans!* They are France, they are the
world. This prudent and intelligent egoism—these are the 'good people' of our time."[44] After his book was published, Tocqueville would
expand on the same subject in another letter to Royer-Collard.[45]

Despite his disillusionment, Tocqueville wrote in 1840 that the
age of revolutions, the great obstacle to the establishment of any
legal and liberal democracy, was about to end (his study of the political parties would soon reinforce the general statement he made on
this subject in the chapter of his book entitled "Why Great Revolutions Will Become Rare"[46]) and the task of construction could begin
(he would have lost that illusion by the time he wrote his *Souvenirs!*). Meanwhile, the book he presented to the public was a peculiar
one in its complex structure and the subtlety of its content. People,
even some of the critics who had praised the first *Democracy* so enthusiastically, found it disconcerting. Three examples of the response
seem to us characteristic of the perplexity and incomprehension in
cultivated circles.

As we know, Villemain had written a laudatory account of the first
Democracy, and the young author had at that time sought his literary
patronage. He reviewed the second *Democracy* in the *Journal des savants*
in May. The first *Democracy,* he wrote, had applied the method of
Montesquieu to America, the second analyzed the mores of democracies in general by means of an abuse of the philosophical method.
And Villemain challenged a number of Tocqueville's "subtle analyses":
that the Americans had a literature different from that of the English,
that they had more general ideas than the latter, that the deformation
of the English language in America was anything other than a phenomenon of aging, that poetry under a democracy had certain specific
characteristics (here he referred to Aristophanes and Milton), that there
were similar customs throughout the whole of the Union, and so on.
Almost his only praise of Tocqueville concerned the latter's fear of the
warmongers (in which Tocqueville's thought complemented Montes-

---

[43]*O.C.* XI, 64.

[44]Letter dated July 21, 1838, *O.C.* XI, 66.

[45]*O.C.* XI, 89–92. On the relationship between Tocqueville and Royer-Collard, see Lamberti, *Tocqueville et les deux démocraties,* vol. 2, 489–500.

[46]This study of the political parties, which appeared in a series of articles in *Le Siècle* in 1843, is
included in *O.C.* III, 2: 95–121.

272

业 业

quieu's) and his having shown that "sovereign power as it increases does not become more secure." This was, indeed, the "affliction of our time." In sum, Tocqueville had dealt with America the way the Church dealt with sacred history, treating it simultaneously as object and as symbol, which made one feel "something of the fatigue that one's eyes feel when they try to look at two separate things at the same time."[47]

Pellegrino Rossi, whose review of the first part of the *Democracy* in the May 21, 1835, issue of the *Journal de l'Instruction publique* had pleased Tocqueville, reviewed the second part in the *Revue des deux mondes*. He harked back with praise to the first part, in which the author had understood that a new principle was transforming the world. In the second part, he said, one searched in vain for such positive conclusions. Whence the "letdown" experienced by the reader. Tocqueville had "opened his hands" too generously to the effects of his principle. His analyses were no doubt sometimes profound, but he should be discussing America more as a historian than as a philosopher; besides, it was America that was moving toward Europe, and not the opposite. For Rossi, democracy was not equality of conditions but equality of rights, which had nothing to fear from individualism.[48]

Sacy's review of the book in the *Le Journal des Débats* did not appear until October 9, 1840. If earlier reviews had only grasped part of the book's underlying conception, Sacy purely and simply misunderstood it. For him, the work attempted to show that American democracy was the prototype of the democracy France would one day have. France would not accept these selfish and utilitarian ways; democracy in France would always be military. But Tocqueville had not shown the current that was pushing France toward democracy, and Sacy ended by praising the established systems of taxation and election that severely limited the size of the electorate. Finally, he apologized for attacking the "suffocating" book of an author whose talent and character he admired.

This last article irritated Tocqueville. The family archives have preserved a draft of a letter which he may not have sent:

I have just received, Monsieur, the issue of *Le Journal des Débats* containing your article on my book. I cannot help expressing to you the painful

[47]Abel François Villemain, "De la *Démocratie en Amérique* par Alexis de Tocqueville," *Journal des savants* (May 1840), 257–63.

[48]Pellegrino Rossi, "De la *Démocratie en Amérique*," *Revue des deux mondes* 23 (September 15, 1840), 884–904.

impression it has made on me. It does not do justice to the most important point, the principal idea, the governing thought of the work, and justice on that point I expected from you above all, Monsieur.

I had become aware that, in our time, the new social state that had produced and is still producing very great benefits was, however, giving birth to a number of quite dangerous tendencies. These seeds, if left to grow unchecked, would produce, it seemed to me, a steady lowering of the intellectual level of society with no conceivable limit, and this would bring in its train the mores of materialism and, finally, universal slavery. I thought I saw that mankind was moving in this direction, and I viewed the prospect with terror. It was essential, I thought, for all men of good will to join in exerting the strongest possible pressure in the opposite direction. To my knowledge, few of the friends of the Revolution of 1789 dared point out these very frightening tendencies . . . Those who saw them and were not afraid to speak of them, being the sort of men who condemned in one fell swoop the entire democratic social state and all its elements, were more likely to irritate people than guide them. The intellectual world was thus divided into blind friends and furious detractors of democracy.

My aim in writing [my] book was to point out these dreadful downward paths opening under the feet of our contemporaries, not to prove that they must be thrown back into an aristocratic state of society . . . but to make these tendencies feared by painting them in vivid colors, and thus to secure the effort of mind and will which alone can combat them—to teach democracy to know itself, and thereby to direct itself and contain itself.[49]

This letter, which we have quoted at length because it defines with clarity the idea that is the key to his book, shows how deeply Tocqueville was affected by the lack of understanding that greeted it. We do not know if he wrote to Villemain and Rossi, but we would not be surprised if his occasional outbursts of ill-humor toward both of these men in later years did not have their source in old hard feelings. Nevertheless, Tocqueville himself had doubts about the value of a book that did not win over the great public. He expressed these doubts in a letter dated August 25 to Royer-Collard, in whose judgment he then had great confidence:

I very often receive responses to the book that I value highly because of the persons who address them to me. But I cannot hide from myself the fact that the book is not much read and not well understood by the great public—by that I mean great in numbers. This silence afflicts me. It gives rise to painful thoughts concerning myself. I ask myself if there is indeed any

[49]Unpublished letter, Tocqueville Archives, file 5.

274

艾 艾

value in this work. I am often driven to doubt it and this doubt leads me to ask myself if I ever did have the ability that people saw in me. For it is not conceivable that a man of some ability could spend four years of his life writing a book without merit.[50]

Royer-Collard, who was rereading the book slowly, responded by both expressing the personal esteem in which he held this "prodigious effort of meditation and patience" and pointing out the causes of the misunderstandings between author and public: "There is not one chapter that could not be different in certain respects from the way you have done it. That, of course, is because of your intention. You set out to imagine, to invent rather than to describe, and invention, within certain limits, is arbitrary." It was in fact Tocqueville's construction of an "ideal type" of society that above all disconcerted his contemporaries.

In England, however, Tocqueville's reputation was solidly established, something rare in those days for a French writer. The very day that Gosselin published the second part of *Democracy in America*, on April 20, it was published in London in Reeve's translation. John Stuart Mill, whose article on the first part of the *Democracy* had appeared in the *London Review*, devoted a long study to the entire book in the October 1840 issue of the *Edinburgh Review*. Since 1835, Tocqueville and Mill had been close friends. Mill, who had already been influenced not only by his father and by Jeremy Bentham but also by the French Saint-Simonians, was attracted by Tocqueville's thought and his method. Students of Mill do not agree on how deep Tocqueville's influence was during these years, and relations between the two men would cool around 1842 after their divergence of opinion on political issues. But Mill's article in 1840 marked the high point of their friendship.

John Stuart Mill saw Tocqueville's book as the first great work of political philosophy devoted to modern democracy. He considered the second part to be of greater significance than the first because it studied human nature in greater depth and because it was ahead of its time. He was in complete agreement with the author on the irresistibility of the movement that was leading the Western world toward equality of conditions, and found that Tocqueville confirmed his own intuition that the democracies of the future would be threatened not by anarchist revolutionary movements but by an ultraconservatism that could arrest

[50]*O.C.* XI, 92–93.

the progress of civilization. He described and attempted to pin down or isolate Tocqueville's ideas concerning the tyranny of the majority and the mediocrity of statesmen in the American democracy. If he said nothing of the social role of religion, about which he certainly disagreed with Tocqueville, he was particularly intent on discussing the prevailing influence of the democratic spirit on attitudes and mores. He himself summed it up as the spirit of the middle classes and was struck by the role of the merchant class as a driving force in modern societies. He thought it was necessary to counterbalance this role through the action of other classes. But despite Mill's reservations, the "governing idea" and the significance of Tocqueville's book appeared to have been perfectly understood. After reading Mill's study, Tocqueville allowed his joy to burst forth: "Of all the articles written on my book, yours is *the only one* in which the author mastered my thought perfectly and was able to display it to others . . . At last I saw myself judged by a very elevated mind that had taken the trouble to penetrate my ideas and subject them to a rigorous analysis."[51] And he added that he was having Mill's article bound in with a copy of the book.

If the second *Democracy in America* had nothing like the success of the first, Tocqueville's image in the eyes of the great public suffered only slightly. A political writer could allow himself to be boring, so long as he appeared serious and profound. Thus, the public did not read him, but felt it was legitimate that his honorable works should win him a place in the Academy. Even though he was affected by his book's partial failure, this was not what turned Tocqueville aside from pursuing a writer's career. Already, in a letter dated November 20, 1838, to Royer-Collard, he had made it clear that he intended to stop writing:

I don't think I'm deceiving myself . . . when I say that nothing has been or is more contrary to my inclinations than to assume the position of an author in the world. That is entirely opposed to my way of judging the things that matter in this life. My firm wish, therefore, after this book is finished, and whatever its fate may be, is to work for myself and not to write for the public anymore unless a very important and *very natural* occasion for doing so presents itself, which is unlikely.[52]

Tocqueville did not have to spell out to Royer-Collard that one of the "things that matter in this life" for him was a future as a politician.

[51]*O.C.* VI, 330.
[52]*O.C.* XI, 74.

276

处 处

Royer-Collard knew it already and spoke ironically of the haste his disciple showed in undertaking a political career. In Alexis's family, there were at least two examples of cases in which the publication of books had made it easier for their authors to enter public life. His cousin Molé's *Essais de politique et de morale* had been read and appreciated by Napoléon, who brought him into the Council of State, and Chateaubriand's *Génie du christianisme* had made him a diplomat. The electors themselves sometimes found it an honor to choose a writer: Lamartine was selected by the electoral college of Béthune because of his works of poetry. How could *Democracy in America*, whose conclusion outlined the guiding principles of a statesman's program, fail to promote its author's career?

What was more, by the time the second *Democracy* appeared, he had already taken the first step. In March 1839, he had been elected deputy from Valognes. We therefore have to backtrack a little to find the starting point of the twelve years in which most of Alexis de Tocqueville's activity was taken up with parliamentary life.

Part III

THE DEPUTY
FROM VALOGNES

16

THE START OF

A POLITICAL CAREER

EVEN IN THE LAST YEARS of the Restoration, when he was still in his early twenties, Alexis de Tocqueville could not conceive of fulfilling his personal destiny in any other way than by active participation in political life. The strength of the family tradition and his father's example set his course in that direction, and so did his own passionate intellectual concerns. There was hardly any distinction for him between his view of himself and his view of the ways in which individuals of his rank had been shaped by France's history in the years since the Revolution. A sort of private dialogue went on between Tocqueville and France, one that in later years he occasionally made public in his speeches in the Chamber (which won him a few gibes and gave him a reputation for being proud). In his innermost being there was an irreducible blend of personal ambition and an aristocratic morality inspired by or inherited from the "great ones" of the past.

Before 1830, his prospects for a career as a statesman were too remote and too uncertain for him to count on it.[1] Comte Hervé had been raised to the peerage, but Hippolyte was the one who would someday inherit the title and the duties that went with it. A younger son had no other recourse than to enter the Chamber of Deputies after gaining an electoral district. Since the Charter of 1814 had fixed the age of eligibility at forty, he would have to champ at the bit until 1845, resigning himself to a career as a magistrate while he waited. Neverthe-

---

[1]We can find occasional unobtrusive traces of the ambitions Tocqueville and Beaumont shared, especially in their early correspondence (for instance, in the letter dated October 25, 1829, *O.C.* VIII, 1: 91–96).

less, sensitive as he was to the passing of time, for the moment he took up the study of politics, with the expectation that a clearer understanding of the great political issues would do much to inform his actions as a statesman. The trip to America made the realization of his hopes possible.[2] The experience he acquired there, together with his writings —quite aside from their bringing him fame—permitted him to enter upon a legislative career better prepared than his contemporaries.

The July revolution had been, among other things, a reaction against gerontocracy. The Charter of 1830 lowered the age at which one was eligible to enter the Chamber to thirty,[3] and this meant that after July 1835 Tocqueville could stand as a candidate for election. Now, *Democracy in America* had appeared in January of that year and had been very successful, as we have seen. Its author was torn between the desire to continue his political studies and the wish to exploit, as soon as possible, a success that would facilitate his entrance into the political world.

Furthermore, the law of June 21, 1833, had made the departmental councils elective, opening a breach in that Napoleonic system of centralization that Tocqueville abhorred. He was not prepared to be a candidate in the general election of 1834, being in the midst of writing his book, but with the new election of one-third of the councillors in October 1836 he thought he might present himself as a candidate for election to a cantonal college, which could be a step toward candidacy in a legislative election. His cousin Le Peletier d'Aunay, who was his mentor at that time along with Royer-Collard, advised him to do this and seems to have made inquiries about a district in the Seine-et-Oise. Tocqueville was also thinking of a canton in the arrondissement of Cherbourg, in the Manche, and asked the advice of the deputy from that arrondissement, Bricqueville, who was Hippolyte's brother-in-law. He gave up the idea after the death of an influential elector who was inclined to support him.[4]

The year 1837 promised to be particularly important. The July monarchy was then at its zenith. It had emerged victorious from the conspiracies that had until then threatened it and cast a shadow over it, and an orderly representative regime seemed to be establishing itself

[2]On the fact that the plan was one of long standing, see above, p. 90.

[3]Article 38 of the Charter.

[4]Unpublished letter from Le Peletier d'Aunay, in the Tocqueville Archives, file 18; unpublished letter from Tocqueville to Bricqueville, ibid., file 72; letter from Tocqueville to Corcelle dated September 26, 1836, *O.C.* XV, 1: 75. Letter to Beaumont dated October 16, 1836, *O.C.* XIII, 1: 108. Unpublished letter to Hervieu dated October 25, 1836 (private collection).

under a firmly entrenched dynasty. The marriage of the Duc d'Orléans   281
to the Princesse Hélène of Mecklenburg seemed to be a good sign for
the future, and the king made it the occasion for granting amnesty to
his political enemies and then inaugurating with great pomp and
ceremony the museum of the Château de Versailles, which symboli-
cally reconciled the glories of the old and the modern France. Comte
Molé, the prime minister, would have liked to take advantage of this
time of euphoria to dissolve, at the end of the regular session, the
Chamber elected in 1834. Everyone was awaiting this decision, which
was delayed by Louis-Philippe's tergiversations. It was not until October 3, by which time the opposition was again gaining strength, that
the king made up his mind to convene the electoral colleges for
November 4.

Alexis de Tocqueville had been on tenterhooks since the spring. He
ardently wished to enter the Chamber, but wanted to be elected
without sacrificing his independence vis-à-vis either the parties or the
government. His cousin the prime minister, whom he encountered
often in the salon of the unofficial "Madame Prime Minister," the
Marquise de Castellane, had great respect for him and, apparently, a
sincere affection. Molé was too subtle to treat this young and easily
offended relative simply as a protégé. His minister of education, Salvandy, a very kind man known for his extreme vanity, hardly had the
same feeling for nuance. He thought to please Tocqueville by including him in the list of those named to the Legion of Honor that was
published on the occasion of the royal marriage.[5] Tocqueville was in
good company—also honored were Hugo, Musset, Sainte-Beuve,
Alexandre Dumas, and Michelet, among others.

Tocqueville, nevertheless, was furious that they had "put this rag
in my buttonhole" and accepted it only on the advice of Le Peletier
d'Aunay and Royer-Collard.[6] He was particularly concerned that it
would be thought he had solicited the favor. He was further enraged
when he saw his name in Le Moniteur among those invited to the
inauguration banquet for the Versailles museum, at which thirteen
hundred guests were to assemble in the presence of the king. The
sub-prefect of Cherbourg started the rumor that Tocqueville had sent
a medical certificate to get out of going and that he was boasting to
right and left—to both Carlists and revolutionaries—about the fact
that he had not gone. Tocqueville forced him to make a public

---

[5]This list of appointments appeared in the June 7 Moniteur. Salvandy had been a friend of Tocqueville's
since his review of the Democracy in Les Débats.
[6]Letter from Royer-Collard, O.C. XI, 32–33.

282
死 死

retraction by threatening to challenge him to a duel, and the sub-prefect made his retraction in a rather craven fashion.[7]

At that time, multiple candidacies were possible. Although in the end Tocqueville ran from only one district, he began or allowed others to begin for him electoral campaigns in four different districts. Two of them had connections with his past, Versailles and the faubourg Saint-Germain, where he had lived until he married, and the other two marked the recent return to his Norman origins that we have already described.

Tocqueville had maintained relations with Versailles society and continued to participate from a distance in the efforts of a few men—mainly doctors, lawyers, and teachers—to create an autonomous intellectual life there. It was men like these who, perhaps at the instigation of Tocqueville himself, decided, in May, to try to send Tocqueville to represent Versailles in the Chamber. One of them, the philosopher Bouchitté, had been connected with the Tocqueville family very early on. In 1837, his brother-in-law, Baudry de Balzac, started a thrice-weekly newspaper called *La Presse de Seine-et-Oise* and Tocqueville, who was a shareholder, published in it the studies of Algeria discussed earlier.[8] The deputy from Versailles, Jouvencel, a rather colorless middle-of-the-road man, had been in office since 1827; but he was growing old and no longer excited much enthusiasm among the electors; it was only with the administration's support that he had been elected in 1834. There was no shortage of liberal candidates in Versailles—a lawyer, a councillor to the prefecture, a deputy mayor, and a pharmacist—and they seemed to be jealous of one another and to cancel one another out. Someone coming from outside and professing a moderate liberalism thus had a good chance. There was a fundamental weakness, however, in putting Tocqueville's name forward: his supporters were intellectuals who did not pay enough tax to qualify as electors.[9]

Most important, one would have to gamble on two uncertainties. The first, whether it was possible to bring together the liberal bourgeoisie of the *quartier* Notre-Dame and the legitimists of the *quartier*

[7]The most detailed account of this little affair can be found in an unpublished letter to Hervieu dated July 4, 1837, to which is attached a copy of Tocqueville's letter to the sub-prefect.

[8]See above, pp. 248–50.

[9]Most of the information about this Versailles candidacy can be found in the Tocqueville Archives, files 12, 17, 18, and 74.

Saint-Louis, who remained faithful to the memory of Comte Hervé 283
and would vote for his son. But the *quartier* Saint-Louis had lost most
of its nobility now that Versailles, since 1830, had become a town like
any other, and Blosseville, who sounded out its intentions where
Tocqueville was concerned, felt that it was not well disposed. The
second uncertainty was whether one could obtain the support of the
prefect for a candidate who chose to remain independent. This prefect,
d'Aubernon, had no anti-Carlist bias; he feared, however, that once
elected, Tocqueville would "vote with Berryer," the legitimist orator
who defended liberal causes. He kept wavering about this candidacy,
and quite understandably, too: it is always unpleasant to fall out with
a recently founded newspaper, and one had to be especially prudent
when a candidate who was not put up by the government was the
beloved cousin of the prime minister, Molé, and of the vice-president
of the Chamber of Deputies, Le Peletier d'Aunay, both implanted in
the department, one in the splendid residence at Champlâtreux, the
other at Mareil. Molé had toyed with the idea of elevating Jouvencel
to the peerage, which would have left a clear place open, then decided
not to. Baudry de Balzac condemned the instability of d'Aubernon's
character, but it seems more likely that the man deliberately muddled
the matter, while remaining unfailingly polite.

When a decision had to be made, in October, d'Aubernon declared
that it was too late for the author of the *Democracy* to be a candidate.
A meeting of the liberal electors on October 31 did not confirm the
candidacy, and Balzac forced himself to keep his mouth shut because
he was not an elector. Tocqueville himself had lost hope, and when
he was asked for an electoral proclamation he evaded the request. On
November 4, 1837, Jouvencel won easily against his opponent, the
liberal lawyer Deschiens.

We know about Tocqueville's candidacy in the 10th arrondissement
of Paris mainly from the letters that Beaumont, who stayed in the
capital from the beginning of September to about the twenty-fifth of
October, addressed to his friend in his house in Normandy. Unfortunately, we do not have Tocqueville's replies.[10]

The 10th arrondissement included the faubourg Saint-Germain and
part of the Latin Quarter. The electoral body was a mixture of resident
aristocrats and men belonging to intellectual circles or the liberal
professions—judges, publishers, lawyers, and the like. Gosselin,

[10]*O.C.* VIII, 1: 230–55.

284
死 死

Tocqueville's publisher, was a "big wheel" in the quarter, and, despite his middle-of-the-road persuasion, seemed ready to push to get one of his authors into the Chamber. In this arrondissement, where legitimism coexisted with the various shades of the opposition—from moderate liberalism to democratic republicanism—the author of a fashionable book could win over the voters of the left, whereas one could hope that the legitimists, "who did not read," would put their trust in his family name. By the end of August, the preliminary maneuvering for this candidacy had begun, with Tocqueville not wanting to be personally involved. The committee of the left that existed then, or at the very least Barrot, seems to have supported this candidacy, but it was Taschereau most of all who endeavored to win prominent figures to the cause. He continued to do this when, the republicans having infiltrated the committee, Barrot withdrew from it, along with the dynastic opposition, to give place to Garnier-Pagès. Tocqueville enjoyed the firm support of *Le Siècle* and Chambolle, and the more reticent, though nevertheless occasionally effective, support of Léon Faucher at the *Courrier français*. [11]

This newspaper posed the problem clearly in its October 11 issue:

We were surprised, yesterday, to see that the city of Paris, which, under the Restoration and in the early period of the July revolution, included in its Chamber the most eminent men representing the nation, has now consented to draw its deputies from lists of unknown names. We are happy to learn that independent electors from the 10th arrondissement of Paris intend to put forward M. Alexis de Tocqueville, author of the fine book *Democracy in America*. The reputable character of M. Alexis de Tocqueville, his great talent as a writer, which has revealed him to be a distinguished interpreter of public affairs, the lofty morality of his doctrines, mark him, for all shades of the constitutional opposition, as a fit candidate to bring them together. M. de Tocqueville is not in the least a party man, he is a man of eminent merit who should be in the Chamber, and the city of Paris will do itself honor in sending him there.

At one point, Tocqueville's candidacy seemed to be taking shape and Victor Lanjuinais, who was a candidate in both this arrondissement and in Brittany, withdrew in his favor. Toward the middle of October, Tocqueville was the only opposition candidate, whereas there were six

[11]Tocqueville and Beaumont condemned Faucher's unstable character. But the latter did not control the newspaper: he had to contend with the influence of Chatelain. See François-Adolphe Chambolle, *Retours sur la vie* (Paris, 1912).

government candidates. But the electors of the 10th arrondissement had more specific requirements than many of the provincials. Not only did they want the assurance that once elected the candidate would accept his mandate but, even more important, they wanted a specific political program from him. Tocqueville, who had done no more than have his electoral circular, addressed to the electors of Valognes, published in *Le Siècle* and *Le Courrier* of October 23 and 25, could not hope to rally the liberals without appearing on November 1 at a scheduled meeting in the School of Medicine, where a number of candidates would describe their programs. At least this is what he wrote to Taschereau on October 17.

By that time, Tocqueville was placing his hopes more and more in the district of Valognes. What he now had to do, therefore, was to use the Paris event to impress the electors of that humble sub-prefecture. Which was the point of the news item published in *Le Siècle* on October 23:

The candidacy which many electors of the 10th arrondissement of Paris had offered to M. Alexis de Tocqueville was gaining numerous votes every day, but since the arrondissement of Valognes (Manche) seemed determined to send the author of *Democracy in America* to the Chamber, he decided, despite the fact that the hope of representing the city of Paris was a flattering prospect, that his duty was to his compatriots. This determination, which is for M. de Tocqueville yet one more claim to their sympathy, leaves it to the electors of the 10th arrondissement to make a new choice.

In the end, a government candidate, Laurent de Jussieu, won in the 10th arrondissement after three rounds of voting. He was the secretary-general of the Seine prefecture, but his name carried some weight with the cultivated public. The liberal vote went to Adrien Lamy, a judge at the Seine tribunal and former mayor of the arrondissement, who obtained only 454 votes as against 590 for Laurent de Jussieu.

There is almost no doubt that from the very beginning Tocqueville attached more value to being a deputy in the Cotentin than in Versailles or even Paris, though the latter tempted him because he would have been entering politics through a large door. There, he was motivated by his eagerness to get ahead; in Normandy, he was completing the return to his origins that he had begun two or three years before.

The château and the village of Tocqueville are situated in the valley of the Saire river, fifteen kilometers east of Cherbourg; the arrondissement of Cherbourg was his home district, and the "natural" one for him to represent in the Chamber.

Its deputy at that time was the Comte de Bricqueville, who in 1834 had won by only eleven votes over his opponent Quénault. Bricqueville belonged to the dynastic left, and was one of those "liberals" still dazzled by imperial times.

He came from an old Norman family and his father had been guillotined. But when he was seventeen, in 1802, he had entered the Ecole Militaire at Fontainebleau and then served practically everywhere, it seems, under the Empire—in Prussia, Spain, Russia. In 1814, when he was a colonel of the lancers, he and his men replaced the Prussian escort accompanying Louis XVIII upon his return, but he resigned his commission immediately afterwards out of hatred for the Bourbons. During the Hundred Days Bricqueville served again, distinguishing himself at Ligny, fighting until the very end in the region of Paris. He had married Coralie de Belisle, sister of Emilie, the wife of Hippolyte de Tocqueville. A letter from Hippolyte to Hyde de Neuville shows that he had tried to induce the latter to stand as a candidate against his brother-in-law. Bricqueville, on the other hand, respected Alexis's character and opinions. Suffering from old wounds, crippled by gout, he promised Alexis he would try to see that he succeeded him in the Chamber and there is no question of his sincerity.

But this succession was in danger. Ever since his defeat by such a narrow margin in 1834, Quénault had been relentlessly kneading his electoral dough. The son of a priest and a nun, he was one of those lawyers who were able to take advantage of the opportunities offered by the 1830 revolution to enter public office. He rose rapidly, and his success would continue. He was a judge in the Seine tribunal in 1830, a department head in the Ministry of Justice in 1833, and in 1837 first rapporteur and then a councillor in the Council of State. He belonged, of course, to the government majority. His most important weapon was corruption. A local newspaper, *Le Pilote de Calvados,* asserted that in the electoral campaign of 1837 he had promised more school scholarships and more posts as justice of the peace than there were in all of France. His only vulnerable point was that at each administrative promotion he was legally required to present himself again before the electoral body. In the end, the electors grew tired of him, and in 1841 Bricqueville returned to the Chamber—more ailing than ever—after a campaign in which Tocqueville had even written his circular for him. Very shortly afterwards, Quénault returned to the Chamber representing Coutances. He was the object of the most sustained political hatred

of Tocqueville's career. The friendship of several years' duration between Tocqueville and Havin, the deputy from Carentan who was one
of the leading figures in the dynastic opposition, had its origin in their
mutual detestation of Quénault.

In June, thinking of withdrawing, Bricqueville began introducing
Tocqueville to the influential electors.[12] Tocqueville apparently made
a good impression on the bourgeoisie of Cherbourg, a circle of lawyers, businessmen, and magistrates who were not insensitive to the fame
of their compatriot and who asked for copies of the *Democracy*—a sign
of culture and seriousness. But the rural electors, the majority, had
prejudices that were very difficult to overcome.

The Carlist members of Tocqueville's family were highly visible;
doubts concerning Alexis's sincerity were kept alive by the distribution
of extracts from the petition on behalf of the Duchesse de Berry and
from his address to the Montbrison court of assizes in defense of Louis
de Kergorlay—two stock items that, until 1848, were brought out
every time he stood as a candidate. And then Quénault's dependents
were everywhere, people for whom he had done favors and especially
those who were expecting favors from a man so well placed in the
government. On September 15, Bricqueville brought together what
amounted to a veritable electoral general staff: Langlois and Sainte-
Colombe, who were members of the departmental council; the doctor
Moulin, mayor of Bricquebec; Clamorgam, soon to be appointed a tax
collector, from Valognes. These were men who before long would
become Alexis's effective supporters. But at this meeting they decided
it was preferable for Bricqueville to take his chances in the election—
that Tocqueville in his place might win votes from Cherbourg's mid-
dle-of-the-roaders, but that he would lose more rural votes than he
could gain in the city. The next day, Bricqueville wrote to Tocqueville, expressing his regret that Tocqueville could not have been present at the meeting, since he would have witnessed the very real respect
which the elite among the electors had for him, but adding something
that all the evidence seems to confirm:

"Little chance for me, less for you. If we lose, we will have upheld
our principles.

"If we are victorious and you are defeated in Valognes, all chances
increase for you, and I withdraw."

Tocqueville was certainly rather put out by this and suspected

[12]The negotiations over the Cherbourg candidacy can be followed through letters that have been
preserved in the Tocqueville Archives (most of them in file 14). Supplementary information can be found
in the correspondence with Beaumont and in the unpublished letters to Hervieu and Langlois.

Bricqueville's wife of scheming. But he yielded to the facts and decided to gamble on his entrance into the Chamber from the district of Valognes alone, where he had also prepared the way for himself.

In this district, the deputy elected in 1834, who was presenting himself as a candidate again, was Comte Polydor Le Marois. He lived five kilometers to the south of Tocqueville, but to the north of the arrondissement of Valognes, near the town of Vicel, in the sumptuous Château de Pepinvast. His father, former aide-de-camp to Napoléon at Arcole and at Austerlitz, had won renown for his defense of Magdeburg in 1814. The year before, he had left his luxurious residence for a gloomy granite mausoleum near the church and cemetery of Vicel. Comte Polydor enjoyed a very great fortune in land, a fortune which, if one is to believe Tocqueville, originated in the rich booty brought back from Germany in the wagons of the imperial army. No one dreamed of pretending that the deputy from Valognes had any intellectual resources. Nevertheless, he had methods of action that were effective under a regime in which the electors were moneyed men: first of all, his fortune itself allowed him to entertain the electoral body at his own expense and gave him great prestige even among people who did not profit from his generosity (such prestige that Tocqueville felt obliged to deposit with a notary, where people could consult them, proofs that he had an income of about twenty thousand francs a year and was therefore not poor!); he had, too, a hearty personal warmth and a strong stomach that allowed him to spend hours banqueting under the marquee during large fairs, as well as a wily and unscrupulous astuteness that we will soon see in action.[13]

For Tocqueville, running against Le Marois, who had voted with the dynastic opposition against the Molé government, was a ticklish business. The committee of the left in its first form, along with Barrot, supported candidates who opposed the government, and in Valognes Tocqueville had to deal with the influence of people now against him who would have supported him in Cherbourg against Quénault and who had come out for him in the 10th arrondissement of Paris. The administration, on the other hand, was looking for a candidate to present against Le Marois. It could have made do with the Baron de Plaisance, third son of the ex-consul Lebrun, a native of Saint-Sauveur and owner of the Château de Chiffrevast. But this retired major was

---

[13]Léon Deries, "Une élection dans l'arrondissement de Valognes," *La Révolution de 1848* 12 (1915–1916), 132–44. See also Charles Pouthas, "A. de Tocqueville représentant de la Manche (1837–1851)," in *Alexis de Tocqueville; livre du centenaire (1859–1959)* (Paris, 1960), 17–32.

not very energetic. He consented to publish an electoral circular whose conformism delighted Mercier, the prefect, who was a model of obedience to the Ministry of the Interior, but he did not bother to spend much time with the electors. He was not the man to win back the district.

Alexis de Tocqueville might be that man. His cousin Molé, who said he wanted to see Alexis in the Chamber even if he had to vote against him every day, saw fit to order the prefect to see that his candidacy was discreetly supported by the civil servants. Aside from the fact that this support risked alienating the independent electors, Tocqueville wanted to enter the Chamber without obligations. On September 12, he complained to Molé about this indiscreet help: "I want to be in a position to conduct a free and independent campaign and I would not be able to do this if I had myself proposed by the government." Molé answered with some irony that in an electoral campaign armies were drawn up under two or three banners and one had to enlist under one of them. He contested the distinction Tocqueville had made in his letter when he wrote that he was appealing to M. Molé as friend and cousin rather than as president of the Council of Ministers. Tocqueville replied with a vehement letter in which he said that he was giving up the illusions he had had about Molé's affection. Molé wrote back that he had been trying to treat Tocqueville "like a son" but that he would do what Tocqueville wanted.[14]

The government would perhaps have remained neutral in Valognes if Le Marois had not taken action on his own account. He went to Paris at the beginning of October and obtained an appointment with the minister of the interior, Montalivet, an old school friend. He acknowledged his opposition in the past, which he attributed to his father's dissatisfaction with the government, and promised that in the future he would stand firmly behind the minister and follow his directions. This maneuver won him the support of the prefectorial administration on the spot, and the more grudging support of the sub-prefect of Valognes, Eugène Clamorgam. He already had the support of the district tax collector of the sub-prefecture, who was his uncle. By keeping his move a secret, he counted on being the government's candidate without ceasing to be that of the opposition as well.

But his calculation was frustrated. At that time, François Buloz, who was the editor of both the *Revue des deux mondes* and the *Revue*

---

[14]Molé's letters are in the Tocqueville Archives. Some of Tocqueville's are published in the *Oeuvres* (Bmt) VI, 74 and 77. See also the amusing story of the meeting of Beaumont and Madame de Castellane, *O.C.* VIII, 1: 235–37.

290 *de Paris,* was being given some financial support by the government,
﴾ ﴿ and, during a conversation with the secretary-general of the Ministry
of the Interior, Edmond Blanc, was told in confidence what Le Marois
had done. Buloz, as Beaumont noted, had his own peculiar way of
keeping secrets. On October 8, he printed the following news item in
the *Revue de Paris:*

We have been hearing stories of those former deputies who, home again
after the dissolution of the Chamber and thinking their reelection imperiled
by their all too frequent votes with the left, have taken the Paris stage in haste
to entreat the Ministry not to leave them out of the government's broad plan
of reconciliation. One in particular came to our notice recently whose name
we will not mention (a name well known in the imperial general staff). It
was impossible not to be a little surprised to see him in Paris at a time when
he was supposed to be hard at work as a provincial candidate, not far from
Cherbourg, busily winning over his electors. But it appears that he had first
to make his peace here. Having made it, he went back home feeling quite
secure but enlisted now under a different banner.[15]

The October 21 issue of *Le Siècle* passed on this news with reservations, and Le Marois felt compelled to respond. He acknowledged that
he had made the visit, but in a very sheepish piece of writing endeavored to challenge the political consequences ascribed to it. All of this
certainly made a bad impression on those electors of Valognes who
read the papers and sought to form their own opinion. Clearly, starting
from this moment, a small but powerful group attached itself to Alexis
de Tocqueville.

However, Le Marois turned his father's fame to advantage by un-
veiling a statue of the general on July 15 in Bricquebec's place du
Marché. There was a parade of the finest companies of the National
Guard of Valognes, a large banquet with a speech by the sub-prefect,
and a light show.

One element of these electoral contests was the publication of
circular letters. The one from Lebrun de Plaisance was rather colorless,
the one from Le Marois concentrated especially on the protection of
Norman animal husbandry against foreign livestock. Tocqueville's
elevated the level of debate. Fully accepting the institutions now
established, he would defend existing liberties against all attacks and
guide France along progressive paths within the framework of the
Charter of 1830, rejecting revolution altogether. But someone calling

[15]*Revue de Paris* 46 (October 8, 1839), 199.

himself an elector who signed his pamphlets "Anonymous"—identified to Tocqueville as a man named Bertrand (who was to write Tocqueville after the election saying that he had been slandered)—made a crude attack on Tocqueville's noble origins and denounced him as a Carlist in disguise. Tocqueville saw these anonymous pamphlets as an occasion to make his position in the electoral body clearer and to justify his role as Kergorlay's attorney. He issued two replies to the pamphlets by "Anonymous."

An elector who seems to have been a sincere convert, to judge from the documents found in the Tocqueville Archives, also published a tribute to Tocqueville which the latter at first distrusted. The regional postmaster of Valognes, who had been won over to the adversaries, blocked the publication of Tocqueville's second response to "Anonymous" and was reprimanded for this by his superiors.

To the rural electors, Tocqueville was depicted as a man of the Cherbourg bourgeoisie, where, as we have seen, he had sympathetic support. Now, the arrondissement of Cherbourg, where Tocqueville was living, was suspected of having dark designs—of scheming to annex two cantons in the arrondissement of Valognes . . .

When it came to the vote on November 4, 1837, Le Marois defeated Tocqueville in the second round by 247 votes to 220, Lebrun de Plaisance having been eliminated in the first round. This victory, noted the sub-prefect, was a victory of "the ruminants over the thinkers."

Tocqueville's family origins had been used against him to the greatest extent possible. The rural electors, lavishly entertained in the taverns of Valognes at Le Marois's expense, had been dragged toward the urns to the cry of "No more noblemen!" and some of them who had come to vote for Tocqueville had had their minds changed by the copious libations. Tocqueville sadly noted their feeling of repulsion against the nobility. "In the minds of these coarse men there was something like the instinctive repugnance Americans feel for men of color." His opinion of the election tallied with that of the sub-prefect: it had been a victory of the animal passions over intelligence.[16]

Such was the case, clearly, but had this alone determined the outcome? At the urging of Montalivet, won over by Le Marois's handsome promises, Molé had decided not to be neutral toward the two candidates. Under the July monarchy the civil servants in the rural districts had considerable power. Le Marois particularly, thanks to his uncle, the district tax collector of Valognes, had the sacred battalion

[16]Tocqueville to Beaumont, November 12, 1837, O.C. VIII, 1: 262–64.

of the tax collectors under his thumb. Their authority to grant delays and offer compromises with the treasury was much greater than it is today and was no doubt particularly appreciated in a Normandy so celebrated for its sense of economy . . . For Tocqueville to be elected, it would have been enough to shift fifteen votes. The knowledge we now have of the electoral files of the July monarchy permits us to assume that administrative actions may have been the decisive factor in the reelection of Le Marois.

But the public, as awareness that Le Marois had played the turncoat spread, was scandalized. This would one day work to Alexis de Tocqueville's advantage. It was therefore with reason that he could say that he had both lost and won.

Le Marois's situation in the Chamber was not exactly comfortable. He had promised his vote to both the government and the opposition and now he had to choose. Even though he kept as quiet as a mouse, even though he was ill for a time, even though he hedged his votes as far as he could, this ambiguous position could not last for long. At the time of the Chamber's vote on the address in response to the king's speech from the throne, at the opening of the 1839 session—a vote that expressed the Chamber's position on overall governmental policy—the Molé government had to face a concerted attack by the newly formed Thiers-Guizot-Barrot coalition and won by only a very narrow margin, 221 votes to 213. Very much weakened, it resigned and on February 2, 1839, the king pronounced the dissolution of the Chamber, with new elections scheduled for March 2. Le Marois now declared himself to be a staunch member of the opposition, one of the "213" that the coalition had pledged to see reelected. In theory, he should have found that he had the support of the opposition headquarters in his district and that the government was against him.

But the situation had been deteriorating for him in the Valognes arrondissement, and not only because his conduct in 1837 had become more and more widely known. His adversaries were organizing. The campaign of 1837 had been heated enough to win Tocqueville zealous supporters who were not ready to give up—important men who were anxious to press the fight against Le Marois's corrupt practices and devious methods without postponing matters until the next election. The entire membership of the departmental council was now on Tocqueville's side, along with most of the councillors in the arrondissement.

They had begun with a petition alleging corruption in the 1837

voting, even though Tocqueville felt the incidents were too minor for
an annulment of the election to be likely. But Le Marois helped to dig
his own grave by circulating a letter from Barrot that "defamed" the
authors of the petition. Barrot denied having written anything of the
sort.[17]

Tocqueville's supporters would have liked to form a central committee that might take up all of the electors' concerns, so that Tocqueville could be involved, for example, in the nominations of justices of
the peace and tax collectors, in the improvement of the lycée, in the
donation of books to a public library—all the services required of a
deputy at that time. Tocqueville rejected the idea of such an organization,[18] but often became involved in dealing with public needs or
individual appointments through the ministries in which he had connections. This was a system he later condemned in his *Souvenirs,* but
in the electoral regime of the July monarchy it was necessary if one
did not want to incur the hostility of a substantial number of electors.

Tocqueville and his advisers, of whom the most active were the
notary Langlois and the naval supply officer Clamorgam, nephew of
the man who was the sub-prefect of Valognes and one of Tocqueville's
supporters in 1837 (for whom Tocqueville would soon get an appointment as tax collector), had set about the conquest of the district
immediately after the elections of 1837. Each canton had one or two
dependable correspondents who would sound out the electors, discover
their inclinations, and then try to get a relative or friend to win them
over. This door-to-door work was done with the help of a list of the
electors that was carefully gone over, name by name. A handwritten
copy arranged by canton and giving the profession of each elector has
been preserved in the Tocqueville Archives. Probably drawn up a little
after the 1839 elections, it enumerates 627 electors and among them
distinguishes 356 for, 125 against, 79 doubtful, and 67 abstaining. Such
painstaking work was apparently not unusual under the July monarchy; it was obligatory in that confined world of the qualified electors.
For Tocqueville, the work fitted in nicely with his penchant for precise
information and statistics. He would later on draw up lists of the
inhabitants of Tocqueville in order to get to know them better and
discover their needs . . .

Let us return to the campaign of 1839. Le Marois wanted, first, to
strengthen his position in Paris by stressing his place among the "213"

---

[17]Barrot's denial is printed in *O.C.* VIII, 1: 269–70.
[18]Unpublished letter from Tocqueville to Langlois dated November 10, 1837, private collection.

so as to take advantage of the general principle that the opposition's central committee would support the candidacy of all the outgoing opposition deputies. He gave a large dance to which the entire opposition was invited. Before the Chamber was dissolved, he had had the official report on the election of the chairman of his committee in the Chamber written by Havin, in order not to be suspected of duplicity. He tried to soften up Barrot, whose honest reactions he feared, by flattering his wife, Agathe, who exercised a not always happy influence over her husband. Then he had it declared in the press that Tocqueville was both a ministerial and a legitimist candidate, which was hardly more contradictory than for Le Marois himself to have been simultaneously for and against the government in 1837! But in spite of these efforts, he found the allusions to his secret connivance with Montalivet at that time to be quite an embarrassment. He had written a letter that set down their mutual obligations in the "synallogmatic contract" (Molé's phrase) agreed upon with the minister at that time, and was quite convinced that the letter was still in existence. His denials could therefore not be too precise for fear that this text would be exhumed, and he limited himself to swearing that he was a man of honor. Yet not everything favored Tocqueville: in the eyes of the leaders of the opposition, the principle that the "213" must be reelected was inviolable. Tocqueville's strongest supporters, Barrot and especially Chambolle, were extremely hampered by it. The latter, after having written an article in favor of Tocqueville in Le Siècle, had to print a retraction, which he put in ambiguous terms, hoping the electors of Valognes would read between the lines. Mignet could not get a restatement favorable to Tocqueville printed in Le Constitutionnel. Tocqueville's relations with the Doctrinaires were already cool and Thiers showed scarcely any enthusiasm at seeing him arrive in the Chamber, not only because of his independent character, but because Thiers feared, wrongly, a collusion between Tocqueville and Lamartine, who was at that time his bête noire.

It was with Thiers's connivance that a real trap opened up before Tocqueville, although the people mainly responsible for it had set it in all innocence. The liberal bourgeoisie of Cherbourg had not given up the idea of having him as their deputy. A petition from eighty electors of that district was addressed to him. But in 1837 Quénault had defeated Bricqueville by 333 votes to 150, and for Tocqueville to give up Valognes for Cherbourg would have been to give up the substance for a shadow. It was a proposal, certainly, that would please the leaders of the opposition, since it would get them out of the awkward situation in Valognes, but it displeased Molé, who favored Quénault. Tocqueville made a show of hesitation but no more, courteously thanked his supporters in Cherbourg, and stood as a candidate solely in the Valognes arrondissement, where he was now a property owner (perhaps the same house we know he later owned in this town) and an elector.

To sustain his local campaign, Le Marois had mobilized a few pens more expert than his own (and perhaps also the help of Quénault) and the polemic of the circulars and the leaflets was rather spirited. But at the very outset he lost an ally from 1837—Gisles, a businessman and the mayor of Valognes, who deliberately changed sides. Havin, like Tocqueville an enemy of Quénault, had no strong desire to see Tocqueville in the Chamber, and in 1837 he had supported Le Marois. At a date during the electoral campaign that we cannot pin down precisely, Havin asked his colleague La Grange, who was Tocqueville's cousin, to meet with Tocqueville. Havin, too, ended the electoral campaign as an ally. Tocqueville's electoral circular, for that matter, was more convincing than the one he had written in 1837, where he introduced himself to the electors of Valognes by describing his achievements, his love of freedom, and his belief that freedom would lead to a gradual amelioration of conditions, and by affirming his loyalty to the institutions now in place and his rejection of both absolute rule and a republic. All this was a little abstract, a literary piece that was a bit subtle for the farmer electors. In 1839, having become their compatriot, he was more direct, and warmer. He reminded them more pointedly that he had served the regime as a magistrate and refuted vigorously the suspicion that he was an aristocrat in disguise: "In all of France and, I daresay, in all of Europe, there is not one man who has demonstrated more publicly that the old aristocracy is dead forever."

He declared himself ready to appear before the assembled electoral body to answer all questions and to respond to any elector who addressed him. In another letter to the electors he made it clear that his position was independent of a ministry that was contending against his rival for the office, one that had broken its promise to that rival and one whose support he himself refused. Thus, he could sum up with convincing clarity:

It is not I who have contributed to bringing about the grave and perilous situation in which we find ourselves, since I had no access either to the councils of the Crown nor to the Chambers. I am a new man who brings

296

to the new circumstances that now exist nothing but a free mind and an ardent and sincere love of representative government and the dignity of our country. Whatever happens, I will maintain this position which I have been put in by circumstances, not only out of respect for myself, but—I am not afraid to say it—out of devotion to my country; for I believe that in the present circumstances, it is important to see deputies enter the councils of the nation who, while in accord with the doctrines of the opposition, do not bring to public affairs the excited passions and the personal grievances of the party man. I am firmly attached to certain principles, but I am not tied to a party. I am even more firmly independent where the government is concerned; I am not a government candidate and I do not in the least want to be one.

Independence, the exercise of free judgment in the Chamber, disavowal of the opposition's intrigues and yet a preference for opposition policies (this offended his cousin Le Peletier d'Aunay): thus Tocqueville defined his position as a candidate.

The Norman electors could understand this language. On March 2, Tocqueville won in the first round by 318 votes to 240 for Le Marois.

Eighty-six percent of the registered electors took part in the voting. This was an unusually high proportion, and shows that political passions had been aroused to a high pitch. Victory went this time to the "thinkers" of the district, who had succeeded in leading the majority beyond its old prejudices against the nobility and who opened up for the frail victor, now thirty-three years old, two immediate prospects. One was to complete, as quickly as possible, his long book. The other was to take up his position at the heart of France's political world.

17

EARLY DAYS IN THE
CHAMBER

TOCQUEVILLE'S success in the election was darkened for him by the defeat of Beaumont in Saint-Calais. As he had been in 1837, Beaumont was narrowly beaten by M. de Montesquiou, *chevalier d'honneur* to the queen. For Tocqueville, this defeat seemed a disaster.[1] Not only had Beaumont been the confidant of his thoughts and the companion of his enterprises for the last ten years, but he was aware that Beaumont was a corrective to some of his failings: a certain hesitation in making up his mind, and above all the lack of amiability that he had already observed in himself in his relations with his colleagues at the Versailles tribunal. He searched in vain to see if there was a deputy of the opposition who had won in two districts; he even intrigued to have M. de Montesquiou raised to the peerage, which would have left the Saint-Calais seat vacant. Finally, the death of the deputy from Mamers, Letronne, opened a place in a district of the Sarthe and Beaumont was elected there on December 15. But from the very start Beaumont did not prove to be the alter ego in the Chamber that Tocqueville had rather naively dreamed of.[2] Allied by his marriage to the Lafayette clan, which had ten members or so scattered through the left and the left center, Beaumont had from the very start a more firmly established parliamentary position than Tocqueville's. He followed a course that was fairly independent of his friend's, while

---

[1]Tocqueville to Beaumont, *O.C.* VIII, 1: 359f.
[2]Kergorlay to Tocqueville, July 27, 1840, *O.C.* XIII, 2: 72.

298
叱 叱

at the same time working with him quite willingly. Beaumont was not without personal ambition of his own and behaved accordingly.

After his election, Alexis de Tocqueville remained in Normandy until March 19, the opening of the session having been fixed for March 25. The electoral campaign had tired him and he took a short rest. But he had to take steps to make it clear what his true political position was. After first listing him as one of those elected by the coalition, Le Journal des Débats described him in its March 7 issue as a ministerialist, perhaps because the king had said he was delighted by his election.[3] Although it would displease Molé, who had been driven out of power by the elections, Tocqueville's responsibility to the men who had elected him obliged him to protest. An article by Chambolle in Le Siècle made Tocqueville's true position clear. Beaumont, and Tocqueville himself, had seen the article in the Débats as more than merely an error of fact. It had the look of an attempt to annex him. For this reason, Tocqueville considered his choice of where to sit in the Chamber an important matter. Corcelle, a good friend ever since his review of the Democracy, had also been elected to the Chamber, from Sées in the Orne. He had gone immediately to Paris, and now he undertook to find Tocqueville the right seat.

In the two Chambers of the July monarchy, the right of the semicircle was occupied by the legitimists, the right center by the ministerialists and the Doctrinaires, the left center by the supporters of Thiers and various small parties, and the left by Barrot's dynastic opposition, flanked by a few "radicals"—republicans, in reality—to the far left. But the boundaries were more flexible then than they are today. The left center in 1839, already overpopulated before the elections, had gained newly elected members. The right, on the other hand, contained empty spaces where certain independents installed themselves, for example Lamartine, who sat very high up, but also men of all persuasions who had not taken care to claim their rightful seats early enough. Quick though Corcelle was, he could not find a place in the left center either for himself or for Tocqueville. Tocqueville, however, was determined to sit there because of the unkind rumors about his legitimism that had been put in circulation among the electors: "In the eyes of those people, the spot where you plant your behind has a primary importance . . . Isn't there some hole at the very top of the left center or on the edge of the left on that side where we could ensconce ourselves?" For lack of anything better, Corcelle had to reserve provi-

sionally two places on the right, which went down badly in Valognes. **299**
As far as his electors were concerned, Tocqueville wrote Corcelle, "the
word 'left' is the only one that has stuck in their minds and that is the
word I wanted to attach to my name so that it would remain attached
to it forever after."[4] Soon, however, he was able to install himself in
seat number 319 on the left center, which had become vacant and
would be his seat from then on, while Corcelle moved into seat
number 11 on the left.

Although he was anchored by his bottom to the left center, Tocqueville did not want to become a member of any existing party. He seems
to have thought rather unrealistically that he could gather around him
deputies disillusioned both by the government's politics and by the
coalition against Molé, and he wrote to Corcelle: "I believe there are
about sixty new deputies. Our future, I think, lies with them especially.
We have to try to do something really new, while at the same time
running with all our strength from the twaddle of the social party."[5]

This last phrase poses the question of the relations between Lamartine
and Tocqueville. On January 19, 1838, Lamartine had proclaimed in the
Chamber the existence of an "immense" social party "in the country
which forms alliances neither with the retrograde passions of the past
nor with the subversive passions of the moment, neither with the
timorousness of the first nor with the anger of the second." Like
Tocqueville, he was thus fundamentally liberal, detesting, on the one
hand, the repressive laws passed by the majority and, on the other, the
Jacobin and Napoleonic traditions that remained alive at the heart of the
left. Like Tocqueville, he thought the dynasty necessary but hoped for
an evolution toward democracy. A short time before, both had been
roused to indignation by the self-serving calculations that brought
about the Thiers-Guizot-Barrot coalition. The principal reproach they
addressed to the parties was that they no longer embodied any great idea,
and Tocqueville could only have applauded Lamartine's fine speech of
October 11, 1838: "Since you cannot return to the past, you must find a
new idea. Don't imagine, Messieurs . . . that everyone is as tired as we are
and fears the slightest change. The generations growing up behind us are
not tired, they want to act and tire themselves in their turn. What have
you given them to do? The nation of France is bored." The domestic
policies that Lamartine then set forth reveal concerns which were, or
which would become, Tocqueville's as well: the separation of Church

---

[4]Tocqueville to Corcelle, *O.C.* XV, 1: 125–39.
[5]*O.C.* XV, 1: 128.

300

匁 匁

and State, reform of the suffrage laws, revision of the tax structure to the advantage of the workers, the liberalization of public education, the abolition of slavery, a broad investigation of poverty for the purpose of eliminating it through the formation of associations, etc. Although the poet was sometimes the bolder of the two men, it was only in matters of foreign policy that their views differed. Must it not have been Lamartine's humanitarian pacifism that Tocqueville characterized as the "twaddle" of the social party?[6]

Lamartine was so sure of the convergence between Tocqueville's ideas and his own that he adopted Tocqueville into the social party in advance, as soon as this imaginary creation took form under its new name of the liberal and social right center. But from the moment he arrived in the Chamber, Tocqueville displayed a prudent reserve toward Lamartine. He himself indicated that his tactics, where Lamartine was concerned, consisted of offering polite words but making no positive commitment, and the presence of Lamartine on the benches of the right had been another reason to avoid sitting there. Between 1839 and 1843, the two men were to go through a roughly parallel evolution: starting with centrist leanings, they would evolve toward the left with the intention of planting some new ideas in Barrot's empty head. For all this, however, they did not associate politically; Tocqueville no doubt feared subservience to a man fifteen years older whose literary fame surpassed his, whose character appeared to him fanciful and undependable, and whose personal ambition seemed unlimited. Vain as he was, Lamartine saw clearly the reasons for his behavior. He wrote in a letter to Beaumont dated October 17, 1843:

I have entered all the areas where I ought to have met you and found myself in accord with you . . . But every time we meet, you have moved away, saying: Careful, he's not one of us, we must drive him away with honors and compliments. Whatever others may think, I have too much good sense not to have noticed this, especially in M. de Tocqueville and in Corcelle. Well! They're wrong and you are too, somewhat. You always assume my ideas are eccentric, idealistic, uncompromising, personal, and that they can't combine with the ideas of others . . . Be assured that on the contrary, nature has made me pleasant, easygoing, conciliatory, and very practical. But with whom should I ally myself if you reject me? Where ideas are concerned, I have no other friends.[7]

[6]See Pierre Quentin-Bauchart, *Lamartine homme politique* (Paris, 1903); Bénoni Tallaguier, *Les Idées politiques et sociales d'Alphonse de Lamartine* (Montpellier, 1954).

[7]Lamartine, *Lettres inédits (1821–1851),* ed. H. Guillemin (Porrentruy, 1944), 75–76.

As Tocqueville was keeping Lamartine and any prospect of an 301 alliance with him at arm's length, he saw with disappointment that the 𝟰 new deputies of 1839 were prudently taking their places in the pre-established cadres of the old parties. At the beginning of his political career, his only intimate associations were with a few friends who would remain loyal to him until the coup-d'état of Louis-Napoléon on December 2, 1851: Corcelle, whom we already know; Combarel de Leyval, a new deputy from Riom, who had moved from legitimism to liberalism and whose southern verve, clumsiness, and periodic spells of indolence astounded Tocqueville but did not prevent his being a loyal and helpful friend; and a little later, Victor Lanjuinais, son of the famous member of the Constituent Assembly, elected in 1838 by a college of the Loire-Inférieure, with a firm character and with a useful competence in political economy. But these few friends did not bring him out of his isolation.

His efforts to win over his colleagues to himself and his ideas seem to have been rather clumsy. He apparently overestimated the reputation of his book and the influence it would give him among the provincial bourgeoisie whose political preoccupations did not always go beyond the most down-to-earth interests. He did not have the right hail-fellow-well-met parliamentary manner, and to others he appeared ambitious and proud. In his preoccupation with general ideas, he would sometimes mistake one man for another, through indifference or distraction or perhaps simply because of his myopia.[8]

In his occasionally muddle-headed haste to take action, he could fall into traps. It was thus that, because he supported a reform of the small electoral colleges, in which corruption was at its height, as well as a very small increase in the electoral body, he joined a committee for electoral reform that had been set up by the radicals, whose program proved to advocate an all but universal suffrage, along with salaries for the deputies and the banning of civil servants from the Chamber. Tocqueville was astonished to see his name among those signed to this program, for at the time it seemed to him the height of demagogy. Barrot and Chambolle rescued him from the blunder by letting him publish a correction in Le Siècle. He quite openly acknowledged the mistake to his mentor Royer-Collard, who was touched by his confession (September 29, 1839).

In the years since 1830, Royer-Collard had come to seem an histori-

[8]See Beaumont's prefatory note to vol. V of his edition of the Oeuvres complètes and also "Fragments et entretiens de Tocqueville avec Nassau Senior," in Eugène d'Eichtal, Alexis de Tocqueville, 263–64.

302

爰 类

cal monument—"made of different clay," as Lamartine said—in the Chambers of the July monarchy. Very tall, his head held high above his high collar and voluminous tie, he would sit perched at the top of the semicircle and direct his sardonic gaze and his scornful smile down at the mediocre discussions going on at his feet. This champion in the great jousting of ideas in the time of the Restoration had, on one last occasion, taken part in the debate on the September laws, in order to defend the liberal principles now under attack by his old friends the Doctrinaires. Since then he had been silent, but his formidable epigrams were repeated in the corridors.[9]

Royer-Collard thought he had found in Tocqueville a true disciple but was disappointed by his eagerness to make a career for himself. After receiving the letter in which Tocqueville confessed he had been, through his own fault, duped by the maneuverings of the far left in the manifesto for electoral reform, Royer-Collard wrote of him to Molé:

> Let us indeed talk about this man. I, too, have a *fondness* for him, even a *weakness,* I like him despite my disappointed expectations. A month ago, he wrote me a very good letter, a due apology for his Barrot campaign, in which he was completely duped. I wrote him a very frank answer, in which I became quite involved, because he provoked me amply by saying to me that he preferred my censure to my indifference. I don't despair of him at all. Le Peletier d'Aunay and I have already been able to stop him from brazenly allying himself with the left.[10]

But on the first of November of that year, in another letter to Molé, Royer-Collard evinces a certain disillusionment: "He needs to be successful. I believe that, in the mixture of which he is composed, although there is more that is good, even much more, he lacks a certain elevation of soul that makes for perfect rectitude."

About the need to be successful with which Royer-Collard reproaches him, we also have the testimony of Tocqueville himself, in a letter to his wife dating from 1841:

> Yesterday, I went to see our old friend Royer-Collard. I found him in pain and weak; he received me like a father; I was truly very touched by this. As is customary for a father, he first preached to me. He told me my only

---

[9]See especially Roger Langeron, *Un conseiller secret de Louis XVIII: Royer-Collard* (Paris, 1956).

[10]Royer-Collard Archives at the Institut de France. Letters from Tocqueville to Royer-Collard dated August 8, 1839, and from Royer-Collard to Tocqueville dated August 17, 1839, *O.C.* XI, 79–83.

defect was that I was too concerned with myself. I admitted that this was   303
true to a certain extent, but I said that if an occasion occurred where I might
forget myself in order to throw myself into something large, he would see
that I was capable of doing so. He answered that he did not doubt it, that
he knew the resources of my soul. He continued in this vein for an hour,
mingling criticism and praise with an infinite grace and goodness. I was at
once full of gratitude for his friendship, full of agreement with the truths
he was telling me, and, in the midst of all that, I could not help smiling inside
to see him keep harking back to himself in order to prove to me that one
should never think of oneself.

In a letter of December 1842 to the Duchesse de Dino, reproduced
by the latter in her famous *Chronique*, Royer-Collard was more specific about his grievances:

You ask me what I make of M. de Tocqueville? He has a fund of honesty
that is not enough for him, that he spends imprudently, but of which
something will always be left; I fear that because of his impatience to arrive,
he will stray into impracticable paths, trying to reconcile what is irreconcil-
able. He uses both his hands at once, giving the right to the left, the left to
us, regretting that he hasn't a third which he would give invisibly.[11]

If the spiteful words reported by the duchesse really date from
December 1842, Royer-Collard had lost sight of his disciple's evolution. At this time, Tocqueville was a resolute opponent of Guizot, not
yet the prime minister but the most powerful figure in the ministry
nominally headed by Soult. Though Tocqueville had not enlisted in
the dynastic left, he now voted most often as it did and showed
deference to Barrot. He had come to realize that a deputy thirty-five
years old who insisted on his right to be independent of all parties
would find the road to any action in the parliament closed to him, and
would be left to sit alone on his bench proclaiming his independence.
For that matter, he had only opted for the left and his somewhat
ambiguous position between Barrot's party and the left center after
painful inner debates and the kinds of hesitations we have seen in him
since 1839.

In America, he had seen the "little parties" with his own eyes, but
people had described for him their memories of the "great parties" of
the preceding generation, at the time of the battles between Federalists
and Republicans. In the Chamber of Deputies of the July monarchy,

[11]Duchesse de Dino, *Chronique* (Paris, 1909), vol. 2, 438.

304
ᚷ ᚴ

he returned to a situation much worse than the battles for or against Jackson. The Thiers-Barrot-Guizot coalition had defeated Molé, but its leaders were fighting over the division of the spoils. All the anticipated government groupings were collapsing in the face of these eleventh-hour demands. The regime and the dynasty were being discredited, and an atmosphere of riot was returning to Paris. This would leave permanent marks, which Tocqueville would denounce from the tribune a little later, on January 18, 1842: "The people have been led to believe that in the political world there are only interests, passions, ambitions, and no ideas . . . I believe that the coalition, with its consequences, was one of the causes of the moral perturbation that reigns in this country."[12] Upon his arrival in the Chamber, he found only shabby conniving, parties that one entered "because of ambition, friendship, or irritation with one's neighbor." The man who had dreamed of a regeneration of political life, the man who was now sorry at times that he had got himself elected, evoked the image of the great parties of earlier days that in France as in America had been united by principles and convictions:

"Will we never see the wind of true political passions rise again . . . those passions that are sometimes violent, hard, cruel, but that are broad in their range, disinterested, fruitful—passions that are the soul of the only parties I understand and to which I would feel willingly disposed to give my time, my fortune, and my life."[13] The day he wrote this to his friend Corcelle, his stomach was troubling him and he was exaggerating somewhat; nonetheless, he found himself extremely irritated by the pedestrian ideas and paltry ruses of the politics of the time.

Still, it was necessary to make a choice between the two profound tendencies that underlay the political struggles of the time: revolution or order. Casimir Périer had grounded his policy on order, and he had been followed in this by each of his successors to the ministry, in a movement that was meant to lead the country gradually to more democratic institutions, one that the dynastic left continued to advocate. Tocqueville understood the situation perfectly, and tried to fathom how his own nature responded to the dilemma it presented. This is the point of an odd text published by Rédier (and since lost) that was written on the back of a page from the rough draft of a speech

[12]This speech appears in Beaumont's edition of the *Oeuvres complètes,* 374–88.
[13]Letter to Corcelle dated October 19, 1839, *O.C.* XV, 1: 139.

on the situation in the Near East, a text that cannot be dated precisely but that clearly belongs to the 1839–1841 period.[14]

The text is headed "My instinct, my opinions." In it, Tocqueville acknowledges that his predilection for democracy is a *"gout de tête,"* an intellectual preference, and that he is "aristocratic by instinct, 'hates' demagogy, the disorderly actions of the masses, their violent and muddled intervention in affairs, the envious passions of the lower classes, their irreligious tendencies."

He adds: "I belong neither to the revolutionary party nor to the conservative party, and when all is said and done I am more attached to the second than to the first. For I differ with the second concerning means but not their end, while I differ with the first concerning both their means and their end.

"Freedom is the strongest of my passions. Voilà, this is the truth."

At the outset of his parliamentary career, Tocqueville held in detestation the illiberal tendencies of a left which still had the musty odors of Jacobinism or Napoleonism. The situation was not the same later, when he believed that the Guizot government, in the years preceding 1848, was also instituting a cunning sort of illiberalism and becoming the instrument of a royal power whose active role Tocqueville, in another text, confessed that he should have acknowledged but could not bring himself to acknowledge out of "hatred for the king."

While waiting to make his choice of a political position, and despite his initial disillusionment, Tocqueville enjoyed the prestige of an "expert." And there were two important issues, both of which seemed pertinent to his "expertise," before the Chamber in 1839 and 1840.

The first was that of the emancipation of the slaves. The author of *Marie,* still engaged with the electors of the Sarthe, was not available, but Tocqueville, who had observed the situation of the blacks in the United States and discussed slavery at length in his *Democracy,* was clearly a knowledgeable authority. Since 1834, he had been taking part in the work of the Society for the Abolition of Slavery, whose president was the Duc de Broglie. The Society gave banquets and exercised a certain influence in political circles.[15]

The need for a decision appeared urgent. In 1833, England had

---

[14]Rédier, *M. de Tocqueville,* 46–48.

[15]On the problem of slavery in general, see Gaston-Martin, *Histoire de l'esclavage dans les colonies françaises* (Paris, 1948), and particularly the *diplôme d'études supérieures* on file at the Sorbonne, Louis Bergeron's *La Question d'esclavage dans les colonies françaises sous la monarchie de Juillet* (Paris, 1950).

306
少 少

declared the emancipation of the slaves in its nineteen tropical colonies, and on August 1, 1838, a million slaves in them had become free men. Certain of the English Antilles islands that had once belonged to France lay within sight of Martinique and Guadeloupe, and French was still spoken in them. How could slavery be maintained under these conditions on France's three "sugar islands"—Martinique, Guadeloupe, Bourbon—and in unpretentious Guiana?

The year before, Hippolyte Passy had presented the Chamber with a plan for gradual emancipation. A committee chaired by Guizot had declared itself favorable to the plan and Rémusat had drawn up a report advocating measures that would prepare the colonies for this radical change. The Chamber was dissolved before the report could be discussed. On June 6, 1839, Tracy took up Passy's proposal in the very same terms (the latter had meanwhile become a minister). A new committee was appointed that chose Sade as chairman and Tocqueville as rapporteur.

Tocqueville's report responded to the anxieties of the colonists by pointing out the impossibility and the dangers of a status quo doomed to be short-lived. It was apparently at his instigation that the committee (whose deliberations have been lost) came to a bolder conclusion than its predecessor's and proposed the immediate and simultaneous emancipation of all slaves. Instead of leaving them for a certain period in the power of their former masters, on whom new obligations would be imposed, the blacks were to be placed—during the years of transition—under the control of the State. The State would act as arbitrator between the former masters and the new freedmen, assigning the blacks, who would be paid wages, to the colonists. A portion of the wages would revert to the State in partial amortization of the indemnities paid to the slaveholders at the time of the emancipation. By thus interposing the power of the State, Tocqueville hoped to prevent the bloody settling of accounts between the two races that had so struck him in the United States.

Tocqueville's report, filed July 23, 1839, was published as a pamphlet by the Society for the Abolition of Slavery. However, it never reached the floor for debate.[16]

A joint committee including both deputies and peers was appointed by the Guizot ministry and presided over by the Duc de Broglie, who presented its conclusions in 1843. But Guizot did not dare put into

---

[16]The text of the report, along with Tocqueville's other writings and speeches on the slavery question, can be found in the *O.C.* III, 1: 41–126.

effect more than a few adjustments in the colonial regime (the Mackau
law of 1845). Guizot would have been happy to have his name attached
to such a reform, but the colonists had powerful advocates close to the
king and the latter opposed the emancipation. In articles published by
Le Siècle in 1843, Tocqueville accused him of this openly. But he also
spoke in favor of the Mackau law: it retained the principle of arbitration between colonists and blacks, and any breach at all in the worm-
eaten edifice of colonial slavery had to hasten its downfall.

In 1840, the Chamber made the problem of prison reform a part of
its order of business. A commission composed of members of parliament and experts, under the auspices of the minister of the interior,
had already, in 1838, examined the question. Rémusat, who was now
the minister of the interior, brought in a bill in May 1840. The
committee appointed to examine it, which also included Gustave de
Beaumont, chose Tocqueville as rapporteur. His report was filed on
June 20, the last day of the session. The minister's plan provided for
a complete recasting of the system of imprisonment and even a reconstruction of French prisons, since he adopted the cell system with
solitary confinement day and night.

Some sort of prison reform did seem necessary because of the
increase in delinquency, especially among recidivists. This was attributed to the communal life in the prisons, which were a "school for
crime." The attempts to impose silence in the workshops in accordance
with the precepts of the Auburn, New York, system—but without
using the whip—had little or no effect.

In 1838, the ministry had consulted the departmental councils concerning the various systems that were under contemplation. A councillor in the Manche, Langlois, a notary and a friend of Tocqueville's,
had asked him for a written opinion. This saw publication in the
Journal de Valognes of September 30, 1838, and was reprinted in various
Parisian journals.

In their *Système pénitentiaire,* as we have seen, Tocqueville and
Beaumont did not express a preference for either the Auburn approach
or the Philadelphia one. Tocqueville, in the edition of the book
published in 1838, came out openly for the Philadelphia system. He
did this without consulting Beaumont, who, informed after the fact,
responded with approval, though his feathers clearly had been a little
ruffled.

Tocqueville's conclusions were favorable to Rémusat's bill. Experience with the Philadelphia system was by now extensive enough to

show up the weakness of the allegation that imprisonment in cells was damaging to the health and to the mental stability of the prisoners. England and Russia had also adopted the system. This solitary imprisonment remained a severe punishment, and that was as it should be. It was more feared by criminals than were the convict prisons, which the draft bill sought to eliminate. It forced the prisoner to work and restored him to society uncontaminated; sometimes it could lead to his moral reform. This harsh system should go hand in hand with a shortening of sentences, and the isolation of the detainees should not be absolute: every prison should provide a teacher and a chaplain and allow visitors.

The prison reform bill did not become law. In 1843, a new committee was appointed, and Tocqueville was at once made the rapporteur. As rapporteur, he brought the matter before the Chamber for debate, though this did not take place until May 1844, and the system of individual imprisonment was adopted. But the resolution was not presented to the Chamber of Peers.[17]

During the first months of 1839, a kind of ministerial anarchy prevailed in the government. The Molé ministry, which had stepped down on March 8, had been replaced by nothing better than a headless ministry composed of civil servants. This situation continued until May 12. On that day, the secret Society of the Seasons, led by Barbès and Blanqui, attempted a surprise attack against the capital that was quickly put down with the loss of some lives. Reaction to this escapade was intense enough to enable Marshal Soult to form, that very evening, a ministry half of which came from the right center and half from the left center, with the big-name party leaders excluded. Tocqueville voted with this ministry, except in the vote that overturned it in February 1840, on the occasion of the endowment plan of the Duc de Nemours.[18] Then, on March 1, Thiers returned to power with a left-center administration.

All his life, Tocqueville felt for Thiers an antipathy that was sometimes tempered, in spite of everything, by the seductively clear and brilliant intelligence of the "siren from Marseilles." This antipathy went back a long way. When, just out of school, he had read the *Histoire de la Révolution française,* the book, which recorded without passing any judgment the successes and failures of the parties, seemed to him the height of immorality. The two men met for the first time

[17]Tocqueville's writings and speeches on penitentiary systems are in the *O.C.* IV, parts 1 and 2, annotated and introduced by Michelle Perrot.

[18]According to his own testimony in his electoral manifesto of June 24, 1842.

in 1836, perhaps at the home of the Duchesse de Dino. Tocqueville's
opinion was modified slightly: Thiers was not systematically immoral,
and if they were equally practical he even preferred good to evil.
Gifted with a superficial and brilliant mind, he made use for his own
purposes of ideas that were neither new nor original, but with an art
for whose oratorical expressions Tocqueville would later express his
admiration.[19] At bottom, this able man was without principles, and
driven only by the necessity to satisfy his own ambition. He was
sometimes right, but one could not trust him. It was always necessary
to be on guard against his will to dominate. Tocqueville overestimated
the Machiavellianism of Thiers but, with ups and downs, he maintained relations with him not only through the "good Mignet," an
intimate of Thiers who was also Tocqueville's friend, but by occasionally frequenting, in the place Saint-Georges, the salon of Madame
Dosne.

The French government, during the brief ministries of Soult and
Thiers in 1839 and 1840, was principally concerned with a crisis in the
Near East that had once more brought to life the eastern question, as
it was then called. To put it briefly, the question was this: With the
Ottoman Empire in decay, which of the European powers was to hold
the dominant position in the Near East? It was a question answered
more than once by acts of war.

In 1833, a temporary equilibrium had been established between
Sultan Mahmud II, the ruler of the Ottoman Empire, and his vassal
in Egypt, Pasha Muhammad Ali. The Convention of Kutahia had
recognized, in 1832, the latter's conquest of Syria, and at the same time
the sultan had been obliged to conclude with Czar Nicholas I, who
had saved the Dardanelles from Egyptian attack, the Treaty of Unkiar
Skelessi, which subjected him to a veritable protectorate.

But in April 1839, encouraged by Lord Ponsonby, the English
ambassador to Constantinople, Sultan Mahmud sent his troops off to
invade Syria. On June 24, they were completely routed at Nezib by
the Egyptian army led by Ibrahim, the pasha's adopted son.

This reawakening of the eastern question brought the chancelleries
of the five great powers (France, England, Russia, Austria, and Prussia)
into a state of alert. Before examining the diplomatic positions adopted
by France, let us take note of the request made by the Soult ministry
to the Chambers for an emergency appropriation to strengthen the

[19]Tocqueville to Royer-Collard, December 6, 1838, *O.C.* XI, 28–30.

310

念 义

French naval force in the Mediterranean. It was on the occasion of the debate on this appropriation, which took place from July 1 to July 3, that Tocqueville stepped up to the tribune for the first time, on July 2, 1839.[20]

No one in Paris knew at this point of the Turkish rout at the battle of Nezib, and the debate bore on the resumption of hostilities with Turkey. It was very broad in range: certain speakers wanted France to keep to her former policy of supporting the sultan, while others, more in accord with prevailing public opinion, supported Muhammad Ali, the champion of "Arab nationhood" and a friend of France. Lamartine proposed dividing up the "cadaver" of the Ottoman Empire into zones of influence for the great powers.

Tocqueville, for his part, attempted to show that France's position was not simple. Russia's interest lay in enfeebling the Ottoman Empire, England's lay in maintaining that empire in order to keep Russia from seizing the Dardanelles and in order to weaken Muhammad Ali, which would permit England to make Egypt a stage on the route to India. France's interest lay in having the sultan independent of the czar, and Muhammad Ali independent of the English. She could therefore not ally herself with either Russia or England in dealing with the eastern question. It did not follow from this that France should remain inactive, but rather that she should act in accordance with her own interests. If Russia took the forfeit of the Dardanelles, France should respond by occupying a spot in Asia Minor. He reminded the Chamber of the policy during the Restoration which, at the time of the Greek War of Independence, had made France the third party to the Anglo-Russian agreement in the Treaty of London of 1827.

This policy of maintaining a French presence in the Near East was in accord with Soult's, who called for the five powers to act in concert to settle the eastern question. Palmerston, in the preliminary negotiations with the French government, showed himself little disposed to leave Muhammad Ali anything in Syria but the south, that is, the Acre pashalik. When the Thiers ministry replaced the Soult ministry on March 1, Thiers judged these negotiations for cooperation among the powers to be a mistake. He was convinced (unlike Tocqueville) of the solidity of the Egyptian power and thought that Muhammad Ali, by negotiating directly with the young sultan who had succeeded Mahmoud as the Ottoman ruler, would obtain more favorable conditions.

---

[20]His speech, which had not been reprinted since its publication in the *Moniteur,* appears, together with his relevant notes, in the *O.C.* III, 2: 255–68.

He therefore let the negotiations with England drag on and sought to encourage mediation between the belligerents on the spot. But Palmerston saw through this game and accepted Russia's proposals for an accord excluding France, to which Austria and Prussia would also adhere. Thus the treaty of July 15, 1840, was concluded: the four powers committed themselves to maintaining the integrity of the Ottoman Empire and undertook to address three summary demands to the pasha of Egypt at ten-day intervals. If he submitted to the first, he would obtain a hereditary title to Egypt and a lifetime title to the pashalik of Acre; if to the second, he would have only Egypt; the third would leave him to the discretion of the sultan. On July 17, this treaty was communicated to Guizot, then ambassador to London, who had in vain warned Thiers of the risk of an Anglo-Russian rapprochement.[21]

Thus pushed to one side, France was overcome by a fever of Anglophobia and chauvinism. Public opinion saw in this treaty a revival of the alliance of 1813. There was talk of fomenting revolution against the rulers of the four powers. But Germany, in the face of threats of intervention by France, demonstrated its Francophobia. The Thiers government, responding to public opinion, called up classes of the army reserves and seemed to be preparing for war. No one knew whether Thiers was bluffing or actually preparing for hostilities in which France would have been alone against the rest of Europe.

Tocqueville, while he found much of the swaggering in the press regrettable and while he affirmed his opposition to any propaganda war that sought to incite revolution abroad, shared the indignation that the treaty aroused. If he felt the situation to be a crisis for the country, he confessed to Corcelle that personally he preferred this stormy atmosphere to the dullness of the "democratic, bourgeois pot-au-feu." He wrote to Thiers on July 31 assuring him of his support:

With respect to Europe, our country is in the most difficult position it has been in since the fall of the Empire. You are its representative and most important guide. What you do in these circumstances must, in the eyes of those who love France and are sensitive to its greatness and its honor, live up to the measure of their support . . .

Permit me to articulate . . . two ideas whose truth seems to me easy enough

---

[21] In addition to the more general diplomatic histories, the *Manuel de la question d'Orient* by Jacques Ansel (Paris, 1923) gives a very clear summary of these events. The matter of the warnings given by Guizot, whose role was misunderstood by his contemporaries, particularly by Tocqueville, is clarified in Ch. H. Pouthas's study, "La politique de Thiers pendant la crise de 1840," in *Revue historique* (1938), 72–96.

to demonstrate. The first is that there is no ministry and even no dynasty that does not run the risk of being brought down if it attempts to make this nation agree to look on calmly while Russia and England *directly,* and with force of arms, put an end to the quarrel between the pasha and the sultan, and bring about the pasha's ruin. The second is that in the state of irresolution and fear that still prevails in the cabinets of all the powers, there is only one means left to prevent a war, and that is to appear very determined to wage it.[22]

And in a letter to Beaumont, Tocqueville goes further, saying that in order to appear determined to make war, one must actually *be* so. True, this was a great risk, not one to be incurred lightly, and he was somewhat afraid of Thiers's "scatterbrained" and "breakneck" spirit. But he saw no other possible attitude than to trust in him.[23]

The crisis reached its height when it was learned that on August 14 an English squadron had seized the Egyptian fleet at Beirut, landed troops, and taken over the fortress of St. Jean d'Acre (now 'Acca, in Israel). Ibrahim proved incapable of a response, to the great disappointment of French public opinion. On October 8, Thiers sent a note to London warning that France would not allow the pasha to be deposed in actuality—to be removed by the sultan—without reacting. For the Chambers, which had been convened, he submitted to the king a speech from the throne that would announce new preparations for war. Louis-Philippe refused to deliver the bellicose address. He dismissed the government and on October 29 summoned to office the Soult-Guizot ministry.

On November 30, 1840, during the Chamber's debate on the address in response to a speech from the throne that accepted the "established facts," Tocqueville gave his second important speech on the eastern question.[24]

First, he stressed the breadth of the question:

What is now taking place in Egypt and in Syria is only at the edge of a vast panorama, only the prelude to a dramatic action on a grand scale. Do you know what is happening in the East? An entire world is changing. From the banks of the Indus to the shores of the Black Sea, in that vast space, every society is being shaken, every religion is growing weaker, the nations are

[22]Bibliothèque Nationale. A fragment of Thiers's reply can be found in Pierre Roland Marcel's *Essai politique sur A. de Tocqueville* (Paris, 1910), 321. The manuscript has not been recovered.

[23]Tocqueville to Beaumont, August 16, 1840, *O.C.* VIII, 1: 422, and Tocqueville to Royer-Collard, August 15, 1840, *O.C.* XI, 91.

[24]This speech, together with relevant notes from the Tocqueville Archives, appears in *O.C.* III, 2: 288–309.

dying, every light is being extinguished, the ancient Asiatic world is disappearing. And we are seeing the European world gradually take its place. In our time, Europe is not merely nibbling away at one corner of Asia as Europe did in the days of the Crusades. It is attacking to the north, the south, the east, the west, everywhere. It is puncturing that ancient world, enveloping it, subduing it.

A great European nation could not fail to take part in this expansion. It could not let itself be pushed to one side, as had happened in the July 15 treaty. This treaty included a clause incompatible with France's honor, the deposition of Muhammad Ali. Now, wrote Tocqueville (who was wrong about this), "the treaty will be carried out to the very end."

But Tocqueville was no less mistrustful of the consequences of the treaty. The English, he believed, were going to establish themselves in the Euphrates valley and in Egypt. It would be necessary to oppose them, and here the continental nations would support France against England.

What he reproached the new Soult-Guizot ministry for was its very inception. It had been called into office to maintain peace and to give up preparations for war: "Any government which cannot wage war is a detestable government."

This government argued the danger of revolution in the case of war. In reality, it was itself leading the way to revolution by wounding the nation's pride, which was the last bond uniting the French people.

Thus, from the very beginnings of the Guizot ministry, Tocqueville manifested toward it a hostility he had not shown its predecessors, and this was because of its foreign policy. In his notes he declares himself ready to compromise on problems of domestic policy if the new government should decide to institute a firm foreign policy.

It was at the end of 1840, then, that Tocqueville began to move toward the left opposition. His parliamentary posture would remain undeclared for some time yet, perhaps because he thought, like many of his colleagues, that the Soult-Guizot ministry was a transitional government that the king would rid himself of once the external crisis had abated. Before the elections of 1842, Tocqueville would draw up a sort of counterprogram in opposition to Guizot's policies. But his initial grievance against the October 28 ministry was that it was humiliating France in the eyes of the world. On the left, he found an attitude similar to his own, with its memories of the great revolutionary and imperial nation still alive—a paradox, when one thinks of how

314

𝓎 𝓎

profoundly Tocqueville distrusted such feelings of nostalgia. But his own nostalgia went back further, to an earlier time: one recalls the emotion with which, in America, he evoked memories of the old French colonial empire. He did not want to wage a war of words fomenting revolution, as the left did, but rather to expand French power in those regions where France might still make a good showing in the world.[25]

Guizot had known Tocqueville since the latter had been his disciple at the end of the Restoration (the Tocqueville Archives contain the summary of a conversation between the two men in 1830). He was too astute a psychologist not to want to gain his affection. When the second *Democracy* was sent to him, he wrote the author: "I take pleasure in your ideas, even when I do not agree with them. Why don't we agree? I find no good reason. I think a good deal of you, sometimes with uneasiness. I do not despair of gaining ground."[26] Much later, under the Second Empire, he would write to him: "I have never understood why you were not one of us." Before the elections of 1842, he confided in a friend of Tocqueville's, saying certain things about the latter that were most likely meant to be repeated to him: "In a long conversation he had about me with one of my friends a few days ago, M. Guizot revealed an extraordinary desire either to bring me over to his side, finally, or to get me out of the Chamber if I persisted in holding to an opposing position."[27]

The ministry chose the second alternative. The elections to the Chamber of July 9, 1842, were preceded by a campaign that was even more heated than that of 1839. The tone was set from Paris by the newspaper *Le Globe,* which ran a whole series of articles on Tocqueville so caustically polemical that there is reason to believe their author may have been Granier de Cassagnac. The articles not only revived the old accusation that Tocqueville was a Carlist in disguise, they also poked fun at his self-conceit, denied that he had any original ideas, and pointed out the grammatical errors in his prose.[28] *Le Globe* was sent, free, to the electors (at Le Marois's expense?) and, in addition, a landowner in the Manche who was on the staff of Duchâtel, the minister of the interior, tried to stir up opposition to Tocqueville by

[25]See above, p. 165.
[26]Roland-Marcel, *Essai politique sur Tocqueville,* 319.
[27]Letter from Tocqueville to Hervieu dated April 23, 1842. Private collection.
[28]Particularly the articles dated June 16, 28, and 29 and July 1 and 5.

sending letters to his tenants.[29] The situation was the reverse of that in 1839: now the government was opposing Tocqueville because it preferred to have as its adversary, once more, the insignificant Le Marois.

But Tocqueville was too firmly entrenched in the Valognes district, having not only the support of the "thinking" elite but also the confidence of a certain proportion of the wealthy farmers. It is not out of the question, either, that a part of the electoral body felt flattered to have a member of the Académie as its deputy. It was a quality label that impressed the provinces.

The turnout of electors at Valognes on July 9 was considerable for an election in a rural area under the July monarchy: out of 741 registered voters, 649 voted, a proportion of over 87 percent. Tocqueville obtained 465 votes and Le Marois only 177. This was a definitive victory. The campaign of 1846 was much calmer and the ministry chose not to become involved. Le Marois ran all the same but obtained only seventy votes.

[29]Tocqueville to Corcelle, June 9, 1842, *O.C.* XV, 1: 142, no. 2.

18

ALGERIA

ALTHOUGH thanks to his reputation as an "expert" Tocqueville had been entrusted while still a freshman deputy with the reports on the plan for emancipating the slaves and the plan for reforming the prisons, he was quite aware of the danger of being frozen into a secondary role. He had not as yet determined his stand in matters of domestic policy, and his first two long speeches in the Chamber, on July 2, 1839, and November 30, 1840, were on the eastern question. The press of events impelled him, of course, for France was caught up in the most intense international crisis the July monarchy had yet experienced. But Tocqueville brought to the debates in the Chamber principles that were the fruit of long reflection.

Like the men of the left and left center, he was aware of the humiliation suffered by the country in 1815 and measured it, in some sense comparatively, by contrasting a France whose frontiers remained those of the Ancien Régime with the other powers, all of which had grown in territory and in strength. A return to the policies of the Revolution and the Empire seemed to him a daydream that could not result in any lasting conquest. His vision, in this arena, went beyond the limits of Europe. Nothing is more characteristic of him in this respect than the conversations he had in 1839 and 1840 with Thiers, of which he has left a summary. For Thiers, the Russian peril weighed on Europe; one could only counterbalance it by an alliance with England. If the Russians took control of Constantinople, which seemed likely, the English should be allowed to install themselves in Egypt. One could placate them in the West by letting them control

Belgium and then, in exchange, annex "the comté of Nice, the Savoy, the Rhine as far as Mainz, Rhenish Bavaria, and the duchy of Clèves."[1] Tocqueville rejected these "whirling thoughts" (which, though less convoluted, were oddly reminiscent of the plan worked out by the Ministry of Foreign Affairs to turn Algeria, just after its conquest, into a bargaining chip so that, through a series of settlements, it would be exchanged for the left bank of the Rhine!). For him, the major policy issue for the European powers was their expansion into Asia, now being assailed on all sides. France should be in a strong position to participate there in a division of territories or zones of influence. For this, it was necessary to maintain a presence in the Mediterranean, "the political sea of our times," whose renewed activity Tocqueville foresaw with clarity. It was therefore necessary to combat the dominance of the English, who were anxious to assure themselves control of the route to the Indies, and to prevent their establishing themselves in Egypt. It was necessary for France to act, in any division of influence in the Near East, the way she had done under the Restoration in the case of the emancipation of Greece.[2] Tocqueville appeared perfectly aware of the displacement of the field of action of France's diplomacy in the time of Chateaubriand and La Ferronays and his ideas followed from that tradition. He affirmed that if France must be active in the Near East in order to force the other powers to allow her her share, she should be the sole mistress of North Africa and, to guarantee that freedom of maneuver, intervene in Spanish affairs. He went so far as to think that France should take over Mahón on the island of Minorca, an indispensable base for France's navy.[3]

All in all, Tocqueville's ideas about French expansion were closer to those of the French imperialists of the Third Republic than to the longing for the Napoleonic continental Empire that continued to rack the left of his time. But if his ideas anticipated the future, their roots went deep into the past. We have seen, in Canada in 1831, how nostalgic Tocqueville was for the colonial empire in America that had been lost under Louis XV.[4] Two years later he muses in a text (Quelques idées sur les raisons qui s'opposent à ce que les Français aient de bonnes colonies) on the possible causes of that failure.[5] In 1840, he

---

[1]Tocqueville Archives, files 77 and 79.

[2]Tocqueville's speeches to the Chamber, July 2, 1839, and November 30, 1840, and many unpublished fragments, particularly rough drafts of articles, in the Tocqueville Archives.

[3]*Travail sur l'Algérie*, O.C. III, 1: 213ff., and unpublished notes on Spain, Tocqueville Archives, file 81.

[4]See above, pp. 134ff.

[5]*O.C.* III, 1: 35–40.

318

𝔵 𝔶

thought that the domination of Algeria was the most important task France had to accomplish. He did not question the legitimacy of such a conquest, having none of the bad conscience on this matter that people of the twentieth century have. He believed, as Kergorlay wrote to him as early as 1830, that France's departure would be followed by the establishment of the English.[6] But above all for France to renounce such an enterprise would be to acknowledge yet another weakness to the world:

> If France were to shrink from an enterprise in which she was faced with no more than the natural difficulties of the terrain and the opposition of little tribes of barbarians, in the eyes of the world she would appear to be yielding to her own powerlessness and succumbing because of her lack of courage. Any nation that readily lets go of what it has taken and withdraws peacefully of its own accord back inside its old boundaries proclaims that the golden age of its history is past. It visibly enters the period of its decline.[7]

Thus did he justify a realist policy: "Once we have committed that great *violence* of conquest, I believe we must not shrink from the smaller violences that are absolutely necessary to consolidate it."[8] Insofar as possible, Tocqueville favored the rule of law and humane administration, but the nation's pride came first.

Among the texts in his hand that we know of, the first mention of Algeria appears back in October 1828: in the face of the ineffectiveness of the blockade that followed the dey's slapping the French consul in the face with his fly whisk, he hoped for a military solution to put an end to "this ridiculous affair."[9] At that moment, public opinion in France was either indifferent or hostile to an African adventure that two small circles—the merchants of Marseilles and Charles X's ultraroyalist entourage—were already hoping for. It was evidently the views of the ultraroyalists that the young magistrate was reflecting at the time.

Once the expedition had been decided upon, Alexis's older brother, Hippolyte, a career soldier, went to some trouble to be a part of the expeditionary body, even being so bold as to approach directly the Duchesse d'Angoulême, who consented to ask Bourmont to take him

[6]*O.C.* XIII, 1: 199.
[7]*O.C.* III, 1: 214.
[8]Unpublished letter to Lamoricière dated April 5, 1846. Archives du Chillon, file V.
[9]*O.C.* XIII, 1: 155.

on as aide-de-camp. Her recommendation was not acted upon, and
Hippolyte remained very angry about this. But Alexis's best friend, his
cousin Louis de Kergorlay, who had graduated from the Ecole Militaire at Metz in 1828 as a second lieutenant in the artillery, was more
fortunate. Assigned to a regiment of foot artillery equipped with light
mountain cannons, he often went into battle in the front ranks and
distinguished himself there. His letters to Alexis remain a remarkable
eyewitness account of the operations involved in the conquest of
Algiers, and of the country and its inhabitants as well. He came back
in August, however, having left the army because he refused to swear
an oath of loyalty to Louis-Philippe. Unfortunately, we have none of
the letters in which Tocqueville, the perpetual researcher, questioned
this exceptional witness.

During his trip to America, he had thought about certain general
questions that could now be raised concerning Africa: relations between conquerors and conquered, relations among different races, the
development of a new country.

When he returned, he very soon found himself thinking about these
problems again. As we have seen, the year 1833 was a year of worries
for him: there was his hesitation at the prospect of marrying Mary
Mottley, his defense of Louis before the Montbrison assizes, his resumption of family relations saddened by a sense of inner exile. Colonists "in yellow gloves," among them the resigned magistrate Vialar,
had already gone off to cultivate large estates in the Algiers region.
Why shouldn't Louis, who seems to have had extensive knowledge of
agronomy, and Alexis, who had at any rate observed in practice the
clearing of new lands in America, go as well? They were on friendly
terms with Lamoricière, who was serving in the army there, and
Tocqueville probably had some contact with Genty de Bussy, the
civilian administrator of Algiers, who would be able to facilitate
matters for them at the start.

The correspondence of the two cousins through September and
October 1833 alludes to the possibility of buying lands in the Mitidja
plain or the valley of the Sahel, and to the advice Lamoricière was
supposed to provide on this subject. Much later, stowing one of his
friend's letters away with several other precious notes, Tocqueville
wrote on a slip of paper in his own hand: "Curious letter from Louis
from 1833 noting our intention of going to Africa." And there exists
a set of questions, also in Tocqueville's hand, dating from the same time
as this correspondence, whose tenor is the following:

We would like M. Silvestre de Sacy to have the goodness to give some information on the following points:

1. Is everyday Arabic a difficult language to learn?

2. How long would it take a man with average ability, if he occupied himself exclusively with this, to acquire the language in such a manner as to be able to speak it usefully for the ordinary purposes of life?

3. Which books would it be most useful to obtain?[10]

Kergorlay was to leave for Algiers as a scout. It seems that Tocqueville anticipated remaining in Paris long enough to write the *Democracy*, which he thought he would be finishing sooner than he actually did. Lamoricière's absence from Algiers at the end of 1833, since he would have facilitated dealings with the Moors, frustrated the prospective colonists more than a little.[11] But we cannot suppose that this alone discouraged them. In fact, we do not know why they abandoned their plan.

We see proof, a little later, of the attention with which Tocqueville continued to follow affairs in Algeria. We have already mentioned how, contemplating getting himself elected deputy from Versailles, he published two very clearly thought out and accurately informed *Letters on Algeria* which appeared on June 23 and August 22, 1837, in *La Presse de Seine-et-Oise*, an ephemeral newspaper of which he was a shareholder. It was a sign of his interest in the colony that he should choose to discuss it on the occasion of his entrance into public life.[12]

As we know, this entrance was postponed to March 1839, when Tocqueville was elected in Valognes. Although he adapted himself to the preoccupations of his Norman electors, which did not include Africa, he did not lose sight of this important affair. In December 1839, Beaumont in his turn was elected deputy, and by the end of the 1840 session at the latest, the two friends conceived the plan of taking a trip to Africa together, continuing the collaboration they had begun in America and England.[13] But the ministry of March 1, 1840, in which Thiers was prime minister and Rémusat, Beaumont's cousin by marriage, minister of the interior, opened other prospects for Beaumont.[14]

In Africa, the governor-general was then Marshal Valée. Although for a long time historians underestimated him, today they are inclined to acknowledge that this "foremost artilleryman in Europe" had great

[10]Tocqueville Archives, file 13.
[11]*O.C.* XIII, 1: 344.
[12]See above, pp. 248–50.
[13]The first mention of this appears in a letter from Beaumont to Tocqueville dated July 20, 1840, *O.C.* VIII, 1: 103–106.
[14]Ibid.

merits, and no doubt they are right.[15] But for all that, in 1840 Valée 321
was a difficult, secretive subordinate in the eyes of the government,
obedient only when he wanted to be, scarcely accounting for his acts,
not very well liked by his underlings and the troops; and his prestige
had suffered from the devastation of the Mitidja in November 1839
by the Hajuta allies of Abd el-Kader, which he had failed to anticipate.
Before committing the resources that resumption of war with the emir
required, the government planned to recall Valée. One very likely
candidate for the post, Bugeaud, had qualities and defects that were the
opposite of Valée's: a clear view of conditions such as only a guerrilla
fighter familiar with the country could have, and a crude vitality that
appealed to the troops. But in the Chamber, Bugeaud was anathema
to the left and even to the left center. Thiers therefore thought of
coupling him with a civil administrator acceptable to liberal circles.
Several politicians in succession were approached, including Gustave
de Beaumont. He was tempted, apparently, but feared a trap (and
perhaps he was not mistaken, to judge from the rather low opinion
of him that Rémusat, ordinarily more kindly, expresses in his *Mémoires*[16]). In any case, Tocqueville, who never liked Thiers and at that
time distrusted Rémusat, pointed out to Beaumont the risks involved
in the undertaking. The plan fell through anyway: Bugeaud proved
to be so arrogant that the government backed off,[17] soon finding itself
up to its neck in the crisis in the Near East. If there should be a general
war, one could not entrust the fate of the colony to a better person
than Valée. Bugeaud's appointment was therefore postponed. He did
not replace Valée until January 1841, under the Soult-Guizot ministry,
which, not having the same reasons as its predecessor for accommodating the parliamentary left, did not pair him with a civilian counter-
weight.

The same international crisis had dissuaded Tocqueville and Beaumont from leaving for Algiers in September 1840, as they had planned.
They were waiting for an anticipated convening of the Chambers,
which, although a little delayed by the change of ministries, took place
on November 6, 1840. The two friends' trip was therefore put off to
the following year.

When, in 1838, Tocqueville had alternated his preparation of the
second *Democracy* with reading works of more general interest, the

---

[15]For works on Marshal Valée, see the biography by Girod de L'Ain (Paris, 1902) and Ch. A. Julien,
Histoire de l'Algérie contemporaine, vol. 1, chap. 3.

[16]Rémusat, *Mémoires de ma vie*, vols. 3 and 4. Especially vol. 4, 84: "[Beaumont] would have made
a very poor minister of the second rank."

[17]Ibid., vol. 3, 429.

322
〆 〆

Koran had figured in this reading alongside Pascal, Machiavelli, and Plato. He read it with pen in hand in Savary's elegant if unfaithful translation. He was far from having the admiration for Mohammed's work that Lamoricière had expressed, and was indignant that the latter had placed it above the Gospel. However, he was not insensitive to the "magnificent images of God that one finds in it constantly." Still, Tocqueville was interested above all in studying the moral influence that a religion exercised on a society. The Christian spirit of American society made democracy possible there, while the Muslim morality that so profoundly impregnated minds and manners crushed man with its materialism and its fatalism.[18] He would later write to Gobineau:

I studied the Koran a great deal, mainly because of our position vis-à-vis the Muslim populations of Algeria and throughout the Near East. I must tell you that I came away from that study with the conviction that by and large there have been few religions in the world as deadly to men as that of Mohammed. As far as I can see, it is the principal cause of the decadence so visible today in the Muslim world, and, though it is less absurd than the polytheism of old, its social and political tendencies are in my opinion infinitely more to be feared, and I therefore regard it as a form of decadence rather than a form of progress in relation to paganism itself.[19]

During the summer of 1840, he was deliberately preparing for his trip in his own way. He put aside the polemical literature to concentrate his study on official texts, which could be presumed to have some objectivity. This was at the time when large compendiums were first beginning to appear, collections like *Le Tableau de la situation des établissements français dans l'Algérie* and *Les Actes du gouvernement*. Through the first, especially, he sought a general comprehension of Algeria on the eve of the conquest: the property system, agricultural and commercial life, taxes, and charities, the system of justice that was so closely tied to religious law. As in America, his analyses gave rise to two different sorts of notes: brief summaries of features of the mores and of characteristic aspects of the institutions; and more developed texts, partial syntheses or judgments. He became aware through these official documents of the frightening arbitrariness that had governed the initial organization of the French colony. Summing up the work accomplished there in the course of the first years (1830–1834), he could not repress his indignation:

[18]The *Notes sur le Coran* are reprinted in the O.C. III, 1: 154–62.
[19]O.C. IX, 69.

It is inconceivable that in our day a nation that calls itself liberal should have established, close to France and in the name of France, a government so disordered, so tyrannical, so meddlesome, so profoundly illiberal—pushing to the limit, just as far as it can go without provoking rebellion—and so alien, indeed, to the most elementary notions of a good colonial regime. Those in power give the impression of a barbarous class, served by the jurists of an ultracivilized and corrupt class and employing the arts of the latter to satisfy its brutish passions. Or rather, one here sees men, generals and administrators, who, after having mortally suffered in their own country under the yoke of public opinion and under the application of the principles of liberty and the rule of law, seize with delight the occasion to act freely at last, far distant now from any hindrances, and to satisfy passions and tastes inflamed by constraint in a country whose exceptional situation serves them as pretext.[20]

This "monstrous state" was put in better order in 1834, but none of the guarantees enjoyed by French citizens existed in Algeria—neither freedom of the press, nor local representation, nor the irremovability of judges, nor formalities governing expropriation. On the contrary, though none of the rights of the citizens of the mother country had been carried over into Africa, all "the constraints of its system of administration" had been transplanted there.

Tocqueville asked himself if such a regime would allow one to do the great things one had dreamed of for Africa. It was as a traveler forewarned that he would visit the colony in 1841.

We can fix the chronology of this trip fairly accurately, thanks to the journal Tocqueville kept and the letters he wrote to his wife.[21] Having left Toulon on May 4 accompanied by Beaumont and his brother Hippolyte, he arrived in Algiers early on the morning of the seventh. Here, once again, he found Corcelle, who was also visiting the colony. Bugeaud had just completed his first expedition, during which he had crossed through the famous Mouzaïa pass to provision Médéa, where Cavaignac was in command. He had completed this expedition after bringing back a rather easy victory against the troops of Abd el-Kader. Back in Algiers, he set about preparing for the great expedition of the year. His initial success had put him in a good humor, and he offered his hospitality to Tocqueville and took him by sea to

[20]O.C. III, 1: 197.
[21]The bulk of the journal was published in the O.C. V, 2: 189–218, and O.C. VIII, 1: 209–12; the few pages discovered since are at the library of the city of Hamburg. Tocqueville's letters to his wife during this period can be found in the Tocqueville Archives, file 18.

324

悠 悠

Mostaganem, where they arrived on the sixteenth, joining Lamoricière, who had come from Oran. Early on the morning of the eighteenth Bugeaud went off to attack and lay waste to the emir's capital, Tagdempt, in the desert, where the latter thought himself safe from the French. Corcelle and Hippolyte left with Bugeaud, and it was a keen disappointment for Tocqueville that he could not accompany them. But his health was already precarious and he yielded to his friends' remonstrances.[22] Beaumont remained with him. The two of them embarked for Oran and Mers El Kébir the same day and, after a stopover at Arzew, were back in Algiers by the twenty-second. A delay on the part of the steamship that was to take them to Bône (now Annaba) allowed them to remain in Algiers investigating the state of the country by talking to public officials and a few Arabists. On the twenty-eighth, they embarked heading east. They visited Bougie (now Bejaïa) and Jijel during stopovers on the twenty-ninth, and landed on the thirtieth in Philippeville (now Skikda). The following day they left for Constantine, three days' journey from Philippeville across pacified country. But that same day or the next, apparently, Tocqueville suffered one of those terrible attacks of dysentery that often accompanied the fevers so common in Africa at that time. He had to be taken back to Philippeville in a cart and from there probably back to Algiers. We find him once again in Toulon on June 11. He had planned a trip of at least two weeks in the province of Constantine, followed by a visit of the same length in Algiers. His illness had caused him to lose a month of experiences in Algeria, and the main part of his investigation was limited to conversations with soldiers and sailors, to five days of interviews in Algiers from the twenty-third to the twenty-eighth, and to the walks in the Sahel that followed his arrival in Algiers. Beaumont, who had counted on finding material for a book in Algeria, sacrificed his plans to take care of his friend.

What Tocqueville had seen was an Algeria where—except for the region around Constantine—the towns, behind their walls and moats, were like islands beaten by the waves of the local uprisings. Only in Oran and Algiers could one roam around the outskirts. A fine road made it possible to cross the Sahel d'Alger, but after six or seven miles one had to stop and, from a hilltop, look down on the Mitidja, now reverted to a wasteland of dwarf palms and swamp, with, in the distance, the silhouette of an Arab rider. To the west, the officers of the engineers had begun "the continuous obstacle," a sort of Great

[22]Letter from Tocqueville to his father dated May 23, 1841, Tocqueville Archives.

Wall of China that was meant to protect France's modest enclave. It 325
would soon be abandoned because it was as dangerous for the men
working on it as it was ineffective in protecting the colonists.

As he had done in America, Tocqueville noted down only those
impressions of the country that might prove useful. To relive, say, the
gathering of the army at Mostaganem, it is necessary to turn to *Les
Français en Algérie,* by Louis Veuillot, who also found himself at
Bugeaud's headquarters just then. During the night of May 17–18,
while the deputy Tocqueville, in the palace occupied by the governor,
was commiserating with himself because he had yielded to his friends
and to good sense and given up the great expedition, Veuillot, a
journalist of the second rank, was being devoured by fleas in a cubicle
of the Moorish bath and impatiently, sleeplessly awaiting the dawn and
his horse.[23]

Tocqueville did write of his astonishment upon his arrival at Algiers' amazing mixture of races and costumes—Arab, Kabyle, Moorish,
Negro, Mahonnish, and French. Each of these races, jostling one
another in streets much too narrow to accommodate them all, spoke
a different language, wore different clothing, and had quite different
sets of customs and beliefs. They all appeared to be involved in feverish
activity. The entire lower city seemed in a state of destruction and
reconstruction. It was "Cincinnati transported onto African soil."[24] He
was sensitive, as he would be in Philippeville, to this activity typical
of a new country, which reminded him of America. But he deplored
the fact that the rules of Moorish architecture were not being respected;
Moorish buildings were "appropriate to the needs of the country and
charming as well." Tocqueville paid particular attention to the construction going on at the ports, especially at Mers El Kébir. All this
was the objective realization of Europe's inevitable expansion beyond
the continent, evidence of how European civilization was taking over
the world.

Like many of his contemporaries, he also admired the natural beau-
ties of the country and shared the illusions rather widely held then
concerning its fertility. From the boat that took him, in marvelous
weather, from Algiers to Philippeville, he sought to divine the life that
filled the mountains, still off limits, that lined the coast. In his articles
of 1837, he had already distinguished between the Kabyles—the Berbers who lived in the coastal ranges—and the Arabs, having a secret

[23]Veuillot, *Les Français en Algérie* (Tours, 1845), chap. 27.
[24]*O.C.* V, 2: 192.

sympathy for the rough and fiercely independent mountain people (he accepted the French raids against the Arabs, but would always be opposed to the military expeditions into Kabylia). From Philippeville, on May 30, he noted down his impressions for his brother Edouard:

A coast such as I have rarely seen in my life. This part of Algeria is infinitely more beautiful than the rest. High mountains plunge down to the sea. These mountains are covered with trees or grazing-ground up to their summits; at every moment they open up to reveal charming cultivated valleys covered with flocks of sheep. This entire immense group of mountains is peopled for the most part by the Kabyles. It is a country of enchantment cultivated by savages. As long as we don't set foot on the territory of these men, they say nothing to us, but woe betide the man who tries to go for a stroll in the beautiful country they inhabit . . . For the rest, they ceaselessly make war among themselves and live, I am told, in a state of utter anarchy, but for all that they have magnificent cultivated land, fine flocks, industries for making cloth, powder, and weapons.[25]

Tocqueville remained, above all, the indefatigable investigator whom we saw plaguing the Americans with questions. He questioned sailors, since part of his time was spent at sea going from one port to another, and also officers, since he was in contact with the army everywhere, and also the public officials in Algiers.

Among the military, he often came across the high-handedness that he had noted in his reading of official documents, and he was to become aware of the "idiotic hatred" of the soldiers for the colonists who were trying to settle in Africa to make money while they themselves had been sent there to shed their blood. It was not until 1846 that Tocqueville would find valuable informants among those officers stationed in the Arab sectors who had made an effort to become familiar with the country. Lamoricière, whom he saw for only one day on this visit, was a precursor of the type. But how many others resembled the colonel in command at Philippeville, who proudly enumerated his acts of terror against the Arabs and boasted of bullying the colonists, in a conversation that provoked Tocqueville to this comment: "Sadly listening to these things, I asked myself what the future of the country could be if it was abandoned to such men, and where this cascade of violence and injustice could end, if not in the revolt of the native population and the downfall of the Europeans."[26]

[25]Unpublished letter dated May 30, 1841.
[26]O.C. V, 2: 217.

The government officials were hardly any better. Under the thumb of the military themselves, they made the weight of administrative regulations felt by those under their jurisdiction, who were abandoned to their mercies without any laws for their own protection. Tocqueville found the officials to be of very low quality, except for the director of public education, Lepècheux, whom Marshal Valée had advised him to see, and Blondel, the head of the finance office, who was also aware of the moral failings in the organization of the colony and with whom Tocqueville seems to have renewed contact later on. The bishop, Monsignor Dupuch, whom he met twice, aroused Tocqueville's sympathy because he was standing up to the governor and had just courageously brought about an exchange of prisoners. But the bishop had something of both "saint and Gascon" in him, and Tocqueville was conscious of the unruliness of a character whose intemperate zeal and excesses hardly suited the delicate post with which he had been entrusted.

Not long after his arrival in Algiers, Tocqueville noted: "Despite the fact that I had read a good deal of material, the actual appearance of the places I had read of astonished me, and as for the inhabitants, I see such amazing differences in their viewpoints at present that I feel a sort of intellectual vertigo."[27]

It was in the following October, as he was slowly recovering at Tocqueville from the illness that had cut short his trip, that he wrote the memoir in which he articulated his position on Algeria.[28] He considered its conquest the most important business France had before her, and was indignant that the Soult-Guizot government treated it as a secondary problem, approaching it without any political doctrine and merely following the suggestions of the various offices of the Ministry of War, which was responsible for administering Algerian affairs.

Beginning in 1842, Tocqueville tried to make opportunities to bring about practical reforms. There was, first, the extraparliamentary commission headed by the Duc Decazes, brought together by the government to study the problems of Algerian colonization. Tocqueville and Beaumont participated enthusiastically in the first sessions and helped determine its agenda. But they soon came to understand that the government had no intention of taking the commission's suggestions into account and immediately decided to withdraw.[29]

Then there was the opportunity in 1845, when Tocqueville was

[27]Letter to his father dated May 12, 1841, Tocqueville Archives.
[28]See *Travail sur l'Algérie*, O.C. III, 1: 213–80.
[29]Tocqueville to Beaumont, December 30, 1842, O.C. VIII, 2: 495.

codirector of the newspaper *Le Commerce*. But his associate and friend Corcelle had ideas concerning Algeria that were quite a bit different from his own and held to them firmly. It appears to have been Corcelle who decided the paper's "Algerian line."

This left the tribune of the Chamber of Deputies. In June of the 1846 session, during the discussion of special appropriations in the budget, a very lively debate on Algeria began in which all the experts on the question took part. In the course of it, Tocqueville gave one of his most eloquent speeches, asserting that until now this question, the most important faced by the country, had been handled merely as chance dictated. He called for the creation of a special Algerian Ministry.

After the 1846 session, Tocqueville, aware of the intensifying troubles in Italy, thought for a time of traveling to the Italian peninsula. But he felt a more immediate need to bring his knowledge of Africa up to date and decided, despite the long bout of illness he had suffered in 1841, to return to Algiers.

Since his earlier visit, the situation had changed significantly. The year 1845 had seen a return offensive by Abd el-Kader, who had wiped out the little force at Sidi Brahim commanded by Colonel de Montaignac. At the same time, the Dahra had risen up in response to the preaching of the fanatic called Bou Maza ("the goat man"). In September, Marshal Bugeaud had had to interrupt his vacation in the Dordogne to return in haste to Algeria. Although a segment of public opinion thought the colony was in grave danger, it had firmly subdued the insurrections. Abd el-Kader was now more a fugitive than a rival, and the tribes, decimated and starving, were everywhere yielding in submission to the French power. In June, Tocqueville had taken note of this before the Chamber: the war was "a burden, an inconvenience, a great deal of trouble, but henceforth no longer a danger."[30]

The future could therefore be looked at afresh. A country that had been altogether pacified no longer needed to be subjected to a military regime—particularly since the growing fame of Bugeaud, whose success with the public was far from a modest one, made the government inclined to limit his powers. The ordinance of April 15, 1845, had already made provision for this by creating a director of civil affairs and by dividing the country into civil, Arab, and mixed zones. But Bugeaud balked at the change and forced the resignation, in August 1846, of the first director of civil affairs, Blondel—whom Tocqueville

---

[30]Speech given June 9, 1846, *O.C.* III, I: 293.

knew, as we have seen—in an attempt to ward off any impediment to the military authority's power.

Even the army now had, alongside the swashbucklers who knew nothing of the country, officers in the bureaus dealing with Arab affairs who were well informed about indigenous life and could give useful opinions on conditions under French rule. Though only fifteen thousand of the European colonists had settled on farms (about one-seventh of the total number of emigrants), they were trying out various systems of planting, and there was, besides, the competition between civilian and military colonization that Bugeaud had anticipated. These early agricultural experiments were thus of great interest, however unrewarding or paltry they might seem.

Tocqueville's first plan was to stay in Algiers and not leave its environs. He had not asked either Corcelle or Beaumont (whom he would only inform of his trip at a late date, their friendship having cooled considerably over the past year) to go with him. Instead, he took along Madame de Tocqueville, who would watch over his health and guard him against the temptation of adventure. We are therefore deprived of any regular correspondence from this trip (Madame de Tocqueville reported the news to the family), a lacuna which is all the more regrettable since only a few fragments remain of the journal kept by Tocqueville.[31] Our main source of information is an article by a journalist, Bussière, who dogged Tocqueville's steps during half his visit and later published an account of his trip.[32]

Tocqueville apparently arrived in Algiers in the first days of November. He went to see the governor, to whom he frankly presented their disagreements. But Bugeaud chose to counterattack with charm. There were other deputies in Algiers: Lanjuinais and Lavergne, both well known to Tocqueville; Béchameil, a seafaring man; and Plichon, a manufacturer, with whom Tocqueville had less to do in Paris, but who were, with Lavergne, his daily companions in the venture proposed to them by the marshal—to go with him by land from Algiers to Oran.

This was how the military excursion was described by Dussert, the sub-director of civil affairs: "Several deputies came to visit Algeria, they were escorted through the whole Arab phantasmagoria, including

---

[31]These fragments are in the library at the University of Hamburg. They contain very detailed observations about the settling of the colonists and the difficulties of developing the lands, as well as lively criticisms of the chaotic bureaucracy.

[32]A. Bussière, "Le maréchal Bugeaud et la colonisation de l'Algérie," in *Revue des deux mondes* (1853), vol. 4, 449–506.

the horsemen's fantasia with rifles blazing, all of it. Powder was thrown (that's the right expression) in their eyes and they went off convinced that they had got to know a country about which they haven't a clue . . . M. de Tocqueville, a very distinguished man . . . was the only one to evade the official stratagems, getting off by himself and away from the tours as much as he could."[33] The itinerary took them through Blida, Médéa, Miliana, and Orléansville. If Bussière's account is correct, the group took six or seven days, apparently from October 20 to 26, to go from Algiers to Orléansville. A stopover in the mountains with France's ally Bou Allem allowed them to appreciate the magnificent hospitality of a great Arab lord. Bugeaud displayed a mixture of goodwill and contentiousness. In Médéa, "he proposed a toast to the army. The remarks he made about it were provocative and seemed almost hostile . . . He praised its discipline, its stoic resignation, its courage—viewed with ingratitude by some, with indifference by others. He tossed out spiteful comparisons here and there, innuendos about the colonists, the Chambers, the government. No one was spared. With a great deal of tact and delicacy, M. de Tocqueville, in his response, was able to avoid anything that could have given a simple toast the appearance of a polemic. He echoed the praise of the army, but he separated out what the marshal had confused, steered clear of innuendoes, and after throwing into the peroration a few felicitous flourishes that outdid the marshal himself, ended by proposing a toast to the union of the civilian forces and the army."[34]

Bugeaud scored some points concerning the country's security: in the Mouzaïa pass, of sinister renown, they met two French workers going on foot, unarmed, from Médéa to Blida. All along the way, his talk amounted to an apologia for the military regime. He pointed out roads and hospitals built by the staff of engineers, gardens cultivated by soldiers, the simplicity and economy of the officers' administration. But at Miliana, he was very much annoyed at having to receive, when his guests were present, a delegation of colonists who had come to demand a civilian commissioner and a justice of the peace. At Orléansville, Marshal Saint-Arnaud, irritated by the presence of the deputies (and in particular, it seems, by Tocqueville), answered the question of the marshal, concerned about "what he had done for the civilian population," by praising the superb organization of the civil militia

[33]Letter from Dussert to Maréchal de Castellane dated January 1, 1847, in *Campagnes d'Afrique: Lettres adressées au maréchal de Castellane* (Paris, 1898), 503.

[34]Bussière, "Le maréchal Bugeaud," 463.

and its rigorous discipline: "At the least neglect of duty, I put them into the grain silo head first. That's what I do for them."[35]

In Orléansville, Tocqueville left the marshal and, with Lieutenant-Colonel Canrobert, crossed the Dahra, which had been only recently subdued, stopped off with a still trembling Kabyle leader, and embarked at Ténès for Oran, where he spent one day with Lamoricière, then returned to Algiers, where he rejoined Madame de Tocqueville on November 30.

Two days later, accompanied by Bussière and escorted by two huntsmen on horseback, he began a week-long visit to the villages of the Sahel and the Mitidja. He made a detailed examination of the basic conditions and organization of the holdings, noting the ravages of fever, the precarious economic situation of many of the colonists, and the deep attachment to the land, despite their setbacks, of a population without which the French colony seemed to him to have no future. This is what comes across in Bussière's account.

But we have no Bussière for the last part of Tocqueville's trip. He had been invited to go to Constantine with his wife by General Bedeau, who was in command there at the time. Embarking on the tenth at Algiers, he suffered the inconvenience of being disembarked and delayed because of heavy weather at Bône. On the fourteenth, he wrote that he hoped to reach Philippeville by sea that evening, where a carriage sent by Bedeau was waiting for him, then to embark for France on December 29. His stay at Constantine is known to us only through a hotel bill preserved in the library of the University of Hamburg. It was thus that he met Bedeau, whom he apparently had not known before. The two men felt an affinity for each other. Tocqueville was critical of Bugeaud for his hostility toward the colo-

[35]Ibid., 471. Saint-Arnaud's impressions are summed up in a letter to his brother dated November 29, 1846 (*Lettres du maréchal de Saint-Arnaud*, vol. 2 [Paris, 1864]): "For five days now, my mind, my legs, and my horses haven't had a rest. My body is less tired than my mind, but confronting a marshal who loves to talk, as well as four deputies and two journalists who question constantly ab hic and ab hoc is too much, I am done in. Anyway, I left on Tuesday, the twenty-fifth, in search of the marshal, who was to the west of Fodda with a squadron. We met up during the day and we dined and bivouacked together. I found him a little indisposed and I left him yesterday in good health. He attributed that happy effect to the contentment he felt in my subdivision. With him he had MM. Tocqueville, de Lavergne, Béchameil and Plichon, deputies, de Broë and de Bussières, men of letters (*Débats* or *Revues des deux mondes*). M. de Tocqueville affected to some degree a profound, rational, methodical sort of observation.

"We had three homeric meals for eighteen people each time, a reception and royal entry at Orléansville, with cannons, troops lining the streets, illuminations, spectacles, etc. All that was missing were bonfires. My hyenas made up for it, and were wildly successful. Marie and Fanny will perhaps have their article in *Les Débats* or the *Revue*. After lunch on Thursday, we split up into two groups, MM. Tocqueville, Béchameil, Lavergne, and Bussières left to embark at Ténès. The marshal, with MM. Plichon and de Broë, came with me to Aïn Méran, whence they set off for Mostaganem."

332

𝄞 𝄞

nists; Lamoricière, despite his fine intellect, was implacably ambitious. Bedeau, more humane, more moderate, was quick to establish regular relations with Tocqueville.[36]

The study made during these three months on Algerian soil was to be used the following year in the two long parliamentary reports published by *Le Moniteur* on May 24, which created a great stir.[37]

On February 27, 1847, the government sent the Chamber two bills, one relating to the special appropriation for Algeria, the other to the creation of military camps that would eventually become sites for civilian colonization, in accordance with a plan of Marshal Bugeaud's.

On a proposition put forward by Gustave de Beaumont, the Chamber voted to entrust the examination of the two plans to a single committee of eighteen members. This committee chose Tocqueville as its chairman and rapporteur.

Not without difficulties. Beaumont ran against him for the position of rapporteur, and it was necessary to win over the members of the committee one by one. Lamoricière supported Beaumont's candidacy. He had been elected deputy from Saint-Calais with the support of Beaumont, who had won a double election, and no doubt thought that Beaumont as the rapporteur on Algerian affairs would reflect his own views with more docility than would Tocqueville.

Conveying the unanimous decision of the committee, Tocqueville caused the entire appropriation for the military colonization to be rejected, which led to the resignation of Governor-General Bugeaud, a result no doubt anticipated by the cabinet when it put forward this plan that was so dear to the marshal's heart. Tocqueville's report on the special appropriation for Algeria underwent a few modifications at the request of his colleagues on the committee, but the picture he presented of the colony corresponded closely to his own ideas. His denunciation of the lack of freedom for civilians led the government to promise free elections in the civilian zones.

In 1849, Tocqueville was chairman of the committee charged with deciding whether to consider the Didier proposal, which moved toward providing a legal framework for the administration in Algeria. He took the occasion to denounce from the tribune one last time the

---

[36]Unpublished letter from Bedeau dated December 18, 1846.
[37]*O.C.* III, 1: 308–408.

incoherence and instability of the regulations that had ruled the colony up to then.[38]

Subsequently, under the Second Empire, Tocqueville did not mention Algeria again—a fact that never ceases to be astonishing—even though his correspondence from 1851 to 1859 is a mine of observations and criticisms of the domestic government of France and its foreign policy. Only from 1837 to 1849, then, can we follow his thoughts through numerous texts. Not all of these, it is true, are equally valuable: concerning the reports of 1847, for example, we know—though the proceedings of the committee have been lost—that Tocqueville made some changes in his initial text at the request of colleagues. At that time, moreover, there were many assertions in his two articles of 1837 that he apparently repudiated.

And yet, taking these writings all together, clear and coherent general ideas emerge from them concerning the conquest, the relationship with the indigenous population, and colonization.

We have seen that, for Tocqueville, Algeria strengthened France's position and allowed it to dominate the western Mediterranean. At the time of his first trip, he admired the bases at Mers El Kébir and Algiers which, in his eyes, justified the conquest. With any rebirth of Muslim independence on the Mediterranean littoral now out of the question, France, if she were to abandon the region, would be succeeded in all probability by England, who would seize the former French territory in Africa and thus round out the conquest of Gibraltar and Malta. Though the bad management of Algerian affairs discouraged Tocqueville from time to time, he never seriously envisaged giving up the colony.

But by 1837, sooner than many of his contemporaries, he understood the impossibility of a limited occupation. The Treaty of the Tafna, whose principle was the unification of the interior of the country by a friendly prince or vassal, seemed to him contrary to the nature of things. How would this prince be able to accept France's ability to block his outlets to the sea?

Once the unification was accomplished, Abd el-Kader would inevitably become France's enemy. What France really had to do was dominate the whole of the country and also implant a population of European farmers in a limited zone. This process of dominating the country should be carried out in tandem with the colonization, each

[38]O.C. III, 1: 429–40.

334

劣 义

bolstering the other, thus discouraging both the natives' hope of driving France out and any possible notion, on the part of a foreign power, of a surprise attack on the coast.

This plan involved making war against Abd el-Kader. Tocqueville did not like war in general, but it did not strike him as an absolute evil. During the crisis of 1840, when France was alone against Europe, he thought war preferable to a humiliating debasement of France and yet, not believing, as some on the left did, in the success of a war of propaganda, he foresaw a defeat. War in Europe was cruel because of the shelling of civilian populations and the blockades. In Africa, its cruelty assumed other forms. Certain officers could easily make it cruel beyond forgiveness by encouraging the massacre of prisoners, and Tocqueville waxed indignant at these pointless acts of violence. But he accepted the raids in which crops were burned, flocks confiscated, and tribes reduced to famine, forcing them to abandon Abd el-Kader. He admired the organization of Bugeaud's mobile columns, which allowed increased scope for the raids and proved their effectiveness. When news of the "smoke-attacks," in which hundreds of natives died in caves—one of them the attack on the Ouled Riah by Pélissier— became known in Paris, and provoked lively reactions, in particular by Montalembert, Tocqueville remained silent.

How should the Arabs be treated after the pacification? In 1837, Tocqueville thought assimilation possible: "There is . . . no reason to believe that the passing of time cannot succeed in blending the two races. God is not preventing it, only human failings can put obstacles in its path."[39] Here we see once again the Tocqueville who could take a sympathetic interest in the Canadian métis, the Tocqueville who later felt indignation at the theories of Gobineau denying the unity of a human race born undivided from a single gesture of the Creator.

But in 1841 his tone changed: the Arabs must not be allowed to forget that they were a defeated people. In his 1847 report, Tocqueville condemned France's excessive generosity, criticized the transport at state expense of pilgrims from Mecca to Egypt, the construction of mosques, the distribution of Legion of Honor rosettes to the natives, and so on. Of course, he spoke up indignantly against the theories of certain newspapers of Algiers that wanted to expel the Arabs, but "it is neither useful nor responsible to allow our Muslim subjects to entertain exaggerated notions of their own importance or to persuade them that we are obliged to treat them in all circumstances precisely

[39]O.C. III, 1: 153.

as though they were our fellow citizens and our equals." France had 335
to retain its political power over them, entrust the natives with secondary powers and, insofar as possible, make use of influences already
existing there. In sum, France owed them strict justice and good
government, that is to say a government that acted not only in France's
interest but in theirs as well.

More generally, Tocqueville wanted to preserve the existing indigenous society but under the external control, to some degree, of the
French authority. This was why, for example, he condemned the fact
that the administration had taken over the Muslims' religious institutions, though he acknowledged the malfeasances of the oukils in charge
of them; but what would be the reaction of French parishioners if an
honest Arab mufti were substituted for their roguish sextons? He went
so far as to refer to the "idiotic glee" of a short notice in the *Tableau*
announcing that at last it was possible to open the "walled houses of
the Moors" to the doctor sent by the registry office. He protested
vigorously against the decline of Constantine's Koran schools that
followed the French settlement.

Once pacification was achieved, therefore, Algeria's society would
be an unequal one: on the one hand, the French and the other Europeans; on the other, natives who would continue to live by the law
of the Koran.

The unequal society thus envisaged hardly seemed to conform to
that divine plan for equality among men described in the *Democracy*. [40]
Certainly the Muslim did not belong to an inferior race, but to an
imperfect civilization, decadent by comparison with the ancient world,
for there were "few religions as deadly to men as that of Mohammed."
But Tocqueville in some sense locked the individual Muslim into that
civilization and did not allow an indigenous elite any prospect of
acceding to the principles of Christian civilization, since he was evidently opposed even to admitting young Arabs to the schools of
France.

Yet Tocqueville did not imagine that Muslim society would remain
fixed. But in what direction would it evolve? He no doubt believed
there would be one evolution for the Kabyles—who had free institutions—and a different one for Arabs in general. In the case of the latter,
he was not sure their ideas and mores would evolve in the direction
of greater enlightenment. In a letter written December 1, 1846, to

[40]See Melvin Richter, "Tocqueville on Algeria," *Review of Politics* 25, 362–98; Michael Hereth, *A.
de Tocqueville, Die Gefährung der Freiheit in der Demokratie* (Stuttgart, 1979).

336

Corcelle, who was concerning himself in a very humane way with the future of the indigenous population, Tocqueville showed that he was not insensitive either to the horrors of the war or to the disarray of the conquered. He spoke up against the ideas of extermination held in parts of the army and added: "What means should be used in order for the two races truly to come into contact? I confess with sorrow that here my mind is troubled and hesitates. I will tell you all I have seen and learned about this subject. Whatever happens, one can be sure that our close proximity will bring about a social revolution among the Arabs that will be extremely difficult for them to work through."[41]

Tocqueville's ideas about colonization were firmer. The goal was to create a population in Algeria that would be an extension of the population of the mother country and subject, insofar as possible, to the same laws.

The implantation of an agricultural population was the basis of this colonization, and in his two trips, Tocqueville inspected with great care the villages of the Sahel and the Mitidja that formed the principal nucleus of it. These villages were created by different methods: Beni-Mered in accordance with the principles of agricultural camps dear to Bugeaud; others in keeping with the system of Colonel Marengo, who had military prisoners build houses and clear a part of the land before turning them over to the civil authority; others following the principle of the director of the interior department at Algiers, Comte Guyot, in which the colonists paid for the land but were provided with construction materials, seed, and livestock. Tocqueville thought these efforts on the part of the administration did more harm than good, and only delayed the moment when the new farmer would find himself face to face with natural difficulties. The role of the State, as he saw it, was to make land grants and to act as intermediary in all cases of land purchases from the natives. Once property was deeded, the State should limit itself to carrying out the cadastral land surveys on which tax assessments were based and setting up a few public services—building roads, digging wells. The military administration could provide indirect support, for example through the purchase of fodder at a price that gave the farmer a fair return.

Tocqueville did not make a formal choice between the system of small-scale colonization in which individuals were given small holdings and the great land grants advocated by Lamoricière, who wanted the State to deal with large companies that would take over the

[41]Tocqueville to Corcelle, Algiers, December 1, 1846, O.C. XV, 1: 222–26.

responsibility of recruiting colonists. Tocqueville's preference ran to the creation of villages in which the landholdings were unequal. This would permit mingling wealthy colonists who had capital with small colonists who had little more than their hands. In this way, a rural society could be freely established which resembled that of villages in the mother country.

But even the problem of European colonization was subordinate for Tocqueville to the question of the body of laws governing persons and property, and he severely criticized the existing state of affairs. In this great Algerian enterprise, two forces—forces that, moreover, were rivals—operated at the expense of the emigrants: the arbitrary rule of the military authority and the centralized administration of the civil authority.

Tocqueville had scathingly denounced the military authority: its expulsion of colonists from Algeria, its expropriation decrees that gave the persons affected only twenty-four hours' notice, its excessive requisitions, and the obtuse hatred of the subordinate officers for the civilian French. But he was perhaps even more scathing toward a civil administration which, far from understanding that the management of a new country called for a simplification of forms and procedures, had multiplied them at will. Tocqueville denounced the twofold centralization to which the colony was subjected: that of the minister of war in Paris, who in addition often had to consult his colleagues, and that of the governor-general in Algiers (at a time when communication between certain towns in the colony and Algiers was even more difficult than communication with Paris). The result was that matters did not go forward very fast, if they were not lost sight of altogether. Tocqueville gave concrete examples of this bureaucratic ponderousness: the chief public official in Constantine could not give an order to the civil engineer of that town. Even if the matter did not have to go all the way back to Paris, which was often the case, he had to advise the governor-general, who would notify the director of public works, who in turn would retransmit the order to Constantine. This cumbersome system was incredibly inefficient. More than a year was required to repair a leak in an aqueduct. Poor people often waited in Algiers for four or five years to gain possession of farm land they had already been granted. In 1847, the administration still had not completed the cadastral survey of the Sahel and the Mitidja.

Private citizens in Algeria were deprived of the protections enjoyed by citizens of the mother country. The fact that judges were not subject to appeal and, even more, the outrageous powers granted the attorney

338

general left the system of justice without any independence. The press was subject to censorship, liberty of education did not exist, there was a total absence of the right to vote even when it came to those lesser judicial bodies with authority to resolve commercial disputes, whose integrity Napoléon had respected.

Individuals were not blameless. The governor-general himself, in five years, had not resided in Algiers for more than two. Many of the public officials were corrupt. But the most serious of the evils the colony suffered was the total absence of leadership. The anarchic spirit with which this great undertaking was conducted could be seen in the successive bodies of regulations that canceled or contradicted each other. Tocqueville thought that in Paris, where the minister of war had too much to do, a Ministry for Algeria should be created that would put in order everything that concerned the laws governing persons and property. In Algiers, a civilian governor-general should be appointed who had limited, statutory powers. More fundamentally, he called for the institution of municipal councils for the Europeans. Such local bodies were, for the liberals of the time, where political liberty was born. These councils would be the germ of what could attract Europeans to a colony: freedoms like those they possessed or sought to possess in their native land.

Thus Tocqueville's long meditations gave rise to a coherent, concrete program for the government, administration, and colonization of Algeria.

Though Tocqueville followed closely the expansion and emigration into new territories (New Zealand, for example) and though he was attentive to the transformations brought about in the governing of well-established colonies (Canada, for example), he never attempted a synthesis of his views on the phenomenon of colonialism in general. But he left us interesting sketches for a study of the greatest colonial achievement of his time, England's empire in India.[42]

This study was no more than a brief episode on the margin of Tocqueville's political career.

In 1840, he demonstrated his interest in India for the first time, an interest that arose from the habit he and his wife had of reading aloud from travel writings almost every evening. As he often did, he consulted Jean-Jacques Ampère, who was for him something of a mine of

[42]Tocqueville's notes on India appear in *O.C.* III, 1: 441–552.

bibliographic information. On September 27, he wrote him that they 339
had been reading books by Alexander Burnes, the former British army 𝕸 𝕸
officer who had published accounts of his travels through India and
Afghanistan:

This gave us, and especially me, a great thirst to know the East better. There
must be other equally instructive modern works, travel writings or histories,
either on Persia, Turkestan, or the Indian peninsula . . . Does there exist a
translation of a good history or description of England's empire in that part
of the world? As for travel writings, there is Elphinstone's, to which Burnes
often refers and which must be intriguing. If your memory and your learning
suggest some ideas to you on this point, it would be a kindness if you would
communicate them to my bookseller, who would buy the books that you
mentioned to him.[43]

But a letter written five days later to Buloz, to whom he had
promised a contribution to the *Revue des deux mondes,* indicates that
he had not first discovered the world of India in Burnes, as his letter
to Ampère might lead one to believe, although Burnes may have
reawakened his interest in the country:

Nothing is less well known in France than the causes that produced and
that sustain the astonishing greatness of the English in India. This subject,
which has always been interesting, is wonderfully so now that all the great
affairs of Europe have their center in Africa. It is particularly so for us now
that we have the colony of Algiers. This subject is therefore connected to
everything that interests and moves men these days . . . I have already
gathered many documents on the position of the English in India; I have
perhaps had more occasion than another to concern myself with it. I ask
nothing better than to do one or two articles on this subject; but I can't
promise these articles immediately, because I would like to do something
worthy of being read by serious people and the material is very difficult.[44]

He could not get down to any serious work before the 1841 session,
which was followed by his first trip to Algeria. Once he was back at
Tocqueville, where he remained ill for several weeks, he wrote to
Buloz on September 12: "My intention is to occupy myself with India
and with you, as soon as the thing is possible. Send me Barchou, please,
and believe, Sir, that quite apart from my desire to deal with an

[43]*O.C.* XI, 145.
[44]Unpublished letter from Tocqueville to Buloz dated October 2, 1840, Lovenjoul Archives.

340

೫ ೫

important and strange subject, I attach great value to doing something that might be pleasing to you."[45] The article on India, planned during the preceding year, was to take the form, then, of one of those long reviews the *Revue* published at that time, in which the author presented his personal views on the occasion of a recently published work—in this instance, Barchou de Penhoen's six-volume *Histoire de la conquête et de la fondation de l'empire anglais dans l'Inde.* Tocqueville read Barchou but did not write the review, even though he was pestered by the author to do so. In truth, Barchou would perhaps have been less disappointed if he had known Tocqueville's opinion of the work, which was no more than a chronicle of events:

I see absolutely nothing in it but a certain knack for narration, a quite secondary quality for the historian. As to the rest, the causes of the events he recounts seem to escape him completely. Not only does he not mention them, he does not even contrive to let one guess them. This is why, instead of bringing out the salient facts in each period, he goes into a thousand details without knowing how to select the most important and without enabling his reader to make the selection himself.[46]

After the sessions of 1842 and 1843, Tocqueville continued to work on India: "It has been a long time since I have worked with as much ardor and enjoyment," he wrote to Reeve. And to Beaumont on October 9, 1843: "Now I'm going to occupy myself with England's empire in India. This work interests me, even amuses me a great deal."[47] This was no doubt the time when, having closed the books he had read, he wrote the rough draft of the first part of the work, which has been preserved for us. But he stopped this project, which he was never to finish, on December 3, the date on which he got back into his parliamentary harness. According to a letter written long afterwards, he gave up writing about India because he had not been able to visit the country.

The Near Eastern crisis of 1840 certainly incited Tocqueville to take a closer interest in England's Indian Empire. He saw Egypt as a landing stage that would permit the Western powers to reach that immense Asian continent destined to fall under the domination of the European states. But he himself pointed out the interest presented by a study of India in its relation to France's conquest of Algeria. At first sight, there

[45]Unpublished letter from Tocqueville to Buloz, Lovenjoul Archives.
[46]*O.C.* III, 1: 512.
[47]*O.C.* VI, 1, 72; *O.C.* VIII, 1: 506.

was an essential difference: Algeria was to be a colony for European 341
settlement; in India, thirty thousand English were governing a million
Hindus. But in both cases, two civilizations whose religions were
radically different were coming into contact. The conquests, which had
been carried out in countries that were already subjected to foreign
rule, could not be held within limits despite the desire of the English
of the eighteenth century and the French of 1830 for a restricted
territorial occupation. Finally, while maintaining the indigenous local
organization of society, the English had superimposed upon it a flexible and competent administrative structure with the home country
retaining, in particular, the power of fiscal control. We should add that
certain passages in the notes on India reveal Tocqueville's sentimental
nostalgia for the empire lost under Louis XV, a nostalgia we have often
encountered in him before: France might have had the great position
in the world which England gained, for the most part, through India:

"*India.* Superb geographical position. From there, England dominates all of Asia. A flash of brilliance that reflects back on the entire
nation. Sense of greatness and power which that gives a whole people.
Financial and commercial considerations are not the only things by
which a nation should judge the value of a conquest."[48]

Tocqueville's plan for the work on India that he intended to write
reveals something of his preoccupations: He would first deal with the
conquest of India and the organization of the conquest. Next, he was
to paint "a picture of the establishment of the English in India as it
is today"; in a third part, he would set out to study the "effects of the
English government on the condition of the Hindus"; finally, the last
part was entitled "How the English empire in India could be destroyed."

Tocqueville wrote no more than a rough draft of the first part.

Europe, Tocqueville tells us, could see in the conquest of India, so
sudden and carried out with such scanty means, nothing but "an
inexplicable and almost marvelous event." And Tocqueville, who with
his master Montesquieu did not think the course of the world was
determined by blind chance, tried to show that, on the contrary, this
conquest was in the nature of things, and was in keeping both with
the state of Hindu society and with a fortunate historical conjuncture.

Hindu society was "in the middle age" of human societies, the age
in which they have lost the energy of barbarians without having
acquired the means of defense of people with an advanced civilization.

[48]*O.C.* III, 1: 478.

342

乡 岁

The Brahman religion, lacking both fanaticism and morality—the only religion in the world that was "worse than a complete absence of belief"—divided this society into castes and paralyzed all common action. Lastly, the local community was the "true social soil of India," leaving the masses indifferent to what was happening above them and preserving them, in the case of conquest, from sinking into anarchy.

Thus India had always been prey to conquerors—a great advantage to a newcomer, all the more so since in the eighteenth century old and new powers in India were embroiled in intestine quarrels that the English were able to exploit. Their only possible rivals, the French—who, like them, had come from the outside—had cleared the way for them and were paralyzed at the decisive moment by the Revolution.

What seemed admirable to Tocqueville, therefore, was not that the English had conquered India with ludicrously small means and uncertain plans, but that they had been able to hold on to it by organizing it in the very midst of the conquest. Pitt's India Act of 1784 had established a balance between the East India Company and the English State which caused the administration to rely on the former, managed by its directors, "twenty-four obscure merchants," while the State actually governed through the Board of Control, without which nothing important could be done, but which in fact brought to the Company the support of British power. "I think it was more difficult to find a nation able to rule India in this manner than to find one able to conquer it."

It was with this homage to the British Empire and Pitt's genius that Tocqueville broke off his draft. The implicit comparison with the bureaucratic, military management of Algeria, and the influence of this study of India on the ideas in his long report of 1847 are obvious.

Concern about the greatness of his country, about the place of the French nation in the world, were preoccupations that Tocqueville asserted almost naively at times. When he cried from the tribune, "I am a devoted servant of my country, but never will I be its lackey,"[49] he was being faithful to the traditions of his ancestors Malesherbes and Vauban, convictions that had prevailed at a time when the nation was incarnate in the royal person. This aspect of his character has sometimes been overlooked by those who see Tocqueville only as he appears in the *Democracy*.

[49]Speech of January 18, 1842, on the Chamber's address.

19

OPPOSITION TO THE GOVERNMENT AND THE QUESTION OF "LIBERTY OF TEACHING" (1842–1846)

THE ELECTIONS of July 9, 1842, were hardly favorable to the government, and during the days following, as the results were appearing in the press, political circles reckoned that its majority, fragile in the last Chamber, would be even more precarious in the new one. But on July 13, these preoccupations—causes for concern for some and hope for others—were cast in the shadow by a tragic incident: the Duc d'Orléans was killed in a carriage accident.

The prince, heir to the throne, was the most popular member of the royal family. The crowds were drawn to his attractive appearance and his easygoing manner, and his broad intelligence and reflective nature had caused him to be appreciated by the elites (and Tocqueville, who could not be said to care for the Orléans dynasty, saw real worth in him). His political tendencies inclined the prince toward a firm foreign policy but a less rigid conservatism in domestic affairs. In the eyes of the opposition, he seemed to understand his time, and because of that helped them to be patient. His death was a dynastic catastrophe. On a throne that was not yet solidly established sat a sixty-nine-year-old king whose heir, the Comte de Paris, son of the Duc d'Orléans, was only five years old.

The possibility of a regency had therefore to be envisaged. The government hoped to gain some control over this eventuality by creating an organic law that would establish, for this and any future exigency, the place of a regency among the institutions of the monarchy. The regency would be entrusted to the prince closest to the throne in the order established by the Charter of 1830. As it happened, this

344

ᛒ ᛔ

was the Duc de Nemours, the oldest of the uncles of the little Comte de Paris, thus excluding the widowed Duchesse d'Orléans, the young Comte's mother, Helen of Mecklenburg. The king and the government sought to rally in support of this law all the dynastic parties in the Chamber, with the exception of the legitimist far right and the radical far left, by making their support a solemn act of Orleanist loyalism.

Thiers, who appeared to be the government's main opponent, was easily won over. He made his peace with the king and set about actively supporting the government. He brought together in his home the principal members of the left center and the left. Tocqueville was present and does not seem to have offered any strong opposition to Thiers's arguments. Barrot apparently went much further: for form's sake, he would vote in favor of an amendment proposing an elective regency, but would then support the government's plan, although he would refuse to speak and would cast his vote in silence.

Yet when the Chamber was convened to discuss the question of the regency, from August 18 to 20, this scenario could not be put into play. On the very first day, Lamartine ascended the tribune. He took the occasion to make a solemn break with the right center and announced that he was in favor of a regency entrusted to the Duchesse d'Orléans. His speech made a strong impression and Guizot felt he had to step up to the tribune immediately afterwards. Tocqueville responded to Guizot and attacked the principle of an organic law, which could only burden the future and encroach on the prerogatives of Chambers still to come. He was willing to see a special law passed that would entrust the regency to the king's uncles, as was provided for in an amendment proposed by Sade, a deputy of the dynastic left. Tocqueville had prepared his speech carefully, accumulating historical examples of expectations which had proved false where regencies were concerned. But he was unsettled by the necessity of answering Guizot, the brilliant extemporizer. Under the circumstances, he was obliged to rely heavily on his notes, and his argument, clear but without warmth, made little impression on the Chamber.[1] No one felt this more than he did, as he wrote to his wife the next day:

I spoke in the Chamber yesterday. The moment was very unfavorable. It was almost six o'clock. The Chamber was impatient. This bothered me. And I thought I spoke horribly badly! From everything I hear people say this

[1]Tocqueville's speech was given August 18, 1842, and printed in the *Moniteur*, pp. 1812–13, on the nineteenth.

morning, it seems that impression of mine was much exaggerated and if
yesterday's speech was not a success, it was not a failure either . . . Yesterday
once again, I discovered that I absolutely lack the talent which, in this
government, is everything, the talent of extemporizing.[2]

That same evening of August 18, Tocqueville hurried over to
Barrot's with a few friends to urge him to speak up against the law.
The following day, Barrot gave an eloquent speech in which he
defended an elective regency and indicated his preference for the
Duchesse d'Orléans. Thiers was surprised by what he considered to be
Barrot's betrayal of his word,[3] and furious at the influences that had
led to this defection. He replied the next day, August 20, with a very
sour speech in which he described the left as being just as incapable of
managing the country as it was of managing itself. The regency law
was voted in by 310 votes to 91, but the debate had not demonstrated
the broad support for the dynasty hoped for by the king.

Thiers had been sincere in his support of this plan: his unquestionable
Orleanist loyalties were reinforced by the misogyny that caused him
to reject the Duchesse d'Orléans. But he believed the Soult-Guizot
ministry had been badly shaken by the results of the elections and he
had every interest in drawing closer to Louis-Philippe in the hope of
becoming the next head of government. Tocqueville's fear of seeing
the entire opposition led in an unforeseeable direction by intrigues on
the part of Thiers—whose Machiavellianism he exaggerated, as we
have seen—was a real nightmare for him. If he himself voiced serious
objections to an organic regency law, the passion he brought to this
was first and foremost directed at thwarting the plots of the skillful
tactician. He thought he had succeeded after Thiers's speech, which
threw the left center and the left into confusion: "In this situation my
friends and I took a loftier position from the practical point of view
than we had earlier because we went in a direction such that the
opposition felt obliged to follow us. In other circumstances, will [we]
be able to impose our feelings, our ideas, our principles on it in the
same way and in this way lead it to place itself on new ground? Only
the future will tell. That is my desire. All my efforts will be in that
direction. Only God knows if they will be crowned with success. The
first step has been taken, I can't say more."[4] And in another letter: "M.
Thiers and his close friends are furious with me and from another side

---

[2]Unpublished letter to his wife dated August 19, 1842, Tocqueville Archives, file 5.
[3]Rémusat, *Mémoires* 4, 28–30.
[4]Unpublished letter to his brother Edouard dated August 24, 1842, Tocqueville Archives.

346

Barrot and Lamartine are making all sorts of advances to me. What I am doing is confusing and difficult; yet I hope with the help of God to get myself out of it honorably."

The first task that Tocqueville set himself was to measure the depth of the wound inflicted by Thiers's insolent speech on Barrot, who was the word incarnate of the left, and on Chambolle, who was "his pen" (poor pen! added Tocqueville) as editor-in-chief of *Le Siècle*. He must have left for Normandy again the very day after the vote on the regency law (August 21), counting on his friends Beaumont, Corcelle, and Combarel de Leyval to keep him informed. They probably took the matter to heart less than he, since he had to ask them again on September 1. On the fifth, Beaumont sent a reassuring answer: Barrot was still embittered and the authoritarian "Agathe" was pushing him into hostilities against Thiers. Chambolle, who had old ties with Thiers, was sorry about this break, but was just as firm, and *Le Siècle* was engaged in a polemic with *Le Constitutionnel*. [5]

At that point, on September 16, Tocqueville decided to write to the two men.

His letter to Barrot[6] was primarily a long diatribe against Thiers. Certainly, the left center and the left could have objectives in common, but with Thiers it was impossible to settle on the limits to an alliance. He attempted to dominate, seeing the opposition only as a "stepping stone" that would allow him to come to power. Although Thiers might want the country to be great, no one in the Chamber was more fundamentally illiberal than he. In reality, he knew nothing but facts, and did not allow for any moral principle in political life.

It was by its moral principles that the left should distinguish itself from him. This was not easy, for the left was composed "of men who are sincere and honest, but violent, not very well informed, with little practical experience, stronger in passions and instincts than in ideas." In sum, Tocqueville was scarcely more indulgent than Thiers toward the behavior of a left that was often more faithful to the revolutionary tradition than it was openly liberal. Nevertheless, it had retained its worship of certain great principles basic to liberalism, and it was these principles that should serve as the basis of its action. Barrot alone, through his magical oratory, his excellent personal qualities, and his deep liberal convictions, could draw the left in the direction of a moderate and honest opposition that would find support in the country

---

[5] *O.C.* VIII, 1, 469–71.

[6] From a copy by Madame de Tocqueville in the Tocqueville Archives. This letter was published by Marcel in his *Essai politique sur A. de Tocqueville*, 336–39.

at large. And Tocqueville sketched out a plan for a "defensive" position on domestic policies in order to counter the abuses of power that
were soon to come. But in one passage of the letter, he revealed his
hand: Sir Robert Peel (who was the statesman he admired most at that
time) had thrust himself upon Britain's mediocre conservative party
with the help of a few friends of high caliber; Barrot should therefore
consider gathering around him what we now call a brain trust. It is
not hard to see who might be the most important figure in it, pouring
suggestions into the "empty head" of the great orator, who would
serve as a spokesman, since the debates on the regency law had proved
that Tocqueville lacked the persuasive qualities that would have allowed him to impose himself.

His letter to Chambolle, written the same day,[7] summarizes and
returns to the same ideas, but with more tact concerning Thiers and
the footsloggers of the left.

Both men answered. Barrot's letter developed at length the theme
of the need for morality in politics, a theme to which he had devoted
his life, and manifested some bitterness against the men who had
wanted to exploit this principle for personal ends, citing Guizot but
also Thiers. Barrot congratulated Tocqueville for having principles
identical to his own, agreed to work with him, but he understood that
the author of the *Democracy* would want to put his ideas into practice
politically and remained silent on that subject. As for Chambolle, he
accepted Tocqueville's offer to write articles for *Le Siècle,* something
Beaumont had already done.[8]

Thus Tocqueville initiated his adherence to the left. He would say
bluntly to other correspondents that he made the move not in order
to adopt the "color" of the left, but to impose his own.[9] This ambition
was clearly revealed in his offers of help to Barrot and Chambolle. It
would arouse some apprehension in them and before long some distrust
within the dynastic left.

The coherent line of conduct that Tocqueville sought to persuade
the left to adopt was to be his own during four years of parliamentary
activity. At the close of 1846, the transformation in political morality,
together with the election of a more conservative Chamber, making
even clearer the deep chasm that lay between the *pays légal* (the

[7] Unpublished, undated letter to Chambolle.
[8] Barrot's answer, dated October 11, 1842, in Marcel, *Essai politique,* 482–86. Chambolle's answer, unpublished, Tocqueville Archives.
[9] Letter to Kergorlay dated October 25, 1842, *O.C.* XIII, 2: 107.

confined political world with its narrowly based suffrage) and the *pays réel* (the popular will in the country at large) would lead him to modify his objectives. The principles he enunciated in 1842 had taken shape little by little in his mind, and the reflections he pursued between the vote on the regency law in August and the return of the Chambers on January 9, 1843, first at Tocqueville and then during a visit to his brother Edouard at Baugy, simply gave them systematic form.

They were worked out in opposition to the policies of Guizot, first against the cravenness with which the October 29 ministry had clutched at an alliance with England and then against its corrupt conduct of affairs, which Tocqueville only seems to have become fully aware of at the time of the July 1842 elections.

Back in Paris a few days later, after describing to his brother his electors' spontaneous demonstrations of affection toward him, he added: "I have fallen back into another world, the real world of politics, but nastier than I have ever seen it. The election made it uncertain that the government commanded a majority, and the liveliness of the intrigues mounted to dupe the new deputies or influence the old was really incredible. As for me, I was quickly overcome by one of the deepest fits of melancholia I have ever experienced."[10] The reaction of wounded patriotism to a foreign policy he thought servile, the reaction of a decent man to rapidly spreading corruption—these were what brought him into opposition to Guizot, and these were the passionately held convictions behind the system of opposition that he elaborated.

Repudiation of the alliance with England was the point of departure for Tocqueville's system where it concerned foreign policy. He had deeply resented the humiliation inflicted on France by Palmerston in 1840, when France was excluded from the Treaty of London, and especially the approval of this humiliation by English public opinion. It was not an episode without consequences, he wrote to John Stuart Mill on March 18, 1841:

It is all very well for the governments to say that all is forgotten. The nation contradicts them in its heart of hearts and for this ill, protocols and diplomatic notes are no remedy. The violent irritation produced by the July 15 treaty is entirely appeased, but what remains is worse, and that is the quiet, profound feeling that there is neither security nor future in an alliance with England,

[10]Unpublished letter to Edouard de Tocqueville dated August 24, 1842, Tocqueville Archives.

that our rivalry of interests is a fact one can no longer deny and cannot bring to an end.[11]

Indeed, what Tocqueville envisaged for France was a maritime and colonial future that would make all accord impossible: "England wants to be not only the first maritime power, but the absolute monarch of the sea. In consequence, she cannot have any real ally among the maritime powers, whoever they may be . . . Her need is not to command but to reign . . . She cannot even let you have two small islands in Oceania." The English aristocracy could maintain itself in power only by guaranteeing work to a burgeoning industrial class, and this it could do only through a monopoly of raw materials and commercial markets.

In sum, it was not England's excesses or France's subordinate role that Tocqueville reproached in the French-English alliance, but the alliance itself. In this, he showed himself to be more unyielding than a Thiers or a Barrot. Unlike many politicians of both the majority and the opposition, he rejected the argument drawn from the similarity of free institutions. Of course, in a particular case (for example, at the time of the arbitrary repressions in the Romagna), the two countries could be in agreement on pleading a humanitarian cause in conformance with the principles of the law of nations. But their own principles were nonetheless radically different. England remained an aristocracy, and its foreign policy was subordinated to material interests that must be satisfied for that aristocracy to remain in power. France, on the other hand, was the "heart and head of democracy," whose strength in the world was tied to the spread of the principles of 1789.

Tocqueville also rejected the so-called decisive argument of partisans of the alliance with England. This alliance, they said, would secure France against any threat from a coalition of the continental powers. But such a coalition was completely improbable. For it to be formed, the princes that represented those powers would have to be moved, as they had once been a century ago, and as they would perhaps be again in some distant future, "by an interest in enlarging their territory." In the present state of Europe, "the great thing for them was to avoid domestic revolutions, with which they were threatened by the results of the French Revolution. In all of continental Europe, the French

[11]Letter to Mill dated March 18, 1841, O.C. VI, 334.

Revolution had caused national policy to be succeeded by dynastic policy, the interest in territorial aggrandizement by the interest in self-preservation."[12]

Isolation was therefore hardly very dangerous for France. But if the continental powers did not pose a threat to her, neither could she conclude an agreement with any of them, except to achieve limited objectives. Someday, perhaps, her trade policy would lead her to conclude agreements on trade with Germany, but that time had not yet come.

Tocqueville's position on domestic policy also became clearly defined through his critique of Guizot's ideas. We are quite familiar with the grounds of this critique through the articles on France's domestic situation that Tocqueville published in *Le Siècle* in January 1843.[13]

Guizot's policy was inspired by the fear of revolutions. His primary aim was to assure France, by all possible means, a stable government. Such a government would direct the nation away from political battles and impel it toward the conquest of material prosperity. In the pacified atmosphere of a country growing rich, the July regime would send down strong roots by virtue of habit alone.

Tocqueville, too, wanted the regime to send down roots, but he opposed the depoliticization of the country. The July regime had issued from the principles of 1789 and 1830, from a love of equality but also from a love of liberty. It was by awakening these sluggish passions that the July regime would find its true strength in the consensus of the great majority of the French people.

Of course, there were two parties hostile to the regime: the republicans and the legitimists. The first included two sorts of men: conservative republicans who were not at all inclined toward a social upheaval, and revolutionaries recruited from the lowest classes, types hardly to be found outside Paris and the manufacturing towns. Tocqueville observed that "revolutions attempted by a single class have always miscarried. As for the legitimist party, it is formed of officers without troops who could not act without a foreign intervention, which they would probably repudiate."

Over against this opposition, the government had an army at its

---

[12]Unpublished notes by Tocqueville, Tocqueville Archives, 83. See also the discussion by Seymour Drescher in his *Tocqueville and England* (Cambridge, Mass., 1964).

[13]These letters, on *La situation intérieure de la France* and addressed to the editor-in-chief of *Le Siècle*, were published in issues of the newspaper dated January 1, 2, 5, 7, 13, and 14, 1843. Two of them were reprinted in English by Seymour Drescher in *Tocqueville and Beaumont on Social Reform* (New York, 1968), 193–200.

disposal, and a centralized administration without parallel in Europe. And most important, those who advocated overthrowing the government were not so much against the institution of the monarchy as they were against the institution of property. Since the French Revolution, France had been the European country in which the middle class was the most highly developed, and the dominant element in that class was the small property owner attached to his holding. The social structure of the country was such that the majority of the French were hostile to any revolutionary adventure. But their natural love of liberty was in conflict with their fear of revolution. It was by exploiting this fear that a series of governments had felled large sections of the liberal edifice constructed in the early 1830s and were even leading France back to the time before the last years of the Restoration. Vigilantly, Tocqueville denounced the successive encroachments of power.

First and foremost, there was the law of April 1834 governing associations, which had strengthened the provisions of the Penal Code without taking any account of the aims of these associations, and which treated infractions of this law as grave misdemeanors to be tried in courts of summary jurisdiction or even—in the case of a threat against the security of the State—in the Chamber of Peers. Shortly afterwards, following Fieschi's nearly successful attempt to assassinate the king, the notorious laws of September 1835 were passed, forbidding a man to call himself a republican, reorganizing the courts of assizes and establishing harsher procedures for trying those found guilty of acts of rebellion (their sentences even being pronounced, when those accused proved insolent, in their absence), and placing further checks on the excesses of the press, with the Chamber of Peers here, too, able to take the place of a jury.

At the time these September laws were under consideration in the Chamber, the aging Royer-Collard had come forward to fight them, opposing his old Doctrinaire friends de Broglie and Guizot. And at that time, Tocqueville had written him an enthusiastic letter, contrasting his attitude, "loyal to the principles of his whole life," to the "inconstancy and turpitudes of the human heart."[14] From then on, opposition to the September laws or acceptance of them would be, for Tocqueville, the touchstone distinguishing the true liberals from those who were not.

But more recent events showed that the work of reaction was continuing. There was the law governing newspapers in the provinces,

[14]Letter to Royer-Collard dated August 28, 1835, *O.C.* XI, 11.

352

茔 茔

the preliminary combing out by prefects of the names on the jury panel, the proceedings instituted on a larger and larger scale against newspapers in order to accuse them of moral complicity in political offenses, the administration's claim that it could subject to prior authorization the Protestant cultural associations of sects not subsidized by the State.

For Tocqueville, all these phenomena were evidence of the antiliberal reaction, which was proceeding hand in glove with the secret and ever-increasing hold the king claimed over the business of government —here, too, returning French political life to the days, which should have been over and done with, of the Restoration.

This regressive movement of the government of the monarchy seemed so important to him that he came to think that a "practical" dynastic opposition should be limited to demanding the restitution of the liberties suppressed or diminished since 1830. In this way, it would be more distinctly separate from the radicals, toward whom the demagogues, the revolutionaries, and those inclined to violence would tend to flock.

Such was the program that Tocqueville, early in 1843, sought to propose for the constitutional left, a coherent program based upon two sources of civic virtue, love of country and love of liberty, but a moderate program that he was careful to keep distinct from the radicals' demands.

Tocqueville was indeed struck by the complexity and originality of French political life. Unlike the Prussian monarchy with its centralized administration, unlike England with its decentralized, representative regime, France's system was a sort of hybrid—one that had never been seen before and that could not be found elsewhere in Europe at that time—between the centralization inherited from monarchical absolutism and a representative regime. This representative regime with an aristocratic origin found itself at the mercy of an electorate drawn from the nonprivileged classes, classes that represented democracy (in Tocqueville's eyes, universal suffrage was not the characteristic mark of democracy). The big problem, in such a state of society, was to enlighten the electorate that represented the democratic factor, to make it conscious of its role in the nation. In this way, it would be possible to prepare for the broader democracy of the ineluctable future by gradual reforms that would avoid the explosions of revolution. But only great parties animated by the civic virtues could play the role of educators of public opinion among this electorate. In sum, it was

Tocqueville's wish that the dynastic opposition, above all else, should elevate these moral convictions to the level of law.[15]

These general principles were to guide Tocqueville's political activities throughout the life of the Chamber elected in 1842, which remained in existence until July 1846.

The parliamentary session of 1843 was the most dismal of the July monarchy. During it, Thiers "gave his party a holiday," never took the floor, worked on his *Histoire du Consulat et de l'Empire*. [16] The most salient debate was on foreign policy, and concerned boarding rights as governed by French-English treaties.[17]

It was a matter of how to organize internationally the suppression of the slave trade, which had been outlawed by the Congress of Vienna. The treaties of 1831 and 1833 between England and France had allowed cruisers belonging to one of the two powers to board any vessel flying the flag of the other in order to verify that it was not transporting slaves from Africa to America. There were to be no more than twice as many English cruisers as there were French patrolling the African coast. But the admission of other powers to the French-English agreement in 1838 required a modification of the treaty. On December 28, 1841, a new text—which did not specify the maximum proportion of two to one between the cruisers of the two nations, and which granted the takings to the captor ships—was accepted by Guizot. At the time of the vote in 1842 on the address in response to the king's speech from the throne, an amendment proposed by a member of the majority asked the government to "safeguard from all attack the interests of our commerce and the independence of our flag." The treaty could not be ratified. Lord Aberdeen, England's foreign minister, contented himself with leaving the protocol open in case France should change her mind.

Tocqueville did not take part in this first debate, but joined in a second one that took place in May 1842. As he saw it, the boarding rights not only constituted an ineffectual solution, they added to the cruelties of the slave trade: the conditions of the captives on board the slave ships were made worse because of the owner's eagerness to sacrifice everything to speed. Tocqueville advocated collective action

---

[15]Tocqueville accumulated numerous notes that make clear his thinking on this point. These appear in the *O.C.* III, 2.

[16]Rémusat, *Mémoires* 4, 48.

[17]See Th.-F. Buxton, *The African Slave Trade* (London, 1839). French translation, 1840.

354

卷 卷

by Europe to oblige the last two countries in which slave markets still remained—Brazil and Cuba—to shut them down.

The Chamber's opposition to the boarding rights was manifested again in 1843, and this time in order to obtain the suppression of the treaties of 1831 and 1833: "We pray for the moment when our commerce will be placed once again under the exclusive surveillance of our own flag." On January 28, Tocqueville spoke, reproaching Guizot for wanting to restore the alliance with England at any price while French public opinion remained exacerbated by the outrage of 1840: "You do not yet really know the people you are trying to lead. Because France, under pressure from all of Europe, submitted . . . you thought she had forgotten."[18] Faced with widespread opposition, Guizot had to settle for negotiating a new treaty that abolished boarding rights.

The determination of Guizot and Aberdeen to achieve an "entente cordiale" was imposed, for better or worse, on the two governments and lent significance to the royal visits of Victoria to the Château d'Eu (September 1843) and of Louis-Philippe to Windsor (October 1844). But even in the months between these two visits there were such outbursts of distrust and hostility in the public opinion of the two nations that more than once war seemed likely. Bugeaud's campaign against the Sultan of Morocco and the concomitant shelling of Mogador by the Prince de Joinville aroused the liveliest fears in England. Worst of all, the news from Oceania led to the violent crisis of the Pritchard affair.

Oceania was opening up, attracting adventurers of all sorts, traffickers, sailors on a spree, escaped convicts from Australia. Whalers cruised its waters and missionaries took up their work there. The whalers wanted to establish bases for their different nations, but it was the ministers of the Gospel more than anyone else who troubled this new world with their rivalries: on the one hand, there were the Methodist pastors backed by the powerful Society of Missions of London, and on the other, Marists or members of the Congregation of Picpus demanding support from France.[19]

England had beaten France to New Zealand, and the French government had sent Admiral Dupetit-Thouars to seize the Marquesas, a

---

[18]*Le Moniteur universel,* January 29, 1843, 162–64, reprinted in *O.C.* (Bmt) IV, 387–409.

[19]On the problem in general, consult J.-P. Faivre, *L'Expansion française dans le Pacifique de 1800 à 1842* (Paris, 1953), and Léonce Jore, *L'Océan Pacifique du temps de la Restauration et de la monarchie de Juillet,* 2 vols. (Paris, 1959).

modest enough compensation. But the Marquesas were close to the 355
Society Islands and it was there that things began to go wrong.

Queen Pomaré, ruler of Papeete, was under the influence of Pritchard—a Methodist pastor, a businessman, and the British consul. Pritchard caused some Catholic missionaries to be expelled from the country and Dupetit-Thouars, alerted to the fact, came and presented Pomaré with a choice between heavy reparations and a French protectorate. In Pritchard's absence, she accepted the latter (September 1842). Dupetit-Thouars left and Pritchard returned. Even though London had raised no objection to the French protectorate, Pritchard caused the queen to reject it. In November 1843, Dupetit-Thouars, coming back to Tahiti, annexed the island. Pomaré fled and her subjects revolted. While the governor, Captain Bruat, fought the rebels in Papeete, his subordinate d'Aubigny secretly locked up Pritchard, instigator of the uprising, in a damp cell where, ill with dysentery, he was not allowed to see his doctor. When Bruat returned, he expelled him.

In February 1844, the French government learned of the annexation, repudiated it in favor of a reversion to the protectorate, and replaced Dupetit-Thouars. This was obviously done to placate the English; the opposition protested. But the crisis became more acute at the end of July, when Pritchard arrived in Great Britain and made known the maltreatment he had been subjected to. Although he was no longer consul to the Society Islands at the time of his expulsion, he had retained that diplomatic function for the other islands. Sir Robert Peel spoke of the "gross outrage" inflicted on England. The press on both sides of the Channel exchanged volleys of insults. The governments reached an agreement by which the French government promised to pay Pritchard the sum of 11,000 francs as compensation for his forced abandonment of his Tahitian trade (he had demanded 100,000)—which, moreover, it did not pay. Naturally, the leftist press was indignant that compensation was being given to an individual who had spilled the blood of French soldiers in "floods."

Tocqueville wrote about this crisis at its height, at the beginning of August 1844, in a series of articles for the newspaper Le Commerce, [20] in which we can see that his thought was influenced by his political partisanship. Before everything else, he blamed the French cabinet, accusing it of having tried to obtain an easy success by occupying a few unimportant islands in Oceania. At little cost to itself, the cabinet

[20] O.C. III, 2: 403–20.

356

𝕏 𝕏

wanted to demonstrate its independence vis-à-vis the English in the eyes of the French public. When easily predictable difficulties arose, it lost face by repudiating the naval officers it had entrusted with taking action on the spot. Tocqueville, who was such a warm partisan of the expansion of French commerce in the world, could see nothing but a pointless action in the takeover of several islands suitable for naval bases. He affirmed, without advancing any proof, that the conquests were useless to French whalers; he made no allusion to the rivalries among the missionaries; he did not conceive that the Marquesas and the Society Islands could be stopovers on the way to California, as certain publicists were proposing at the time—though he knew what hung in the balance between Mexicans, Americans, English, and Russians on the Pacific coast of North America and asserted that France had an interest in what came to pass there. He foresaw a very dark future for France's occupation of Tahiti. The instinctive reaction of Tocqueville, who was caught unawares by the event, was partisan. His hostility to Guizot blinded him to a part of the problem.

Five months later, taking the matter up again in the course of the Chamber's discussion of the address in response to the speech from the throne, he treated it with more breadth and serenity. The Tahitian affair had in some sense been integrated into the collection of facts that, in Tocqueville's eyes, made the alliance with England an illusory enticement.[21]

Tocqueville restrained himself from blaming the British temperament, as other orators did. It was the very structure of English society that prevented it from making the concessions that would have maintained an equal alliance. The British Isles had two workers for every farmer—a proportion unique in Europe—and their aristocratic government could maintain itself in power only by controlling the sources of raw materials and the outlets for manufactured products throughout the entire world.

Nevertheless, in the long run Britain's dominion over the seas was in danger. Here, Tocqueville revived an argument by the Prince de Joinville that had caused a furor the year before.[22] The technical revolution of steam power was going to allow four-fifths of all ships' crews to be eliminated, and Great Britain would thus lose the advantage it derived from its superabundant population of sailors.

---

[21]Session of January 20, 1845, *Le Moniteur universel* of the twenty-first, 124–26.
[22]Article in the *Revue des deux mondes*, "De l'état des forces navales de la France," May 15, 1844, 708–46. An anonymous article whose author was known to everyone.

The ideas expressed in this speech of January 1845 represented the culmination of Tocqueville's reflections over the past several years.

During the period from 1833 to 1840, Spain was being torn apart by the first Carlist war. The pretender, entrenched in the provinces of the North, represented monarchical absolutism and for this reason enjoyed the sympathies of the continental powers. The constitutional party was supporting the regent María Cristina, mother of the little queen Isabella II. England, France, and Portugal had signed the Quadruple Alliance Treaty with her in 1834. But Spanish liberals were split into two parties, moderates and progressives, both fighting ardently for power, the first sympathizing with France, the second with England, and the alliance signed by France and England eliminated neither the distrust nor the reciprocal intrigues in the peninsula. In 1840, General Espartero, conqueror of the Carlists, drove María Cristina out and seized the regency with the connivance of the progressives. Already ill disposed toward France, he was exasperated by the pretension of the new ambassador, Salvandy, in delivering his letter of credentials directly to the queen.

Tocqueville could not help following the events in Spain closely. He attached too much value to Mediterranean problems and to the conquest of nearby Algeria, which seemed to him France's most important concern. In 1842 and 1843, at the time of the crisis in relations between France and Spain under Espartero, he studied, pen in hand, the tormented development of the events of the past ten years and tried to isolate their main lines. Civil war and party hatreds had turned the army into an autonomous force and put power within reach of a victorious general. The pattern was not unlike that of the French Revolution. But France could have prevented this had she seen fit to cut short the time of troubles whose long duration brought on the social conditions that led to the dictatorship. Tocqueville articulated this conviction in a speech given from the tribune of the Chamber on March 28, 1843, during part of which he used notes he had been gathering over the past few months.[23]

The governments led by one or the other of the two liberal parties during María Cristina's regency were too weak and too hotly contested by the party in opposition to survive without the support of a foreign power. The moderates, who most often won the elections, were the natural allies of France and they needed French help. In 1836, the Whig

---

[23]These notes, held in the Tocqueville Archives, are published in *O.C.* III, 2: 389–95.

administration governing England was so uneasy over the Carlist threat that even it wanted France to intervene.

Thiers was in favor of this fairly safe military intervention, which would have put an end to the civil war and consolidated French influence. The king rejected it because "it was a complicated business." France's friends in Spain were discredited and obliged to yield power to the friends of England. A ridiculous affair of protocol ended in France's quarreling with Espartero, who could perhaps have been won over. Guizot tried to justify France's inertia, saying that France was no longer in the situation of 1714. Of course, said Tocqueville, but the current situation was worse. England, absolute mistress of the seas, could launch an army into Spain that would force France to put a military guard on the Pyrenees frontier.

Thus, fear of a war with England sharpened Tocqueville's interest in Spain. As Espartero was driven from power a few months after Tocqueville's speech, Tocqueville, though he apparently did not lose sight of affairs on the peninsula, stopped making such detailed analyses of the events taking place there.

Tocqueville's preoccupation with the need to combat the maritime and commercial supremacy of England was behind his position on the problems of Texas and Oregon. The friendship of the United States, a maritime power second only to England, could help France maintain the freedom of the seas against England, without France's even having to conclude an alliance. The expansion of the United States was therefore of primary importance to France. Yet in 1842, Guizot had joined the English in opposing the annexation of Texas by the United States, provisionally rejected by the American Senate at the time Tocqueville put his thoughts in writing (toward the beginning of 1846), but soon to become inevitable. France's position, the excuse for which was the attempt to achieve a balance among the powers installed in North America, had no other motive than to favor England in her negotiations with the United States by giving the latter to understand that it could not count on France's traditional friendship. Guizot was in the course of repeating the same maneuver with respect to Oregon and, at the time of the discussion of the address in response to the speech from the throne in 1846, Tocqueville prepared to denounce it from the tribune. Thiers, "to my great displeasure, did me the honor of stealing my turn to speak," he wrote. For other reasons, he was prevented from speaking a few days later, but his unpublished notes preserve for us the spirit of this speech that was never delivered.[24]

Oregon was then an immense, loosely defined territory that since 1818 had been provisionally held under joint occupation by the English and the Americans. It was visited by fur hunters working for the English Hudson's Bay Company, but more and more American colonists were settling there. The English and the Americans hoped to end the joint possession by dividing up the territory, but their views on the future frontier differed radically. Tocqueville insisted that in this question, which threatened the peace, Guizot's declaration in advance that France was neutral was hostile to the Americans and contrary to France's interests: "The question of Oregon is in general not clearly understood. What is happening there? Are these two great nations fighting over a few square leagues of wilderness? No, the question is immense: immense for England, immense for America, important even for us . . . Are we indifferent as to whether we find American or English ports on the Pacific Ocean? Today, the Pacific Ocean is entirely in the hands of the English or of the half-civilized republics of Spanish America." Tocqueville was not thinking, as were certain journalists, of a French settlement on the Pacific coast, but believed that allying herself with America would help France free the ocean from English domination. Even as late as March 23, 1848, though this was at a time when his feelings of hostility to England had softened considerably, he was to shout out during a democratic banquet at Cherbourg: "The earth is free but the sea is still a slave. A single nation rules there, not only as dominator but as tyrant. A single nation has insolently appropriated for itself what was the common domain of all nations . . . Let the French Republic and the American Republic stretch their great arms across the seas that separate them, let them give each other their hands, and the sea will be free. To achieve this, there will not even be need for a war."[25] It was in that year, 1848, that the frontier was established by a compromise between the conflicting aims of 1845 that separated American Oregon from British Columbia; in that year, too, California was taken away from Mexico.

·   ·   ·

[24]In a letter dated January 21, 1846, to Clamorgam, Tocqueville wrote: "I was the one who was supposed to speak yesterday on America. But M. Thiers did me the honor of trying to steal my turn to speak, and succeeded, to my great displeasure." In *Alexis de Tocqueville als Abgeordneter, Briefe an seinen Wahlagenten Paul Clamorgam (1837–1851)*, ed. by Joachim Kühn (Hamburg, 1972), 105.

[25]Speech printed in the *Journal de Cherbourg*, March 23, 1848.

360

卍 卍

Where domestic policy was concerned, Tocqueville in his parliamentary activities did not take up the economic problems that were at the forefront in these years of rapidly developing capitalism and the building of canals, roads, railways. Yet these problems were not unfamiliar to him. For the departmental council of the Manche, he wrote a heavily documented report on the Paris–Cherbourg railway. He tells us that through this study he formed his own opinion on the question of free trade and came to support a moderate protectionist policy. It might therefore seem surprising that his political notes contain only a brief economic study of the competition between cane sugar and beet sugar, a question debated numerous times since the days of the Empire. Probably intentionally, where domestic policy was concerned Tocqueville confined himself to questions of pure policy, or, rather, of political morality.

As he stated in the program published by *Le Siècle* in January 1843, his aim was not the reform of institutions. No doubt he took advantage of the discussion of the law regulating haulage to attack the extension of administrative jurisdiction, but it was in a rather disillusioned fashion that he recited this old liberal refrain.[26] His liveliest criticism of institutions, because it took up directly the prevailing mores in political life, bore on the inadequacy of the powers granted to local elected bodies. What actually resulted from this? "A sad apathy and an indifference that is all but universal have taken the place of political activity. If nothing is done to get out of this rut, one can predict that the country will not only remain stationary . . . but even that it will present the deplorable spectacle of a march to the rear."

Defending political morality meant being on guard to make sure that cunning actions of the government and administration did not shift the law in an illiberal direction.

Two speeches by Tocqueville seem to us characteristic examples of this intellectual approach in quite different areas. One is on the application of the law governing the Paris fortifications, the other on the harassment of the Protestants of the "revival."

The law on the Paris fortifications, born of the crisis of 1840 and passed the following year, provided for the protection of the capital by a continuous surrounding wall that had separate forts standing before it. Tocqueville had voted against the law, without having wanted to take part in the discussion. But the law's application seemed suspect to him. An entrenched camp had been created at Vincennes, and

[26]Speech given April 23, 1843, printed in *Le Moniteur universel* of April 24.

at Saint-Maur sixty-six hectares of land—about a quarter of a square mile—had been leveled to make room for a vast complex of military establishments. In Tocqueville's judgment, it was no longer the enemy who was threatened by this concentration of troops kept separate from the civilian population. The spirit of the law had thus been changed altogether by a simple decision on the part of the executive power. Paris was menaced by "soldiers massed in great numbers and permanently established in and around Paris, [by] soldiers shut up behind ramparts and separated from the civilian population." He smelled a government ruse and called for explanations.[27]

The second problem has nothing in common with the preceding one except for Tocqueville's denunciation of the government's cunning. Guizot did not confine himself to individual victories, he attempted victories we would describe as categorical. Whence his maneuvers to win over the lower-level clergy in order to undermine legitimist influences. It was for this reason that a fund existed for paying bonuses to ecclesiastics "who distinguished themselves." But there was something more serious: parishioners who quarreled with their parish priests would turn to pastors of the "revival," who were themselves often at odds with the orthodox Protestant consistories. Through a dubious interpretation of the law, prefects went to the aid of the parish priests by closing religious premises and entering into prosecutions. Thus Tocqueville, even though he preferred the Catholic Church to the Protestant sects, opposed the Protestant Guizot to defend the freedom to honor God in one's own way without prior authorization by the police.[28]

In an address to the Chamber, Tocqueville recalled Guizot's speech of 1837 during a banquet in Mézidon, in which he openly affirmed to his Norman electors the government's right to give priority in its favors to those who voted for it.[29] He was indignant at this cynicism, but preferred it to the underhanded distribution of individual favors that created constituencies for the deputies of the majority and debased the unique experiment being conducted by France under the July monarchy: the attempt to make administrative centralization, representative institutions, and democracy work together.

This defense of the liberties born in 1830 would have been the

[27]Speech given March 2, 1844, and published in *Le Moniteur universel* on March 3, 480.
[28]Speech given April 28, 1845, and printed in *Le Moniteur universel* on April 29, 1130.
[29]It was during the discussion on the secret funds (session of March 2, 1843) that Tocqueville referred to Guizot's speech to his electors from the canton of Mézidon, on October 3, 1837 (*Le Moniteur universel* of March 3, 1843, 349–50).

principal focus of Tocqueville's political activity if he had not been drawn into the controversy that reanimated the parties from 1844 to 1846—the dispute over liberty of teaching.

The Charter of 1830 contained a promise that liberty of teaching would be guaranteed. By this was meant, principally, that the schools operated by the Catholic Church, primary and secondary, would be given free scope to teach in their own way without being made subject to all regulations of the secular authority. The promise had been fulfilled for primary education by the Guizot law of 1833. But it seemed much more important at that time to stabilize the entire regime of secondary education, for it schooled the children of the prosperous classes from which the electors came—the only French citizens who had full civic rights and a role in the government of the country. The monopoly of the University established by Napoléon remained the rule, and the University controlled secondary schools as well as the advanced institutions of learning. But Napoléon had had to compromise with things as they were and recognize the existence of private schools and boarding schools. These continued to be authorized by the University in a generous fashion, to judge from the figures given at the end of 1843 by Villemain, then minister of education, in his report to the king. Alongside 43 *collèges royaux* and 311 *collèges communaux*, with in all 53,864 students, there were 984 private schools and boarding schools with 38,176 students. But in the case of some of these schools and even some of the *collèges communaux*, one could not speak of secondary studies, which were being pursued, according to Villemain's report, only by 72,161 students. There were in addition the 113 ecclesiastical secondary schools, the *petits séminaires,* for which an ordinance of 1828 had fixed the maximum number of students at 20,000. On this point, the regulation of 1828 was respected, since at the end of 1843 the students in these schools numbered 18,524, but the other requirements (the wearing of soutanes by pupils aged fourteen and older and the appointment of school principals) had been evaded by the bishops, who administered the *petits séminaires* as they pleased.

The University gave official recognition to the completion of studies by conferring the baccalaureate degree, but in order to be awarded the degree it was necessary to produce a certificate attesting to the fact that the student's last two years had been spent in an establishment directly subordinate to the University or in a private school offering the full curriculum (there were about a hundred of these)—unless

studies had been pursued in the student's own home, an exception that 363
lent itself to fraud. Officially, in any case, students in the ecclesiastical 艸 艸
secondary schools had no access to the baccalaureate, nor did those in
the boarding schools that did not send their upper-level students to
follow the course offered in one of the acceptable *collèges*.

In 1837, Guizot proposed a law favorable to the liberty of teaching
that was passed with restrictive amendments by the Chamber of Deputies but never presented to the Peers, either because of Guizot's departure from the ministry or because the partisans of liberty of teaching
considered that the restrictions imposed by the Chamber had enfeebled
the law. Villemain proposed a new text to the Chamber in 1841 that
hardly favored liberty of teaching at all, and which was not reported
out of committee (Tocqueville was a member of the committee).
Finally, in 1844, a new plan of Villemain's was passed by the Chamber
of Peers and sent to the Chamber of Deputies.

The political climate was much worse than it had been in 1837. A
war was now going on at full tilt between the University and the
Church. Hostilities had been opened by violent ecclesiastical pamphlets, the most celebrated of which were those by Abbé Combalot
and the Jesuit Deschamps, and by a few pastoral letters from the
bishops. Since the close of 1842, Louis Veuillot had been editor of
L'Univers and devoted a column each day to attacks on the University
monopoly of education. In reply, certain members of the University
faculties attacked the dogma or the morals of the Church, making the
Jesuits, whose presence in France was barely tolerated, their special
target. The course that Michelet and Quinet devoted to the Jesuit order
at the Collège de France in 1843 made a great stir.[30] The newspapers
of the left—*Le Constitutionnel, Le Courrier,* and *Le Siècle*— outdid one
another in their mockery of religious practices and their expatiations
on the moral lapses of the clergy. Initially, the attacks of the ecclesiastics against the University centered on the teaching of philosophy, on
the laxness of the University's moral principles, and on the prevailing
irreligious atmosphere in the schools, which weighed on the con-
sciences of the children. (The eclectic philosophical system of Victor
Cousin, then the dominating figure in French education and philosophy, embodied an official idealism that professed no more than a
somewhat contemptuous respect for Catholic dogmatics.) The Church,

---

[30]Quinet and Michelet published the courses on the Jesuits they offered during 1843–1844 in 1845. On
the war between the University and the Church, see P. Gerbod, *La Condition universitaire en France au
XIXe siècle* (Paris, 1966).

364

卐 卐

at first stunned by the shock of the revolution of 1830, had since gained ground in society, and, in order to obtain the liberty of teaching that certain advocates were demanding be as complete "as in Belgium," it magnified incidents that were probably untypical. In any case, it was not possible to enact liberty of teaching into law before the formation, toward 1843, of a Catholic party centered on Charles de Montalembert to which, despite their taste for tranquillity, most of the bishops felt obliged to give their approval.

It was primarily from the aspect of the struggle between the secular world and the Church that Tocqueville examined the question of liberty of teaching when he spoke in 1844 on the Chamber's address in response to the speech from the throne. Disagreeing with the opinion that malevolent political passions were dying out, he said that the battle had simply moved to a new terrain:[31]

Listen to the parties to this dispute. Are those on the one side really asking for no more than liberty of teaching? Don't their words go so far as to attack freedom of thought itself, the very principle of lay education in France, where it is guaranteed? Listen to the other side and you will see that they no longer confine themselves merely to speaking of the University and its rules, but that once again they are attacking religion itself, and the general principles, the general rules, on which it is based.

What is going on here, gentlemen? I will tell you: it is nothing more nor less than war, the old war so fortunately interrupted for ten years, which is beginning again at every point of contact, and which is spreading, if I may use the expression, along the entire battlefront it occupied before.

In an article written a few months later, Tocqueville showed the depth of his disappointment: "For our part, we never gave up hope of seeing the Church and the new society become reconciled with each other. We hoped for it and above all we ardently desired it. It seemed to us that each of them might have drawn from that union the strengths that they lacked."[32]

Tocqueville was saying once more—his conviction here had not changed since he wrote *Democracy in America*— that a religion, a moral force independent of the State that could elevate the preoccupations of the great mass of the people above their petty interests, was indispensable to the functioning of a democratic society:

[31]Speech on the address given January 17, 1844. *Le Moniteur universel* for January 18, 92–94.
[32]Article from *Le Commerce,* reprinted in *O.C.* III, 2. A portion of the articles on religious liberty was published by Mme. A. M. Battista in *Lo spirito liberale e lo spirito religioso* (Milan, 1975).

"What is democracy if not the constant and powerful effort made by society to ameliorate, elevate, and give moral substance to the lives of each of its members, to come to the aid of all the unfortunate, to reach out a hand to all forms of misery?"

Tocqueville did not fear, as the left did or pretended to, that a Catholic party might take control of the State. But the Church, attacked in its turn, could throw itself into the arms of the powers-that-be, and he accused Guizot of reckoning on this. The Church would then be discredited, as it had been under the Restoration, and its moral function in a society that had no alternative to Catholicism and that could not do without a body of beliefs would be lost. With the abandonment of beliefs would come skepticism, a factor in the decline of all civilizations.

And this decline would first take the form, necessarily, of political tyranny.

Alluding to the destruction brought on by the philosophy of the eighteenth century, he added: "After this carnage of all authorities in the social world, in the hierarchy of classes, in the family, in the political world, one cannot survive without an *authority* in the intellectual and moral world; if it is lacking there, it will have to be found somewhere else where I do not want it, either in a new class hierarchy or in massive political power. We will need soldiers and prisons if we abolish beliefs."

Either through self-interest or through confusion of mind, the war between the Church and the University had become inextricably involved with the principle of liberty of teaching, which was linked to something far above it, the liberal principles of 1789 which recognized in man rights anterior and superior to those of the State. It was connected to the idea "of a great society in which freedom would exist not only for a few but for all, in which all feelings, all ideas could manifest themselves and come forward by turns to be offered to the good sense of the nation." In a personal admission of a sort seldom found in his writings, he added that it was this idea, opening a new era in the annals of humanity, and not the substitution of the government of one class for that of another, that had converted him, brought up as he had been according to other principles, to the spirit of 1789. Before the war between the Church and the University had confused matters, it was the men of the dynastic left who were truly imbued with this spirit—Destutt de Tracy, Sade, Chambolle. They, together with the University teacher Saint-Marc Girardin, had best defended liberty of teaching during the debates on the Guizot plan.

366
𝖄 𝖄

In concrete terms, the objective of liberty of teaching for Tocqueville was not simply to permit the clergy to bring up the children of Catholic families. He was intensely interested in the question of curriculum. He had read and taken notes not only on Ambroise Rendu's *Code universitaire*, but also on the books of Victor Cousin and Saint-Marc Girardin.[33] He was prepared to concede to the latter that an elite should be brought up in the culture of antiquity and Greek and Latin literature, but, as he had already noted in the *Democracy*, this could only be a very small elite. He believed, like Lamartine, that secondary teaching should seek out new paths better adapted to the modern world. It was in this way above all that free teaching should compete with the University and that it could be capable of preventing the latter from humming along in a routine determined by tradition. He believed the University was capable of reacting to that competition. With the capital of superior minds that it possessed, it could respond victoriously to this challenge. The variety of subjects offered to young Germans seems to have struck him particularly, through the studies done by Cousin and Girardin. He thought it would be good to have the same variety of educational offerings in France, adapted to the diversity of French society. He showed as much interest in ensuring the freedom of secular education as he did in the demands made on behalf of clerical education. And he condemned the abuse inherent in the privileged regime of the *petits séminaires:* they should be subject to the same laws as the rest and emancipated from the capricious guardianship of the bishops.

More generally, for free establishments to be innovative, they had to be able to commit themselves without hindrance to approaches other than that of the University, for which there was no salvation outside the established humanities curriculum. Tocqueville did not anathematize public education as the Catholic party did, but like that party he opposed the control exercised by the University hierarchy over teachers and students in the private schools. So that, suspect as his proposals made him in the eyes of those who sought to attain liberty of teaching in the way Montalembert wanted it, he became even more suspect in the eyes of those like Cousin and Thiers who wanted to continue the ascendancy of the University by indirect means.

[33]Ambroise Rendu, *Code universitaire, ou lois status et règlements de l'université royale de France,* 2nd ed. (1835). Victor Cousin, *De l'instruction secondaire dans le royaume de Prusse, Oeuvres,* vol. 3 (Brussels, 1841), and *Recueil des principaux actes du ministère de l'Instruction publique, du 1er mars au 29 octobre 1840.* Saint-Marc Girardin, *De l'instruction intermédiaire et de son état dans le midi de l'Allemagne* (Paris, 1835).

Thiers, in fact, was taking advantage of circumstances to make an active reentry into political life. Not only had the attacks of the clergy roused the indignation of the dynastic left as well as the left center, but on this point a part of the right center was also evading Guizot's attempts at making peace between the factions, starting with the editorial board of the *Journal des débats,* the usual organ of the cabinet. An anticlerical policy based on the defense of the University monopoly — this was a program that would win over to Guizot's successor a majority that would necessarily have to include a fraction of the right center. "It is time to lay Voltaire's hand on these people," proclaimed the astute parliamentary tactician. "These people" were primarily the Jesuits, still very unpopular with the public, and Thiers was merely applying the formula ironically articulated during the Restoration by Benjamin Constant: "One is quite wrong to be at a loss for an opposition; when one has nothing, well!—there are always the Jesuits. I ring for them like a valet: they always come."

Tocqueville understood Thiers's maneuver perfectly. He denounced it in an article that his friend Corcelle would stop him from publishing:[34]

The constitutional left cannot hope to succeed the current government right away. M. Guizot's first heirs will obviously be chosen from among other ranks than ours. Now, what is the visible interest of all those who can hope to succeed the current government? Their visible interest is that at the moment they arrive in power, the religious question should have become the most important domestic matter and, if possible, the only one preoccupying people's minds, exciting their passions, and agitating their souls. Now it is in this area that they have the most chance of pleasing the opposition, without losing the support of the current majority. It will always be much easier for them to hunt down Jesuits than to permit electoral reform or parliamentary reform. Their obvious interest is therefore in concentrating the entire attention of the country on the religious question alone.

This article was written in August 1844, after Thiers had succeeded in being appointed rapporteur of the Chamber's committee to examine the Villemain plan and had filed his report on July 23. But as soon as the maneuver that was to lead to this result became apparent in the middle of June, Tocqueville had denounced it angrily in a letter to Barrot:[35]

[34]Article meant for *Le Commerce,* in the Tocqueville Archives.
[35]Unpublished letter to Barrot, Tocqueville Archives.

Returning home, my dear friend, I find *La Patrie,* in which I learn that all independent men should join together to bring M. Thiers into the committee so that he can *defend their opinions* there. This morning, *Le Siècle* branded as counterrevolutionary and ultramontanist any writing that did not reflect M. Thiers's opinion in this matter. I imagine that this is going to be the tone in which these two newspapers, which call themselves newspapers of the left and particularly of M. Barrot, are going to conduct their polemic . . . That they insult us in honoring M. Thiers, that they place in his hands alone the management of this important affair and treat him as the very personification of our party—this, I confess to you, is what fills me with pain and indignation . . . I don't know what you are planning to do, but as for me, I will not bow my head to this third-rate dictatorship and I will not let myself impose, through it, doctrines that are not only contrary to the liberalism of the present day, but to that of all time.

On June 18, although one group of deputies named Tocqueville a member of the committee, another chose Thiers, and Thiers was appointed rapporteur.

His report, filed on July 23, accepted liberty of teaching, but imposed conditions for faculty appointments that were then difficult to fulfill for graduates from the new institutions who sought teaching or administrative positions, and subjected these conditions to very strict supervision by the University. Members of the *Congrégations* were, of course, not permitted to teach. Students in the *petits séminaires* were no more able to sit for the baccalaureate now than they had been in the past. In order to win over the bishops, Thiers proposed granting them eight thousand scholarships, an offer the bishops had the good sense to refuse. The spirit of the report was an apologia for the Napoleonic University and for classical studies; certain ideas of Tocqueville's, like that of confining the teaching of philosophy to logic, were held up to ridicule. The discussion of the plan, in this mutilated form, never took place. Villemain, already overwhelmed with family worries, suffered greatly because of the polemics that his plan unleashed. In December, his reason became unhinged and he took a pile of paving stones from the place de la Concorde to use against some Jesuits who wanted to do him harm. Guizot hastily replaced him by Salvandy, who deferred yet again the realization of liberty of teaching.

After his recognition that he could not persuade the Chamber through his own eloquence and after the letter to Barrot of September 1842 proposing close cooperation, Tocqueville had attempted, as we will see further along, to publish a newspaper. Here, too, he failed. 369 Despite these temporary discouragements, he was nevertheless prepared to attempt the experiment of a new party.

By the time a new Chamber was elected on August 1, 1846, he had acquired a certain weight in the political world and definitely cut an original figure. Let us interrupt the story of his career for a moment to attempt a portrait of the man, who had by now reached full maturity, a portrait based on the testimony of his contemporaries and his own confidences.

20

TOCQUEVILLE

IN PRIVATE LIFE

ALEXIS DE TOCQUEVILLE had his portraitist, Théodore Chassériau, and the best iconographic accounts we have are the portrait drawn by Chassériau in 1844 and his large painting on canvas shown at the Salon in 1850. The two men did see each other socially, although Tocqueville seems to have been closer to Frédéric, the painter's brother, who was in the Naval Ministry and later on became the rapporteur of the Council of State. How did these relationships begin? We can only note that the father of the two Chassériaus had been a protégé of Chateaubriand's, who, while minister of foreign affairs, once used him for a secret mission.

As for Chassériau's large portrait of Tocqueville, it was possibly undertaken by the painter out of gratitude. In his book *Le Palais du Conseil d'Etat et de la Cour des Comptes,* Marius Vachon tells us the following anecdote, which he had from Frédéric Chassériau:

One evening, Frédéric and Théodore Chassériau were visiting M. Alexis de Tocqueville in his home. Tocqueville said to Frédéric that his brother seemed sad.

"That's true," answered M. Frédéric Chassériau. "They are going to refuse his request to do a mural painting in a Paris monument."

"Who has the final authority?" asked M. Alexis de Tocqueville.

"The minister of the interior."

"Ah!" replied M. de Tocqueville, "is that all! I'll take care of it. Reassure your brother."

M. Vitet, a deputy, was a very close friend of the minister of the interior,

Comte Duchâtel, and his adviser where art was concerned. M. Vitet had submitted his candidacy to the Académie Française, of which M. Alexis de Tocqueville was a member.

"My dear friend," the Academician said to him. "One good turn deserves another. I promise you my vote on condition that Chassériau gets his mural without fail."[1]

This anecdote is confirmed by a note of recommendation from Tocqueville. At the time Vitet was elected in 1845, however, only the top of the stairway of the Cour des Comptes was being discussed. A countess interceded with Guizot later on so that the painter could have the whole stairway: Chassériau's biographer, Bénédite, believes the countess was Madame de Tocqueville.[2] This does not seem very likely. What seems certain is the interest taken by Tocqueville in Chassériau's career and art. There was something temperate and balanced in Chassériau's romanticism that suited the esthetic predilections we can discern in Tocqueville. He must have been quite content to sit for the painter. And Chassériau has left us a portrait which confirms the most reliable accounts of Tocqueville's appearance.

Antoine Rédier met several old men before the First World War who had known Alexis de Tocqueville well. One was an American living in Paris, Edward Childe. The author of the *Democracy* was frequently present at his mother's salon, and after her death made efforts to guide him in his choice of a career. Tocqueville's family archives have preserved a note in which Edward Childe makes a date with Rédier to talk about that time, which, he says, he cannot recall without a feeling of melancholy. Unfortunately, Rédier has not left us any record of their conversation. On the other hand, he did ask an old Norman, Lécrivain, to describe the man he had known a half century earlier and he quotes this portrait:

"His face was pale; his black eyes showed you his great energetic soul; his voice was very sonorous and his words always marked by the loftiest reason. His hair, which was a beautiful jet black, fell in silky curls around his neck; he usually wore a soft felt hat on his head; his hands were small and thin, his fingers long and tipped with long nails."[3]

This rather overpolished description is not without value; it lets us

---

[1]M. Vachon, *Le Palais du Conseil d'Etat et de la Cour des Comptes* (Paris, 1879), 20.

[2]L. Bénédite, *Théodore Chassériau, sa vie et son oeuvre* (Paris, 1939), 318–19.

[3]Rédier, *M. de Tocqueville*, 145.

see the energy that emanated from this frail man, so noticeable to his compatriots from the Cotentin.

Custine, who met Tocqueville in 1841, portrays him, on the other hand, as ill at ease in the company of someone he did not know, and interprets this uneasiness in an unkindly way. He brings out the somewhat morbid childishness of Tocqueville's looks:

> I have met M. de Tocqueville, the author of *La Démocratie américaine*. He is a puny, thin, small man, still young. There is something of the old man about him and also something of the child, he is the most naive of ambitious men. His gaze is charming, but lacks frankness, his mouth is old and ill shaped, his skin color is bilious, his expressive features would have captivated me if they had not disturbed me so much. One can see that he gives his words more than one meaning and that his opinions are weapons to attain his goal. Such is the new star on our political horizon as he appeared to me.[4]

Charles de Rémusat in his *Mémoires* describes similar features in his portrait of the man as he was in the same year, though with perspicacity and sympathy rather than ill will. Rémusat's observations about Tocqueville are often penetrating. Let us confine ourselves here to what he says of Tocqueville's appearance:

> He was a small, slight man with an agreeable, regular, but sickly face shadowed by a mass of curly brown hair that preserved an air of youth about him; his sad, unanimated features assumed more expression when he talked. The livid pallor of his skin was an early sign of organic ailments and led malicious people to suspect him of being bilious, envious and everything that follows from that. He was not at all so; only a little mistrustful, often in pain, often discouraged about himself.[5]

We have evidence of Tocqueville's poor health even in his youth. There were periods of relief, and, except for the attack of pleurisy he contracted during a spell of terrible cold, the trip to the United States coincided with one of them, as did the writing of the first *Democracy*. But the whole of his active life was darkened by migraines, intolerable attacks of neuralgia, difficult digestion, stomach cramps lasting more than a week. In 1853, under the care of Dr. Bretonneau, some of the pain of these conditions seems to have been eased yet the doctor could not arrest the deterioration of Tocqueville's health during his last years.

[4]*Lettres de Custine à Varnhagen von Ense,* February 22, 1841, 420–21.
[5]Rémusat, *Mémoires* 4, 45.

Until 1850, he was a fragile man, quite often confined to his bedroom 373
by slight illnesses but still, in 1849, bearing the heavy burdens of the ⚜ ⚜
Ministry of Foreign Affairs without his health's seeming to suffer from
it. Things changed in March 1850 with the first serious pulmonary
attack, when he began to spit blood and seemed to be dying. Despite
periodic remissions, he would never again be altogether well. His
friends, used to his being in bad health, apparently did not understand
that he was now seriously ill. Tocqueville died at Cannes in April 1859
of the disease that had first manifested itself in 1850, probably a slowly
developing pulmonary tuberculosis.

But except for these last years, Tocqueville's life was not that of a
man chronically ill. His body, "puny" though it may have been, bent
to the demands of his will without too much fatigue. In America,
Tocqueville spent days on horseback or in carriages with no suspension
on execrable roads. Besides these exceptional performances, he was a
good swimmer, a fair hunter despite his myopia, and most of all a great
walker, who, during his rambles in Normandy, would push through
the thickest hedges in that wooded countryside rather than deviate
from his straight line.[6]

Yet there was something a little pathological about his irritability
in domestic life. Obsessively punctual, almost always tense and impatient, he reacted to his wife's British phlegm with sudden, lively rages.
Most striking of all, perhaps, were the periodic swings in his moods,
which varied sharply along with the state of his health, leading him
from exaltation to dejection and back again.

In his periods of euphoria, he allowed himself to be carried away
by an enthusiasm that made him lose his sense of reality. After the
great success of the *Democracy,* he already saw himself playing a
grand role in affairs of state. After the quarrel between Barrot and
Thiers in 1842, he saw himself as Barrot's *éminence grise,* leading the
left toward new ideas. More often, he knew states of depression. He
thought of changing his life completely, quitting politics altogether,
after Louis-Napoléon's overwhelming victory in the presidential
election of December 10, 1848. He left unfinished several studies
promised in good faith to Buloz or others, growing discouraged and
unsure of their value.

"By nature, I have great distrust of myself," he said, and when he
was appointed minister of foreign affairs, Saint-Priest noted unkindly
the mixture of pride, shyness, and fear with which he accepted the

[6]Ampère, obituary article, *O.C.* XI, 443.

374

ᛉ ᛉ

post.[7] His wife judged him astutely when she compared him to a compass needle oscillating ceaselessly before becoming fixed. This lack of confidence in himself made him sensitive to criticism and praise alike "much more than was reasonable," he confessed to Madame Swetchine, with whom he tried to be perfectly sincere.

It was this uneasiness that seems to have made him secretive and shy in his youth. In his Versailles days, the fluency of speech of his inseparable friend Beaumont eclipsed him somewhat. "Gustave de Beaumont was as witty as he was pleasant; he had solid qualities of heart and a vivacity of spirit that contained much grace and gaiety; Tocqueville, on the other hand, was cold, reserved, self-controlled to the point of calculating his actions as well as his associations": this was how Blosseville saw the two friends.[8] Cavour, who met them in 1835 in London, made similar sorts of observations, despite his enthusiasm for the *Democracy*. [9] But Tocqueville's uneasiness in the world was soon to disappear, it seems, when he became fully aware that he was an author preceded everywhere by the stir his book had created. Thenceforth, he could be simple or modest without affectation, and that was the impression he left on those he met shortly after 1835. It was in such terms that Madame d'Agoult described him in 1857 to her son-in-law Emile Ollivier, with whom he was going to dine.[10]

Yet there was a counterbalance to this uneasiness of temperament in Tocqueville: a great good sense that made him seek to achieve no more than what was possible. He did not believe, for example, that the democracy which would develop in the future had to be imposed without any transitional period, and his moderate views took circumstances into account, allowing for a gradual evolution over time at a pace that certain commentators have felt he let be excessively slow. If his imagination was vivid, Tocqueville's reason remained realistic and prudent.

He tended to subject his analysis of facts to a classic discipline. From among the facts registered by an almost unrivaled memory, he would first separate out the germinal ideas, then articulate them with a soberness of style that was almost anachronistic in the romantic era, then deduce their consequences and determine their effects.

The rigor with which Tocqueville developed his conclusions has given him a reputation as a prophet. Two characteristic examples of

[7] Letter from Saint-Priest to Barante in Barante, *Souvenirs* (Paris, 1840–1901), vol. 7, 451.
[8] Passy, *Le Marquis de Blosseville,* 107.
[9] Whyte, *Cavour,* 122, 129.
[10] J. Vier, *La Comtesse d'Agoult et son temps,* vol. 5, 97.

these "prophecies" have been proposed by critics for the admiration   375
of his readers:

—The comparison between the United States and Russia, two
nations which by different paths, that of democracy and that of despotism, were moving toward a shared dominion over the world. This
passage, which concludes the first *Democracy,* is brilliant, rich in well-
turned phrases. But Tocqueville was only giving striking form to a
widespread idea—and one that was suggested by the facts, to anyone
who had witnessed the extraordinary development of America and
who had seen the Cossacks in Paris in 1815 when they were bivouacked
in the courtyard of the Tuileries—a fearful sight even to the czar's
allies.

—His speech of January 27, 1848, in which he announced that the
wind of revolution was rising. Tocqueville, who wanted to shake up
the sluggishness of parliamentary circles, was giving vigorous expression to an opinion one tended to encounter among other observers
sensitive to the torpor of the July regime, to the revival of national
movements, and to the economic crisis. Here, too, he merely summed
up a trend of thought in a forceful way.

Naturally, Tocqueville was struck by the great movement toward
democracy throughout the Christian world. But his profound originality was to show that men could either organize this movement so
that it fostered free societies or resign themselves to a new form of
despotism. The hope that the first solution would be achieved gave him
confidence at times in the future, and fears of the second inspired the
Democracy's darkest pages. In the same way, under the Second Empire,
he lamented men's resignation and then, several months later, foresaw
the rebirth of freedom.

Tocqueville tried to look forward, to discern the possibilities. He
clung to the conviction that man would remain free to choose between
these possibilities. According to the times, he was more or less optimistic or more or less gloomy, but he never despaired or gave up.

He was no more a misanthrope than he was a fatalist. Certainly, he
showed no indulgence when it came to analyzing the psychological
mechanisms of his contemporaries, and his *Souvenirs* form a gallery of
not very flattering portraits of his friends, alongside ferocious ones of
his enemies.[11] He could be vindictive enough, but there was also a
certain verve, a sense of caricature in him that we must take into

[11]M. Bressolette, "Tocqueville, mémorialiste féroce," *Littératures* 19 (1972), 61–69.

376

卐卐

consideration. And the painter did not flatter himself any more than he did his models.

For the rest, he forgave Beaumont his sometimes devious moves during their political life and proved, to the few he adopted as close friends (Stoffels, Kergorlay, Beaumont himself) to be reliable, faithful, and tactful throughout their long association. In a much more general sense, he loved his fellow men. He was to say to Loménie that he could never converse with a man without being aware of the original equality of the species. This was a profound instinct in him, and he was wounded by Gobineau's celebrated book on the inequality of the human races.

He was "touched," he told Loménie, by the good opinion that his Norman compatriots had of him, and added, "I am aware that something of that good opinion is merited. I have made many mistakes in my life, but I have truly loved justice and men and I hope that this will cause me to find grace before God."[12]

Rémusat has written quite correctly that Tocqueville broke with legitimism, not with the legitimists. Among many men who have gone over from a conservative milieu to an opposing party, there is harmony between their reason and passions in repudiating their original milieu. But Tocqueville was not in the least a man who harbored ill-feeling, and one could say that the further his reason took him from his own people, the more he respected their feelings and even their prejudices. It is only through very discreet allusions that we know that one part of his family anathematized him, that he did not dare attend the funeral of the father of Louis de Kergorlay, one of the most hot-blooded Carlists of his time. In the papers Tocqueville left behind, we have found no trace of any complaint at having been treated in this way. On the contrary, the public man of the July monarchy retained his modest family piety and continued to express his admiration for these relatives who were once close to the court of the Bourbons and continued to be faithful to the Bourbon cause. A letter to his wife written in 1846 seems revealing in this regard:

I went to spend the evening with the duchesses yesterday. I found these two small old women sitting on the same sofa, all alone in a large salon on the ground floor. It was really desperately sad. The Duchesse de Narbonne

---

[12]L. de Loménie, "Publicistes modernes de la France, Alexis de Tocqueville," *Revue des deux mondes* 21 (May 15, 1859).

was in pain and my aunt was still out of sorts and depressed. They both received me very affectionately, and when I asked the Duchesse de Narbonne, after my aunt left, if it would be suitable to come back to pay my aunt another visit, she said yes, and that her sister had a great liking for me. I will therefore return.[13]

One might think this was a matter of his being more attached to traditional conceptions of family ties than he was to the nobility as a class. But his identification with the nobility sometimes showed itself in a pure state. In 1849, the Second Republic appointed the Comte de Tanlay, from the solid nobility of Bourgogne, as prefect of the Manche, succeeding a series of bourgeois prefects in Saint-Lô. Tocqueville, who had as yet met him only once, wrote him in connection with an administrative matter and added:

I only ask you to make a distinction between M. de Tanlay and the prefect . . . I am writing not so much to the prefect as to the first . . . Our common origins, traditions, habits, and social position give me the sort of confidence in the first that I confess to you I have never had the habit of showing to the various representatives of the powers-that-be that we have had in the department over the last ten years.[14]

Tocqueville, who refused to adorn himself with his title of comte, which he felt was old-fashioned, remained attached by his most intimate feelings to the way of life of these aristocrats of the West, whose tradition he had taken care to pass on to his nephew Hubert. It was with nostalgia that he wrote to his wife in 1858, apropos of the upheaval in social relations brought about by the inevitable progress of democracy:

We will not be replaced, as I often tell myself sadly . . . We are part . . . of a world that is passing. An old family, in an old house that belonged to its forefathers, still enclosed and protected by the traditional respect and by memories dear to it and to the surrounding population—these are the remains of a society that is falling into dust and that will soon have left no trace. Happy are those who can tie together in their thoughts the past, the present, and the future! No Frenchman of our time has this happiness and already few can even understand it.[15]

[13]Unpublished letter to his wife dated August 19, 1846.
[14]Unpublished letter, Tocqueville Archives, file 97.
[15]Unpublished letter to his wife, May 4, 1858.

378

𝕵 𝕴

Tocqueville's family origins provided him with a natural entrée into the great legitimist salons—in the home, for example, of the Duchesse de Rauzan, whose salon was a continuation of the once famous salon of her mother, Madame de Duras, and who not only received brilliant society in the evening, but also welcomed select notables from the world of literature or politics in the afternoon. Tocqueville was also received in the world of the old legal aristocracy, with which he was connected through his cousins, by people like the Séguiers, the d'Aguesseaux, and old Chancellor Pasquier, the friend of Madame de Boigne, whom, at the end of his life, Tocqueville took pains not to sadden in his description of the Ancien Régime.[16] But under the July monarchy, he was above all a privileged habitué of the salon of Madame de Castellane, the adviser and companion of his cousin the Comte de Molé. He liked the "slightly sugary" conversation of the lady, "for whom it was as difficult to tell the truth as for a crab to walk forward" (Mérimée). Molé himself, about whose conniving mind Tocqueville had no illusions, seemed to him the embodiment of the delicate courtesy of an earlier day and an artful, witty conversationalist. But he had also been introduced by Royer-Collard into another great political salon of the time, that of the Duchesse de Dino, presided over by Talleyrand, whose oracular statements politicians came to drink in.

He frequented, at least from 1835 on, the famous salon of l'Abbaye-au-Bois. The German Gans, who published an article on Madame Récamier's salon early in 1836, portrays him there:

Across from [Cousin] is a young man with a pale and rather sickly face. He is shown a gentle deference and a good deal of attention. He talks about England and America as a man who has endeavored to study them. In his manner, there is a grace and a politeness to which the present generation of Frenchmen seems to attach less value than the preceding one. "Who is that young man?" I asked my companion, for I had been struck by him. "That is M. de Tocqueville" was the answer. "He's the one who has just published a very remarkable book about the United States . . . He is much sought after and well liked; all the salons want to have him."[17]

Not all of these salons were marked by such seriousness. Tocqueville frequented that of an old marquise whom Armand de Melun describes thus without revealing the hostess's identity:

---

[16] Letter to Ampère dated January 7, 1857, *O.C.* XI, 359.
[17] E. Gans, "Le salon de madame Récamier," *Revue de Paris* (February 7, 1836), 237–42.

In the least devout dwelling of the faubourg Saint-Germain, where dinners
were given every Friday, where the meats were prepared with meticulous
and by no means penitential care, where the mistress of the house, very old,
had the manners of a dowager of the Ancien Régime and the spirit and ideas
of the eighteenth century, where, among the guests, Tocqueville and Mérimée could be found, already distinguished in literature and politics, where
one also encountered the most amusing and the least orthodox of storytellers,
I was often invited and made welcome.[18]

It seems certain that Tocqueville, through a desire to become better
acquainted with Europe as a whole, often frequented foreign salons in
Paris. Although he does not seem to have been in the home of Madame
de Lieven, he did visit the other Russian ladies: Princesse Bagration
and, later, Madame de Circourt, whose want of practical sense irritated
him, but whose husband he liked to consult, for he was a walking
dictionary and an erudite and talkative man; then Madame Swetchine,
for whom he felt a deferential friendship that caused him to tolerate
the devotees of her salon for whom he had little respect.[19] Under the
July monarchy, he frequented the salon of Princesse Belgiojoso. Here
he was interested in the mixture of international guests, although he
had many bad things to say about the princesse.

In his *Souvenirs,* he tells of his meeting in 1848 with George Sand,[20]
whom he did not know since he had not been associating with the
literary bohemia. This may be so, but all the same, he had often visited
the home of Madame Ancelot,[21] whose reputation was not unblem-
ished, and addressed an embarrassed refusal to her when she tried to
dedicate one of her works to him, for fear of what people would say.
When the mistress of the house herself portrayed, in a *tableau vivant,*
the tragedienne Rachel in the role of Racine's Hermione, surrounded
by the habitués of the salon, Tocqueville was among them along with
Madame Récamier, Chateaubriand, Jouffroy, Stendhal, Considérant,
and others.[22]

Aside from the salons in the strict sense, Tocqueville was also a
member of a few associations. Some of these were austere, like the
Society for the Abolition of Slavery and the Society for Christian

[18]A. de Melun, *Mémoires,* ed. Comte Le Camus (Paris, 1891), vol. 1, 153.
[19]The correspondence between Tocqueville and the Circourts appears, ed. A. P. Kerr, in *O.C.* XVIII.
The correspondence with Madame Swetchine, ed. Pierre Gibert, appears in *O.C.* XV, 2.
[20]*Souvenirs, O.C.* XII, 149–50.
[21]V. Ancelot, *Un salon de Paris, 1824–1864* (Paris, 1866); H. Martineau, *Stendhal et le salon de madame
Ancelot* (Paris, 1932), 76.
[22]H. Martineau, ibid.

Morality, where a Protestant tone prevailed. But he also took part in much more informal weekly dinners at the Palais-Royal, in company with Quinet, Sainte-Beuve, Montalembert, Corcelle, Ampère, and others.

There was, then, a sort of worldly elite with which Tocqueville maintained regular relations. Included in this elite were politicians like Thiers, Lamartine, Rémusat, Corcelle, and Salvandy; great lords, foreigners on their way through town, like von Humboldt, Disraeli, and Cavour; men of letters, like Ampère, Ballanche, Vigny (with whom he seems to have been quite close[23]), Balzac no doubt, and Mérimée, whom he encountered everywhere with mixed feelings of amusement and annoyance.

In the salons, Tocqueville was a brilliant if somewhat irregular talker. The subject had to please him, and the circle of people could not be too large. He also knew how to listen and was attentive to the reactions of the people he was talking to. The Comte de Chambrun, who saw him alone in 1858, noted: "Every time, he would place me in full light the better to observe, in my face, the effect of his words, whereas he himself always sat in shadow, like the oracles."[24]

Paris life was succeeded by country life during the summer and fall. At the farthest extreme of the Cotentin, in the fertile valley of the Saire, the Château de Tocqueville was tucked away in the greenery of meadows and woods; in the distance, from the second floor, one could see the sea. When Tocqueville took possession of it in 1836, it consisted of a large main house with a reddish-brown roof flanked by heavy towers and overlooking a courtyard surrounded by outbuildings. The château had been uninhabited, except for brief visits, since 1790. Tocqueville and his wife became attached to the old house, and up to the end of their lives continued to try to make it more comfortable and cheerful.

Nearby was the landed property from which most of their income was derived. Madame de Tocqueville was the one to discuss the leases; her British obstinacy allowed her to come out on top in bartering with the Norman peasants.

It has often been said that Tocqueville was poor. This is true only in the context of the social rank he occupied. Under the July monarchy, he paid from 1,800 to 2,000 francs in taxes and his income can be estimated at about ten times that sum. This was much too little to

[23]E. Dupuy, *A. de Vigny, Les Amitiés* (Paris, 1912), passim.

[24]A. de Pineton de Chambrun, *Nos historiens, Guizot, Tocqueville, Taine* (Paris, 1888).

maintain a pack of hounds, beautiful carriages and horses, or girls from
the Opéra. But with a bourgeois life-style in Paris, the Tocquevilles
were able to enjoy the ease of landed proprietors in the country, and
they entertained fairly often in the house they had acquired in Valognes.

Tocqueville loved this rural life. At the time he was preparing
L'Ancien Régime, he wrote, with the touch of irony about himself one
so often finds in him: "Writer before lunch, farmer afterwards, I find
that these two ways of living make up something complete which I
am attached to despite the monotony. I have seriously gotten back to
work on my book and I am building a magnificent pigsty. Which of
these two works will outlast the other? Alas, I have no idea, to tell
the truth. The walls I am giving my pigs are good and solid."[25]

In Tocqueville's writings, "my country" most often has a local sense,
and refers to his home in the Cotentin. It was here that his life
preserved or regained the radiance of one of those "great lives" characteristic of the aristocratic ages. But two areas within it must be distinguished: the area close to the château, corresponding to the village of
Tocqueville, where family traditions had been revived, and the department of the Manche. At the château itself, bread was distributed to the
poor in the traditional way each week, and the chatelain visited the
sick. During times of crisis, as in 1848, even though his revenues were
somewhat diminished, Tocqueville gave work to a number of the
villagers. The mayor of Tocqueville was the descendant of old syndics
from before the Revolution: one felt back in the life of an earlier time.
This was merely an illusion, and Tocqueville knew it better than
anyone.[26] A certain laughable incident provided a characteristic example. The Tocquevilles' pew in the parish church was in the choir, and
a rumor went around that during mass the priest accorded the chatelain
the privilege of a special wave of incense from the censer. Several
documents in the Tocqueville Archives mention this serious affair, and
Tocqueville wrote to his electoral agent, the tax collector Clamorgam:
"Do you think that after speaking out for the great movement for the
equality of man, I would demand the exclusive right to strut about
between the verger and the cantor and cause myself to be blackened
with smoke like a fox in its hole?"[27] Though he grumbled, Tocqueville
did not take this foolishness lightly and moved from the choir to the

---

[25]Fragment of a letter published by Loménie, "Publicistes modernes," 424.

[26]Loménie, "Publicistes modernes," passim.

[27]Letter to Clamorgan dated January 1, 1839. Kühn, *Tocqueville als Abgeordneter,* 31, text corrected
against the original.

nave, "where he will be less, feudally speaking, but greater where warmth is concerned."

In 1848, when they went to vote in the chief town of the canton, the electors were lined up two by two in alphabetical order, and Tocqueville modestly placed himself under the letter T. It was at the insistence of his compatriots that he gave them a little speech before the vote. Each of them had prepared his ballot before leaving home, and one farmer said to him after the poll: "Monsieur de Tocqueville, you seem tired. And yet we were all carrying you in our pockets this morning." A remark made in 1857 by the coachman who was taking Louis de Loménie to Tocqueville, and that amused him, conformed fundamentally to the truth: "The people like Monsieur de Tocqueville very much, and he is very grateful to them for it."

But the deputy from Valognes also had interests and duties that extended to the whole arrondissement. Tocqueville spent part of the summer traveling through it, going from dinner to dinner despite his stomach troubles, not only out of a desire to win votes, and not even in order to find out the needs of the region, but to inform all these local notables, landowners, magistrates, and civil servants of the great political interests of the country. Even though he sometimes grumbled, he did not dislike meeting these men, quite often cultivated or erudite—more diverse, in any case, than the rural society of our times. And the way in which he took part in the work of the departmental council and conceived his obligations to it is a sign of his attachment to local life.

The representative of the twin cantons of Saint-Pierre-Eglise and Montebourg to the departmental council was Sivard de Baulieu, councillor in the Cour des Comptes, who belonged to a livelier opposition than that of Tocqueville. Six months before the elections of December 1842, he indirectly asked Tocqueville if he was going to stand as a candidate. Tocqueville was evasive, thinking that he might offend one of the notables of the canton likely to oppose Sivard, about whose activity the electors were not very happy. But a little later, Tocqueville allowed the rumor to spread that although he was not a candidate, he would not refuse any votes that might be given to him. This Norman prudence did not prevent his being elected, and in a letter to Havin he seems quite surprised at Sivard de Baulieu's displeasure![28]

Once elected to the departmental council, he took his job seriously.

[28]E. Lhommédé, *Un département français sous la monarchie de Juillet; le Conseil général de la Manche et Alexis de Tocqueville* (Paris), 9–10.

He studied all the texts relative to such an assembly, played an impor-   383
tant role in the discussions, and allowed himself to be overwhelmed   ꠶ ꠶
by reports on important local issues like the construction of the Cherbourg–Paris railroad and the elimination of the revolving boxes at the
entrance to foundling hospitals in which infants could be left. The
culmination of his active career in the department and certainly for him
one of the high points of his public life was his tenure as president of
the departmental council in 1849, 1850, and 1851.

It is odd to note that Tocqueville, at ease in the salons or the
academies as well as in the departmental council, was much less so in
the Chamber of Deputies. It seems that here he felt clothed in the same
anonymity that had troubled the young magistrate of Versailles when
he first went out into the world. He also seems to have found somewhat distasteful the superficial and facile camaraderie that is the rule
in such assemblies. With his mind focused on the issues under discussion, he was lost when it came to more covert intrigues, and he
bewildered his colleagues: people took as haughtiness what was no
more than abstraction aggravated by myopia. One day Beaumont
remarked upon this to him and he became immediately warm toward
Durand (de Romorantin), who must have been surprised by an effu-
siveness which, moreover, had no sequel.[29] But his livid skin color was
thought to be the outward sign of an ambition grown rancid. Thiers,
seeing him on the tribune on January 27, 1848—the day Tocqueville
spoke of the rising wind of revolution—said to Rémusat that this was
clearly a wicked man (he would soon change his opinion and, in the
presence of Nassau Senior, pay homage to the purity of his patriotism).
All in all, he was hardly liked, and his colleagues sometimes took
pleasure in not appointing him to committees he wanted to be part of.

He was not able to make an immediate impression in his speeches;
he had neither the aplomb of a Guizot nor the urgent rhetoric of a
Berryer nor the clear ease of a Thiers. He detested bombast, and the
eloquence of a Montalembert was particularly antipathetic to him. His
speeches were closely argued but without warmth, and we have seen
how he hesitated to approach the tribune.[30]

Nevertheless, at the end of the July monarchy Tocqueville was not
as isolated as was claimed by Beaumont, whose conscience was perhaps
not very easy. His influence extended beyond the small circle that had
at first gathered around him. He appeared to be the negotiator best

[29]G. de Beaumont, in a conversation with Nassau Senior, *Correspondence and Conversations with Nassau-William Senior 1834–1859*, ed. C. M. Simpson (London, 1872; New York, 1960), 12, p. 265.
[30]G. de Beaumont, *Notice sur Alexis de Tocqueville*, O.C. (Bmt) V, 59–63.

384

placed between the two scissions of right and left that threatened to break up the fixed structures of the parties. The mobs that took to the streets quickly made these attempts at parliamentary regroupings a thing of the past. But the Revolution of 1848 would also reveal, to Tocqueville's own surprise, how solid his position was in the department of the Manche.

A writer celebrated in his own time and a notable figure in political life, Tocqueville had a personality too complex to be readily summed up by the mere description of its principal features. Anxiety was a dominant trait in him, but he responded to this anxiety with action that conformed to a moral rule. He never doubted life's seriousness.

His anxiety had in it both religious disquiet and the anguish of an acutely sensitive social and political conscience.

Religious skepticism was the most private of his contradictions. He disguised it as best he could. His wife did not know of it. At Tocqueville, he attended mass and vespers. (What was he thinking about, standing or sitting in the *seigneur*'s pew, while the farmers of Lower Normandy, as he has told us himself, called upon the Lord with their discordant bawling?) He had declared once and for all that not every man had the means to resolve the metaphysical problem on his own, but this dimension could not easily be eliminated from the outlook of an intellectual of the romantic era. In his American journal, he spoke of doubt as one of the three great evils, along with illness and death, and he would confide his qualms to no one but Madame Swetchine, who seemed to him "saintliness and genius combined."

He blamed the *philosophes* of the eighteenth century for having attacked the old *Credo*. He had read Lamennais, he had heard Lacordaire at Notre-Dame, and he felt estranged from the Catholicism of his time. "The greatest enemy of Catholicism since Voltaire is Montalembert," he dared to write. The ultramontanism that made of the bishop of Rome a sacred figure, the appetite for miracles, the private devotions—all these seemed to him to be a degradation of the old religion. Here we have yet another paradox: though he worshipped man's liberty, he also remained sensitive to a Christian tradition that hardly credited it.

We know the broad vision of the evolution of Christian societies that filled Tocqueville with "religious terror": they were being ineluctably drawn by the divine will toward the state of democracy. But within this state, men would be able either to resign themselves to despotism, or to organize societies based on human freedom. At that point, in the political action laying the groundwork for the future, there would be a choice between good and evil, thus a fundamental duty requiring of every citizen that he work to bring about freedom.

It was the cult of freedom that guided Tocqueville as writer and as man of action. For him, the necessity for freedom was an article of faith drawn directly from the experience of life, and its grounds were beyond discussion. It was something more sacred than Benjamin Constant's individualism and much closer to the Pauline freedom of the children of God. It was this freedom that would assure the harmony of the future democracy, if that democracy did not founder beneath an evil dictatorship. But for this, it would be necessary for the citizens to have been shaped by the ethical molding of religion. And the religion most capable of molding men whose souls were free was, through the discipline of its dogma, Catholicism. It was far from Tocqueville's way of thinking to conceive of a religion that could be imposed upon the people while the elites were free of it; the leaders must share in the common faith. But the remarkable thing is that Tocqueville himself did not share in it. He believed in God and in a future life, and to this limited spiritualist *Credo* he added a sense of the superiority of Christian morality. He was, in fact, closer to the Unitarianism of someone like Channing than he was to Catholicism, for all his advocacy of its exceptional social virtues.

This advocacy, in any case, implied a hierarchy of values in which private virtues had a negligible place beside public duties. He could not forgive the Church under the Second Empire for not taking a stand against the regime, and Madame Swetchine had to remind him that the Church also had as its mission the salvation of the faithful.

"To live for the sake of living has no interest for me," Tocqueville once wrote. Even his most banal personal ambitions were situated within a broader perspective: to collaborate in the work of providence that marked a new creative stage in making the conditions of men equal, and to do so while preserving, at the heart of the new democratic civilization, that free will, sign of man's greatness, without which he would be merely a fallen creature.

21

FROM *LE COMMERCE*

TO THE "YOUNG LEFT"

AT THE START of his political career, Tocqueville had thought to gather around himself new deputies who were unwilling to take part in the usual party intrigues and ready to adopt firmer principles and a stricter political morality. This illusion was most probably a consequence of the *Democracy*'s success, still fresh, which had at once turned him into something of a celebrity. But within the microcosm of parliament the glamour of intellect counted for little without the power of eloquence. Solitary figures who would otherwise find little support in the Chamber were able to arouse both controversy and admiration through their impassioned words. Tocqueville always felt some jealous rancor toward the great orators—men like Montalembert and Lamartine. He had nothing of their talent. He could reduce whatever problem he was considering to its essentials by means of a somewhat abstract logical process, but his overly austere manner of speaking did not capture the Chamber's attention.

He therefore had to try to act within the framework of the parties. As we have seen, he chose to ally himself with the dynastic left, the "Barrot assembly." His ulterior motive was to play a special role in it. In his public life, he was encountering an old personal problem: to influence others, he had always needed a go-between. Beaumont, who had played this role in many instances for the past ten years, had abandoned it upon his entry into parliamentary life. Why should Tocqueville not feed ideas to the agreeable Barrot? Unfortunately, Barrot was too devious and too imbued with the sense of his responsibilities as head of the opposition. He was to observe, much later on, that he had not appreciated Tocqueville's true value at that time.

387
𝕏 𝕏

During the 1843 session, while Thiers stood aloof from political life, Tocqueville was not able to be an effective force in the Chamber. He was still one of the notable figures of the opposition, but somewhat off to one side, surrounded by a few friends. After that session, he wrote Kergorlay that his situation was not a good one. He wanted to change the spirit of the institutions, he said, rather than the institutions themselves. The conservatives did not want to change anything at all, and the left center, with which he would have been in agreement, wanted to employ means and put forward men he found repugnant. The "lively left," on the other hand, wanted profound changes, and it was for this reason that Lamartine had made himself the apostle of electoral reform. Tocqueville's position was too subtle to have any impact on many of the deputies, who were on the whole a mediocre lot. In his response, Kergorlay suggested what was probably a good tactic: to harry the government each time it put forward a concrete measure that chipped away at any freedom.[1] Unfortunately, this was hardly practicable for Tocqueville, because it called for the ability to extemporize upon demand and also for a consistently hearty physical condition—both of which he lacked, the second perhaps even more than the first.

For that matter, the split between Thiers and Barrot could not last. For a long time, Thiers had hoped that the king, tiring of Guizot, would turn to him, and that he would inherit the majority that had supported Guizot. By 1844, he felt that this was an illusion and that his only chance of returning to power was through an alliance between the left center and the left. Accomplices went to work. One was Duvergier de Hauranne, who saw in a coalition of these two parties of the dynastic opposition a guarantee that the representative government would continue to function in loyal support of the monarchy. More important were the *ministrables* of both parties—those whose rank and prestige gave them reason to think they would be considered for ministerial positions in the event of a victory of the left. Among these, Beaumont seems to have been one of the most active agents of reconciliation.

Tocqueville also stressed the role of Abbatucci, the "master in-

---

[1]Letter to Kergorlay dated October 19, 1843, and letter from Kergorlay dated October 31, 1843, *O.C.* XIII, 2: 126–35.

388
彡 彡

triguer," a friend of Thiers and like him a great admirer of Napoléon, who joined Barrot's piquet party every evening. In any case, by the end of 1843 the left had at its head a planning group consisting of ten members, five from the left (Barrot, Beaumont, Tocqueville, Abbatucci, and Havin), and five from the left center (Thiers, Rémusat, Vivien, Billault, and Duvergier de Hauranne). A year later, what amounted to a contractual agreement on running the government was signed by Thiers and Barrot. But as early as the beginning of the 1844 session, Tocqueville must have agreed to make his peace with Thiers and subject his own actions to collective discipline. The columns of *Le Siècle* would no longer have been open to him had he not accepted that discipline.

The course we have just described seems to us to explain the desire that he and several of his friends had to acquire a newspaper of their own.

An opportunity soon presented itself to put this plan into effect. On March 19, 1844, Tocqueville learned that *Le Commerce,* a newspaper of radical tendency that specialized in commercial and industrial news, was up for sale. The very same day, he wrote to his brother Edouard to ask his advice, and his letter shows us how the affair looked to him:[2]

As you know, there is a fairly widely read newspaper called *Le Commerce.* An opportunity has presented itself to me and my closest friends in the Chamber to take over this newspaper and make it the regular vehicle for our ideas. You can sense what an immense advantage it would be thus to possess and use each day one of the main channels of public information. But to do this, we must find 150,000 francs. As you are well aware, neither I nor even most of my friends could produce such a sum. To obtain it, we have thought of addressing a few very respectable major interests which have scarcely been represented in the press up to now. Agriculture, first of all. We have thought that it could be very useful for farmers to be assured of having their complaints heard or their ideas expressed in one of the large Paris newspapers, and we imagine that perhaps that interest might help us find the necessary capital.

On June 29, a development corporation was formed for the newspaper. A landowner, Tamisier, took twenty-seven of the fifty shares; six deputies from the opposition—Dezeimeris, Corcelle, Tocqueville, de Viard, Lanjuinais, and Combarel de Leyval—together with two law-

[2]Unpublished letter to his brother Edouard dated March 19, 1844.

yers, divided up the rest. An administrative council was created that included Tamisier, Combarel de Leyval, Corcelle, Roche, and de Viard. The administration was at first directed by Dezeimeris, a deputy from the Dordogne and an expert on agricultural matters. He left the newspaper in early February 1845 and was, we believe, replaced by Roche, though Dezeimeris continued to publish articles sporadically after that. Beginning in February, other articles were signed E.T., which probably stood for Edouard de Tocqueville. An editorial board was formed that included Tamisier, Corcelle, Tocqueville, Dezeimeris, and Combarel de Leyval. Apparently, Tocqueville's proposals were not always approved by this board, even though he was its most influential member.

Tocqueville was thus not in charge of the entire enterprise. To judge from the documents and letters that have been preserved, its history seems to have been a troubled one, involving rivalries among journalists, "oddballs" that other interests tried to slip onto the editorial staff, financial conflicts between the administrator Roche and the cashier.[3]

The editorial staff does not seem to have been very stable. In the beginning, the editorials, which were at that time called the *premiers Paris,* were entrusted to Arnold Scheffer. Scheffer was from a Dutch family whose members had come to France in 1815; he was the brother of the painter Ary Scheffer, then very famous and a member of Lafayette's circle. It was in Ary's studio that Arnold was appointed editor-in-chief of *Le Commerce* during a conversation with Tocqueville and Corcelle. Corcelle was the oldest of Scheffer's friends; their association dated back to their youth, when they had both fought for the Carbonari cause. Arnold Scheffer very quickly won Tocqueville's respect by his disinterestedness and loyalty. But he was a lackluster journalist, an intellect that lacked a sense of proportion. His articles exasperated Corcelle, and Tocqueville, while defending him against his old friend, recognized his inadequacy. The solution seemed to be to give him an associate editor, Forgues, who had contributed to *Le National* and who, under the name of "Old Nick," had earned a certain fame. Forgues knew England well, had published translations and written newspaper columns, but his attempt at being political editor was not a success. Scheffer ceased to be the newspaper's regular editor, though he retained a sort of general authority over the contributors. A note from March 1845 alludes to the replacement of Michel by

---

[3]This information is taken from two files, one in the Tocqueville Archives and the other in the d'Harcourt Archives.

390

Urbain as editor of the political page. Urbain is almost certainly the picturesque mulatto, a Saint-Simonian and a convert to Islam, who wrote for many papers and contributed to *Débats*. He was a close friend of d'Eichtal, whom Tocqueville knew well and who contributed a few letters from Greece. An examination of the Urbain archives, however, seems to have shown nothing to indicate that he was a contributor to *Le Commerce*.[4] However that may be, a note from the end of March 1845 shows the editorial staff of the paper being distributed as follows: Urbain in charge of the political page, Michel in charge of the commercial page, Thomas the *feuilleton* (the features page), and Forgues the theaters. We also know a few of the other contributors, for instance Burat, who was to send letters on industry from Germany.

It is easy to establish when the new team took over the newspaper. On July 24, 1844, *Le Commerce* published a manifesto, quite possibly by Tocqueville, on the goals it had set for itself. It would continue to be concerned with industrial and commercial news while broadening its perspective with news from abroad, but it would give a good deal of space to defending agricultural interests, as was guaranteed by the presence of Dezeimeris. Politically, the newspaper would not be "so ridiculous as to speak in the name of a new party," but would be one more organ for "the great national party which has ceaselessly worked, through all the vicissitudes of a half century of revolutions, to establish political liberty and equality before the law." Although *Le Commerce* was associated with Barrot's constitutional opposition, it would not be hostile toward the left center. The harmony of the opposition was a harmony of different shades of opinion; its essential goal was to win the country's respect for that opposition. There was, therefore, more concern for the immediate present than for the future. Two days later, on July 26, Arnold Scheffer's first editorial complemented this statement of intention in a fairly banal fashion.

If we can be quite precise about the birth of the new newspaper, the date of its death is harder to pin down. It seems to have begun a slow decline very early on. We know that in 1844 it lost disquietingly large numbers of subscribers. In 1845, we can trace the progress of the hemorrhaging through the following figures: on August 6, there were 3,549 subscribers, that is, 600 less than on January 1. The company was already dissolved: Combarel de Leyval had given up a share (or perhaps all his shares) to an owner who was himself a straw man for an

---

[4]Urbain's papers are divided between the Archives d'Outremer (Aix-en-Provence) and the Arsenal library. See Latéfa Bousdraoui, *Urbain Thomas Ismail*, typed dissertation (Paris VIII, 1977).

advertising company that called for dissolution on May 27, 1845. The
public notices at the time of the creation of the joint-stock company
had not been in conformity with the law, and Tocqueville's business
adviser counseled letting the business go without waiting for a trial,
"given the present disaccord among the interested parties and the
disrepute into which the newspaper has fallen." Tamisier, the majority
stockholder, was entrusted with selling the paper. Unfortunately, he
went about it rather inefficiently. After refusing an offer of 200,000
francs, he sold it in November for 110,000 francs. If we are correctly
interpreting a fragment of an account handed down to us, Tocqueville
lost slightly over 4,500 francs, or about a quarter of his yearly revenues.
Yet his complaints, which are unsupported by figures, would lead one
to suppose that his losses were greater. It was only in 1847 that the final
liquidation of the defunct company took place. But as early as May
1845 Tocqueville was thinking of leaving the paper; he ceased to play
any sort of role there on June 30.

It is not very easy to discover what exactly Tocqueville did during
the period of eleven months and seven days when he exercised a sort
of patronage at *Le Commerce.* We have not been able to recover his
correspondence with Scheffer, an important source, fragments of
which were used in a work on Ary Scheffer.[5] The articles in the paper
were anonymous, as was the general rule in those days, and Tocqueville
was strict in respecting the anonymity he had promised certain of his
contributors. Even Scheffer did not know the identity of some of
them, and he was the only person authorized to pass on to the printer
the articles Tocqueville wrote.

Yet we know of Tocqueville's efforts to give the newspaper new
life because of two initiatives of his. The first was his undertaking to
publish letters from unusually well-informed correspondents abroad,
"a practice . . . which constitutes the greatest merit of the English
newspapers and . . . is absolutely lacking in ours." For his English
correspondent, he first approached Disraeli, who could not promise
more than an occasional contribution, then came to an agreement with
the radical Charles Buller, member of the House of Commons, who
had accompanied Lord Durham to Canada and had been the principal
author of the latter's famous report on the colony. Every two weeks,
Buller sent a letter from England. For his American correspondent,
Tocqueville turned to Franz Lieber, the translator of *Le Système pénitentiaire,* with whom he had remained in contact since his trip to the

---

[5]Marthe Kolb, *Ary Scheffer et son temps* (Paris, 1937).

392

新 新

New World. Lieber sent four monthly letters. Tocqueville asked Lanjuinais, who was traveling in Spain, to find a correspondent from that country; Lanjuinais himself, it appears, wrote down some impressions, but there was only one letter from Madrid. Tocqueville also failed to find a regular correspondent in Germany; news from Switzerland, on the other hand, was abundant and came from a variety of sources.

The attempt to find good foreign correspondents was in harmony with Tocqueville's own interests. But his second initiative was inspired by fashion and the public demand for good serialized novels, the *romans-feuilletons*. He felt constrained to enter into negotiations that were less than completely successful: with "that pig of a literary man," Balzac, but Tocqueville wanted something other than the *Courtisanes;* with Alexandre Dumas in the hope of getting *Le Bâtard de Mauléon,* but the book was unfinished. The newspaper had to settle for second-rate authors. There was also some thought given to putting the literary editorship in the hands of the Vicomte d'Arlincourt, Balzac's whipping-boy, but the idea was apparently never followed up. To humor his young friend Gobineau, Tocqueville took six columns of his literary criticism, but did not think much of them and reproached Gobineau especially for devoting an article to Alfred de Musset, a second-rate literary subject. Yet these columns were what survived the oblivion into which the newspaper fell, since with one exception they were reprinted by M. Martineau.[6]

As for Tocqueville's own contribution, it is hard to separate it out, as we have already said. Of his political friends who embarked on this venture, Combarel de Leyval very quickly lost interest, and Lanjuinais showed only a moderate enthusiasm for it. The case was not the same for Corcelle, whose special domain was Algerian and Moroccan affairs, but whose finicky intransigence could not tolerate the slightest divergence of opinion; in consequence, minor quarrels took place in which he threatened to quit the paper, and Tocqueville had to agree to withdraw articles of which Corcelle did not approve.

During the summer of 1844, Tocqueville and Corcelle were busy launching the newspaper and remained in Paris until August 8, when Tocqueville returned to the Manche; shortly afterwards, Corcelle underwent an operation, then returned to the Orne.

During his brief stay in Paris, Tocqueville wrote an article on liberty

[6]These columns appear in the collection of pieces by Gobineau entitled *Etudes critiques 1844–1848* (Paris, 1927).

of teaching and a few editorials on the Pritchard affair. Absorbed in local politics during the summer, he sent only one article, but wrote two series on liberty of teaching and the debate on the proposed law on education of 1837. Back in Paris on November 6, he must have finished in haste his long report on the usefulness of the Paris–Cherbourg railway. He not only had to examine commercial statistics, but had to talk with cattle drivers and butter merchants—"I who am accused of treating problems in too abstract a manner," as he remarked ironically. He nonetheless took up work on the newspaper again.

The feeling spread through political circles that *Le Commerce* was on its way out, and that the ambition quite correctly attributed to Tocqueville of wanting to turn it into an important journal of opinion was ending in failure. Tocqueville thought he could discern his enemies' malicious joy, and for him it was a sharp blow to his self-esteem.

On November 24, he published a signed article on administrative centralization. Even though he had written a few days earlier that he would contribute only signed articles, either this was a pretense or he soon changed his mind, because on November 29 he published an unsigned article on the religious question that was followed, in December, by others on the same problem and on liberty of teaching.

Tocqueville's stated intention was to lift up *Le Commerce* by a stroke of brilliance so that it would be distinguished by its originality from other opposition newspapers. In his November 29 article, he criticized *Le Constitutionnel* and *Le Siècle* for devoting themselves primarily to attacks against the clergy and to the ridicule of religious practices. This was to brush to one side as of no importance the opposition's program of reforms, and to play the game of a candidate to succeed Guizot as head of government who might thus be able to extend his majority to include the conservative benches of the far right. In other words, the two principal newspapers of the left saw themselves accused of turning themselves over to Thiers lock, stock, and barrel. This imputation put Chambolle in a rage and during the following days *Le Commerce* was embroiled in an even sharper controversy with *Le Siècle* than with Thiers's avowed supporter, *Le Constitutionnel.* Now, for the last six months, Gustave de Beaumont had been a member of the overseeing board of *Le Siècle.* He wanted to wait until he had completely filled this temporary mandate before rejoining Tocqueville at *Le Commerce,* or at least that was his manifest intention. He abruptly changed his mind because of the broadsides this newspaper fired at *Le Commerce,* and quit *Le Siècle,* though he announced his resignation in a public letter that was full of praise for Chambolle. Tocqueville was not at all grateful for this act and remembered only the form it took. Chambolle had exasperated him by attacking him in his most sensitive spot, his legitimist origins, to which, it was insinuated, he remained secretly loyal. *Le Siècle* also reprinted a rumor started the July before by *Le Constitutionnel* according to which Tocqueville was prepared to accept the votes of the deputies of the majority to be appointed rapporteur of the law on secondary education instead of Thiers. A very lively exchange of letters took place between him and Beaumont, and it seems clear that this was their first quarrel in eighteen years of friendship. They were reconciled, but their relations continued to be affected by the consequences of this storm of abuse until 1848.[7]

In December, *Le Commerce* was in fact engaged in polemics on two fronts—against *Le Constitutionnel, Le Siècle,* and *Le National* on the one hand, and against *L'Univers* on the other. If Tocqueville was not the author of all the *Le Commerce* articles, their inspiration was obvious, and he at least provided their outlines. Nevertheless, this campaign, which had been intended to show the public that there existed a constitutional left independent of Thiers, appeared to the bulk of the leftist deputies, including, it seems, Barrot, as a regrettable attempt at a split.

After this outburst, Tocqueville continued to occupy himself with the newspaper, as Beaumont attests on January 10 in a letter to Ampère: "Tocqueville is in better health than ever, despite the fatigue caused him by *Le Commerce,* of which he is more or less the only one in charge, and he writes extremely remarkable articles. I don't know if you knew about the circumstances in which I separated from *Le Siècle* without joining our friends from *Le Commerce.* My isolation, which will necessarily be long, was the only thing possible."[8] What was Tocqueville writing in *Le Commerce* at that time? It has not been possible to determine which pieces were his. One would like to know what position he adopted in March during the newspaper's campaign against the Jesuits. If he had scarcely any liking for the famous Society, he nevertheless did not show such a lively hostility to it in his notes.[9] His influence at *Le Commerce* was not the only influence, and we are inclined to think it diminished even before his departure. It is possible, for that matter, that after his departure the regular editors asked

---

[7] On this polemic, see the letters between Tocqueville and Beaumont in December 1844, *O.C.* VIII, 1: 544–55.

[8] Ampère papers in the Institut de France.

[9] Rédier (*M. de Tocqueville,* 149–50) has identified Tocqueville as the author of an article in *Le Commerce* on the Jesuits of Lucerne, though we doubt that this is actually the case.

Tocqueville for an article now and then, for the political line laid down by him seems to have remained more or less in place during the transitional period during which a buyer was being sought for the paper.

Tocqueville did not think that his project was going to end in utter failure. Since the founding of *La Presse* by Emile de Girardin, since Guillemot's transformation of *Le Siècle* in 1836 into a cheap newspaper with wide circulation, the world of the dailies had been undergoing a profound change. Guillemot, who after leaving *Le Siècle* had been head of one of the departments in the Ministry of Finance, resigned from his post in April or May to found, with the help of one Dutacq, a financier who was also no novice where the press was concerned, a new newspaper that would absorb several existing ones, including *Le Commerce* and *Le Pays*. This daily, *Le Soleil,* [10] was to have the format of the London *Times,* far superior to that of the French papers of those days, and was to be a combination political paper, trade paper, medical journal, journal of public education, scientific journal, legal journal, administrative paper, and literary paper. Tocqueville had confidence in Guillemot and respected his intelligence and character, and Guillemot's success at *Le Siècle* had been clear. He agreed to join the editorial board of the future newspaper along with two friends and fellow deputies, Ferdinand de Lasteyrie and Corne, and thus to be in a position to exert a strong influence on its policies without having either to write for the paper or to purchase shares (Tocqueville's associates in the *Le Commerce* experiment, Combarel, Lanjuinais, Corcelle, and of course Beaumont, had nothing to do with this new attempt). But in the end, the enterprise could not bring together sufficient capital, for financial reasons that Tocqueville described on November 13 to his friend Corne:[11]

We collected at first more than four million in stock subscriptions, but instead of asking for immediate part payment from each subscriber we waited until the precise figure we wanted to reach was attained. Time passed. Then came the business crisis that is presently affecting the principal centers, London and Paris. Money was scarcer, panic spread through all the joint-stock companies, and when at last we wanted to request a first payment from our subscribers, a large number of whom had no doubt merely wanted to gamble

---

[10]The prospectus for *Le Soleil* is in the Bibliothèque Nationale. See also the Tocqueville-Beaumont correspondence, *O.C.* VIII, 1: 556–68.

[11]Unpublished letter to Corne dated November 13, 1845. Rédier copy, Tocqueville Archives.

in our stocks, we found their purses empty or closed. Only six or seven thousand francs were produced. One would need two million to undertake such a large enterprise.

Tocqueville remained bitter, and believed that his position had been shaken—not in his district, but in the political world. He thought that henceforth the opposition press would keep silent about his speeches and acts, would put him under "a pneumatic bell," that he had provoked strong hatreds against himself among his colleagues. He harbored resentment against Beaumont, who had urged him on to this attempt, then abandoned him. He despaired at seeing Thiers reign as head of the opposition, with even Barrot now joined more firmly than ever to his fortunes. But in the same letter to Corne, he added:

> I have done everything a man could do to create, in this country, a newspaper that would represent or uphold everything I believed and still believe to be the true, great spirit of the French Revolution . . . I have broken with part of my family, with beloved attachments and precious memories, to embrace the cause and the ideas of '89. Having made such great sacrifices for my opinions, I will certainly not deny them out of fear of the malevolence of the press and the sly hostility of our good friends in the opposition. I will uphold these doctrines as long as I am in the Chamber, with all my power and all my strength, at all costs, even if I should be the only one to do so.

Was the failure of Le Commerce as serious as Tocqueville thought it was? Whatever the case, he recovered fairly quickly, to judge by the fragment of a letter that is unfortunately dated only with the year 1846: "I was able to get back on my feet by myself after the terrible shock that the Commerce business . . . dealt to my fortune."[12] By the beginning of the 1846 session, he wanted, for the first time, to be a member of the budget committee and was elected to it. This desire itself seems to be a sign of his new political outlook. Until now he had confined his interests to purely political problems. But the study of the plan for the Paris–Cherbourg railway caused him to come into close contact with the development of the industrial infrastructure. He associated the crisis of the newspapers with that of the banking centers that developed in 1845. He could not be unaware of the fact that these jolts in the economy imposed severe hardships on the working classes.

[12]Fragment of letter to his wife, 1846, Tocqueville Archives.

Here were converging events that must have led Tocqueville to entertain the thoughts about economics and society that he expressed on the
eve of the 1848 Revolution.

During the summer of 1846, Tocqueville had a more immediate
preoccupation, the elections set for August 1. He was not worried
about being reelected. The Guizot ministry, after having contemplated
running Gisles, the mayor of Valognes, against him, was not contesting
the election at all, not only because his situation was too strong, but
because a sort of sympathy had formed between him and Duchâtel, the
minister of the interior. Tocqueville foresaw victory for the government, and wrote Beaumont on July 20:

Either I am very much mistaken, or the opposition will suffer serious losses
in this election . . . [I] gather [this] . . . from the general state of the country
and the physiognomy of the parties . . . I think . . . very deep-lying causes,
not subject to direct influence when the decisive moment comes, determine
the results of a general election. I believe the conservative party will increase
notably in the Chamber. The result will probably be that it will split and
that in one form or another a neo-conservative party will be created that may
well overturn the cabinet.[13]

Yet Tocqueville was surprised nevertheless by the election results
—not because the conservatives gained about thirty votes in the Chamber but because the left center suffered hardly any losses while the
dynastic left lost important members, de Viard and especially Corne,
defeated in Douai, whose probity and independence Tocqueville respected.

Though deep-lying causes had led to the victory of the right center,
the cycle of corruption admitted almost openly by Guizot—giving
compensations to districts which had elected docile deputies so that
they would be reelected—also had something to do with it. During
a brief summer session (August 18–September 4), the procedure of
verifying the qualifications of the members of the Chamber was
marked by stormy battles. Tocqueville, usually so careful to spare
individuals, stood up on the tribune and attacked the election of
Delangle, chief public prosecutor of the Court of Cassation, the nation's highest court, and future minister under Napoléon III, who had

[13]Letter to Beaumont dated July 20, 1846, *O.C.* VIII, 1: 577.

398

𝕰 𝕸

won by a single vote in Cosne.[14] Demolishing the quibbling arguments of a committee report in Delangle's favor, Tocqueville pointed out how the local courts had put justice itself in the service of the candidate, going so far as to set free the imprisoned relatives of one of the electors. His speech, more serious in tone than heated, emphasized the danger of enslaving justice in the liberal State. It was not as an enemy of the government, it was as a descendant of the judges in the parlements of the Ancien Régime that he denounced such a scandal from the tribune.

This was not, however, the salient interest for Tocqueville during the brief extraordinary session. The main question was whether the new Chamber would offer the possibility of freeing the country from the rivalry of "those two jealous individualities," Guizot and Thiers. On August 18, he wrote to his wife:

The whole future has been engulfed in thick fog until now. The newcomers want to do new things, but don't know how to go about it without ceasing to be conservatives. As for the old ones, Thiers and Barrot, they seem more closely tied to each other than ever. But Billault, if I can credit his language, and Dufaure, if I can credit the speech you allude to, are determined to seize the first occasion to raise their own flag. My liberation in political life will depend on this combination. For at present I am a slave. However it may be, this wrangling will not lead immediately to a dramatic rupture. The session will be too short. But I consider it very probable that it will take place at the next session.

Tocqueville was noting signs of thaw in the two blocs, which had been rather frozen on the eve of the elections. For him there was no question of joining the neo-conservatives. But within the left center itself, Dufaure, a great orator, honest, independent, at odds with Thiers, and Billault, an incisive opponent of Guizot who had repelled Thiers's advances when he was asked to be part of a sort of phantom cabinet, and, in addition, a practical man and a skilled politician, had some notion of creating a "new left."

This new left outlined its first plans in a meeting at the end of the short session at which Tocqueville could not be present. For several years now, he had felt some sympathy for the curmudgeon Dufaure —of whom it was said that he was the very model of an even temper, since his temper was always bad—and Dufaure seems to have felt a certain sympathy for him in return. In 1845, Le Commerce supported

---

[14]Speech of August 22, 1846, Le Moniteur universel of August 23, 2217–18.

Billault against Le Peletier d'Aunay when he was candidate for a vice-presidency in the Chamber.

Tocqueville, passing through Paris at the end of September 1846 on his way to Algiers, met with Dufaure, with whom he had already had a long conversation at the end of August. Between these two conversations, he wrote a letter to Dufaure which is of some interest.[15]

Tocqueville agreed that the program of the new party should not be established on new principles; it would have for its foundation liberty and equality in the tradition of 1789. But it would present the sort of clean face Tocqueville had been vainly dreaming of since he entered political life, "an association of a few men of talent and good heart who would not involve themselves in intrigue . . . but work at what there was to be done for its own sake."

As for the studies thus carried out together, they would bear on "a certain number of reforms, either administrative or social," that had been up to now left to the most mediocre deputies. On this subject, Tocqueville's point of view was the same as Dufaure's, and he added:

I also think, as you do, that above and beyond day-to-day politics there is a great, patriotic stance to be adopted as regards the people, properly speaking, and that the greatest future is in this area. Up to now, all matters having to do with the well-being of the lower classes have been abandoned either to the selfish, unintelligent scorn of the conservative majority—a sort of new nobility that hardly concerns itself with the people . . . any more than its predecessors did—or to the dreams and passions of the utopians. A party that took it upon itself as its principal mission to work politically and actively for the moral and material well-being of the lower classes, without indulging their prejudices or inflaming their passions, would assume a new role that would be at the same time a great one.

The 1847 session of the Chambers did not open until January 12, and the discussion of the address in response to the speech from the throne did not take place until February 1. It was during the February 2 session that the new left made its existence felt in a vote on an amendment to the address.

In the text of the address, the king and the government were congratulated for bringing about the marriages celebrated the preceding October 10, between Queen Isabella of Spain and her cousin the Duke of Cadiz, and between her younger sister the Infanta Louisa Fernanda and the Duc de Montpensier, the youngest son of Louis-

[15]Unpublished letter to Dufaure from 1846; draft in the Tocqueville Archives.

Philippe. This double marriage eliminated a Coburg pretender supported by England, and Palmerston, who had returned to the Foreign Office in July 1846, declared that France had violated the agreements concluded at Eu at the time of Queen Victoria's visit to the King of France. Without examining the question in depth, we can point out that the left center and the left, so hostile until then to the entente cordiale between England and France, now deplored the fact that it had been broken. It was in opposition to this about-face of Thiers's that Dufaure and Billault proposed a paragraph adding to the congratulations of the majority of the Chamber the hope that this diplomatic success would not be bought by concessions to England. Neither Thiers nor Guizot could accept this amendment; it cast doubt on how long the success would last.

The amendment, defended first by its authors and then by a brief speech from Tocqueville[16] saying that it was consonant with Barrot's teachings, to which Barrot himself, in his present political position, no longer adhered (which earned Tocqueville a sharp reply), garnered only twenty-eight votes out of two hundred. The scission brought about by the new party within the left center and the left drew away only a very small number of men.

In the course of this session, Tocqueville was busy with the two long reports on Algeria that we have already discussed. He was named rapporteur on March 8 and submitted his conclusions on May 27, then defended them before the Chamber. He thus did not take part directly in the discussions on parliamentary reform and electoral reform. He was more in favor of the latter than he had once been, no doubt because he had been taught something by the corruption revealed in 1846, but he would have liked to balance the extension of the electoral body somewhat by instituting a two-stage vote.

The rejection of all reform by the Chamber gave rise, as we know, to the campaign of the banquets. The first was held July 9, 1847, at the Château Rouge, and there were similar demonstrations throughout France. The "father of the banquets" was Duvergier de Hauranne, an intimate of Thiers's, but the two men attracted others from the left center, the dynastic left, and the radicals. Thiers did not involve himself, but his newspaper, Le Constitutionnel, advocated the banquets, and Tocqueville, in his Souvenirs, compared Thiers's attitude to that

---

[16]Speech by Tocqueville on the Spanish marriages, of February 2, 1847, Le Moniteur universel of February 3, 104.

of Barrot in the following terms: "He remained motionless and mute
in Paris, while Barrot crisscrossed the country, alone, in every direction
... giving ... long speeches and bearing some resemblance, I thought,
to those beaters that make a great noise so as to bring the game within
range of the marksman who lies in wait."[17]

Tocqueville, invited to the Château Rouge banquet, avoided going,
and soon after, Dufaure, asked to preside over the banquet at Saintes,
responded with a very stiff refusal. The new left stayed away, as did
Thiers's immediate circle, but for a different reason—its mistrust of the
agitation throughout the country that the campaign was encouraging.
It formed what one deputy from the Manche called "the fasting
opposition."[18]

Dufaure's plan for using the time between the session of 1847 and
that of 1848 was a different one. He intended to write a manifesto that
would be published at the opening of the 1848 session. In it, he was
to propose a whole gamut of measures, with tax reform the most
important, that might bring some relief to the working classes.

Tocqueville's notes show that since his letter of the autumn of 1846
he had continued to be concerned with this problem. He agreed, in
October 1847, to write a preamble to the manifesto. Dufaure gave up
the project for reasons we do not know, perhaps simply because he was
"awkward with a pen in his hand." We have only two rough drafts
of Tocqueville's text, and they overlap in places. One is entitled
"Financial Question," the other "On the Middle Class and the People."
Beaumont published the first in his edition of the *Oeuvres complètes,*
giving it the title of the second.

Tocqueville's point of departure was the torpor of political life,
which ever since the abolition of privileges had been confined to a
single class, the middle class. This state of affairs could not last, and
the political awakening of the working classes would culminate in a
challenge to the last remaining privilege, the right of property.
Tocqueville did not question the political capacity attributed to the
middle class, but he foresaw a new revolution if the middle class did
not carry out a whole series of reforms for the benefit of the masses:

What might be done for the people falls into several categories:
A reduction of the public charges it is asked to bear, including everything—military service, legal costs. This is what I am particularly concerned

---

[17]*Souvenirs,* O.C. XII, 43.
[18]Unpublished letter from Abraham Dubois to Tocqueville, Tocqueville Archives.

with. It is a great deal, but it is not enough. It is an indirect way of coming to the aid of the poor.

Let us see what the direct ways are:

1) Establishing institutions meant for its special use, ones that would serve as a means of education and make greater financial security possible: savings banks, credit institutions, free schools, laws limiting the length of the workday, infant schools, charity workshops, mutual relief funds.

2) Finally, coming directly to the aid of the poor by relieving their misery through the expenditure of tax funds: almshouses, relief committees, poor taxes, and the distribution of produce, of work, of money.

In short, three means of coming to the aid of the people:

1) Relieving it of a part of its public responsibilities or, at the least, only burdening it proportionately.

2) Making available to it institutions that can allow it to get out of its difficulties and to become more prosperous.

3) Coming to its aid and assisting it in its need.

For ten years, since writing his *Mémoire sur le paupérisme,* Tocqueville had not given much thought to social questions. But his reflections on the ways in which the country's narrowly based political system—the *pays légal*—seemed to have become enmired in quicksand, together with his reading of Saint-Simon, Fourier, Owen, and Louis Blanc (unfortunately, he did not keep the notes in which he summed up their doctrines), now led him to these establishments for social assistance that were a departure from the liberal doctrines of political economy. They appear to have been, for Tocqueville, an obligatory complement to the political democratization of society. Unlike most of the dynastic opposition, the new left was clearly sensitive to the innovative trends of thought that industrialization and the economic crisis had stimulated in the *pays réel*—the real country, something quite distinct from the narrow political world of the *pays légal.*

The speech Tocqueville gave before the Chamber on January 27, 1848, caused the greatest stir of all his speeches and has remained the most famous.[19] Though he revealed only a fraction of what was on his mind in his denunciation of the government for encouraging by its policies lower moral standards in the nation as a whole, he nonetheless warned that small, selfish, closed world of the *pays légal* that it stood in danger of being bowled over by the rising wind of revolution.

Dufaure reproached him for having played upon the fear of revolu-

[19]Speech of January 27, 1848, *Le Moniteur universel* of January 28, 211–12. Tocqueville included this speech in the last edition of *Democracy in America* published during his lifetime. An English translation appears in *Democracy in America,* tr. George Lawrence, ed. J. P. Mayer (New York, 1966), 749–58.

tion and Tocqueville himself acknowledged that in order to impress 403
his listeners he had exaggerated the dangers. Less than a month later,
he found that he had been a prophet.

As we know, the troubles that led to the revolution arose over the
issue of the organization and then the interdiction of a last banquet
planned for February 22 at the Champs-Elysées.

The disquiet expressed by Tocqueville on January 27 was shared by
other politicians. The neo-conservatives, for the most part new deputies, reproached Guizot for his immobility. About forty of them were
prepared to join with the new left in overturning the Guizot ministry
if their colleagues of the new left could succeed in persuading the
organizers of the banquet to cancel it. Tocqueville was asked to draft
the joint agenda that would trip Guizot up. Let us note this passage
from one of the variants of his text: "Our principal duty will be to
make sure that the government does not withdraw the support of its
own example from public and private morality."[20] Rivet, a friend of
Dufaure and Tocqueville, was sent to Duvergier de Hauranne, but did
not succeed in persuading him to cancel the banquet.

On February 23, Guizot resigned. One after another, Molé, Thiers,
and Barrot (whose footsteps Gustave de Beaumont was dogging, already seeing himself as a minister) failed in their attempts to quell the
disturbance.

Tocqueville, who did not consider himself a likely ministerial candidate, was present, more as an onlooker than as an actor, at the session
of the Chamber of Deputies which saw the fall of the monarchy.

[20]Tocqueville Archives, 92.

Part IV

TOCQUEVILLE AND
THE SECOND REPUBLIC

22

THE REVOLUTION OF 1848

ON FEBRUARY 24, 1848, Tocqueville was present at the session of the Chamber of Deputies during which, after the abdication of Louis-Philippe, the Duchesse d'Orléans presented the little Comte de Paris and tried to have herself proclaimed regent. In Tocqueville's eyes, Lamartine was the only parliamentary orator capable of defending this solution by urging it on the crowd that was invading the Assembly. He began encouraging him, but soon saw that the poet's silence concealed other thoughts, and when Lamartine did actually step up on the tribune he proposed the republic. Soon the Duchesse d'Orléans had to leave the Chamber, which was breaking up. Conforming to the old revolutionary ritual, the radical leaders were going to proclaim the republic and form a provisional government at the Hôtel de Ville.[1]

Tocqueville was now no more than the observer of a revolution, trying to catch a glimpse of the future. Soon, he would write that he had always thought republican institutions would eventually come to exist, but by gradual evolution.[2] The revolution filled him with uneasiness and sadness. Its deeper meaning seemed to him to be the uprising of the proletarians against a right of property that had been the guarantee of the social order for thousands of years. Paris and her riches seemed to have been given over to them, and a moderate government was hardly capable of restraining their instincts, sharpened

[1]*Souvenirs, O.C.* XII, 69–77.
[2]Circular to the electors of the Manche, 1848.

408

𝕶 𝕷 by socialist writings, and this opened a formidable cycle of anarchy and despotism for France's future.

As far as the near future was concerned, Tocqueville was perhaps more preoccupied by the probable internationalization of the movement and the war that could arise from it. Since 1845, he had followed attentively the troubles in Switzerland, the less distinct movements in Italy, and the general state of affairs in Germany. In 1846, he had hesitated between the fact-finding trip he was to take to Algeria and a trip to the Italian peninsula. He now also thought that, as in 1830, the Paris riots could reopen the Belgian question.

On the twenty-fifth, he spent all day alone plunged in his black thoughts. In the evening, Ampère, keeping an appointment that Tocqueville had forgotten, arrived at his house for dinner. Ampère was one of those generous liberals who, for the past two days, had allowed themselves to be swayed by the ideals of trust in the people and the creation of a fraternal republic. He had just proclaimed his brand-new enthusiasm before his listeners in the Collège de France. He tried to repeat this declamatory speech to Tocqueville, whose dark mood changed into violent anger; the good Ampère was never to forget the storm of abuse he received then.[3]

A letter dated March 7 shows Tocqueville to be somewhat calmer. News from abroad indicated that war was not very likely; "the news one gathers from all parts of France tells us that the most profound tranquillity reigns everywhere, that nowhere is there any serious disorder, that there is an immense aspiration toward order on the part of all classes"; one could assume that the future Constituent Assembly would have a moderate majority. But if one could see the possibility of emerging from the political difficulties, the economic and financial difficulties remained "formidable." Here lay the true danger for the government.[4]

For the moment, it was necessary to support this provisional government, which was dominated by moderate republicans, in its attempt to maintain order and keep the peace. Tocqueville had no feelings of hostility against the legalist republicans, whom he carefully distinguished from those who advocated violent action. He had a continuing personal relationship with Lamartine, and this was strengthened by the relationship between their English wives. Naturally, he spoke ill of the public man, who often irritated him, but acknowledged his courage

[3]*Souvenirs, O.C.* XII, 88–89.
[4]Letter to Clamorgam dated March 7, 1848. Kühn, *Tocqueville als Abgeordneter,* 121–25.

and good sense. He had good relations with the Arago tribe, and, what
was more surprising, with Garnier-Pagès, who had spent several days
at Tocqueville the summer before. The publisher for this little moderate republican group, Pagnerre, was at that time reissuing the *Democracy*. With the dynastic problem gone, there was nothing fundamental
separating Tocqueville from these people, and if *Le National* was not
favorable to him, this was apparently due mainly to the want of
sympathy between Tocqueville and the editor-in-chief, Marrast.

Universal suffrage was proclaimed on March 2, and on the fifth, the
provisional government decreed the election of a Constituent Assembly by vote from department lists, but with vote splitting possible, the
elected members being the candidates who had obtained the most votes
within the limit of the seats to be filled. The former members of the
dynastic opposition debated with themselves whether the wisest course
of action was to retire to private life or to stand as candidates in order
to give the future assembly the benefit of their experience. Although
Tocqueville might observe Thiers's vacillations with irony, he was
faced with the same dilemma.

After some hesitation, he convinced himself that his duty was to try
to reenter public life; having been a deputy during a period of calm,
it would have been an act of desertion to return to private life now
that election to the legislature presented possible dangers. Though he
would not solicit votes, he would put at the disposal of his fellow
citizens "his time, his fortune, and his life," a nuance that events
quickly obliterated, for he soon undertook a campaign to get himself
elected. He continued to say that he would be happy not to be elected,
but we may believe that in this case he lacked his usual insight into
himself. Although political life had already rewarded him with some
discouraging moments, the habits of a man who for nine years had
devoted his thoughts and actions to public office had become second
nature by now.

The department of the Manche was a part of the "reactionary
Western bloc" which in actuality encompassed quite diverse collective
attitudes. There were regions in which old loyalties were still stirred
by memories of the Revolution, like the lower Maine, the Anjou, or
the Vendée, where the nobility continued to enjoy the confidence of
the peasants. This was not at all the case in the Manche. If Tocqueville
was popular in the Cotentin, it was because he had made people forget
his role of chatelain and now projected the image of an important
public figure rebaptized by the principles of 1789. In the Manche, the
public abhorred the memories of feudality; people there were both

410

ﾐ ﾐ

egalitarian and conservative. They did not miss Louis-Philippe—"it was a good thing in his case and he certainly deserved it"[5]—and nothing more effectively demonstrates how few roots the July dynasty had in the country. But the increase in taxes, the stories of enduring anarchy in the capital, and especially the threat to property rights had caused growing fear among the country people; the owner of the smallest plot of land felt a solidarity with the large rural landowners.

True, the new powers-that-be were represented in the department by reassuring individuals. Ledru-Rollin, minister of the interior in the provisional government, had sent representatives of the Republic to the administrative headquarters in the chief towns of all the departments, commissioners who were endowed with full powers to dismiss and appoint civil servants, and the behavior of these men varied widely from place to place. In Saint-Lô, "by an amazing effort," Havin had managed to get himself appointed. This notary had been one of the moderate members of the dynastic opposition, though the son of a member of the National Convention. It was on his arm that the Duchesse d'Orléans had left the Chamber of Deputies on February 24. Ledru-Rollin tried to diminish the effect of his decision by appointing as Havin's adjunct Vieillard, the only "radical" deputy from the Manche before 1848. But Vieillard, a sincere, learned republican, who had been tutor to the brother of Louis-Napoléon, allowed himself to be dominated by the authoritarianism and cunning of Havin, who governed the department until the meeting of the Constituent Assembly.

But although Tocqueville might approve of Havin's moderate government, the way it was exercised could make his candidacy more difficult. After having come to an understanding on the policies to follow in the department, the two men had had a falling out in September 1846. Tocqueville could expect nothing good from such a devious character. The department of the Manche had to elect fifteen deputies, and a kind of tacit agreement divided them by arrondissement; the arrondissement of Valognes would have two representatives on the list, unofficially backed by the government commissioners. Obviously, Tocqueville had to be one of these two; but he also wanted a colleague who would not overshadow him, and he very soon selected Boulatignier, the rapporteur in the Council of State and originally from the arrondissement, who had already performed many services for the electors; he was a good jurist with very moderate opinions, who

[5]*Souvenirs, O.C.* XII, 106.

accepted the Republic but would make a career for himself under the Empire.

On March 14, Tocqueville arrived in Valognes, the natural center of his sphere of influence, and settled in the Hôtel du Louvre, which still exists today. He had been "struck while on the road by the tranquillity of the province"; in Valognes itself, the dominant feelings were fear and a growing hatred of Paris. There was, nevertheless, a "lively" party that was attempting to galvanize the workers, led by the lawyer Clément. Apart from such small minorities, the region as a whole was going along with the rituals of the day in which a kind of imitation of English political habits mingled with memories of the Revolution: the people organized open-air political debates and met at banquets of several hundred, clubs were formed in which people called one another "citizen." Tocqueville was sometimes uneasy about these changes, but each event that caused him worry proved trivial. To cite one example: the most progressive of the workers' clubs of the Cherbourg arsenal did not seem inclined to vote for him; Hippolyte de Tocqueville went to harangue them and they ended up applauding his brother's name.

But to become deputy from the Manche, elected by universal suffrage, was not so easy. Though Tocqueville saw himself right away as the hope of the moderate liberals and also of his old conservative adversaries (Le Marois urged people to vote for him), the "lively" party hesitated between supporting and opposing him.

On Sunday, March 19, he had his first contact with universal suffrage. In the marketplace of Valognes, at noon, he extemporized a short speech in the open air. He himself was moved, and some of his listeners were in tears. Then he headed for Cherbourg, where a banquet for fifteen hundred people took place at three o'clock, presided over by the commissioners of the Republic.[6]

The commissioners had not invited him and Havin greeted him coldly without asking him to sit at the official table. Tocqueville, without touching any of the dishes—his stomach was troubling him—mingled with the crowd. But after the commissioners had read a short speech (Havin was incapable of improvising as much as three sentences) and another speaker had offered a toast to the memory of Bricqueville, Tocqueville hastened to the platform and launched into an extemporaneous speech that has been preserved for us by *Le Journal*

---

[6]For Tocqueville's electoral campaign at Valognes, we have used two very important sources, both unpublished: file 92 of the Tocqueville Archives, and Tocqueville's almost daily letters to his wife.

412

de Cherbourg. He later wrote that this speech was a bad one, and it is clear that for once in his life he was something of a demagogue. He mentioned his relationship with Bricqueville, preached union among citizens and among nations, and in conclusion proposed a toast to the union of France and the United States against England's domination of the seas. This speech was an immense success, eclipsing that of the commissioners and showing to what an extent Tocqueville, in the arrondissement of Cherbourg, was a man at home on his native ground.[7]

That Sunday, March 19, 1848, was an important day in Tocqueville's life. His family had once been leaders of the nobility of the Cotentin; for ten years, he himself had had the support of the notables of the region. Now the people of the peninsula were identifying with him and publicly returning the affection he felt for them. That night, he went to sleep in his beloved Tocqueville; the next day he wrote to his wife:

When I found myself squarely in this place again, the only place dear to me in this world . . . I felt an extraordinary tug at my heart and (something I dare say only to you), I cried like a child . . . In the time that we are living in now, such outbursts of emotion are not good. They drain one's energy. I hope to avoid them henceforth. For I need all my strength. I am at one and the same time dismayed and moved to see the hope that this whole population puts in me, even though I have no power over their fate. It seems as though I hold their whole future in my pocket; and yet who can do anything today for the future of anyone in this great game of chance that France is playing?[8]

The following Sunday, questioned by some of his adversaries, he had to explain his political position. His answers, revised by him and published, bear on the sincerity of his republicanism and on his refusal to take part in the campaign of the banquets. He took pride in his perceptiveness, declaring that most of the participants would have stayed away if they had been able to foresee the revolution that resulted from it. These explanations seemed unanswerable, and one speaker who tried to recall the days of privileges and feudal rights was hooted down by the crowd.[9]

The following week, the departmental council met in extraordinary

[7] *Le Journal de Cherbourg,* March 23, 1848.
[8] Unpublished letter to Madame de Tocqueville, March 30, 1848.
[9] Alexis de Tocqueville's answer to the president of the electoral committee of Valognes, *Journal de Valognes* of March 31, 1848.

session at Saint-Lô. We do not know very much about it, beyond what 413
was noted in the *Souvenirs* about the servility of the old councillors
of the Guizot majority toward Havin, whom they had kept from being
president of their assembly since 1844. But it was during this session
that the lists were made up for the election to the Constituent Assembly.

In truth, hundreds of lists were making the rounds of the department. But the only ones that had any weight were those drawn up by
the government's commissioners, by the old majority, by the clergy,
by the legitimists, and by the progressive republicans. These lists tended
to include a few known personalities in the hope that they would pull
along with them the lowly but ambitious men who had drawn them
up. Thus, Tocqueville found himself on almost all the lists; paradoxically, Havin's resentment almost resulted in his exclusion from the
most useful list, that of the commissioners. In the end, he was on it,
but placed in the fifteenth position. But in Valognes, the lawyer
Clément moved heaven and earth in an attempt to be designated in
place of Boulatignier, the candidate supported by Tocqueville, who
complained of his lack of energy.[10]

On March 17, the elections to the Constituent Assembly had been
postponed from April 9 to April 23. On April 2, Tocqueville, back
from Saint-Lô, presided over a democratic banquet at Saint-Pierre-Eglise and gave another speech there. Then he returned to Paris, where
the agitation worried him and where he had left Madame de Tocqueville in ill health. It was also a way for him to avoid last-minute
intrigues and solicitations. He did not go back to Tocqueville until the
nineteenth.

When universal suffrage was first instituted, voting took place in
the chief town of the canton, and the various communes were admitted
by turns into the voting hall.[11] The government's commissioners had
given the order to the mayors to organize their flocks into rows by
alphabetical order and to put themselves at the head of the column,
together with the local police force, to make the trip. The voters of
Tocqueville organized themselves in this way on the morning of the
twenty-fourth to go to Saint-Pierre. The story of the event is told on
a well-known page of the *Souvenirs:* how Tocqueville modestly took
his place in the ranks at the letter *T,* the walk in the pouring rain, the
short speech he gave before reaching Saint-Pierre in response to the

[10]Numerous electoral lists exist in file 92 of the Tocqueville Archives.
[11]P. Bastid, *L'Avènement du suffrage universel* (Paris, 1948).

general demand, the discipline the troop of villagers maintained throughout. After the vote, Tocqueville, without waiting for the results, hurried back to the capital.[12]

It was in Paris that he learned he had been elected. He was third in the department, after the two commissioners, with 110,704 votes (Havin had 119,817 and Vieillard 117,756). Boulatignier was the eighth elected and des Essarts, a judge in Caen whom Tocqueville had supported despite his "red" aspects because he was a friend of Beaumont's, was the fifteenth, with 46,794 votes. Tocqueville had hoped for no more than fifth place, but had outstripped two colorless candidates he had thought would receive almost unanimous approval. He obtained nine-tenths of the votes cast, but worried over a few local defections in the Cotentin.

The Constituent Assembly met on May 4. On the fifteenth, it was invaded by the people, led by the heads of the clubs, and the twenty-third to the twenty-sixth of the following month were the celebrated Days of June, the bloody civil war that broke the socialist revolution.

The sequence of events between May 4 and June 26 that led to civil war forms the central episode of the second part of the *Souvenirs*. Tocqueville's account of this time is one of the most valuable, even though the author was a committed witness and hostile to the new revolution.

The course of this second revolution had something almost inevitable about it, as Marx stressed: "The February republic was won by the workers with the passive support of the bourgeoisie. The proletarians regarded themselves, and rightly, as the victors of February, and they made the proud claims of victors. They had to be vanquished on the streets, they had to be shown that they were worsted as soon as they fought, not with the bourgeoisie, but against the bourgeoisie."[13] A de facto problem since February: an immense concentration of workers, often without employment or living on an allowance from the national workshops, masters of a Paris from which the army had been withdrawn; confronting these masses, an Assembly gathered from the country beyond Paris that by a great majority was not revolutionary. We do not have to assume some sort of bourgeois plot, or a plot to seize power conceived by the heads of the secret societies, in order to see how this situation would lead naturally to civil war. We do know that the conflagration was sparked by the Constituent Assembly's

---

[12]*Souvenirs*, O.C. XII, 114.

[13]Marx, *La Lutte des classes en France, Oeuvres* 2 (Paris, 1948), 57–58. English translation, Marx, *Class Struggles in France (1848–1850)*, tr. anon. (New York: International Publishers, 1964), 55.

attempt to disperse into the countryside or send into the army a large   415
proportion of the workers from the national workshops.

Public opinion grew cognizant of the danger immediately after the
elections. In Valognes, Tocqueville's friends had bid farewell to him
with tears in their eyes, promising to fly to the aid of the Constituent
Assembly if its existence was threatened. For Tocqueville, there was
no choice. The defense of freedom had to be by way of respect for
legality, democratically expressed, and one could not compromise with
a de facto power that made bold to use the centralized administration
still in place to control the country as a whole. What was being
challenged was the right to property, and if Tocqueville had doubts
about the liberal axiom—traditional since Locke—that property was
a right natural to man and prior to society, he felt the right was
indispensable to a peaceful society and irreplaceable in the state of
civilization of his time. Those who were threatening it were barbarians
whose greed for the goods of others had been fired up by the socialist
preachers who, when they were sincere, belonged in an insane asylum.
Tocqueville had a few instances of this before him, but in the violence
of the conflict, he lost the objectivity he sometimes showed toward
certain of these theories, especially those of the Saint-Simonians.[14]

What was most striking about the June Days was their character of
class struggle. The natural leaders of the movement were all arrested
on May 15. And yet the proletarian Paris of the eastern part of the city
rose up as one, while the worker minorities in the western *quartiers*
were coming to the boil.

But the revolutionary movement had weaknesses that would bring
about its defeat:

—The cadres of the secret societies were split between Jacobins well
prepared for rioting but not true socialists and socialist theoreticians
who lacked experience in the field.

—The men in the provisional government were lucky: they had
drafted into the Garde Mobile—the security police—twenty thousand
young proletarians no more than fifteen to twenty years old who
remained loyal to their units, disowning the bonds of blood and
affection that almost all of them had with the insurgents.[15]

—Finally, the movement remained confined to Paris. It had re-

---

[14]Beyond the arguments in the *Souvenirs,* there exist in the Tocqueville Archives unpublished notes
on the challenge to the right of property.

[15]Tocqueville insisted on the role of the Garde Mobile in a conversation with Senior, *Correspondence
and Conversations with N. W. Senior,* published by Mrs. Simpson (London, 1872), and reprinted at New
York in 1968, vol. 1, 48.

cruited its members in a milieu artificially swollen by the conjunction of the industrial revolution and centralization. The provinces were, on the whole, opposed to another revolution. The uncertainties that this second revolution brought with it caused great fear at first, but now the dominant feeling was: "This has gone far enough!"

The "foolishness" of the 1848 revolutionaries had helped to produce this isolation of Paris. If, instead of merely repeating the events of 1793 and proclaiming a division of property, they had proclaimed the abolition of debts, they would have rallied to their cause a part of France that was swarming with indebted landowners.[16]

Tocqueville depicted the bitterness of the struggle. But he also tried to understand the new members of the extreme left, the Montagnards of this second revolution, sitting in the Assembly alongside men from the old parties: men of a new sort, their minds nourished on café talk and newspaper articles, their argot embellished with insulting or jovial exclamations. In his *Souvenirs,* he is not very hard on a man like Ledru-Rollin, who symbolized them, even though he had fomented an insurrection against the government to which Tocqueville belonged. Tocqueville was sometimes much more acrimonious in his depictions of men who were politically closer to him.

Nevertheless, the *Souvenirs* and the letters dating from this period are severe toward the June insurgents. Even though Tocqueville wrote that the people of Paris were dying of hunger, he condemned the greed of these men with as much harshness as he did the attempts of the middle class to exploit the State during the preceding regime. One would like to discover in his writing some of the accents of pity shown by men like Armand de Melun or Ozanam. But such feelings were rare, not to be found among the old republicans, and the Assembly as a whole rejected any attempt at a solution other than military victory.

The June Days disposed Tocqueville to adopt a conservative policy of order. This old adversary of the September laws voted, on June 24, against the declaration of the state of siege but soon regretted it. And his reversal of position was a considerable one, when one thinks of the program of social reforms he drew up the year before. He now voted against the limitation of the workday to ten hours, against the abolition of the salt tax, in favor of continuing to allow men called for military service to hire substitutes instead of making military service obligatory for all—and, of course, against amnesty for those convicted during the June Days.

[16]*Souvenirs, O.C.* XII, 112–16.

Tocqueville was not merely a spectator and judge of what was happening. The work of the Constituent Assembly was, by definition, to give the country a Constitution. In order to perform this essential task, it was decided to select a committee of eighteen members, each of whom was to be chosen by a simple majority of the Assembly. Out of a total membership of nine hundred, the Assembly had a center of more than five hundred made up of republicans "from the eve of the revolution," most of whom were very moderate. They did not make a party issue of the election of the committee except to exclude legitimists. The vote, therefore, was largely a test of the prestige of those elected.

The first day of the voting, May 17, only six men were elected: Cormenin (657 votes), whose reputation as pamphleteer, under the signature of Timon, was even greater now because of the fact that he had just published a draft Constitution; Marrast, editor-in-chief of *Le National,* one of the victors of February and afterwards mayor of Paris (646 votes); Lamennais, who had also just published a draft Constitution (552 votes); and three other men who were publicists or politicians of the old opposition: Vivien (517 votes), Tocqueville (490), and Dufaure (395). It was not until the next day that Beaumont and Dupin were elected, and the day after, Barrot. All in all, the committee was made up of ten moderate republicans, two representatives of the far left (Lamennais and Considérant), and six old Orleanists. But Tocqueville's election on the first day of the voting was an indication of the respect the republican establishment had for the author of *Democracy in America.*

The period in which the Constitution was drafted can be broken down into three phases: from May 20 to June 19, the committee worked out a preliminary draft; this draft was then communicated to the floor committees of the Chamber, each of which delegated one member to convey their observations back to the committee drafting the Constitution (July–August); these observations led the committee to revise its draft in a more conservative direction. On August 30, the revised draft was filed with the Assembly, introduced by a report by Marrast, and examined by the Assembly from September 4 to November 4, the date on which it was promulgated. It is interesting to note that the president, Cormenin, who had criticized the work of his colleagues, was "fired" by them and took no part in the debates before the Assembly, nor did the rapporteur; because most of the committee members were not very eloquent, their work, which established repub-

418

ᕽ ᕽ

lican institutions, was explained or defended by old Orleanists—
Dufaure, Vivien, Barrot, and Tocqueville.

Tocqueville in his *Souvenirs* had harsh things to say about the
committee's work. He condemned the incompetence of most of its
members and pointed out the underhanded dictatorial procedures of
Cormenin, who would present articles already drawn up in full and
try to get a vote on them immediately. Reading over the debates
hardly gives the impression that its members held very coherent views;
as for the method followed by Cormenin, it had been imprudently
suggested by Beaumont.[17]

However, the first session was marked by an effort to leave beaten
paths. Barrot suggested beginning by organizing the local communes,
which were close to the individual man and his family, before going
on to the powers of the State. He was supported by Lamennais, who
remained faithful on this point to the doctrine of *L'Avenir*. Their only
backing within the committee came from Tocqueville. Lamennais
resigned and Tocqueville, sent to persuade him to come back, was
unsuccessful. The committee then reverted to the traditional schema of
its predecessors.

Tocqueville's contributions, both within the committee and during
the discussion in the Assembly, bore essentially on three points: the
right to work, the existence of two Chambers, and the election of the
president of the Republic by popular vote.

The right to work was the great victory the workers expected from
the 1848 revolution; for them it had the force of myth, balancing the
right to property. On May 23 and 24, the committee discussed it
passionately, without Tocqueville's saying anything. The preamble of
the text presented to the Assembly, more cautious than the version
dating from before the June Days, merely said—in its Article 8—that
the Republic should "through fraternal assistance assure the livelihood
of needy citizens, either by procuring them work within the limits of
its resources, or, when there was no family, by giving aid to those not
in a condition to work." This set forth the duty to offer assistance but
without any precise obligation on the part of the State, and an amendment by Mathieu, from the Drôme, proposed substituting this paragraph: "[The Republic] recognizes the right of all citizens to
education, work, and assistance." This gave rise to one of the most
extended debates. The amendment was fought by Tocqueville, Duver-

---

[17]The official proceedings of the 1848 Constitution committee, filed in the National Archives (under
the shelf-mark 918), and often analyzed, have so far remained unpublished.

gier de Hauranne, Thiers, Dufaure, and Goudchaux, and supported by 419
Ledru-Rollin, Arnaud de l'Ariège, Billault, and others. It was rejected.

Tocqueville's speech on September 12 immediately broadened the discussion: recognition of the right to work led to the socialization of society, and it was therefore socialism itself that he was denouncing. The latter, in its different forms, had three constant principles: the worship of material goods, the abolition of private property, and the suppression of individual liberty. It was as remote as possible from the values exalted by the French revolution. The revolution of 1848 would deny the ideas of 1789 if it established socialism. It ought to confine itself to the concrete realization of the ideas of 1789, thus showing itself to be both democratic and Christian, which this draft did by recognizing the duty to broaden charity and give it a societal organization.[18]

Bicameralism had also been the subject of discussions within the committee. The public was so convinced that the existence of two Chambers would destroy the unity of popular sovereignty—which seemed a hasty and false conclusion to Tocqueville—that even Dufaure and Beaumont went over to the notion of a single Chamber, with only Barrot, Vivien, and Tocqueville defending the "lost cause" of the two Chambers. Tocqueville especially stressed the example of America, all of whose states possessed two houses, some after having experimented with just one, which showed that the system had nothing specifically aristocratic or British about it. Tocqueville's American friends had encouraged him to stand fast on the issue of the two chambers, in particular J. C. Spencer[19] (Thiers also received similar advice from America).

The debate in the Assembly took place from September 25 to September 27. Tocqueville, fallen ill, could not give the speech he had prepared. His notes reveal its central argument:[20] it was necessary to "fight the chronic disease of democracies—instability, capriciousness, and tyranny on the part of the legislative power," and for that, to "slow down popular movements. The ruling principle of democracy is that nothing is to be done despite the people and apart from the people, and not that the people can immediately realize every desire." Tocqueville acknowledged that a single assembly, in the France of 1848, would be an instrument not of the Terror but of anarchy, of bad government.

The cause of bicameralism being a lost one, it was necessary to

[18]Speech of September 12, 1848, *Le Moniteur universel* of the following day.
[19]Letter from Spencer to Tocqueville dated June 10, 1848, Tocqueville Archives.
[20]Tocqueville's notes are in the Tocqueville Archives, file 92.

endeavor to counterbalance the impulsive acts of a single assembly in other ways. And Tocqueville, both within the committee and in his speech of October 5, would defend the principle of the election of the president of the Republic by the people.[21] He stepped up to the tribune after the future communard Félix Pyat, who viewed this mode of election as a more fearful "consecration" than that of the kings, and the creation of a two-headed monster standing at the pinnacle of the Republic. Tocqueville responded that there could be no question of dividing the sovereignty which was the Assembly's prerogative. But only election by the people would ensure, within a limited sphere, the autonomy of the executive power. The double responsibility of the president and the ministers, a new principle which he seems to have initiated, appeared to him to guarantee that the president would not be able to exceed his powers as determined by law. We know that it was a speech by Lamartine that caused the triumph of the notion of election by the people, and we know as well what followed from it—the election of Prince Louis-Napoléon as president of the French Republic, his coup d'état, and the authoritarian regime of the Second Empire. Tocqueville was not the last to ironize over that institution he had taken such pains to ensure and define.

These three speeches were associated in one overall design: to determine the most important features of the French society of the future. The latter already had, like American society, the mores of a democracy of small property holders. To give it a framework of free and moderate institutions, capable of ensuring its political stability; to see that it avoided, in this way, the risk of further revolutions, was to assure the country the best possible chance for the future.

We have noted the vote of the Constituent Assembly in favor of Vivien, Tocqueville, and Dufaure at the time of the election to the committee to draft the Constitution, and we have also noted the dominant part played by them in the explanation of the draft to the Assembly. Tocqueville's two speeches on the election of the president and on the right to work caused a great stir, especially the second, which was published in numerous pamphlets. Indeed, it was the former general staff of the "young left" of 1847 that continued to work together on current political problems. Mention is made of regular meetings of eight men, but in fact there were ten or twelve taking part

[21]Speech on the election of the president given October 5, 1848, *Le Moniteur universel* of the sixth, 2724–25.

in this sort of "brain trust" in which Tocqueville, for several years   421
now, had seen a means of having an effect on the parties. Billault had
probably already distanced himself from this little group, and Beaumont had reentered the fold. There was only one new member, Freslon, a great lawyer, the representative from the Maine-et-Loire, and
a republican from before the revolution, though very moderate, who
became close to Tocqueville in the Constituent Assembly and would
remain one of his most faithful friends until Tocqueville's death.

A coterie? Of course, but its influence derived not only from the
quality of its members, but from its strategic position as intermediary
group between the party of the republicans from before the revolution,
which was being eroded, and the party of order, which was recovering
under the impetus of the leaders who had regained their seats and their
aplomb, the "Burgraves" Thiers, Molé, and Berryer.

Following the June insurrection, Eugène Cavaignac, the general
who had put it down, was invested with the executive power. The son
of a member of the regicide Convention and the brother of Godefroy
Cavaignac, the republican leader who had died quite young, this
former officer in Africa was nevertheless more or less a stranger to
political circles. To form his ministry, he had called upon his companions in arms—Bedeau, who remained only a few days, and Lamoricière, who, appointed to the Ministry of War, was one of his principal
advisers. For the rest, he had drawn on the clan that gravitated around
Le National, Godefroy's old newspaper; these were decent men, often
rather second-rate, who nevertheless sometimes frightened the public;
they were rapidly worn down once in power. Cavaignac, irresolute
and politically timid as he was, felt it necessary to call on more
experienced politicians, and it was quite natural that he should turn to
the Dufaure group, which was sincerely attached to the Republic. On
August 7, he took a first step in this direction by sending Gustave de
Beaumont to London as minister plenipotentiary. But it was not until
October 13 that he proceeded, after many attempts, to reform his
cabinet: Sénart was replaced in the Interior by Dufaure, Recurt in
Public Works by Vivien, Vaulabelle in Education by Freslon.[22] It
seemed that this last post was to have gone to Tocqueville, but Cavaignac felt that his speeches showed him to be too far to the right, and
he also harbored some resentment against him for not having supported
election of the president of the Republic by the Assembly.

However that may have been, Tocqueville had reasons for being

[22]Letter from Tocqueville to Beaumont, dated October 11 and 12, 1848, *O.C.* VIII, 2: 59–65.

422

𝕶 𝕸

"unhappy," and he was. Cavaignac asked him to be France's representative in the Anglo-French mediation, which was to take concrete form in a conference in Brussels entrusted with ensuring the peace between Austria and the Piedmontese defeated at Custozza. Tocqueville allowed himself to be convinced that if this mediation actually took place, it would be a great role to play on the European stage. He eagerly examined the files of the Ministry of Foreign Affairs which the good-hearted but mediocre Bastide opened to him without restriction, and conferred with Lord Normanby, then with Sir Henry Ellis, possibly his future British colleague.[23]

December 10, the date of the election of the president by universal suffrage, was approaching. Tocqueville did not believe Cavaignac would win, for one very simple reason: he was the very incarnation of the Republic and public opinion had turned against the Republic. Louis-Napoléon, on the other hand, was supported by the Burgraves and had rallied around him all the opposing tendencies. Yet Tocqueville fought for Cavaignac locally in the Manche, although he was annoyed that a campaign poster in favor of Cavaignac by thirteen deputies from the Manche bore his signature without anyone's having consulted him.

Nevertheless, the magnitude of Louis-Napoléon Bonaparte's success—by a margin of very nearly three to one over all his opponents—exceeded Tocqueville's expectations. Perhaps he had hoped that none of the candidates would gain an absolute majority, which would have given the Constituent Assembly the power to choose among the three who had obtained the most votes.

Tocqueville immediately resigned from the mediating mission he had been preparing for (the Brussels conference never did take place), while Beaumont left the London embassy. In a fit of discouragement, Tocqueville thought of withdrawing from public life at this point, then of not running for the future Legislative Assembly. But once again, he finally decided to continue pursuing his political career.

On December 20, the prince-president had formed a cabinet presided over by Barrot and recruited from among the party of order, in which the presence of Falloux in Education marked the reentry of the legitimists into government affairs. The only moderate republican in the cabinet resigned after a few days.

There was therefore a latent conflict between this ministry and the

[23]The notes taken by Tocqueville at the Ministry of Foreign Affairs on Italian affairs will be published in the O.C. III, 3.

Constituent Assembly with its republican majority. And the republi- 423
cans tried to prolong the struggle by alleging that the Constituent
Assembly could not disband before passing the organic laws that were
to complete the Constitution.

Dufaure, Tocqueville, and his friends were against such systematic
opposition. They thought that if it was continued the Assembly, in
formal disaccord with public opinion, would eventually be discredited.
The Rateau proposal, whose author was a lawyer from Bordeaux and
a friend of Dufaure's, fixed the elections to the Legislative Assembly
for the month of March. The whole of the small group Tocqueville
belonged to approved the second reading, which was passed by a
majority of only four votes.[24]

When it came under discussion, Lanjuinais, with Rateau's agreement, introduced an amendment that softened its tenor: the Constituent Assembly would vote a law on the organization of the Council
of State, another on the responsibility of the president and the ministers, and another on elections to the Legislative Assembly. The Lanjuinais proposal had been written and signed in Tocqueville's home and
at his own table.[25]

For Tocqueville, the months of January and February 1849 were a
time of very fragile health, as is attested by the leaves of absence he
had to ask from the Assembly. In this state of sickly torpor, he lost
touch even with the affairs of his own department.

At this time, Tocqueville was not a staunch adversary of the new
administration, nor did he avoid contact with the new president.
Vieillard, with whom he was then on excellent terms, served as an
intermediary, although we do not know if he was the one who
suggested to the prince that he woo Tocqueville or whether the prince
himself had already felt it would be valuable to win over the author
of the *Democracy*. In any case, on March 16, Tocqueville wrote to his
regular electoral agent, Clamorgam, who had been part of the liberal
opposition under the July monarchy and was now a fanatical partisan
of the president:

It seems that the friends of the president in our country resent me more
than the president himself. The latter, in fact, pays me all sorts of attentions.
I had remained quite aloof, naturally, as befitted a man who had voted and

---

[24]Letter dated January 24, 1849, to Clamorgam. Kühn, *Tocqueville als Abgeordneter*, 141–42.
[25]Letter dated February 17, 1849, to Clamorgam, ibid., 146.

taken action against him and was not sorry for it. I had confined myself to leaving my name at his home on the first of January, like the rest of the Assembly. He has invited me to every party he has given since that time, and the day before yesterday I received and accepted an invitation to dine at his home. I sat next to him at the table and for the first time we were able to talk at length. I took the opportunity to try and form an opinion of him. As you know, I have some perspicacity in understanding men. Yet despite this, I still am unable to paint the intellectual portrait of this one. A secluded education and several years in prison have given his appearance and speech a discretion that leaves the observer at a loss. I have therefore put off drawing any conclusions.[26]

The approach of the elections brought Tocqueville back to local affairs.

The department of the Manche was being subjected to the reactionary measures of Faucher, minister of the interior, and the people in place before the February revolution were trying to avenge themselves for the disturbance it had caused them. In January, the prefect Le Hodey, Havin's tool, had to give up his spot in Saint-Lô to Tanlay, who attempted to slow down local purgings. Among those sacrificed were the sub-prefect of Cherbourg, Ozenne, and the sub-prefect of Valognes, Lerat, both local lawyers appointed in 1848. At Valognes, the new appointee was a young man from a family in the Midi, an acquaintance of Rémusat's who seemed to be tying his fortune to Tocqueville's. Several comical incidents had to be untangled: the Abbé Couppey, principal of the *collège,* denounced the professor of rhetoric, Canivet, as a dangerous "red," and succeeded, through his calumnies, in having him suspended by the prefect, Tanlay, and the rector, the Abbé Daniel. Apparently, Canivet's greatest crime was that he had presided over one of Tocqueville's meetings. The prefect, duly enlightened, tried to replace Couppey by Canivet at the *collège,* but the people of Valognes wanted a man in a soutane as principal! Clamorgam's methods were less devious than those of the ecclesiastic: prolonging a discussion of the municipal council into the street, he ruffled the mayor. The latter organized a demonstration of workers singing the *Marseillaise* around the liberty tree. One can understand Tocqueville's desire to wage his electoral campaign from afar and not mix in these "chamberpot wars." In any case, the "Havin era" was well and truly over for the department of the Manche and ended in the last days of

[26]Letter to Clamorgam dated March 16, 1849, ibid., 151.

August at a meeting of the departmental council. Adulated in 1848 by the most conservative members of the council, Havin was now replaced as president by Tocqueville in Tocqueville's absence—he had been detained by his ministerial duties. Havin tried to salvage the situation by bidding for the vice-presidency but was defeated by Vieillard.

Tocqueville had another reason for not becoming directly involved in the elections to the Legislative Assembly. The lists, much more than they had been for the Constituent Assembly, would be those of opposing parties. The list of the party of order, which supported the president's administration, was composed of old conservatives of the time of Guizot, along with legitimists. That of Havin was composed of men faithful to the Republic but hostile to the new administration. In addition, there were lists that were more or less "red." Tocqueville, who found himself on almost all the lists, did not want to take sides. He was against all systematic opposition to the cabinet in place, but remained attached to the republicans, with whom he had fought side by side against "anarchy." He did not give in even to the entreaties of the sub-prefect, who asked him to publish at least one manifesto, and on May 7 left for Germany, whose atmosphere he was eager to observe in the midst of its own revolutionary events.

This rather ambivalent attitude threatened, for that matter, to work to his disadvantage. The party of order in the Manche had found a new leader, Daru, attached by his past experience to the Empire, a future member of the Institute and a man whose liberalism and intelligence Tocqueville respected. Daru had entered the Assembly in January on the occasion of a special election. Havin's departure left the position of the big man of the department empty, and Daru was ready to fill it. Tocqueville, in a fit of ill humor, declared that the problem did not concern him, but that should be taken with a grain of salt.

The votes of his compatriots, on May 13, fully validated Tocqueville's position in the department. Many fewer voters took part than in the election for the Constituent Assembly, but Tocqueville garnered a vote from almost every one of them. He found himself at the head of the list with 82,404 votes; Daru followed with 77,491; Vieillard, who had gone over to the party of order along with the prince-president, received 75,084 votes. Boulatignier had withdrawn to become a councillor of state. One saw old veterans of the July monarchy returning to the Legislative Assembly—Le Marois or Noël-Agnès —alongside the legitimist Duparc. The man elected with the least votes was the astronomer Leverrier, with 56,674. Havin, who had kept his position at the top of the republican list, obtained only 24,761 votes, and none of the others on his list received anything close to 20,000.

This was a victory for the party of order, but an even clearer personal victory for Tocqueville. In 1849, he was unquestionably the big man of his home territory.

23

MINISTER OF

FOREIGN AFFAIRS

THE ELECTIONS for the Legislative Assembly were held on May 13, 1849. On the following day, the ministry headed by Odilon Barrot that had been formed on December 20 of the previous year was in a state of crisis. Léon Faucher, the minister of the interior, resigned. Barrot also wanted to remove the minister of foreign affairs, Drouyn de Lhuys. Lastly, for months he had been the only one to speak from the tribune in defense of the work of the executive power, since the only other orator in the ministry, Falloux, was a legitimist and thus hardly had the ear of the Constituent Assembly.

The makeup of the new Legislative Assembly seemed to require changes in the cabinet. The party of the moderate republicans, which had had a majority in the Constituent Assembly, was the big loser, with no more than 80 elected out of 750 members. The Mountain, on the other hand, still had almost 200 seats, only a relative success but one that dismayed the new majority. The latter, the conservative party of order, had more than 450 seats, including 150 legitimists.

It would have seemed logical to form a government in which the different factions of the party of order were represented. Molé had proposed this to Thiers, de Broglie, and Berryer, but these Burgraves had dodged the suggestion. Thiers, in particular, preferred an administration he could control without having to make compromises, and Rémusat, after agreeing to replace Drouyn as minister of foreign affairs, drew back in the face of Thiers's reservations.

Some thought was given to calling on Marshal Bugeaud (who would die on June 20 of cholera) but not only did Bugeaud have a rather muddled mind, but his name alone was enough to provoke the republicans. Bugeaud would have preferred to be minister of war, but he would have been unable to get along with Changarnier, who was in command of both the National Guard and the First Military Region and seemed indispensable to the maintenance of order in the capital. Bugeaud was enticed away by the prospect of playing a great role as the commander of the Army of the Alps.

Barrot was approached again, and he now insisted that Dufaure be brought into the ministry. The prince-president had no desire to give Dufaure the Interior, where he had been on the eve of December 10, but he yielded. Dufaure insisted that Tocqueville and Lanjuinais also be brought in. Tocqueville would have liked the Ministry of Education; ever since 1844, the achievement of liberty of teaching had been one of his principal concerns. Now, in January Falloux had created an extraordinary commission to study this reform, and the ultra-Catholic party's ostracism of Tocqueville had kept him off it. It would have been a pretty sort of revenge to take Falloux's place, but the latter, who was needed in the ministry in order to maintain good relations with the legitimists and the religious party, refused to change portfolios; personally disinterested, he stayed on as the Church's man in the Ministry of Education. On the other hand, he finally agreed to the replacement of his friend Buffet in Agriculture and in Commerce, which isolated him in the new team: now, as he said to Dufaure and Tocqueville, he would be not their colleague but their prisoner.[1]

Since he could not have Education, Tocqueville was offered Foreign Affairs, which he accepted with some trepidation. And yet he was not as much of a novice as has sometimes been said; since his entrance into public life, he had studied international problems with fervor. The year before, he had been designated French mediator in the Austro-Sardinian conflict and in preparation for the planned conference at Brussels had examined the Italian files at the ministry. He had just come back from Germany, where he had gone to observe the revolutionary movements for himself.

Barrot limited the reform of the ministry to these changes. Passy remained in Finance, the mediocre General Rulhières in War, Tracy in the Navy, and Lacrosse in Public Works.

The most salient feature of the new ministry was that except for Barrot, its prominent members had all supported Cavaignac at the time

---

[1]*Souvenirs*, O.C. XII, 206; Falloux, *Mémoires d'un royaliste*, 1, 480.

of the presidential election, some very quietly, like Falloux, and some quite flamboyantly, like Dufaure.

What was more, with an Assembly that was farther to the right, this ministry was farther to the left than its predecessor. It was drawn essentially from the rather slender fringe between the party of order and the attenuated group of republicans from before the revolution. It could only obtain a majority through the tolerance of the leaders of the party of order, who had also not given up advising the prince-president directly. The ministers could not entertain any great illusion about their political longevity; they knew they were on "a leaky ship."[2]

What had permitted this second Barrot ministry to exist was the fear of the Mountain among the ranks of the majority. The latter could see the "reds" taking to the streets to decide the question of universal suffrage. They sought to rally the moderate republicans to the defense of legality. The fact was that within parliamentary circles, confidence in Dufaure's firmness of character and loyalty was a feeling shared by the center, the right, and the moderate left; it allowed Dufaure to appear as society's savior. But Tocqueville foresaw that Dufaure and his friends would become "useless, as soon as we have reestablished order, and embarrassing" because "we will represent, in the position of power, the idea of a moderate and reasonable republic, which almost no one wants, everyone desiring something more, less, or different."[3]

So long as they remained moderate, Barrot himself was not particular about whether or not his associates carried a republican flag. In the negotiations Barrot held to form the government, Tocqueville shows him gathering ministers as a hen gathers her brood, "without worrying too much whether this was a brood of ducks or chicks."[4] And the equal respect felt for republican institutions by the members of his team had different motivations. Tocqueville thought that a representative regime with a stable and hereditary head of the executive would have been a better solution for the country. But the idea, dear to Thiers twenty-five years later, that the Republic was the least divisive regime for France, was an axiom that Rémusat pointed to as a prudent rule in 1849.[5] Given the mediocrity or the revolutionary instincts of the

[2]Tocqueville to Beaumont, September 4, 1849, *O.C.* VIII, 2: 169.
[3]On the atmosphere in which the government was formed, see the *Souvenirs*, *O.C.* XII, 201–203.
[4]Ibid., 206.
[5]Rémusat, *Mémoires* 4, 405.

majority of the republicans, the attempt to save the Republic had to be made without the help of most of them.

One could not contemplate winning the legitimists over to republican institutions, since their principle was personal loyalty to the sovereign. But a Republic that gave them liberty of teaching would thereby show regard for the rural constituencies of their leading figures and cause itself to be accepted, for all practical purposes, by men whose immediate hopes of a restoration were almost purely theoretical. Within the cabinet, Tocqueville was the natural link between his other colleagues and the legitimists' representative, Alfred de Falloux. The relations between Dufaure, a "true bourgeois from the West and an enemy of the nobility and the priesthood," and Falloux, an exquisitely polite gentleman from Angers, have been vividly depicted in the *Souvenirs* as a natural antipathy rife with misunderstandings.[6] A friend of Dufaure's, Tocqueville was "of the same breed as Falloux" and endeavored, not without difficulty, to reconcile them. In attempting this, he won the sympathy of Falloux, whom he supported in spite of the reservations of his colleagues when Falloux tried to obtain a pardon for the legitimists of the Vendée who had been imprisoned after the attempt of the Duchesse de Berry in 1832. It appears that Falloux and the legitimists avoided putting obstacles in Tocqueville's path when he tried to gain liberal concessions in Rome. This was more than a simple agreement to cooperate: as we have seen, despite everything that divided him from the legitimists Tocqueville had retained a sincere affection for the milieu of his origins that facilitated his relations with the party.

There was a much more pressing threat to the Republic, and that was the very person of its president. Tocqueville did his best to disarm this threat as far as he could. He mixed in the circle of "idiots" and "hussies" who made up the Bonaparte family, and the hotheads who formed the bulk of the prince's former fellow adventurers. The prince knew little about concrete problems, possessed a rather crazy imagination, was endowed by his birth with a fatalistic belief in his star, had nothing respectable about his morals, was completely lacking in eloquence when it came to expressing his ideas, and above all, was difficult to construe. But on the whole, he was better than he was made out to be by the party leaders who had pushed him into the presidency because they were planning to use him. Capable of affection and gratitude, he could also be persuaded to modify his actions. Although

[6]*Souvenirs, O.C.* XII, 223–24.

he might stubbornly hang on to a few intangible principles, he did not 431
mind being deterred from acting upon them and was even capable of 𝟪 𝟪
feeling repentant.

Dufaure and Passy wounded him cruelly by showing how little they
valued his opinions; Falloux, on the other hand, knew how to capture
his attention. Tocqueville regularly gave him an account of European
affairs and explained the reasons for the decisions he made. When
Tocqueville felt he had to resist the prince's choices or whims, he
justified his resistance. The result of these relations was a somewhat
mistrustful sympathy on Tocqueville's part and a livelier sympathy on
the part of the president, evidence of which he would give later. From
that moment, Tocqueville felt it would be unrealistic to think of
removing the prince from public life immediately after his term as
president. Yet there was no question of helping him in the coup d'état
planned by his entourage and probably by the prince himself as well.
In a country's institutions, the princes of various dynasties could serve
as "tools," and even though this one could not govern alone and was
sometimes ungovernable, one could no doubt make him useful in an
important decorative position which would be pleasing to him because
of his indolence. This is how we construe the plan referred to in a
rather enigmatic passage of the Souvenirs. [7]

Naturally, the Ministry of Foreign Affairs absorbed most of the time
and energy of its new chief. Tocqueville needed a man he could trust
as his private secretary, and he chose Arthur de Gobineau.

He had known the man since 1843, when he had made use of him
to provide précis of works by French and German philosophers for a
report he planned to present at the Institute. In 1844, Gobineau had
contributed a few articles to Le Commerce. In 1847, Louis de Kergorlay
had asked Tocqueville for his opinion of Gobineau and Tocqueville
wrote him: "He's a fine fellow . . . born into our class"; he was
sometimes superficial and flighty "but when I used him, I saw that his
heart was much worthier than his mind and that the principles guiding
his conduct were straighter and firmer than those guiding his pen or
his tongue."[8] At that date, Tocqueville did not seem to know of
Gobineau's early great successes in the literary world. The year 1848
had been a lean one for the writer, with assignments from the newspa-

[7]Ibid., 286. And to Clamorgam (Kühn, Tocqueville als Abgeordneter, 139): "I can't possibly tell you to
what degree I don't give a f— for all [these royal or imperial races] without exception . . . I therefore
have no prejudice against the tool you are offering me."
[8]Letter to Kergorlay dated August 23, 1847, O.C. XIII, 2: 203.

432

🙊 🙊

pers no longer coming in. Starting in September, he had been collaborating with Kergorlay on the *Revue provinciale,* which, despite some promising articles, was to fail after a year for financial reasons. By asking his help, Tocqueville brought Gobineau out of a nearly destitute state (with a salary of seven thousand francs a year and lodgings in the ministry!)—but would be able to count on the devotion of this "slogger" who, "rising at five o'clock, had no time to eat, no time to sleep, and not a minute to himself." A few days after Tocqueville's resignation from the ministry, d'Hautpoul, who saw to the affairs of the ministry for a time, would appoint Gobineau secretary to the embassy at Berne, thus fulfilling the promise of his old boss to bring him into the diplomatic corps. Gobineau would thereby get to know the Near East and the Orient, which were to be the inspiration for his later works of fiction. He would always remain deeply grateful to Tocqueville in spite of their intellectual differences, and during this particular time he appears to have been an absolutely devoted private secretary.[9]

Tocqueville did not have a very high opinion of the diplomatic staff he found when he arrived at the ministry: on the one hand, there were the rather cautious or undistinguished diplomatic agents who because of these virtues had escaped the 1848 purge; on the other, there were the republicans from before the revolution, sympathizers with the revolutionary movements taking place throughout Europe, who had been given diplomatic missions in many instances simply in order to get them out of the way.

The most important post, that of ambassador to London, was vacant because of the resignation of Admiral Cecille. Tocqueville gave it to his own predecessor, Drouyn de Lhuys, with whom he had had good relations for a long time. When Guizot had deprived Drouyn of his position as undersecretary in the ministry because he had voted in the Chamber against the Pritchard indemnity, *Le Commerce* had protested with an article that may have been by Tocqueville, and the latter had also recalled the affair in his speech of January 28, 1848. Drouyn was an experienced informant, self-possessed, wary, and dependable.

In July 1849, the Czar of Russia having recognized the Republic, an ambassador to Russia had to be appointed. Tocqueville's choice was Lamoricière, whose petulance could be dangerous in the Legislative

[9]J. Boissel, *Gobineau* (Paris, 1981), 121–22.

Assembly; Lamoricière was favorably received in Saint Petersburg and, having been "trained by Arab diplomacy," was useful there.[10]

In Vienna, France had only a simple chargé d'affaires, Delacour. Tocqueville thought of transferring Rayneval from Naples to Vienna, but Rayneval's wife did not want to leave Italy; then he thought of Rémusat, who declared that he felt he was "decidedly unsuited to action."[11] The president then suggested to Tocqueville that he appoint Beaumont, who had left London on December 10 and who, while he was ambassador there, had made some very insulting remarks about him. Beaumont was well liked in Vienna, as he was everywhere, but arrived there too late to be very useful to the government.

It was in central Italy that the choice of a new ambassador became a pressing need. We will see how very complex the situation of the Papal States was. France's diplomatic interests there were entrusted jointly to the Duc d'Harcourt, ambassador to the Holy See, and Rayneval, ambassador to Naples and France's representative at the Gaeta conference—and also, in point of fact, to General Oudinot, commander of the French expeditionary force. Tocqueville sent Corcelle to unify the approaches of these men, which were sometimes at odds. He must have been reminded of the unpleasant dealings he had had at Le Commerce. Corcelle, a recent convert to Catholicism, allowed himself to be enthralled by the charm of Pius IX, and in October, Tocqueville confessed to Beaumont:

The Rome affair is still causing me a lot of concern and embarrassment. I have to keep an eye constantly on Corcelle. The idea that you and I had to send him there was not a good one . . . He takes care to point out what he sees as contradictions on my part which don't exist except in his imagination, or rather, in his desire not to follow my exact instructions. It's well worth the trouble of hiring one's best friends as diplomatic agents, so that they can leave such documents in the boxes of the ministries.[12]

Between Corcelle, who did not obey the minister's instructions, and Oudinot, who did not understand them (and whom Tocqueville could not get rid of until very late), the difficult Rome affair could only cause vexations for the government. As we shall see, it eventually caused its downfall.

[10]Souvenirs, O.C. XII, 221.
[11]Unpublished letter from Rémusat in the Tocqueville Archives.
[12]Letter to Beaumont dated October 12, O.C. VIII, 2: 200.

434

𝒦 𝒴

Tocqueville attempted to keep himself provided with accurate information on the various problem areas in Europe. Official representatives like Thouvenal in Athens who sent him clear and vivid reports were very few. He therefore turned to unofficial agents but with no great illusions about their reliability, writing on the file enclosing their reports: "Letters . . . which prove only one thing, and that is how little these secret agents, whom diplomacy makes use of and who cost a good deal, do to earn their money."[13] Yet he gathered information by various means. One agent in Paris regularly received messengers from the Dual Monarchy and kept Tocqueville up to date on the last stages of the Hungarian revolt (the only one for which Tocqueville felt a private sympathy that he had to suppress as minister). A certain Jacob, who had rather strange handwriting, slowly worked his way down from Schaffhausen to Rome, describing the rout of the Baden revolutionaries, sounding out the morale of the Swiss army, observing the extortion practiced by the Austrians in their legations, portraying the French soldiers as they greeted ecclesiastics with catcalls in the streets of the Eternal City. Colonel Callier, a graduate of the Ecole Polytechnique who had been recommended by Lamartine and a soldier who dreamed of leaving the army for the diplomatic corps, gave Tocqueville more valuable information. Certain travelers communicated their impressions to the minister, including John Lemoinne, a journalist from Les Débats in whom he manifested a good deal of confidence, and Boulatignier, his alter ego in the delegation from the Manche to the Constituent Assembly. These unoffical sources, who transmitted information to the minister which did not bear the embassy stamp, made Corcelle feel his functions were being duplicated and he took it badly. The minister sought informants everywhere, from every rank. In the case of Prussia, the most important was Adolphe de Circourt, who had carried out a mission to that country in 1848 and written an interesting report for Lamartine. Tocqueville asked this versatile legitimist writer, who was very familiar with German affairs, for a report on Germany that turned out to be less interesting but seems to have sealed the friendship between the two men.[14]

At the end of the July monarchy and also, with even greater reason, in 1848, when he was appointed French mediator with an English

[13]Tocqueville Archives, file 104.
[14]Ibid.; see also Les Lettres du colonel Callier, ed. A. B. Duff and M. Degros (Paris, 1950).

colleague in the Austro-Sardinian conflict, Tocqueville would not   435
have indulged in the sorts of attacks he had launched from the tribune   ⚹ ⚹
of the Chamber against the conciliatory policy just after the 1840 crisis.
Starting in 1847, he agreed that in the policy of entente with the
English, "the basic strategy was a good one."[15] He now acknowledged
that France's foreign policy should not endeavor to give French pride
those satisfactions he had reproached Guizot for not being able to give.
There was a gap between public opinion, which lingered over the great
memories of France's European role in the days of Revolution and
Empire, and the real possibilities for action. Since February 1848, those
at the head of the Ministry of Foreign Affairs—Lamartine, Bastide, and
Drouyn de Lhuys—had stood firm against the insistent urgings of the
firebrands who called for France's intervention even where her help
had not been sought. Tocqueville wanted France to attain greater
prominence in Europe, but he approved of his predecessors' discretion.

In the troubled Europe of 1849, the most important interest was the
maintenance of the peace. On June 15, Tocqueville affirmed this broad
principle in response to Mauguin's peremptory questioning. Every
year, Mauguin loomed up on the tribune to reveal a plot against France
on the part of the sovereigns of Europe, and this time he predicted the
arrival of the Russians. Tocqueville took this as an excellent opportunity to proclaim that peace was necessary and that it was not at that
moment threatened.[16]

War, in the present circumstances, would not only be a disaster for
the French Republic, "it could bring with it, not only for us, but for
the whole of the civilized world, a frightful catastrophe," at a moment
in history "when societies are trembling on their foundations." A
coalition against France seemed impossible: England wanted to keep
the peace, the German powers had never been so divided, and although
the Russians had established themselves in the Principalities and were
participating in the repression of the Hungarian uprising, their ambitions remained limited.

In September 1848, studying Palmerston's policy, Tocqueville had
noted "England's sincere desire to keep the general peace as long as
possible, its resolution not to become involved in war until the last
possible minute, but to hold back with everyone else and not to let
itself be carried away by anything." Within these limits, a collaboration between France and England—to settle the Italian conflicts, for

---

[15]Letter to Corcelle dated September 29, 1847, *O.C.* XV, 1: 240.
[16]June 15 session, *Le Moniteur universel* of June 16, 2155.

436 example—was possible. Palmerston was thinking of replacing Piedmont's friendship with the traditional friendship of Austria, and Tocqueville saw quite clearly that in maintaining a firm entente with France Palmerston was seeking to limit her influence[17] (though he did not know that the English statesman had unfairly called him a "crazy man" who had brought on the revolution in France).

A continental coalition had never been possible without England. What was more, Germany was in a state of confusion following the refusal of the imperial crown by the King of Prussia, who had been offered it by the Frankfurt parliament. The latter was no longer anything more than a rump parliament that had fallen under the domination of extremists. The struggle was continuing between this revolutionary Germany, whose center continued to be Frankfurt, and the Germany of the princes, led from Berlin by the King of Prussia, freed of the internal convulsions of his states. Austria, absorbed by the Hungarian war, was, for the time being, almost absent from Germany's space. Tocqueville was wagering on the victory of the Germany of the princes over the Germany of the revolution. But he foresaw that in the end Austria would return to the German sphere, and there would be a settling of accounts with Prussia. These upheavals in Germany required the greatest vigilance, but Tocqueville thought it should be a discreet vigilance, that France should refrain from anything resembling an offensive move toward the Rhine. France should not give any aid to Prussia's enemies, but at the same time it should not side with Prussia. His policy where Italian affairs were concerned also avoided profiting from the current troubles of Prince Schwarzenberg, the Austrian prime minister.

Italian affairs imposed more precise duties on the minister of foreign affairs than did those of Germany. The tradition according to which France endeavored to counterbalance Austria's influence here was still alive, as the debates concerning the occupation of Ancona under the July monarchy had shown. Tocqueville was aware that since the February revolution France's influence had grown weaker in the north and the south of Italy, and that the only field of action that remained was central Italy.

In the north, the King of Piedmont, Charles Albert, had tried to take advantage of the Hungarian war to liberate Lombardy from Austria. Soundly defeated by the Austrian field marshal Radetsky at Novara (March 25), Charles Albert had abdicated in favor of his son, Victor

[17]Tocqueville Archives, file 109.

Emmanuel. Austria offered an armistice, but Piedmont tried to wangle advantages in central Italy in exchange for giving up its claims to Lombardy. At that point, Schwarzenberg threatened to break the armistice, without taking the role of the French and English mediation into account. Tocqueville immediately summoned Hübner, the Austrian ambassador to Paris, and, pretending not to know the language of diplomacy, gave him a sound scolding. Actually, Schwarzenberg merely wanted to force Piedmont to negotiate, without risking a general war, and on June 15 he reopened negotiations. He contented himself with the payment of an indemnity, with no annexation of territory. But he rejected all mediation where Venice was concerned. The bombardment of Venice began June 13 and forced it to capitulate August 22.

In southern Italy, the King of Naples, Ferdinand II, refusing to allow a renewal of mediation by the French and English admirals between the rebellious Sicilians and himself, reestablished his authority in the island during the month of May.

In central Italy itself, the revolutionary movements were giving way under pressure from Austria: in Tuscany, for instance, the return of the grand duke was expected at the end of May.

But here the great affair was the Roman revolution. This problem of foreign policy was to dominate the entire life of the second Barrot cabinet (June 2 to October 31). It was in solidarity with the Roman revolutionaries that the Mountain tried to take over Paris on June 13, and it was the relative failure of French diplomacy in Rome that gave Louis-Napoléon the pretext for breaking with his ministers.

It is thus important to go over the circumstances in some detail.[18]

Pope Pius IX had tried to establish a constitutional regime in 1848, but his prime minister, Count Pelligrino Rossi, had been assassinated on November 15 and the Pope himself had fled Rome several days later. He had confided in France's ambassador, the Duc d'Harcourt, his desire to take refuge in France, but, following secret intrigues, had reached Gaeta in the Kingdom of Naples, whence, in January 1849, he appealed to the Catholic nations for help. Rome had indeed become a republic with a Constituent Assembly and with a triumvirate, dominated by Mazzini, as its executive power. Groups of revolutionaries, now being hunted down all over Europe, were arriving in the Eternal City, and since April 27 Garibaldi's charismatic power had filled them

---

[18]G. Mollat, *La Question romaine de Pie VI à Pie IX* (Paris, 1932); A.-M. Ghisalberti, *Roma di Mazzini a Pio IX* (Milan, 1958).

438

☙ ☙

with new life. Yet the Roman Republic had only a precarious foothold. From Austria, Naples, and Spain contingents had been sent or would soon be on their way to occupy parts of the Papal States. On April 16, Barrot had asked the Constituent Assembly for a special appropriation to finance sending a French expeditionary force there. He portrayed this intervention as an attempt at mediation between the Pope and his rebellious subjects. In fact, from the very outset his intention was equivocal: to counterbalance the influence of Austria, to restore the Pope's temporal power, and to impose liberal institutions on central Italy. The leader of the expedition, General Oudinot, landed at Civitavecchia on April 24, presented himself in Rome "as a friend" on the thirtieth, and was repulsed with losses. The Constituent Assembly blamed the Barrot government, but the president kept it in office. Drouyn de Lhuys sent Ferdinand de Lesseps to negotiate a modus vivendi between the French army and the Romans. But he was recalled by the minister for having exceeded his instructions and the order to take Rome was sent secretly to General Oudinot on the eve of the convening of the Legislative Assembly.

Tocqueville—who had voted in favor of the appropriation for the expeditionary force on April 16—learned of this secret order when he returned from Germany and accepted his post in the Ministry of Foreign Affairs only on condition that he would not have to justify the Roman policy of his predecessor. As far as one can judge, he condemned the order to attack the city more because it was untimely or premature than for any deeper reasons. Falloux reports that before Toqueville entered the ministry he thought the Romans should have been consulted on the reestablishment of the Pope's temporal power.[19] But once the affair was undertaken (even if he thought it wrongly undertaken) it was necessary to support it in order not to lose face. To avoid that risk, he would not hesitate to propose intensifying hostilities if necessary in order to curtail the sort of lengthy siege that would make France look ridiculous. It is perhaps fortunate for Rome that it yielded before the dispositions Tocqueville ordered could be carried out. On July 1, he wrote to Corcelle:

I'm not hiding from myself the fact that from this moment on, the true responsibility for the Rome affair rests on our heads. I bear this responsibility courageously, as a duty, but with great anxiety and profound sadness. If Rome is sacked and half destroyed as a consequence of this equivocal expedi-

[19]Falloux, *Mémoires* 1, 475.

tion of doubtful value, we will hardly be excusable in the eyes of history. **439**
This sort of work is for the Austrians. Earlier mistakes without number have
led us—though we were not the ones who made them—to this terrible
alternative: either to deliver Rome to all the horrors of war, or to withdraw
covered with shame, defeated by the very men who have been put to flight
on all the battlefields of Italy for the past eighteen months. The first would
be a very great misfortune, but the other would be a frightful disaster and,
for my part, I have no hesitation.[20]

French policy could, nevertheless, find one justification, that of
imposing a constitutional regime on the Papal States. This idea was an
application of the principle expressed in the *Democracy,* that modern
liberty and the Church must be enabled to coexist if the moral equilibrium of the future democratic society is to be assured. The negotiation
of the Roman affair was therefore a test of one of Tocqueville's
fundamental ideas: "If the sovereign pontiff, though scarcely restored
to power, works to reestablish abuses that even absolutist Europe no
longer wants, if he institutes harsh measures that history does not
pardon even in the case of secular princes, it is the Catholic Church
that would be not only weakened but dishonored throughout the
entire world."

On the very day, June 3, that Tocqueville moved into the ministry,
Oudinot attacked the Romans' advanced positions on the right bank
of the Tiber and came up against the first great wall defending the
heights of the Janiculum that overlooked the city. A month of strict
siege was necessary in order to take possession of the bastions that
crowned these heights. Hostilities then ceased and the French entered
Rome on July 2. The military operations seem to have been very
poorly carried out, though they at least had the merit of not having
damaged any important monument, no matter what was alleged in the
noisy protests orchestrated by the British consul.

The news of the renewal of hostilities was the signal for a day of
revolution in Paris. On June 11, Ledru-Rollin stepped up on the
tribune and asked that the president of the Republic and his ministers
be formally accused of violating Article 5 of the Constitution, which
stated: "[France] shall never use its strength against the liberty of any
people." Ledru-Rollin's speech ended in a call to arms. Barrot answered with a justification of past policy, as had been agreed, but
Tocqueville the next day showed his continuing solidarity by refusing

[20]Letter to Corcelle dated July 1, 1849, *O.C.* XV, 1: 293.

440

཰ ཱ

all access to documents to anyone who advocated resorting to force. On the thirteenth, he was with Dufaure when, the uprising having broken out, the latter decided to declare a state of siege. But this demonstration by the "reds" was quickly suppressed by Changarnier.

It was shortly after the taking of Rome that the diplomatic corps came to the fore in order to decide upon the conditions for restoring the Pope. It had two fields of action, Rome and Gaeta.

In Rome, the organization established by France's occupation had mortgaged the future. Tocqueville would have liked to obtain the collaboration of a moderate liberal party, of men who had participated in the first reforms of Pius IX. Such a party could not be found, and the men who would have been capable of being part of it were avoiding contact with France for fear of assassins. General Oudinot had moved precipitately, taking no precautions, to turn over his essential powers to a triumvirate of cardinal legates who had presented themselves to him in the name of the Pope. He restored officials compromised by their role in the old regime, and his blundering actions ended by making it impossible to turn the life of the city in a new direction. Tocqueville could only fulminate against his "prodigious stupidity."[21]

It was at Gaeta that the principal match was being played out between Antonelli, the cardinal secretary of state, and the representatives of the four Catholic powers. From the former, one could expect underhanded chicanery, like his challenge to Corcelle's powers and his obstinate resistance to reforms. But Tocqueville had received certain assurances from Schwarzenberg, whom he had endeavored to convince that a liberal regime in the Papal States would give Venetian Lombardy a more peaceful neighbor than the hated traditional one. It does not seem that Esterhazy, the Austrian representative at Gaeta, gave enthusiastic support to the reforms, nor did the Spanish representative, Martínez de la Rosa, whose liberal past had led Tocqueville to count on him. Corcelle and Rayneval (who took Corcelle's place when he became dangerously ill) seem, too, to have been less than explicit about the views of their minister. From Paris itself, the nuncio transmitted information from individuals belonging to the party of order or the religious party (even though Falloux was personally loyal) which encouraged the cardinal secretary of state in his resistance. Tocqueville tried having Corcelle appeal directly to the Pope, who received him splendidly but had little but sweet words to offer him.

The dilatory conduct of the Roman court exasperated Tocqueville.

[21]Unpublished letter to Lamoricière dated August 28, file 104 of the Tocqueville Archives.

France could not consent to be so ridiculed and abused, he said, and 441
he sometimes thought of creating a scandal. His feelings were shared ⚶ ⚶
by the prince-president, who on August 12, in a letter to his aide-de-
camp Edgard Ney, declared that France, the liberator of the people
everywhere, had not sent out her soldiers in order to restore papal
absolutism, and expressed his indignation that a manifesto published by
the cardinal legates had not found it appropriate to thank his army.
Tocqueville and Falloux believed that this letter, whose terms they did
not disapprove of, would reach only a limited public, but Louis-
Napoléon, after trying to have it printed in Le Moniteur romain, had
it printed on September 7 in Le Moniteur universel.

On August 6, Tocqueville had been addressed in the Legislative
Assembly by Arnaud de l'Ariège. This representative, a fervent Catholic, sat with the Mountain. He reproached the minister for having
compromised both religion and democracy, with no result, in the
Roman affair, all in order to reestablish a temporal power of the Pope
that was not necessary to the independence of the Catholic Church.
Tocqueville replied by recalling the aims of France's intervention and
by affirming the need, for the present, to restore the temporal power.
"For my part, I am convinced that in the present state of things, there
is no other way, today (I do not know what the chances are for the
future, but politicians must concern themselves above all with the
present and the immediate future), there is no other way, today or in
the immediate future, to make the sovereign pontiff independent than
to allow him a temporal power." And the whole last part of Tocqueville's speech is an appeal to Pius IX's conscience, reminding him of
his liberal actions in 1848 and the resultant prestige for Catholicism
in the rest of the world. It is unlikely that there was any connivance
between his challenger and himself on the content of the question, since
Arnaud, while keeping his tone lofty, almost theological, had not
spared the minister's policy. But this concern for harmony between
democracy and religion had awakened a sympathetic response in
Tocqueville: he made him a gift of his portrait.[22]

It was through the Motu proprio of September 12, to which was
added the publication of an amnesty,[23] that Pius IX determined upon
the measures that would allow him to reenter his capital. These two
texts were deeply disappointing to Tocqueville.

[22]Arnaud de l'Ariège's speech and Tocqueville's answer can be found in Le Moniteur universel of August
7, on pages 2606–7 and 2608–9, respectively. On Arnaud's interesting personality, see J.-B. Duroselle,
Arnaud de l'Ariège et la démocratie chrétienne, typed thesis, 1959.
[23]The text of the Motu proprio and that of the amnesty are reproduced in the O.C. XV, 1: 434–36.

Even though he had been surprised, when France's troops entered the Eternal City, at the absence of any demonstration of loyalty to the Holy Father, Tocqueville thought that Pius's Roman subjects would accept his return without displeasure if that return was disassociated from the restoration of the defunct, detested clerical regime in place prior to 1848. But the *Motu proprio* made no gesture toward granting the hoped-for institutional reforms. It did establish local and provincial elected authorities, and created both a Council of State and an Assembly. But creation of the Assembly appeared to the French government to offer a false promise. Its members were chosen from different categories of citizens, but the Pope could add to it anyone he pleased, thus taking away with one hand what he had given with the other. Above all, Tocqueville did not hide his "irritation" at the fact that, despite promises made in the negotiations, the Assembly would not vote on the budget and would have only an advisory role, which would make of any constitutional regime a mere illusion. There was also no promise of any laicization of the administration, and the promises for a reform of the courts were so vague as to be meaningless. Already, the Inquisition had been restored. Corcelle assured him that the Inquisition was no longer anything more than a name; he did not suspect that Tocqueville had taken care to study and take notes on the entire judiciary organization of the Papal States.[24]

The amnesty decreed by the Pope exasperated Tocqueville much more. He called for the texts of all the amnesties granted after revolutionary movements by lay princes and found only one, that of Ferdinand VII of Spain, in 1823, as restrictive as that of Pius IX. Whole categories of citizens were excluded from it and the definitions of these categories could easily be broadened. All members of the Constituent Assembly, even those hostile to the Republic, were excluded from the amnesty, as well as all the "regimental commanding officers" of the Roman army. Tocqueville considered the execution of such an act a challenge to France's honor. He took steps to offer the Roman exiles decent asylum in France and reprimanded Corcelle for having tolerated certain of the amnesty's measures.

Nevertheless, on October 18, at the opening of a debate on Roman affairs connected to the vote on appropriations for the occupation—a law for which Thiers was rapporteur—Tocqueville had to present to the Legislative Assembly a description of the measures taken. He

---

[24]Unpublished notes (file 104 in the Tocqueville Archives) which will be published in vol. III, 3, of the *O.C.*.

protested vigorously against the amnesty, expressing the desire that its execution should be merciful, and assured his listeners that though the *Motu proprio* might be insufficient it did contain the seeds of reforms that could develop later. In answer to questions from the left, he could not say that the achievements of the expedition were illusory. The majority of the Assembly was content with the reestablishment of the temporal power and, with Thiers, considered the *Motu proprio* an acceptable basis for the institutions of the Pontifical State. Tocqueville, however, reminded his listeners—and endorsed it as the government's true position—of the president's letter to Edgard Ney, his aide-de-camp, in which he protested against the policies of the Pope and which, when published in the *Moniteur,* had caused a sensation.[25]

Thiers, on the other hand, had said nothing of the president's letter in his report, and Louis-Napoléon had been deeply wounded by this. He wrote a letter to Barrot which, without showing any disagreement with his ministers, ended in a sort of challenge to the majority of the Legislative Assembly. Barrot, after some hesitation, did not read it out to the Assembly and this left the president unhappy.

On October 31, the president resolved to get rid of those ministers who offended him by their personalities and prevented him from freeing himself of the Assembly because that seemed unconstitutional to them. He replaced them by understudies: the brother of Odilon Barrot, "Barrot Cain," in Interior; General d'Hautpoul, the most conspicuous character in the new cabinet, in War; General Ducos de la Hitte in Foreign Affairs. With a tone that was already imperial, Louis-Napoléon communicated these changes to the Assembly.

In two letters dated November 1 and 2, the first addressed to an unidentified correspondent and the second to Beaumont,[26] Tocqueville had this to say about the event:

Through these different incidents, you will also have noticed already the governing idea in all this, which is simply the desire to avoid what is called the guardianship of the National Assembly, whichever side may try to assume it. Imperial harping and nothing more, for the moment, the crow trying to imitate the eagle, but a clear augury of an impending crisis. All the parties in the Assembly are angered by the insolent message that was read yesterday, despite the fact that no one wants to provoke a fight between the Assembly and the president. This fight seems inevitable to me sooner or later, given the dispositions, desires, and especially the instincts of men . . .

[25]*Le Moniteur universel* of September 7, 2837.
[26]Unpublished letter, Tocqueville Archives, file 97. Letter to Beaumont, *O.C.* VIII, 2: 232.

Up to now, the small-scale coup d'état hasn't been very successful and is not taken seriously, even though it seems to be a very serious symptom of the future. Yet I expect it to be followed by a fairly widespread calm for some time.

Tocqueville was right. Although this intrusion on the part of the prince-president into the relations of his ministers and the Assembly was dangerous in the long run, Louis-Napoléon, satisfied with having affirmed his personal authority, did not push his advantage farther and his new government showed no propensity to impose reforms on the Pope that were repugnant to him.

Tocqueville, on the other hand, remained personally marked by this experience in the diplomatic world. He had been exasperated by the hypocrisy of the Roman court. Catholic by tradition and habit, he felt almost none of the veneration for Pius IX expressed by believers of his time: "What a shame you're a Protestant!" Corcelle wrote to him one day, and this remark indicates a very real difference in their sensibilities. For Tocqueville, the private virtues of the Holy Father did not count for very much compared to the want of acumen that chained him to the tortuous policies of his secretary of state. From that time on, there was an anticlerical acerbity in him, perceptible in his correspondence, that he had not shown before. It would continue to be evident under the Second Empire.

The Rome expedition did not, however, absorb all the time and energy of the minister of foreign affairs. He also took part in settling an international crisis over the refugees from Constantinople.

In September 1849, troops loyal to the Hapsburgs had just crushed the Hungarian uprising with the help of one hundred and fifty thousand Russians who had crossed the Principalities and Transylvania to come to their aid. The survivors of the conquered armies, four thousand Hungarians, along with eight hundred Polish volunteers out of the corps of ten thousand who had joined the Hungarians, were seeking asylum in Turkey. Among these were Kossuth and several Polish generals. The fugitives were trying to escape the brutal Austrian repression. It was the czar, however, who wrote a threatening letter to the sultan demanding that the refugees be handed over to their conquerors. The sultan refused, since the English ambassador, Stratford Canning, had already promised him the support of Great Britain. France's ambassador, General Aupick, also encouraged the Turkish government to resist. In Vienna, Schwarzenberg could only back Russia's demand, even though, at that moment, he was primarily interested in German affairs, where Prussia, taking advantage of Austria's absence from the scene, had been trying to acquire more territory.

The Western powers asked themselves what the czar's move meant. Was he trying to satisfy the Russian military, who dreamed of taking revenge on the Polish traitors? In the opinion of Lamoricière and Tocqueville, this was the most probable interpretation, and subsequent events appeared to prove them right. Was he trying to profit from this incident to lean on Turkey with all his weight and resume his march toward Constantinople? This hypothesis could not be entirely dismissed. Palmerston's reaction was both energetic and prudent.[27] On October 2, he assured the Turkish ambassador to London of England's moral and, if necessary, material aid. But in the diplomatic protests he initiated, he endeavored to retain a certain cordiality in order not to wound the czar's honor. While asking France to take similar steps, he did not wish the two countries to act in accord, putting it out that France had been moved to respond by Turkish representations in Paris.

Tocqueville was indignant at the serious violation of international law represented by the Austrian and Russian move. But he still had a bad memory of the Piedmont alarm in July: Palmerston had promised a purely moral support in case of a war by Piedmont and France against Austria, since England did not have the same interests as France in northern Italy. Tocqueville pointed out that England had more interests than France in the eastern question and that, in addition, in case of a general war England risked only its fleet while France risked its very existence. While protesting in St. Petersburg and in Vienna, he would have liked there to be a delay before the French Mediterranean fleet was sent to join that of Admiral Parker, which was going to take up position in the Bay of Besiktas, close to the Bosporus strait. But Lord Normanby, the English ambassador in Paris, had talked with the president, who had promised that the two fleets would join forces, a move that prefigured his policy on the eve of the Crimean War, when he sought an alliance with England. The cabinet shared the president's opinion.

Actually, the crisis was easily dealt with. On October 16, the czar received Fuad Effendi, the sultan's envoy, and consented to allow the refugees to be interned in Turkish fortresses, where they were to

---

[27]Donald Southgate, *The Most English Minister . . .* (New York, 1966), 259–61.

445

remain for two years. As a gesture toward British opinion, Palmerston made a public protest to St. Petersburg and would have tried to do the same to Vienna, but here, Ambassador Ponsonby chose not to go along with his government, which he treated in an offhand manner. France's protests, which were not joined to those of England, would provoke no bitterness either in Nesselrode or in Schwarzenberg.[28]

Tocqueville was visibly humoring Schwarzenberg. And in this, one can see a characteristic sign of his political conceptions. As we know, Tocqueville, who believed in the triumph of democracy, had never spoken out for anything but prudent, progressive reforms. In the same way, he believed in the eventual triumph of German unity and was not at all alarmed by it, since he was convinced that the Russians threatened to submerge Central and Western Europe, and a strong Germany could be a barrier against this. For the present, he saw, quite correctly, the developing conflict between Austria and Prussia for hegemony in Germany and thought that Austria would reestablish its dominance. He was soon proved right.

Affairs in the New World also occupied Tocqueville's attention.

There was a diplomatic incident with the United States. The ambassador to Washington was Major Guillaume-Tell Poussin, whose book, copied from the *Democracy*, had already displeased Tocqueville. Poussin and the secretary of state, John Middleton Clayton, had exchanged rather discourteous letters over some minor matters, and Clayton had asked for Poussin's recall. Under these conditions, Tocqueville felt he could not receive William Cabell Rives, the new ambassador of the United States to Paris. In the end, since Drouyn had already dismissed Poussin, the incident could be smoothed over, and this was done under Tocqueville's successor. "But what animals these Americans are!" Tocqueville exclaimed, aware of how ironic it was that his administration should have been marked by a deterioration of relations with the United States.

But the most serious affair in the New World was that of the Río de la Plata.[29]

France and England had been engaged in a conflict with the Argentine dictator Juan Manuel de Rosas since 1832. The two powers together had blockaded the Río de la Plata, but had realized the

[28]The *Souvenirs,* silent about the Roman question, discuss the affair of the refugees from Constantinople at some length (*O.C.* XII, 255–63).

[29]On this matter, see Carlos Pereyra, *Rosas y Thiers, la diplomacía europea en el Río de la Plata* (Madrid, 1919), and J. F. Cady, *Foreign Intervention in the Río de la Plata* (Philadelphia, 1929).

ineffectiveness of their action. Palmerston had then concluded a sepa-   447
rate treaty with Rosas that became final in January 1849.

France remained in the state of hostilities with Rosas, no longer
because of the status of its nationals in Buenos Aires, but over the
problem of the Oriental Republic (Uruguay). The former president
of the Republic, Oribe, an ally and in some sense a vassal of Rosas,
had, since 1842, been laying siege to Montevideo, where the current
president, Fructuoso Rivera, was able to keep going only because of
a foreign legion made up mainly of Frenchmen. But pessimistic rumors
were circulating about how much longer the city would be able to
withstand the siege. Many Frenchmen had left it to go to Buenos Aires.
The year before, Bastide had sent Admiral Le Prédour to the spot and
the admiral, convinced of the desperation of Montevideo's situation,
had prepared two agreements, one with Rosas (April 4, 1849) and one
with Oribe (May 15). The ratification of these agreements was therefore to be submitted to the Legislative Assembly. It was a serious
problem which Tocqueville asked Beaumont to study, and which he
himself reexamined in its entirety, pen in hand, also making notes
about the advantages and disadvantages of different solutions.[30]

The refusal to negotiate resulted not only in an army and a fleet
being sent to the aid of Montevideo, but also in the settlement in
Uruguay of a first contingent of five thousand colonists, planting the
seed of a "new Algeria" in South America. Already, a Society for the
Colonization of Uruguay had been created in Paris. Palmerston was
concerned about it, and Tocqueville gave him to understand that, now
that England had withdrawn from the affairs of the Río de la Plata,
this matter was beyond his competence. Thiers became enthusiastic
about the new project. But Tocqueville felt that these plans were not
very wise; he wanted to ratify the Le Prédour treaty and was prepared
to make improvements in it. In Argentina, Rosas was no longer
persecuting the French; he implicitly recognized Uruguay's independence and, having become wiser with advancing age, would no doubt
keep his promises.

It was not until January 1850 that the Legislative Assembly examined the Le Prédour treaty. Despite the minister's opinion, it was
rejected. Tocqueville had prepared a speech supporting his successor,
but, for reasons we cannot discover, did not give it.

The solution to the la Plata affair was unexpected. In 1850, Brazil

---

[30]Beaumont's note on the situation in 1849 is included in the O.C. VIII, 2: 133–62. Tocqueville's
unpublished notes on the subject will appear in vol. III, 3.

led a coalition of allies against Rosas, who, with his friend Oribe, went into exile in England in 1852.

Tocqueville's actions as minister have been severely judged by some. "What is . . . important is that this great thinker, this great writer, was not a useful minister," wrote Augustin Cochin to Montalembert after Tocqueville's death.[31] Even during the time when he was minister, neither the press of the party of order nor that of the republican opposition was very kind to him. The English press seems to have shown him more indulgence.

We must first point out how difficult it is to judge a foreign minister on the basis of only five months in office. He is inevitably hostage to the major international affairs of the day, even when he considers it a mistake to have become involved in them; and he is necessarily the heir to his predecessor's decisions.

Tocqueville's great failure, of course, was that he was unable to force Pope Pius IX to create liberal institutions in Rome, but when he took over the direction of the negotiations he appears to have thought there was little chance of success. In another area, that of the refugees in Constantinople, although his position was less prominent than Palmerston's he had the clear merit of triumphing more quietly than his English colleague and thus preserving good relations with Russia and Austria.

What probably remains Tocqueville's greatest accomplishment as minister was to have maintained the peace in Italy through good relations with Austria. On September 25, the London *Times* offered the opinion that it was because of the abilities of Schwarzenberg and Tocqueville that war had been avoided. Of course, Austria did not give France strong support in the Gaeta conferences that were meant to secure from the Pope the reforms which both nations had agreed were desirable. This seems to have been less a matter of bad faith on Austria's part than of her catering to the Holy See, and Tocqueville himself felt that one could hardly grab Pius IX by the throat in order to get more from him. Obviously, it is not certain that the Pope could have governed tranquilly with a constitutional regime, but Tocqueville was right to foresee the impossibility of the papacy's maintaining itself by reinstituting the abuses of the past, and the presence of a French garrison in Rome until 1870 was the proof.

[31]Unpublished letter in the Cochin Archives.

24

THE END OF THE REPUBLIC

SOON AFTER the presidential message of October 31, in which Louis-Napoléon, after paying a few compliments to his ministers, noted that the cabinet had not "sufficiently maintained order within France and upheld her dignity abroad," Tocqueville wrote a letter of protest in the name of his former colleagues in which, without breaking with the prince-president, he appealed to the court of public opinion to give its verdict on the president's decision and assured him that they were ready to continue working with him in the interest of the nation but under the supervision of the Assembly, "the sole trustee of the will of the people." In the end, the dismissed ministers felt it was more dignified to keep silent than to address this collective letter to the president.[1]

Nevertheless, their discontent could not escape Louis-Napoléon's attention. As he often did after an outburst, he made a gesture of appeasement. This consisted of a letter to Tocqueville, a rather unusual move since it bypassed Barrot. His reason for it seems sincere: "You are one of those with whom I feel most sympathy." He asked Tocqueville to act as his intermediary with his former colleagues, whom he had let go for political reasons. He had had no intention of ruffling the feelings of men "whom he liked and respected." Tocqueville answered, on November 7, that he had left the ministry with no regrets, but added that the censure contained in the message, which had been seen as such by the public, had wounded him personally. He

[1]The rough draft of this letter is in the Tocqueville Archives, file 97.

450

〻〻

thanked the president for the interpretation he had given it and went to make peace the next day by appearing at the president's reception. He did not return to the Elysée Palace after that, but asked Vieillard to say on his behalf that the reason for this was that he wanted to nip in the bud any possible malicious interpretations.[2]

The character of the Barrot cabinet of June 2, drawn "from the minority of the majority," had given rise to persistent intrigues against it. But because of the conditions of its dismissal and the replacement of the noteworthy men who comprised it by obscure minor figures, the cabinet was missed by the Assembly, which was also the target of the president's authoritarian act. Tocqueville noted, not without humor: "Never has a fallen ministry had fewer enemies. The intriguers who attacked us, thinking they would take our places, are biting their fingernails, and the bulk of their friends, seeing that they have been led to fight the wrong battle, are attempting to voice their regrets that they were not more sympathetic to us."[3] The result of all this was an estrangement between the president and the majority, now aware of the possibility of a sudden coup d'état. The former ministers remained noncommittal, refraining from any attack on the new government so as not to bring on a reconciliation between the government and the main body of the party of order, and even in April 1850 Tocqueville, consulted by Lamoricière, tried to dissuade the fiery general from attacking the minister of war, since the support he would draw from the left in such an enterprise would make the majority suspicious of him.[4] Thus, just after the fall of the ministry, Tocqueville's parliamentary activity was limited: nevertheless, he was rapporteur of the Didier proposal to provide Algeria at once with its own laws, in application of Article 109 of the Constitution. On January 12, 1850, he spoke from the tribune in this regard and was appointed a member of the ad hoc committee.

As the weeks went by, however, he became aware that the majority of the Legislative Assembly were tending to draw closer to the president. It was swayed by a livelier, more lasting feeling than its distrust of Louis-Napoléon, and that was fear of the "reds"; it was particularly dismayed by the progress of socialist ideas in the army. The majority of the party of order became less and less submissive to the voice of its leaders, whether Orleanists or legitimists. Above all, it wanted a strong power that would protect it from "anarchy," without, for all

[2]Tocqueville Archives, file 104.
[3]Tocqueville to Beaumont, November 2, 1849, *O.C.* VIII, 2: 235.
[4]Tocqueville to Lamoricière, April 29, 1850, Chillon Archives, file 10.

that, wanting to see the Empire reestablished. Tocqueville perceived
that under these conditions all the prince-president needed was a very
ordinary talent in order to channel the current to his own advantage
and bring about a coup d'état without violence. The future seemed to
him more uncertain than ever.

He had reached this point in his thinking when his public career was
interrupted by illness. As we know, he had been very tired in the spring
of 1849 and found himself confined to bed when he was made minister
of foreign affairs. In that office, he did a considerable amount of work,
neglecting his personal affairs, which he set about putting in order
again in November. In the weeks that followed, although his wife was
obliged to stay in bed for a month, his own health did not seem bad.
But in March 1850 it broke suddenly. He was absent from the Assembly starting on the sixth, and on the eleventh requested a six-month
leave of absence because of illness. He spat blood for the first time, in
what appears to have been the beginning of the slowly developing
tuberculosis that was to cause his death nine years later. We do not
know many details of his illness. On March 15, Faucher wrote to
Reeve that there was no hope; on the nineteenth, that Tocqueville was
better. But it was not until the first days of April that Tocqueville
wrote a few lines of thanks to Barrot, who had come by several times
seeking news of him. There was no question of resuming his political
activity: on June 2, he left for Le Havre, embarked there for Cherbourg, and was at Tocqueville by June 4. His wife, too, was convales-
cent, but she recovered her strength more rapidly than he did, as
though the air of the Cotentin reminded her of her "native air."

Political action thus dropped abruptly out of Tocqueville's life. It
was this sudden interruption of activity, more than a sense of the
seriousness of his illness, that consigned him once again to that metaphysical distress that was perhaps one of the secret motivating forces
that hurled him into political activity as a diversion. From his Normandy retreat, he wrote Corcelle:

I have never had such difficulty bearing the weight of the obscurity that
surrounds all things of the other world; never have I felt such need of the
foundation, the solid ground on which life ought to be built . . . A few days
before I left Paris, I had thought of having a long, serious conversation with
[Abbé Coeur] on the terrible problems of human life. I asked him to come;
he came, and I said nothing to him about what was occupying my mind.
What would he have said that I hadn't said to myself a hundred times without
being able to create a complete and absolute conviction? . . . I am convinced

that one has to be born with the faculty of faith and that all that happens with age is the development of a seed that the soul already carries within it at birth.[5]

But although he might banish these thoughts, which only led "to a great, bottomless, black hole in which man's opinions tumble about in confusion," Tocqueville still felt the need to take stock of his own life and his way of leading it.

The first thing he saw was that he felt old and the declining period of his life was now beginning. He therefore had to make the best possible use of the years that remained to him. Which led him to ask himself if the ten years during which he had devoted most of his energies to public life had not had something illusory about them. It was certainly true that he had recently been involved, however briefly, in important affairs. But Tocqueville, skeptical, anxious, questioned further. Were these important affairs anything but merely the vicissitudes of an extended revolutionary period? He confessed he had been wrong to believe, after 1830, that the crisis separating the old world from the democracy of the future was over: "When I saw that democracy, after destroying all privileges, had reached the point of confronting only the very ancient and necessary privilege of property, I thought that, like the ocean, it had at last found its shore. A mistake! It is clear today that the tide is continuing to move, that the sea is rising; that not only have we not seen the end of the immense revolution that began before our own time, but the child born today will very likely not see it either. What is involved here is not a modification, but a transformation of the social body—but to attain what? In truth, I don't know, and I believe this is beyond the intelligence of everyone."[6] Nevertheless, for the present, French society possessed enough living strength to resist serious crises.

The project of writing his *Souvenirs* about the recent past was connected to these thoughts. It was in July 1850 that Tocqueville wrote the first part: "In my present solitary situation, I am reduced to turning my thoughts toward myself for a time, or rather toward calling back to mind the contemporary events in which I have been an actor or of which I have been a witness."[7] It was not only for the pleasure of portraying these, but in order to sort out the "confused features that make up the indistinct physiognomy of our time" that Tocqueville

[5]Tocqueville to Corcelle, August 1, 1850, *O.C.* XV, 2: 29.
[6]Unpublished notes, Tocqueville Archives, file 92.
[7]*Souvenirs, O.C.* XII, 29.

undertook this task. He also wanted these *Souvenirs* to be a "mirror" in which to observe himself. But we should not necessarily believe him when he declares that they are not destined for the public, even if one thinks it was for his own personal satisfaction that he chose the appropriate adjective from among several possibilities and cut out digressions for the sake of a balanced tone. No doubt he did not intend to release them to the public during his lifetime. But his reflections on his age led Tocqueville to a concern for what posterity would think of him. If posterity was still reading the *Democracy* and the new work that he was beginning to contemplate, it would be quite surprising if this same posterity were not also curious about his account of his time. Tocqueville, who was a great reader of memoirs, knew this sort of curiosity well. But, prudent Norman that he was, he envisaged the forgetfulness of future generations and rather hypocritically declared that he wanted to keep secret a work that would perhaps not interest them.

During that summer of 1850, he borrowed a collection of newspapers in Valognes and reviewed the February crisis that had swept away the monarchy. With a little perspective, he went on with the analyses he had already made in 1847 and 1848 of the vices and weaknesses of the July regime at its end. He saw it as the government of a single class for its own profit, broken by the unexpected irruption of popular forces into that closed universe. Though he confined himself to an account of the contingent day-by-day changes, he situated them in the tragic acceleration of the revolutionary thrust. And because the actors in the theater of the monarchy behaved with the disarray of burlesque marionettes as they confronted the crowds, Tocqueville was able to draw unforgettable caricatures.

One link with politics survived, however, during that summer of 1850: the departmental council. The year 1848 had seen Havin brought to the presidency by councillors who, Tocqueville noted maliciously, did not even dare speak ill of him among themselves, for fear he might hear of it. The year 1850—here we have one instance of it—was the year for local dignitaries to have their worst fears realized. Havin had been soundly defeated in the election for the Legislative Assembly, and in the departmental council a number of his former courtiers had assured Tocqueville's election. They had even preferred Vieillard over Havin as vice-president. The minister of foreign affairs had not been above making the trip to Saint-Lô to enjoy his local triumph. Asked to support a request by the mayor of Cherbourg, who wanted the prince-president to come visit the large works of the arsenal, he had been happy to do it. In the summer of 1850, after a tour of the East,

454

𝕏 𝕏

where he had been coldly received, the prince-president went off to Normandy in a barouche. On August 6, he was in Cherbourg for a three-day visit, during which Tocqueville, reelected president of the departmental council, held forth at length for his benefit. Tocqueville added to his words of welcome an expression of the department's most important need—a railway link to Paris. The president responded graciously and showed publicly the esteem and friendship he felt for the president of the departmental council.[8] The latter accompanied him in his visit to the port and took part in the banquet that followed. Louis-Napoléon was full of friendly attentions, though he did not bring up political problems. One can assume that from that time on he understood that Tocqueville was not a man who would take part in anything underhanded, but that he should be courted in order to make use of him later, when the passions aroused by a coup d'état had died down. For the present, Tocqueville was not unaware of the increase in local prestige that the attentions of the president were giving him. He was annoyed that Le Journal de Valognes, in its account of the festivities at Cherbourg, did not immediately print the speeches. The brief session of the departmental council, the festivities in Cherbourg, with the interviews, the speeches, the contact with the crowd, had tired Tocqueville, who lost the use of his voice, suffering from pain in his larynx. He was forced to recognize the obvious fact that the serious crisis in his health was not yet over. Before he could think of resuming an active life, he had to consult the doctors who had treated him in March, and particularly Dr. Gabriel Andral. The Tocquevilles therefore left the Cotentin at the end of September for Paris. The doctors told him that the right lung had healed but that his illness required a winter of rest in a Mediterranean climate. Tocqueville, persuaded that the president would not attempt anything while the Chambers were in session and that this calm would last all winter, resigned himself to leaving for Italy, though not without occasional moments of uneasiness.

The trip was an arduous one. On November 1, 1850, Tocqueville stopped over in Dijon; it was not until November 9 that he embarked at Marseilles. At the port of Genoa, the ship took on a great many English passengers who had just learned that the quarantine of the port of Naples had been lifted. In these crowded conditions, the ship went through such a violent tempest on its southward coastal passage that

[8]These speeches are printed in the O.C. (Bmt) IX, 572–73.

Tocqueville thought the ship, with all its passengers, was lost.[9] The 455
Tocquevilles landed at Civitavecchia and slowly made their way to
Naples by land. They were there by November 21, but gave up their
earlier plan to embark for Palermo. On December 12, they rented a
house in Sorrento "placed halfway up a hillside, very dry and comfortable," from which they could go out directly into the countryside.
Ampère joined his friends there in January and did not leave them until
March 7, 1851, or thereabouts; they themselves embarked for Marseilles, no doubt at Naples, on April 14. Ampère would later describe
this visit in the article he wrote for *Le Correspondant* upon the death
of his friend:

We lived in a house situated above the road, a little before Sorrento, on the
lowest slopes of the mountain; from a terrace roof, one saw, to the right,
Naples and Mount Vesuvius; to the left, the eye plunged into valleys filled
with orange trees whose fruit sparkled in the sun and from whose midst rose
domes, bell towers, white villas; it was a magical prospect. What fine, subtle,
lofty things I heard him say on that terrace! Then we would take long walks
in the mountains, for, frail though he was, he was a great walker; and in order
to follow the straight line that seemed to be his natural course he would cross
over a hedge, a ditch, sometimes a wall, if he had to. We would stop in some
beautiful spot, with the sea before us and the Naples sky over our heads.
Then, out of breath, we would rest a few moments, and our conversation
would begin again . . . That winter, the heavens, which have since been so
much harsher, blessed us with remarkably beautiful and gentle weather, even
for the climate of Naples. Almost every day, we were able to take these walks,
so priceless to us, and we were joined for several weeks by a man very highly
respected in England and of an untiring liveliness of wit, Mr. Senior. Our
walks would end in gathering a large bouquet for Mme de Tocqueville of
the broad-petaled violets that grew by the edge of the paths, for she was
confined to her terrace by poor health.[10]

One of the subjects of Tocqueville's very diverse and always original conversations with Ampère and Senior was that of the *Souvenirs*
of 1848, which he had resumed writing in the latter two weeks of
December 1850.

At Tocqueville, he had recalled his expectations in 1847 and given
an eyewitness account of the days of February. Now he continued his
reflections on that event, but with a broader perspective. He described
how Paris had become France's busiest manufacturing city and how the

[9]Letter from Tocqueville to Beaumont dated November 24, 1850, *O.C.* VIII, 2: 326–27.
[10]*O.C.* XI, 443.

456
㟢 㟢

political consciousness of the working class had been awakened by socialist preaching. For a revolution to take place, it had been necessary for these "general causes [to be] made fruitful by accidental events," a conclusion he would remember when he came to write *L'Ancien Régime et la Révolution*. But what struck him and remained for him the essential character of the Revolution of 1848 was the fact that it was directed against society and not the government, the fall of the July monarchy being merely one more contingent event. The most important episode was that of the June Days, a "slaves' war" that had broken out when the proletariat was threatened with losing the dominion over Paris it had enjoyed since February.

This aspect of class struggle characterized only the Paris revolution. The feeling in the provinces was quite different. Tocqueville's visit to Normandy in April for his electoral campaign had allowed him to experience directly the fact that not only was there a difference of attitude between the provinces and the capital; there was, for the first time, mutual hatred. And it was for this reason that the Constituent Assembly had been able to overcome the workers' uprising in Paris: it had all of France as its reserve army. Tocqueville stopped his writing in Sorrento after completing his account of that crucial June. In the midst of describing these great events, he spoke with a sort of bitter derision about the drafting of the Constitution, in which he had participated. Although he was prepared to defend that Constitution in a legalist spirit, he did not have much faith that it would last. With the perspective he gained at Sorrento, the Republic did not seem to him either stable or a suitable regime for a France that remained centralized and in which, as a consequence, the executive would always be powerful. He was not without remorse at having stepped up on the tribune in defense of the election of the president of the Republic by universal suffrage.

For even in Sorrento he maintained a link with Paris and kept up to date, with a delay of two weeks, on French political life, thanks for the most part to Beaumont's letters. It was so tumultuous, and changed its appearance so much from one day to the next, that asking Tocqueville's advice could seem futile. He himself felt this, though he counseled, on the whole, an attempt at reconciliation with the president, but without reducing the legislative power. In March, the prince-president considered bringing back Barrot. Louis-Napoléon expressed concern to Beaumont about Tocqueville's recovery, and Barrot was willing, if Tocqueville's health permitted, to entrust him once again with Foreign Affairs. A friend of Tocqueville's advised him at that

point to consolidate his relations with Paris. But in fact, another   457
scheme prevailed, the Faucher ministry of April 10.   ℀ ℀

If Tocqueville felt tied to politics still, he contemplated loosening
this tie. His meditations of the previous summer on his maturity and
decline led him to the conclusion that he must write a book: he would
be remembered more for what he had written than for what he had
done. The work he was contemplating was a historical meditation on
Napoléon, an episode of the great drama of the French Revolution
which, as events were proving, was not yet over. In short, Tocqueville,
whose interest in history sprang not out of imaginative curiosity or
a desire to resurrect the past but from the need to explain his own
time—to explain it to himself, so to speak—was contemplating the
notion of ceasing to participate in the accidental episodes of day-to-day
political life in order to attain to something more essential. We will
later observe the various transformations of this first seed of L'Ancien
Régime. [11]

Tocqueville asked Kergorlay's and Beaumont's advice, wrote to
Stoffels, and spoke to Ampère about this project. "He was still looking
for the most appropriate form for this work, which he felt to be crucial
for his reputation, because he hoped for a great success." He knew from
experience that he could not carry on with both composing such a
work and leading a political life. He thus had some notion of abandoning politics in the near future. Would he have done so if what
happened on December 2 had not taken place?

On his return to Paris, he was immediately caught up again in
political life. He found the situation had worsened since his departure
six months earlier. The Constitution, which forbade two consecutive
terms for the president, had so brought it about that in May 1852 there
would be elections for both the presidency and the Legislative Assembly, only a few days apart. No one thought that Louis-Napoléon
would step aside with good grace, and the party of order was convinced that the "reds" would take advantage of the power vacuum to
attempt an insurrection. These prospects paralyzed business as well as
political life.

The prince-president was still hesitating, not about what he should
do, since he was determined to remain in power and had no doubt that
the majority of the French people wanted him to remain, but over
ways and means.

[11]See below, Chapter 26.

458

灺 灺

On May 15, he summoned Tocqueville and had a talk with him.[12] Tocqueville, with some mental reservations, described to him the three ways by which he could manage to remain in the Elysée Palace:

—A coup d'état, an idea Tocqueville dismissed, trying to persuade the president that it would probably be a failure.

—Illegal reelection by universal suffrage in May 1852. In principle, Tocqueville dismissed this idea also. But in fact, his correspondence shows that he felt this course was the most probable. He resigned himself to it, hoping that the president's majority would be less than that of 1848. However, he was afraid that the generals of the Assembly, especially Lamoricière, would then launch a civil war. This danger seemed more formidable to him than an uprising provoked by the Mountain.

—Modifying the Constitution. For this, the Legislative Assembly would have to declare, by a three-quarters majority, the need to elect a new Constituent Assembly. Such a vote appeared to be quite difficult to obtain, not only from the republicans but also from the Orleanists. Even some of Tocqueville's friends, for instance Dufaure, were against it. Nevertheless, it had to be tried.

It is possible, though his notes do not say this, that the May 15 talk made Tocqueville decide to become a candidate for rapporteur of a plan for revision of the Constitution. He would thus make a prominent reentrance into public life, from which he had been standing somewhat aloof since his return. His health, indeed, remained delicate. He rented, in the first days of June, a house in Versailles—Grille du Grand Montreuil—which stood on the property of his friend Rivet. He came to Paris for the important sessions of the Assembly.

A petition signed by 233 members had called for the revision of the Constitution. A committee to study the various proposals for revision was then chosen in the floor committees and Tocqueville was made a member of it. This committee met from June 10 to July 8. On June 25, Tocqueville was elected rapporteur by eight votes as against five for the Duc de Broglie, one for Corcelle, and one for Barrot. The latter seems to have become rather ill-tempered and accused Tocqueville of having intrigued to win his appointment.

On July 8, Tocqueville read his report to the Assembly and concluded in favor of the election of a Constituent Assembly that would

<hr />

[12]The Tocqueville Archives contain a summary of this conversation, though it is unfortunately incomplete. It was published as an appendix to the *Souvenirs*, *O.C.* XII, 288–89.

proceed to an overall revision of the Constitution, not excluding even   459
the republican form itself.

After debates that took place from July 14 to July 19, during which
Barrot spoke in favor of the project and Dufaure against it, the revision
was voted in with 446 in favor and 278 against, among whom were
not only the Mountain and the republican left, but also the pure
Orleanists, all the African generals, and most of Tocqueville's friends,
except for Corcelle and Beaumont. In order for the project to be
adopted, a majority of three-quarters of the 724 votes, or 543 votes,
would have been required.[13]

At that time, certain friends of Tocqueville's were very interested
in the possibility that Louis-Philippe's third son, François d'Orléans,
Prince de Joinville, might run for president. Now that the Duc
d'Orléans was dead, the prince was no doubt the only one of Louis-
Philippe's sons who enjoyed any real popularity and he had always
passed for an adversary of the conservative party under the July
monarchy. But it seemed quite difficult to create a broad movement
in favor of him; Thiers and Le Journal des débats were refraining from
any commitment. Tocqueville saw this candidacy only as a useful way
to lessen the prince-president's majority and declared that he himself
would vote for him, but without promising the sort of public support
Dufaure seemed prepared to advocate. It is quite possible that Dufaure
was restrained from going further by his friend Tocqueville.

While waiting for the opening of the session, scheduled for November 4, Tocqueville, in his Versailles solitude, resumed the Souvenirs.
This time, he did not write as a witness of the great revolutionary days
of 1848, telling what he had seen, but as the minister of foreign affairs,
passing over the year between June 1848 and June 1849 to draw a
perceptive picture of the life of the ministry of June 2, 1849, and
describe certain of the problems with which he had had to deal. The
account was quite incomplete, for although he went on, rather compla-
cently, about the matter of the refugees in Constantinople, he said
almost nothing of the Roman affair that had taken up the better part
of his time and energies.

Yet the prorogation period of the Assembly, from August to November 1851, was not empty politically. Expressing the uneasiness of
the public, the departmental councils continued, despite the vote in the
Chamber, to call for revision of the Constitution. Seventy-nine out of

---

[13]Tocqueville's report, presented to the Chamber on July 8, was published in O.C. (Bmt) IX, 574–606.

460

ᴚ ᴚ

the eighty-four councils issued resolutions calling for revision, including that of the Manche after a speech by Tocqueville, who had been elected president for the third time.[14] It was at his instigation that the same departmental council called for the abrogation of the law of May 31, 1850, that had so mutilated universal suffrage.

The campaign for revision was not destined to succeed. Before the resumption of legislative work on November 4, the prince-president declared that he too was in favor of abrogating the law of May 31, which resulted in the resignation of Faucher and the government of April 10, for whom this law was the holy of holies. A new government was formed on October 27 with General de Saint-Arnaud as minister of war. The coup d'état was close at hand.

Tocqueville was of course one of the protesting deputies on the morning of December 2. He was among the members of the Assembly driven out by the regiment from the Bourbon Palace and took part in the session they held, with more than two hundred present, at the town hall of the 10th arrondissement near the present-day Carrefour de la Croix-Rouge, as Victor Hugo (who was not there) tells in *L'Histoire d'un crime:* "M. de Tocqueville, who was ill and who could be seen leaning back against the corner of a window, took a piece of bread from a soldier that he shared with M. Chambolle" and, when the representatives were transferred to the Orsay barracks, "M. de Tocqueville, ill, threw his coat on the floor in the recess of a window and lay down. He stayed lying thus for several hours."[15] But then Tocqueville, along with Barrot and the Duc de Broglie, was among the several representatives whom Colonel Feray, Bugeaud's son-in-law and Salvandy's cousin, put up for the night in his parlor while the others lay crowded together in the attics of the barracks.

The next day, he was in the contingent of fifty representives transported to Vincennes in a prison carriage. It was not until the evening of December 3 that Eugène, his valet, managed to join him. The same evening, he received a release order signed by the prefect of police, a favor due to the intervention either of his friend Janvier or of Chassériau, the painter's brother. He refused to leave before his colleagues.

Most of the latter were freed on the morning of the fourth. Tocqueville had accepted this captivity, which he had anticipated for a long time, with great calm, like "a man who has done his duty," more

---

[14]The resolution of the departmental council of the Manche (August 28, 1851), proposed by Gaslonde, and the deliberations on the subject can be found in *L'Annuaire de la Manche* of 1852, 198–222.

[15]These two allusions to Tocqueville in *L'Historie d'un crime* can be found respectively on pages 67 and 76 of vol. 8 of the edition of the *Oeuvres complètes* of 1968.

concerned about his wife than anything else, since she was also, it   461
appears, in bad health. The coup d'état of December 2 put an end to   𝒴 𝒴
a period of his life that had begun almost thirteen years before. He
never forgave the man who had brought this about for the affront to
representative government and the consequent loss of civil liberties.

On December 14, he gave his opinion of the event in a letter
addressed to a compatriot of the Manche—perhaps the mayor of
Tocqueville—who had asked for news of him:

What has just happened in Paris is abominable, in form and substance, and
when the details are known, they will appear even nastier than the event as
a whole. As for the event itself, it was contained as an embryo in the February
revolution, like a chick in an egg. For it to emerge, all that was needed was
enough time for the incubation. As soon as socialism appeared, one should
have predicted the reign of the sword. One engendered the other. I had been
expecting it for a long time, and even though I am filled with shame and
sorrow for our country and great indignation over certain acts of violence
and certain contemptible actions that exceeded all bounds, I feel little surprise
and no inner confusion . . . The nation, at this moment, is mad with fear
of the socialists and a passionate desire to regain its well-being. It is incapable
and, though I say it with much regret, unworthy of being free . . . This nation
which has forgotten over the last thirty-four years what bureaucratic and
military despotism is like . . . is getting a taste of it once again, and this time
without the seasoning of greatness and glory.

Part V

INTERNAL EXILE

25

TOCQUEVILLE AND

THE SECOND EMPIRE

TOCQUEVILLE'S parliamentary career had been brutally shattered by the coup d'état of December 2. But he thought it a duty, in the face of the lies of the government-inspired press, to reaffirm the truth concerning the events of that day and their causes. It was impossible, of course, to publish any contradiction whatsoever of the official account in France itself. But although the English press for the most part had accepted the explanation that the president had done no more than anticipate a surprise attack against his person engineered by the Legislative Assembly—or, if not that, then he'd moved to ward off the threat of the "reds" seizing power in 1852—it would not refuse to publish the account of a member of the opposition with Tocqueville's credentials. His friend Harriet Lewin Grote, the wife of the historian George Grote, happened to be in Paris and agreed to take the text of his article back to England. She gave it to Henry Reeve, who made the translation and saw to its publication in the *Times* on December 11. This long article, after exonerating the Assembly for taking measures other than defensive ones in regard to the executive power, revealed the contents of two precious documents that had been concealed from the curiosity of the police: the summary of the meeting held by the Assembly at the town hall of the 10th arrondissement, including a list of the 218 protesting deputies, almost all men of the right and the center, some of whom were known and respected across the Channel, and the decree drawn up by the High Court of Justice, which, meeting quietly, had removed the president from office for abuse of authority and been able to pass its sentence before the arrival of the commissioner of police. Although the article was of course published in the *Times* anonymously, its text was corroborated by indisputable official documents.[1]

At almost the same moment, an account of the action taken by the National Assembly appeared in London. It was a pamphlet, written in French, entitled *Récit de la conduite qu'a tenue l'Assemblée nationale au 2 Décembre 1851;* a copy was found among Tocqueville's papers. It cannot have been written by him, because its judgment of Dupin's actions is favorable and this is a conclusion that Tocqueville, in his concern for the truth and his scorn for the man, would have been incapable of expressing in print even in order to cover his traces. But the pamphlet proves to have been drawn from the best sources and it may even contain certain things that Tocqueville said. It denies the bold lie of the French newspapers that neither the Duc de Broglie nor Dufaure nor Tocqueville had been arrested, and stresses the fact that Tocqueville refused to be released before his colleagues.

There was one last civic function for Tocqueville, however: the departmental council. He presided once more at a small session held in March 1852, but, learning that henceforth departmental councillors would be required to swear an oath of allegiance to the new regime, he published a letter of resignation addressed to his electors of the canton of Montebourg. In it, he skirted any explanation of his real motive, because he foresaw the possibility that one day it would perhaps be necessary to enter the departmental council by swearing an oath of allegiance in order to fight the government, and he did not want to cast any aspersion on those councillors who thought taking the oath compatible with a certain independence. The following July, elections for the departmental councils were held and Tocqueville refused to be a candidate. This position of principle caused him considerable distress:

All of this particular consequence of December 2 is the part that has affected me personally in the most painful way. In my department, I had a position that offered only untroubled charms, one of considerable authority in the important affairs of this part of the world—a sort of rule by men concerned for the personal well-being of those in their charge, quite independent of political opinions. What came out of that side of public life cast a reflection on private life and made it more agreeable.[2]

[1] *The Times* of December 11, 1851. The French original has been lost, but a retranslation of the English text is included in *O.C.* VI, 119–29.
[2] Letter to Beaumont of May 1, 1852, *O.C.* VIII, 3: 45.

Vieillard, a former representative of the Manche in the Constituent   467
Assembly and the Legislative Assembly, after having been a republican   𝕏 𝕏
deputy under the July monarchy had become friends with Tocqueville,
especially after 1848. He was a personal friend of Louis-Napoléon's,
having formerly been his brother's tutor and having been somewhat
involved in the prince-president's own education as well. He was a
senator in the new regime (and the only one who dared vote against
the restoration of the Empire). On December 5, he had appeared at
Tocqueville's home conveying apologies from Louis-Napoléon for the
arrest of December 2, and he harbored no grudge for having been
shown the door. He continued to feel friendly toward Tocqueville,
who had helped him become vice-president of the departmental council in 1849, and undertook to maintain Tocqueville in his local situation. In July 1852, he came unexpectedly to spend the day at the
Château de Tocqueville, where the conversation scarcely left the topic
of eighteenth-century literature.[3] He then suggested to Louis-Napoléon that Tocqueville be excused from taking the oath. Tocqueville
would have consented to this, but there were protests—easy enough
to understand—from Persigny, then minister of the interior. The
following year, Vieillard sounded Tocqueville out on behalf of the
emperor to see if he would consent to resume his post as minister of
foreign affairs, an incident that is very revealing of a personality trait
of Louis-Napoléon's that Tocqueville had observed back in 1849—that
he was less forgetful of courtesies shown him than he was of abuse.
Naturally, Tocqueville refused to serve the authoritarian Empire.

He made a point, on May 23, 1857, of attending Vieillard's funeral.
"Everyone in the official world was there, and I had the satisfaction
of turning my backside to several former friends who were offering
me their faces." His picture of the hypocritical indignation that seized
the elite of the regime when it was announced that the burial would
be secular is so ferociously vivid that it makes one sorry this was
Tocqueville's only direct contact with court circles and the upper levels
of the imperial administration.[4]

In the deputation from the Manche of 1848, there was another
representative who owed his election to Tocqueville, and that was
Boulatignier, the second deputy from Valognes. In 1849, Boulatignier,
accepting the new regime, had chosen to become a member of the
Council of State. Tocqueville would have forgiven him for this if he

[3]Letter to Beaumont dated July 16, 1852, O.C. VIII, 3: 61–64.
[4]Letter to Ampère dated May 25, 1857, O.C. XI, 57–80.

468

卍 卍

had not voted affirmatively in the deliberation on the confiscation of the goods of the Orléans family. "From your seat as judge . . . you cover with the false image of justice the greatest and least excusable despoiling that has taken place in France since the worst days of our great Revolution," he wrote to his old friend. The pain this act of Boulatignier's caused him kept him from sleeping.[5] For it was the fact that decent men were going over to the other side that scandalized and deeply troubled Tocqueville. When he learned, on the other hand, that Dupin, whom he had already described in his *Souvenirs* as a "monkey" and a "jackal," had been won over, he felt the satisfaction of seeing a logical process reach its conclusion. Yet skill in collecting honors or lofty positions by means of platitudes irritated him. He despised Cormenin and Troplong, those former liberals who now presided over the Council of State and the Supreme Court of Appeal, the chief administrative body and the highest court of the new regime, and he showed a stubborn resentment toward Billault and Stourm, defectors from the old "young left." Of the literary men, he was harder on Senator Sainte-Beuve, though he called him an "insignificant rogue," than he was on Senator Mérimée, whom he made fun of, but who, after all, had bounced the empress on his knee when she was a child. He retained some affection for Gobineau, despite all the irritation he felt over Gobineau's theories, so hostile to human liberty. After having wanted to see him withdraw from the diplomatic world, he understood that Gobineau was making a career of it. He himself wished that men who did not share the new ideology of the Empire would serve it faithfully, but without asking favors or making illegitimate requests. In order to help his nephew Hubert enter the diplomatic world, he applied to Drouyn de Lhuys, who was once again a minister.

He even accepted certain services that helped him in his preparation of *L'Ancien Régime*, services zealously performed by civil servants who had taken advantage of the change of regime: Taschereau, the director of the Bibliothèque Nationale, the librarian Haureau, and the director of the National Archives, Chabrier, who, it was true, had remained fairly independent.

But Tocqueville's emotional life was bounded by his friendships with those former companions in his political battles who were now in internal exile and dispersed throughout the country. Beaumont first of all, who had retired to the small estate of La Borde in Beaumont-

[5]Unpublished letter to Boulatignier dated November 8, 1852. Copy in the Tocqueville Archives.

sur-Dême (Sarthe) and was pluckily struggling to recover a comfortable way of life very much jeopardized by the encumbered inheritance of his father-in-law, Georges de Lafayette, and who was absorbed in the education of his children, the oldest of whom, Antonin, would make a career for himself in the Army of Africa. Tocqueville would have liked Beaumont to have a more active intellectual life, and exchanged with him a German newspaper that made it possible, despite the frequent seizures of the paper at the border, to find out what people in the rest of the world were thinking. One of the last pleasures of his life would be seeing the republication of Beaumont's book on Ireland, brought out by the author. And there was Corcelle, more and more absorbed in his Catholic faith, the only one to whom Tocqueville sometimes confided his metaphysical qualms, though at the same time he would tease Corcelle gently for his excessive piety. Rivet, a model of loyalty, who had become an administrator of railways in the West. Lanjuinais, traveling and studying monetary problems, biding his time until he emerged as an opposition deputy under the liberal Empire. Dufaure and Freslon, who had taken up their lawyer vocations again, Freslon as well informed as it was possible for an opponent of the regime to be; he combined a solid understanding of history with strong ties of friendship in many circles, and he had a preferred place among Tocqueville's friends. Lastly, Ampère, who, unoccupied since the death of Madame Récamier, had attached himself to Tocqueville's household and until 1857 would stay with him for long periods. He was still in good form, applying himself to too many different studies to write a great book, but a true "intellectual volcano," the most eloquent of talkers, the most agreeable of guests. In these friendships, Tocqueville made the comparison, for himself and his friends, to "the Jews of the Middle Ages, who needed to live together in order to recover a homeland."

His family relationships had become somewhat strained, not with Comte Hervé, who died on June 9, 1856, at the age of eighty-three, in the small house in Clairoix, near Compiègne, where he had been spending his summers for several years, and whose death, more or less unexpected, plunged Alexis into profound grief, but with his brothers Edouard and Hippolyte.

In truth, the time of intimacy, of long visits to Baugy, the home of "the Edouards," was several years in the past now. "The Hippolytes" had beautified their residence at Nacqueville, to the west of Cherbourg, but there had been no visits between the two households since 1846. The lack of good feeling between Madame de Tocqueville

470

𝔂 𝔂

and her sisters-in-law had only paved the way for an estrangement now aggravated by political differences.

In 1852, Edouard de Tocqueville stood as a candidate in the legislative elections in the Oise. His electoral circular (which one newspaper unfortunately printed over the signature A. de Tocqueville) formally expressed approval of the coup d'état and the regime it had instituted. On February 14, Tocqueville wrote an indignant letter to his brother: "The ruination of liberty, of that sacred and noble cause to which I have devoted my life, my renunciation of public life, the humiliation of my country, the exile of my friends or their voluntary dispersal, have not, I believe, been as bitter to me as the profound schism between us ... We no longer agree either in our hatreds, or our hopes, or our fears."[6] Tocqueville continued to show his affection for his nephews, and Edouard went to Cannes during the last days of his brother's life. But the subjects that most passionately concerned Alexis were forbidden in their conversations.

The situation with Hippolyte was no different, but in Alexis's eyes, it was Hippolyte's wife, Emilie, who was responsible:

My poor Hippolyte . . . has become as tractable, as perfectly submissive, zealous, and obsequious, as he was once a liberal and a demagogue. Citizen Tocqueville burns to be a senator or, if such a lofty ambition is forbidden him, he at least hopes that the glory of being a deputy will sooner or later be within his reach. In this hope, he becomes so insipid that it irritates me, but he is so good that I reproach myself for having become irritated. From time to time, I very crudely give him a piece of my mind and am then angry with myself for having done it. It would be fairer to tell his wife what I think, for she is the one who holds sway and rules the roost now without even permitting him the appearance of authority that such despotism can afford to concede. As long as the husband hadn't a penny and was good for nothing, the wife left him in his corner, but now that he is rich and may begin to have a salary, she has come along and taken control of everything.[7]

Thus, following the aftermath of the coup d'état, Tocqueville returned to private life and an emotional world in which generous loyalties to his old friends were conjoined with bruised feelings within his family.

· · ·

[6]Letter to his brother dated February 14, 1852, cited by Rédier, *M. de Tocqueville*, 227–30.
[7]Letter to Beaumont, January 22, 1858, *O.C.* VIII, 3: 536.

Two actions, quite distinct from each other, marked the farewell to his political career. One was the adoption of a position for the long term, a sort of provisional commitment to the future. The other was a reflection, in retrospect, on the relation between practical politics and theory.

471 ⚘ ⚘

The first was a letter to the Comte de Chambord dated January 14, 1852. In this letter, Tocqueville expressed the idea that the only possible alternative to the imperial despotism was a liberal monarchy to which the legitimate sovereign, who represented a traditional guarantee of order, had a better chance of winning over the French than anyone else. And Tocqueville, without trying to outline a precise political program, indicated its indispensable foundations: individual liberties, national representation, free and public parliamentary debate, and freedom of the press.[8]

This letter must be seen in the context of the attempts made to merge the different branches of the royal family after the end of the monarchy in 1848, attempts at which moderate Orleanists like Salvandy worked very hard. As we know, the upshot was no more than a semi-reconciliation between the Comte de Chambord and his cousins, the sons of Louis-Philippe. In 1850, Guizot had been asked for his opinion and had advised the Comte de Chambord to adopt openly a parliamentary regime. The coup d'état of December 2 had given new ardor to the partisans of merging the branches, and in his biography of Berryer Charles Lacombe gives us information that throws light on Tocqueville's letter.[9]

The Duc de Levis, representative of the Comte de Chambord, had been introduced to Tocqueville by Corcelle, who also took him to the homes of Barrot, Vivien, Rivet, and Dufaure. In short, it was in the name of his friends that Tocqueville, who had been their spokesman several times, wrote his letter. Corcelle also took part in meetings on the merging that brought together Salvandy, Broglie, Montebello, Duchâtel, and the legitimist Moulin, secretary of this unofficial committee. Berryer, Guizot, and Tocqueville apparently followed the work that was being done without participating in it. On March 22, 1852, Tocqueville tried to demonstrate to Rémusat, still in exile, that it was the only possible alternative to the government in power and

---

[8]This *Lettre au comte de Chambord* is dated January 14, 1852. It was published by *La Gazette de France* on November 23, 1871, then by Rédier, *M. de Tocqueville,* 244–53. The Tocqueville Archives contain a rough draft of it, the Kergorlay Archives a copy.
[9]Charles Lacombe, *Vie de Berryer* 3, 227ff.

472

ﺀﻼ ﺀﻼ

begged this faithful supporter of the Duchesse d'Orléans to come over to their side.[10] It was to these efforts to bring about a merging that Tocqueville was referring on May 13 of that year when, reaffirming that it was the only practical course, he wrote to Corcelle in deliberately obscure terms: "Naturally, I am leaving aside what has so preoccupied you during recent times and which has been very important and is even still very important, because of the influence of the fact on the attitude of the parties."[11]

For several years, with a hope that became more and more slender, Tocqueville would keep himself informed as best he could about the attempts at merging. Starting in 1852, he no longer believed in the possibility of a republic made stable by the simple strengthening of the executive. As we have seen, in 1849 he was contemplating such a regime, but the necessary "tool" had turned into a despot. It seemed to him that the specific remedy for this new anarchy would have to be sought in one of the old dynasties that still had enough prestige to counterbalance the impulses of the people, but for this, it was necessary to join their present union to the force of tradition.

According to Kergorlay, Tocqueville's letter to the Comte de Chambord had no more than a polite reception. And it is true that among the papers of this old legitimist friend the following note exists, in his hand, accompanying a copy of the letter:

"It seems that the Comte de Chambord simply expressed out loud the feeling that this piece of writing was interesting and contained things of value. But he confined himself to that and gave no indication that he saw it as a document of far-reaching significance."[12]

On April 12, 1852, Tocqueville, in his capacity as president of the Académie des Sciences Morales et Politiques, was to give an account of the essays that had been sent to the Academy on the subjects it had offered for competition the previous year, and then announce the prizes.[13] He preceded the awarding of the prizes with a preamble in which he examined the relations between political science and the art of governing. At one time, he said, he had viewed the former as the road that led to the latter. Now, after he had spent twelve years in politics, his ideas were less rigid. Practical politics had a certain autonomy and required different qualities of public men than did the study

[10]Unpublished letters, de Rémusat Archives, Lafitte-Vigordame.
[11]O.C. XV, 2, 53.
[12]Kergorlay Archives, note in the hand of Louis de Kergorlay.
[13]Speech given during the annual public session of the Académie des Sciences Morales et Politiques by M. de Tocqueville, president of the Academy (April 3, 1852).

of societies. Yet these societies could nonetheless be analyzed, from many points of view, by human sciences as exact as those applied to individual human beings.

Tocqueville was giving a sort of last testament as he left public life, and he may have been remembering that, during the time when he frequented his salon, Talleyrand had taken advantage of the occasion, when he offered a eulogy before this same Academy, to present a final statement of the principles guiding diplomacy. Tocqueville, at the same time that he was taking his leave of the theater of action, implicitly revealed that he was going back to work on one of those great studies that allow the pervading tone of an epoch to be understood.

None of this stood in the way of his sharing in the disarray of the liberal elites, a disarray that would manifest itself during the authoritarian Empire by opposing reactions. There were the optimists, or the men who tried to fool themselves, proclaiming that "this" would not last, could not last, because it was contrary to reason and the spirit of the century. There were pessimists like Rémusat, returned from exile, who remarked that the government was not the culprit, that it was laying down a lasting foundation for itself with the full consent of the majority of the French people. Some of these pessimists spoke of an irremediable decadence, evoking the great precedent of the Byzantine Empire.

Tocqueville rejected this analogy: "Your Romans were dead, while we are asleep," he wrote to Ampère, and, without being more specific, he said that the French nation had occasionally experienced such periods of sleep in the past.[14] In a general way, he believed that this sleep would be a long one. He was struck by the difference in mentality between the men of his generation, with their aspirations to justice, and those of the generation that followed, with its hunger for material well-being. "The first," he wrote to Barrot (October 26, 1853), "are already like those antediluvian monsters one sees in the cases of natural history museums, while life belongs to another race. But," he added, "the present race will also pass and will be replaced by another that will be more like us than like it, I'm convinced. But will we ourselves witness this new transformation? I doubt it. Some time will have to go by to obliterate the deplorable impressions left by these last few years and for the French to return, I won't say to a passionate love of

473

474

৯ৎ ৯ৎ

liberty, but to that pride in themselves, to that habit of speaking and writing freely, that need to at least call their obedience into question, which is in the spirit of the century and in the oldest instinct of their race."[15]

This hope in the future did not soothe Tocqueville's bitterness, a bitterness which was like a constant ache in the soul, sometimes dull, sometimes piercing, which he could not escape except through work. In June 1853, alluding to the progress of *L'Ancien Régime et la Révolution,* he wrote to Freslon: "In this way I have managed to get out of myself, myself being a very bad lodging. But try as I may I can't prevent myself hearing, even in the midst of my work, the muffled echo of contemporary events. I manage to be calm, but not cheerful." And, four months later, to the same correspondent: "You don't want me to be sad. That's brave advice, but how to follow it? How can one help being sad at seeing this nation, always the same, so refractory toward freedom and so biddable in servitude, not only tolerating its fetters but shaking them as though in triumph and kissing them in ecstasy."[16] It was also with great sadness that he crossed the frontiers of his country, on his return from Germany in 1854, from England in 1857. Nevertheless, he remained on the lookout for weaknesses that could bring about the decline or the fall of the system, and had never followed with so much interest the economic and monetary crises. He watched foreign policy as closely as he could, even though he said that the powers-that-be would not be able to make a fatal error until the day when there were no longer any declared opponents of the regime left within the country. In every regime, Tocqueville insisted, the confidence gained through a series of successes created the conditions for its downfall. But Tocqueville, with his varying moods, did not have an unalterable opinion on this subject. One can find, in his hand, false predictions side by side with keenly perceptive analyses of the strengths and weaknesses of the Empire. Nevertheless, his most consistent view, expressed as early as 1852, was that this regime would continue without laying the basis for anything, a general idea which history would confirm. Tocqueville described the imperial regime, in sum, as a new variety of historical accident, a sort of pause in the revolutionary process that was leading France, together with Europe as a whole, toward democracy. He wrote on November 24, 1853: "The revolutionary era has not come to an end either here or elsewhere, and

---

[15]*O.C.* (Bmt) VII, 300–302.
[16]Letter to Freslon dated June 9, 1853, *O.C.* (Bmt) VI, 209, and September 23, 1853 (unpublished, copy by Beaumont in the Tocqueville Archives).

this is still no more than an episode in the great drama that is not even 475 close to coming to its conclusion. Even those who are playing out the present farce have no faith that it will have a long run."

Yet its revolutionary roots were what assured the imperial regime the broad popular base that made it, like the imperialism of ancient Rome, a regime of country people and soldiers. In a letter of May 5, 1852, to Lamoricière, Tocqueville insisted on the role of the regular army since December 2, a role without precedent since it did not even exist in the time of the great Napoléon: "The army is the dominant class in this phase of our long revolution, as the old nobility was the dominant class of the Restoration, the bourgeoisie the dominant class of the July government, and the workers the dominant class under the Republic."[17]

The French were not so much enthusiastic about the new regime as "submissive" to it. On the whole, France was "tired, enervated, half rotten," and asked only "to serve under whoever would assure its material well-being." And this malady, in the form of fear of the "reds," had struck the upper classes as well as the lower: "It is not the farmers, the bourgeois, the shopowners only, who, so long as they are assured tranquillity and the sale of their produce or their merchandise, are happy to sacrifice the freedom, the dignity, the honor of their country." The same cowardice could be found in the salons of Paris, which were full "of so-called gentlemen and pitiful little weaklings who were so very afraid of 1852, who trembled so much for their incomes that really what has just happened, what is still happening, the ignominy of this new regime, fills them with joy."

Of all the adherents of the imperial regime, Tocqueville particularly resented the old legitimists and those devoted to the Church. Up to now, the first had laid claim to a loyalty based on honor, the second professed a morality based on human dignity. The hypocritical betrayal of their convictions by both groups outraged Tocqueville.

The old legitimists feared nothing so much as the return of the king, now reconciled with the Orléans, a return that would be accompanied by liberal institutions. They were quite content with an absolutism that assured their local positions. "Nothing proves so clearly how the dearth of public offices in which they have been living for twenty-five years has given them a ravenous hunger for this kind of food." They were "like certain believers [who] seek for Heaven while spending as much

---

[17]Unpublished letter, from a Rédier copy in the Tocqueville Archives.

476
苌 苌

time as possible in this vale of tears." The most absurd pretexts served them as alibis, like the so-called testament of Louis-Napoléon that was supposed to have designated the Comte de Chambord as his successor. And to the duchesse who said she liked Bonaparte because it seemed he was going to erect a commemorative ex-voto in the Temple, Tocqueville answered dryly that one owed some courtesy to those whose heritage one had confiscated. The fact that rural France was being officered by members of the nobility who served the regime by putting aside their principles angered Tocqueville profoundly. And he understood the orders to stand aloof from such activity given—often in vain—by the Comte de Chambord.

Tocqueville felt just as lively a resentment against the clergy, who, at the instigation of *L'Univers,* were making a headlong rush into servitude. For him, this was a subject of profound affliction: "I am saddened and disturbed more than I ever have been before when I see in so many Catholics this aspiration toward tyranny, this attraction to servitude, this love of force, of the police, of the censor, of the gallows."[18] Madame Swetchine tried in vain to make him concede that the clergy were more obliged to inculcate private virtue than they were civic virtue. He could not accept the bishops' flattery of this "new Constantine," this "envoy of the Almighty"—for a sovereign surrounded, as Changarnier put it, by "crooks and pimps." To one of those intrepid sycophants, Monsignor Daniel, with whom he had had good relations under the Republic, he wrote:

I wonder if there is not some danger for religion in siding with the new power and recommending it in the name of God. Even in my own time, I have seen the Church confusing its cause with that of the first Emperor in the same way. I have seen it shielding the Restoration with its word in the same way, and it did not seem to me that it profited from this course of conduct. In a country like ours that is undergoing a revolution, the judgments made on the powers-that-be of a given moment cannot be unanimous; in these unhappy times it is not merely a matter of censuring the government's acts. One questions its morality, its laws. In France today, there are still a great many men who regard it as an act of conscience not to recognize the new power. I believe one could not deny that among them there are several who, by the range of their intellect and the integrity of their lives, often by the sincerity of their faith, are the natural allies of the Church . . .
Even among those who approve of the course now being taken by those in power, how many respected the beginnings? To break oaths that were

[18]Letter to his brother dated February 14, 1852, cited by Rédier, *M. de Tocqueville,* 227–30.

sworn and sworn again so freely and so solemnly; to overturn by violence laws that one was duty bound to respect; to massacre unarmed men in Paris in order to inspire a healthy terror and forestall any resistance . . . These acts . . . are absolutely condemned by universal morality . . .[19]

Montalembert's support of the coup d'état particularly exasperated Tocqueville. They had known each other for a long time, had taken part in the same weekly dinners in the 1830s. The "mountebank" side of the man had always annoyed Tocqueville, who had not in the least approved of the creation of a Catholic party. But on October 10, 1852, this very impulsive man published a courageous pamphlet entitled *Les Interêts catholiques au XIXe siècle*. Despite their quarrel, he sent a copy to Tocqueville. Although their differences of opinion continued, the two men henceforth enjoyed a fundamental agreement that expressed itself in a few very beautiful letters. Tocqueville set the tone:

What you have just done is in the service not only of ordinary liberty but perhaps even more of religion . . . It is a great act that deserves not only the thanks but the gratitude of those who resented you most after December 2. This letter would lose its merit in your eyes if I did not add that I was one of those men.

I have never been more convinced than I am today that only liberty . . . and religion, through a combined effort, are capable of raising men out of the mire in which democratic equality naturally plunges them as soon as one of these two supports is lacking.[20]

But the Catholic closest in sentiments to Tocqueville was Monsignor Dupanloup, who extolled liberty in a pastoral letter dated December 2, 1852, and whose triumphant election to the Académie Française in 1854 would be taken for a vigorous act of opposition.

These attitudes inspired in Tocqueville a sort of repulsion for the worldly life of Paris that was rather new in him. In the salons, conversation battened off rumors of which one knew no more in the evening than one had in the morning. In these salons, one was more and more likely to meet uninteresting people (he sighed when he remembered the brilliant society of his youth) or adherents of the new order of things. He wrote to Madame de Circourt—in a rather cutting

---

[19]Letter to Monsignor Daniel dated March 4, 1858. Tocqueville's copy in the Tocqueville Archives. Partial publication without name of addressee by Beaumont, *O.C.* (Bmt) VII, 490–92.

[20]Letter dated December 1, 1852, Montalembert Archives.

478

𝕷 𝕸

way, given the actual eclecticism of her salon: "Put on one side all the good people who are nothing more than well-meaning fools and on another all the intelligent people who are nothing more than witty rogues or—what is perhaps worse, seeing how many of them there are—merely quite ordinary souls slightly ornamented or prettied up by their wits. I ask you to count on your fingers what is left, and won't this give you a certain desire to go off into the wilderness?"[21]

There were, of course, a few special salons, but for Tocqueville, Paris was now, aside from the Bibliothèque Impériale and the Archives, primarily the seat of the two Académies he belonged to. It was essential to maintain their liberal majorities. Not only did the "perpetual" secretaries, Villemain and Mignet, launch anguished appeals at every election to their right-thinking colleagues, but men like Guizot and de Broglie responded to this reminder with the same passion with which they had formerly governed. Tocqueville himself was one of the proponents of the Barrot candidacy for a place as correspondent in the Académie des Sciences Morales, a candidacy that annoyed the government. Barrot was elected by a majority of two votes, Tocqueville having come in from Compiègne to vote even though he was ill, and Beaumont from his distant manor. Wrath descended on the Institute at that point. It was given a new set of rules, and within the guilty Academy the government appointed ten members on its own authority. Received in rather the same way as the professors appointed under the Vichy regime were received by colleagues who had been recruited by election, these members of the "garrison" were apparently pitifully humble. The Institute, in general, remained the last bastion of liberalism.

Was it any better in Normandy than in Paris? Tocqueville doubted it, often comparing the province to a cave into which no ray of light could penetrate now that papers no longer printed any objective news. People talked about nothing but their private affairs. They were uneasy at heart but had a dread of showing their fear, and for Tocqueville this was the worst sort of fear. He had good relations with his Norman neighbors, but during his wanderings he did not attempt to make new friends. In the course of the year he spent at Tours, where châteaus and salons would have been open to him, he visited only the archbishop, the very moderate Cardinal Morlot, and the archivist, who thought as he did politically.

Yet he could not help taking an interest in politics from a distance.

[21]Letter dated October 31, 1854, *O.C.* XVIII, 216.

Thus, after censuring the tergiversations of the emperor and calling the 479
reopening of the eastern question no more than a monks' quarrel (over
the possession of the keys to the churches of the Holy Sepulcher), he
gave his approval, in principle, to the war with Russia, though at the
same time he lamented the frightful cost of the Crimean campaign and
felt some anger that the English army, coming from a country that had
free institutions, should show itself to be inferior to the French. Despite
Faucher's insistent urgings, he believed, and wrote as much to Barrot,
that the present danger for France was no reason to give one's support
to the government. It was enough to do nothing that would be harmful
to the country in time of war.

It would be tedious to enumerate all of Tocqueville's criticisms of
domestic policy. There is, however, one point worth noting: he did
not see the usefulness of the policy of great public works, the "Hauss-
mannization" of Paris in particular, and his opposition on this point
reminds one of Montesquieu's incomprehension confronting the ur-
banism of Tourny, the administrator of Bordeaux.

From 1852 on, Tocqueville's life was organized around the writing
of his book, *L'Ancien Régime et la Révolution*. Yet circumstances having
nothing to do with this work imposed certain obligations on him,
sometimes stringent ones.

There was his health, first of all. As we have seen, in the spring of
1850 he suffered a grave pulmonary crisis in which he spat blood, and
this was followed by a slow and incomplete recovery at Sorrento the
following winter. Another attack, a very serious one, occurred in the
autumn of 1852. Tocqueville, stricken with pleurisy, remained in bed
for at least two months, from October to December. He left the place
de la Madeleine for a sunny and sheltered house in the rue de Cour-
celles, which apparently did not prevent his having relapses in January
and February. Deciding the Normandy summer would be too rainy,
he settled in Saint-Cyr, near Tours, not far from the celebrated Dr.
Pierre Bretonneau, whom he trusted, and he remained there for a year.
But these were grave crises. We know from certain references in his
correspondence that his stomach often gave him problems, and he
suffered many bouts of flu and bronchitis. He was sensitive to changes
of season, to the cold, to wind, and to rain, a series of intermittent signs
which, despite Beaumont's statements, point to a latent illness that
continued until the final crisis, when he once again spat blood, in June
1858.

Another imperative was the state of Tocqueville's finances. He was
not a rich landowner, as we have seen, but a comfortable landowner

480

彪 彪

who had to watch his spending more than many people of his class. The loss of his salary as representative in the Assemblies of the Republic, which amounted to nine thousand francs, deprived him of almost a third of his income. We do not know whether the rent from his farms, which made up the greater part of this income, kept pace with the rise in prices at the beginning of the Empire—not very successfully, no doubt. Certainly the household maintained a way of life that was modest for its time, though not for ours, with three servants and the upkeep of a château. After 1856, his share of the inheritance from Comte Hervé would augment these resources. The household's financial situation would probably have been better if Tocqueville had not bought stocks and bonds in railways in the United States which yielded no interest because of the economic crisis there that began in 1856. But, at least before 1856, each exceptional expenditure had to be compensated for by some savings. After the stay in Germany in 1854, for instance, the Tocquevilles lived in a very modest house in Compiègne, then in an apartment in the rue de Fleurus in Paris whose meanness made their friend Mélanie de Corcelle indignant.

It was in the course of a vagabond existence that had none of the seasonal rhythm of the years of his political career that Tocqueville was to write his *Ancien Régime*. For almost three years (from September 1852 to July 1855), he did not go to Tocqueville, and from the time of the coup d'état to the publication of *L'Ancien Régime* (June 16, 1856), he spent altogether only slightly more than twenty months in Paris. These displacements and the sort of life they necessitated were closely bound up with the genesis of *L'Ancien Régime*. We will therefore not try to separate them in the following chapter.

26

L'ANCIEN RÉGIME
ET LA RÉVOLUTION

ONE MONTH AFTER the publication of *L'Ancien Régime et la Révolution* in June 1856, Tocqueville wrote to Montalembert: "The book I have just published and its sequel have been rolling around in my head for better than fifteen years. The plan ripened and the shape was set during a grave illness I suffered in 1850; I can say that since then I have thought of it constantly."[1]

Tocqueville is usually precise when he makes a statement about his own chronology, and in this case other letters, though they are less precise, confirm what he says. He would thus have first thought of writing a book on the Revolution around 1841. The year before, he had published the second part of the *Democracy;* for two years, he had been deputy from Valognes and was already feeling some dissatisfaction with this job in the parliament he had gone to such trouble to win for himself, an attitude characteristic of his temperament. Finally —and this could well be a clearer sign, given his propensity to go thoroughly into any subject he tackled—when he was elected to the Académie Française on December 23, 1841, he found himself obliged to prepare, for the following April, the eulogy for Lacuée de Cessac, his predecessor, and to do this, had to delve into the history of the First Empire. But other preoccupations deflected him from this path: his interest in the conquest of Algeria led him to sketch out a book on the English rule in India. Most important, in 1842 he was drawn by the illusory hope of playing a great political role within the liberal

---

[1]Unpublished letter dated July 10, 1856, Montalembert Archives.

opposition, and, getting more and more caught up in political activity, did not begin to slow down until 1850. It was thus especially in the moments of lassitude and doubt of the sort he often experienced that he would give thought to reentering the literary world with a work on the Revolution. Nevertheless, it would be difficult not to make a suggestive comparison: beginning in 1825, he had contemplated studying American democracy without, apparently, putting his ideas down on paper. Between 1841 and 1850, he dreamed in the same way of this new work. When one admires the confidence with which he conducted his American investigation, when one marvels at the sure instinct with which he found his way through the archives of the eighteenth century, is it not possible to think that these long periods of preliminary meditation determined the organization of his work?

We can pin down precisely the moment when he decided to carry out his intention of writing on the Revolution. Three letters to his most intimate friends, Kergorlay, Beaumont, and Stoffels, dated December 15, 26, and 30, 1850, impart this information, and two plans from the same period constitute the germ of the future work.[2]

Tocqueville was then in Sorrento, recovering slowly from the chest ailment that, as we have seen, endangered his life the previous March. In contrast to his daily life in the Assemblies of the Republic, this stay at Sorrento was a period of rest in which he could withdraw from the press of events.

At the time, he was recording in his *Souvenirs* those events in which he had been caught up since February 1848. But the work was not enough for "the activity of his mind," which his solitude had overstimulated. He asked himself about the future of public life in France and became more deeply aware of the fragility of this liberal Republic to which he had given his full support. At the same time, he sought to envisage his own future. Despite his recent rise in the political world and the chance that he might resume his position as minister, about which his correspondents kept him informed, he considered himself more a writer than a statesman. Since 1840, he had published only brief occasional texts, and yet it was as a writer that he had some chance of leaving "a mark" on the world. But "life's boundaries are revealing themselves more clearly and drawing closer, and one must therefore hurry."

Tocqueville was incapable of writing on a subject that did not

[2]See *O.C.* II, 2, critical note introducing this volume, 12–13.

impassion him to the point of anguish. Form and style, which he controlled with such severe exaction in his writing, were only tools, and his thought, fed by an ethic that took seriously all the actions of life, was incapable of being casual or random. Although he admired Michelet's great talent, he did not have that temperament of the historian which makes him a curious visitor of cemeteries and evoker of their ghosts. Capable though he was of bringing scenes of the past to life, he had no taste for retelling them. Of this past, all that really interested him was what was still involved in the present and could throw light on it. Tocqueville as historian took over from Tocqueville as politician just as the politican had taken over from the observer of democracy. His conception of the slow movement of civilization had not essentially changed, but his experience of the world and of men had made it more complex and in certain respects more somber. Progress toward democracy, steady on the other side of the Atlantic, continued in France only through the tumultuous episodes of a revolution that had been going on now for sixty years. In 1830, Tocqueville had succumbed to the illusion that this revolution was over. The events of 1848 had proved that it was not over by any means, and Tocqueville compared this sexagenarian revolution to a sea that continued to rise without either himself or any of his contemporaries being able to see the shoreline that would mark a limit to the fearful tide. The drama of public life tended to become identified, for Tocqueville, with his own inner drama. By endeavoring to comprehend for himself this crucially important problem, he would expose and confront the latent disquiet of the public at large. With his customary insight into himself, he acknowledged that he sought such an encounter with the public out of his desire for popular acclaim and his hope of repeating the success of the *Democracy,* as if such success were the concrete sign of the "mark" he would leave on the future.

In itself, the French Revolution was not a new subject. On the eve of 1848, the curiosity of the public about it had been revived by three books greeted with approval or enthusiasm: Lamartine's *Histoire des girondins,* the beginning of the *Histoire de la Révolution française* by Michelet, and Louis Blanc's *Histoire de la Révolution.* Of course Tocqueville had not waited for this trend in public opinion before becoming interested in the subject himself. As we know, he had published in 1836 his *Etat social et politique de la France avant et après 1789* and planned to follow it with another panel devoted to post-revolutionary France. He did not do this, but had assembled the

484

꠱ ꠲

materials for it.[3] Difficult though it is to find out what he was reading and the sources of what he wrote, one can be sure that he already had very firm notions about the period that extended from the reign of Louis XV to the fall of Napoléon. As we know, upon leaving his *collège* he had read Thiers's *Histoire de la Révolution française,* which he had found shockingly amoral.[4] Since 1845, Thiers had brought out the successive volumes of the *Histoire du Consulat et de l'Empire,* which Tocqueville, with his usual lack of goodwill toward the author, judged to be too much centered on military events with a "ridiculous . . . claim to an understanding of the profession of war."[5] He took the measure of the empty rhetoric of the *Histoire des girondins,* but we do not know if he was aware of the polemics that had preceded it, on the rehabilitation of Robespierre in connection with Esquiros's book.[6] He had read with admiration Michelet's *Histoire de France,* but he does not seem to have written to the author (with whom we have reason to believe he was no longer on very good terms) at the time of the publication of the *Histoire de la Révolution,* though it would be quite extraordinary if he had not read it. It is less certain if Louis Blanc's history was among the books of Blanc that he was familiar with. But he could not have been unaware of the *Histoire de la Révolution* by his friend Mignet, or of a book that is forgotten today, the *Histoire du règne de Louis XVI pendant les années où l'on pouvait prévenir la Révolution* [the history of the reign of Louis XVI during the years when the Revolution might have been prevented], by François-Xavier Droz (1839); he set great store by the author, who had presented a copy of the book to him, and the problematics of the work are somewhat comparable to those of *L'Ancien Régime.* Between Tocqueville's book and Madame de Staël's *Les Considérations sur la Révolution française* there are some resemblances that seem to prove he had read it attentively, but as far as we know, he never spoke of it. In any case, he was not unaware of the importance of the forty volumes of *L'Histoire parlementaire de la Révolution* by Buchez and Roux (1833–1836), which, in fact, provoked a veritable revolution in the historiography of the period. He was concerned about having them at hand, and ended up buying them.

For a long time, too, Tocqueville had approached the study of the period from the Ancien Régime to the Restoration in a more direct way. Since his youth, memoirs had been appearing that reflected the

---

[3]See above, 246–47.
[4]See above, 308.
[5]Letter to Kergorlay dated December 15, 1850, *O.C.* XIII, 2: 231.
[6]*Histoire des Montagnards,* 2 vols. (Paris, 1847).

tormented fate of the preceding generation; the public's interest in these personal histories is shown by the great quantity of them, with fabricated or falsified memoirs swelling the numbers of the genuine accounts. Tocqueville had read and reread most of them. He made this clear in his answer to a letter from Ampère, unfortunately lost, in which the latter suggests that he choose from a list those which he wants to be sent. The only one Tocqueville was unfamiliar with was the *Mémoires* of the Marquis de Ferrières.[7]

At his death, he was to leave behind him a rich collection of revolutionary newspapers; *cahiers* of the States-General containing lists of grievances and proposals for reform; speeches, addresses, and other printed matter from the same period. No doubt he acquired many of these at the time he was writing his book, but nothing prevents us from thinking that some of them were already in the library of the château de Tocqueville, and that he could have been familiar with them earlier.

Whatever the case, his reflections before he set to work writing led him to two decisions: to take as a subject an episode of the Revolution, and to treat this with a different approach from that of historical narration:

> For a long time, I have had the thought . . . of choosing, from the long stretch of time which extends from 1789 to the present and which I continue to call the French Revolution, the ten years of the Empire . . . The more I think about it, the more I believe that this period would be a very apt choice. In itself, it is not only great, but singular, even unique . . . What is more, it sheds a bright light on the period that preceded it and on the one that follows.[8]

What interested Tocqueville was the way the period of the Revolution, in the narrow sense of the word, gave rise to a new order—and, beyond that, to those structures, whose strength and rigidity he had experienced in the course of his political career, that the Empire had bequeathed to the France of his time. To place the Empire in that double perspective, "I would no doubt lay out the events and I would follow their thread, but my main business would not be to narrate them; my aim, above all, would be to explain the salient events, showing the diverse causes that produced them and the consequences that emerged from them."[9] Thus, it would be a combination of history

---

[7]Letter to Ampère dated October 2, 1856, *O.C.* XI, 347.
[8]Letter to Kergorlay dated December 15, 1850, *O.C.* XIII, 2: 231.
[9]Ibid., 232.

486
𝕾 𝕾

and the philosophy of history closely enmeshed, the difficulty of which Tocqueville did not hide from himself. His great model remained the *Considérations sur les causes de la grandeur des Romains et de leur décadence,* but Montesquieu's task had been easier, since he was working on a remote history, pruned of all secondary events, whereas for a recent period, and a period of ten years, the crucial facts were still entangled in detail.

Already at Sorrento, in December 1850, Tocqueville set down on paper two plans for the projected work. In them, he emphasized the conjunction of exceptional circumstances with the extraordinary genius of Napoléon and insisted on his work as lawgiver. It was clear that he did not intend to relate the stupendous military epic of the Empire. He jotted down a few scattered observations, the fruit of his reflections during walks in "the mountains of Sorrento."[10]

Once he was back in Paris, he was unable to get down to serious work: first of all, he presented in the Legislative Assembly the report on the plan for revising the Constitution; then, in the autumn, he finished writing his *Souvenirs.* But after the coup d'état, having returned to private life, he found that the active preparation of the projected work was the best remedy for the profound sadness that filled him, and soon he devoted himself to it with a passion.

It was the project he had conceived in Sorrento that Tocqueville now endeavored to realize. He had attached great importance to the "point of departure" in his study of American political society, and it was therefore natural that he should begin his new book by analyzing the causes of the coup d'état of 18 Brumaire. But this choice had also been determined, as he acknowledged, by the resemblance between the two seizures of power, the uncle's and the nephew's.

Thiers had given a perceptive and colorful account of the immediate causes of 18 Brumaire and its carrying out in Volume 8 of his *Histoire de la Révolution française,* minutely documented by the stories of the survivors and the memoirs of the time.

Without neglecting the same sources, Tocqueville directed his research toward a deeper explanation of the crisis that had permitted the coup d'état to take place. In the official texts (particularly the unpublished register of the deliberations of the Directoire), he studied the disintegration of the regime, and he gathered material about party hatreds and the general disaffection with the Republic consisting of

[10]*O.C.* II, 2: 301–304.

accounts in pamphlets from the years III, IV, and V that he found in   487
cartons at the Bibliothèque Nationale. Above all, he gave the event a   ※ ※
broad social significance: why did this disaffection with the directorial
regime not lead the French people to want the return of the Ancien
Régime? Because, Tocqueville answered in his notes, the masses had
won by the Revolution. And, not content with seeking evidence of
this in the pamphlets of the time, he was to be the first to make an
effort to provide figures for the economic gains that the great classes
of the country, especially the peasantry, were able to derive from the
Revolution.

He attempted to evaluate the absorption of rural debt by the depre-
ciation of the Revolution's paper currency, the alleviation brought
about by the disappearance of feudal privileges, and the conditions of
purchase of the national property.

He thus raised large problems for which only the historians of the
twentieth century would be able to propose solutions. But this makes
it no less striking to see Tocqueville consider, before anyone else,
making a comparison between the inventory of properties the Con-
stitutent Assembly had ordered drawn up in 1790 and the land registers of his own time—and to see him, unable to carry out such a
study of the shifting of properties on a large scale, do so within the
narrow framework of the parish of Tocqueville and its immediate
environs.

Thus, the breadth of his social perceptions was the most valuable
part of the two chapters written from July to September 1852—"Why
the Republic was ready to receive a master" and "How the nation
while ceasing to be republican remained revolutionary"—while they
were animated by the vibrant style of a man who had just been through
a conflict analogous to the one he was describing.[11]

He had left Paris in June for the soothing solitude of Tocqueville,
where it was easier to escape from political preoccupations. Ampère,
who had left for North America from Southampton on August 27,
1851, was back in Paris in May 1852 and came to Tocqueville to write
down his impressions of America for the readers of the *Revue des deux
mondes:* "M. Ampère . . . is working on an account of the trip he has
just taken to the United States; he is occupying the top of one tower
and I, for my part, am scribbling away down below him on the second
floor. From time to time, we meet in the library and, in the presence
of Mme. de Tocqueville, who forms the only audience, we read each

[11]*O.C.* II, 2: 269–98.

488

乄乄

other what we have done, we comment, criticize, praise, and the time passes agreeably."[12]

Tocqueville's concern with seeking, beneath the surface of events, more profound historical developments caused him to depart from the narrow chronological framework he had fixed for himself at Sorrento. If the peasantry, in Brumaire of the year VIII, disillusioned by the anarchy of the Directoire, preferred a new dictatorship to the return of the old order, that was in part because of the memory of the feudal charges laid on them in the past. It was therefore necessary to go back to the Ancien Régime in order to understand their mentality. What was more, we know that one of Tocqueville's essential ideas was that centralization, still in place, constituted an obstacle to a free democracy in France. He had fought this centralization in vain during his political career. Thiers, who admired it, construed it as an offspring of the imperial genius. Back in 1835, in the *Democracy,* Tocqueville had spoken out against this conception: "It is not right to say that centralization sprang from the French Revolution. The Revolution perfected it but did not create it. The taste for centralization and the mania for regulations date in France from the time when lawyers came into the government; that takes us back to the time of Philip the Fair. Both these things have grown steadily since then."[13] But if Napoleonic centralization was only the blossoming of such a long evolution, one was carried back, in order to explain it, quite far into the past, and Brumaire was an illusory point of departure.

Even though he did not explain this development in his work clearly, saying merely, in September 1852: "I don't know how to find my way through this ocean of the French Revolution," he tended more and more to abandon his readings on the Consulate and the Empire in favor of pursuing research on the Ancien Régime. A handwritten note, dating from December 1852, may perhaps mark a decisive moment in this change of approach: "I am returning Thibaudeau's Memoirs on the Consulate to the Bibliothèque without having read them; to be resumed when I go back to this period." It seems he never afterwards returned to it; the few texts on the Consulate and the Empire, dating from the spring of 1853, are only easily gathered gleanings, taken for whatever purpose they might serve.

At the beginning of 1853, he was working in the Archives of the Hôtel de Ville, no longer in existence today, and in April noted with

[12]Letter to Reeve dated August 8, 1852, *O.C.* VI, 134.
[13]*O.C.* I, 2: 447. *Democracy,* 723.

disappointment that the documents from the old *généralité* of Paris (as the district overseen by a finance officer was called under the Ancien Régime) only rarely went back earlier than 1787:

"These cartons contain few documents from before 1787 and starting at that time, the old administrative constitution changes profoundly and one enters into the transitional and not very interesting period separating the administration of the Ancien Régime from the administrative system created in the Consulate and which still rules us today." A surprising sentence, but one that reveals how little interest he had in the purely revolutionary convulsions, instead concentrating all his attention on a comparison between the administrative structures of the Ancien Régime and those of his own time.[14]

Nevertheless, it was not without some regret that he abandoned his original plan. In June 1853, he was only thinking of a sort of introductory chapter, about thirty pages long, on the Ancien Régime. Even in 1856, in a note oddly entitled "Original idea, earliest sense of the subject, to be reread now and then to return me to the main path of my thoughts," he would reaffirm his desire to center the whole drama of the Revolution on the figure of Napoléon. Nevertheless, he sought to explain the most distant origins of the drama in a very long introduction that spanned whole centuries and that was typical of the sort of introduction people would write in those days. For this, he thought of taking his research back to the first great vanquisher of the feudal lords, King Louis XI.

As we noted in the preceding chapter, in 1853, for reasons of health, Tocqueville had to give up his plan to spend the summer in the Cotentin and on June 1 settled in Touraine for a year. Beaumont had taken it upon himself to look for an establishment that would suit the Tocquevilles and handled negotiations with the owner of the furnished house they chose, the difficult Dr. Mège.

This house, "Les Trésorières," which still stands, is situated at Saint-Cyr-lès-Tours, on the north bank of the Loire, which is joined at that spot by a little tributary, the Choisille. The valley thus formed enjoyed what we would today call a microclimate, whose pleasant qualities had been what primarily attracted the Tocquevilles. "Its main quality . . . is that it possesses a temperature of an unchanging softness: not a breath of unpleasant wind can penetrate there . . . I believe it is the only spot in the Loire basin that is equally sheltered from all the winds

[14]Tocqueville's rough drafts, notes, and outlines for *L'Ancien Régime* are in the Tocqueville Archives, files 42–44.

490

of the north and the northwest and even the west."[15] The house itself was fairly spacious and, if the rooms in which the Tocquevilles had lodged their servants were infested with bedbugs[16]—a fact that Dr. Mège had refrained from mentioning—the rest of the house was wholesome and sunny; besides, it seems that the insecticide campaign waged by Madame de Tocqueville destroyed or at least decimated the adversary. In any case, there were two rooms available for visiting friends, one of which, a room on the ground floor, was fitted out as a study, eventually to be occupied by Ampère. The Tocquevilles remained aloof from the society of Touraine, and saw only the archbishop, Monsignor Morlot, and the archivist Charles de Grandmaison, who tells us that Tocqueville lived in a house "whose owner had had the unusual idea of decorating it with busts of many sages and great men placed between the windows. Before the house, which faces south, a lawn surrounded by beautiful trees forms a small park beyond which extends a vast kitchen garden and orchard with broad paths intersecting at right angles. The background is dominated by a triple row of linden trees."[17]

The proximity of Tours, the "last houses" of which could be seen from Les Trésorières, had been part of the reason for choosing the place. It was about two and a half miles away from the prefecture, which housed the archives containing all the files of the intendants —the provincial administrators of the Ancien Régime—and also contained what was for Tocqueville another treasure, a particularly hard-working archivist, Charles de Grandmaison, who had studied at the School of Paleography and Librarianship in Paris. Grandmaison had found the archives of the intendants in a chaotic state when he arrived in Tours, and had just completed classifying them when Tocqueville appeared.

The two men had already met, when Grandmaison was still in Paris interning under the librarian Haureau, whom Tocqueville knew well. Grandmaison began by advising Tocqueville to limit his research to the eighteenth century. During the whole summer, Tocqueville would arrive every day at noon carrying a large black portfolio that recalled his former duties. He would chat with the archivist for a quarter of an hour, stopping abruptly when the time was up, with his usual somewhat finical punctuality, and start work.

[15]Beaumont to Tocqueville, April 19, 1853, O.C. VIII, 3: 107–12.
[16]Tocqueville to Beaumont, June 4, 1853, ibid., 128–29.
[17]Charles de Grandmaison, *Alexis de Tocqueville en Touraine* (Paris, 1893).

Toward the end of the year, he was to reduce his visits to one or 491
two a week, when he began writing. Grandmaison, who followed
the thread of his preoccupations from one day to the next, who in
particular understood his concern to comprehend administrative
practices and customs as well as the regulations, would prepare the
files for him to examine. To protect this illustrious client from the
curiosity of the local residents, which, during the first days, had
brought unaccustomed visitors to the Archives, he had set Tocqueville up in his own office, which was a narrow little passageway with
a beautiful view over the gardens of the prefecture. Mutual trust
grew up between the two men all the more easily because Tocqueville understood that Grandmaison was anything but a fervent partisan of the Second Empire. Later, when Grandmaison sought the
appointment to a vacant place in the Archives Nationales, Tocqueville recommended him to the director, Chabrier, but the latter was
obliged to select instead a protégé of the empress. When he sent
Grandmaison a copy of L'Ancien Régime, Tocqueville wrote to him:
"Without you and your archives, I would never have been able to
write the book I have just published. Nothing I found in my earlier
studies has any connection with it. With you, I found the train of
ideas I was looking for . . . It was our conversations, specifically, that
enabled me to fix my mind on ideas that afterwards became the
fountainhead of all the rest." Even if there is some hyperbole in these
thanks, there is no doubt that Charles de Grandmaison saved the
author of L'Ancien Régime a good deal of time by pointing his
research in useful directions.

Tocqueville read from many other sources besides those of the
archives. These sources were no longer simply memoirs yielding him
"the feeling of the time"—he knew many of them already, and with
his admirable memory, he retained the essence of them—but heavy
tomes on law, on feudalism, on the theories of the physiocrats. Jok-
ingly, he wrote that he was now capable of teaching a course at the
Collège de France on the institutions of the old France, adding that
the most important part of his task was to understand the spirit in
which these institutions functioned.[18]

In November 1853, he attempted to sketch out his introductory
chapter, the idea for which he had conceived before he left Paris, and

---

[18]Notes in the Tocqueville Archives, file 43. Letter to Corcelle dated September 17, 1853, O.C. XV, 2: 79–81.

492

彩 彩

which had by now split into two chapters. Around January 1, 1854, he wrote to Ampère:

I have written the first chapter of the book, or rather I've done a rough draft of it. Its object is to show what the real purpose of the Revolution was, and which features set this Revolution apart from mankind's other great upheavals. I have already begun the second chapter, in which I want to explore the reasons why this general revolution began in France rather than elsewhere, and what gave it among us the particular features that distinguish it from all the other revolutions that were its sequel.[19]

But the idea that Tocqueville had just dealt with in his first chapter would be the idea governing all of Book I in the 1856 volume—a short section, it is true. The ideas he wanted to deal with in the second chapter would be developed throughout the twenty chapters of Books II and III of *L'Ancien Régime et la Révolution*. Describing these in the last paragraph of Book I, Tocqueville used almost exactly the same terms in which he had indicated the subject of his second chapter in the letter above: "But why did this Revolution, in preparation everywhere, threatening everywhere, break out in France rather than elsewhere? Why did it have certain characteristics among us that were not found anywhere else or that appeared elsewhere only in part? This second question certainly deserves to be asked; the object of the following books will be to examine it."[20]

The growing importance that Tocqueville was attaching to the study of the Ancien Régime is apparent in a letter dated March 7, 1854, to his brother Edouard in which he summed up what he had done and what he meant to do while in Touraine. His analysis of the society of the Ancien Régime was to be the first part of the work he planned that would cover, when it was complete, the periods of the Revolution and the Empire:

I have devoted the entire year to doing what has never been done, studying the Ancien Régime and finding out what even the contemporaries of the Ancien Régime did not know, how things stood in those times; what were the political practices, the rules . . . I think that from this study I have derived a great many facts and new insights that not only explain why this great Revolution took place in France; why it assumed the character it had; but even why many events took place that have occurred since and from which

[19]Tocqueville to Ampère, *O.C.* XI, 231–32.
[20]*L'Ancien Régime et la Révolution*, *O.C.* II, 1: 96.

we have inherited a host of habits, opinions, and inclinations which we think   493
are new and which have their roots in the government of the Ancien Régime.   𖤐 𖤐
It is this first part that will be, I repeat, finished by the time I leave here.
And if that proves to be the case, my time will not have been wasted. For
I had to plunge into an immense amount of preparatory work in which I
was almost always feeling my way. My intent is not to go beyond two
volumes. I am afraid I have begun with my cake. For the early days of the
Revolution, it will still be fairly easy for me to procure the documents I need.
But when I come to the Empire, I fear that the petty passions of the
government now in power will close all the openings through which light
might have reached me.[21]

Tocqueville's illusions about the possibility of being done with the
Ancien Régime before leaving Tours remind one of the period from
1836 to 1839 when he was sure he would soon be done with the second
Democracy. These illusions are particularly surprising given the fact
that he wanted to submit his hypothesis—that the Revolution had to
break out first in France rather than in any other country in
Europe—to the test of a historical comparison. It was for a similar
reason that he had observed England's political institutions before
publishing the *Democracy*. But a rereading of Blackstone showed him
that there were too many differences between France and England in
the eighteenth century for the comparison to be fruitful. On the other
hand, he thought that in Germany he would still be able to find living
examples of feudal traditions analogous to those that remained at the
end of France's Ancien Régime. He also wanted to analyze why
Germany's impulses toward revolution, so visible before 1789, had
come to nothing. Lastly, he proposed to study the reactions that the
French regime had provoked in Germany. He decided to visit the
country before continuing with the writing of his book.

He had made only one brief trip to Germany before, in May 1849,
when he had witnessed the death throes of the Frankfurt parliament.
We do not know exactly how much interest he took in German affairs
before 1848, though we can be sure that English life and politics were
more familiar to him at that time. But as the minister of foreign affairs
he had followed Germany's upheavals attentively and although he had
wagered on an imminent restoration of the Austrian hegemony, he
took great interest in Prussia, whose future rise to power he seems to
have divined. He also had a growing interest in Germany's intellectual
life, perhaps because of the influence of Ampère, who, at the Univer-

[21]Letter to Edouard, *O.C.* (Bmt) VI, 251–52, corrected text.

494

࿊ ࿊

sity in Bonn in 1826, had studied with Barthold Niebuhr and Wilhelm Schlegel, and had once visited the aged Goethe. His friend Kergorlay had had some notion of writing a book about Germany, and Beaumont had also thought of writing on Austria. He shared a good deal of interest in Germany in his friendship with Circourt, who had been charged with a mission to Berlin in 1848 and had associated with Frederick William IV and his court, and who, after transmitting information to Lamartine in 1848, had given Tocqueville when he was minister a report on Prussia. He knew personally the geographer Alexander von Humboldt, the philosopher Christian Brandis, who was a correspondent of the Institute, and perhaps the celebrated jurist Friedrich von Savigny. He deliberately sought the acquaintance of the historians Christian von Bunsen, former ambassador to London, and Leopold von Ranke.

In addition, Tocqueville set about studying the German language, which he did not know though his wife spoke it correctly. Starting on October 14, 1853, he shared with Beaumont a subscription to the *Kölnische Zeitung,* and in Tours took German lessons from "a chubby-cheeked pedant."

The Tocquevilles arrived in Bonn, where they had decided to make their first stop, on June 19.[22] They took rooms in the best hotel, the Goldener Stern, but were soon to rent a furnished apartment in Coblenzerstrasse, between the Rhine and the Hofgarten, on the grounds of the University. They were welcomed most amiably. The day after their arrival, Brandis invited them to a party being given in honor of Bunsen, who was passing through town:

The University was there en masse, females as well as males . . . At nine o'clock, we had to sit down to table before an immense supper of which we didn't touch a thing, but which the natives ate like the Germans of the sixteenth century. Everyone there was extremely friendly to us. But we were introduced to so many people in succession that we left in a daze and our heads were full of a university chaos which we haven't been able to emerge from since . . . In sum, we were delighted by the evening. I will now try to see all these people again separately and extract from them all that I can.[23]

Beyond this, we have little idea which people Tocqueville—very embarrassed because he spoke the language badly, although he read it

---

[22]K.-J. Seidel, "Tocqueville Forschungsaufenthalt in Bonn 1854," *Rheinische Vierteljahr-Blätter* 41 (1977), 283–97.

[23]Letter to Ampère dated June 21, 1854, *O.C.* XI, 245–47.

more or less fluently—talked to in Bonn. Among them were the jurist
Hälschner, a correspondent of Ampère's and defender of the autonomy
of Rhenish law, and the Swiss Charles Monnard, whose bilingualism
made him useful. But we know from Tocqueville's own statements
that he saw many people we have no way of identifying.

Here, he did not make use of archives for his research. But he had
access to a very rich library, and the librarian, in order to make
Tocqueville's work easier, relaxed his rules about lending books. In
truth, these Bonn Germans had scarcely any civic spirit, but this was
more a consequence of their indifference than of a princely tyranny.
The mood was more relaxed here than in France, and private life had
its tranquil charms. There was at least one salon in which one might
enjoy the pleasures of the mind, presided over by Madame d'Oriola,
née Maximiliane von Arnim, along with her sister Armgart. These
were the daughters of the celebrated Bettina von Arnim, whom the
Tocquevilles just missed meeting, since she arrived in Bonn a few days
after they returned to France.[24] Armgart had stayed in Paris in 1850
in the home of the Circourts, and it was they who had given the
Tocquevilles an introduction to her. Colonel d'Oriola was a distinguished intellect, the son of a Portuguese ambassador who had become
a citizen of Prussia; but what a wealth of memories were evoked in
Tocqueville by the two sisters in particular, daughters of Achim von
Arnim, nieces of Clemens von Brentano and of Savigny, raised in the
atmosphere of the great romantic salons of Berlin, that of Rahel
Varnhagen von Ense and that of their mother, who was still faithful
to the cult of Goethe twenty-two years after his death. They had lived
through the events of 1848 in Berlin itself, though they had not shared
their mother's enthusiasm for the revolution.

But if Tocqueville learned a good deal about eighteenth-century
Germany in the library and would derive from his reading a few
interesting notes for L'Ancien Régime, Bonn was in that part of Germany in which the vestiges of feudalism had probably been most
completely effaced. In order to find traces that were still in being, it
would be necessary to go farther east, which was why Tocqueville
planned a second stage in the journey, to visit Dresden and Berlin. He
prepared this part of the trip with great care. Not only was he anxious
to see politicians, but he asked Circourt to give him the names of
specialists in law and feudal customs in those cities. Kergorlay had some
friends in Mecklenburg, and Tocqueville had him send a letter of

[24]Drewits, *Bettina von Arnim*. French translation, Paris, 1982.

introduction so that he would be invited to the home of a lord (we do not know which one) where the feudal world was living on amid its own ruins.

Madame de Tocqueville had the annoying habit of falling ill when traveling and thus upsetting projected itineraries. This time was no exception. On August 6, in Bonn, she had an attack of rheumatism of the wrist and thumb that forced her to carry her right arm in a sling. It had perhaps been unwise of the couple to live so close to the Rhine, where the damp air and fogs often brought on this ailment. However that may be, instead of leaving for Dresden, on the seventeenth they were obliged to go to Wildbad, a minuscule watering place lost in the Black Forest whose baths were supposed to be efficacious. Tocqueville was furious that his trip had been spoiled; he claims he hid this from Mary, but that is not altogether certain. The great lover of long walks was horrified by the pine-covered mountains, and the human landscape hardly seemed more cheerful to him: "We are living in the midst of such a great number of hunchbacked, stoop-shouldered, one-armed, lame, and legless people that I begin to think that a man who is solidly planted on both legs and has the use of both arms is the exception in the human race."[25] Ampère, who had left Rome to go join them in Dresden, learned of their change in plans, turned left at Vienna, and went up the Danube to spend a week with them and return to France in their company. On the banks of the Rhine, Tocqueville had met some Englishmen, Reeve and Lewis, but their ill will toward Russia provoked him. On his way through Brussels, he had seen the exiled generals Bedeau and Lamoricière again. The latter and his wife, whom they were supposed to meet up with again in Dresden, learned of the visit to Wildbad and came before they left, to spend two days with them in Göttingen. At the end of September, Tocqueville returned sadly to the French Empire.

On November 6, after a brief visit to his father, he settled in Compiègne in a small, light, dry house on the edge of the forest and stayed there until April 3, 1855. This was a particularly severe winter, and Madame de Tocqueville recovered very slowly from her rheumatism, the cold sometimes forcing the two of them to take refuge together in the warmest room. Nevertheless, even when it was snowing, Tocqueville would escape from the "hovel" to take long walks in the forest. He saw no one in Compiègne and went to Paris only

[25]Letter to Corcelle dated August 29, 1854, O.C. XV, 2: 110.

for the rare sessions of the Academies, the reception for Monsignor
Dupanloup at the Académie Française or the election of Barrot as
corresponding member of the Sciences Morales. He worked relentlessly
and was now determined to write a separate volume on the end of the
Ancien Régime. He had more than a thousand pages of notes and was
returning to the drafts he had done at Tours. Despite his working at
it day in and day out, he was unable to finish the book before he left
Compiègne. One chapter, which afterwards split into two ("How men
of letters became the most prominent politicians in the country toward
the middle of the eighteenth century and the effects of this" and "How
irreligion was able to become a general and dominant passion among
the French of the eighteenth century"), presented difficulties which he
did not manage to overcome. He once again plunged more thoroughly
into his thoughts about these very general themes and endeavored to
express them in a classically pure style.

From April to June, the Tocquevilles lived in Paris again, in a
modest apartment in the rue de Fleurus which had been put in order
for them by the Lagden sisters, the two Englishwomen who had taken
charge of Mérimée's life and with whom Madame de Tocqueville
seems to have had fairly close relations. Tocqueville deliberately put
his files aside and, by way of diversion, studied the statutes of the *pays
d'Etats,* the outlying provinces that were still being administered by
an assembly of the Three Estates in the eighteenth century when the
highly centralized royal administration prevailed in Paris and the
provinces of the center. This study gave rise to the appendix to
L'Ancien Régime on Languedoc. Apropos of the difficult chapter we
mentioned, he had noted down as he was leaving Compiègne: "Once
I'm back in Paris, I fear that in the midst of the broken-up life I'm
leading, I won't be able to recover the succession of my ideas and the
energy with which to express them. I will therefore postpone resuming
my work until I am at Tocqueville. Then it will be necessary to look
the whole chapter over again and reshape it all at once."

After a brief visit to Beaumont-la-Chartre, where he read aloud
several chapters, and to Beaufossé, Corcelle's home, he arrived at
Tocqueville at the beginning of July. He had not been back there for
three years, and the surroundings of the château looked rather like a
wilderness. He spent several weeks pruning hedges, filling ditches, and
planting shrubs, while Madame de Tocqueville invested the savings
accumulated since their return from Germany in making the château
less gloomy and more comfortable. Nevertheless, despite his mediocre

498

⚹ ⚹

health, working "obstinately, passionately, and sadly," he finished revising the volume in January 1856 and on February 16 began negotiating with Michel Lévy, who had become the principal publisher for the liberal writers.

The title of the work still remained to be decided upon. Tocqueville had thought of "La Révolution"; Michel Lévy and Ampère leaned toward "La Révolution Française." We do not know who suggested the title *L'Ancien Régime et la Révolution,* which everyone came to favor. After Beaumont, however, observed that this title was appropriate only for the first volume, Tocqueville answered on March 22: "If I continue my work I will obviously go back, for the book as a whole, to the more general title I had first chosen."

Tocqueville's father and brothers had taken an active part in going over the manuscript of the first *Democracy.* There was no longer any question of this as far as Tocqueville's brothers were concerned, and for a long time Tocqueville had kept from his father the fact that he was writing a book, after having dodged his father's request for help in soliciting reviews for his own book on the reigns of Louis XV and Louis XVI, one that Tocqueville probably did not value very highly. Kergorlay was taken up with industrial business, Ampère was leaving again for Rome. Beaumont agreed to read with a critical eye, at the same time that Tocqueville did, the galley proofs sent by the printer Didot.

An unforeseen misfortune delayed the publication of *L'Ancien Régime et la Révolution* for some days. This was the quite sudden death of Comte Hervé. On June 16, however, Michel Lévy put the book on sale.

L'Ancien Régime et la Révolution is divided into three parts (even though Book III was not detached from Book II until the first republication).

The first part is an attempt to define the significance of the Revolution. Louis Blanc had seen it as a revolt of the individual against authority (and fixed its point of departure at the condemnation of Jan Hus, the Czech religious leader, in 1415!). Michelet had defined it as the advent of a new world based on justice and replacing an old world subject to the arbitrary divine will. Tocqueville denied that the Revolution had the character of either an anarchic revolt or an anti-Christian crusade. Certainly it had exalted the citizen, in an abstract way, above particular societies. It had thus assumed an international character in its propaganda, which made it resemble a great religious

revolution. But its goal had been to abolish "the political societies   499
which for several centuries had reigned unopposed over most of the   ℣ ℣
peoples of Europe and which are customarily called by the name of
feudal institutions, in order to substitute a simpler and more uniform
social and political order based on equality of conditions."[26]

For Tocqueville, it thus had a sociopolitical character. Furthermore,
this Revolution, rather than a sudden mutation, was the acceleration
of a movement that was already under way throughout Europe. It was
therefore necessary to explain why the Revolution had broken out in
France rather than elsewhere, and this was the problem that dominated
the second part of the work.

In France, the breaking up of the feudal institutions—which when
they were all of a piece had constituted the *seigneurie* (the powers and
authority of the *seigneur,* the feudal lord)—was more advanced than
anywhere else in Europe. There was no more serfdom, there were no
longer *corvées* (unpaid labor for the *seigneur*) on the domain. The
peasant, moreover, had often become a small proprietor with land of
his own. Nonetheless, this *seigneur,* who no longer had any functions
or responsibilities, continued to enjoy privileges, in contrast to the
former vassals who were now his neighbors. This state of affairs
provoked hatred on the part of the former vassals, who bestowed the
name of *hobereau*— the smallest of the birds of prey—on these country
gentlemen of modest means. Tocqueville gives a striking description
of the way in which this hatred came to be:

I ask you to imagine the French peasant of the eighteenth century—or
rather, the one you know today, for he is still the same. His condition has
changed, but not his mentality. See him as the documents I have quoted from
portray him, so passionately in love with the land that he puts all his savings
into buying it and buys it at any price. To acquire it, he must first pay certain
dues, not to the government but to other landowners in the neighborhood
who are as much strangers as he is to the administration of public affairs, and
almost as powerless as he. At last he takes possession of it; he plants his heart
in it along with his grain. This little piece of earth that he possesses in his
own right in this vast universe fills him with pride and a feeling of independence. Yet now these same neighbors come along, wrest him from his field
and force him to go to work elsewhere without pay. If he tries to protect
his plantings against the animals they hunt, the same neighbors make him take
down his fences; they wait for him at the river crossing and make him pay
a toll. They find him again at the market, where they make him pay for the

right to sell his own produce; and when, having returned to his farm, he wants to make use of the wheat he has put aside for his own needs, this wheat which grew under his own eyes and was harvested with his own hands, he cannot do so until he has sent it to be ground in the mill and baked in the oven of these same men. It is to provide them with unearned incomes that he gives up part of the income from his own little domain, and these charges are imprescriptible and irredeemable.

Whatever he does, he encounters these inconvenient neighbors all along the way, disturbing his pleasures, interfering with his work, eating what he produces; and when he has finished with them, others turn up, dressed in black, and take away the better part of his harvest. Imagine the condition, the needs, the character, the passions of this man, and calculate, if you can, the treasures of hatred and envy that are stored up in his heart.[27]

The deficiency of the nobility, which was not able, as the English nobility was, to absorb new men or to adapt to new tasks, was a fact heavy with consequences. For "when a people has destroyed the aristocracy within its midst, it runs toward centralization as though of its own accord," Tocqueville wrote, revealing a pessimism that had hardly existed in the first *Democracy*. In France, all the free institutions whose origins dated back to the Middle Ages had died out, from the meeting of the *seigneur*'s court to the States-General, including the free administration of the towns and the modest parish meetings.

Thus, a sort of void was created, within which the monarchy could organize a centralized regime. "This was a work of patience, of skill, and of the passage of time, rather than one of compulsion and the arbitrary exercise of power. At the moment the Revolution broke out, almost nothing had as yet been destroyed of France's old administrative edifice; another had, so to speak, been built underneath it."

And Tocqueville enumerated the principal organs of this new edifice—the king's Council, the comptroller-general, the intendants, and the "exceptional" courts. He described their principal modes of action: the trusteeship of local administrative bodies, the system whereby all cases that involved the administration were taken before a special court. He summed up the new structure in the following terms:

A single body placed at the center of the kingdom, which regulates public administration throughout the country; the same minister directing almost all internal affairs; in each province, a government representative who oversees every detail of administration; no secondary administrative bodies what-

[27]*O.C.* II, 1: 106.

soever, or only bodies that cannot take action without prior authorization; "exceptional" courts that judge cases in which the administration has an interest and protect all its agents. What is this, if not the centralization that we know? Its forms are less sharply delineated than today, its procedures less coordinated, its operation not as smooth, but it is the same entity.[28]

This political organization which excluded the subject from all participation in the management of public affairs and sometimes even intervened in the management of his own affairs profoundly marked the society of the end of the Ancien Régime.

The nobility, no longer having any functions in the rural world, had fled, almost everywhere, to the court or the towns. Its members were growing poor and clung all the more fiercely to their privileges. The order of nobility was becoming a closed caste anxious to maintain a clearly marked boundary separating it from all those not of noble birth.

As for the bourgeoisie, it was busy getting rich. The upper bourgeoisie was not only equal in fortune to the nobility, but had enjoyed the same education and possessed the same ideas. It thirsted for the privileges of precedence or income that came with certain positions, and bought offices that the monarchy, always short of cash, put up for sale—no matter how trifling and precarious the prerogatives might be. The upper bourgeoisie wanted to distinguish itself from the petty bourgeoisie of the artisans, but both had become divided up into small, often minuscule groups whose social horizon hardly extended beyond the group itself.

When Tocqueville wrote in *L'Ancien Régime* that the French, isolated as they were from each other, had never resembled each other so closely, he was thinking only of those classes that would one day be privileged by their payment of substantial property taxes to participate in elections as candidates or electors—the citizens of the *pays légal*. For the country people made up a class quite distinct from these. Abandoned by the nobility, seeing everyone flee from their midst who had the wherewithal to live apart from the land, they constituted the great mass of the French population, ignorant and rude, who had no recourse but to submit to the high-handed ways of those in power. The country people were the ones who had to pay the *taille* —the direct tax levied by the king on his subjects—for which the collectors, themselves chosen from among the peasantry, were held personally

[28]*O.C.* II, 1: 127.

responsible. They were the ones who did the work of the royal *corvées,* the days of obligatory unpaid labor that went far beyond the upkeep of the roads. They drew lots for service in the militia, when a "good number" was not always secure protection. Tocqueville had shown in the first chapter of Book II what still remained of feudal burdens on the peasants. In the last chapter he returned separately to what was arbitrary, oppressive, and ruinous for them in the new monarchical organization. This structuring of the book is not easy for the reader, but it reveals the author's indignation over an absolutism that had its harshest effect on the very social class that had no means of defending itself through useful debate or by alerting public opinion.

For there existed, for the other classes, a sort of liberty that expressed itself in the mores. Despotism, which was still young (Tocqueville shared Madame de Staël's opinion that in France freedom was old and despotism new), did not have the self-assured confidence in its convictions and actions that was clearly apparent to his readers in 1856. If the rules were stern, their execution was lenient. And it was the established custom for those under administrative rule to launch blunt-spoken, unsparing verbal attacks on the powers-that-be. Furthermore, there were still guarantees for individuals: the spirit of solidarity most clearly visible in the clergy, the judiciary authority of the *parlements,* whether this authority was confined to these courts' particular province or encroached upon the political domain.

In Book III, Tocqueville examined the Revolution's most immediate causes, which had arisen since the mid-eighteenth century.

It was at about this time that the *philosophes* began to exercise an authoritative power over public opinion. Having no more practical political experience than their readers and thus being incapable of distinguishing the useful from the harmful in the monarchical system, they offered very diverse plans for reconstruction, but "all of them thought it right to substitute simple, elementary rules deriving from reason and from natural law for the complex, traditional customs that ruled the society of their time."[29] And since the Church rested upon tradition, remained tied to the old powers-that-be, and endeavored to prevent the expression of the *philosophe*'s ideas, it was against the Church and the beliefs it taught that their most lively attacks were directed.

The work of the *philosophes* was not hostile to the royal power.

[29]*O.C.* II, 1: 194.

Tocqueville analyzed in greater detail the political ideas of the physio-crats who sought to establish a "democratic despotism."

Without analyzing its causes, he noted an awakening toward 1770 of the spirit of liberty. It was this spirit which, joined to the spirit of equality, gave rise to the principles of 1789. But it could not create a lasting liberal democracy, and for sixty years the French were to attempt to place "liberty's head on the body of a slave," and then, out of weariness, they let liberty go:

> When the love of the French for political liberty reawakened, they had already formed certain notions concerning government which were not merely out of harmony with the existence of free institutions. They were all but contrary to them.
>
> The French had accepted, as the ideal social system, a people with no other aristocracy than the government officials, and a single all-powerful administration that would run the State and act as the guardian of private individuals. Though they wanted to be free, they did not intend to depart from this original notion; they simply tried to reconcile it with the notion of liberty . . .
>
> It was this desire to introduce political liberty into the midst of institutions and ideas that were foreign or contrary to it, but to which we were already accustomed or for which we had already developed a taste, that over the last sixty years produced so many fruitless attempts to establish free governments, followed by such disastrous revolutions, to the point where finally, tired out from so many efforts, disheartened by such arduous and sterile labors, aban-doning their second goal to return to their first, many Frenchmen have been reduced to thinking that life under a master, in which all men are equal, has something pleasant about it. And so it is that today we find our political views resemble those of the physiocrats of 1750 infinitely more than those of our fathers of 1789.[30]

A conclusion that would be pessimistic to the point of fatalism if Tocqueville did not have faith in the French temperament, capable of the best as well as the worst and able to reestablish a government and free institutions at the least expected moment.

L'Ancien Régime presented a sociopolitical picture of France before 1789 and stressed the imbalances in it which necessarily led to the Revolution. It is easy to point out what is missing from the book, or moments when its affirmations are too categorical—to criticize, for instance, the view of the feudal order that the book presupposes. It is

[30]*O.C.* II, 1: 216.

504

nonetheless certain that the analysis was very fresh and remains today one of the great systematic explanations of the revolutionary phenomenon.

As he carried his manuscript to Paris at the moment of the meeting of the Congress of Paris, which seemed to be the triumph of imperial politics, Tocqueville was full of apprehension: "Who is going to have any time to read or take an interest in reading, amid all the fanfare celebrating the proclamation of peace,"[31] he wrote to Ampère. He recounted to his wife what his thoughts were during one night of insomnia:

I said to myself that the ideas in my book were of a kind that would please no one. The legitimists would see it as a dreadful description of the Ancien Régime and of royalty. Believers like Corcelle would find little sympathy for the Church in it. Revolutionaries would discover little liking in it for all the cheap finery of the Revolution. Only the true friends of liberty would enjoy reading it, and these can be counted on the fingers of one's two hands.

However, *L'Ancien Régime et la Révolution* had an indisputable success. The author's friends were reminded of the triumph of the *Democracy* in 1835, "minus the surprise." The rather unfavorable critic of *La Presse* wrote, "It is worth noting that the publication of this book has produced a certain excitement." And the very imperialist *Revue contemporaine,* transforming into a defense of the regime its double review of *L'Ancien Régime* and a contemporary work by Rémusat, titled the review "The Imperial Government and the New Opposition." The public continued to be eager to read the book right up to the death of Tocqueville, who wrote to Ampère on November 16, 1858: "Have I told you that we are bringing out a fourth edition of *L'Ancien Régime?* Two thousand copies, twenty-five hundred francs to the author as with the earlier editions. That makes almost nine thousand volumes printed in less than three years."[32]

If a part of the public reproached Tocqueville for not reaching a clear enough conclusion, discerning readers found in the book a diagnosis of the ailment that had brought on the collapse of representative institutions in France. Despite its internal quarrels, the whole liberal family was united in its support: Barrot, Montalembert, Duvergier de Hauranne, Mignet, Cousin, and the rest.

L'Ancien Régime contained an implicit manifesto against the wor-

[31]Letter to Ampère dated February 1, 1856, *O.C.* XI, 307–308.
[32]Letter to Ampère, *O.C.* XI, 413.

ship of authority and the worship of money. Tocqueville, on his 505
pessimistic days, believed that the public was no longer interested in
anything but the fluctuations of the stock exchange and the trappings
of luxury. The success of his book gave him proof that this was not
true, and it surprised and delighted him. If the book did not provoke
a reawakening of opinion, its success at least showed that certain
religious and moral values persisted in the depths of the public consciousness. Some of the responses, like a letter from the "youth of the
Ecoles," appear to have pleased the author greatly.

In the state of closely watched freedom in which the periodical press
found itself, one could not expect a very broad acceptance of the book.
In *Le Constitutionnel,* one of the pillars of the regime, there was a
hostile article by Paulin Limayrac. The role of *Le Siècle* was to give
the government a conventionally leftist response, but the animosity of
its director, Havin, toward Tocqueville had free rein: four different
articles attempted to persuade readers that Tocqueville was nostalgic
for the Ancien Régime. Tocqueville detested that "trimmer" Désiré
Nisard and certainly did not hide his feelings from him when they met
at the Académie, and Nisard was the one who reviewed *L'Ancien
Régime* in *La Patrie,* exuding a fairly perfidious gall despite a few
words of praise. In *La Presse,* Adolphe Peyrat praised Tocqueville for
his liberal sentiments, but accused this "overrated" author of not
adding anything new to the work of his predecessors; the article was
a curious one, unfavorable to Tocqueville but also to the regime, and
including the statement: "There are periods in which to meditate on
the past is to work for the future."[33]

The best of the articles hostile to *L'Ancien Régime* was a magazine
piece by Forcade La Roquette, half-brother of Achille de Saint-Arnaud
and future minister, in the *Revue contemporaine.*[34] While recognizing
the merits of the book, he vindicated the imperial regime (of the First
and Second Empires) for having created an order that guaranteed
everyone's security.

But the flatterers of the regime were not the only ones to attack the
book: "It will be admired by everyone and will not satisfy anyone,"
Pontmartin had written. In *Le Correspondant,* Vicomte de Meaux,
son-in-law of Montalembert, described the objections of the strict
legitimists.[35] Tocqueville had not seen the benefits of absolutism, had
exaggerated the decline of the nobility, and had above all misunder-

[33]These reviews are cited in a list found and published by Peter Mayer, *O.C.* II, 1: 335–37.
[34]*Revue contemporaine et athénáeum français* 39 (1856), 5–29.
[35]*Le Correspondant* 39 (November 1856), 254–82.

stood the spirit of the Revolution, a spirit of pride and revolt: the polemics of the admirers of the past, but a review that treated the author with great care and respect and acknowledged his gifts.

There was much more praise in the review in *L'Assemblée nationale* by another legitimist, Pontmartin.[36] His two articles contained a few reservations, but emphasized not only the freshness of Tocqueville's ideas but the originality of a style that expressed "many thoughts in few words." And the author concluded: "This liberty that he cherishes would be certain to triumph, and this time its triumph would surely be our newest and most beautiful conquest, if all of M. de Tocqueville's contemporaries understood it the way he does."

The two principal liberal organs, *Le Journal des débats* and the *Revue des deux mondes,* gave *L'Ancien Régime* strong support.

Le Journal des débats had announced the book's publication in an article signed by Sacy but actually written by Beaumont. Tocqueville expected that later a more detailed review would be written by Ampère. But Villemain, who no longer wrote for the press and whose great reputation was at its height, offered his own services. Ampère deferred to him and on July 1 Villemain published an analysis of the book in which he emphasized all its new ideas and praised it brilliantly and without reservation.[37]

Both Rémusat and Loménie wanted to review the book for the *Revue des deux mondes;* Loménie yielded to Rémusat, though with bad grace. Rémusat's article was more personal, more thorough than Villemain's, full of comparisons with England, which Rémusat knew well, and was, according to Tocqueville, the best thing that had been written about his work. Nonetheless, he found Rémusat at fault for not having made enough of the connections between the new book and the *Democracy.*[38]

The provincial press also published reviews (in a handwritten note, Tocqueville listed eight). The one in *La Gironde* by Lavertujon pleased him so much that he asked the author to come make his acquaintance.[39]

L'Ancien Régime had been translated into English by Reeve while still in proof, and its success seems to have been as great in England as it was in France. Important journals in Germany gave it long reviews, and it was as the author of *L'Ancien Régime* that Tocqueville's name now quickly became known in Russia.

[36]*L'Assemblée nationale,* July 5 and 12, 1856.
[37]*Le Journal des débats,* July 1, 1856.
[38]*Revue des deux mondes,* August 1, 1856.
[39]Unpublished letter in the archives of the Arsenal.

Tocqueville had thus, less than three years before his death, made a notable reappearance as a writer before the public. Even his political adversaries felt themselves obliged to pay homage to his character and talent in their criticisms. As for his liberal friends, they gave free rein to their enthusiasm and joy. The powers-that-be were quite taken aback.

27

THE AFTERMATH OF

L'ANCIEN RÉGIME

IN JUNE 1856, two very different events marked Tocqueville's life: the publication of *L'Ancien Régime* and the death of his father. When we compare the very abundant correspondence of the years that followed 1856 with that of the years before, we have the impression that, all in all, Tocqueville's nature became somewhat gentler. In any case, his daily round underwent substantial changes, as he himself observed.

We are familiar with the anxiety it caused him to make his reappearance before the public as a writer. In 1856, his need to regain the sympathy or the admiration of his readers was particularly acute. Their response could be a sort of appeasing of the private doubt he felt about the value of the work. But *L'Ancien Régime* was received so enthusiastically and greeted with such signs of esteem that one was reminded of the great success of 1835. He was able to take more pleasure in it this time, because while before he had viewed this literary success as one stage on his way to a career as statesman, he now only wanted to resume his rank in the literary world. He felt a certain solidarity with the liberal generation of men in their fifties and sixties, whom their successors accused of having conducted the affairs of the country badly, when he himself found it far superior to the younger generation, in which, rather unfairly, he saw no signs of new life. Though Lamartine, an uneven poet, might now be sinking into "alimentary rhapsodies," his contemporaries, established since the days of the July monarchy, seemed to Tocqueville to be the leading figures still in France's literary world:[1] Cousin, despite the strangeness of some of the subjects he chose; Villemain, the greatest critic; Mignet and Thiers, historians still producing a large output; Duvergier de Hauranne himself, who was defining for the future the history of the representative regime in France; Rémusat, the great essayist; and Montalembert, who, deprived of the tribune, had become an unrivaled pamphleteer. *L'Ancien Régime* had taken its place in the constellation of works by the liberal opposition and shone there with a brilliance all its own. When that holy of holies of the liberal school, the *Revue des deux mondes,* seemed threatened with a trial, he exerted himself to predispose the judges in its favor.

He had also never been happier about the successes of his old political friends: Dufaure had risen to a place of eminence in the Paris bar; Rivet had gone back into business and was involved in the railways; and he tended to nudge the lazy ones like Lanjuinais or Beaumont, who were not showing the public what they were capable of. He had always been a tactful friend, but now he became a devoted one, successfully managing the difficult matrimonial negotiations that allowed Corcelle's daughter to become Madame de Chambrun. Certain accounts—too few, it is true, for one to draw any general conclusions from them—depict him as cheerful, relaxed. His feelings for the imperial regime remained unchanged, but he evinced less harshness and more irony toward the "rascals" who had gone over to it.

Despite the fact that Comte Hervé was eighty-four years old at the time of his death, the loss was an extremely painful one for Alexis. Even though he had sometimes grumbled about the narrow horizons of his father's household during the last few years, his filial attachment to the old man ran very deep. The death of the head of the family brought the brothers closer together, but their political differences stood in the way of a renewal of the old intimacy. Tocqueville saw another cause for the relative coldness, and that was the conduct of his two sisters-in-law, especially Emilie, Hippolyte's wife; but it is quite clear that Mary's feelings for them were not warm. She had tolerated, without a great deal of grace, the association with her father-in-law. Now that she was nearly sixty, she was more jealously possessive of the exclusive affection of her husband, who, turning to her in his need for tenderness, yielded to her preferences. She was also becoming more

[1]Letter from Tocqueville to Gobineau, September 16, 1858, *O.C.* IX, 297.

510
⚶ ⚶

and more of a stay-at-home and loved her rest; this was in part explained by her poor health: kidney complaints, attacks of rheumatism, throat ailments. Rédier supposes that she had become neurasthenic, which is quite plausible. It also seems that in her last years she was much more involved than in the past with her own family. In 1857 and 1858, the Tocquevilles paid a visit to Chamarande to be near her aunt, Mrs. Belam, who was ninety years old. In 1857, during his trip to England, she asked Alexis to do something that was rather humiliating for him. He went to see Sir Charles Wood, first lord of the admiralty, to ask that his brother-in-law Joe be appointed port captain, a favor that the minister kindly granted him. Madame de Tocqueville also became more conscious of her British origins, to a degree that surprised her husband. She formed a friendship with the British consul at Cherbourg and his daughters. She lost sleep over the Great Mutiny in India in 1857 and followed passionately the gradual reestablishment of English authority in the colony.

The château and estate of Tocqueville were the center from which she governed things and people, her husband occasionally intervening to soothe conflicts with the latter. It was she who prescribed the household's long stays in the Cotentin. Tocqueville became resigned to them. In earlier times, he wrote, he could not have done without the capital and its salons, but now he was acquiring a taste for this somewhat monotonous life. He examined himself to see if he had become more sensible, but feared that he had only become older. At the time of the trip he made to England in 1857, which had an almost triumphal aspect, he wrote to his wife how eager he was to return quickly. For a long time, he had had a real affection for his country neighbors; now raising sheep, fattening pigs, fertilization trials with guano occupied a larger and larger place among his preoccupations. Before the publication of his book in 1856, he would rise as usual before six, devote the morning to his mental work, and then spend the afternoon in the fields, for instance directing the group of workers who were making over the grounds of the château. After dinner, in keeping with a habit of many years' standing, he and his wife would read aloud together.

The château of Tocqueville thus became the center of their life. From June 25, 1856, the date of his return after the publication of L'Ancien Régime, until his final departure on September 28, 1858, Tocqueville spent twenty-two and a half months there and his wife a little more. She was not at all inactive. Starting in 1855, she had undertaken to make the interior comfortable. From 1856 to 1858,

larger projects were pursued on the grounds, which had somewhat 511
resembled a swampy woods. Ditches were filled and trees cut down. 𖤐 𖤐
A sheltered walk was laid out, and Ampère was assured that he would
be able to smoke his cigar there protected from the weather without
getting his feet wet. A greenhouse was built. The best methods of
constructing animal enclosures were studied, so that livestock could be
kept from invading the courtyard. Hedges and young trees were
planted. The overgrown expanse in the middle distance, as far as the
cultivated fields beyond, was converted into meadow. The inheritance
Tocqueville had received from his father helped pay for this work, but
every penny of the royalties he earned (a sum which was not negligible, since Lévy was giving him one franc per volume) was poured into
it as well.

Several visits broke the monotony of this daily life without upsetting its rhythm. The couple wanted Ampère to come for as long as
possible. His conversation was brilliant, he appreciated the good dishes,
and he joined Madame de Tocqueville at billiards. He still had the heart
of the twenty-year-old he had been when he fell in love with Madame
Récamier, then forty. Now he had established a sort of "sentimental
domesticity" in relation to Madame Guillemin, daughter of the rich
banker Cheuvreux, whose health required that she live in Italy, where
her parents had followed her. He was a "confiscated man," Tocqueville
complained, and in fact, Ampère lived in Italy from the beginning of
1857 to April 1859, when he landed in Marseilles to learn of Tocqueville's death.

Though they could not have Ampère, they received visits from old
friends of the days of the July monarchy—the Beaumonts, the Corcelles, Lanjuinais, Rivet, and in 1857 the Loménies, who had counted on
finding Ampére there, whereas he had remained in Italy. Most of the
guests stayed for a week or two. For some, there were stages along the
way to or from that far corner of the Cotentin: at Beaufossé in the Orne,
Corcelle's place; at Broglie with the duke; or at Val Richer with Guizot,
who was visited by Reeve and his family—they had just spent two
weeks at Tocqueville—shortly after Reeve finished his translation of
L'Ancien Régime. Traveling conditions were transformed by the Paris–
Cherbourg railway line, which opened in July 1858. The inauguration
of the railway coincided with that of the great docks of the port of
Cherbourg, and the festivities, marked by a meeting between Queen
Victoria and Napoléon III, went on from the fourth of August to the
eighth. Six hundred English and French vessels had been brought
together in the roads, and Tocqueville took his guests of the moment,

512
𝕏 𝕏

the Beaumonts and Rivet, to admire the maneuvers of this immense fleet from the top of the towers of Tourlaville, the Renaissance château that belonged at that time to his brother Edouard, and from the rocks of Fermanville that bounded the roads toward the east.

But if Tocqueville's daily life seemed calm, if the lively wit of the author of the *Souvenirs* was less often turned on his fellow men, he nevertheless remained an uneasy soul. Perhaps the death of his father and that of his uncle Rosanbo, expected for several years, led him to concern himself more with religious problems, as did also, perhaps, the very fact that his existence was no longer filled with the preoccupations of public life, as it had been before. Back in 1850, after the serious illness that had threatened his life and at the moment of going away to convalesce, he had summoned Abbé Coeur, a well-known theologian and a friend who would soon become Bishop of Troyes, to discuss fundamentals of the faith; then, afraid of reaching some conclusion, he had talked to the ecclesiastic about other things. We have considered his letter of February 26, 1857, the most explicit confession of his loss of the Catholic faith in his youth and a profession of the faith he now held, which was altogether a spiritualist one; the month before, on January 24, he had defended to Gobineau—who had taken this as nothing but irony—those men who were not convinced of the Christian truths and yet had a "filial tenderness" for Christianity. Letters to Corcelle from the same period expressed both his desire to believe and his incapacity for belief. His attitude was summed up, finally, in a letter dated January 18, 1858, to an old friend, the philosopher Louis Bouchitté, who had published a book on the proofs of God's existence. Bouchitté had written him a letter in which he affirmed that man could know God through his heart and through his mind, and Tocqueville had answered him: "All the rest is nothing compared to that question," but, after recalling that he believed in providence and divine justice, he added that there existed a "depth" that he could not touch: "that is the why and the wherefore of the world, the plan of this creation of which we know nothing, not even our bodies, even less our minds; the ground of the destiny of this singular being whom we call man . . ."[2]

· · ·

[2]Letters to Corcelle dated August 1, 1850, *O.C.* XV, 2: 29, particularly the passage cited above on page 460; to Madame Swetchine dated February 2, 1857, ibid., 314–35; to Gobineau dated January 24, 1857, *O.C.* IX, 276–78; to Bouchitté dated January 18, 1858, *O.C.* (Bmt) VII, 476–77. Bouchitté's letter is in the Tocqueville Archives, file 17.

For a long time, Tocqueville had grieved over not having a child 513
of his own, and it was natural that this sorrow should increase with 烬 烬
the years. He bestowed most of his affection on his nephew Hubert,
one of his brother Edouard's sons, who had begun a diplomatic career
first in Vienna, then in Berlin. He wrote him letters in which he
endeavored to transmit the family traditions to him and to orient his
intellectual life. He had respect for this nephew's serious qualities, but
felt he was too good, with a morality that was too orderly. Despite
his affection for him, he reproached him with not being enough like
what he himself had been thirty years earlier, with not having inherited
his adventurous fervor.

He was more conscious than ever of time passing. He talked more
about his youth, about his past as a politician. He sometimes declared
that old age had brought him serenity, but this serenity was often
touched with melancholy. For instance, he wrote from Paris to his
wife, apropos of the attentions he was being shown by librarians and
archivists: "When I was writing *Democracy in America,* I had none of
these advantages, but I had youth, I had faith in a cause, and the hope
that allowed me to do without the kindliness of librarians and the favor
of archivists. Cuvier created an admirable work in a garret . . . My
own garret was a small room in the rue de Verneuil where I worked
away in profound obscurity at a book that was to bring me out of that
obscurity."[3]

The letters Tocqueville received after the publication of *L'Ancien
Régime et la Révolution* often expressed the hope that the rest of the
work would appear soon. He himself, in his foreword, had committed
himself to following "the course of this Revolution" and to showing
how, after the enthusiasm of 1789, the French had come to resign
themselves to "a power stronger and more absolute than the one
the Revolution had overthrown." He added: "Part of this book has
been roughed out, but it is still unworthy of being offered to the
public."[4] This last statement was a pure product of his imagination.

In that summer of 1856 he felt the need to rest a little and step back
from his book. He thought of doing some work that was rather
marginal to his main preoccupations, but that would not take him too

[3]Unpublished letter dated April 18, 1858.
[4]*O.C.* II, 1: 73.

far away from them: he promised Buloz that for the *Revue des deux mondes* he would write a study of Friedrich Perthes, a German who went from admiring 1789 to favoring the nationalism of 1814. He read through the first volume of the biography Perthes's son had written, and took some fragmentary but carefully written notes.[5] Then he declared that he was unsuited to enclosing his thoughts within the framework of a magazine article, and, despite his desire to show his interest in the *Revue,* abandoned the project.

He slowly went back to work at writing the sequel to *L'Ancien Régime.* He decided against the original project of commenting on the Consulate and the Empire, to devote himself to the Revolution proper. The problem was to bridge the gap, as it were, between *L'Ancien Régime,* which he had just published, and the two chapters of 1852 on the causes of 18 Brumaire, which were still unpublished. This could only be done by following a chronological plan. But for Tocqueville, this was a new kind of work: *L'Ancien Régime* was a picture of France on the eve of the Revolution, as the *Democracy* of 1835 had been a sociopolitical picture of America. To follow the course of events was to make the change from sociologist to historian.

He had no intention of limiting himself to narrating the succession of events that shaped the Revolution. In his book, these would be merely the infrastructure of the changes of opinion of the French or of certain classes of the French. Whence a very great difficulty in determining his subject. Tocqueville had the impression that it constituted a shapeless body that could not be grasped because of the veils that hid it. On September 20, 1856, he analyzed the problem in a letter to Freslon:

> The difficulty of my present undertaking is . . . much greater than those I have encountered before. If I draw back too far from the details of the events and deal only with the movement in the nation's ideas and attitudes during the revolutionary epoch (which is my subject, properly speaking), I am indefinite and elusive; if I draw too near the details, I fall into an immense ocean that has nevertheless been well explored in all of its reaches and is thoroughly known. The very sight of it makes me dizzy . . . I haven't yet come to that half-light that allows one to glimpse the country and ask the inhabitants to point out one's road.[6]

[5]These notes have been published in the *O.C.* II, 2: 255–65.
[6]Unpublished letter.

A letter to Beaumont written more than a year later (December 6, 1857) shows that he had made some progress, but did not yet feel in control of his project:

> To handle [my subject] in a new way is an all but chimerical notion, and to do nothing but repeat commonplaces that we have heard since the day we were born is impossible for me. I would die of boredom myself before the book could bore my reader. What is more, I must interweave ideas and events, I must say enough about the events to make the ideas comprehensible and make the reader feel how interesting or important they are, and yet I must not write a history properly speaking . . . I can see, I think, the object that I want to portray; but the light illuminating it wavers and does not yet allow me to grasp the image well enough to be able to reproduce it.[7]

Nevertheless, by that date he had chosen the sources that seemed to him essential in order to carry out his plan. In a letter written October 6, 1856, to George Lewis, the very erudite chancellor of the exchequer, he described the reasons for his preferences: "Since my object is much more to portray the changes in attitudes and ideas that successively produced the events of the Revolution than to recount these events themselves, I need historical documents a good deal less than I need writings in which the spirit of the times is revealed at each step of the way: newspapers, pamphlets, private letters, administrative correspondence."[8]

Tocqueville had heard that the British Museum possessed an unrivaled collection of these documents and asked his correspondent if this was true. The latter confirmed it, and Tocqueville decided to take a trip to London the following year.

But shortly after he wrote this letter, he learned, no doubt through Ampère, that in 1855 the Bibliothèque Impériale had published a catalogue of its printed material on the history of France. Before this date, it was impossible for historians to establish a serious bibliography of the ephemeral publications that were contemporaneous with the last days of the Ancien Régime and the Revolution. Now one could do so easily and find out everything the library contained, which, though less significant than the wealth of the British Museum, still formed a considerable mass of material.[9] This was fortunate for Tocqueville,

---

[7]*O.C.* VIII, 3: 522.
[8]*O.C.* (Bmt) VII, 410.
[9]See Ledos, *Histoires des catalogues imprimés de la Bibliothèque nationale* (Paris, 1936).

516

寒寒

especially since his good relations with the administrator Taschereau and several other librarians allowed him rather astonishing special privileges: "I have been shown extreme kindliness, particularly at the Bibliothèque Impériale, that singularly facilitates the work I can do in the country. They have given me a copy of the printed catalogue containing all the works relating to the Revolution. In this book, I indicate all those I need, and they send them to me. Many of them are pamphlets or unbound documents. They have sent me as many as one hundred fifty at a time. This is what is called helping people," he wrote to Beaumont on February 1, 1857, and a few days later, he told Freslon that he had just read through fifty pamphlets in three days.[10]

At this time, Tocqueville's reading bore on the period 1787–1790. In April 1857, he and his wife left the Cotentin to spend several weeks at Chamarande, near Mrs. Belam, the old aunt who had raised Mary. The château, no doubt built by Mansart, had become the property of a Paris merchant who had ruined the gardens, destroying flower beds and statues in order to cultivate potatoes, and who rented out apartments. In October, the whole property was bought back by the Duc de Persigny, who thus became the Tocquevilles' landlord, but, in order to restore the whole estate, he brought in a crowd of workers who put them to flight in the spring of 1858. During the period of April to June 1857, Tocqueville spent the weekends at Chamarande, which is only forty kilometers from Paris, and starting Monday evening or Tuesday morning spent three or four days in Paris, working primarily on completing his documentation at the Archives.

He had not, however, given up his trip to London. He arrived there on June 19 and seems to have remained in England until July 24. He admired the mass of pamphlets on the revolutionary epoch that the British Museum contained, but nothing was catalogued and he would have had to spend six months finding his way around the collection. He fell back on the State Paper Office: the diplomatic correspondence of the years 1787–1793 was not available to the public, but Lord Clarendon, the minister of foreign affairs, made an exception in his favor. He was thus able to convince himself that the assertion that England had deliberately encouraged France's revolutionary troubles was an absurd, apocryphal story. All this was rather disappointing: "My trip to England will certainly have had some pleasures, but I won't derive much profit from the documents," he wrote his wife.

[10]Letter to Beaumont, O.C. III, 3: 457; to Freslon, unpublished letter, Tocqueville Archives.

The "pleasures," on the other hand, were extremely flattering. *L'An-* 517
cien Régime had had an extraordinary success in the world of the ☙ ☙
English aristocracy and among English intellectuals. Tocqueville was
a most sought-after guest, and was deluged with invitations to dinner
as soon as he arrived. He refused them all—even that of Lord Palmerston—wanting to rest after his research by dining alone at the Athenaeum Club, but almost every day he had to have lunch at the homes
of prominent figures in the aristocracy or the political world (at the
beginning of his visit, he found himself, as in 1835, with Mérimée and
noted maliciously that the latter's title as senator of the Empire did not
keep him from being placed to the left of the mistress of the house
while he, Tocqueville, sat on her right[11]) and go into society in the
evening. A fragment of a letter to his wife gives the tone of the
welcome he received: "Yesterday, I was invited to dine with Lord
Granville. I refused. But Lady Granville wrote me to ask me to come
in the evening, at least. I went. Many of the principal ministers were
there, and several of the greatest ladies of England. It seems that my
book had been the subject of conversation at dinner. So that everyone
was freshly 'sharpened up,' as they say, on the subject. Thus, when I
made my entrance I was so completely surrounded, caressed, praised,
that I didn't really know where to hide."[12] Old Lord Lyndhurst,
survivor of another age, told him that he had written the book of the
century. Through Lord Clarendon as intermediary, Prince Albert
asked to meet him, saying that there was no one he wanted so much
to meet. On the day and the hour proposed, Tocqueville had already
promised to lunch with Reeve at the home of the Duc de Nemours,
who had, through Reeve, expressed the desire to see him. Prince Albert
consented to put the meeting off to the next day.[13]

Tocqueville escaped from London several times to go see his friends
the Grotes in the country and to visit the two great estates of Lord
Hatherton and Lord Radnor, where he was shown around by the
owners.

At the end, Sir Charles Wood made available to him a small ship
from the British fleet which took him by night from Portsmouth back
to Cherbourg, causing great amazement among the local inhabitants
when he landed, probably on July 25, at eight in the morning. An
English newspaper revealed to its readers that a ship of the British navy
had taken back to Cherbourg a top-ranking French official who had

[11]Unpublished letter to his wife dated June 29, 1857.
[12]Unpublished letter to his wife dated June 27, 1857.
[13]On this meeting see the *O.C.* VI, 1, appendix: 353.

518

𝕊 𝕊

come to settle the details of a meeting between Queen Victoria and Napoléon III.

Tocqueville had found himself once again among the English aristocracy with whom he felt so close an affinity. He had also rediscovered the love of liberty so lacking in his own country. Before 1848, he had fought English imperialism, then had been shocked by the favor shown the French despot in that free country. But how could such a welcome not have made him describe England as a second homeland? We should not be at all surprised that he so energetically sided with the English against the mutinous Hindus: for him, this was a struggle between civilization and barbarism. He remained clear in his mind about the mistakes of British policy and the defects of British pride (as his letters to Reeve show) but at the end of his life, friendships with the English played a more important role than ever in his correspondence.

The trip to England, originally conceived as a working visit, had become a sort of intermission in the work in progress, which had to be resumed when Tocqueville returned. It was not until the end of October that he felt ready to write Book I of the new volume, and he gave his time to this until January 1858. The seven chapters that composed it took the reader from 1787 to the meeting of the States-General in May 1789. The author intended to return to them later, as was his usual practice, in order to give them final form. He was not able to do so.[14]

These rough drafts have great interest, nonetheless. In them, Tocqueville first pointed out the connections between the French Revolution and the profound intellectual disquiet that then pervaded Europe. He next showed that in France the privileged orders were the first to revolt against the royal power. Once the latter was defeated, the apparent union of the social classes behind the Assembly of Notables or the *parlements* that had led the assault was superseded by a conflict between the third estate (the bourgeoisie) and the privileged orders of the nobility and clergy—an expression of the social structure analyzed in *L'Ancien Régime*. Sometimes—and this was the greatness of the spirit of 1789—the sense that the revolution was being carried forward for the benefit of all mankind masked this conflict between the classes.

No one before Tocqueville had made the connection between the ideas evolving in Europe as a whole and the event of the French

[14]They are printed in the *O.C.* II, 2: 33–139.

Revolution. It was also quite new to stress the "aristocratic revolution"   519
of the years 1787 and 1788. Neither Michelet, absorbed in his vision   ꙮ ꙮ
of a people rising on a day of justice, nor Thiers, who had narrated
events without going below the surface of things, had seen the importance of this. Perhaps the only one who had sensed it was Madame de
Staël, a witness as much as a historian, in her *Considérations sur la
Révolution française*. But no one had brought out with such energy the
immediate origins of 1789 or seen that a "great revolution" had, in fact,
preceded the meeting of the States-General.

At the moment he was writing this book, Tocqueville was already
preparing the following one, on the States-General and the Constituent
Assembly. He was using the great compilation of Bouchez and Roux,
the forty volumes of their *Histoire parlementaire de la Révolution,* as well
as contemporary newspapers and letters from deputies to their constitu-
ents. For a more thorough study of the crucially important role of Paris
and a clearer understanding of the anarchy in the provinces, he judged
this printed documentation insufficient. In April 1858, he journeyed to
Paris to consult the Archives on the deliberations of the municipal
authorities, the correspondence of Jean-Sylvain Bailly and Lafayette,
that of the minister of the royal household, and the reports of the
provincial administrations.

But in May, discouraged by his throat and stomach ailments and
overwhelmed by solitude, he could not manage to find a way of
organizing his subject, and his mood would swing from rare moments
of enthusiasm to fits of discouragement. He decided to return to
Tocqueville, putting more thorough work off until later.

The book on the Revolution was to go no further, and it is easy
to see that Tocqueville was far from having realized his plan. Except
for the spacious preamble that appeared in 1856—*L'Ancien Régime et
la Révolution*—only nine chapters had reached the stage of rough
drafts, more or less advanced, by 1859: seven on the immediate origins
of the Revolution and two on the accession of Bonaparte. Especially
in the case of the first seven, which included unwritten passages,
lacunae that were supposed to be filled with quotations, the author
certainly would have made rather substantial revisions.

For the rest, there exist only reading notes and scattered reflections.
All in all, not much on the Consulate and the Empire, a good deal
more on the beginnings of the Revolution. But there are major subjects
that are scarcely represented: the Legislative Assembly, the Committee
of Public Safety. Tocqueville never systematically studied the revolutionary war that changed the entire history of the period. Certain

opinions which he jotted down hurriedly, on the Terror or the Empire, can only be considered working hypotheses, and are not the expression of definitively acquired convictions.

Although these lacunae are accounted for by the circumstances, it is nonetheless surprising to find almost nothing about two important topics.

First, there is no discussion of the influence of war on the development of the revolutionary ideology. At the time, there was already little question of the importance of the role played by the wars of the Ancien Régime in the centralizing of monarchical power. As a deputy, Tocqueville had said that he was against wars that sought to impose a political regime on the enemy, but that he would find it easy enough to accept a war, even under very unfavorable circumstances, if it were a question of defending the nation's honor. The changes that war, that major disease of the body politic, could bring about in the institutions of the country waging it seem to have largely escaped him.

The second lacuna, even more surprising, is the absence of any substantial note on the Jacobins. Here, one cannot suspect Tocqueville of having misunderstood the problem. All his life, his thinking had been haunted by the existence of "this new race, of revolutionaries," who had spread throughout the world thanks to the French Revolution.

As early as the time of his trip to America, he had noted how different the men of 1793 were from true democrats; in his youth, he could not fail to evoke with pain the memories of the Convention. Under the July monarchy, he had met survivors of that time and their successors, within the very heart of the dynastic left and the groups of radical members he was close to in the spectrum of the parties. He studied their mores with interest under the Second Republic. What seems to have caused him difficulty was discovering the underlying reasons for their behavior and their passions. When and how did these men deviate from the shared ideals of 1789? Tocqueville sometimes seems to suspect that some influence was exerted on the formation of the Jacobin ideology by the social and agrarian troubles of the beginnings of the Revolution; he also saw the new interests that could lead to a fanatical defense of the Revolution. But he does not seem to have reached a firm conclusion in this area.

It is true that he sometimes wrote nothing about the very problems that occupied his thoughts the most. In this case, he was no doubt waiting until he had had a chance to examine the pamphlets and newspapers of the period of the Convention, something he was never able to do.

28

CANNES

TOCQUEVILLE'S health was never very good, as we have seen. From his youth on he had suffered from troubles with his digestive system, and these were in part responsible for his irritability and his tendency to become emotional. But the state of his health did not prevent him from successfully carrying out the difficult American journey, when he had only one bout of serious illness and quickly recovered from it. While he was a deputy during the July monarchy and the Second Republic, his health was fragile and he sometimes had to keep to his room, but only for a few days and not for long stretches. The first real sign of deterioration in his health was the terrible crisis in March 1850, when he spat blood and seemed on the point of dying.[1] As we have seen, he recovered from this very slowly after the winter of 1850–1851, which he spent at Sorrento. But in July 1851 he found himself unable to complete the reading of his report to the Assembly on the revision of the Constitution. From that time on, the presence of a slowly developing tuberculosis could be detected in his right lung. In 1853, a serious crisis of which we know very little forced him to spend a year in Touraine. He was treated by Dr. Brettoneau, but mainly, it seems, for stomach troubles which the doctor would soothe temporarily with a cure-all he was very fond of, silver nitrate and belladonna. Over the course of the following years, there was a series of crises and remissions. Tocqueville's correspondence alludes to many throat inflammations, flus, and attacks of bronchitis that dragged on

[1]See above, page 372.

and then were more or less cured. Beaumont thought that Tocqueville was very wrong to spend the winters of 1855, 1856, and 1857 in the Cotentin, where the cold was accompanied by dampness and storms. But Beaumont was no more aware than Tocqueville himself and their other friends of the gradual deterioration of his condition, although it is obvious to anyone who reads through his correspondence. For years, Tocqueville's health had been so unstable that no one realized that the disease was steadily making headway.

But in April 1858, Tocqueville, who had gone to Paris to work on the sequel to *L'Ancien Régime,* suffered from such stomach and throat problems and then felt so ill by the middle of May that he gave up his researches and returned to Tocqueville. Around June 20, he spat blood: "Eight years ago, a terrible illness had begun in the same way. I thought I was having another attack of it. My wife was even more convinced than I. She sent in all haste for my brother, who lives near Cherbourg, and a doctor. It was, however, an isolated episode. But since that time I have not been the same man. Today I am still not back in the saddle [July 23]."[2] In August, however, he received friends; but, aware of suspicious noises in his chest, he went to Paris on September 13 to consult the celebrated doctors Andral and Charruau. They diagnosed bronchitis in the right lung and prescribed blistering for three weeks. Charruau sent the patient back to Tocqueville, whence he returned on September 28 for the application of the third plaster, for which Charruau substituted a caustic. Even though the doctors claimed to note an improvement in the patient's condition, they ordered him to spend the winter in the south and, faced with Madame de Tocqueville's abhorrence of going by sea to Italy, Andral assured Tocqueville that Cannes would be just as good. Madame de Tocqueville went to join her husband in the capital, and they left for Cannes on October 28.

The trip was extremely difficult, even though it was made in small stages. On October 28, the Tocquevilles slept in Dijon, on the twenty-ninth at Lyon, on the thirtieth at Valence, on the thirty-first at Aix. Here, they rested on November 1 and left the next day for Cannes, where they arrived the evening of the fourth. They had left the railway at Lyon, and at Aix had found very mediocre hired carriages in which to continue on their way. "In the valley of the Rhône we were caught in the midst of a hurricane from the north that removed the bridges

[2]Letter to Mrs. Grote, *O.C.* (Bmt) VI, 449–50.

from the river while we were traveling along its banks. Since then, the 523
cold has not left us. The mountains surrounding us here are covered
with snow and it freezes every night." During the last leg of the trip
snow fell all the way from Fréjus to within sight of Cannes. Tocqueville was reminded of the fate of those many invalids who had been
sent to the South too late and died in inns along the way. The sudden
arrival of that winter of 1858–1859, whose brutality is also attested to
in Mérimée's *Correspondance,* made him aware of his extremely weak
condition. He arrived in Cannes, he wrote on the sixth to his brother
Edouard, "so exhausted that it would have been impossible for me to
go any farther . . . Even here it freezes every night and the mountains
are white. But this extraordinary weather can't last. The countryside
is admirable and we couldn't have been luckier in our house."[3]

The site of the villa "Montfleury" is now swallowed up in the
agglomeration of Cannes. At the time, it lay a little more than a mile
to the east of the town, in the midst of orange and lemon groves
halfway between the heights of the Croix-des-Gardes and the sea. The
spot was relatively sheltered, and the ocean breezes carried the fra-
grance of flowers. The view out over the bay and the Ile Sainte-
Marguerite was magnificent. The house faced south and was
approached by an alley lined with date palms and cypresses. It was
large, designed for two families, and when the Tocquevilles were there
alone, they left six rooms unoccupied.

Cannes was becoming a fashionable resort. Mérimée, who arrived
January 1, 1859, and stayed there until about February 20, noted that
it "was becoming more civilized every day, even too much so," and
predicted that the construction of the railway, which was being ac-
celerated because of the possibility of war in Italy, would lead to an
invasion of people from Marseilles. For the moment, it was still an
aristocratic resort, frequented by a few great notables of the imperial
regime, a few Russians, and especially a large colony of English. The
two men who had discovered its charms, Woolfield and above all Lord
Brougham, were there. Tocqueville had quarreled with Brougham
fifteen years before, at the time when, in connection with the matter
of boarding rights off the African coast, Brougham had accused him
of "marvelous ignorance" in a speech that had led to an exchange of
quite acerbic public letters. Nevertheless, Senior, informed of Tocqueville's situation, had written to Lord Brougham to suggest a reconcilia-

---

[3]Unpublished letters to his brother Edouard, dated November 1 and 6. Letter to Beaumont dated
November 11, *O.C.* VIII, 3: 603–605.

tion that would appear spontaneous.[4] Brougham paid Tocqueville a visit, and although they had hardly any conversations, the Englishman's rich library helped Tocqueville to fight off boredom during the times when he was able to read. Even though he could hardly converse except in a low voice, Tocqueville received Baron von Bunsen several times. He continued to take an interest in political events, and the great affair of the day was the possibility of a war in which France would intervene as Piedmont's ally against Austria in order to liberate Venetian Lombardy. Upon his arrival in Cannes, Tocqueville thought that Napoléon III, after having acted in a threatening way, would draw back before the prospect of a conflict. Bunsen, former ambassador from Prussia to London, up-to-date about French military preparations, believed the war would take place and seems to have induced Tocqueville to share his conviction.

But even their few associations with the outside world were intermittent for the residents of the villa "Montfleury." After arriving at Cannes in a worrisome state of exhaustion, Tocqueville was immediately subjected to a week of exceptional cold. Afterwards, periods of mild, sunny weather alternated with days of rain and spells of cold. In any case, life was organized around the patient according to the care he had to be given. The trip had made Madame de Tocqueville ill; she hardly recovered at all during their stay; her throat was in such bad condition that she was forbidden to speak, and her eyes were equally bad, so that she had to remain in darkness for days at a time. The care she could give her husband was therefore quite insufficient, despite her willingness to give it. He was visited regularly by two doctors, Dr. Sève, who had been recommended to him before he left Paris, and Dr. Maure, from Grasse, a former colleague from the Assemblies of 1846 and 1849 and a friend of Thiers, who had taken the initiative of writing to ask him to go see Tocqueville, an attention for which Tocqueville expressed his gratitude to the former statesman. Occasionally, one of the doctors slept at the villa "Montfleury." But the patient was normally watched over by two nuns from the Congrégation du Bon-Secours, Sister Valérie and Sister Gertrude, who took turns, day in day out, caring for him. In his last days, beginning on April 10, he had the help of a young medical assistant, Thadée Dujardin-Beaumetz, no doubt sent by Corcelle. If Tocqueville could not continue to think of his work as he had hoped to when he left Paris, his mind could not remain without food, and starting in November, he hired a reader:

---

[4]Senior to Brougham, unpublished letter in the London University Library.

"I had ordered some books that I had wanted to read for a long time 525 and that I hadn't happened to find earlier. In the evenings, when reading was difficult for me, I made up for it by having a reader. In Cannes I discovered a sort of seminarist, who comes to spend part of the evening here with us to read out loud. This future member of the priestly tribe is a great milksop. Because the roads that lead to our house are rather deserted in the evening, he never fails, even though he is nineteen years old, to make his mama come with him, and she knits in the antechamber while her son gives us French prose in a Provençal accent. All in all, he doesn't read badly and this is a great resource."[5]

Tocqueville also had the moral support of his brothers. Hippolyte spent nearly three months at Cannes starting from the beginning of December and came back for Alexis's last days. Edouard, who at first had to remain with his wife because she was also ill, took her to Nice and then came at least twice to stay at the villa "Montfleury"; he was there, together with his son Hubert, when Alexis died.

Friends of Tocqueville also offered to come. The presence of Corcelle, it seemed to him, would be more of an encumbrance than a blessing, and he dissuaded Corcelle from making the trip. But on March 4, Tocqueville, who had refused an earlier offer from Beaumont, appealed to him in these terms:

"My dear friend, I don't know if anything has ever cost me so much to say as what I am going to say to you: *I ask you to come.* We are here alone: Hippolyte has flown off; Edouard is at Nice on the point of doing the same. . . . My wife's state of mind frightens me, my friend. She is suffering, suffering more than she has for a month; she is visibly reaching the last extremity of her physical and *moral* strength; this state is engendering in her soul ideas, feelings, sorrows, and dreads that might end by leading her spirit anywhere . . ."[6] Beaumont hurried to him and remained in Cannes until April 6.

On April 9, Louis de Kergorlay came to take over from Beaumont. Until then, Louis had been kept away by his wife's health and the death of one of his children, at an early age. As soon as he was able, he came to Alexis and spent the last week of Alexis's life with him. As we have said, Ampère was in Rome. He was not aware that his friend was gravely ill, though this was by now well known in Paris. In March, he decided to come, taking advantage of Madame Guillemin's im-

[5]Tocqueville to Ampère, December 5, 1858, *O.C.* XI, 415.
[6]Letter to Beaumont dated March 4, 1859, *O.C.* VIII, 3: 615.

526

光 光

proved health. On the 9th of April, probably before Kergorlay's arrival, Tocqueville wrote Ampère the last letter he was to write in his own hand:

My dear friend, what you tell me in your last letter fills me with delight; I tell you this without standing on ceremony. My joy will never have been so great at seeing you again, even though I have never been less capable of enjoying your society. For my wife's throat is in pitiable condition and almost always requires her to use a slate. As for me, I can no longer set one foot in front of the other; I am obliged to speak in a soft voice and very little. Readings that go on for very long soon render me incapable of listening. Nevertheless I say to you: Come, come, for nothing is more selfish than true friendship, like another feeling one doesn't even name any longer, especially in my present position. Your bed is going to be made up this instant, and your neighbor will be the only inhabitant of the house who can speak, Edouard.[7]

Ampère had already left Rome when this letter arrived there. He landed at Marseilles on April 17, happy at the prospect of seeing his friend again. It was there that he learned that Tocqueville had died the day before.

In Cannes, Tocqueville had experienced periods of crises and remissions, as often happens with tuberculosis. Judging from the documentary evidence, it seems the disease became more generalized: there were stomach troubles and a loss of appetite that prevented him from eating, and very sharp intermittent pains in his bladder. From the beginning Dr. Maure felt his case was hopeless, though the other doctor maintained some hope for a long time.

At the beginning of November, the invalid's recuperation from his trip had gone slowly. He did begin to feel better, however, and thought he was on the way to recovery at the end of the month, when his brother Hippolyte left the Cotentin to come to Cannes. Perhaps Hippolyte's departure was the source of the news that appeared in the newspapers of the West and was taken up by *La Patrie* on December 1, 1858, and *La Gazette de France* on the second, that Tocqueville was dangerously ill. During the days that followed, he wrote a number of letters reassuring his friends.

In early January, Tocqueville's condition worsened again. On January 7, Mérimée wrote to their mutual friend Madame de Boigne:

"It isn't easy to know just how M. de Tocqueville is. He sees

[7]*O.C.* XI, 423–24.

absolutely no one; neither does his wife. His brother's feeling about it is sometimes good, sometimes bad. Of the two doctors who are treating him, one thinks he is lost, the other has some hope. He spat blood not long ago, then the day before yesterday he was a little better."

On the eighteenth, Mérimée seemed even more pessimistic as he gave news to Edward Ellice: "Here, we have poor Tocqueville very ill with bronchitis and an ulcerated lung. I truly fear he will never leave this part of the country." And on the twenty-fifth, he wrote again to Madame de Boigne: "Poor Tocqueville is alternately better and worse. I have seen his doctor, who is an intelligent man and a friend of M. Thiers. He told me there was no hope, that one of his lungs was tubercular and already ulcerated. His morale is weak. He is depressed about his condition and completely lacking in energy. I don't really know if energy would be of any use to him. Nevertheless, perhaps he ought to try some Madeira."[8]

In reality, the month of January had been disastrous and had weakened the invalid further. In February, he was a little better; he stopped spitting blood and his appetite returned; he was able to take short walks or at least go warm himself in the sun in the cypress-lined alley that led to the villa, leaning on the arm of one of the two nuns. But from March on, it seems there were new crises, which the doctors of those days called the "work of the springtime." Very much weakened, Tocqueville lost consciousness briefly and then died on April 16 at seven in the evening.

All the letters he had written from Cannes exuded optimism, and although he complained of his bad health and confessed that January had been the one month out of his whole life that should be marked with a black cross, he never seems to have feared that he was mortally ill. There is no doubt that victims of tuberculosis do tend to maintain this optimism up to the very end. And those who witnessed his stay at Cannes, his brothers and Beaumont, confirm that, perceptive as this man was, he was not aware of his true condition.[9] They are no doubt right, but all the same, one can ask oneself if it is not possible that Tocqueville concealed his fears. Before leaving Paris, he had apparently wanted to see Beaumont privately, and Beaumont may have hidden the truth later to spare Mary, who was convinced that her husband had really not had any fear that his death was imminent. The account given

[8] Mérimée, *Correspondance générale*, 2nd series, vol. 3 (1859–1860), 20 (to Madame de Boigne), 24 (to Edward Ellice), and 35 (to Madame de Boigne).
[9] See in particular Beaumont, notice of the O.C. (Bmt) V, 116.

by Mérimée, in whom Dr. Maure confided, shows him to be, on the
contrary, quite uneasy.

Few problems have provoked such controversy, occasionally passionate controversy, as that of Alexis de Tocqueville's religious convictions.

Among commentators who view Tocqueville as a Catholic, there
are two schools: those who affirm that he was always a believer, and
those who have tried to demonstrate that in the very last weeks or even
the last days of his life, he returned to the Christian faith.

We do not believe that Tocqueville can be considered to have been
a believer during the course of his life. It is not impossible that there
were occasional brief returns to the faith of his childhood, but there
is now too much evidence in the *Oeuvres Complètes* that he did not
have faith for it to be possible, in our opinion, to persist in maintaining
that he did. He regretted it, of course, because he had kept an affectionate attachment to the Catholicism of his childhood. He continued,
for that matter, to attend mass on Sundays, at least in Tocqueville, for,
like many nonbelieving notables of that time, he did not want to
sadden the curé or scandalize the other parishioners. We have also
advanced the hypothesis that a more acute religious uneasiness appeared
in him starting in 1856, perhaps after the death of his father. Madame
de Tocqueville, on the other hand—and of this we have a good deal
of evidence—became a fervent Catholic after her abjuration of Protestantism in 1835, devout and not very tolerant.

For Alexis, therefore, the problem open to discussion is the following: In the spring of 1859, did he hold to the Catholic faith and
Catholic doctrine?

What has given rise to the controversy is an account by Gustave de
Beaumont. In his preface to Tocqueville's *Oeuvres et Correspondance*,
which he published in 1860, Beaumont wrote: "Tocqueville's end was as
Christian as his life. People have spoken of conversion, and this is
wrong; he did not have to convert, because there had never been the
slightest trace of irreligion in him."[10] Then Beaumont weakened this
affirmation by saying that Tocqueville had always been "troubled by
many doubts" and that his religious faith was a part of his political faith.

After examining the manuscript pages of this preface, we think we
have uncovered the cause of the difficulty that the wording of the
passage presents. There exists a prior version that Beaumont did not

[10]*O.C.* (Bmt) V, 120.

destroy and that shows what he was thinking before Madame de   529
Tocqueville (in all probability) asked him to modify it:

Shortly before his death, his wife led him gently around to the subject of
confession:

"Don't ever speak to me of confession—ever! Ever! No one will ever
make me lie to myself and make a pretense of faith when I don't have faith.
I want to remain myself and not stoop to telling lies." His wife took the
subject up again tenderly; same response; he added: "It is not the confession
in itself that I find repugnant; on the contrary, I would find it very sweet;
it is one of the most beautiful and admirable things in the Christian religion—this humbling of one's pride, this avowal of one's weaknesses, and this
outpouring of the heart, emptying itself entirely into another soul so as to
be purified there. But the first condition of the Catholic confession is faith
in all the dogmas of the Catholic Church; and it is these dogmas—which
my reason has always challenged—that I do not want to acknowledge or
approve when in reality I still do not accept them!" Insisting again with the
same gentleness, Madame de Tocqueville pointed out that no such profession
of faith in the dogmas was required of anyone making his confession. And
after she had come back to this subject several times, she did actually persuade
him that the priest to whom he would confess would not ask anything more
of him than his sincere repentance. Later, he himself summoned M. le curé
of Cannes, to whom he opened his heart in such touching terms that this
worthy priest was profoundly moved. Never had a soul so noble, so great,
so admirable even in its failings, revealed itself to him. Tocqueville had begun
with a general confession of his sins. When he prepared to go into detail,
M. le curé of Cannes stopped him and told him he did not want to hear
anything more.

A few moments later, since nothing but a complete and more detailed
confession of his sins would entirely soothe his soul, he entreated his dear
wife, that soul so worthy to receive his entire confession, to finish the priest's
work and hear the detailed confession that he needed to make; Madame de
Tocqueville appointed the next day for it, and begged him to rest and take
joy in the peace of his conscience.

This was what he did, but nothing more, and it was in these conditions
that he received communion at the same time as the beloved companion of
his life. Shortly after, when he himself was telling me about this serious event
in his life, he depicted to me in admirable terms the happiness this Christian
communion had brought him, saying that it had created yet another bond
between his dear wife and him, the only one lacking to make their union
complete.[11]

[11]This text, which is in the Tocqueville Archives, file 52, was communicated to J. J. Chevallier, who
published it as a footnote in the O.C. IX, 13–14.

530
𝕴 𝕾

In a conversation with Senior, Beaumont was more categorical about the fact that Tocqueville had not truly converted: "He died with his doubts, I know it."

Rédier and Lukacs have challenged Beaumont's testimony and suspected him of bad faith.[12] Lukacs has pointed out that in editing his friend's texts, Beaumont altered them. This is certainly the case, but he did it—often clumsily—either to spare Tocqueville certain posthumous resentments or to make his style more polished. After reading all the copies and corrections of texts attributable to Beaumont, we have not seen any in which he knowingly altered anything in Tocqueville's thought, which he admired. Rédier, for his part, had cited against Beaumont the letter to Madame Swetchine that Falloux wanted to publish and that was burned. But this suppression was ordered by Madame de Tocqueville, influenced by a misguided devotion (as unpublished texts prove) and if there survives a copy in the hand of Madame de Beaumont, who copied texts for her husband, it was most likely not without the knowledge of Gustave, who very probably participated in this "pious fraud." For that matter, although Beaumont was not a believer, he does not seem to have had the antireligious passions attributed to him.

However, there are facts that tend to allow with more likelihood the possibility of a conversion. There can be no doubt about the conversation in which Tocqueville said to his brother Edouard that he intended to do his paschal duty (that year, Easter fell on April 24) and to his nephew Hubert that in the future he would take more interest in religious matters. He did not say these things merely in order to be pleasant to Edouard and Hubert, though that was certainly part of it. We believe that in these conversations, he was showing the desire to attempt the elucidation, in the future, of this religious question which had deeply troubled him for several years and concerning which his illness had no doubt made his anxiety more acute.

Above all, there are the facts to which Beaumont alludes, the meetings with the curé of Cannes, the confession and the communion. We also know that Dupanloup, when he came to see him, celebrated mass in his room and that this could hardly have been a simple act of politeness on the part of the Bishop of Orléans, even though he greatly

---

[12]Rédier, *M. de Tocqueville*, 291–99. J. Lukacs, "The Last Days of A. de Tocqueville," *The Catholic Historical Review* 50 (July 1964), 155–70. The first of these authors obtained a statement from Sister Gertrude, one of the two sisters who attended Tocqueville at Cannes. The second came upon the observations written down concerning Tocqueville's last days in the collection of the Congrégation du Bon-Secours, which constitute an interesting and sincere testimony, but one of doubtful perspicacity.

respected Tocqueville and liked his liberalism. As for the curé of 531
Cannes, Tocqueville had first shown him the door, then asked him to
visit. The curé performed at least the one mass in the sick man's room,
at which Tocqueville took communion, after having confessed, in
company with his wife. Rédier affirms that an ecclesiastic could not
do this for someone who did not have the faith without committing
a sacrilege. Even though we are no more of a theologian than Rédier,
this seems to us inaccurate: Tocqueville could in all truth affirm his
desire to have faith. And the doctrine of the Church seems to us to
be that the sacraments can infuse the grace of God necessary to have
this faith. Such is, at least, the interpretation that one can give the
"liberalism" of the curé of Cannes. In stating that Tocqueville had
taken communion in order to create a new emotional bond with his
wife, Beaumont was telling the truth, but not the whole truth, because
he himself probably did not feel the desire to believe or the attachment
to the Church that Tocqueville felt. Despite appearances, therefore,
these facts do not imply an intellectual conversion to Catholicism.

Several texts published in the years following Tocqueville's death
have sought to convince the public of his conversion. We will not
examine the inconclusive controversies they provoked, but will note
that the two best informed of Tocqueville's friends remained silent.

One was Kergorlay, who lived close to Tocqueville for the whole
of the last week. We know that Tocqueville confided his most intimate
thoughts to him, and when Rédier says that Beaumont could not know
what Tocqueville's attitude was after he left Cannes, he is forgetting
that it is hardly possible that he did not hear from his friend Kergorlay
about the last moments of their mutual friend.

The other was Corcelle. He had chosen the medical assistant whom
Tocqueville had close to him during the last week of his life. The
d'Harcourt Archives contain a letter to Corcelle written by this man,
Dujardin-Beaumetz, in which he gives a precise account of Tocqueville's last hours. It does not appear to allude to a religious end, which
is surprising given Corcelle's preoccupations. The essential part of it
reads as follows:

I am sorry to announce to you the death of your excellent friend, Monsieur
de Tocqueville. On Friday, he had two attacks of suffocation made frightful
by the harshness of the mistral, which had been blowing for three days.
Nevertheless, the night was fairly good. In the morning, Monsieur de
Tocqueville felt a little better. But alas! Our illusions were no sooner born
than they died away. A terrible attack, two hours long, was followed by such

532

a deep calm that I was afraid we had arrived at one of those periods in which it seems that nature is resting from her past fatigues and renewing her forces for the last struggle. I must have imparted these fears to MM. Hippolyte and Edouard de Tocqueville. As the day went on, his respiration, pulse, and vital forces decreased one after another. M. de Tocqueville was able to receive his brothers and M. L. de Kergorlay and say a few affectionate and good words to them, without being aware that he was so close to the moment of farewell. Madame de Tocqueville did not leave her husband's bedside; he remained calm, was able to talk a little, listen to a short reading. From time to time a little distress and some fits of coughing, and toward five-thirty the last attack began. Forgive me, Monsieur, for afflicting you with these details. I can affirm to you religiously that we did everything we could to relieve M. de Tocqueville and sustain his hope. But God alone is all powerful, it pleased Him to withdraw from us His helping hand. All that remains to us—alas!—is to adore His will and to weep over the mortal remains of a superior soul whom He took back into His bosom.[13]

Corcelle, who was sometimes given to indiscreet proselytizing, has nowhere alluded to a Christian end for Tocqueville, whose feelings he was well aware of before Tocqueville left for Cannes. This silence appears to us, in the light of the public controversies, quite significant.

We do not believe, therefore, in Tocqueville's deathbed conversion. We are inclined to think that he died in a feeling of communion with a religion that Abbé Lesueur had once taught him to love, without accepting its dogmas. But the biographer, in this domain, must base his opinions on what his hero has communicated to others. In the case of a mind as active, as passionate, as secret as that of Alexis de Tocqueville, we will not be so bold as to assume any certainty about his last thoughts. There are intimate reaches of the spirit that compel one to silence.

After a religious ceremony at Cannes, Tocqueville's coffin was taken back to Paris, where it was laid in the crypt of the Eglise de la Madeleine, and from there transported to Tocqueville, where he was buried on May 10.

Tocqueville had wanted to be laid to rest in the cemetery of the little village he had loved so much, and he had also asked that a simple wooden cross mark his grave. Corcelle and Ampère, who had accompanied his widow from Cannes, were there that day alongside his

[13]This letter is in the d'Harcourt Archives.

family. No one from the government was present to pay homage, but an immense crowd had gathered, led by children from the schools Tocqueville had founded. Five years later, Madame de Tocqueville was laid to rest beside him.

EPILOGUE

TOCQUEVILLE'S work had a surprising fate. At the time of the author's death, he was famous in France, England, the United States, and even Germany. His reputation suffered an eclipse from 1880 to about 1930, but since then there has been a renaissance that now places him in the ranks of the political theorists most discussed in countries of broad culture.

We will not follow the ups and downs of this posthumous life.[1] Let us only note that Tocqueville found a larger and larger audience as the great social ills of the modern world—totalitarianism, the alienation of man within the consumer society, the omnipotence of an anonymous bureaucracy—have been revealed. Because he denounced these evils, Tocqueville seems to be our contemporary,[2] and his work is rich enough so that his interpreters during the Hitler years did not stress the same truths as do those of our own day.[3] At a time when democratic societies were still young, he drew up an inventory of the dangers they held within them—seeds that were destined to germinate, grow, and bear fruit. And his denunciations of these dangers, made in fear and trembling, had at times a strongly pessimistic tone. But there was confidence as well that man might win through by the exercise of that freedom which distinguishes the human species from all other

[1]Madame Françoise Mélonio is preparing a thesis on the reception of Tocqueville's work in France.
[2]The expression is J. P. Mayer's.
[3]See the excellent commentaries by R. Nisbet, "Many Tocquevilles," *American Scholar* 46 (1976–1977), 59–75.

creatures. Though man may yield and submit, he remains capable of rousing himself and again taking up the struggle.

Tocqueville was not only the author of a book about America that marked an epoch and another on the origins of the French Revolution whose great merits are being rediscovered. Writing never seemed to him an end in itself, just as "living for the sake of living" had no interest for him. Born at a time when the old aristocratic world was falling into ruin, he wanted to preserve, not the privileges, but the duties he found in his heritage—such as he considered them to be—in order to incorporate them into the new society. The realization of this social duty formed the essential unity of his moral life and welded together his thought and his actions. This lofty ethic did not prevent his character from having contradictions and failings (an ambition that was sometimes petty, an excessive desire to win reputation). By temperament, he was unequally gifted as political writer and statesman. Endowed with a sharp lucidity inspired by an exacting search for the truth, he was also, despite his great good sense, paralyzed by scruples and doubts.

It has often been said that he was a liberal "not like the others." What seems to us to distinguish him from many of his contemporaries was his very keen sense of solidarity with mankind. This opinion may surprise the reader who remembers the acidulous sketches of friends and enemies in the *Souvenirs* or the bitterness he sometimes showed over his personal failures. And yet, when Tocqueville said that he believed he must be justified in the eyes of God because he had loved men, he judged himself accurately. He did not feel this affection only for humanity in general, like certain lovers of mankind for whom it serves as a cover for detesting the people around them, but also for the men he associated with, and he felt this affection in a hierarchical order opposite to that of his teacher Montesquieu: first his family, then the Normans of the Cotentin, then the French, then the rest of the world . . .

It was this devotion to the public weal that defined a body of written work that embraced the most unequal subjects, from reports to the departmental councils to considerations on the future of Christian societies. It went hand in hand with the conviction that a society, if it is to bring its members happiness, must be committed to making the choice between good and evil, and it must be a conscious, informed choice.

Tocqueville's work is neither abstract nor cold. It is imbued with

536

🌿 🌿

the passion that animated the man, though kept in check by an altogether classical control of thought and style. This passion was, indeed,
the moral energy that the Ancients and Montesquieu understood by
"virtue," but Tocqueville's conception of the role of the citizen was
the highest possible: to contribute to the providential work of creation,
for that work, if it is to be fulfilled, depends upon the exercise of man's
will in freedom.

BIBLIOGRAPHICAL

NOTE

Numerous works devoted to Tocqueville, like those of Fabian, Gargan, and Drescher, include detailed bibliographies. In republishing the *Democracy in America* in Reeve's translation, Phillips Bradley has provided as an appendix to his bibliography the list of different editions of the book in all languages (1960). Even more important, in his Italian edition of the same work, Nicola Matteuci has added a very complete *nota bibliografica* (1968). A selected and annotated bibliography of 273 titles has been published by André Jardin and Françoise Mélonio in the Actes du Colloque de Gummersbach, brought out under the direction of Michael Hereth and Jutta Höffken with the title *Zur Politik in der Demokratie* (Baden-Baden, 1981), to which we would like to refer the reader.

Since that date, the following volumes have been added to Tocqueville's *Oeuvres Complètes,* published by Editions Gallimard:

Volume III, *Ecrits et discours politiques,* two volumes, ed. André Jardin.

Volume IV, *Ecrits pénitentiaires,* two volumes, ed. Michelle Perrot.

Volume XV, *Correspondance d'Alexis de Tocqueville et de Francisque de Corcelle et Correspondance d'Alexis de Tocqueville et de Madame Swetchine,* two volumes, ed. Pierre Gibert.

Volume XVIII, *Correspondance d'Alexis de Tocqueville avec Adolphe de Circourt et avec Madame de Circourt,* ed. A. Patricia Kerr.

Two important works have also appeared since 1981: the thesis by Jean-Claude Lamberti, *Tocqueville et les deux démocraties,* (P.U.F., 1983), the first state thesis in France devoted to Alexis de Tocqueville, and a brilliant little book by Pierre Manent, *Tocqueville et la nature de la démocratie* (Julliard, 1982). We should also draw attention to the appearance of Xavier de la Fournière's *Alexis de Tocqueville, un monarchiste indépendant* (Paris, 1981); Richard Reeves's *American Journey, Travelling with Tocqueville in Search of Democracy in America* (New York, 1982); and Pierre Michel's *Un mythe romantique, les Barbares, 1789–1848* (Lyons, 1981), which includes a chapter entitled "Démocratie et Barbarie: Tocqueville," 267–92.

A great many articles have appeared or been brought to our attention since 1981. We can cite only a few of them:

Raymond Aron, "Tocqueville retrouvé." *Tocqueville Review,* Fall 1979, 8–23; Roger Boesche, "Tocqueville and *Le Commerce:* A Newspaper Expressing Unusual Liberalism." *Journal of the History of Ideas* 44, no. 2 (April–June 1983): 277–92; E. Botto, "Libertà politica e libertà morale nel pensiero di Tocqueville." *Rivista di filosofia neoscolastica* 73, no. 3 (1981): 497–511; H. V. Brogan, "Tocqueville and the American Presidency." *Journal of American Studies* 15, no. 3 (December 1981): 357–75; L. Diez del Corral, "Tocqueville y Royer-Collard, Historia económica y pensamiento social." *Estudios en homenaje a Diego Mateo del Peral* (Madrid, 1983): 75–86; E. T. Gargan, "The Silence of Tocqueville on Education." *Historical Reflections* 7, nos. 2–3 (1980): 565–75; A. Lebacqz, "De Tocqueville à Valéry Giscard d'Estaing."

538

兆 兆

Revue des deux mondes (January–March 1982): 350–55; E. Martonyl, "Une contribution à l'étude du vocabulaire politique du XIXe siècle. L'usage du terme 'égalité des conditions' par Tocqueville." *Acta Romanica* 5 (Szeged, 1978): 235–49; F. Mélonio, "La religion selon Tocqueville, ordre moral ou esprit de liberté." *Etudes* (January 1984) 73–88; L. Orr, "Tocqueville et l'histoire incompréhensible, l'Ancien Régime et la Révolution." *Poétique* 13, no. 49 (February 1982): 51–70; E. Pessen, "Tocqueville's Misreading of America, America's Misreading of Tocqueville." *Tocqueville Review* 4, no. 1 (Spring–Summer 1982): 5–22. F. Riccobono, "Osservazioni su eguaglianza e democrazia in A. de Tocqueville." *Rivista internazionale di filosofia del diritto,* series 4, vol. 54, no. 4 (1977): 887–903; J. T. Schleifer, "Tocqueville and American Literature: A Newly Acquired Letter." *Yale University Library Gazette* 54, no. 3 (1980): 129–54; J. T. Schleifer, "Tocqueville and Religion, Some New Perspectives." *Tocqueville Review* 4, no. 2 (Fall–Winter 1982): 303–21; C. Zuckert, "Not by Preaching: Tocqueville on the Role of Religion in American Democracy." *Review of Politics* 43, no. 2 (1981): 259–80.

André Jardin
December 1983

INDEX

541